C0-GFQ-309

STUDIES IN HONOUR OF CLIFFORD EDMUND BOSWORTH

VOLUME II

Clifford Edmund Bosworth (Photo: Christine Norbury).

STUDIES IN HONOUR OF CLIFFORD EDMUND BOSWORTH VOLUME II

The Sultan's Turret: Studies in Persian and Turkish Culture

EDITED BY

CAROLE HILLENBRAND

BRILL
LEIDEN · BOSTON · KÖLN
2000

LUTHER SEMINARY
LIBRARY
2375 Como Avenue
St. Paul, MN 55108-1447

DS62
.S88
v.2

This book is printed on acid-free paper.

Die Deutsche Bibliothek - CIP-Einheitsaufnahme

Studies in honour of Clifford Edmund Bosworth:
The Sultan's turret / ed. by Carole Hillenbrand - Leiden ; Boston ; Köln : Brill, 1999
Vol. 2. The Sultan's turret. Studies in Persian and Turkish culture. - 1999
ISBN 90-04-11075-5

Library of Congress Cataloging-in-Publication Data

Library of Congress Cataloging-in-Publication Data is also available

ISBN 90 04 11075 5

© Copyright 2000 by Koninklijke Brill NV, Leiden, The Netherlands

All rights reserved. No part of this publication may be reproduced, translated, stored in a retrieval system, or transmitted in any form or by any means, electronic, mechanical, photocopying, recording or otherwise, without prior written permission from the publisher.

Authorization to photocopy items for internal or personal use is granted by Brill provided that the appropriate fees are paid directly to The Copyright Clearance Center, 222 Rosewood Drive, Suite 910 Danvers MA 01923, USA. Fees are subject to change.

PRINTED IN THE NETHERLANDS

o:39323082

Awake! For Morning in the
Bowl of Night
Has flung the Stone that puts the
Stars to Flight:
And Lo! the Hunter of the East
has caught
The Sultan's Turret in a Noose of
Light.

The Rubaiyat of Omar Khayyam
trans. Edward FitzGerald (1st version)

CONTENTS

EDITOR'S PREFACE

Every attempt has been made in this volume to follow the editorial conventions laid down in Volume I of this *Festschrift*, edited by Professor Ian Netton, and to achieve reasonable consistency amongst the very diverse contributions in this volume. While most contributors followed a modified EI^2 transliteration system, I have nevertheless respected the wishes of some contributors in this matter. "A foolish consistency is the hobgoblin of little minds" and it is indeed no easy task to juggle transliteration systems which embrace Pahlavi, Persian, Arabic and Ottoman and modern Turkish. Some well known proper nouns have not been transliterated. American and British spelling conventions have both been observed.

I should like to thank Ian Netton for his enthusiastic collaboration in producing this unusually wide-ranging *Festschrift*, Lesley Scobie for her secretarial help, and all those at Brill who have been involved in this volume, above all Peri Bearman for her initial support and Julie Plokker and Jan Fehrmann for seeing the volume through to publication.

Carole Hillenbrand

EDITOR'S TRIBUTE TO EDMUND BOSWORTH

When the suggestion was made to Edmund Bosworth that he should receive a *Festschrift* from his colleagues in Islamic studies, he responded with his customary enthusiasm. Indeed, it was he who chose the contributors to the *Festschrift* amongst friends whom he cherishes and fellow-scholars whom he respects. I believe that this volume, dedicated to Persian and Turkish studies, is a fine contribution to scholarship in this field as well as a true reflection of Edmund Bosworth's abiding interest and research in these areas of the Islamic world.

Michael Wickens has provided an eloquent and comprehensive appreciation of Edmund's personality and scholarly achievements. I will therefore confine myself to a few personal reminiscences and observations of my own.

Over the many years that I have known Edmund I have always been impressed by his prodigious energy and enthusiasm for every project he undertakes and by his genuinely wide-ranging interests within his field. Nor is he self-seeking and mean with his knowledge—he is always willing to impart bibliographical information to others and to encourage those who are just starting their apprenticeship in Islamic studies. His own standing in the field received timely recognition in his election as Fellow of the British Academy in 1992 but his reputation extends far beyond the borders of the UK and Europe. Despite his scholarly persona, Edmund is happy to be teased; indeed, he himself has a puckish sense of humour which he rarely reveals to his colleagues but which makes him a delightful companion outside working hours.

Edmund's life-long interest in medieval Islamic history and thought has not prevented him from enjoying outside interests. He is a devoted husband, father and grandfather and a pillar of his local church. He finds time for regular visits to his alma mater, St John's College, Oxford, to collect books, to pursue his passion for Victoriana and for gardening, and perhaps above all to pace the Scottish hills and the Isle of Arran with a youthful vigour and speed that leaves his companions gasping for breath.

This volume is offered to Edmund in gratitude and affection.

Carole Hillenbrand

HOMAGE TO EDMUND BOSWORTH

G.M. Wickens

In the normal way of things I would have hoped to offer a (more or less!) traditional academic article for the *Festschrift* in Bosworth's honour, but age and health problems have colluded to frustrate my purpose. However, by the kind accommodation of the editor of this volume, I am allowed to pay a direct tribute from personal experience, and from the heart, rather than obliquely by way of research and reasoned argument.

In those studies associated with the Middle East and the Islamic world, over the last 40 years or so, Edmund Bosworth has played a part of unique significance and force. Virtually no other scholar of our day, in the whole Western world, has contributed so much, in so many areas, and at such diverse levels. And all this he has done without forfeiting any of his qualities as a human being, for he is essentially what the Irish are reputed to call "a lovely man" and Yiddish-speakers a *mensch.* There are, in my own experience, only a small minority of academics about whom this could be sincerely said, but I should be most surprised if any—let alone many—would rise up to contest, or even qualify, such a judgment in this case. Should such there be, "bad cess" to them anyway! If Bosworth has been at all driven by ambitions, they have been reasonable, controlled, and always directed towards the practical end of "getting a job done".

But for the moment I will leave aside the strictly personal. I suppose that virtually any of Edmund Bosworth's colleagues in the field, if asked to label him succinctly, would designate him as a "historian" and the "longtime British editor of the new *Encyclopaedia of Islam*". Yet while such categorisations would be valid in essence, they would convey a most inadequate idea of this scholar's stature and breadth.

In the first place, in his work as a historian, he is that rarity, a "straight" historian (a First Class in Modern History at Oxford) who—after "auditing" various Middle Eastern courses while at Oxford and then working for two years as a Civil Servant—went on, while no longer in his first youth, to the serious academic study of Middle

Eastern culture and languages. This he did in the Edinburgh school, gaining another First Class degree and finally the Ph.D. (Most historians, and other discipline-based scholars, in our field have—for various reasons—found this an impossibly hard row to hoe, and consequently must get along as best they can without a convincing mastery of all the tools. At the same time, those who do fully possess such tools have to pursue their work in areas of history, sociology, philosophy, and so forth without ever meeting complete "disciplinary" acceptance in most cases. The overall work done is rarely negligible, but the situation on both sides is far from ideal.)

Secondly—and by no means unrelated to both his personality and his earlier career-paths—Bosworth is an unusually wide-ranging historian. For the most part his "period" is pre-modern, but he could not rightly be classified as a medievalist, certainly not in any restricted sense. His "geographical" interests have tended towards Iran and Central Asia, but are not limited to those areas by any means. (It should be particularly remarked that he has played an outstanding part in the great Columbia Ṭabarī project, as both editor and contributor: this could be seen as a happy union of all his professional talents.) Again, his historical bent, while ostensibly political (or religio-political, as is necessarily the case in addressing the world of Islam), takes into its purview social conditions, economic structures, both the high culture and the sub-cultures—and much else besides. And always his investigations and conclusions rest on the solid foundations of primary documents and texts, not merely on translations or secondary works.

Thirdly, and not least, Bosworth writes lucidly, even elegantly, and in an unfailingly interesting manner. Those scholars who have had occasion to consult professionally his close on 20 books, and his hundreds of articles—that is to say virtually everyone in the field—must often have lingered to enjoy the experience for its own sake, for here is not a trace of the turgidity, dullness, and desiccation which some regard as the essential hallmarks of sound scholarship. I do not know if he at all subscribes to G.M. Trevelyan's apprehension of Clio as the traditional "muse", but—with all his scientific accuracy and objectivity—he certainly remains a humanist in the best classical sense.

In his work as a pivotal editor of *EI*², Edmund Bosworth has performed prodigies of heroic endeavour, miraculously preserving in the process his sanity and even a charitable and boyish good-humour. It is difficult to imagine the project having stayed alive, let alone prospered as it has, without his vital contribution. If only his magic touch could be invoked in *all* such ventures!

All who have edited even a very modest collection or two are likely to retain acute, and often excruciating, memories of their dealings with contributors on the one hand and publishers on the other. With the former there are the "no shows", the promised articles or chapters that simply never arrive; while others arrive late, often impossibly so. There are the mildly or severely substandard offerings, requiring some surgery or, in extreme cases, a gentle quietus. Then, again, there come the hobby-horses, not infrequently ridden to the wildest lengths. Still more difficult to handle are the prima donnas, those who demand special treatment or insist on their perfect ability to "perform" in a language not their own and all too imperfectly mastered. And so on and so forth; and however lucky editors may be with many of their contributors, these substantial minorities must always be reckoned with, especially in a project of such vast and enduring proportions as the *Encyclopaedia.* Yet I have rarely heard Bosworth refer to such trials and vexations other than casually and obliquely, much less in a tone of complaint or sympathy-seeking. His evident integrity and sincerity, his decency and tact, his serious and generous concern—all these have surely been drawn on heavily, constantly, and to good effect with all but the most recalcitrant. One thing I do know: on numerous occasions he has had no choice but to write or rewrite the needed material, at very short notice, in a modern version of the ancient accomplishment of *irtijāl.* In such circumstances, it is not the least of his virtues that he could always muster the energy, the pragmatic good-sense, the dedication, and the professional expertise to perform this uncalled-for exercise. Such benevolent denizens are rarely encountered in the groves of academe, not only because they are few in number but by virtue also of their inherent shyness and modesty.

On the other side of the editing operation, I believe Bosworth's experience with the publishers to have been reasonably good, partly perhaps due to the terms under which the project was conceived and set up, and partly as an intrinsic factor of the publishers' own longstanding professional and specialised experience. But as we all know, publishers, their own in-house editors, and printers can all and always—at least potentially—introduce problems of their own, often not to be resolved without confrontation and compromise in which the rôle of the academic editors must be crucial and ultimately decisive. To Edmund Bosworth's qualities so far enumerated must here be added clarity of thought and firmness of decision.

To turn now from the scholar and the editor, the public figure known to all concerned with the culture of the Middle East and the world of Islam, to some more personal impressions of my own. My personal knowledge of Bosworth goes back some thirty years.

In the mid-60s, when I was striving to build the new Department of Islamic (later Middle East and Islamic) Studies at the University of Toronto, I was sufficiently taken with what I had seen and heard of Bosworth and his work to invite him to Toronto as a professorial Visitor for one year. It was clear enough that, in doing so, I hoped (if everything proved satisfactory on both sides) to convert the visiting appointment into a substantive one as soon as practicable. (My hopes were shared by my own colleague Roger Savory, who had himself followed such a course a few years earlier with what has remained a most notable success to the present day.) In the event, and for various reasons, fortune did not favour us, and Bosworth returned to Britain, but for some while the decision did seem to hang in the balance. Over the years since then, he (often accompanied by his wife Annette) has come back to us on several occasions, sometimes to give a guest-lecture or two, but also to visit his old colleagues and other friends. In this way he has remained *au courant* of developments at the University and in the Toronto area generally (to say nothing of Canada at large) to a degree that few, if any, non-residents could claim to be.

His "visiting" year (1965–6) was a remarkable professional and personal success, with all the attributes mentioned above coming fully into play—even at his then relatively young age. Having myself weathered (and later experienced vicariously) the several problems faced by foreign scholars trying—if only half-heartedly in some cases—to adapt to the Canadian social and academic scene, I was filled with admiration at Edmund Bosworth's smooth entry and assimilation. He truly has the gift for making, in the literal sense of the term, "the best" of any situation. With colleagues and students alike his popularity was immediate and sustained. He worked assiduously in all areas (teaching, research, and even "administration"), never—like some "visitors"—treating his appointment as a sinecure and a quasi-vacation with pay, not to say, "a bit of a lark". Moreover, his industry would have counted for much less, had it not been grounded in a quick intelligence and the ability to absorb and apply. With all his natural Yorkshire frankness, his many questions and comments were patently intended to elicit information to be put to practical use, so as to save himself and others from embarrassing misunderstandings: he never, to my knowledge, committed the very common, and deeply resented, cardinal sin of patronising Canadians and telling them how things were done in Britain, especially at Oxbridge. I suspect that this was because, again, he quickly appreciated that many Canadians, native or immigrant, in fact already knew such things by personal experience of Britain, the USA, and other lands and had already come to conclusions of their own.

Nor was the success of this period confined to his academic life, for he displayed a like keenness to get to know Canadians and Canadian life generally. I had been fortunate to secure for him and his family a year's rental on the house of another colleague, in West Toronto. Such arrangements sometimes bring heartaches on all sides, but I believe this was a virtually unqualified good-deal. Certainly, I had rightly judged both parties to be "reasonable people". (A few years later, and there might have been the extra advantage of the rapid-transit subway-extension to that area, as he himself wryly observed on a subsequent visit.) Helped partly by their Anglican affiliation, the Bosworths rapidly gained a place in the local community, and I gather that many of the friends then made are still visited whenever Edmund and Annette come to Toronto. Indeed, their "socialisation" has extended beyond Toronto and its region into Ontario generally and other parts of Canada as well. Ironically, I must admit that they have made a much more wholehearted "go" of this than I myself have ever done.

Had they stayed, there is little doubt that (as with the Savorys and a few others) theirs would have been one of the most notable cases of assimilation on record from that golden age of European immigration into Canada, the 1950s and '60s. As in other societies and academic institutions in the Western world, they would have had to contend later with a decline, a loss of quality, and even some decay; but their coping with these problems in their native land would suggest that they would have survived philosophically, not to say optimistically and positively, in Toronto equally well.

Edmund may be unaware (unless our tongues have slipped) that he is still fondly and familiarly remembered at Toronto as "Bozzy"—a sort of cross between Dickens' "Boz" and Disraeli's "Dizzy", which in itself perhaps lends a reassuring 19th-century flavour to one who is otherwise "always up with the latest", and even often "ahead of the game". Annette too is most kindly recalled, but (as she may be relieved to hear) without any sobriquet of her own. No doubt, though, she has picked up one or more in the course of life with Edmund, always a ready man with a quip or an apt turn of phrase!

Floreant ad multos annos!

BIBLIOGRAPHY OF THE WORKS OF C.E. BOSWORTH

Abbreviations

AHR	American Historical Review, Washington, D.C.
Azure	Azure. The Review of Arab Arts and Culture, London
BEO	Bulletin d'Etudes Orientales, Damascus
BiOr	Bibliotheca Orientalis, Leiden
BJMES	British Journal of Middle Eastern Studies, Durham, Abingdon
BJRUL	Bulletin of the John Rylands University Library, Manchester
BSOAS	Bulletin of the School of Oriental and African Studies, London
Bull. BSMES	Bulletin of the British Society for Middle East Studies, Oxford, Exeter
CAJ	Central Asiatic Journal, The Hague, Wiesbaden
CT	Cahiers de Tunisie, Tunis
DMA	Dictionary of the Middle Ages, New York
EHR	English Historical Review, London
EI	Encyclopaedia of Islam, new edn., Leiden
EIr	Encyclopaedia Iranica, New York and London, New York and Costa Mesa, Calif.
EW	East and West, Rome
GMS	Gibb Memorial Series, London
IJMES	International Journal of Middle East Studies, Cambridge
IOS	Israel Oriental Studies, Tel Aviv
IQ	The Islamic Quarterly, London
Iran, JBIPS	Iran, Journal of the British Institute of Persian Studies, London
Isl.	Der Islam, Berlin
JA	Journal Asiatique, Paris
JAH	Journal of Asian History, Wiesbaden
JAOS	Journal of the American Oriental Society, New Haven, Conn.
JESHO	Journal of the Economic and Social History of the Orient, Leiden
JIS	Journal of Islamic Studies, Oxford
JNES	Journal of Near Eastern Studies, Chicago
JOAS	Journal of Oriental and African Studies, Athens
JRAS	Journal of the Royal Asiatic Society, London
JSS	Journal of Semitic Studies, Manchester
MEJ	Middle East Journal, Washington D.C.
MESA Bull.	Middle East Studies of America Bulletin, Tucson
MW	The Muslim World, Hartford, Conn.
OLZ	Orientalistisches Literaturzeitung, Berlin
St. Ir.	Studia Iranica, Paris and Leiden
TLS	The Times Literary Supplement, London
ZDMG	Zeitschrift der Deutschen Morgenländischen Gesellschaft, Wiesbaden

1959

1. *EI* vol. I, art. "Bahrā'".

1960

2. "The rise of the Karāmiyyah in Khurasan", MW, L (1960), 5–14.
3. "Ghaznavid military organisation", Isl., XXXVI (1960), 37–77.
4. *EI* vol. I, arts. "Bi'r Maʿūna", "al-Bishr", "Buʿāth", "Buzākha".

1961

5. "The early Islamic history of Ghūr", *CAJ*, VI (1961), 116–33.

1962

6. "The imperial policy of the early Ghaznawids", *Islamic Studies. Journal of the Central Institute of Islamic Research*, Karachi, I/3 (1962), 49–82.
7. *EI* vol. II, art. "Djaʿda (ʿĀmir)".
8. Review in *JRAS* (1962), 86: Hans L. Gottschalk, *Al-Malik al-Kāmil von Egypten und Seine Zeit*, Wiesbaden 1958.

1963

9. *The Ghaznavids, their empire in Afghanistan and eastern Iran 994:1040*, Edinburgh University Press 1963, pp. xii + 331. Reprinted Munshiram Manoharlal, Delhi 1992. Second edition, with updated bibliography, Librairie du Liban, pp. xii + 335, Beirut 1973.
10. "A Turco-Mongol practice amongst the early Ghaznavids?", *CAJ*, VII (1962), 237–40.
11. "The titulature of the early Ghaznavids", *Oriens*, XV (1962), 210–33.
12. "The section on codes and their decipherment in Qalqashandī's *Ṣubḥ al-aʿshā*", *JSS*, VIII (1963), 17–33.
13. "Early sources for the history of the first four Ghaznavid sultans", *IQ*, VII (1963), 3–22.
14. "A pioneer Arabic encyclopaedia of the sciences: al-Khwārizmī's 'Keys of the sciences'", *Isis*, LIV, no. 175 (1963), 97–111.
15. "Some historical gleanings from the section on symbolic actions in Qalqašandī's *Ṣubḥ al-aʿšā*", *Arabica*, X (1963), 148–53.
16. *EI* vol. II, art. "Djudhām".
17. Reviews of U. Heyd (ed.), *Studies in Islamic history and civilisation*, Scripta Hierosylimitana IX, Jerusalem 1961, in *JSS*, VIII (1963), 116–19; E.E. Elder and W. Mc E. Miller (ed. and tr.), *al-Kitāb al-aqdas or the Most Holy Book of Mīrzā Ḥusayn ʿAlī Bahā'u'llāh*, in *JRAS* (1963), 93–4; G.E. von Grunebaum, *Modern Islam, the search for cultural identity*, Berkeley and Los Angeles 1962, in *ibid.*, 114–15.

1964

18. "On the chronology of the Ziyārids in Gurgān and Ṭabaristān", *Isl.*, XL (1964), 25–34.
19. "A *maqāma* on secretaryship: al-Qalqashandī's *al-Kawākib al-durriyya fī 'l-manāqib al-badriyya*", *BSOAS*, xxvii (1964), 291–8.
20. "Some new manuscripts of al-Khwārizmī's *Mafātīḥ al-ʿulūm*", *JSS*, IX (1964), 341–5.

21. *EI* vol. II, art. "Fīl. As beasts of war".
22. Reviews of Kemal R. Faruki, *Islamic jurisprudence*, Karachi, 1382/1962, in *JRAS* (1964), 75–6; Leonard Binder, *Iran, political development in a changing nation*, Berkeley and Los Angeles 1962, in *Man*, no. 160 (July–August 1964), 127–8.

1965

23. "Language reform and nationalism in modern Turkey, a brief conspectus", *MW*, LV (1965), 58–65, 117–24.
24. "Notes on the pre-Ghaznavid history of eastern Afghanistan", *IQ*, IX (1965), 12–24.
25. "An embassy to Maḥmūd of Ghazna recorded in Q̱āḍī Ibn az-Zubair's *Kitāb adh-dhakhā'ir wa 't-tuḥaf*", *JAOS*, LXXXV (1965), 404–7.
26. (with Sir Gerard Clauson) "Al-Xwārazmī on the peoples of Central Asia", *JRAS* (1965), 2–12.
27. *EI* vol. II arts. "G̲hazna", "G̲hulām. ii. Persia"; "G̲hūr".
28. Reviews of Roderick H. Davison, *Reform in the Ottoman empire 1856–1876*, Princeton 1963, in *IQ*, IX (1965), 56–8; Arsenio Pacheco, *Historia de Jacob Xalabin*, Barcelona 1964, in *ibid.*, 58–60; J.J. Saunders, *A history of mediaeval Islam*, London 1965), in *JRAS* (1965), 149–50; S.M. Stern, *Fāṭimid decrees, original documents from the Fāṭimid chancery*, London 1964, in *JSS*, X (1965), 303–5.

1966

29. "Maḥmūd of Ghazna in contemporary eyes and later Persian literature", *Iran, JBIPS*, IV (1966), 85–92.
30. *EI* vol. III, arts. "Ḥād̲j̲ib. iii. Eastern dynasties"; "Ḥarb. v. Persia".
31. Reviews of Gianroberto Scarcia, *Ṣifat-nāma-yi Darvīš Muḥammad Ḫān-i Ġāzī. Cronaca di una crociata musulmana contro i Kafiri di Laġmān nell'anno 1582*, Serie Orientale Roma XXXII, ISMEO, Rome 1965, in *EW*, N.S. XVI (1966), 340–2.

1967

32. *The Islamic dynasties, a chronological and genealogical handbook*, Islamic Surveys 5, Edinburgh University Press 1967, pp. xviii + 245. Russian tr. P.A. Gryaznevich, *Musulmanskie dynastii*, Moscow 1971. Persian tr. Farīdūn Badrā'ī, *Silsilahā-yi khāndānhā-yi islāmī*, Tehran 1350/1971, repr. 1371/1992. Turkish tr. Erdoğan Merçil and Mehmet İpşirli, *Islâm devletleri tarihi (kronoloji ve soykütüğü elkitabı)*, Istanbul 1980. Arabic tr. Ḥusayn 'Alī al-Labūdī, *al-Usar al-ḥākima fi 'l-Islām, dirāsa fi 'l-ta'rīkh wa 'l-ansāb*, Kuwait 1992. French tr. Yves Thoraval, *Les dynasties musulmans*, Paris 1966.
33. "Military organisation under the Būyids of Persia and Iraq, *Oriens*, XVIII–XIX (1965–6), 143–67.
34. *EI* vol. III, arts. "Hiba. 1. The Caliphate"; "Hindūs̲h̲āhīs"; "Ḥiṣār. iii. Persia".
35. Reviews of J.W. Spain, *The Pathan borderland*, The Hague 1963, in *Oriens*, XVIII–XIX (1965–6), 441–3; Karl Jahn, *Rashīd al-Dīn's History of India*, The Hague 1965, in *JRAS* (1967), 44–5; Alessio Bombaci, *The Kufic inscription in Persian verses in the court of the royal palace of Mas'ūd III at Ghazni*, ISMEO, Centro Studi e Scavi Archeologici in Asia, Reports and Memoirs V, Rome 1966, in *EW*, N.S. XVII (1967), 126–7; Max Klimburg, *Afghanistan, das Land im historischen Spannungsfeld Mittelasiens*, Vienna and Munich 1966, in *JRAS* (1967), 38–9; J.A. Boyle, *Grammar of modern Persian*, Wiesbaden 1966, in *JSS*, XII (1967), 325–6.

1968

36. *Sīstān under the Arabs, from the Islamic conquest to the rise of the Ṣaffārids (30–250/651–864)*, ISMEO, Centro Studi e Scavi in Asia, Reports and Memoirs XI, Rome 1968, pp. xi + 145.
37. *The book of curious and entertaining information. The Laṭā'if al-ma'ārif of Tha'ālibī. Translated with an introduction and notes*, Edinburgh University Press 1968, pp. ix + 164.
38. Ch. 1 "The political and dynastic history of the Iranian world 1000–1217", in J.A. Boyle (ed.), *The Cambridge history of Iran. V. The Saljuq and Mongol periods*, Cambridge 1968, 1–202.
39. W. Barthold, *Turkestan down to the Mongol invasion*, third edition with an additional chapter hitherto unpublished in English translated by Mrs. T. Minorsky and edited by C.E. Bosworth, and with further Addenda and Corrigenda by C.E. Bosworth, GMS, N.S. V, London 1968, pp. xxxii + 573.
40. "The development of Persian culture under the early Ghaznavids", *Iran, JBIPS*, VI (1968), 33–44.
41. "The armies of the Ṣaffārids", *BSOAS*, XXXVI (1968), 534–54, Arabic tr. A.J. Nājī, "Jaysh al-Ṣaffāriyyīn", in *Majallat Kulliyyat al-Ādāb, Jāmi'at Baghdād* (1972), no. 7, pp. 189–261.
42. Reviews of Mary Catherine Bateson, *Arabic language handbook*, Washington D.C. 1967, in *JSS*, XIII (1968), 311–13; *Atti del terzo congresso di studi arabi e islamici, Ravello 1–6 settembre 1966*, Naples 1967, in *ibid.*, 315–16; S.M. Stern (ed.), *Documents from Islamic chanceries*, Oxford 1965, in *JRAS* (1968), 181.

1969

43. "The Ṭāhirids and Arabic culture", *JSS*, XIV (1969), 45–79.
44. "The Ṭāhirids and Persian literature", *Iran, JBIPS*, VII (1969), 103–6.
45. "Abū 'Abdallāh al-Khwārazmī on the technical terms of the secretary's art, a contribution to the administrative history of mediaeval Islam", *JESHO*, XII (1969), 113–64.
46. "An alleged embassy from the Emperor of China to the Amīr Naṣr b. Aḥmad, a contribution to Sāmānid military history", in Mujtaba Minovi and Iraj Afshar (eds.), *Yād-nāme-ye īrānī-ye Minorsky*, Tehran 1969, 17–29.
47. *EI* vol. III, art. "Īdhādj or Māl-Amīr".
48. Reviews of H. Horst, *Die Staatsverwaltung der Grosselǧūqen und Ḫorazmšāhs (1038–1231)*, Wiesbaden 1964, in *Oriens*, XX (1967) [publ. 1969], 242–4; Camille Hechaïme, *Louis Cheikho et son livre «Le christianisme et la littérature chrétienne en Arabie avant l'Islam»*, Beirut 1967, in *JSS*, XIV (1969), 136–8; Freeland Abbott, *Islam and Pakistan*, Oxford and Ithaca 1968, and W. Montgomery Watt, *What is Islam?*, London 1968, in *Asian Review*, II/2 (January 1969), 162–4.

1970

49. V. Minorsky, *Ḥudūd al-'ālam. The regions of the world, a Persian geography 372 A.H.–982 A.D.*, second edition, with the Preface by V.V. Barthold translated from the Russian and with additional material by the late Professor Minorsky, edited by C.E. Bosworth, GMS, N.S. XI, London 1970, pp. lxxxiii + 524.
50. "A propos de l'article de Mohamed Khadr, "'Deux actes de waqf d'un Qaraḫānide d'Asie Centrale'" *JA*, CCLVI (1968) [publ. 1970], 449–53.
51. "An early Arabic Mirror for Princes: Ṭāhir Dhū l-Yamīnain's epistle to his son 'Abdallāh (206/821)", *JNES*, XXIX (1970), 25–41.
52. "Dailamīs in central Iran: the Kākūyids of Jibāl and Yazd", *Iran, JBIPS*, VIII (1970), 73–95.

53. "A dramatisation of the Prophet Muḥammad's life: Henri de Bornier's *Mahomet*", *Numen*, XVII (1970), 105–17.
54. Arts. on Islamic history and historical geography in *The Encyclopedia Americana*.
55. *EI* vol. III, arts. "Ikhshīd", "Ilek-Khāns or Ḳarakhādnids", "Ildeñizids or Eldigüzids", "Ili", "Ilyāsids", "Inʿām".
56. Obituary of S.M. Stern, *Iran JBIPS*, VIII (1970), p. ix.
57. Reviews of R.M.N.E. Elahie, *The life and works of Yāqūt al-Ḥamawī*, Lahore 1965, in *IJMES*, I (1970), 184–6; Muhammad Shafi, *Wāmiq-o-Adhrā*, Lahore 1967, in *ibid.*, 186–7; Fuat Sezgin. *Geschichte der arabischen Schrifttums*. Bd. I, *Qur'ānwissenschaften – Ḥadīt – Geschichte – Fiqh – Dogmatik – Mystik, bis ca. 430 H.*, Leiden 1967, in *JSS*, XV (1970), 130–4; A.K. Sanjian, *Colophons of Armenian manuscripts 1301–1480*, Cambridge, Mass. 1979, in *ibid.*, 142–3; D. and J. Sourdel, *La civilisation de l'Islam classique*, Paris 1968, in *ibid.*, 270–1; S.J. Shaw (ed.), *International Journal of Middle East Studies*, I/1 (1970), in *ibid.*, 271–2.

1971

58. *Iran and Islam. In memory of the late Vladimir Minorsky*, ed. C.E. Bosworth, Edinburgh University Press 1971, pp. xvi + 574.
59. 'The Banū Ilyās of Kirmān (320–57/932–68)", in *ibid.*, 107–24.
60. "The Turks in the Islamic lands up to the mid-11th century, in Cl. Cahen (ed.), *Philologiae turcicae fundamenta*, III, Wiesbaden 1970 [publ. 1971], separately printed, pp. 20.
61. "Manuscripts of Thaʿālibī's *Yatīmat ad-dahr* in the Süleymaniye Library, Istanbul", *JSS*, XVI (1971), 41–9.
62. Two arts. on Turkish personages in *The McGraw-Hill Encyclopedia of World Biography*.
63. Reviews of K.M. Röhrborn, *Provinzen und Zentralgewalt Persiens im 16. und 17. Jahrhundert*, Berlin 1966, in *Oriens*, XX (1968–9) [publ. 1971], 459–60; Ataullah Mansour, *In a new light*, London 1969, in *European Judaism*, V (Winter 1970–1), 51; H.J. Kissling *et alii*, *The Muslim world, a historical survey. Part III. The last great Muslim empires*, Leiden 1969, in *MEJ*, XXV (Winter 1971), 106–7; P.M. Holt, A.K.S. Lambton and Bernard Lewis (eds.), *The Cambridge history of Islam*, 2 vols. Cambridge 1970, in *South Asian Review*, V/1 (October 1971), 79–81; E. Wiedemann, *Aufsätze zur arabischen Wissenschaftsgeschichte*, 2 vols. Hildesheim 1970, in *JSS*, XVI (1971), 277–8; Kuthayyir 'Azza and al-Ṣanawbarī, *Dīwāns*, ed. Iḥsān 'Abbās, Beirut 1971, 1970, in *ibid.*, 278–9; H. Loebenstein, *Katalog der arabischer Handschriften der österreichischen Nationalbibliothek. Neuerwerbungen 1868–1968, Teil I*, Vienna 1970, in *ibid.*, 281–2.

1972

64. J.L. Burckhardt, *Arabic proverbs*, repr. Curzon Press, London, and Rowan and Littlefield, Totowa N.J. 1972, with an introduction by C.E. Bosworth, pp. i–iii.
65. "Christian and Jewish religious dignitaries in Mamlûk Egypt and Syria: Qalqashandī's information on their hierarchy, titulature and appointment", *IJMES*, III (1972), 59–74, 199–216.
66. "Some correspondence in the John Rylands University Library concerning John Lewis Burckhardt and Lady Hester Stanhope's physician", *BJRUL*, LV/1 (Autumn 1972), 33–59.
67. "Rajā' ibn Ḥaywa and the Umayyad caliphs", *IQ*, XVI (1972), 36–80.
68. "Ṣanawbarī's elegy on the pilgrims slain in the Carmathian attack on Mecca (317/930): a literary and historical study, *Arabica*, XIX (1972), 222–39.
69. "William Lithgow: a seventeenth century traveller in the Near East", *Memoirs*

and Proceedings of the Manchester Literary and Philosophical Society, CXIV (1971–2), no. 1 [publ. 1972], 1–21.

70. Ch. "Islamic history" in Derek Hopwood and Diana Grimwood Jones (ed.), *Middle East Libraries Committee. Middle East and Islam. A bibliographical introduction*, Zug-London 1972, 55–72.
71. Reviews of H. Busse, *Chalif und Grosskönig, die Buyiden im Iraq (945–1055)*, Beirut 1969, in *al-Abḥāth*, Beirut, xxii (1969) [publ. 1972], 103–7; E.I.J. Rosenthal, *Studia Semitica*, 2 vols. Cambridge 1971, in *IQ*, XV(1971) [publ. 1972], 143–5; A.A. Abd Dixon, *The Umayyad caliphate 65–86/684–705 (a political study)*, London 1971, in *ibid.*, 208–10; M.A. Shaban, *Islamic history* A.D. *600–750 (*A.H. *132), a new interpretation*, Cambridge 1971, in *ibid.*, XVI (1972), 105–7; G. Vitestam, *Kanz al-mulūk fī kaifiyyat as-sulūk . . . ascribed to Sibṭ ibn al-Djauzī*, Lund 1970, in *JNES*, XXXI (1972), 61–3; *Serie onomasticon arabicum*, Parts 1–3, Paris 1971, in *JSS*, XVII (1972), 154–6; J. Penrice, *A dictionary and glossary of the Kor-ân*, repr. London 1971, in *ibid.*, 161–2; H.S. Karmi, *al-Manar, an Arabic-English dictionary*, London and Beirut 1970, in *ibid.*, 276; Fuat Sezgin, *Geschichte des arabischen Schrifttums*, Bd. III, *Medizin – Pharmazie – Zoologie – Tierheilkunde bis ca. 430* H., Leiden 1970; Bd. IV, *Alchimie – Chemie – Botanik – Agrikultur bis ca. 430* H., Leiden 1971, in *ibid.*, 277–9.

1973

72. "Islamic history", in D. Hopwood and Diana Grimwood-Jones (eds.), *Middle East and Islam, a bibliographical introduction*, Bibliotheca Asiatica 9, Zug 1972 [publ. 1973], 55–72.
73. "Barbarian incursions: the coming of the Turks into the Islamic world", in D.S. Richards (ed.), *Islamic civilisation 950–1150*, Papers on Islamic History III, Oxford 1973, 1–16.
74. "A Mamlūk text on the orthographical distinction of *ḍād* and *ẓā*'", *Parole d'Orient*, Kaslik, Lebanon, 111 (1972) [publ. 1973], 153–69; also in J.M. Barral (ed.), *Orientalia hispanica, sive studia F.M. Pareja octogenario dicata*, I, *Arabo-islamica*, Pars prior, Leiden 1974, 135–49.
75. "The heritage of rulership in early Islamic Iran and the search for dynastic connections with the past", *Iran JBIPS*, XI (1973), 51–62; also in *Iranian Studies*, XI (1978), 7–34.
76. "The tomb in Cairo of John Lewis Burckhardt", *JSS*, XVIII (1973), 259–66.
77. "'Ubaidallāh b. Abī Bakra and the 'Army of Destruction' in Zābulistān (79/698)", *Isl.*, L (1973), 268–83.
78. *EI* vol. IV, arts. "Isfarāyīn"; "Ismā'īl b. Aḥmad"; "Ismā'īl b. Nūḥ"; "Ismā'īl b. Sebüktigin"; "Ispahbadh"; "Ispahsālār, Sipahsālār"; "Iṣṭabl. v. Persia".
79. Reviews of Joel Carmichael, *The shaping of the Arabs: a study in ethnic identity*, London 1969, in *JRAS* (1972) [publ. 1973], 61; J. Aubin (ed.), *Le monde iranien et l'Islam*, I, Paris 1971, in *ibid.* (1973), 169–70; Simon Digby, *War-horse and elephant in the Delhi Sultanate: a study of military supplies*, Oxford 1971, in *ibid.*, 178–9; *Israel Oriental Studies*, Jerusalem, I (1971), in *JSS*, XVIII (1973), 169–74 (with T. Muraoka); Merlin S. Swartz, *Ibn al-Jawzī's Kitāb al-Quṣṣāṣ wa 'l-Mudhakkirīn*, Beirut 1971, in *ibid.*, 178–81; Hassanein Rabie, *The financial system of Egypt* A.H. *564–741/*A.D. *1169–1341*, Oxford 1972, in *EHR*, LXXXVIII, no. 348 (1973), 618–19; M. Gaudefroy-Demombynes, *Mahomet*, 2nd ed. Paris 1969, in *OLZ*, 68. Jahrgang (1973), no. 7–8, 375; P.M. Holt, A.K.S. Lambton and Bernard Lewis, *The Cambridge history of Islam*, 2 vols. Cambridge 1970, in *IQ*, XVI (1972) [publ. 1973], 205–9; F. Rosenthal, *The herb. Hashish versus medieval Muslim society*, Leiden 1971, in *ibid.*, 209–11.

1974

80. *The legacy of Islam*, second edition, edited by the late Joseph Schacht with C.E. Bosworth, Oxford 1974, Arabic translation *Turāth al-Islām*, 2 vols., Kuwait 1st ed. 1978.
81. "Islamic frontiers in Africa and Asia. (b) Central Asia", in *ibid.*, 116–30.
82. "Caliphate, Empire of the", in *Encyclopaedia Britannica*, 15th edition, Chicago 1974, *Macropaedia*, III, 623–45.
83. "The Qur'anic prophet Shuʿaib and Ibn Taimiyya's epistle concerning him", *Le Muséon*, LXXXVII/34 (1974), 425–40.
84. Obituary, "Sir Gerard Clauson (1891–1973)", in *Bull. BSMES*, I/1 (1974), 39–40.
85. *EI* vol. IV, arts. "Istiʿrāḍ, ʿArḍ"; "al-Ḳabḳ"; "Kābul"; "Kābulistān"; "Ḳābūs b. Wushmagīr b. Ziyār".
86. Reviews of Ludwig W. Adamec, *Afghanistan 1900–1923, a diplomatic history*, Berkeley and Los Angeles 1967, in *Oriens*, XXIII–XXIV (1970) [publ. 1974], 542–4; S.D. Goitein, *A Mediterranean society. The Jewish societies of the Arab world as portrayed in the documents of the Cairo geniza*, I, *Economic foundations*, Berkeley and Los Angeles and Cambridge 1967, in *OLZ*, 69. Jahrgang (1974), no. 3–4, 168–9; P.M. Holt, *Studies in the history of the Near East*, London 1973, in *BSOAS*, XXX (1974), 223; Ḥasan-i Fasāʾī, *Fārs-nāma-yi Nāṣirī*, tr. H. Busse, *History of Persia under Qājār rule*, New York and London 1972, in *IQ*, XVII (1973) [publ. 1974], 102–4; H. Gaube, *Arabosasanidische Numismatik*, Handbuch der mittelasiatischen Numismatik Bd. II, Brunswick 1973, in *JSS*, XIX (1974), 135–7; J.D. Pearson and Ann Walsh, *Index Islamicus, Third Supplement 1966–70*, London 1972, in *ibid.*, 319–20; Sir Hamilton Gibb, *The life of Saladin from the works of ʿImād ad-Dīn and Bahāʾ ad-Dīn*, Oxford 1973, in *ibid.*, 320; Thābit b. Sinān *et alii*, *Taʾrīkh akhbār al-Qarāmiṭa*, ed. Suhayl Zakkār, Beirut 1391/1971, in *al-Abḥāth*, XXIV (1971) [publ. 1974], 148–9.

1975

87. *A catalogue of accessions to the Arabic manuscripts in the John Rylands University Library of Manchester, with indices*, Manchester 1974 [publ. 1975], pp. 85.
88. Chs. 3 and 5, "The Ṭāhirids and Ṣaffārids" and "The early Ghaznavids" in R.N. Frye (ed.), *The Cambridge history of Iran., IV. From the Arab invasion to the Saljuqs*, Cambridge 1975, 90–135 and 162–97.
89. "Recruitment, muster and review in medieval Islamic armies", in V.J. Parry and M.E. Yapp (eds.), *War, technology and society in the Middle East*, London 1975, 59–77.
90. "Henry Salt, Consul in Egypt 1816–27 and pioneer Egyptologist", *BJRUL*, LVII (Autumn 1974) [publ. 1975], 69–91.
91. *EI* vol. IV, arts. "Kāfiristān"; "Kākūyids"; "al-Ḳalkashandī"; "Ḳandahār"; "Ḳanghlï"; "Kannanūr"; "Kānpur"; "Ḳarā Bāgh"; "Ḳarā Khiṭāy"; "Ḳarā-Köl".
92. Reviews of Heinz Gaube, *Ein arabischer Palast in Südsyrien, Ḫirbet el-Baiḍa*, Beirut 1974, in *JSS*, XX (1975), 130–1; Bernard Lewis, *Race and color in Islam*, New York 1971, in *ibid.*, 133; al-Balādhurī, *Ansāb al-ashrāf*, IVA, ed. Max Schloessinger and M.J. Kister, Jerusalem 1971, in *ibid.*, 270–1; Dickran K. Kouymjian (ed.), *Near Eastern numismatics, iconography, epigraphy and history. Studies in honor of George C. Miles*, Beirut 1974, in *ibid.*, 281–3; J. Riley-Smith, *The feudal nobility and the Kingdom of Jerusalem*, London 1973, in *IQ*, XVII (1973) [publ. 1975], 185–7; Heinz Gaube, *Die südpersische Provinz Arraǧān/Kūh Gīlūyeh*, Vienna 1973, in *ibid.*, 184–5; R.W. Bulliett, *The patricians of Nishapur, a study in medieval Islamic social history*, Cambridge, Mass. and London 1972, in *ibid.*, XVIII (1974) [publ. 1975], 47–8; Bernard Lewis (ed. and tr.), *Islam, from the Prophet Muhammad to the capture*

of Constantinople. I. Politics and war. II. Religion and society, New York 1974, in *ibid.*, 48–50; Sir George Robertson, *The Kafirs of the Hindu-Kush*, repr. Karachi 1974, in *ibid.*, 50–1.

1976

93. *The mediaeval Islamic underworld, the Banū Sāsān in Arabic society and literature, Part 1. The Banū Sāsān in Arabic life and lore*, Leiden 1976, pp. xiv + 1–179 + *11, Part 2. *The Arabic jargon texts.* The Qaṣīda sāsaniyyas *of Abū Dulaf and Ṣafī d-Dīn*, Leiden 1976, pp. vii + 181–361 (English), pp. 1–100 (Arabic) + 4 pp. facsimiles.
94. Ch. 2, "The historical background of Islamic civilisation", in R.M. Savory (ed.), *Introduction to Islamic civilisation*, Cambridge 1976, 15–31.
95. Ch. 8, "Armies of the Prophet: strategy, tactics and weapons in Islamic warfare", in Bernard Lewis (ed.), *The world of Islam. Faith, people, culture*, London and New York 1976, 201–24.
96. "The Khwarazmian historical background to Bīrūnī's life", in *The commemoration volume of Biruni International Congress in Tehran. B. English and French papers*, Tehran 1976, 11–27.
97. "The Kūfichīs or Qufṣ in Persian history", in *Iran, JBIPS*, XIV (1976), 9–17.
98. "The Prophet vindicated: a Restoration treatise on Islam and Muhammad", *Religion, a Journal of Religion and Religions*, VI (1976), 1–12.
99. "The Arabic manuscripts in Chetham's Library, Manchester", *JSS*, XXI (1976), 99–108.
100. "Rudyard Kipling in India", *Arbeitspapiere, Betriebswirtschaftliches Institut der Friedrich-Alexander Universität Erlangen-Nürnberg*, 1976, pp. 25.
101. *EI* vol. IV, arts. "Ḳarluḳ"; "Karrāmiyya"; "al-Ḳāshānī"; "Kath".
102. Reviews of J. Prušek, *Dictionary of oriental literatures*, 3 vols., London 1974, in *JSS*, XXI (1976), 205–6; J.D. Pearson. *A bibliography of pre-Islamic Persia*, London 1975, in *ibid.*, 206–7; Fuat Sezgin, *Geschichte des arabischen Schrifttums*, Bd. V, *Mathematik bis ca. 430 H.*, Leiden 1974, in *ibid.*, 214; F.E. Peters, *Allah's commonwealth*, New York 1973, in *ibid.*, 228.

1977

103. *The later Ghaznavids, splendour and decay. The dynasty in Afghanistan and northern India 1040–1186*, Edinburgh 1977. Reprinted Munshiram Manohavlal, Delhi 1992.
104. *The medieval history of Iran, Afghanistan and Central Asia*, Variorum Reprints, London 1977, pp. iv + 374.
105. "Orientalism and orientalists", in Diana Grimwood-Jones *et alii* (eds.), *Arabic Islamic bibliography. The Middle East Library Committee guide*, Hassocks, Sussex 1977, 148–56.
106. "Al-Jabartī and the Frankish archaeologists", *IJMES*, VIII (1977), 229–36.
107. "Jewish elements, in the Banū Sāsān", *BiOr*, XXXIII/5–6 (Sept.–Nov. 1976) [1977], 289–94.
108. "The Tübingen Atlas of the Near East", *Bull. BSMES*, IV (1977), 115–16.
109. *EI* vol. IV, arts. "Khʷāf"; "Khaladj i. History"; "Khalkhāl".
110. Reviews of M. Mitchiner, *The multiple dirhams of medieval Afghanistan*, Sanderstead, Surrey 1973, in *JRAS* (1977), 124–5; Fuat Sezgin, *Geschichte des islamischen Schrifttums. Bd. II. Poesie bis ca. 430 H.*, Leiden 1975, in *JSS*, XXII (1977), 234–5; Titus Burckhardt, *Art of Islam: language and meaning*, and Ayşe Parman, *Geometric concepts in Islamic art*, London 1976, in *ibid.*, 245–7; Robert Attal (ed.), *A bibliography of the writings of Professor Shelomo Dov Goitein*, Jerusalem 1975, in *ibid.*, 247; Ch. Pellat, *Ibn al-Muqaffaʿ, mort vers 140/757, «Conseiller» du calife*,

Paris 1976, in *ibid.*, 253–4; E. Ashtor, *A social and economic history of the Near East in the Middle Ages*, London 1976, in *EHR*, XCII, no. 364 (1977), 638–9; Wolfgang Behn, *The Kurds in Iran, a selected and annotated bibliography*, London and Munich 1977, in *Bull. BSMES*, IV (1977), 121–2; M.A. Shaban, *Islamic history, a new interpretation. 2. A.D. 750–1055 (A.H. 132–448)*, Cambridge 1976, in *TLS* (21.7.77), 84.

1978

111. "William Lithgow of Lanark's travels in North Africa 1615–16", *JSS*, XXIII (1978) [= *Studies in honour of F.F. Bruce*], 199–215.
112. "Al-Ḫwārazmī on theology and sects: the chapter on *kalām* in the *Mafātīḥ al-ʿulūm*", *BEO*, XXIX (1977) [1978] (= *Mélanges offerts à Henri Laoust*), 85–95.
113. *EI* vol. IV, arts. "Khārān"; "Kh^{w}ārazm"; "Kh^{w}ārazm-Shāhs"; "Khāṣṣ Oda"; "Khaybar"; "Khayma. iv. In Central Asia"; "Khayrpūr"; "Khāzin"; "al-Khazradjī".
114. Reviews of J. Sadan, *Le mobilier au Proche Orient médiéval*, Leiden 1976, in *JSS*, XXIII (1978), 141–2; M.W. Dols, *The Black Death in the Middle East*, Princeton 1977, in *MESA Bull.*, XII (1978), 41–2.

1979

115. "Al-Maqrīzī's exposition of the formative period in Islamic history and its cosmic significance: the *Kitāb an-Nizāʿ wa 't-takhāṣum*", in Alford T. Welch and Pierre Cachia (eds.), *Islam: past influence and present challenge. In honour of William Montgomery Watt*, Edinburgh 1979, 93–104.
116. "The 'Protected Peoples' (Christians and Jews) in mediaeval Egypt and Syria", *BJRUL*, LXII/1 (Autumn 1979), 11–36.
117. "The interaction of Arabic and Persian culture in the 10th and 11th centuries", *al-Abḥāth*, XXVII (1978–9) [1979], 59–75.
118. Obituary, "Professor J.A. Boyle", in *Iran, JBIPS*, XVII (1979), pp. i–ix.
119. *EI* vol. V, arts. "Kherla"; "Khokand"; "Khōst"; "Khudjand"; "Khudjistān"; "Khulm"; "Khurāsān"; "Khuttalān"; "Kilāt"; "Kimäk"; "Ḳimār".
120. Reviews of D. Grimwood-Jones, D. Hopwood and J.D. Pearson (eds.), *Arabic Islamic bibliography*, Hassocks, Sussex and Highland, N.J. 1977, in *JSS*, XXIV (1979), 134; A.J. Cameron, *Abû Dharr al-Ghifârî. An examination of his place in the hagiography of Islam*, London 1973, in *ibid.*, 145–6; J.D. Pearson (compiler), *Index islamicus, Fourth Supplement 1971–1975*, London 1977, in *ibid.*, 318; J. Landau, *Abdul-Hamid's Palestine*, Jerusalem 1979, in *BSOAS*, XLII (1979), 591; "Man's religious Quest: a review of Open University materials, section on Islam", in *Religion*, IX (1979), 132–5; George Lenczkowski (ed.), *Iran under the Pahlavis*, Stanford 1978, in *International Journal, Canadian Institute of International Affairs, Toronto* (1979), 512–13; Gustav Meiseles, *Reference literature to Arabic Studies, a bibliographical guide*, Tel Aviv 1978, in *Bull. BSMES*, VI (1979), 138–40.

1980

121. "The nomenclature of the Persian Gulf", in A.J. Cottrell (General Ed.), C.E. Bosworth, R.M. Burrell, K. McLachlan and R.M. Savory (eds.), *The Persian Gulf states. A general survey*, Baltimore and London 1980, pp. xvii–xxxiv.
122. "The poetical citations in Baihaqī's *Taʾrīkh-i Masʿūdī*", *XX. Deutscher Orientalistentag . . . 1977 in Erlangen. Vorträge* = Suppl. IV to ZDMG, Wiesbaden 1980, 41–56.
123. "The influence of Arabic literature on English literature", *Azure*, no. 5 (Spring 1980), 14–19; Arabic tr., "Taʾthīr al-adab al-ʿarabī fi 'l-adab al-inkilīzī", *al-Maʿrifa*, Damascus, nos. 191–2 (February 1978), 199–215.

124. *EI* Vol. V, arts. "Kis̲h̲"; "Ḳi̊s̲h̲laḳ"; "Ḳisma"; "Ḳi̊z"; "Ḳi̊zi̊l"; "Ḳum"; "Kōhāt"; "Körfüz"; "Kōtwāl"; "Koyl"; "Ḳozan-Og̲h̲ullari̊"; "Ḳubād̲h̲iyān"; "Ḳūčān"; "Ḳufṣ"; "Kūh-i Bābā"; "Ḳuhrūd"; "Ḳūla"; "Ḳūlam"; "Ḳuld̲j̲a"; "Kumīd̲j̲īs"; "Ḳūmis". *Supplement*: "ʿAbd al-Raḥmān b. Ḥassān"; "Arg̲h̲iyān"; "Aʿyās"; "Bādgīr"; "Bād̲h̲ām"; "al-Bad̲h̲d̲h̲"; "Bahāʾ al-Dawla"; "Banīd̲j̲ūrids"; "Bāriz, D̲j̲abal".

125. Reviews of A.J. Butler, *The Arab conquest of Egypt and the last thirty years of the Roman dominion*, 2nd edn., Oxford 1978, in *JSS*, XXV (1980), 126–7; Qāsim al-Sāmarrāʾī (ed.), *al-Thaʿālibī, Laṭāʾif al-ẓurafāʾ*, Leiden 1978, in *ibid.*, 136–7; J. Brugman and F. Schröder, *Arabic studies in the Netherlands*, Leiden 1979, in *ibid.*, 303–4; Max van Berchem, *Opera minora*, 2 vols., Geneva 1978, in *BSOAS*, XLIII (1980), 139–40; J. Richard, *La Papauté et les missions d'Orient au moyen âge (XIII–XIV siècles)*, Rome 1977, in *EHR*, XCV, no. 375 (April 1980), 410; F. Rosenthal, *Gambling in Islam*, Leiden 1975, in *OLZ*, LXXV/5 (1980), 468–9; J. Lassner, *The shaping of ʿAbbasid rule*, Princeton 1980, in *TLS*, 19.9.80, 1042.

1981

126. *Al-Maqrīzī's "Book of contention and strife concerning the relations between the Banū Umayya and the Banū Hāshim"*, JSS Monograph no. 3, Manchester n.d. [1981].

127. "The terminology of the history of the Arabs in the Jāhiliyya, according to Khwārazmī's 'Keys of the sciences'", in S. Morag, I. Ben-Ami and N.A. Stillman (eds.), *Studies in Judaism and Islam presented to Shelomo Dov Goitein on the occasion of his eightieth birthday*, Jerusalem 1981, English vol., 27–43.

128. "Al-Maqrīzī's epistle 'Concerning what has come down to us about the Banū Umayya and the Banū 'l-ʿAbbās'", in Widād al-Qāḍī (ed.), *Studia Arabica et Islamica. Festschrift for Iḥsān ʿAbbās on his sixtieth birthday*, Beirut 1981, 39–45.

129. "The rulers of Chaghāniyān in early Islamic times", *Iran, JBIPS*, XIX (1981), 1–20.

130. "A mediaeval Islamic prototype of the fountain-pen?", *JSS*, XXVI (1981), 229–34.

131. "Some observations on Jerusalem Arabic inscriptions (ad Levant XI (1979), 112–37", *Levant*, XIII (1981), 266–7.

132. *EI* Vol. V, arts. "Ḳun"; "Ḳunduz"; "al-Ḳunfud̲h̲a"; "Ḳungrāt"; "al-Kurd̲j̲"; "Ḳurḥ"; "Ḳurra b. S̲h̲arīk"; "Kurram". *Supplement*: "Bas̲h̲kard"; "Biyār"; "Buḳʿa"; "Dabīr"; "Dabūsiyya"; "Dandānḳān"; "D̲h̲āt al-Ṣawārī"; "D̲h̲ikrīs"; "D̲j̲ād̲j̲arm"; "D̲j̲alālābād"; "D̲j̲and".

133. Art. "Bettlerwesen. IV. Islamische Welt", *Lexikon des Mittelalters*, Band 2, Lieferung 1, Munich 1981.

134. Reviews of Afaf Lutfi al-Sayyid Marsot (ed.), *Society and the sexes in medieval Islam*, Malibu 1979, in *JRAS* (1981), 77–8; B.G. Bloomfield (ed.), *Middle East studies and libraries. A felicitation volume for Professor J.D. Pearson*, London 1980, in *ibid.*, 207; M.J.L. Young, *Catalogue of oriental manuscripts. VII*, Leeds [1979–80], in *JSS*, XXVI (1981), 141; Fuat Sezgin, *Geschichte des arabischen Schrifttums*, Bd VI. *Astronomie bis ca. 430 H.*, Leiden 1978, in *ibid.*, 141–2; B. Lewin, *A vocabulary of the Hud̲ailian poems*, Gothenburg 1978, in *ibid.*, 147–8; J. Spencer Trimingham, *The influence of Islam upon Africa*, 2nd edn. London, New York and Beirut 1980, in *ibid.*, 167; Heinz Gaube, *Arabische Inschriften aus Syrien*, Beirut and Wiesbaden 1978, in *BSOAS*, XLIV (1981), 369–70; Elizabeth M. Sartain, *Jalāl al-Dīn al-Suyūṭī. I. Biography and background. II. "Al-Taḥadduth bi niʿmat allāh"*, Cambridge 1975, in *OLZ*, LXXVI no. 3 (1981), 266–8; Dorothee Metlizki, *The matter of Araby in mediaeval England*, New Haven and London 1977, in *ibid.*, LXXVI no. 6 (1981), 564–5; A.G. Walls and Amal Abu 'l-Hajj, *Arabic inscriptions in Jerusalem, a handlist and maps*, London 1980, in *Azure*, no. 8 (1981), 43.

1982

135. *Medieval Arabic culture and administration*, Collected Studies CS 165, Variorum Reprints, London 1982, pp. iii + 358.
136. "The concept of *Dhimma* in early Islam", in B. Braude and Bernard Lewis (eds.), *Christians and Jews in the Ottoman empire, the functioning of a plural society*, New York and London 1982, I, 37–51.
137. "James Elroy Flecker's vision of the East", *Azure*, no. 11 (1982), 10–14.
138. *EI* Vol. V, arts. "Ḳuṣdār"; "Kutāhya"; "Ḳutayba b. Muslim"; "Ḳut̲h̲am b. al-ʿAbbās"; "Kwatta"; "Laḳab". *Supplement*: "D̲j̲irga"; "Ekinči b. Ḳočkar"; "Eličpur"; "Fak̲h̲r-i Mudabbir"; "Faḳīr of Ipi"; "Fasāʾī"; "Fayd"; "Firrīm"; "al-G̲h̲iṭrīf"; "Gūmāl"; "al-G̲h̲azzī"; "Gurčānī"; "Hazārad̲j̲āt"; "Hazāras"; "Ḥudūd al-ʿālam"; "al-Ḥusaynī"; "Ibn al-Balk̲h̲ī"; "Ibn Dārust"; "Ibn Farīg̲h̲ūn"; "Ibn Nāẓir al-D̲j̲ays̲h̲"; "Ibn Saʿdān"; "Īlāḳ".
139. *EIr*, vol. I, arts. "Āb-e Istāda"; "Ābāda"; "Abarqūh. 1. History"; "Abaskūn"; "ʿAbbasid caliphate in Iran"; "ʿAbd-al-Ḥamīd b. Aḥmad"; "ʿAbd-al-Malek b. Nūḥ"; "ʿAbd-al-Malek b. Nūḥ b. Naṣr"; "ʿAbd-al-Rašīd, Abū Manṣūr"; "ʿAbd-al-Razzāq Maymandī"; "ʿAbdallāh b. Ṭāher"; "ʿĀbedī"; "Abhar"; "Abharī"; "Abīvard".
140. *DMA*, vol. I, arts. "Alamūt"; "Alpigin".
141. Reviews of G.E. von Grunebaum, *Themes in medieval Arabic literature*, ed. D.S. Wilson, London 1981, in *JRAS* (1982), 55; R. Peters (ed.), *Proceedings of the Ninth Congress of the Union Européenne des Arabisants et Islamisants*, Amsterdam 1978, Leiden 1981, in *ibid.*, 191; Peter B. Golden, *Khazar studies. An historico-philological enquiry into the origins of the Khazars*, Budapest 1980, in *BSOAS*, XLV (1982), 179; Daniel Pipes, *Slave soldiers and Islam. The genesis of a military system*, New Haven 1981, in *AHR*, LXXXVII/1 (April 1982), 508–9; *Occident et Orient au Xe siècle. Actes du IXe Congrès de la Société des Historiens Médiévistes . . . (Dijon, 2–4 juin 1978)*, Paris 1979, in *EHR*, XCVII, no. 383 (April 1982), 401–2.

1983

142. Ch. 16, "Iran and the Arabs before Islam", in Ehsan Yarshater (ed.), *The Cambridge history of Iran. III. The Seleucid, Parthian and Sasanian periods*, Part 1, Cambridge 1983, 593–612.
143. Ch. 23, "The Persian impact on Arabic literature", in A.F.L. Beeston *et alii* (eds.), *The Cambridge history of Arabic literature. Arabic literature to the end of the Umayyad period*, Cambridge 1983, 483–96.
144. "Ǧihād in Afghanistan and Muslim India", in Joel L. Kraemer and Ilai Alon (eds.), *Religion and government in the world of Islam. Proceedings of the colloquium held at Tel Aviv University 3–5 June 1979* (= *IOS*, X (1980) [publ. 1983]), 149–58.
145. "William Lithgow of Lanark's travels in Greece and Turkey, 1609–11", *BJRUL*, LXV/2 (Spring 1983), 8–36.
146. *EI* vol. V, arts. "Lamg̲h̲ānāt"; "Lanbasar"; "Las Bēla"; "Las̲h̲kar-i Bāzār"; "Lawḥ"; "Linga"; "Liṣṣ".
147. *EIr* vol. I, arts. "Abnāʾ"; "Abū Aḥmad b. Abī Bakr"; "Abu 'l-ʿAlāʾ ʿAṭāʾ"; "Abū ʿAlī Aḥmad b. Sādān"; "Abū ʿAlī Dāmġānī"; "Abū Bakr b. Ṣāleḥ"; "Abū Esḥāq Ebrāhīm"; "Abu 'l-Fatḥ Yūsof"; "Abu 'l-Fazl Tāǰ al-Dīn"; "Abu 'l-Ḥasan Esfarāʾinī"; "Abu 'l-Ḥasan Kāteb"; "Abū Kālīǰār Garšāsp I and II"; "Abū Manṣūr Farāmarz"; "Abū Naṣr Aḥmad"; "Abū Naṣr Fāmī"; "Abū Naṣr Fārsīī"; "Abū ʿObayda Maʿmar"; "Abu 'l-Q̲āsem ʿAlī b. Ḥasan"; "Abū Sahl K̲ojanda"; "Abū Ṣāleḥ Manṣūr b. Esḥāq"; "Ādāb al-ḥarb wa 'l-Šaǰāʿa"; "Adab al-Kāteb".
148. *DMA*, vol. III, art. "Commander of the Faithful".

149. Arts. on Islamic history and historical geography in *The Encyclopedia Americana.*
150. Reviews of C.H. Beckingham, *Between Islam and Christendom,* London 1983, in *JSS,* XXVIII (1983), 381–2; R. Israeli (ed.), *The public diary of President Sadat,* 3 parts, Leiden 1979, in *ibid.,* 388–9; J.D. Pearson (comp.), *Index islamicus 1976–80,* 2 vols., London 1983, in *ibid.,* 389; Chr. Décobert and Denis Gril, *Linteaux à épigraphes à l'oasis de Dakhla* (= Suppl. aux Annales Islamologiques, cahier no. 1), Cairo 1981, in *JRAS* (1983), 104; Hugh Kennedy, *The Abbasid caliphate, a political history,* London and Totowa, N.J. 1981, in *EHR,* XCVIII, no. 388 (July 1983), 652–3; H.H. Roemer and A. Noth (eds.), *Studien zur Geschichte und Kultur des Vorderen Orients. Festschrift für Bertold Spuler zum siebigsten Geburtstag,* Leiden 1981, in *MESA Bull.,* XVII/1 (July 1983), 68; Susan J. Staffa, *Conquest and fusion. The social evolution of Cairo A.D. 642–1850,* Leiden 1977, in *OLZ,* LXXVIII no. 1 (1983), 58–9; H.R. Idris and K. Röhrborn, *Regierung und Verwaltung des Vorderen Orients in islamischer Zeit* (= Hdbuch. der Orientalistik, Abt. 1, Bd. 6, Abschn. 5, Teil 1), in *ibid.,* LXXVIII no. 5, 476.

1984

151. *Qajar Iran, political, social and cultural change 1800–1925. Studies presented to Professor L.P. Elwell-Sutton,* ed. Edmund Bosworth and Carole Hillenbrand, Edinburgh University Press, Edinburgh 1984, pp. xxv + 414 (Foreword by E.B., pp. xiii–xvi).
152. W. Barthold, *An historical geography of Iran,* tr. Svat Soucek, edited with an introduction by C.E. Bosworth, Modern Classics in Near Eastern Studies, Princeton U.P., Princeton 1984, pp. xv + 285.
153. "Madyan Shuʿayb in pre-Islamic and early Islamic lore and history", *JSS,* XXIX (1984), 53–64.
154. "An early Persian Ṣūfī: Shaykh Abū Saʿīd of Mayhanah", in R.M. Savory and D.A. Agius (eds.), *Logos islamikos. Studia islamica in honorem Georgii Michaelis Wickens,* Pontifical Institute of Mediaeval Studies, Toronto 1984, 79–96.
155. "The coming of Islam to Afghanistan", in Y. Friedmann (ed.), *Islam in Asia. I. South Asia,* Jerusalem 1984, 1–22.
156. "Les études islamiques et historiques en Grande-Bretagne, aux Etats-Unis et au Canada", *CT,* XXX, nos. 121–2 (1982) [publ. 1984], 235–50.
157. Arts. on Islam in John R. Hinnells (ed.), *The Penguin dictionary of religions,* Allen Lane, London 1984 (91 entries).
158. *EI* vol. V, arts. "Mā warā al-nahr. 2. History"; "Maʿalt͟hāyā".
159. *EIr* vol. I, arts. "Afšīn"; "Aḥmad b. Asad"; "Aḥmad b. Fażlān"; "Aḥmad b. Moḥammad b. K͟alaf"; "Aḥmad b. Moḥammad b. Ṭāher"; "Aḥmad b. Neẓām al-Molk"; "Aḥmad b. Qodām"; "Aḥmad b. Sahl b. Hāšem"; "Aḥmad Inaltigin"; "Aḥmad K͟oǰestānī"; "Aḥmad Šīrāzī"; "Aḥrār"; "Aḥsan al-taqāsem"; "Ahvāz. i. History"; "ʿAǰā'eb al-mak͟lūqāt. i. Arabic works"; "Aǰam"; "Ak͟bār al-dawla al-salǰūqīya"; "al-Ak͟bār al-ṭewāl"; "Ak͟lāṭ. i. History"; "Ak͟sīkat͟"; "Āl-e Afrāsīāb"; "Āl-e Afrīḡ"; "Āl-e Borhān"; "Āl-e Elyās"; "Āl-e Farīḡūn"; "Āl-e Ma'mūn"; "Āl-e Moḥtāǰ"; "ʿAlā' al-Dawla ʿAlī"; "ʿAlā' al-Dawla Moḥammad"; "ʿAlā' al-Dīn ʿAlī"; "ʿAlā' al-Dīn Atsïz"; "ʿAlā' al-Dīn Ḥosayn J̌ahānsūz"; "ʿAlā' al-Dīn Moḥammad".
160. Review of ʿAbd al-Raḥmān Muḥammad al-Tawwāb, *Stèles islamiques de la nécropole d'Assouan, II (nos. 151–300),* Cairo 1982, in *JRAS* (1984), 124–5.

1985

161. *EI* vol. V, arts. "Ma'āt͟hir al-umarā'", "Mābeyn"; "Mad͟hḥid͟j"; "Mad͟jd al-Dawla"; "Madyan S͟huʿayb"; "Māhīm"; "Mahisur. 1. Geography and history".

162. *EIr* vol. I, arts. "ʿAlī b. Farāmarz"; "ʿAlī b. Ḥarb"; "ʿAlī b. Maʾmūn"; "ʿAlī b. Masʿūd"; ʿAlī b. ʿObaydallāh"; "ʿAlī Qarīb"; "ʿAlītigin"; "Alptigin"; "Altuntaš"; "ʿĀmel"; "ʿAmīd, Abu ʿAbdallāh"; "Amīr"; "Amīr-i Ḥaras"; "Amīr al-Omarā'. I. The early period"; "Amīrak Bayhaqī"; "Āmol. I. History"; "Āmol (Āmūya)"; "ʿAmr b. Layṯ"; "ʿAmr b. Yaʿqūb".
163. *DMA*, vol. V, arts. "Games, Islamic"; "Ghāzān (Khan), Mahmūd"; "Ghaznavids"; "Ghūrids". Vol. VI, art. "Islamic administration".
164. Reviews of D.O. Morgan (ed.), *Medieval historical writing in the Christian and Islamic worlds*, London 1982, in *JRAS* (1985), 77–8; P.M. Holt (tr.), *The memoirs of a Syrian prince, Abu 'l-Fidā', Sultan of Ḥamāh (672–732/1273–1331)*, Wiesbaden 1983, in *ibid.*, 193–4; Barbara D. Metcalf (ed.), *Moral conduct and authority. The place of* adab *in South Asian Islam*, Berkeley, Los Angeles and London 1984, in *Asian Affairs*, XVI (1985), 319–20.

1986

165. "The land of Palestine in the late Ottoman period as mirrored in Western guide books", *Bull. BSMES*, XIII/1 (1986), 36–44.
166. Ch. "Islamic history", in Paul Auchterlonie (ed.), *Middle East Libraries Committee. Middle East and Islam. A bibliographical introduction, Supplement 1977–1983*, Zug 1986, 29–33.
167. *EI* vol. VI, arts. "Maḥmūd b. Muḥammad b. Malik-Shāh"; "Maḥmūd b. Sebüktigin"; "Maḥmūd Yalawač"; "Māhūr" (with J. Burton-Page); "Mākān b. Kākī".
168. *EIr* vol. II, arts. "Anārak"; "Anbār"; "ʿAnbarī"; "ʿAnbarīān"; "Andeǰān"; "Anūšervān b. Ḵāled"; "Anūšervān b. Manūčehr"; "Anūštigin Garčaʾī; "ʿAqdā"; "ʿArab. i. Arabs and Iran in the pre-Islamic period"; "Arāk. i. History"; "Araxes. ii. Historical perspective"; "Ardabīl. i. History"; "Ardakān-e Fārs"; "Ardakān-e Yazd"; "Ardašīr-e Ḵorra"; "ʿĀreż".
169. *DMA* vol. VII, art. "Kurds".
170. Reviews of Yūsuf Rāġib, *Marchands d'étoffes du Fayyoum au IIIe à IXe siècle d'après leur archives (Actes et lettres). I. Les actes des Banū ʿAbd al-Muʾmin*, Cairo 1982, in *OLZ*, LXXXI, no. 5 (1986), 484–5; Martin Strohmeier, *Seldschukische Geschichte und türkische Geschichtswissenschaft. Die Seldschuken im Urteil moderner türkischer Historiker*, Berlin 1984, in *MESA Bull.*, XX (1986), 84–5.

1987

171. *The History of al-Ṭabarī. An annotated translation.* Vol. XXXII. *The reunification of the ʿAbbāsid Caliphate. The Caliphate of al-Maʾmūn* A.D. *812–833/*A.H. *198–213*, State University of New York Press, Albany 1987, pp. xvii + 281.
172. E.W. Lane, *Arabian society in the Middle Ages*, repr. Curzon Press, London, and Humanities Press, Totowa N.J. 1987, with an introduction by C.E. Bosworth, pp. v–vii.
173. R.A. Nicholson, *Translations of eastern poetry and prose*, repr. Curzon Press, London, and Humanities Press, Totowa N.J. 1987, with an introduction by C.E. Bosworth, pp. vii–ix.
174. "James Elroy Flecker: poet, diplomat, orientalist", *BJRUL*, LXIX/2 (Spring 1987), 359–78.
175. "The Byzantine defence system in Asia Minor and the first Arab incursions", in M.A. Bakhit (ed.), *Proceedings of the Second Symposium on the history of Bilād al-Shām during the early Islamic period up to 40* A.H.*/660* A.D. *The Fourth International Conference on the history of Bilād al-Shām (English and French papers)*, I, Amman 1987, 116–24.

176. *EI* vol. VI, arts. "Makka. 2. From the 'Abbāsid to the modern period" (with A.J. Wensinck); "Makrān"; "al-Malik al-'Azīz"; "al-Malik al-Raḥīm"; "Malik-Shāh"; "Ma'mūn b. Muḥammad".
177. *EIr* vol. II, arts. "'Arż, Dīvān-e"; "Arzenjān"; "Asad b. Sāmānkodā"; "Asadābād"; "Aš'arī"; "Asāwera"; "Asb. iv. In Afghanistan"; "Asfār b. Šīrūya"; "Asfezār"; "Asfījāb"; "'Askar Mokram"; "Astarābād. i. History"; Aštīān"; "Āṯār al-belād". In vol. III, arts. "Atrak"; "Atsïz Ğarča'ī"; "Āva".
178. Reviews of Shaikha Haya Ali Al Khalifa and Michael Rice (eds.), *Bahrain through the ages: the archaeology*, London and New York 1986, in *Archaeology Today* (March 1987), 46; 'Afīf 'Abd al-Raḥmān, *Mu'jam al-shu'arā' al-jāhiliyyīn wa 'l-mukhaḍramīn*, [Beirut] 1403/1983, and *Mu'jam al-amthāl al-'arabiyya al-qadīma*, [Beirut] 1405/1985, in *JSS*, XXXII (1987), 219–20; Ahmed Hebbo, *Die Fremdwörter in der arabischer Prophetenbiographie des Ibn Hischam (gest. 218/834)*, Frankfurt 1984, in *ibid.*, 220–1; Fuat Sezgin, *Geschichte des arabischen Schrifttums*, Bd. IX, *Grammatik, bis ca. 430 H.*, Leiden 1984, in *ibid.*, 384–5; Peter Clark, *Marmaduke Pickthall, British Muslim*, London 1986, and Marmaduke Pickthall, *Saïd the fisherman*, in *ibid.*, 395–6.

1988

179. "The Arabic manuscripts", in Margaret Gibson and Susan M. Wright (eds.), *Joseph Mayer of Liverpool, 1803–1886* (Society of Antiquaries of London, Occasional Papers (New Series), XI), London 1988, 162–4.
180. *EI* vol. VI, arts. "Mangrōl"; "Mānī b. Fāttik"; "Manōhar"; "Marāfiḳ"; "Marand" (wih V. Minorsky).
181. *EIr* vol. III, arts. "Āzādbeh b. Bānegān"; "Āzādvār"; "Azerbaijan. iv. Islamic history to 1941"; "Baban"; "Bādgīs"; "Bāfq"; "Bahrāmšāh"; "Bājarrān"; "Bākarz"; "Balāḏorī"; "Bal'amī, Abu 'l-Fażl Moḥammad"; "Balāsāgūn. ii. In the Islamic period"; "Balāsānī"; "Balk. ii. History from the Arab conquest to the Mongols"; "Banākaṯ"; "Banū Sāsān"; "Barda and bardadārī. iii. In the Islamic period up to the Mongol invasion. v. Military slavery in Islamic Iran"; "Barda'a".
182. *DMA* vol. X, art. "Saffārids". Vol. XI, arts. "Sebüktigin"; "Seljuks of Rūm"; "Tāhir ibn al-Husain"; "Tāhirids".
183. Reviews of 'Abd al-Raḥmān Muḥammad 'Abd al-Tawwāb, *Stèles islamiques de la nécropole d'Assouan, III (nos. 301–450)*, Cairo 1986, in *JRAS* (1988), 170–1; J.J. Witkam (ed.), *Manuscripts of the Middle East. A journal devoted to the study of handwritten materials of the Middle East*, I, Leiden 1986, in JSS, XXXIII (1988), 314–17; Widād al-Qāḍī, *Bishr b. Abi 'l-Kubār al-Balawī, numūdhaj min al-nathr al-fannī al-mubakkir fi 'l-Yaman*, Beirut 1405/1985, in *ibid.*, 318–19; M.H. Burgoyne, with D.S. Richards, *Mamluk Jerusalem. An architectural study*, London 1986, in *ibid.*, 349–51; Muhsion D. Yusuf, *Economic survey of Syria during the tenth and eleventh centuries*, Berlin 1985, in *OLZ*, LXXXIII, no. 6 (1988), 698–9; G.R. Hawting, *The first dynasty of Islam. The Umayyad caliphate* 661–750, London 1986, in *Bull. BSMES*, XIV (1988), 195–6; K.N. Chaudhuri, *Trade and civilisation in the Indian Ocean, An economic history from the rise of Islam to 1750*, Cambridge 1985, in *ibid.*, 197–8.

1989

184. *Bahā' al-Dīn 'Amilī and his literary anthologies*, JSS Monograph no. 10, Manchester 1989, pp. ix + 128.
185. *The History of al-Ṭabarī. An annotated translation.* Vol. XXX. *The 'Abbāsid Caliphate in equilibrium. The caliphates of Mūsā al-Hādī and Hārūn al-Rashīd A.D. 785–809/A.H. 169–193*, State University of New York Press, Albany 1989, pp. xxvii + 365.

186. "A note on *taʿarrub* in early Islam", *JSS*, XXXIV (1989) (Published to celebrate the seventieth birthday of Edward Ullendorff), 355–62.
187. "Al-Khwārazmī on the secular and religious titles of the Byzantines and Christians", *CT*, XXXV, no. 139–40 (1987) (Numéro spécial. Mélanges Charles Pellat), 28–36.
188. "A Janissary poet of sixteenth-century Damascus: Māmayya al-Rūmī", in C.E. Bosworth, Charles Issawi, Roger Savory and A.L. Udovitch (eds.), *The Islamic world, from classical to modern times. Essays in honor of Bernard Lewis*, Princeton 1989, 451–66.
189. "The intrepid Victorian lady in Persia. Mrs. Isabella Bishop's travels in Luristan and Kurdistan, 1890), *Iran, JBIPS*, XXVII (1989), 87–101.
190. "The sword of Islam threatens the pen of Moslem critics", *Newsday*, Melville, Long Island, N.Y., 27.2.89.
191. Obituary: "Martin Hinds, 1941–1988", in *Bull. BSMES*, XVI (1989), 118–20.
192. *EI*² Vol. VI, arts. "Mardāwīdj b. Ziyār"; "Mārdīn. 2. The Ottoman and modern periods" (with V. Minorsky); "Marghīnān": "Marḥala"; "Marw al-Rūdh"; "Marw al-Shāhidjān" (with A.Yu. Yakubovskii); "Marwān I b. al-Ḥakam"; "Marwānids"; "al-Marwazī, al-Sukkarī"; "al-Marwazī, Sharaf al-Zamān"; Mashhād; "al-Masīḥ" (with A.J. Wensinck) "Ma'ṣir"; "Masʿūd b. Maḥmūd"; "Masʿūd b. Muḥammad b. Malik-Shāh"; "Masʿūd Beg"; "Mawdūd b. Maḥmūd".
193. *EIr* Vol. III, arts. "Barīd"; "Barkīāroq"; "Barskān"; "Bayhaq"; "Bayhaqī, Ebrāhīm b. Moḥammad"; "Baylaqān"; "Baytuz"; "Bayżā"; "Begging. In the early centuries of the Islamic period"; "Begtoğdï"; "Begtuzun"; "Bīār"; "Bilgetigin"; "Bird, Isabella L."; "Bīrūnī, Abu Rayḥān. i. Life"; "Bīsotūn, Abū Manṣūr"; "Boğrā Khan"; "Bojnūrd. ii. History"; "Böri"; "Bū Ḥalīm Šaybānī"; "Bukhara. ii. from the Arab invasions to the Mongols."
194. *DMA*, vol. XII. arts. "Transoxania"; "Yaʿqūb ibn Laith".
195. Reviews of W. Eilers, *Iranische Ortsnamen*, Vienna 1987, in *JRAS* (1989), 153–4; W.D. Kubiak, *Al-Fustat. Its foundation and early development*, Cairo 1987, in *Bull. BSMES*, XVI (1989), 57; U. Haarmann (ed.), *Geschichter der arabischen Welt*, Munich 1987, in *ibid.*, 87; Ekkehard Rotter, *Abendland und Sarazener: des okzidentale Araberbild in seine Entstehung im Frühmittelalter*, Berlin and New York 1986, in *ibid.*, 87; V. Christides, *The conquest of Crete by the Arabs (ca. 824)*, Athens 1984, in *OLZ*, LXXXIV, no. 5 (1989), 568–70.

1990

196. "Al-Khwārazmī on various faiths and sects, chiefly Iranian", in *Textes et Mémoires. Vol. XVI. Iranica varia. Papers in honor of Professor Ehsan Yarshater*, Leiden 1990, 10–19.
197. *EI*² Vol. VI, arts. "al-Mawṣil. 1. History up to 1900" (with E. Honigmann); "Mawsim" (with A.J. Wensinck; "Maybud"; "al-Maybudī"; "Mayhana"; "Maymana"; "Maymandī" (with M. Nāẓim); "Maymūn-Diz"; "Māzandarān" (with R. Vasmer"; Mazār-i Sharīf"; "Mazyad, Banū"; "Merzifūn" (with F. Babinger). Vol. VII, arts. "Mihrān"; "Mīkālīs"; "Mikhlāf; "Milla" (with F. Buhl); "Mīr Djumla"; "Mīr Ḳāsim ʿAlī"; "al-Mirbāṭ".
198. *EIr* vol. IV, arts. "Čāč"; "Čağānīān"; "Čağānrūd"; "Čağrī Beg b. Dāwūd"; "Capital cities. ii. In Islamic times". Vol. V, "Čašnīgīr".
199. Reviews of Ihsān ʿAbbās, *Shadharāt min kutub mafqūda fi 'l-ta'rīkh*, Beirut 1408/1988, in *JSS*, XXXV (1990), 164–6; J.J. Witkam (ed.), *Manuscripts of the Middle East . . .*, II (Leiden 1987), in *ibid.*, 375–6; W.H. Behn, *Index Islamicus 1665–1905. A bibliography of articles on Islamic subjects in periodicals and other collective publications*, Millersville, Pa. 1988, in *ibid.*, 378–9; A. Photopoulos (ed.), *Journal of Oriental*

and African Studies, Athens, vol. I (1989), in *Bull. BSMES*, XVII (1990), 62; D.N. Maclean, *Religion and society in Arab Sind*, Leiden 1989, in *ibid.*, 62–3.

1991

200. *The History of al-Ṭabarī. An annotated translation.* Vol. XXXIII. *Storm and stress along the northern frontiers of the ʿAbbāsid caliphate*, State University of New York Press, Albany 1991, pp. xxi + 239.
201. *A commentary on the Qurʾān . . . prepared by Richard Bell, ed. C.E. Bosworth and M.E.J. Richardson*, 2 vols., JSS Monograph no. 14, Manchester 1991, pp. xxii + 608, 603.
202. Ch. 10, "Administrative literature", in M.J.L. Young, J.D. Latham and R.B. Serjeant (eds.), *The Cambridge history of Arabic literature. Religion, learning and science in the ʿAbbasid period*, Cambridge 1990 [publ. 1991], 155–67.
203. "Ghars al-niʿma [b.] Hilāl al-Ṣābiʾ's Kitāb al-Hafawāt al-nādira and Būyid history", in A. Jones (ed.), *Arabicus Felix, Luminosus Britannicus. Essays in honour of A.F.L. Beeston on his eightieth birthday*, Reading 1991, 129–41.
204. "Farrukhī's elegy on Maḥmūd of Ghazna", *Iran, JBIPS*, XXIX (1991), 43–9.
205. "Some remarks on the terminology of irrigation practices and hydraulic construction in the eastern Arab and Iranian worlds in the third–fifth centuries A.H." *JIS*, II (1991), 78–85.
206. 14 articles in J.R. Hinnells (ed.), *Who's who of world religions*, London 1991.
207. Obituary, "Joan Allgrove 1928–1991", in *Iran, JBIPS*, XXIX (1991), p. v.
208. *EI*^{2} Vol. VII, arts. "Muʿammā" "Muʿāwiya II"; "Muʾayyad al-Dawla"; "Mudawwara"; "Mudjāhid. 2. In Muslim Indian usage"; "Mughals. 5. Commerce and European trade connections with Mughal India" (with W.H. Moreland); "al-Muhallabī, Abū Muḥammad al-Ḥasan" (with K.V. Zetterstéen); "Muḥammad b. ʿAbd Allāh b. Ṭāhir" (with K.V. Zetterstéen); "Muḥammad b. Hindū-Shāh"; "Muḥammad b. Maḥmūd b. Malik-Shāh"; "Muḥammad b. Maḥmūd b. Sebüktigin"; "Muḥammad b. Malik-Shāh"; "Muḥammad b. Waṣīf"; "Muḥammad Bakhtiyār Khaldjī"; "Muḥammad Farīd Bey"; "Muḥammad Shāh b. Djahān-Shāh"; "al-Muḥillūn"; "al-Muhtadī" (with K.V. Zetterstéen); "Muḥtādjids"; "Mukārī"; "Muḳāsama. I. In the caliphate"; "Muḳāṭaʿa. i. In the mediaeval caliphate".
209. *EIr*, Vol. V, arts. "Central Asia. iv. In the Islamic period up to the Mongols"; "Češt".
210. Reviews of S.A. al-Durūbī (ed.), *Sharḥ maqāmāt Jalāl al-Dīn al-Suyūṭī*, Beirut 1409/1989, in *JSS*, XXXVI (1991), 185–6; Annemarie Schimmel, *Islamic names*, Edinburgh 1989, in *ibid.*, 364–5; Sajida Sultana Alvi (tr.), *Advice on the art of governance: Mauʿizah-Jahāngīrī of Muhammad Bāqir Najm-i Sānī, an Indo-Muslim Mirror for Princes*, in *Bull. BSMES*, XVII (1990) [1991], 222–3; Youssef M. Choueiri, *Arab history and the nation state. A study in modern Arab historiography 1820–1980*, London 1989, in *ibid.*, XVIII (1991), 110–11; Paul Lunde and Caroline Stone (ed. and tr.), *The meadows of gold: the Abbasids*, London and New York 1989, in *ibid.*, 139–40; Reinhard Eisener, *Zwischen Faktum und Fiktion, Eine Studie zum Umayyadenkalifen Sulaimān b. ʿAbdalmalik und seinem Bild in den Quellen*, Wiesbaden 1987, in *OLZ*, LXXXV, no. 4 (1990) (publ. 1991), 446–8; Gregor C. Kozlowski, *Muslim endowments and society in British India*, Cambridge 1985, in *Isl.*, LXVIII (1991), 154–6; Irfan Shahîd, *Byzantium and the Arabs in the fifth century*, Dumbarton Oaks, Washington D.C. 1989, in *AHR*, (1991), 1179–80.

1992

211. "The city of Tarsus and the Arab-Byzantine frontier in early and middle ʿAbbāsid times", *Oriens*, XXXIII (1992), 268–86.

212. "Byzantium and the Syrian frontier in the early Abbasid period", in *Bilād al-Shām during the Abbasid period . . . Proceedings of the Fifth International Conference on the history of Bilād al-Shām . . . 1410/1990*, English and French section, ed. M.A. Bakhit and R. Schick, Amman 1412/1991 [1992], 54–62.
213. "The early Islamic period of Iranian history: an overview", *Arab Journal for the Humanities*, Kuwait vol. XXXIX, 10th year (1992), 386–400.
214. "Greeks and Arabs: clash and concord between two world civilisations", in *Euro-Arab understanding and cultural exchange, Euro-Arab seminar organised by the Secretary-General of the Council of Europe, Strasbourg, 14–15 November 1991. Contributions* [Strasbourg 1992], 63–9.
215. *EI*² Vol. VII, arts. "Mukhattam"; "al-Muḳtadir" (with K.V. Zettersteén); "al-Muktafī" (with K.V. Zettersteén); "Munādī"; "Munādjāt"; "Mungīr"; "Mu'nis Dede"; "Mu'nis al-Faḥl"; "Munshī"; "Munṣif"; "al-Muntaṣir"; "Murādābād" (with J. Allan); "Murghāb"; "Murīd"; "al-Mūriyānī"; "Murshid"; "al-Musʿabī"; "Muṣādara. 2. In the administrative terminology of the mediaeval Islamic caliphate"; "Musāwāt"; "Musawwida"; "Mūsh" (with J.H. Kramers); "al-Mushaḳḳar"; " Mushīr al-Dawla"; "Mushrif. 1. In the Arab and Persian lands"; "Muṣṭafā Pasha, Bayraḳdār" (with J.H. Kramers); "al-Mustaʿīn" (with K.V. Zettersteén); "al-Mustakfī"; "Mustakhridj"; "Mustawfī" (with R. Levy); "Müstethnā Eyāletler"; "al-Muʿtaṣim"; "Mutaṭawwiʿa"; "al-Muʿtazz"; "al-Muṭīʿ"; "al-Muttaḳī"; "Muwādaʿa"; "al-Muwaḳḳar"; "Muẓaffarpur"; "Nābulus" (with F. Buhl); "al-Nadjaf" (with E. Honigmann); "Nadjīb al-Dawla"; "Nadjībābād"; "Nagawr" (with J. Burton-Page); "Nahr. 1. In the Middle East"; "Nā'īn"; "Nakhčewān" (with V. Minorsky); "Naḳīb. 1. In early Islamic history"; "Nangrahār"; "Narāḳ"; "Narmashīr"; "Narshakhī"; "Nasā"; "Nashīṭ"; "Naṣībīn" (with E. Honigmann); "Naṣīḥat al-mulūk".
216. *EIr*, Vol. V, arts. "Chorasmia. ii. In Islamic times"; "Codes".
217. Reviews of P.A. Andrews (ed.), *Ethnic groups in the Republic of Turkey*, Beiheft zum TAVO, Reihe B (Geisteswissenschaften), Nr. 60, Wiesbaden 1989, in *JRAS*, 3rd Ser., vol. II (1992), 79–80; Denis Sinor (ed.), *The Cambridge history of early Inner Asia*, Cambridge 1990, in *ibid.*, 123–4; Leonor Fernandes, *The evolution of a Sufi institution in Mamluk Egypt. The Khankah*, Berlin 1988, in *OLZ*, LXXXVI, no. 5 (1991), 534–5; K.N. Chaudhuri, *Asia before Europe. Economy and civilisation of the Indian Ocean from the rise of Islam to 1750*, Cambridge 1990, in *BSOAS*, LV (1992), 345–6.

1993

218. "Byzantium and the Arabs: war and peace between two world civilisations", *JOAS*, III–IV (1991–2) [1993]. 1–24.
219. "Abū ʿAmr ʿUthmān al-Ṭarsūsī's Siyar al-thughūr and the last years of Arab rule in Tarsus (fourth/tenth century)", *Graeco-Arabica*, V (1993) (= Fourth International Congress on Graeco-Oriental and Graeco-African Studies), 183–95.
220. "Bahā' al-Dīn ʿĀmilī in the two worlds of the Ottomans and Safavids", in *Convegno sul thema La Shīʿa nell' impero ottomano (Roma, 15 aprile 1991), Accad. Nazionale dei Lincei, Fondazione Leone Caetani*, Rome 1993, 85–105.
221. "The Hon. George Nathaniel Curzon's travels in Russian Central Asia and Persia", *Iran, JBIPS*, XXXI (1993), 127–36.
222. (with Gerd Rispling) "An ʿAyyār coin from Sīstān", *JRAS*, 3rd Ser., Vol. III (1993), 215–17.
223. *EI*² Vol. VIII, arts. "Nicobars"; "Nihāwandī"; "Nishāpūrī"; "Nithār. 1." "Nīzak, Ṭarkhān"; "Niẓām"; "Niẓām al-Mulk" (with H. Bowen); "Niẓām al-Mulk Čīn Kilič Khān"; "Niẓām-i Djedīd" (with F. Babinger); "Niẓāmiyya"; "Nūba. 2 History. (b) From the Ayyūbid period to the 16th century" (with S. Hillelson);

"Nūḥ (I) b. Naṣr"; "Nūḥ (II) b. Manṣūr"; "Nūn. 2. In Turkish"; "Nūr al-Dīn Arslān Shāh"; "al-Nūsharī"; "Nuṣratābād"; "al-Nuwayrī, Muḥammad b. al-Ḳāsim"; "Ob"; "Oghul" (with F. Babinger); "Ordūbād"; "Ordu. 1. In early Turkish and then Islamic usage"; "Orkhon"; "Orta"; "Othmānlī. I. Political and dynastic history. 1. General survey and chronology of the dynasty; IV. religious life"; "Ötüken"; "Özbeg b. Muḥammad Pahlawān"; "Pā'" (with R. Levy); "Pādishāh" (with F. Babinger); "Pahlawān"; "Palānpūr"; "Pamirs"; "Pandjhīr"; "Pāndú'ā" (with C.C. Davies); "Parendā"; "Parwīz, Khusraw (II)"; Paṭrīk"; "Payghū"; "Penče"; "Pendjik"; "Peshāwar (with C.C. Davies); Philby, H.St.J."; "Pickthall, M.M."; "Pīrī-zāde"; "Pīshdādids"; "Pishpek"; "Posta. 1."; "Pūstneshīn"; "Rādjā Ganesh"; "Radjʿiyya"; "Rādjmahāl".

224. *EIr* Vol. VI, art. "Courts and courtiers. iii. In the Islamic period to the Mongol conquest".

225. Reviews of Martin Hinds, *An early Islamic family from Oman. Al-ʿAwtabī's account of the Muhallabids*, Manchester 1991, in *JOAS*, III–IV (1991–2) [1993], 258; Robert L. Redfield (ed.), *Turko-Persia in historical perspective*, Cambridge 1991, in *JIS*, I/4 (1993), 97–9; Ross E. Dunn, *The adventures of Ibn Battuta, a Muslim traveller of the fourteenth century*, Berkeley, Los Angeles and London 1986, in *ibid.*, 109–10; ʿAḍud al-Dīn ʿAbd al-Raḥmān al-Ījī, *Risālat Adab al-baʿth wa 'l-munāẓara*, ed. Mū'il Yūsuf ʿIzz al-Dīn, Riyāḍ 1412/1991, in *al-ʿUṣūr al-Wusṭā, Bull. of Middle East Medievalists*, V/1 (1993), 21; R.B. Serjeant, *Customary and Sharīʿah law in Arabian society*, Variorum, London 1991, in *JRAS*, 3rd Ser., Vol. III (1993), 118; D.E.P. Jackson *et alii* (eds.), *Occasional papers of the School of Abbasid Studies, University of St. Andrews*, No. 2, Edinburgh 1988, in *JSS*, XXXVIII (1993), 167–8; G.J. Roper (compiler and ed.), *Index Islamicus 1981–1985*, 2 vols., in *ibid.*, 171–2; Moshe Gil, *A history of Palestine 634–1099*, Cambridge 1992, in *EHR*, CVIII, no. 428 (1993), 668–70; Shmuel Moreh, *Live theatre and dramatic literature in the medieval Arabic world*, Edinburgh 1992, in *TLS*, 15.1.93; Richard Williams, *The first thousand Penguins, a bibliographical checklist*, Dragonby, Lincs. 1987, and *idem*, *Pan books, 1945–1955, a bibliographical checklist*, Dragonby 1990, in *Analytical and Enumerative Bibliography*, Northern Illinois University, de Kalb, Ill., V/2 (1991) [1993], 115–20.

1994

226. *The history of the Saffarids of Sistan and the Maliks of Nimruz (247/861 to 949/1542–3)*, Columbia Lectures on Iranian Studies 8, Costa Mesa and New York 1994, pp. xxvi + 525.

227. "Abū Ḥafṣ ʿUmar al-Kirmānī and the rise of the Barmakids", *BSOAS*, LVII (1994), 268–82.

228. "Rulers of Makrān and Quṣdār in the early Islamic period", *St. Ir.*, XXIII (1994), 199–209.

229. "Arab attacks on Rhodes in the pre-Ottoman period" (Eng. and Greek tr.), in *Rhodos 2400. Diethnes synedrio* 1993, Rhodian Historical Society, Rhodes 1994, 205–15.

230. "Seductive Orient voices. Arabic influences in the art and letters of 19th century Britain", in Michel Barbot (ed.), *1492. L'héritage culturel arabe in Europe. Actes du colloque international organisé par le G.E.O. (Strasbourg) et le C.R.E.L (Mulhouse) (Strasbourg-Mulhouse, 6–8 octobre 1992)*, Strasbourg 1994, 24–33.

231. "Irish and British contributions to Arabic and Islamic studies since 1800", in Kevin J. Cathcart (ed.), *The Edward Hincks bicentenary lectures*, Dublin 1994, 178–94.

232. *EI*² Vol. VIII, arts. "Rāfiʿ b. Harthama"; "Rāfiʿ b. al-Layth"; "Rafsandjān";

"Ragh̲ūsa. 2. History after 1800"; "Rā'iḳa"; "Ra'īs. 2. In the sense of 'mayor' in the eastern Islamic lands"; "Ra'iyya. 2. In the mediaeval Islamic world"; "Rām-Hurmuz" (with V. Minorsky); "Rāṇā Sāṇgā"; "Rangoon"; "Rash̲t" (with B. Nikitine); "al-Rass"; "Rawalpindi" (with C.C. Davies); "Rawandiz" (with B. Nikitine); "Rawsh̲aniyya" (with D.S. Margoliouth); "Rawwādids"; "Rāyčūr"; "Rayy. 2. Archaeological monuments" (with V. Minorsky); "Riḍā"; "Riḍwān b. Tutush̲"; "Rifā'iyya"; "Rizḳ, 1. As a theological concept, and 3. In military terminology"; "Rūdh̲bār"; "Rūdh̲rāwar"; "al-Rūdh̲rāwarī"; "al-Ruhā" (with E. Honigmann); "al-Rukh̲kh̲adj̲"; "Rukn al-Dawla" (with H. Bowen); "Rūm. 2. Relations between the Islamic powers and the Byzantines"; "Rūm Ḳal'esi" (with E. Honigmann); "Rūpiyya" (with J. Allan); "al-Ruṣāfa. 1. and 2."; "Rustāḳ"; "Rūznāma"; "Sa'ādat 'Alī Kh̲ān" (with C.C. Davies); "Sabandj̲a"; "Sabīl. 1. As a religious concept"; "Sābūr b. Ardash̲īr"; "Sabzawār"; "Sādj̲ids"; "Ṣadr. 1. In Transoxania".

233. *EIr* Vol. VI, arts. "Dandānqān"; "Dargazīnī"; "Dawā(t)dār"; "Dawraq"; "Dayr al-'Āqūl"; "Daysam Kordī"; "Dehestān"; "Dehestānī".

234. Reviews of H. Halm, *Das Reich des Mahdi*, in *OLZ*, LXXXIX no. 1 (1994), 70–1; Farhan Ahmad Nizami (ed.), *Journal of Islamic Studies*, Oxford, I (1990), in *JSS*, XXXIX (1994), 391; R. Marín-Guzmán, *Popular dimensions of the 'Abbasid Revolution. A case study of medieval Islamic social history*, Cambridge, Mass. 1990, in *Arabica*, XLI (1994), 134–5; Walter E. Kaegi, *Byzantium and the early Islamic conquests*, Cambridge 1992, in *BJMES*, XXI (1994), 252–3.

1995

235. "E.G. Browne and his *A year amongst the Persians*". *Iran, JBIPS*, XXXIII (1995), 115–22.

236. *EI*[2] Vol. VIII, arts. "Ṣaff, 1. In religious practice, 2. In military organisation"; "Ṣaffārids"; "Safīd Kūh"; "Safīd Rūd"; "Safīna. 1. In the pre-modern period. (a) Pre-islamic and early Islamic aspects (with H. Kindermann), (b) The Mediterranean, (c) The Mesopotamian-Kh̲ūzistān river systems, (d) The Arabian Sea and Indian Ocean shores"; "Sahāranpūr" (with T.W. Haig); "al-Sahmī"; "Sa'īd b. al-'Āṣ"; "Sa'īd Pash̲a"; "Ṣā'ifa. I. In the Arab-Byzantine warfare"; "al-Ṣaḳāliba. 2. In the central lands of the caliphate"; "Saḳḳi̊z"; "Salāma b. Dīnār"; "Sālār" (with V.F. Büchner); "Saldj̲ūḳids. I. Historical significance, II. Origins and early history, III. The various branches, V. Administrative, social and economic history, VII. Literature. 2. In Anatolia"; "Salgh̲urids"; "al-Ṣāliḥiyya"; "Salm b. Ziyād b. Abīhi"; "Salmās"; "Sāmānids. 1. History, literary life and economic activity"; "Samarḳand" (with H.H. Schaeder); "al-Samāwa"; "al-Samhūdī"; "Samrū Begam" (with S. Digby); "Ṣamṣām al-Dawla". In Vol. IX, "Sanandadj̲" (with V. Minorsky); "Sandabīl"; "Sandj̲a"; "Sandj̲ar"; "Saracens. 2. In mediaeval European usage"; "Sarakh̲s"; "Sarandīb"; "Sārangpur"; "Sarāparda"; "Sardāb"; "Sardhanā"; "Sarḥadd"; "Sārī"; "Sarūdj̲" (with M. Plessner); "Sarwistān"; "Sāsān, Banū"; "Sāwa" (with V. Minorsky); "Sawdj̲-Bulāḳ" (with V. Minorsky); "Savdj̲i̊, Sawdj̲i̊" (with F. Babinger); "Sayābidj̲a"; "Ṣaymara"; "Sayyid"; "Sebüktigin"; "Sh̲abānkāra" (with V.F. Büchner); "Sh̲abānkāra'ī" (with P. Jackson); "al-Sh̲ābushtī"; "Sh̲addādids"; "Sh̲āh Malik"; "Sh̲āh Rūd".

237. *EIr* Vol. VII, art. "Derham b. Nażr".

238. Reviews of O. Hulec and M. Mendel (eds.), *Threefold wisdom: Islam, the Arab world and Africa. Papers in honour of Ivan Hrbek*, Prague 1993, in *JSS*, XL (1995), 189–90; Alan H. Jutzi (ed.), *In search of Sir Richard Burton. Papers from a Huntington Library symposium*, San Marino, Calif. 1993, in *ibid.*, 392;, Thomas Naff (ed.),

Paths to the Middle East: ten scholars look back, Albany 1993, in *JRAS*, 3rd Ser., vol. V (1995), 93–4; R.B. Serjeant, R.L. Bidwell and G. Rex Smith, *New Arabian Studies*, I, Exeter 1993, in *ibid.*, 266–7; Sukumar Ray, *Bairam Khan*, Karachi 1992, in *ibid.*, 303–4; Farhad Daftary, *The Assassin legends. Myths of the Isma'ilis*, London 1994, in *Graeco-Arabica*, VI (1995), 367–9; Faḍlullāh b. Rūzbihān Khunjī Iṣfahānī, *Tārīkh-i 'Ālam-ārā-yi amīnī*, text ed. John E. Woods, abridged tr. V. Minorsky, London 1992, in *JAOS*, CXV (1995), 555; A. Fodor and A. Shivtiel (eds.), *Proceedings of the colloquium on popular customs and the monotheistic religions in the Middle East and North Africa, Budapest, 19th–25th September 1993*, Budapest 1994, in *OLZ*, XL no. 2 (1995), 187–8.

1996

239. *The New Islamic dynasties. A chronological and genealogical manual*, Edinburgh University Press and Columbia University Press 1996, pp. xxvi + 389.
240. *The Arabs, Byzantium and Iran. Studies in early Islamic history and culture*, Variorum Reprints, CS Series 529, Aldershot 1996, pp. xii + 320.
241. "Arab attacks on Rhodes in the pre-Ottoman period", *JRAS*, 3rd Ser., vol. VI (1996), 157–64.
242. "Notes on the lives of some 'Abbāsid princes and descendants", *The Maghrib Review*, XIX/3–4 (1994) [1996] (Hommage à André Miquel), 277–84.
243. "The Isma'ilis of Quhistān and the Maliks of Nīmrūz or Sīstān", in F. Daftary (ed.), *Mediaeval Isma'ili history and thought*, Cambridge 1996, 221–9.
244. "Arabic influences in the literature of nineteenth and early twentieth century Britain", in J.R. Smart (ed.), *Tradition and modernity in Arabic language and literature*, Richmond, Surrey 1996, 155–64.
245. "Islam in Central Asia and the Caucasus", in Azim A. Nanji (ed.), *The Muslim almanac. A reference work on the history, faith, culture, and peoples of Islam*, Gale Research Inc., Detroit 1996, 83–9.
246. Arts. on mediaeval Islamic personages in Alexis Savvides (ed.), *Enkuklopaidiko prosōprographiko lexiko byzantinēs istorias kai politismou* ("Encyclopaedic prosopographical lexicon of Byzantine history and civilisation"), I, Aamr – Alphios, Athens 1996.
247. *EI*² Vol. IX, arts. "Shahrazūr"; "Shakarkhelda"; "Shakkī" (with V. Minorsky); "al-Shām. 1. Geography, 2. History (a) to 1918 (with H. Lammens). (b) From the end of the First World War to the end of the Mandate"; "Shammākha"; "Shāpūr" (rulers); "Shār"; "Sharaf al-Dīn 'Alī Yazdī"; "Sharīf Pasha" (with J.H. Kramers); "Shehir Ketkhudāsi"; "Shikārī" (with T.W. Haig); "Shimshāṭ"; "Shīrwān" (with W. Barthold); "Shīrwān-Shāh" (with W. Barthold), "Shīz" (with J. Ruska); "Shōlāpur"; "Shughnān"; "Shūl", "Shūmān"; "Shūrā. 1. In early Islamic history"; "Shuraḥbīl b. Ḥasana"; "Shushtar" (with J.H. Kramers); "Shuwa. 1. History"; "Sībī"; "Sidhpūr"; "Sighnāḳ"; "Si'ird. 1. History (a) The pre-Ottoman period"; "Sikandar But-Shikan"; "Sikhs. I. General. 4. History after 1849"; "Sikka. 1. Legal and constitutional aspects".
248. *EIr* Vol. VII, arts. "Dīnār, Malek"; "Dīnavar"; "Dīwān. ii. Government office"; "Ebn Abī Ṭāher Ṭayfūr".
249. Reviews of Raoul Curiel and Rika Gyselen (eds.), *Itinéraires d'Orient. Hommages à Claude Cahen*, in *JRAS*, 3rd Ser., vol. VI (1996), 83–7; Willem Floor, *The Dutch East Indies Company (VOC) and Diewel-Sind (Pakistan) in the 17th and 18th centuries (based on original Dutch records)*, Karachi-Islamabad 1993–4, in *ibid.*, 121–2; R.L. Bidwell, G.R. Smith and J.R. Smart (eds.), *New Arabian studies, 2*, Exeter 1994, in *ibid.*, 233–4; Jean Aubin and Jacqueline Calmard (eds.), *Européens en Orient au XVIII*ᵉ *siècle*, Paris 1994, in *ibid.*, 250–1; Shireen Moosvi (tr. and ed.),

Episodes in the life of Akbar. Contemporary records and reminiscences, New Delhi 1994, in *ibid.*, 266–7; W. Montgomery Watt, *Islamic creeds, a selection*, Edinburgh 1994, in *JSS*, XLI (1996), 197; *The Byzantine and early Islamic Near East. I. Problems in the literary source material. Papers of the First Workshop on Late Antiquity and Early Islam*, Princeton 1992, in *ibid.*, 348–50; Bernd Radtke, *Weltgeschichte und Weltbeschreibung im mittelalterlichen Islam*, BTS 51, Stuttgart 1992, in *ibid.*, 354–6; G.S.P. Freeman-Grenville, *The Islamic and Christian calendars A.D. 622–2222 (A.H. 1–1650). A complete guide for converting Christian and Islamic dates and dates of festivals*, Reading 1995, in *ibid.*, 378–80.

1997

250. "The study of Islam in British scholarship", in Azim Nanji (ed.), *Mapping Islamic studies. Genealogy, continuity and change*, Berlin-New York 1997, 45–67.

251. "Thaʿālibī's information on the Turks", in Rudolf Vesely and Eduard Gombár (eds.), *Zafar nāme. Memorial volume of Felix Tauer*, Prague 1996 [1997], 61–6.

252. Articles on Islamic personages in Alexis Savvides (ed.), *Enkuklopaidiko prosōpographiko lexiko byzantinēs istorias kai politismou*, Vol. II, Alphios – Antiocheus, Athens 1997.

253. *EI*² Vol. IX, arts. "Simaw"; "Sīmdjūrids"; "Simnān"; "al-Ṣīn. 1. The name. 2. The present distribution of Muslims in China and a characterisation of Islam there. 3. Geographical and historical information to the year ca. A.D. 1050" (with M. Hartmann); "Sind. 1. History in the pre-modern period" (with T.W. Haig); "Sindabūr"; "Sindān"; "Sipāhī. 1. In the Ottoman empire"; "Sīr Daryā. 1. In the early and mediaeval periods" (with W. Barthold); "al-Sīradjān"; "Sīrāf"; "Sirhind"; "Sīstān"; "Siwri Ḥiṣār" (with J.H. Kramers); "al-Siyālkūtī"; "Siyāsa. 1. In the sense of statecraft . . ."; "Ṣofta"; Śrīrangapaṭṭanam"; "Su"; "Su Bashi̊" (with J.H. Kramers); "Subayta"; "al-Subkī" (with J. Schacht); "Sudjān Rāy Bhandārī" (with Mohammed Shafi); "Ṣūfiyānā"; "Sufyānids"; "al-Ṣughd" (with W. Barthold); "Sulaymān Mountains"; "Sulaymān b. ʿAlī b. ʿAbd Allāh"; "Sulaymān b. Yaḥyā"; "Sulaymāniyya. 2. Since 1920"; "Süleymān Čelebi"; "Sulṭān. 1. In early Islamic usage and in the central lands of Islam" (with J.H. Kramers); "Sulṭān al-Dawla"; "Sulṭānābād"; "Sulṭāniyya. 1. History" (with V. Minorsky); "Sūmanāt"; "Sumatra"; "Sumerā"; "Sūrat" (with T.W. Haig); "Sūrs or Sūrīs"; al-Sūs" (with M. Streck); "Sūyāb"; "Swāt".

254. *EIr* Vol. VIII, arts. "Ebn Bābā Kāšānī"; "Ebn al-Balkī"; "Ebn Dārost, Majd al-Wozarā Moḥammad"; "Ebn Dārost, Tāj al-Molk Abu 'l-Ḡanā'em"; "Ebn Fūlād"; "Ebn Karmīl"; "Ebn Kordādbeh"; "Ebn Morsal"; "Ebn Rosta"; "Ebrāhīm b. Masʿūd"; "Ebrāhīm Inal".

255. Reviews of Amikam Elad, *Medieval Jerusalem and Islamic worship: holy places, ceremonies, pilgrimage*, Leiden, etc. 1995, in *BSOAS*, LX (1997), 132–3; R. Amitai-Preiss, *Mongols and Mamluks. The Mamluk-Ilkhānid war, 1260–1281*, Cambridge 1995, in *JIS*, VIII (1997), 99–102; H.A.R. Gibb and C.F. Beckingham (trs.), *The travels of Ibn Baṭṭūṭa A.D. 1325–1354, Vol. IV*, Hakluyt Society, London 1994, in *JSS*, XLII (1997), 191–2; Maya Shatzmiller, *Labour in the medieval Islamic world*, Leiden 1994, in *ibid.*, 437–9; Mervyn Hiskett, *The course of Islam in Africa*, Edinburgh 1994, in *ibid.*, 195 6; Devin DeWeese, *Islamization and native religion, in the Golden Horde: Baba Tükles and conversion to Islam in historical and epic tradition*, University Park, Pa. 1994, in *JAH*, XXX (1997), 61–2; G.R. Smith, J.R. Smart and B.R. Pridham (eds.), *New Arabian studies 3*, Exeter 1996, in *JRAS*, 3rd Ser., Vol. VII (1997), 287–8; Louis Alexandre Olivier de Corancez, tr. E. Tabet, introd. R.M. Burrell, *The history of the Wahabis from their origin until the end of 1809. The founders of Saudi Arabia*, Reading 1995, in *ibid.*, 296–7.

1998

256. M.S. Asimov and C.E. Bosworth (eds.), *History of civilizations of Central Asia. Vol. IV. The age of achievement: A.D. 750 to the end of the fifteenth century.* Part 1. *The historical, social and economic setting*, UNESCO, Paris 1998, pp. 485. Sections by C.E. Bosworth: Introduction, 19–21; Ch. 1, Pt. 1, "The appearance of the Arabs in Central Asia under the Umayyads and the establishment of Islam", 23–5; Ch. 4, "The Ghaznavids", 95–117; Ch. 7, "The Seljuqs and the Khwarazm Shahs. Pt. 2, The consolidation of the Seljuq Sultanate in Iran (1055–1118)", and Pt. 3, "The Eastern Seljuq Sultanate (1118–57) and the rise and florescence of the Khwarazm Shahs of Anūshtegin's line up to the appearance of the Mongols (1097–1219)", 155–76; Ch. 14, "The Delhi Sultanate. Pt. 2, The Delhi Sultanate, 1316–1526", 279–91; Conclusion, 421.
257. Articles on Classical Arabic Literature in *Encyclopedia of Arabic literature*, ed. Julie Scott Meisami and Paul Starkey, Routledge and Kegan Paul, London and New York, 2 vols. 1998.
258. Articles on Islamic personages in Alexis Savvides (ed.), *Enkuklopaidiko prosōpographiko lexiko byzantinēs istorias kai politismou*, Vol. III, Antiochos-Apsimaros, Athens 1998.
259. *EI*[2] Vol. X, arts. "Taʿarrub"; "al-Ṭabarī, Abū Djaʿfar Muḥammad b. Djarīr"; "Ṭabaristān"; "Ṭabarsarān"; "Ṭabas"; "Tabrīz. i. Geography and history" (with V. Minorsky); "Tādj al-Dīn Yildiz"; "Tādjīk. i. Etymology and early linguistic development of the term"; "Tadjmīr"; "Tadmur"; "Ṭāhir b. al-Ḥusayn"; "Ṭāhirids. i."; "Ṭahmāsp. ii."; "Ṭahmūrath"; "Taḥṣīl"; "al-Ṭāʾiʿ" (with K.V. Zettersteen); "Takht-i Ṭāwūs"; "Takrīt" (with J.H. Kramers); "Taḳsīṭ"; "Ṭālaḳān. 1, 2"; "Ṭalḥat al-Ṭalaḥāt"; "Tālīkōtā"; "Tamīm b. Baḥr"; "Ṭarābī, Maḥmūd"; "Ṭarābulus al-Gharb. 5. From 1835 to the present day"; "Ṭarābulus al-Shām. 1. History up to the Mamlūk period" (with F. Buhl); "Ṭarāz"; "Tardjumān"; "Ṭarsūs"; "al-Ṭarsūsī"; "Ṭarṭūs" (with E. Honigmann); "Ṭārum" (with V. Minorsky).
260. *EIr* Vol. IX, arts. "Elwell-Sutton, L.P."; "ʿEmād al-Dawla, Abu 'l-Ḥasan ʿAlī"; "ʿEmād al-Dīn Marzbān"; "Eqlīd"; "ʿErāq-e ʿAjam(ī)"; "Esfarāyen"; "Eškāš(e)m"; "Esmāʿīl b. Seboktegīn"; "Esmāʿīl b. Aḥmad Sāmānī".
261. Reviews of Anthony McNicoll and Warwick Ball *et alii*, *Excavations at Kandahar 1974 and 1975. The first two sessions at Shahr-i Kohna (Old Kandahar) conducted by the British Institute of Afghan Studies*, Oxford 1996, in *JRAS*, 3rd Ser., Vol. VIII (1998), 111–13; Jean-Michel Mouton, *Damas et sa principauté sous les Saljoukides et les Bourides (468–549/1076–1154): vie politique et religieuse*, Cairo 1994, in *ibid.*, 263–5; Hilal Ahmad Zubairi (ed.), *Dr. Ishtiaq Husain Qureshi memorial volume, II*, Karachi 1994, in *ibid.*, 275–6; Audrey Burton, *The Bukharans. A dynastic, diplomatic and commercial history 1550–1702*, London 1997, in *JIS*, IX (1998), 305–7; Saul Shaked, *From Zoroastrian Iran to Islam. Studies in religious history and intercultural contacts*, Aldershot 1995, in *JSS*, XLIII (1998), 188–9; Michael Carney, *Britain in pictures. A history and bibliography*, London 1995, in *Analytical and Enumerative Bibliography*, Northern Illinois University, De Kalb, Ill., N.S. IX (1995) [1998], 254–7; Robert Chenciner, *Daghestan, tradition and survival*, Richmond 1997, in *TLS*, 31.7.98, p. 27; and in *JOAS*, IX (1997–8), 159–61.
262. Obituary, "Professor Charles Beckingham", *The Daily Telegraph*, 14.10.98.

In the press

263. *The History of al-Ṭabarī. An annotated translation.* Vol. V. *The Sāsānids, the Byzantines, the Lakhmids and Yemen*, tr. and annotated by C.E. Bosworth, State University of New York Press, Albany 1999.

264. C.E. Bosworth and M.S. Asimov (eds.), *History of civilizations of Central Asia*. Vol. IV. *The age of achievement: A.D. 750 to the end of the fifteenth century*. Part 2, *The achievements*, UNESCO, Paris 1999.
265. Article "Vladimir Minorsky", in *The new dictionary of national biography*, O.U.P., Oxford.
266. Articles on Middle Eastern and Indo-Muslim topics in *The companion to military history*, ed. Richard Holmes and Christopher Bellamy, O.U.P., Oxford.

LIST OF CONTRIBUTORS

Çiğdem Balim-Harding	University of Manchester
John Carswell	London, formerly of Sothebys
Farhad Daftary	The Institute of Isma'ili Studies, London
François de Blois	Royal Asiatic Society, London
Heinz Gaube	University of Tübingen
Colin Heywood	School of Oriental and African Studies, University of London
Robert Hillenbrand	University of Edinburgh
Peter Jackson	Keele University
Bernard Lewis	Princeton University
J.P. Luft	University of Manchester
Denis MacEoin	Newcastle-upon-Tyne
Wilferd Madelung	University of Oxford
Ulrich Marzolph	Enzyklopädie des Märchens, Göttingen
Julie Scott Meisami	University of Oxford
David Morgan	School of Oriental and African Studies, University of London
S. Soucek	Princeton University
Luke Treadwell	University of Oxford
Ehsan Yarshater	Columbia University
Yaqub Zaki (James Dickie)	The Muslim Institute for Research and Planning, London

THE LAST OF THE ANATOLIAN NATIONALISTS: NURETTİN TOPÇU

Çiğdem Balım-Harding

Anadoluculuk (Anatolianism) developed in Turkey during World War I, as a reaction to Islamism, Ottomanism and Pan-Turkism, and before and during the War of Liberation the Ottoman literati saw it as the uniting force. Nüzhet Sabit's (1883–1919) journal *Vazife* (1909) carried expressions of love for Anatolia and of the need to save Anatolia above all. He proposed a non-aggressive, non-oppressive nationalism, counter to both the Young Turks and Ziya Gökalp.[1] During 1917, among the members of Türk Ocağı (Hearth of the Turk) (1911), a movement known as "narrow Turkism" or "Turkeyism" was born. Its leader was the historian Mükrimin Halil Yınanç, and the other prominent figures included Hilmi Ziya Ülken, Haluk Nihat Pepe, and Reşit Kayı. Later, Nihat Özön's journal *Dergâh* (1921–1923), in opposition to Ziya Gökalp's Durkheimian and positivist sociology, promoted an essentially Bergsonian philosophy through writers like İsmail Hakkı Baltacıoğlu, Mustafa Şekip Tunç, and Mehmet Emin Erişirgil. Although they had their differences, the authors who published in *Dergâh* were united in their opposition to Ziya Gökalp and also in their support of the War of Liberation in Anatolia. They agreed that the success of the Anatolian people against the occupying forces was realized not because of "positivism", but because of their "élan vital". Other well known writers in the journal included Yahya Kemal Beyatlı, Fuad Köprülü, Yakup Kadri Karaosmanoğlu, Falih Rıfkı Atay, Halide Edip Adıvar, Ruşen Eşref Ünaydın, Abdülhak Şinasi Hisar, Kemalettin Kamu, Ahmet Hamdi Tanpınar, Hasan Ali Yücel and Ahmet Kutsi Tecer.

In 1924, the journal *Anadolu* was founded by Mehmet Halit Bayrı, with Mükrimin Halil Yınanç writing on history, Ziyaeddin Fahri Fındıkoğlu on folklore, Hilmi Ziya Ülken on culture and Mehmet Halit Bayrı on folk poetry. Poems by Necip Fazıl Kısakürek and Ahmet Hamdi Tanpınar were also published. For the writers in this journal,

[1] Hilmi Ziya Ülken, *Türkiye'de Çağdaş Düşünce Tarihi*, 342.

a nation needed first of all a homeland within definite borders, then a common history. Homeland was the entity which one would die for, even if it did not bring material gain to the individual. This mystical quality found its best expression in Remzi Oğuz Arık's *Coğrafyadan Vatana* (From Geography to Homeland).[2]

However, after the War, the movement gradually assumed an even more mystical and epic dimension, and *Anadoluculuk* was left to those who saw Anatolia as the source of a cultural and political revolution, as opposed to Kemalism which was essentially an urban intellectual ideology. While the state policy of the new Republic (Kemalism) accepted Anatolia as the homeland, and in theory also accepted the potential of the rural population, it aimed to create a new secular culture and new identity for the Turkish Republic. It accepted positivism and modernism. *Anadoluculuk*, on the other hand, defended the position that the unlikely victory of the Anatolians in the War had stemmed from their spiritual power, and the source of this power was in the magical combination of the Oghuz Turks who had come to Anatolia in 1071, and Islam. It celebrated the "purity" and "traditional spirituality" of rural positivism in the face of modernity and the decadence of urban industrialism and life style.

Nurettin Topçu was the most influential figure of *Anadoluculuk* during its final phase, and synonymous with the journal *Hareket* (Action) which he himself founded and published between the years 1939–42, 1942–43, 1947–1949, 1952–53 and 1966–1975. He became the honorary *hodja* of dozens of students who later took an active part in Turkish politics. As such, he may be thought of as one of the last great teachers in the traditional sense of the word in the days before the media largely took over face-to-face oral interaction and transfer of ideas. Although he published vigorously, much of his teaching depended on his power as an orator during meetings with his disciples. In the personalities of teachers like Topçu, the warm, affectionate, traditional relationship between leader and disciple was recreated in an urban setting.

A self-styled philosopher and mystic, Topçu was more complicated and demanding in his teachings than his contemporaries. He was educated in France and knew the history of Western philosophy and arts well. When we consider that his listeners were mostly young

[2] Remzi Oğuz Arık, *Coğrafyadan Vatana.*

students from Anatolian villages who had come to İstanbul for higher education during the 1940s and 1950s, Topçu must have been their window to the rest of the world, introducing them to Western authors and philosophers and to Christianity, as well as to his own version of Anatolian history, and presenting them with concepts they had not met before. His power over his students was later expressed by one of them:

> When he talked of the misery and the poverty of the Anatolian people and especially of the Anatolian villager, which was more widespread in those years, our feelings of responsibility used to be aroused and we used to feel the need to search why and how our nation was reduced to this state and [the urge] to evaluate and judge events and people in the course of history.[3]

In this article, which is about Topçu's life and ideas, I hope to document the messages and representations that dozens of young people received from him. Topçu's teachings will also shed light on the last phase of *Anadoluculuk* in Turkey. I will refrain (as far as possible) from judging the contents of his teachings.

Topçu's life

Nurettin Topçu was born in 1909 in İstanbul to a family of rural origin. His father was from Erzurum and had a butcher's shop in İstanbul. Before the war he had originally been a merchant dealing in grain and cattle between Erzurum and İstanbul, but like many others the War had not been kind to him. He lost his business and two sons during the Balkan Wars. Nurettin's mother, whom Nurettin worshipped, was Ahmet Efendi's second wife, and no doubt much younger than him. Fatma Hanım was from Eğin, where Nurettin was later to spend his summer holidays walking in the countryside. Nurettin had an older brother Hayrettin (b. 1906).

During World War I, Nurettin was in elementary school. His friends later describe him as a quiet, introvert child who collected books and newspapers in a wooden chest. His father did not smile much except for the times when the school master praised Nurettin's intelligence.[4]

[3] Ali İhsan Balım, "Kaybettiğimiz idealist Topçu", 48.

[4] As reported by Sırrı Tüzeer in Mustafa Kutlu "Nurettin Topçu için bir biyografi denemesi", 112.

The year Nurettin started high school his father died. Left without an income, the family rented out part of their house and the older brother Hayrettin left school in order to earn the keep of the family. Nurettin continued his education at Vefa, and later İstanbul Lisesi. No doubt the love and admiration of Nurettin for his mother deepened when the young woman was left to bring up on her own two young boys. From all accounts, the older brother must have acted as the head of the family and protector for Nurettin. This protection would continue later into their adulthood, where one brother would be always the more practical and worldly than the other. Hüseyin Avni Ulaş,[5] an old time friend of the family, was then in İstanbul and no doubt during his formative years Nurettin witnessed the misfortunes of this fierce opponent of Atatürk and listened to his accounts of Republican political history in the making. The beginnings of his mistrust and distaste for politics, political parties and even democracy reflected in his teachings in later years must have started at this age. His admiration for Mehmet Akif, to whose poetry he was introduced in elementary school, must also owe much to Ulaş, who was a good friend of the poet.

In 1928, Nurettin received a state scholarship to continue his education in France. Future Nationalist activists such as Remzi Oğuz Arık, Ziyaeddin Fahri Fındıkoğlu, were already in France when Nurettin arrived and he became especially close friends with Arık. Topçu attended the Bordeaux Lycée for two years and like Fındıkoğlu,[6] it was here that he met Maurice Blondel who was to have a lasting effect on his world view. Blondel became Topçu's source of inspiration and admiration. In fact, Topçu later founded a journal and named it after Blondel's "action" concept: *Hareket.*

After attending Strasbourg University where he studied philosophy and art, Topçu received his doctorate in philosophy from the Sorbonne. Before the end of 1934, Topçu was back in Turkey and began to teach philosophy at Galatasaray Lisesi. However, 1935 was a year

---

[5] Hüseyin Avni Ulaş (b. 1887, Erzurum) fought on the Caucasian front during World War I. He was one of the conveners of the Erzurum Conference. As an MP in the First National Assembly (1920) he was a renowned opponent of Mustafa Kemal and his authority. After 1923 he was not re-elected to Parliament. He made abortive attempts to set up opposition parties until he died in 1948, a sad and broken man. For an account of his life see Muammer Çelik, *Hüseyin Avni Ulaş*; and Ali Fuad Başgil, *Hüseyin Avni Ulaş*.

[6] Hilmi Ziya Ülken, *Türkiye'de Çağdaş Düşünce Tarihi*, 482.

full of events for him. He married Ulaş's step-daughter Fethiye Hanım and at the same time he lost his job at Galatasaray and was appointed to İzmir Atatürk Lisesi. The reason for this sudden change of appointment was a usual one for the times: despite the requests of the headmaster, Topçu had refused to pass some of the students. In return, the angry influential headmaster had Topçu removed from his school.

In İzmir, Topçu's marriage ended. There is nothing about this brief marriage in the written sources but Topçu never married again. In fact, until his death, he lived with his mother and she was probably the only woman in his life. In 1939, he started to publish his monthly journal *Hareket*.[7] It was a short-lived attempt because in the fourth issue, he published his short story *Çalgıcılar* (Musicians) which was about an imaginary leader who had made himself into a deity. It was openly a mockery of the single-party regime and of President İnönü. Topçu soon found himself in Denizli (one of the favourite exile locations of the state for the opponents of the regime). It was the one and only time that he would write such a juvenile attack against the regime.

His childhood friend Sırrı Tüzeer used the influence of a *hodja* to bring Topçu back to İstanbul.[8] Topçu now taught at Haydarpaşa Lisesi but these were turbulent times for the young teacher full of the vigour of his education in France. He aspired to be a philosopher and an academic and no doubt would have been better placed at a university. Meanwhile he was searching to find a means of reconciling East and West. He was tormented with questions that he could not answer. On the one hand, he was under the influence of Ulaş and Mehmet Akif in his opposition to the regime; on the other, he could not find the mysticism he yearned for in the everyday application of Islam. The country was poor and the single-party regime in Turkey had created a group of political elites which were far from perfect. During his quest, the same friend who had helped him to come to İstanbul proposed taking him to meet Abdülâziz Bekkine of Zeyrek, the Nakşibendi shaykh of Zincirlikuyu. Nurettin was unwilling and very sceptical at first but this encounter was to be most

---

[7] The financial support for the journal came from the state which since 1929 was financing the publication of newspapers and journals in order to increase the use of the Latin alphabet and to aid literacy and no doubt also to spread the ideals of the Republic.

[8] Sırrı Tüzeer in Mustafa Kutlu, "Topçu için bir biyografi denemesi", 119.

influential on his life. Topçu is later reported to have said about Bekkine

> If I had not met him, I would not have understood Mohammed.[9]

He became a frequent visitor of the *hodja* and spent long hours talking with him. During this period, Bekkine had attracted a circle of educated young disciples around him[10] and it was through this circle that Topçu met other young people who were closer to himself in their upbringing and thought. There is no account of whether after the death of Bekkine, Topçu was as close to Mehmed Zahid Kotku who followed Bekkine in the order. Bekkine became in many ways the role model for Topçu.

In 1942, Topçu started to publish *Hareket* again and wrote most of the articles in the journal himself. However, names like Münif İslamoğlu (later MP), Mehmet Kaplan (later professor of Turkish), Cahit Okurer (teacher and later MP) were also seen. Topçu joined İstanbul University briefly for two years and worked under Hilmi Ziya Ülken preparing a study of Bergson.[11] He was not given tenure and had to leave.[12] Meanwhile, since his return to İstanbul, the house which he shared with his mother had become the meeting place of colleagues, friends, and young university students. These were either his students from lycees, or university students mostly of rural origin, who had come to İstanbul to study. It is not difficult to imagine the lost, hungry souls and minds of this youth who were searching for a community, like the ones they had left behind. If one also realizes that neither media nor communications were developed in the Turkey of the 1940s, the environment that teachers like Topçu provided for them was perfect. It was oral, warm and sincere as opposed to the alien nature of the ideology and social structure imposed by the state. Through the words of the *hodja*, they were introduced to philosophy, history, literature and even arts. The conviviality, fellow feeling and affection between a sufi master and his disciples were revitalized.[13] Topçu and his close disciples did not take part in the activities of

---

[9] Emin Işık, "N. Topçu ve din adamları", 87.

[10] Ruşen Çakır, *Ayet ve Slogan*, 19.

[11] He published this study in 1968. Nurettin Topçu, *Bergson*.

[12] In the university appointment system of the times, the tenure of a new member had to be voted. Nurettin Topçu lost this voting with 13 for, 12 against and 1 abstained.

[13] Şerif Mardin, "Culture and the Intellectual".

the Pan-Turkists led by Atsız and Togan during the 1940s and were not prosecuted like the latter during a time of purge. During 1948, Topçu was an active speaker at the meetings of Türk Kültür Ocağı (Hearths of Turkish Culture)[14] spreading his ideas which combined Sufi mysticism with Anatolian nationalism.

In 1950, Demokrat Parti (Democrat Party) won the elections, an event which marked the official end of the single-party regime in Turkey. At first Topçu was very hopeful of the new politicians. They promised a rule which would give supremacy to the Anatolian peasant over the urban Republican elite. Soon, however, Topçu began to see the new cadre as being no different from their predecessors. He was not close to the Party and he was not a member of Remzi Oğuz Arık's Türkiye Köylü Partisi (Countrymen Party of Turkey) either. Now he was active in the new Türkiye Milliyetçiler Derneği (Association of the Nationalists of Turkey) which housed the Pan-Turkists as well as Topçu's Anatolian nationalists. He was accepted as the spiritual leader of the Association. While he taught part-time at the İmam Hatip Okulu (clergy training school), he met Celâl Hoca (Celâleddin Ökten) and the two stayed closed friends until the death of Ökten in 1961.[15] Among the things they shared was a strong distaste for the material world.

Relations between the Democrat Party and Türkiye Milliyetçiler Derneği were not very close, but, prior to the 1960 coup, the Party approached the Association for support. They wanted to unite young people with nationalist and Islamic tendencies to support them against the army and the liberals. Topçu was not for action, for which it was too late anyhow. He was, however, very much against a military takeover and was especially upset that the Pan-Turkist Colonel Türkeş had played one of the major roles in the coup. After 1960, he worked for the establishment of Adalet Partisi (Justice Party) and even accepted to become a candidate from Konya during the 1961 elections. Adalet Partisi won the elections but Topçu was not elected. He was not upset. He had never meant to get involved in active politics. However, almost sixty of his disciples and sympathizers were elected as MPs. The early days looked hopeful. The new MPs visited

[14] Hearths of Turkish Culture were set up in 1946 to spread Turkish culture and to protect it from external ideologies. For a history of nationalist organizations and associations in Turkey see Landau, *Pan-Turkism in Turkey*.

[15] For Celâleddin Ökten see Milliyetçiler Derneği, *Celâl Hoca: hayatı ve şahsiyeti*.

Topçu in groups and asked for his advice, but as time went on, their visits ceased:

> Some of them claimed: "Politics has its own laws and these can be learned through active politics. Hodja [i.e. Topçu] is a spiritual man, and a man of intellect. He is not a man of action."[16]

In 1963, at a time when Türkiye Milliyetçiler Derneği had fourteen branches in Turkey, Topçu had to leave the Association with a group of close followers. During one of his talks Topçu had given a name to his utopian social order and it was "Islamic Socialism". The reaction of the members was "We are Muslims not Socialists" and he was shunned by the Association. According to Ercüment Konukman, who left the Association with him, Topçu had always advocated this ideal social order without giving it a name. It was a socialism which accepted a history of a thousand years in Anatolia, an authoritarian state, belief in the eternity of the soul, and an economic system founded on social justice.[17]

Topçu returned to his journal *Hareket* with a broken heart. He taught at İstanbul Lisesi until his retirement in 1974. He had undoubtedly been a very talented teacher. Later one of his students wrote:

> In the beginning I found him a little harsh, stern and intolerant as a teacher. Later I discovered the deep and real love he had for his students. Beneath his discipline which seemed to have no tolerance, he was a teacher who loved his students, who could see his students' inner lives; more importantly, he was able to make the students love boring philosophy lessons. . . . . [he had] a style of expression which excited the students, sometimes made them dream, but all the time a magical expression which carried you along. . . . I heard stories about Topçu as a teacher from his past and present students. Even those who later had opposing views to his, all agree with my impressions about him as a teacher.[18]

Topçu's cancer was not diagnosed until it was too late. He died on 10 July 1975 in İstanbul.

---

[16] Ercüment Konukman, "Nurettin Topçu hocamızın ardından", 69.
[17] Ibid., 69.
[18] Orhan Okay, "Nurettin Topçu: bir idealistin ölümü", 46.

Topçu's Utopia

Defining the ideal human being takes up a large section of Topçu's writings. His definitions "will-power" and "freedom" are important concepts. He defines the ideal man as someone who has found real freedom through the control of his mental powers. However, because he lives in a constant tension between matter, which wants to make him a slave, and meaning, which gives him freedom, he is in a state of constant anguish from the resulting tension. Material (body) is the enemy of the soul; its cage from which the soul must escape to freedom. But will-power is necessary for freedom. For Topçu, Bergson and Spinoza had made the same mistake about "freedom". Freedom is not in thought, but in action:

> In modern philosophy, Maurice Blondel who is a master of Christian epistemology. . . . has shown the real source of freedom in his philosophy of action. He says that human action which is realized with divine will, will definitely be free. Blondel has said "action is a synthesis of God and man" and defined action as "[action is when] one changes the material and oneself".[19]

Man should be aware of his inner self and should have the freedom to control all actions dependent on it. "Will-power" is the inner strength by which man resists the temptations of the outside world. Gandhi and Christ had allowed their bodies to suffer and through suffering had strengthened their will-power. They taught mankind that virtue can be reached only through suffering.

This belief in suffering brings Topçu closer to Christian mysticism and to the teachings of Mevlâna, enabling him to make peace between different religions. In fact, Topçu explains his positions in an article about Mevlâna:

> The clergy who are not able to realize the secret of *Vahdet-i vücut* (monotheism), accept two different entities when they say that God is outside this world. According to them, we know this world with personal experience but we do not know God. We accept God's existence through our faith. However, the basis of their faith is not personal experience but derives from the testimony of the Prophet and the Qur'ān. Hence, God is presented to us from outside through inculcation. He is not personally experienced. However, the understanding of God

[19] Nurettin Topçu, *Kültürümüzün Meseleleri*, 96.

> in *Vahdet-i vücut* erases the duality of God and universe. It claims that one can get to know God directly by living in this world.[20]

Topçu's ideal man is deeply religious. However, he does not differentiate between religions, since all religions are systems of ethics and nothing, not even science, has autonomy outside ethics. Separating science, ethics and metaphysics has given rise to the social disease known as "positivism". Topçu accuses the likes of Ziya Gökalp (and hence the Republican ideology) of adopting positivism in order to imitate the West but without knowing its real meaning. This is because they are not capable of differentiating between "thought" and "activity". "Scientific thought" and "scientific activity" are not the same thing. "Scientific thought' is more important and nobler than "scientific activity" itself:

> The miracle which has raised the soul of the European to the skies since the Renaissance is "scientific thought" which the East has not been able to identify with. "Scientific thought" is not "science". It is the ability to do science. Science is passed on through books, whereas "scientific thought", is an ore born of faith in the truth present in souls.[21]

Topçu's ideal man rejects institutions based on dogmatic principles. For Topçu, ethical decay in society is so extensive that even Islam has decayed and become another institution with dogmatic principles. Therefore it has to be saved and made to go back to being a dynamic power again. This will not happen through "critical thinking" which would lead to opposition and dogma. Only mysticism is salvation, because Sufism rejects dogmatism in religion and turns religion into an "action". In the same manner, because the *Sharīʿa* is formalist, dogmatic, and static, it is unnecessary:

> It has been a long time since we lost the divine spirit which is the core of Islam. For centuries, for the clergy, religious life has stopped being the belief in a divine source and has turned into a relationship of benefit and a legal system.[22]

He also writes:

---

[20] Nurettin Topçu, "Mevlâna'da âlem ve insan", 50.
[21] Nurettin Topçu, *Kültür ve Medeniyet*, 48.
[22] Ibid., 19.

> [The *Shari'a*] is neither the source of religious life, nor the essence of religion. Just like the laws which are the applicators and regulators of good and bad values which control our lives, the *Shari'a* is the law of religion and its regulator according to each period in time. Laws which do not have the flexibility to fit changing times and communities cannot live; in the same manner, the *Shari'a* which is shaped to last an eternity, cannot walk at the same pace with humanity. Islam, which has the ability to accommodate the real necessities of each period in time, today has lost all its power of life because it has been stripped of its divine values in the hands of a clergy composed of bigots, fortune-tellers and the superstitious.[23]

Topçu's perfect individuals do not live alone. Through their common belief and understanding of life, they form a collective entity. This is his "cemaat" (community) as opposed to the "cemiyet" (society) of Ziya Gökalp. For Topçu, society (cemiyet) means a crowd of undefined, faithless individuals devoid of personal will-power, whereas community (cemaat) is composed of individuals who have sacrificed their individualism and materialism to meaning. Topçu's individualism comes from the fact that his community is composed of individuals who have individually high morals and eternal souls.

Despite his spirituality, Topçu accepts the importance of the material world, and proceeds to define first his understanding of what a nation is and then his ideal economic and social system. First, Topçu criticizes Islamism, Ottomanism and Pan-Turkism:

> Islamists thought that they could create a national power with the remnants of the age of *umma* and forgot the real national history born of common geography and economy. They did not realize that labour that is action is the first and foremost core of will-power in man. . . . . . Ottomanism made the history and fate of people inseparable from that of a family and its glory and honour. . . . . . Pan-Turkists confused the notion of race with the notion of nation. In reality, just as there is no Latin nation, no Germanic or Slavic nation, there could not be a Turan nation. . . . Isn't thinking that, without the unity of matter, a unity of spirit would happen, as unfortunate as believing in the existence of spirit without matter? They named the nation of their utopia after their race and looked for the elements of a nation in the sources of the race. [On the other hand] they disclaimed the constructive value of a common race in the creation of the national entity. There must be

[23] Nurettin Topçu, "Din hayatı", 70.

> political reasons in this incredible denial of Ziya Gökalp's. For him, a common land is not a nation-making element . . . he assumed that the Oghuz who live in Turkey, Azerbaijan, Iran and Khorezm are a nation.[24]

It is not the case that Topçu denies the necessity of "a common race" for a nation. But this "common race" for him is the Oghuz Turk of Anatolia. He also very gently insinuates in his attack on Ziya Gökalp that the well-known leaders are not from Anatolia and therefore not of the same race.

According to Topçu, what makes a group of people a nation is the sum of their missions around common ideals which can only be spiritual. To come from a common race is not enough; race on its own is a material notion, it has no content and no life. Life-giving sources of each nation are different from each another. For the Turks this has been Islam. Islam has given the Oghuz Turks the love for the divine which joined them forever. Yet, common geography and history are also necessary because they prepare the background for being a nation. Like the forefathers of *Anadoluculuk*, Topçu accepts 1071 as the beginning of Turkish history. This is the date that the Oghuz Turks entered Anatolia and ended their nomadic lives; they became farmers and began to practise a common religion which gave them love and soul. Topçu's ideal man is a farmer because the most exhalted form of existence is found in agriculture. By becoming Muslims and farmers, the Oghuz Turks fulfilled this ideal. They left behind their nomadic days and, in the purity of the agricultural life, they joined their natural abilities with the mysticism of "Anatolian" Islam. In lyrical romanticism, he praises the supremacy of the Anatolian farmer of the 11th century:

> The Islam of the nomadic Arab who lived in the desert took on a new identity in the soul of the Anatolian farmer. . . . . It is necessary to know that these people who joined their future with the land had higher spiritual and ethical qualities than the Arabs and the Central Turkmen tribes, because the Anatolian was not a nomad like the Arab or the Central Asian Turk. Because a man who lives tied to the land is someone who carries the continuous responsibility of a reality. . . . This man is not the sly nomadic merchant who reaches to the land for material gains and then leaves it. He is a farmer who feels that he comes closer to God every day as his ties to the land get stronger.[25]

---

[24] Nurettin Topçu, "Bizde milliyet hareketleri", 146.
[25] Ibid., 150.

Topçu accepts that the nomadic Oghuz learned agriculture from the previous Anatolians going back all the way to the Hittites. Topçu's nationalism admits to this reality and accepts the notion of cultural influence. For something to be accepted as "national", it does not have to be created by that particular nation. According to Öğün,[26] his romanticism on the one hand, and his flexibility in accepting reality on the other, are among the elements which make Topçu a "populist" like Ziya Gökalp whom he criticizes bitterly.

In Topçu's interpretation of history, Anatolia lived its golden age in the hands of the Seljuqs and during the early days of the Ottomans, and illustrated the perfect trinity of man-earth-God. However, after its early years, the Ottomans fell into the hands of materialism. They used *ghaza* to bring them riches and material gain. They forgot the land and the farmer. When they expanded the lands of the Empire, they embraced peoples from other lands and allowed their own people, the Anatolian people, to suffer in poverty, while the foreign elements governed the Empire and rose to the highest administrative positions. The Anatolian villager was used to support the aims of the state. Meanwhile the clergy also rotted. They cheated the people and abused the good will of the Anatolian:

> Anatolia did not give birth to any social classes, because the spiritual power which gave it its soul during its creation did not come to the assistance of Anatolia, nor was the material power created by this country left in the hands of its own children. Hence, neither the intellectuals of Auguste Comte by whom he wanted Europe to be led, nor the industrialists that Saint-Simon wanted as rulers, were born in Anatolia. As long as there were those who lived off the labour of the nation and the revenue derived from the work force of the Anatolian villager, it would not have been possible to establish the power of the people in Anatolia.[27]

And as for more contemporary times:

> After losing World War I, Anatolia went to war for independence. On the war front, the sword was victorious. However, it was the spirit of the people that was victorious. We did not exalt the victory of the soul to the skies like a flag. Instead of celebrating the spirit of the

[26] Süleyman Seyfi Öğün, *Türkiye'de Cemaatçi Milliyetçilik ve Nurettin Topçu.*
[27] Nurettin Topçu, "İçtimai sınıflar", 81.

> people who went to war, we celebrated the *efeler* who came back from the war, and using victory, joined in the pillage.[28]

While it is impossible to mistake whom Topçu means by the word "efeler", i.e. the non-Anatolian commanders and their men, Topçu is actually against all people and powers who, according to him, have usurped the Anatolian villager for their own material gain. He is angry at the non-Anatolian and non-Muslim minorities of the Ottoman Empire who were not villagers and who had occupied the highest positions in the administration. The Crusaders and the armies of Timur, merchants and capitalists, are all enemies. He does not hide his anti-Semitism. He dislikes the Jews because they are merchants and capitalists.

After all his anger at the enemies of the people (capitalists, Jews, minorities in the Ottoman Empire, etc.) whom he attacks with the same fierceness as he embraces spirituality, he advocates love. He believes that even a seemingly bad man has

> the right to love goodness and, moreover, has a secret hope to be good . . . A bad man is a man without hope. . . . We can save people from their despair . . . Where despair is not cured, vengeance takes over. Vengeance is born from despair. Vengeance is the enemy of compassion and love. . . .[29]

Like Gandhi, whom he praises and regards as one of the Messiahs of the world because of his non-violent, non-physical forms of protest, Topçu is against technology and industrialization. For him technology enslaves the soul of man and makes him addicted to material. In this context, a struggle against industrialization becomes a struggle against capitalism and against all its representatives. Topçu's attitude to Westernization revolves around this hostility towards industrialization. He claims that the Westernization movements in the Ottoman Empire (and in the world in general) were and are doomed to fail because the ethics of the West cannot be separated from the technology of the West and that one can not borrow the technology of the West on its own:

> The Western mind and the entity called "the Westerner" is the whole of its literature, music, ethics and family life and it is not possible to separate these from the technology of the West.[30]

[28] Nurettin Topçu, "Mes'uliyet hareketi", 125.
[29] Nurettin Topçu, "Millet ve komünism", 9.
[30] Nurettin Topçu, "Avrupa", 189.

However, unlike many nationalists and Islamicists, Topçu does not think that "Western ethics" are the enemy. For him "ethics" are universal and systems of ethics are religions, all of which are viable. Western Christian spirituality is perfectly adequate and is to be celebrated. The real problem in the world is one of spiritual versus material:

> [In Europe] the delicate Christian spirituality collided with the crude and coarse materialism of the colonialist industrialist. . . . The power of soul and faith of Pascal who can be regarded as the most sincere representative of Christ in Europe; the work ethics of Kant; the heart and love of nature in Rousseau which created romanticism and brought excitement and fire to tired hearts . . . all these have been products of the Christian spirit in Europe. However, from time to time the machine wanted to drown the voice of the heart and the faith and it has been successful.[31]

Hence, if the machine takes over in any part of the world, spirituality is lost. The cause of it all is the positivist and materialist mentality. However, technology is acceptable as long as it fits the native culture of the people and this is the reason why Turkey cannot import technology from the West:

> The West praised technology and we tagged on with admiration to the tail of this caravan. We imitated the values which sprang from Europe's own entity and the products of its own genius. . . . As a result of this disaster, which has been going on for over a century, we are alienated from ourselves. . . .[32]

Topçu was accused of being a "communist" (but not a fascist) by the more Pan-Turkist fractions of the Nationalist movement. However, he is in fact against Russian communists whom he sees as carrying the same spirit as the capitalist imperialist Russians. For him, the communists, hiding behind the mask of social justice, are as materialistic as the imperialists. And because communism was born out of capitalism, the real enemy of the people is capitalism. Topçu thinks that communism will cease to exist for a while but unless the capitalist oppression is melted in a system of justice, the vengeance of communism will not leave humanity alone. It is this vengeance which

[31] Ibid., 191.
[32] Nurettin Topçu, "Milli kültürümüz ve garplılaşma meselesi", 195.

will destroy the spiritual unity of humanity which ties it to God.[33] Topçu dislikes the physical revolutionary aspect of communism which is fired with vengeance. According to him, revolution and physical violence would bring oppression, and oppression of one kind cannot be overcome with oppression of another kind.

It is not difficult to see that what Topçu is advocating has been inspired by a long line of philosophers and thinkers such as Rousseau, Fichte, Nietzche, Giovanni and Hegel, nor that he would naturally admire national socialism. In fact, in one of his articles, Topçu singles out national socialism among all the different kinds of socialisms but criticizes the Germans for claiming to be a "master race".[34] According to him, in an ideal system, there would be a strong state which would play the role of regulator and carry out strict moral policing. His system would be realized in three phases: first of all, a socialist society would be established. Then the people would be trained and educated, then the morals and the culture of Islam would be revitalized by going back to its true sources.[35] Since his socialism would be based on agriculture, a "land reform", which would make an end of the oppression of the big land owner, would be realized. The formation of cooperatives would keep the farmer in his village and at the same time give him the opportunity to cater for and protect his material needs. In various articles he talks about the details of his utopia including education, justice, health and economy. The young people who would realize his dream of perfect order would have to be of a very special kind:

> The architects of tomorrow's Turkey, will be the miners of the spiritual front who will leave the pleasures of life aside and give their hearts to the love of giving life, who will work with patience and determination yet without ostentation and affection. . . . These able young people who will be capable of self-sacrifice of every kind will not ask for a reward in return for their services from the people they serve; [but] will present their work to eternity and they will hear the echoes of their work from eternity.[36]

---

[33] Nurettin Topçu, *Komünizm Karşısında Yeni Nizam.*
[34] Nurettin Topçu, "Sosyalizm ve şekilleri".
[35] Nurettin Topçu, "Sosyalist cemiyet nizamı".
[36] Nurettin Topçu, *Yarınki Türkiye*, 10.

Afterwards

Following Topçu's death, one of his colleagues said:

> Nurettin Topçu was too mystical for me. This mysticism was removed from the realities of the land. I did not believe that [his] ideas would solve the problems of Turkey.[37]

It is not certain how many of his sympathizers and listeners understood or approved of what Topçu advocated. However, they all accepted that on a personal level Topçu practised what he preached. He bought material goods with reluctance, prayed in private, never changed a decision that he made; his will-power was very strong, he loved nature, and he preferred to walk almost everywhere because he hated cars.[38]

Despite the fury and anger which quite often bursts from his writings, his students, whose interactions with him were mostly oral, do not remember him preaching hatred. Quite the opposite:

> Who could explain in such a terse manner and convince his audience that love for mankind should be the primary element of our actions and thoughts?[39]

Topçu remains one of the great orators who influenced many young minds of an era.

Bibliography

Arık, Remzi Oğuz, *Coğrafyadan Vatana*, Ankara, 1969.
Balım, Ali İhsan, "Kaybettiğimiz İdealist Topçu", *Hareket* 112 (1976), 48–50.
Başgil, Ali Fuat, ed., *Celâl Hoca*, İstanbul, 1962.
Çakır, Ruşen, *Ayet ve Slogan*, İstanbul, 1990.
Çelik, Muammer, ed., *Hüseyin Avni Ulaş*, Erzurum, 1996.
Güvenç, Bozkurt, Gencay Şaylan, İlhan Tekeli, Şerafettin Turan, eds., *Türk-İslâm Sentezi*, İstanbul, 1994.
Işık, Emin, "N. Topçu ve din adamları", *Hareket* 112 (1976), 84–89.

---

[37] Interview with Mehmet Kaplan, in "Kırk Yıllık Hareket", 66. Mehmet Kaplan was one of the architects of the *Türk-İslâm Sentezi* (Turk-Islam Synthesis) of the 1970s which was accepted as the official state policy of culture in the 1980s. About *Türk-İslâm Sentezi* see Bozkurt Güvenç, et al., *Türk-İslâm Sentezi*; İbrahim Kafesoğlu, *Türk-İslâm Sentezi*; Mehmet Kaplan, *Büyük Türkiye Rüyası*.

[38] Hayrettin Topçu in Mustafa Kutlu, "N. Topçu için bir biyografi denemesi", 120.

[39] Ali İhsan Balım, "Kaybettiğimiz idealist Topçu", 48.

Kafesoğlu, İbrahim, *Türk-İslâm Sentezi*, İstanbul, 1985.
Kaplan, Mehmet, *Büyük Türkiye Rüyası*, İstanbul, 1969.
Konukman, Ercüment, "Nurettin Topçu hocamızın ardından", *Hareket* 112 (1976), 64–71.
Kutlu, Mustafa, "Nurettin Topçu için bir biyografi denemesi", *Hareket* 112 (1976), 110–120.
Landau, Jacob M., *Pan-Turkism in Turkey*, London, 1981.
Mardin, Şerif, "Culture and the intellectual" in *Cultural Transitions in the Middle East*, ed. Şerif Mardin, Leiden, 1994, 189–213.
Milliyetçiler Derneği, *Hüseyin Ayni Ulaş*, İstanbul, 1958.
Okay, Orhan, "Nurettin Topçu: bir idealistin ölümü", *Hareket* 112 (1976), 42–7.
Öğün, Süleyman Seyfi, *Türkiye'de Cemaatçi Milliyetçilik ve Nurettin Topçu*, İstanbul, 1992.
Topçu, Nurettin, *Kömünizm Karşısında Yeni Nizam*, İstanbul, 1960, "Millet ve kömünizm", 5–10; "Sosyalizm ve şekilleri", 17–21.
———, *Ahlâk Nizamı*, İstanbul, 1961, "Din hayatı, 69–77.
———, *Yarınki Türkiye* (İstanbul: Yağmur Yayınları, 1961), "Bizde milliyet hareketleri", 142–52; "İçtimai sınıflar", 71–81; "Mes'uliyet hareketi", 124–8; "Avrupa", 187–193; "Milli kültürümüz ve garplılaşma meselesi", 194–205.
———, "Sosyalist cemiyet nizamı", *Hareket* 11 (1966), 16–7.
———, *Bergson*, İstanbul, 1968.
———, *Kültür ve Medeniyet*, İstanbul, 1970.
———, "Mevlâna'da âlem ve insan", *Hareket* 97 (1974), 53–59.
Ülken, Hilmi Ziya, *Türkiye'de Çağdaş Düşünce Tarihi*, İstanbul 1994.
Yenihaber, Asım, "Kırk yıllık Hareket", *Hareket* 1 (1979), 64–7.

A YOUNG MAN ABROAD
SIR THOMAS HERBERT'S TRAVELS TO PERSIA IN 1626 A.D.

JOHN CARSWELL

Before describing Sir Thomas Herbert's youthful trip to Persia in 1626, it is appropriate to sketch in the major events of his colourful and extremely varied life.[1] He was born in York in 1606, to a well-established merchant family, and baptised in the church of St Crux, the same church where he was to be buried seventy-six years later. He was an undergraduate at Oxford but he never took a degree. Instead, he moved to London where he was taken under the wing of his kinsman, William Herbert, Earl of Pembroke. Pembroke was a friend of Shakespeare, and had influence at the court of Charles I. It was through Pembroke that Herbert secured a place in the retinue of Sir Dodmore Cotton, just about to depart as Ambassador to the Shah of Persia.

Cotton sailed in 1626, along with Sir Robert Sherley and his wife, and the young Thomas Herbert. They travelled round the Cape of Good Hope and across the Indian Ocean to Goa, arriving ten months later when they disembarked at Gombrun. The company then travelled overland by Shiraz and Persepolis to Isfahan. Finding Shah Abbas was in residence at Ashraf, they then proceeded north to the Caspian Sea. Diplomatically, the audience with the Shah proved unsatisfactory, and the party retreated via Qazvin. Here both Cotton and Sherley were taken ill and died, which put something of a damper on the enterprise. Herbert was also sick but recovered thanks to an ill-intentioned dose of Shiraz wine, administered by a malevolent servant who had something quite else in mind than a restorative. After obtaining a *firman* for right of passage from the Shah, Herbert and

---

[1] My initial interest in Herbert was concerned with the illustrations in his travel-book, and how he attempted to describe and draw the unfamiliar; these thoughts were published in two articles in *Art and Archaeology Research Papers*, "East and West: A Study in Aesthetic Contrasts", Part I, *AARP* 2, (1972), 77–87; Part II, *AARP* 3, (1973), 82–98. The ideas were further developed in a lecture given at the Windsor Festival in 1995, which was the genesis of the present contribution.

the surviving members of his expedition got back to the Gulf and set sail for home. They returned by way of Ceylon, Mauritius and St Helena, and after many more adventures arrived back in Plymouth three years later, towards the end of 1629.

Back home, Herbert hoped to benefit once more from Pembroke's patronage, but the Earl inconveniently dropped dead just before he was due to meet him for dinner. His brother Philip, his successor, does not seem to have been much help, although he was Lord Chancellor. Thomas Herbert retired to the country and married in 1632. He wrote the first account of his travels in 1634,[2] followed by a second edition in 1638. The Civil War changed his fortunes. Pembroke joined the Parliamentary faction, and Herbert found himself attached to his suite, to accompany the captive King. Charles took to Thomas Herbert, and made him Groom of the Bedchamber; for the last two years of his life they were close companions, and Herbert was profoundly influenced by the King's character; he became a convinced Royalist for the rest of his life. He accompanied Charles from St James Palace to his execution in Whitehall, and Charles gave him several personal mementoes including his pocket-watch.

After this incident Herbert again retired from the scene and did not return to London until the Restoration. He was rewarded for his loyal sentiments with a baronetcy in 1660. He took a house in Petty France in Westminster, but during the Plague prudently retired to York. A much-expanded version of his travels appeared in a third edition, published in 1665, and a fourth and final edition came out in 1667. Meanwhile the work had been translated into both French and Dutch. Besides his travel writings, his account of the last days of King Charles' life would itself have been enough to earn him a place in literary history.[3] In York he indulged in antiquarian pursuits, and in 1666 gave twenty manuscripts to the Bodleian at his old university, including Wycliffe's Bible. From all this it is clear that Herbert lived an exceptionally varied life during a colourful and eventful period of English history. It is within this framework that one must place his youthful journey to Persia as a young man of twenty.

[2] *A relation of some yeares travaile, begunne Anno 1626, into Afrique and the greater Asia, especially the territories of the Persian Monarchie, and some parts of the oriental Indies . . . of their religion, language, habit . . . and other matters concerning them. Together with the proceedings and death of the three late ambassadours: Sir D[odmore] C[otton], Sir R[obert] S[herley] and the Persian Nogdi-Beg . . . By T. H[erbert] Esquier*, London, 1634.

[3] Herbert, *Threnodia Carolina.*

* * * * *

Of the four versions of his travel-book, two were relatively youthful products, the first written when he was twenty-eight and revised four years later. Then came the extraordinary interlude when he was Charles' minder. The third edition was produced when he was fifty-nine, and the fourth was published when he was seventy-one, the product of his mature years. Comparing the four editions it is intriguing to see how he completely changed the text, not only by adding new material but also rephrasing the smallest details. The first version has the vivid impact of experience set down at speed. Later, there is more the impression of emotion set down in tranquillity, with extra material furnished from his own memories and other sources. In his introduction he refers to his difficulties as a writer:

> My desire to see, took away my sight, as it fares with those who are suddenly taken with a killing beauty, or gaze upon the Sun. Yet some glimmering I have observed, like an ill-sighted man, who sees with Spectacles or Perspectives.

Thomas, Lord Fairfax wrote an introduction to the second edition and put it rather differently. In an appalling verse addressed to the Reader, he muses:

> *Here thou at greater ease than he,*
> *Mayest behold what he did see,*
> *Thou participate his gains,*
> *But he alone reserves the pains,*
> *He traded not with luker sotted,*
> *He went for knowledge and he got it.*

An indication of Herbert's insular, indeed chauvinistic attitude to what he encountered may be gleaned from the engraving on the title-page. (Figure 1) At the top left is a frank expression of his horror at native goings-on, in this case a scene of naked fireworshippers, presumably Zoroastrians presided over by the Devil incarnate. (Figure 2) And at the top right we have a familiar scene illustrating a point of view, alas still with us to this day—the innocent virgin, Europe, clasping a cross and sitting on a Knole chair, being attacked by ruthless Turks armed with scimitars. (Figure 3) No chance of a swift entry into the Common Market here.

But by far one of the most interesting aspects of Herbert's work is that he tacitly acknowledges the inadequacy of words alone to convey his experiences, and his stress on what things actually looked

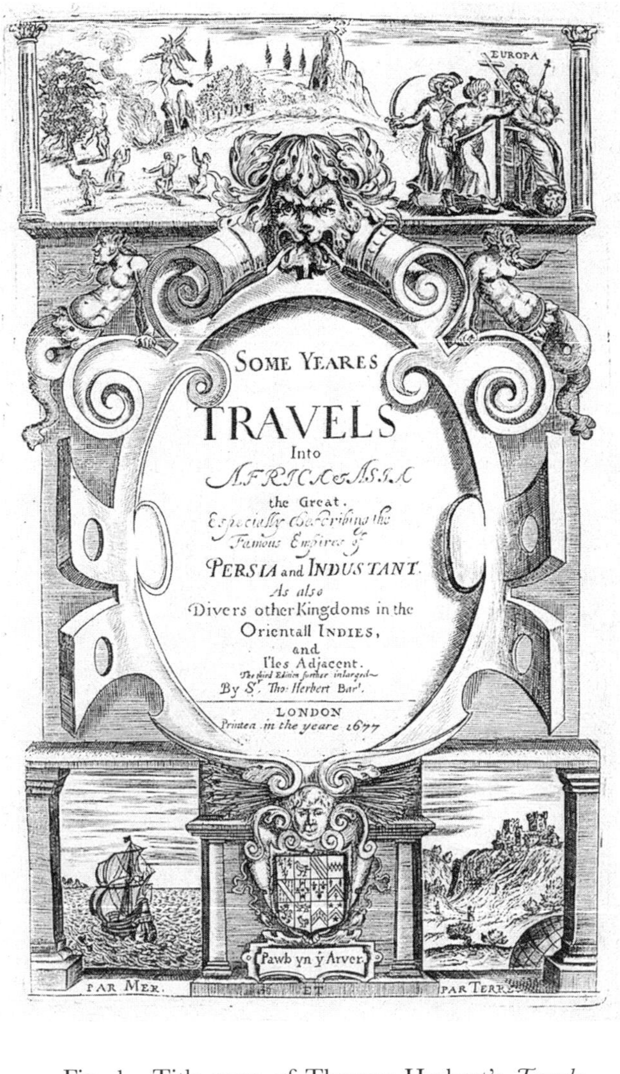

Fig. 1 Title page of Thomas Herbert's *Travels*

Fig. 2 Detail of title page, *top left*

Fig. 3 Detail of title page, *top right*

like. This led to the inclusion of numerous engravings throughout the text, which he tells us are after his own drawings made on the spot, in what he calls his "table-book" or journal. He is rightly diffident about their artistic merit; as he says, they were "not drawn by Phidias". But fortunately most of them were engraved by an almost equally inept printmaker, so some hard facts survive untrammelled by a fancy style. He had a remarkable curiosity about the landscape and its inhabitants, the strange flora and fauna, architecture and antiquities. He even made a brave attempt at reproducing foreign scripts, such as the Persian alphabet and ancient cuneiform.

* * * * *

Now for the voyage itself. He set off from Deal on Good Friday, 1626, in an East India sailing-ship, in a convoy of similar vessels. Twenty-nine days later they were still struggling across the Bay of Biscay in a huge storm. He must have been a good sailor for he describes it all quite cheerfully:

> plowing the liquid seas in merriness made us the sport of danger, struggling with such mighty waves and deep seas as off-times seemed to make us climb up mountains of salt water, and were straitway precipitated headlong as it were twixt cloven seas, a good while heaven and earth seeming undivided.

They sighted Porto Sancto, then passed by the Azores, and the Canary Islands. The ancient inhabitants he tells us:

> knew no God but Nature, were ignorant of the use of fire, shaved with flint stones, gave their children to be nursed by goats, cultured the earth with Horns of Oxen, abominated the slaughter of beasts, and used women in common.

Thanks to the civilising threat of the Spanish Inquisition they were converted to Christianity and Grand Canary became the seat of the Inquisitor. To compensate for their lot Herbert tells us that they had an abundance of good things such as:

> goats, beefs, asses, hogs, barley, rye, rice, a variety of flowers, grapes and other excellent fruits, and sugar-houses in which to boil cane sugar.

Sailing down the coast of Africa all was not well aboard. There were tornadoes and the sailors got wet through manning the sails and had to get into their beds:

Fig. 4 A Sharke Fish

> resting their weary bodies in wet, nasty cloaths, thereby breeding many diseases as fevers, calentures, fluxes, aches, scurvy and the like.

When they were becalmed the men swam in the sea and Herbert takes the occasion to describe the hungry sharks; as he says,

> many have been devoured by this ravenous fish and more suffered in their members, whose shape take thus resembled (though mistaken in his posture by the ingraver). (Figure 4)

Further on, the weather did not get any better:

> the stinking rain is no sooner in the sea, but a whirlwind usually circles with such violence . . . that oft-times the waves rebound top-gallant height.

Nor did the natives improve either; describing the inhabitants of Angola:

> for colour they may well cry chimney-sweep; unlike them in this, they are of no profession, except rapine and villainy make one.

There is an amusing story of the bawdy antics of the ladies of Angola and how they revenged themselves on the Moon, which they thought was the cause of their monthly troubles:

> here the female sex each new moon defy pale *Cynthia*, imagining her to be the cause of their distempers, which to comply with the weaker sex, the men threaten with their shafts, as if they could reach that planet, albeit distant from them no less than one hundred and twenty thousand miles.

The engraving accompanying this story is marvellously uninhibited, with the Angolan wearing a curly bonnet and his genitals neatly tied with a bow, not unreminiscent of Joe Alessandrio's antics in Andy Warhol's movie, *Flesh.* (Figure 5)

On the way to the Cape, seen and duly drawn were boobies, which perched on the yard-arm of the ship and lived up to their name by letting the sailors easily take them. Further on there was an abundance of penguins, which Herbert classifies as,

> a degenerate Duck, for using both sea and shore, it feeds in the one, breeds on the other, is very fat and oily, and some adventure to eat them. (Figure 6)

—which he does not recommend. There were large numbers of seals, as big as:

> the greatest sort of mastiffs, and something like them in visage; and in voice out-bark them.

There were also crocodiles, otters and mannatees to wonder at, quite apart from whales which:

> like so many floating islands accompanied us, and after guize thundered out our welcome . . . these Leviathans are indeed the largest, not only of all fish in the sea, but of all creatures . . . the body is thick and round, which the savages eat, but the merchants covet them rather for profit, one usually giving out twelve tons of oil . . . [to mate] belly touches belly, in bringing forth they have but one at a time . . . like the elephant.

They then came to the Cape of Good Hope and anchored in Souldanja Bay. Herbert claims the engraving of the local inhabitants is based on his own drawing, saying:

"I present the reader so well as I was able to draw them". (Figure 7) Here he vents a full flood of Western prejudice:

> by way of dress some have all their skull, some half others leave a tuft atop. Their ears are extended by links of brass . . . arms and legs loaden with volontary shackles of brass, iron and ivory . . . and about their necks the raw guts of beasts . . . the rest of their body is naked save for a thong of leather . . . and the women give suck, the uberous dugg being stretched over their naked shoulder . . . their language is apishly founded, with whom tis thought they have unnatural mixture . . . so as considering the resemblance they bear with baboons, which I could observe kept frequent company with the women.

Fig. 5 An Inhabitant of Angola

Fig. 6 A Pen-gwin

In the background Herbert draws the Table Mountain—looking just like a table.

Rounding the Cape, they sailed up the East African coast past Madagascar, which he states is unquestionably the greatest island in the world:

> the island is rich in minerals and marquisite, gold, silver, iron and copper, buffaloes, antilopes, deer, goats, milk, hens, eggs, wheat, barley, rice . . . oranges lemons, limes, plantains, sugarcane, ginger and coconuts . . . here also are lizards and chameleons . . . [exceptionally, the natives are] strong, active and courageous . . . black, at no time shading their bodies from the parching sun, delighting to their bodies all over with grease proud to see their flesh shine, the stink never offending them. They are delighted with sports and novelties, hunting, hawking, fishing and dancing.

They sailed north through the Comores and Herbert drew the profile of Mozambique and "Meotty's Isle", the present day Mayotte. They were accompanied by an armada of dolphins:

> glittering in the ocean with a variety of beautiful colours . . . they were glad of our company, many miles in an eager and unwearied pursuit frisking about us. (Figure 8)

Fig. 7 A Man and Woman of the Cape of Good Hope

They came to the island of Mohelia, and here the inhabitants are:

> perfect black . . . with big lips, flat noses, sharp chins, large limbs, and in mode affecting Adam's garb, with a few plantain-leaves vailing their modest parts.

Herbert concedes, after a discourse on why blacks are black:

> now this difference from us in colour and garb was to either a deformity; our habit and white complexion being as strange and unpleasant to these negroes, as their blackness was to us.[4]

[4] The writer can verify this. When I visited the Maldive Islands in 1972 with

Fig. 8 Dolphin

He describes the products once more; tobacco, arecca, betelnuts, animals and fruits, fish and turtles, and three fruits he singles out for special attention:

> the banana, the fruit a golden yellow, and relished like a Windsor pear, so delicious it melts in one's mouth, good for urine but bad for fluxes, and too liberally eaten disposes to dysenteries. The coconut is like a man's skull, yielding a quart of ambrosia, the kernel enough to satiate the appetite of two reasonable men.

The tree also has a variety of uses, and once again his cousin Pembroke sums it up with another ghastly verse:

> . . . the Indian Nut alone,
> Is cloathing, meat and trencher, drink and can,
> Boat, cable, sail, mast, needle, all in one.

Finally he describes toddy, the fermented product of the palm tree, and the delight of many a South Asian man to this day;[5] he says:

> toddy for colour resembles whey, but tastes like Rhenish; at first draught it is uncouth, but every draught tastes better than other; a little makes men merry, much inebriates; in the morning it is found laxative, in the evening costive; at midnight dangerous.

He also says that the Mohelians do not have ships or boats, but canoes hewn out of a single tree trunk big enough for three men,

---

my wife and family and spent a month on Male, then little visited by foreigners, every day when we emerged from our house there were shrieks of laughter and giggles at the colour of our pink skins.

[5] And also women; see Michael Ondaatje, *Running in the Family*, 1983, 12, for an account of a bibulous session drinking toddy with his sister and Aunt Phyllis in the Governor's house in Jaffna.

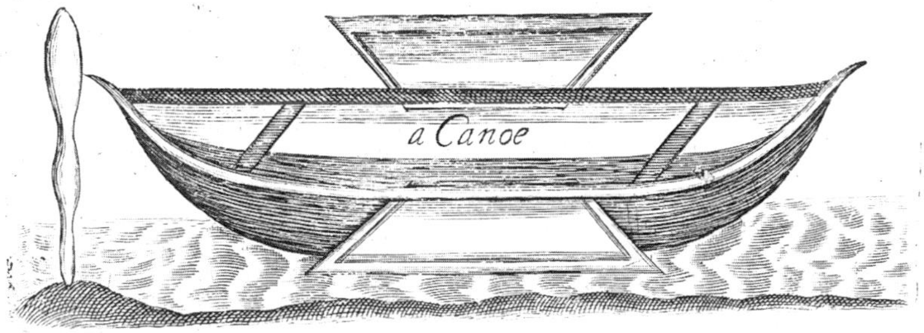

Fig. 9 A Canoe

and he gives a sketch of this unusual craft. (Figure 9) Sailing northwards they were becalmed and:

> the greatest recreation we had was of such large shoals of flying fish as their interposing multitude for some time darkened the sun. (Figure 10)

Three weeks later they were off the coast of Goa in southern India, and one can only surmise they had been swept across the Indian Ocean by the south-east monsoon.[6] This was not the direction they were aiming at, so now they had to make their way up the coast of India past Chaul to Surat. Here the Persian ambassador Nadj Ali Beg, whom they were conveying with them back home, died. Herbert speculates that he in fact committed suicide, unable to face the reprimand of Shah Abbas, who would have learned of his diplomatic ineptitude in England by message overland from Aleppo before he was due to arrive.

Herbert's lengthy description of Surat and the English and Dutch colonies there is an excuse for a series of observations about India and its inhabitants in general. He tells how the Banyan merchants pitch their tents at Swalley Road on the coast down river from Surat, and sell calicoes, China-satin, porcelain ware, cabinets of mother of pearl, ebony, ivory, agates, turquoises, heliotropes and carnelians, as well as more humble supplies of rice, sugar, bananas and Arack. He gives a lengthy description of the Hindu religion and the rule of the Brahmin priesthood. And in his drawing of a Banyan merchant he

[6] It should be remarked that this is only thirty years later than Ahmed ibn Majid revealed the secret of direct navigation across the Indian Ocean to the Portuguese.

Fig. 10 A Flying Fish

includes a typical idolatrous shrine, which he says are often placed under banyan trees. The idols are:

> ugly-faced, with long black hair, goggled eyes, wide-mouthed with forked beard, everyway so mishapen and horrible as somewhat resembles the old obscene forms of Pan and Priapus.

Further on he discourses on the Parsees and their practice of exposing their dead to be eaten by vultures:

> the corpses are conveyed in a round building, flat on top and plastered, in the middle of which is a hole made to let in the putrefaction of the melted bodies, laid naked and exposed to the sun's rage and the appetite of ravening birds. (Figure 11)

It was a rare way of burial and:

> the dislike of the Parsees expressed at my taking a view of this golgotha made it appear that they do not delight that it should be seen by foreigners.

From Surat, they took another ship to the Persian Gulf, and finally arrived off the coast of Arabia. They stopped at Hormuz where:

Fig. 11 The Burial place of the Parsees in India

> the houses were exceedingly neatly furnished with gilded leather, and with Indian and Chinese rarities, the Bazaar was rich and beautiful, the churches [that is, mosques] splendid, and both within and without the castle so regularly built . . . that none exceeded it throughout the Orient.

The final port of call was Gombrun, and at Sir Dodmore Cotton's command Sherley went ashore and acquainted himself with the Sultan, to obtain a *firman* for safe passage to proceed overland to the court of Shah Abbas. The captain signalled their departure by firing a hundred cannon, and mounted on a richly apparelled Arab horse the Ambassador was ceremoniously conveyed to the Sultan's palace,

> where in a delightful chamber the floor was spread with a Persian carpet as big as the chamber itself . . . [they were entertained] with a very neat collation of sweetmeats and *pilaf*, choice Shiraz wine and music both of that country and from our ships.

Here follows yet another description of a couple, this time a typical Persian pair from the Gulf, and remarks about their dress and nudity, though he does quote another author who states that:

> the naked American women do not so much incite to wantoness or appear as libidinous, as European women by the magic of their eyes, mimick dress, painting, patching and gestures of several immodest fashions and loose inventions.

Indeed Herbert is fascinated by appearances, and his drawing even includes a little sketch of a nose jewel.

The Ambassador's party set off overland on twelve horses and twenty-nine camels, tenting on the way and occasionally making use of caravansarays:

> a building resembling and empty college . . . of great use seeing these parts have no inns.

Travelling through the villages they were occasionally entertained, for instance by the chief magistrate of Larr. They finally arrived in Shiraz, which Herbert says is the second town in Persia for magnificence and

> the houses are all of sun-dried bricks, hard and durable but not very lofty, flat and terraced above, having balconies and windows curiously trellised.

They feasted in Sultan Shah Ali Beg's mansion, where:

> his dining room was high and wide and spacious, the walls embossed with gold and wrought with imagery . . . the windows of painted glass, the floor spread with curious carpets. Few or none here are without their gardens.

There were fifteen mosques, and Herbert attempts to find words to describe their splendour, such as one where:

> the outside was varnished and wrought with knots and poesies [it had two minarets] round and coupled at the top, garnished with great art and cost, from whose tops the clear-voiced boys sing every twenty-four hours eulogies to their prophets Ali and Mohamet.

Fig. 12 Detail of Wenceslas Hollar's engraving of Persepolis (1663)

They were entertained by the Duke of Shiraz, and:

> no part of the world has wine better than Shiraz . . . many bottles and flagons were emptied

and afterwards on mounting his horse, the Duke fell back, and was only saved by the Ambassador who had by chance upheld him. Sir Dodmore Cotton next day received twelve horses as a recompense, and the Duke's hospitality was never-ending; it was a month before they were finally able to set off again.

The first stop was at the ruins of Persepolis, which were described by Herbert in the greatest detail. The engraving in the third and last editions of his travel-book was by Wenceslas Hollar, who had been sent by the Duke of Arundel to sketch antiquities. (Figure 12) A comparison with the site as it has today survived shows that he did not do a bad job. As Herbert says, eastwards near the stairs are:

> four strange beasts carved in stone, not such beasts as are in nature but rather than as an issue from the poet's brain . . . . these quadrupeds stand two by two . . . two look toward the stair . . . and the other two have their face turned towards the hill. One is like an elephant, the second a rhinocerus, the third a flying griffin, and the fourth disfigured.

Fig. 13 Cuneiform characters

Herbert was very curious about the inscriptions he saw, and includes a drawing of a panel of cuneiform in his work, which he says nevertheless cannot be read. (Figure 13)

Riding on to Isfahan, they received a royal welcome, except Shah Abbas was not there. Nevertheless, there was a cavalcade of four thousand horses:

> kettledrums, fifes, timbrels, dancing-wenches and hocus-pocus and other antics past my remembrance.

The Armenian colony, settled since 1604 in the suburb of New Djulfa across the River Zanderud south from Isfahan, entertained the Ambassador and his party. The leader of the community, Khodjar Nazar, had them to a party in his house, which still stands to this day:

> The flagons and bowls in his house were all of gold . . . vials of sweet water for perfume, and glasses of Shiraz wine emptied for our entertainment . . . a Christian he professes to be but his house was furnished with such ugly beastly pictures, such ugly postures as are indeed not fit to be remembered . . . . pity these Christians living among infidels are so past shame.

A more appreciative account of another party in the same house was given just a few years later in 1639, by Olearius, the Duke of Holstein, who was also a guest of the Khodjar:

> we found an open hall . . . where we were entreated to sit down on the ground . . . the cloth, which was of gold and silver brocade, was covered with all sorts of fruits and conserves and we drank a certain prepared water . . . having taken away the fruits, they laid an Indian cotton cloth and the meat was brought up, in silver dishes . . . we had

> hardly eaten so much as allayed our first hunger, when we were conducted to another hall, which looked into the garden. It was arched all about and there were on the walls pictures representing most women of the world dressed according to their countries . . . the floor was covered with rich tapestry . . . and cushions of flowered satin . . . in the midst of the hall there was a fountain, of white marble, the water covered with flowers and beset all about with flagons and bottles of wine . . . we had the divertisment of music and dancing . . . the whole day was spent thus, till the Ambassadors perceiving night approach took leave of their hosts, but they pretending to conduct us out of the house brought us to the other side of the garden, where we found the cloth laid and all sorts of meat, flesh, fish, pies, fruits and conserves . . . it is not imagined we could have eat ought. Having with much ado taken our leave, thus we concluded that day, which I must confess was one of the most pleasant we had in all our travels.[7]

Herbert described Isfahan in detail, giving a sketch of yet another couple, this time Georgians. (Figure 14) He made a plan of the maidan, the entrance to the bazaar at the bottom, the Masjid es-Shah at the top, the King's House (the Chihil Sutun palace) on the left and the Lutfallah mosque on the right, although these are reversed in the engraving. He also sketched the tower of skulls, a monument to the rebellion in 1500 by the inhabitants of Isfahan, when Shah Tahmasp put to death 30,000 citizens and built the column as a salutary reminder of what happens if you do not pay your taxes.

After a fortnight in Isfahan, they learned that Shah Abbas was at Ashraf, and set off north towards the Caspian. There are more sketches to accompany his narrative—an old Persian (Figure 15), and an inhabitant of Hyrcania. He remarks that the natives were for the most part exceedingly courteous and hospitable to strangers. His map of the Caspian Sea is somewhat muddled, but gives a general idea of the lay of the land. At this point his descriptions are all second-hand, but he manages to include a drawing of an Uzbek. And there is a strange elevation of a caravansaray at Tabriz. (Figure 16) When they arrived at Qazvin, Sir Dodmore Cotton attempted to make direct contact with the Shah, but was thwarted by his minister, Mahomet Ali Beg. Disheartened at the ultimate failure of his mission, Sir Robert

[7] This is an abbreviated version of the detailed account given by Adam Olearius, *Voyages . . .*, London, 1669, of his visit in 1637. For the full text, see J. Carswell, *New Julfa*, Oxford, 1968, 81.

Fig. 14 A Georgian man and woman

Fig. 15 An old Inhabitant of Persia

Fig. 16 A Caravansaray, Tabriz

Sherley took ill and died. Only a few days later, the Ambassador himself succumbed. Thomas Herbert and what was left of the party set off home. After they obtained another *firman*, they travelled south by Qum and Kashan. Herbert himself was also horribly sick:

> I was like a skeleton, and reduced to such weakness that scarce any man could be more enfeebled . . . in this sad condition and misery I was forced to travel three hundred miles hanging upon the side of a camel in a cage resembling a cradle.

It was at this moment that his servant attempted to finish him off with a dose of wine, which beverage had been forbidden him by the Shah's doctor. It put him out for twenty-four hours; he was then violently sick and fell into a deep sleep, which was the beginning of his recovery. In a few months he became perfectly well and strong again, but not before the servant robbed him of his cash and his linen. Much of Herbert's book from this point onwards is speculative, concerned with local history and customs rather than an account of his travels, and the illustrations bear this out. They came again to Swalley by boat, then sailed down the West coast of India, and here his objective descriptions and drawings are resumed. He draws the profile of Mount Ely with Cannanore in the distance. He visits Calicut and Quilon and then Ceylon. He describes Masulputanam, but whether he visited the Coromandel coast is not clear. At this point there is much padding, with descriptions of South-east Asia, China and Japan.

It is not until he is on his way back across the Indian Ocean that he resumes his first-hand account. They stopped at Mauritius, of which he gives a panoramic view. There is also an illustration of a bird, a bat, a coconut-tree and a palmetto looking rather like a pair of pleated serviettes. (Figure 17) A charming drawing shows in diminishing scale a Dodo, a Hen and a Coccatoo Parrot. He is also good at fish—a torpaedo, or cramp-fish; a predatory remora, and what he calls an eagle fish but must have been a giant ray. We also get another whale and a long poem in its honour. The last drawing is of St Helena. Battered by bad weather and tornados they made it back to the Atlantic, sailed past the Azores and were driven by storms too close to the French coast for their pleasure. (Figure 18) However, a few hours more gave them the comfortable sight of their own country. He concludes:

Fig. 17 A Coco-tree, A Batt, A Tropique Bird, A Palmeto-tree

and we came to anchor at Plymouth and returned God hearty thanks for our preservation.

Thomas Herbert's drawings are a valuable addition to his book. In a way, his diffidence about his artistic ability enhances their value, for it indicates an attempted objectivity. More important still he acknowledges the necessity for accurate visual recording. Today such an attitude is taken for granted, but in this respect Herbert was one of the pioneers. Through his drawings and descriptions he has left us with a vivid and original record of his youthful adventure.

Bibliography

Carswell, J., "East and West: a study in aesthetic contrasts", Part I, *AARP* 2, (1972), 77–87; Part II, *AARP* 3, (1973), 82–98.

Carswell, J., *New Julfa: the Armenian churches and other buildings*, Oxford, 1968.

Herbert, T., *A relation of some yeares travaile, begunne Anno 1626, into Afrique and the greater Asia, especially the territories of the Persian Monarchie, and some parts of the oriental Indies* . . ., London, 1634.

Ondaatje, M., *Running in the family*, 1983.

Fig. 18 All at sea—detail of title page, *bottom left*

THE MEDIEVAL ISMĀʿĪLĪS OF THE IRANIAN LANDS

Farhad Daftary

A major Shīʿī Muslim community, the Ismāʿīlīs have had a long and eventful history dating to the middle of the 2nd/8th century. After obscure beginnings in southern Iraq, the Ismāʿīlī *daʿwa* or mission spread rapidly to eastern Arabia, Yemen, Syria, and other Arab lands as well as North Africa where the Ismāʿīlīs founded their own state, the Fāṭimid caliphate, in 297/909. Meanwhile, the Ismāʿīlī *daʿwa* had been extended to many regions of the Iranian lands, from Khūzistān in southwestern Persia and Daylam in the southern shores of the Caspian Sea to Khurāsān and Transoxania in Central Asia. Belonging to a variety of ethnic groupings and socio-cultural milieux, the Ismāʿīlīs in time elaborated diverse intellectual and literary traditions in Arabic, Persian and Indic languages. At present, the Ismāʿīlīs are scattered in more than twenty-five countries of Asia, the Middle East, Africa, Europe and North America.

Of all the Ismāʿīlī communities which have survived to our own times, those of the Iranian lands and Yemen have had the longest continuous histories. This study, presented respectfully to Professor C. Edmund Bosworth who has so meticulously studied over several decades the history and cultures of the peoples of the Iranian lands, aims to provide a historical overview of the medieval Ismāʿīlī communities of these lands and their prominent *dāʿīs* or missionaries, who were also their community's scholars and authors. The Iranian Ismāʿīlīs are primarily Persian-speaking and, since 487/1094, have belonged to the majoritarian Nizārī community of Ismāʿīlism. The Iranian Ismāʿīlīs, now situated mainly within the borders of Iran, Afghanistan and Tajikistan as well as in Hunza and other northern areas of Pakistan, along with the Khoja Ismāʿīlīs of Indian origins and other Nizārī Ismāʿīlīs of the world, currently acknowledge H.H. Prince Karim Aga Khan IV as their forty-ninth imam or spiritual leader.

The Early Period

On the Imam Jaʿfar al-Ṣādiq's death in 148/765, the Imāmī Shīʿīs who had acquired their prominence in his imamate, split into various groups. Later Imāmī heresiographers identify two of these Kūfan-based splinter groups as the earliest Ismāʿīlīs. One group, the so-called "pure Ismāʿīliyya", denied the death of Ismāʿīl, Jaʿfar al-Ṣādiq's eldest son and original heir-designate, and awaited his return as the Mahdi or *qāʾim*. A second group, acknowledging Ismāʿīl's death in his father's lifetime, now recognized Ismāʿīl's son Muḥammad as their new imam; this group became known as the Mubārakiyya, named after Ismāʿīl's epithet of al-Mubārak (the Blessed One).[1] Few details are known about the subsequent history of the early Ismāʿīlīs until the middle of the 3rd/9th century. Soon after 148/765, when the bulk of the Imāmiyya recognized the imamate of Ismāʿīl's half-brother Mūsā al-Kāẓim (d. 183/799), later counted as the seventh imam of the Twelver Shīʿīs, Muḥammad b. Ismāʿīl left the permanent residence of the ʿAlids in Medina and went into hiding to avoid ʿAbbāsid persecution, initiating the *dawr al-satr* or period of concealment in early Ismāʿīlī history. It is certain that Muḥammad b. Ismāʿīl spent the latter part of his life in Khūzistān, where he had some following in addition to the bulk of the Mubārakiyya who lived clandestinely in Kūfa. In fact, Khūzistān in southwestern Persia remained the scene of the activities of early Ismāʿīlī leadership for several decades.

On the death of Muḥammad b. Ismāʿīl, not long after 179/795, the Mubārakiyya themselves split into two groups. A majority, refusing to accept his death, now acknowledged him as the Mahdi, while an obscure group traced the imamate in his progeny. Modern scholarship has revealed that for almost a century after Muḥammad b. Ismāʿīl, a group of his descendants worked secretly and systematically as the central leaders of the earliest Ismāʿīlīs to create a unified and expanding Ismāʿīlī revolutionary movement. These leaders, whose Fāṭimid ʿAlid genealogy was in due course acknowledged by the Ismāʿīlīs, did not for three generations claim the Ismāʿīlī imamate openly in order to safeguard themselves against ʿAbbāsid persecution. The first of these leaders, Muḥammad b. Ismāʿīl's son ʿAbd Allāh, had in fact organized a reinvigorated Ismāʿīlī *daʿwa* around the cen-

---

[1] See Nawbakhtī, *Kitāb firaq al-Shīʿa*, 57–58, 60–61; al-Qummī, *Kitāb al-maqālāt* 80–81, 83, and Daftary, "The Earliest Ismāʿīlīs", 214–245.

tral doctrine of the bulk of the earliest Ismāʿīlīs, viz., the Mahdiship of Muḥammad b. Ismāʿīl. Leading an anti-ʿAbbāsid revolutionary movement in the name of a hidden imam who could not be tracked down by the ʿAbbāsid agents did indeed hold obvious advantages for ʿAbd Allāh and his next two successors, who took every precaution to hide their own true identities as the central leaders of the Ismāʿīliyya. ʿAbd Allāh, a capable organizer and strategist, spent his youth in the vicinity of Ahwāz in Khūzistān. He eventually settled down in ʿAskar Mukram, then an economically flourishing town situated some forty kilometres to the north of Ahwāz. Today the ruins of ʿAskar Mukram, to the south of Shūshtar, are known as Band-i Qīr. ʿAbd Allāh lived as a wealthy merchant in ʿAskar Mukram, from where he decided to organize an expanding Ismāʿīlī movement with a network of *dāʿīs* operating in different regions. Thus, Khūzistān represented the original base of operations for what was to become the successful Ismāʿīlī *daʿwa* of the 3rd/9th century. Subsequently, ʿAbd Allāh was forced to flee from ʿAskar Mukram due to the hostilities of his enemies; he eventually settled down in Salamiyya, in central Syria, where the secret headquarters of the early Ismāʿīlī *daʿwa* now came to be located for several decades.

The efforts of ʿAbd Allāh to reorganize the Ismāʿīlī movement began to bear concrete results from around 260/873 when numerous *dāʿīs* appeared simultaneously in southern Iraq and in different parts of Persia. Al-Ḥusayn al-Ahwāzī, who converted Ḥamdān Qarmaṭ in the Sawād of Kūfa, was a Persian *dāʿī* and a close associate of ʿAbd Allāh. Ḥamdān Qarmaṭ, then, organized the *daʿwa* in southern Iraq, where the Ismāʿīlīs became known as the Qarāmiṭa, named after their first local leader. Ḥamdān's chief assistant, and one of the most learned *dāʿīs* of the early Ismāʿīlīs, was his brother-in-law ʿAbdān who himself hailed from Khūzistān. ʿAbdān recruited and trained numerous *dāʿīs*, who were dispatched in due course to various regions around the Persian Gulf. Amongst such *dāʿīs*, who were of Persian origins and operated in different parts of Persia, particular mention may be made of Abū Saʿīd Ḥasan b. Bahrām al-Jannābī, a native of the port of Jannāba (Persian, Ganāva) on the northern shore of the Persian Gulf. Abū Saʿīd was initially active with much success in southern Persia, before being dispatched to Baḥrayn in eastern Arabia, where he spread the *daʿwa* successfully among the indigenous bedouin tribesmen and the Persians residing there. He eventually founded the independent Qarmaṭī state of Baḥrayn which lasted for almost two centuries. There was also

ʿAbdān's own brother al-Maʾmūn, who was appointed as *dāʿī* in Fārs, where the Ismāʿīlīs were evidently called the Maʾmūniyya after him.[2]

The initiation of the *daʿwa* in the west-central and northwestern parts of Persia, the region designated as the Jibāl by the Arabs, also dates to the early 260s /870s, or possibly earlier, as the Imāmī scholar al-Faḍl b. Shādhān who died in 260/873 had already written a refutation of the Ismāʿīliyya (Qarāmiṭa) in Persia. The *daʿwa* in the Jibāl was initiated by a certain *dāʿī* called Khalaf al-Ḥallāj, who was sent there by the central leader of the Ismāʿīlī movement. Khalaf established himself in the village of Kulayn, in the district of Pashāpūya near Rayy (to the south of modern-day Tehran), where an important Imāmī community already existed; and the area of Rayy continued to serve as the base of operations for the *daʿwa* in the Jibāl. The earliest Ismāʿīlīs of Rayy became known as the Khalafiyya, named after their first local leader. Khalaf was succeeded as the chief *dāʿī* of Rayy by his son Aḥmad and then by the latter's chief disciple Ghiyāth, a native of Kulayn. Ghiyāth extended the *daʿwa* to Qumm, another important Imāmī centre in Persia, Kāshān, Hamadān and other towns of the Jibāl. Ghiyāth also initiated the *daʿwa* in Khurāsān. However, the efforts of these early *dāʿī*s of Rayy to mobilize rural support for insurrectional purposes, as attempted by Ḥamdān and ʿAbdān in Iraq, proved futile. The Persian *dāʿī*s soon adopted a new policy, addressing their message to the ruling classes. After its initial success in the Jibāl, this policy was also implemented in Khurāsān and Transoxania. It was in accordance with this policy that Ghiyāth converted al-Ḥusayn b. ʿAlī al-Marwazī, a prominent *amīr* in the service of the Sāmānids in Khurāsān. As a result, large numbers in the districts of Ṭāliqān, Maymana, Harāt, Gharjistān and Ghūr, under the influence of this *amīr* who later became a *dāʿī* himself, also converted to Ismāʿīlism. Ghiyāth's chief deputy was the learned theologian Abū Ḥātim al-Rāzī, a native of Rayy, who in time became the fifth *dāʿī* of the Jibāl.[3]

As a result of the efforts of ʿAbd Allāh, later designated in the Fāṭimid sources as al-Akbar (the Elder), and his successors, a unified

[2] Al-Daylamī, *Bayān*, 21.

[3] The most detailed account of the initiation of the Ismāʿīlī *daʿwa* in the Jibāl, Khurāsān, and Transoxania is contained in Niẓām al-Mulk, *Siyar*, ed. Darke, 282–295, 297–305; English trans., Darke, 208–218, 220–226. See also Stern, "The Early Ismāʿīlī Missionaries", 56–90, reprinted in Stern, *Studies in Early Ismāʿīlism*, 189–233.

and dynamic Ismāʿīlī movement had by the early 280s/890s completely replaced the earlier Kūfan-based splinter groups. This movement was centrally and secretly directed from Salamiyya. The Ismāʿīlīs now referred to their religio-political campaign and movement as *al-daʿwa al-hādiya* (the rightly guiding mission), or simply as the *daʿwa* (the mission), in addition to using expressions such as the *daʿwat al-ḥaqq* (the summons to the truth). The Ismāʿīlīs were then united around the doctrine of the Mahdiship of Muḥammad b. Ismāʿīl, whose imminent return was expected. Centred on the advent of the Mahdi, the restorer of true Islam who would establish the rule of justice in the world, the Ismāʿīlī movement of the second half of the 3rd/9th century had much messianic appeal for different underprivileged groups. Indeed, Ismāʿīlism now appeared as a movement of social protest against the oppressive rule of the ʿAbbāsids and their social order. The early Ismāʿīlī movement achieved particular success among the Imāmī Shīʿīs of Iraq and Persia who were left without an imam and in a state of disarray on the death of their eleventh imam, al-Ḥasan al-ʿAskarī, in 260/873–874. At the same time, the fragmentation of the ʿAbbāsid state and the various peripheral challenges posed to the authority of the ʿAbbāsid caliph by a number of new dynasties, such as the Ṣaffārids of Sīstān, had made it possible for the Ismāʿīlīs and others to launch their own insurrectional activities.

The Ismāʿīlī movement was rent by a major schism in 286/899. In that year, the then central leader of the movement, the future founder of the Fāṭimid state ʿAbd Allāh al-Mahdī, claimed the imamate openly for himself and his ancestors, the same individuals who had actually led the Ismāʿīlī movement after Muḥammad b. Ismāʿīl. ʿAbd Allāh al-Mahdī had now in effect introduced continuity in the Ismāʿīlī imamate. He also explained that the same leaders had always regarded themselves as the true imams, but as a form of *taqiyya* or dissimulation they had not divulged their true status in order to safeguard themselves against ʿAbbāsid persecution. In other words, the propagation of the Mahdiship of Muḥammad b. Ismāʿīl had been, we are told, no more than a decoy adopted by the central leaders of early Ismāʿīlism, who evidently also used various pseudonyms and posed as the *ḥujja*s or chief representatives of the hidden Mahdi.[4]

[4] On ʿAbd Allāh al-Mahdī's reform and its consequences, see Madelung, "Das Imamat", 43–65, 69 ff., and Daftary, "A Major Schism", 123–139.

The reform of ʿAbd Allāh al-Mahdī split the unified Ismāʿīlī movement of the time into two rival factions in 286/899. The loyal Ismāʿīlīs, later known as Fāṭimid Ismāʿīlīs, accepted the reform and maintained continuity in the imamate. This loyalist camp included the bulk of the Ismāʿīlīs of Yemen, as well as those of North Africa and Egypt. On the other hand, a dissident camp rejected ʿAbd Allāh al-Mahdī's declarations, and retained their original belief in the Mahdiship of Muḥammad b. Ismāʿīl. Henceforth, the term Qarmaṭī came to be applied specifically to the dissident Ismāʿīlīs, who did not acknowledge ʿAbd Allāh al-Mahdī and his predecessors, as well as his successors in the Fāṭimid dynasty, as their imams. Centred in Baḥrayn, the dissident Qarmaṭī faction initially also comprised the communities of Iraq and most of those situated in the Jibāl, Khurāsān and Transoxania.[5]

The Fāṭimid Period

The foundation of the Fāṭimid caliphate in 297/909 in North Africa marked the crowning success of the early Ismāʿīlīs. The religio-political *daʿwa* of the Ismāʿīliyya had finally led to the establishment of a state or *dawla*, which lasted for more than two centuries until 567/1171. The Fāṭimid victory, indeed, represented the long-awaited fulfilment of a Shīʿī ideal which had been frustrated by numerous defeats after the brief rule of ʿAlī b. Abī Ṭālib (d. 40/661), the first Shīʿī imam. In line with their universal aspirations, the Fāṭimid caliph-imams did not discontinue their *daʿwa* upon assuming power. But it was not until the second half of the 5th/11th century that the Fāṭimid *dāʿīs* working in the central and eastern lands of Islam succeeded in winning a growing number of converts within the dominions of the ʿAbbāsids, and their Būyid and Seljuq overlords, as well as in territories ruled by the Ṣaffārids, Ghaznawids and other dynasties emerging in the eastern Iranian lands. These converts acknowledged the Fāṭimid caliph as the rightful Shīʿī imam of the time. All the surviving Qarmaṭī communities, outside of Baḥrayn, too, had by then either disintegrated or switched their allegiance to

[5] On the early history of these Qarmaṭī communities, and their relations with the Fāṭimids, see Madelung, "The Fatimids and the Qarmaṭīs of Baḥrayn", 21–73; W. Madelung, "Ḳarmaṭī", *EI*^{2}, vol. 4, 660–665, and Daftary, "Carmatians", 823–832.

the Fāṭimid Ismāʿīlī *daʿwa*, whose central headquarters were located in the royal city of Cairo founded by the Fāṭimids themselves.

Educated as theologians at special institutions of learning in Cairo, the Fāṭimid *dāʿīs* were at the same time the scholars and authors of their community. They produced the classical texts of the Ismāʿīlī literature on a multitude of exoteric (*ẓāhirī*) and esoteric (*bāṭinī*) subjects, also developing the Ismāʿīlī *taʾwīl* or esoteric exegesis to its fullest extent. The *dāʿīs* of the Fāṭimid period, especially those operating secretly in the Iranian lands, also elaborated distinctive intellectual traditions, and made important contributions to Islamic civilization.

ʿAbd Allāh al-Mahdī (d. 322/934) and his next two successors in the Fāṭimid dynasty were preoccupied with establishing and consolidating the Fāṭimid state in North Africa. It was only with the fourth caliph-imam al-Muʿizz, who conquered Egypt in 358/969 and transferred the seat of the Fāṭimid state there, that the Fāṭimids could begin to concern themselves effectively with their *daʿwa* activities. At any rate, before leaving Salamiyya permanently in 289/902, al-Mahdī had already dispatched a certain Abū ʿAbd Allāh al-Khādim to Khurāsān as the first chief *dāʿī* there. The *dāʿī* al-Khādim established his secret headquarters at Nīshāpūr sometime during 290–300/903–913. He propagated the *daʿwa* on behalf of ʿAbd Allāh al-Mahdī, while Ghiyāth had earlier introduced Ismāʿīlism to Khurāsān on behalf of the hidden Mahdi Muḥammad b. Ismāʿīl. It was under such confusing circumstances that both factions of Ismāʿīlism came to be represented in Khurāsān. Be that as it may, al-Khādim was succeeded, around 307/919, by the *dāʿī* Abū Saʿīd al-Shaʿrānī who converted several notables of the province. The next chief *dāʿī* of Khurāsān was the already-noted al-Ḥusayn b. ʿAlī al-Marwazī, who is a well-known *amīr* in the annals of the Sāmānid dynasty.[6] In his time, the provincial seat of the *daʿwa* was transferred from Nīshāpūr to Marw al-Rūdh (present-day Bālā Murghāb in northern Afghanistan).

The *dāʿī* al-Marwazī appointed as his successor Muḥammad b. Aḥmad al-Nasafī, a learned theologian and philosopher who hailed from the vicinity of Nakhshab (Arabicized, Nasaf), a town in Central Asia. The *dāʿī* al-Nasafī, who is generally credited with having introduced a form of Neoplatonic philosophy into Ismāʿīlī thought,

[6] Gardīzī, *Zayn al-akhbār*, 148–149; *Taʾrīkh-i Sīstān*, ed. Bahār, 290–294, 300–302; ed. Ṣādiqī, 158–160, 165–166; English trans., *The Tārikh-e Sistān*, tr. M. Gold, 233–237, 243–244; Mīrkhwānd, *Rawḍat al-ṣafāʾ*, vol. 4, 40–42, and Barthold, *Turkestan*, 241–245.

transferred the seat of the *daʿwa* to Transoxania, where he had been advised to go by his predecessor in order to convert the dignitaries of the Sāmānid court. After a brief period in Bukhārā, the Sāmānid capital (in present-day Uzbekistan), al-Nasafī retreated to his native Nakhshab, from where he was more successful in penetrating the inner circles of the Sāmānid regime. Subsequently, al-Nasafī settled down in Bukhārā and, with the help of his influential converts at the court, including Ashʿath, the private secretary, won over the young Sāmānid *amīr* Naṣr II b. Aḥmad (301–331/914–943). Encouraged by his successes, al-Nasafī now began to preach openly in Bukhārā, while extending the *daʿwa* also to Sīstān (Arabicized, Sijistān) through one of his subordinate *dāʿīs*. The *dāʿī* al-Nasafī reaffirmed the Mahdiship of Muḥammad b. Ismāʿīl in his *Kitāb al-maḥṣūl*, which also contained a new emanational cosmological doctrine based on Neoplatonic philosophy. It seems that al-Nasafī's *al-Maḥṣūl* gained widespread acceptance within the various Qarmaṭī circles and it played a major part in unifying the Qarmaṭīs of the Iranian lands who, by contrast to the Qarmaṭīs of Baḥrayn, lacked central leadership.

The fortunes of the *dāʿī* al-Nasafī and the *daʿwa* in Khurāsān and Transoxania were reversed in the aftermath of the revolt of the Turkish soldiers who were in alliance with the Sunnī *ʿulamāʾ* of the Sāmānid state. Under the *amīr* Naṣr II's son and successor, Nūḥ I b. Naṣr (331–343/943–954), al-Nasafī and his close associates were executed in Bukhārā in 332/943, and their co-religionists were severely persecuted. The Sunnī *ʿulamāʾ* of the Sāmānid state had now in fact declared a *jihād* or holy war against the Qarmaṭī "heretics". Despite these setbacks, however, the *daʿwa* survived in Khurāsān and Transoxania under the leadership of al-Nasafī's son Masʿūd, nicknamed Dihqān, and then other chief *dāʿīs*, notably Abū Yaʿqūb al-Sijistānī.

In the meantime, Abū Ḥātim al-Rāzī had assumed office during 300–310/912–923 as the fifth *dāʿī* of Rayy. He extended the *daʿwa* to Ādharbāyjān and Daylam, which in medieval times referred to a number of Caspian provinces including Daylamān, Gīlān, Ṭabaristān (Māzandarān) and Gurgān. Abū Ḥātim was particularly successful in converting several local rulers, starting with Aḥmad b. ʿAlī, the governor of Rayy during 307–311/919–924. In the aftermath of the conquest of Rayy by the Sunnī Sāmānids, however, Abū Ḥātim went to Ṭabaristān where he sided with Asfār b. Shirawayh (d. 319/931) against the local Zaydī Imam al-Dāʿī al-Ṣaghīr. Abū Ḥātim converted Asfār and soon acquired many followers in Ṭabaristān and other regions of northern Persia which were then ruled by this Daylamī *amīr*. Abū Ḥātim also converted Asfār's chief lieutenant Mardāwīj b. Ziyār (d. 323/935), who later rebelled against his master and founded the Ziyārid dynasty of Ṭabaristān and Gurgān. The famous disputations between the *dāʿī* Abū Ḥātim and the physician-philosopher Abū Bakr Muḥammad b. Zakariyyāʾ al-Rāzī reportedly took place in the presence of Mardāwīj.[7]

Abū Ḥātim, like al-Nasafī, evidently belonged to the dissident Qarmaṭī branch and did not recognize the imamate of his contemporary ʿAbd Allāh al-Mahdī. Indeed, he corresponded with Abū Ṭāhir al-Jannābī, the leader of the Qarmaṭī state of Baḥrayn, and like the latter was expecting the appearance of the Mahdi in the year 316/928. Abū Ḥātim may even have claimed to have been the lieutenant of the hidden Mahdi. At any rate, as Abū Ḥātim's date for the emergence of the Mahdi proved wrong, Mardāwīj turned against the *dāʿī* and his community. Subsequently, Abū Ḥātim sought refuge with Mufliḥ, a local ruler in Ādharbāyjān, and died in that northwestern region of Persia in 322/934. On Abū Ḥātim's death, the Qarmaṭīs (Ismāʿīlīs) of the Jibāl were thrown into disarray and their leadership eventually passed to ʿAbd al-Malik al-Kawkabī who resided in Girdkūh, near Dāmghān, the future Nizārī Ismāʿīlī stronghold, and a certain Isḥāq residing in Rayy. The latter *dāʿī* may perhaps be identified with Abū Yaʿqūb Isḥāq b. Aḥmad al-Sijistānī, the *dāʿī* al-Nasafī's disciple and successor in Khurāsān.

It was due to Abū Ḥātim al-Rāzī's successes in Daylam that the *daʿwa* also spread to the Rūdbār of Alamūt or Daylamān, the traditional seat of the obscure Justānid dynasty. One of the earlier Justānid rulers, Wahsūdān b. Marzubān, had built around the middle of the 3rd/9th century the fortress of Alamūt, which was to become the central headquarters of the Nizārī Ismāʿīlī *daʿwa* and state. The Justānids traditionally supported the Shīʿism of the Zaydī ʿAlid rulers of Ṭabaristān. Mahdī b. Khusraw Fīrūz, known as Siyāhchashm, who succeeded his father at Alamūt soon after 307/919, was the first Justānid to embrace Ismāʿīlism of the dissident Qarmaṭī kind.[8] After being defeated by Muḥammad b. Musāfir, the founder

[7] Al-Kirmānī, *al-Aqwāl*, 2–3.

[8] On the Justānids, who are variously treated by a few medieval chroniclers of the Caspian provinces, including Ibn Isfandiyār, Awliyāʾ Allāh Āmulī and Ẓahīr al-Dīn Marʿashī, see Madelung, "Abū Isḥāq al-Ṣābī", especially 52–57, reprinted in his *Religious and Ethnic Movements*, article VII, and Bosworth, *The New Islamic Dynasties*, 145–146.

of the powerful Musāfirid dynasty of Daylam, Siyāhchashm sought refuge in 316/928 with his co-religionist Asfār b. Shirawayh. But he was soon murdered by Asfār who aspired to add Rūdbār to his own dominions. After Siyāhchashm the Justānids came to be eclipsed by the vigorous dynasty of the Musāfirids or Sallārids, who ruled over parts of Daylam as well as Ādharbāyjān and Arrān.

In 330/941, the founder of the Musāfirid dynasty, Muḥammad b. Musāfir who had held the castle of Shamīrān in Ṭārum, was deposed by his sons Wahsūdān and Marzubān. Both of these Musāfirids were converted by the *dāʿīs* of Rayy, and numismatic evidence from the year 343/954–955 confirms that they adhered to Qarmaṭism and acknowledged the Mahdiship of Muḥammad b. Ismāʿīl rather than the imamate of their contemporary Fāṭimid caliph-imam, al-Muʿizz.[9] Wahsūdān b. Muḥammad (330–355/941–966) remained at Shamīrān and governed Ṭārum, while his more influential brother Marzubān (330–346/941–957) soon conquered Ādharbāyjān and Arrān, as well as Armenia and other parts of Transcaucasia as far as Darband, and began to rule over the expanding Musāfirid dominions from his own seat at Ardabīl in northwestern Persia.

After the demise of the Sājids in 317/929, who governed on behalf of the ʿAbbāsids, Ādharbāyjān had become the scene of rivalries among various independent local rulers, including Mufliḥ, a former Sājid officer who gave refuge to Abū Ḥātim al-Rāzī and who may have been one of the *dāʿī*'s converts. By 326/938, the Khārijī Daysam b. Ibrāhīm al-Kurdī had established his own control over Ādharbāyjān. In the aftermath of a rupture between Daysam and his vizier Abu'l-Qāsim ʿAlī b. Jaʿfar, the latter fled to Ṭārum in 330/941 and entered the service of the Musāfirids. Originally serving the Sājids as a financial administrator, Abu'l-Qāsim had also been active secretly as a Bāṭinī (Qarmaṭī) *dāʿī* in northwestern Persia. He was instrumental in encouraging his co-religionist Marzubān b. Muḥammad's conquest of Ādharbāyjān, where he had earlier converted numerous Daylamī notables and army officers in the service of Daysam. It was also at Abu'l-Qāsim's instigation that the bulk of Daysam's army, including

[9] See Stern, "Early Ismāʿīlī Missionaries", 70–74. On the Musāfirids, see the following works by Minorsky: *Studies in Caucasian History*, 159–166; *History of Sharvān and Darband*, 27, 60–62, 71, 76, 85, 112, and "Musāfirids", *EI*², vol. 7, 655–657. See also Madelung, "The Minor Dynasties", 224–225, 231 ff., and Bosworth, *New Islamic Dynasties*, 148–149.

many Qarmaṭī converts, deserted him and switched their allegiance to Marzubān. Soon, Marzubān appointed the *dāʿī* Abu'l-Qāsim as his own vizier; and he was now permitted to preach the *daʿwa* openly with much success throughout the Musāfirid dominions. The well-informed Ibn Ḥawqal, who may himself have been a secret Fāṭimid *dāʿī* and who visited Ādharbāyjān around the year 344/955, reports on the existence of a large Bāṭinī (Qarmaṭī) community there.[10] Qarmaṭism evidently survived under the later Musāfirids, who were eventually obliged to withdraw to Ṭārum. After submitting to the Saljuqs, the Musāfirid dynasty was finally overthrown by the Nizārīs of Alamūt who incorporated Shamīrān and other fortresses of Ṭārum into their own network of mountain strongholds in Rūdbār.

In the meantime, Qarmaṭism had persisted in Khurāsān and Transoxania in the dominions of the later Sāmānids. The sources have preserved some fragmentary information on the *dāʿī*-authors operating secretly in the eastern Iranian lands after al-Nasafī and his son. There were the *dāʿī*s Abu'l-Faḍl Zangurz and ʿAtīq, as well as Abu'l-Haytham Aḥmad b. al-Ḥasan al-Jurjānī, an Ismāʿīlī philosopher and poet from Gurgān, and his disciple Muḥammad b. Surkh al-Nīsābūrī. There was also Abū Tammām, an obscure *dāʿī* from Khurāsān who belonged to al-Nasafī's dissident school. Paul Walker in his recent studies has shown that Abū Tammām, in fact, produced what may well be the only Ismāʿīlī heresiography on Muslim sects.[11] Above all, mention should be made of Abu Yaʿqūb Isḥāq b. Aḥmad al-Sijistānī who led the *daʿwa* in Khurāsān, and Sīstān, his original base of operations.[12] He may also have headed the *daʿwa* in the Jibāl, in succession to Abū Ḥātim al-Rāzī, as well as in Iraq.[13] A contemporary of the Fāṭimid caliph-imam al-Muʿizz, the *dāʿī* al-Sijistānī was executed as a heretic by the order of the Ṣaffārid *amīr* of Sīstān, Khalaf b. Aḥmad (352–393/963–1003),[14] not long after 361/971, the date of completion of one of his last books.

[10] Ibn Ḥawqal, *Ṣūrat al-arḍ*, 348–349, 354. See also Miskawayh, *Tajārib*, ed. and trans. Amedroz and Margoliouth, Arabic text, vol. 2, 31–37, 62–67, 115, 135–136, 148–154, 166–167, 177–180, 219–220, English translation, vol. 5, 33–41, 67–74, 118, 140–142, 156–164, 178–180, 192–195, 233.

[11] See Walker, "Abū Tammām" 343–352, and his "An Ismaʿili Version", 161–177. See also Bosworth, *The History of the Saffarids*, 292–293.

[12] For the most comprehensive modern studies of al-Sijistānī's thought and intellectual contributions, see Walker, *Early Philosophical Shiism*, and his *Abū Yaʿqūb al-Sijistānī*.

[13] Ibn al-Nadīm, *Kitāb al-fihrist*, 240–241; English trans., 472.

[14] See Bosworth, *Saffarids*, 301–337.

A learned theologian and philosopher, the *dāʿī* al-Sijistānī was also a prolific writer; and it is mainly on the basis of his numerous extant works that modern scholars have now begun to study an important tradition of philosophical theology developed by the *dāʿīs* of the Iranian lands, particularly in Khurāsān, during the 4th/10th century.[15] This tradition of learning, which in fact represented a distinctive "Iranian school" of philosophical Ismāʿīlism, was evidently initiated by al-Nasafī. The *dāʿī* al-Nasafī, and his successors, wrote for the ruling elite and the educated strata of Muslim society in Khurāsān, and this may explain why they attempted to express their theology in terms of the then most modern and intellectually fashionable philosophical terminologies and themes, without however compromising the Shīʿī essence of their religious message. Drawing on a type of Neoplatonism then current among the educated circles of Khurāsān, these *dāʿīs* of the Iranian lands elaborated complex metaphysical systems of thought, amalgamating in an original manner their Shīʿī theology with a Hellenized system of emanational Neoplatonic philosophy. A Neoplatonic cosmology, with the universal intellect (*ʿaql*) and soul (*nafs*) as the first and the second originated beings created by the command of an unknowable God, was an important part of their systems; and this new cosmological doctrine gradually superseded the earlier mythological cosmogony of the pre-Fāṭimid Ismāʿīlīs. Al-Sijistānī was perhaps the foremost Shīʿī Neoplatonist of his time, and his writings are extremely valuable not only for understanding philosophical Ismāʿīlism but also for discovering how Neoplatonic themes came to be originally adopted by Muslim thinkers.

It is interesting to note that the leading Iranian *dāʿīs* of the early Fāṭimid times wrote on a multitude of theological issues; they also disagreed among themselves and engaged in a long-drawn disputation over certain aspects of their doctrines. Abū Ḥātim al-Rāzī, who himself adopted Neoplatonism, wrote his *Kitāb al-iṣlāḥ* (*Book of the Correction*) to correct certain ideas found in al-Nasafī's *Kitāb al-maḥṣūl* (*Book of the Yield*), while al-Sijistānī wrote his *Kitāb al-nuṣra* (*Book of the Defence*) to defend al-Nasafī against Abū Ḥātim's criticisms. Subsequently,

[15] For al-Sijistānī's writings, see Poonawala, *Biobibliography*, 82–89, and Walker, *al-Sijistānī*, 104–118. Only one of al-Sijistānī's books, the *Kitāb al-yanābīʿ*, containing the major components and themes of his metaphysical system, has been translated into English; see Walker, *Wellsprings*, 37–111; for the Arabic text and partial French translation of this work, see Corbin, *Trilogie ismaélienne*, text 1–97, translation 5–127.

Ḥamīd al-Dīn al-Kirmānī, another learned *dāʿī* belonging to the same "Iranian school" of philosophical Ismāʿīlism, acted as an arbiter in this disputation in his *Kitāb al-riyāḍ* (*Book of the Meadows*).[16]

The Fāṭimid caliph-imam al-Muʿizz (341–365/953–975), as noted, was the first member of his dynasty who found it possible to concern himself with the affairs of the Fāṭimid Ismāʿīlī *daʿwa* outside the Fāṭimid dominions, where Qarmaṭī communities had continued to flourish with their own *dāʿīs* undermining the success of the Fāṭimid *dāʿīs*. In this connection, and in order to win the support of the eastern Qarmaṭīs, al-Muʿizz also attempted a limited doctrinal rapprochement with the Qarmaṭīs, including a partial endorsement of the Neoplatonic cosmological doctrine propounded by the Iranian *dāʿīs*. As a result of these efforts, al-Sijistānī was won over to the side of the Fāṭimid *daʿwa*, which henceforth began to preserve his books. At the same time, the dissident communities under the leadership or influence of al-Sijistānī also switched their allegiance to the Fāṭimid al-Muʿizz, recognizing him as the rightful imam of the time. These developments marked a turning point in the stagnating fortunes of the Fāṭimid *daʿwa* throughout Khurāsān, Sīstān, Makrān and other eastern parts of the Iranian world.

Al-Muʿizz won an important victory also in Sind, where through the conversion of a local ruler an Ismāʿīlī state was established around the year 347/958. The rulers of this state, centred at Multān, recognized the suzerainty of the Fāṭimid caliph and recited the *khuṭba* in his name rather than for the ʿAbbāsid caliph. Large numbers of Hindus converted to Ismāʿīlism in this state which was effectively uprooted in 396/1005, when Sultan Maḥmūd of Ghazna invaded Multān and made its Ismāʿīlī ruler a tributary. Soon afterwards, Sultan Maḥmūd began to massacre the Ismāʿīlīs of Multān and other parts of his domains, also frustrating renewed Ismāʿīlī attempts to re-establish their local rule in Sind.[17] However, Ismāʿīlism survived clandestinely the Ghaznawid persecutions in northern India, where the Ismāʿīlīs later received the protection of the Sūmras, an Ismāʿīlī dynasty which ruled independently in Sind from Thatta for almost

[16] See Corbin, *Cyclical Time*, 151–193; Madelung, "Aspects of Ismāʿīlī Theology", 53–65, reprinted in Madelung, *Religious Schools*, article XVII, and Daftary, *The Ismāʿīlīs*, 234–246.

[17] See Stern, "Ismāʿīlī Propaganda", 298–307, reprinted in his *Studies*, 177–188; Hamdani, *The Beginnings*, 3 ff.; Bosworth, *The Ghaznavids*, 52–53, 76, 199–200, 235, and Halm, *The Empire of the Mahdi*, 385–392.

three centuries. Despite the efforts of al-Muʿizz and the Fāṭimid *daʿwa*, Qarmaṭism persisted for a while longer in certain parts of the Iranian lands, notably Daylam, Ādharbāyjān, and western Persia, as well as in Iraq. Above all, al-Muʿizz failed to win the support of the Qarmaṭīs of Baḥrayn, who were to pose a serious obstacle to the extension of Fāṭimid rule to the central and eastern lands of Islam, beyond Syria and Palestine.

The Fāṭimid *daʿwa* was systematically intensified in the Iranian lands under al-Muʿizz's next two successors in the Fāṭimid dynasty, al-ʿAzīz (365–386/975–996) and al-Ḥākim (386–411/996–1021). By this time, the Fāṭimids had realized the difficulty of extending their rule over the eastern regions of the Muslim world, and in fact a stalemate had by then developed between them and the Būyids, who were still the real masters of the ʿAbbāsid state. Nevertheless, the Fāṭimids did not abandon their universal aspirations, aiming to be acknowledged as imams by all Muslims. It was in the pursuit of this objective that the Fāṭimids retained and, indeed, intensified their *daʿwa* activities in the Iranian lands, especially under al-Ḥākim who also concerned himself with the organization of the *daʿwa* as well as the training of the *dāʿīs*. The Fāṭimid *dāʿīs*, including many from Persia and other eastern lands, now received elaborate instructions at the "House of Knowledge" (Dār al-ʿIlm), founded by al-Ḥākim in a section of the Fāṭimid palace in 395/1005, and other institutions of learning in Cairo. Among the lesser known Iranian *dāʿīs* of this period mention may be made of Aḥmad b. Ibrāhīm al-Nīsābūrī, who wrote the only known Ismāʿīlī treatise of the genre of *adab al-dāʿī* on the ideal *dāʿī* and his attributes.[18]

By far the most eminent Ismāʿīlī theologian and *dāʿī* of this period was Ḥamīd al-Dīn Aḥmad b. ʿAbd Allāh al-Kirmānī, who was also the most accomplished Ismāʿīlī philosopher of the entire Fāṭimid period. As his *nisba* indicates, al-Kirmānī was probably born in the Persian province of Kirmān. He later maintained his contacts with the Ismāʿīlī community of Kirmān, addressing at least one of his treatises to a subordinate *dāʿī* in Jīruft in that province. In time, al-Kirmānī became the chief *dāʿī* in Iraq, in addition to heading the *daʿwa* in central and western parts of Persia, known as the ʿIrāq-i

[18] Al-Nīsābūrī's treatise entitled *al-Risāla al-mūjaza al-kāfiya fī ādāb al-duʿāt* has not survived directly, but it has been preserved in full in later Ismāʿīlī sources; see Poonawala, *Biobibliography*, 91–92.

ʿAjam; hence his honorific title of *ḥujjat al-ʿIrāqayn*, the *ḥujja* or chief *dāʿī* of both Iraqs. As the most learned theologian of the time, al-Kirmānī was called to Cairo in 405/1014 to refute on behalf of the Fāṭimid *daʿwa* the extremist doctrines propounded by the founders of the Druze movement and religion. Later, he returned to Iraq where he composed his principal work, the *Rāḥat al-ʿaql* (*Quietude of the Intellect*), in 411/1020 and where he died soon afterwards. It was mainly due to al-Kirmānī's efforts that several influential local *amīr*s of Iraq were won over to the side of the Fāṭimids, preparing the ground for later successes of the Fāṭimid *daʿwa* in the East.[19]

A prolific writer, al-Kirmānī produced some forty treatises.[20] He expounded the Ismāʿīlī Shīʿī doctrine of the imamate in several of his works. He also defended the Fāṭimids against the polemical attacks of the Zaydīs of Persia and other adversaries. As a philosopher, al-Kirmānī was fully acquainted with Aristotelian and Neoplatonic philosophies as well as the metaphysical systems of the Muslim philosophers (*falāsifa*), notably al-Fārābī and his own contemporary Ibn Sīnā (Avicenna), whose father and brother had converted to Ismāʿīlism in their native Transoxania. It was in al-Kirmānī's metaphysical system that philosophical Ismāʿīlism attained its summit, reflecting a distinctive synthesis of Shīʿī theology, Hellenistic traditions and gnostic doctrines. In his system, fully elaborated in the *Rāḥat al-ʿaql*, al-Kirmānī also propounded what may be regarded as the third stage in the development of Ismāʿīlī cosmology in medieval times.[21] In his cosmogonic doctrine, al-Kirmānī replaced the Neoplatonic dyad of the intellect and soul in the spiritual world, which had been adopted by his predecessors in the Iranian school of philosophical Ismāʿīlism, by a series of ten separate intellects in partial adoption of al-Fārābī's Aristotelian cosmic system.

The Fāṭimid *daʿwa* continued to be propagated successfully in the eastern lands, even after the ardently Sunnī Seljuqs had replaced the Shīʿī Būyids in 447/1055 as the effective rulers of the ʿAbbāsid state. Indeed, by the early decades of the reign of the Fāṭimid caliph-imam al-Mustanṣir (427–487/1036–1094), Fāṭimid Ismāʿīlism had

---

[19] See Daftary, *The Ismāʿīlīs*, 186–197; Walker, "The Ismaili Daʿwa", 161–182, and Halm, *The Fatimids and their Traditions*, 35 ff., 53–54, 71–78.

[20] Poonawala, *Biobibliography*, 94–102, and van Ess, "Bibliographische Notizen", 255–261.

[21] For a comprehensive study of al-Kirmānī's thought, as expounded mainly in his *Rāḥat al-ʿaql*, see De Smet, *La Quiétude de l'Intellect*.

been established in many parts of the Iranian world, where Qarmaṭī communities had almost completely ceased to exist. The Fāṭimid *dāʿīs* were now particularly active in Iraq and various parts of Persia, notably Fārs, Iṣfahān, Rayy, and other areas of the Jibāl. In Khurāsān and Transoxania, too, the *daʿwa* had become more successful after the downfall of the Sāmānids in 395/1005, when the Turkish Qarakhānids and Ghaznawids divided the former Sāmānid dominions between themselves. This is attested by the fact that in 436/1044 Bughrā Khan, the ruler of the eastern Qarakhānid kingdom established over the lands of the middle Syr Daryā valley, ordered the massacre of a large number of Ismāʿīlīs who had been converted by the Fāṭimid *dāʿīs* operating in his territories. The Fāṭimid *daʿwa* had been active also in the western territories of the Qarakhānids, in Bukhārā, Samarqand, Farghāna and elsewhere in Transoxania. There, Aḥmad b. Khiḍr, the local Qarakhānid ruler, was executed in Samarqand in 488/1095 (or earlier in 482/1089) on the accusation of having converted to Ismāʿīlism.[22]

The most prominent Fāṭimid *dāʿī* of al-Mustanṣir's time was al-Mu'ayyad fi'l-Dīn al-Shīrāzī. He was born around 390/1000 in Shīrāz, in the province of Fārs, into a Daylamī Ismāʿīlī family. His father had acquired some influence in the Būyid circles of Fārs where he eventually seems to have headed the *daʿwa*. Al-Mu'ayyad succeeded his father, and in 429/1037 entered the service of the Būyid Abū Kālījār Marzubān (415–440/1024–1048), who ruled over Fārs and Khūzistān from his capital at Shīrāz. The subsequent decades until 451/1059 in al-Mu'ayyad's career are well-documented in his autobiography.[23] At any rate, he soon converted Abū Kālījār himself and many of his courtiers as well as a large number of the Daylamī troops in the service of the Būyids. Al-Mu'ayyad's success in Fārs brought about hostile reactions spurred on by the caliph at Baghdad, obliging the *dāʿī* to emigrate permanently from Shīrāz in 435/1043. He arrived in Cairo in 439/1047, and soon began to play an active part in the affairs of the Fāṭimid state and *daʿwa*. Later, al-Mu'ayyad played a key role as an intermediary between the Fāṭimids and Arslān

---

[22] Al-Maqrīzī, *Ittiʿāẓ al-ḥunafā'*, vol. 2, 191–192; Ibn al-Athīr, *al-Kāmil*, vol. 9, 211, 358, and vol. 10, 112 ff., 165–166, and Barthold, *Turkestan*, 251, 304–305, 316–318.

[23] See al-Mu'ayyad fi'l-Dīn al-Shīrāzī, *Sīrat al-Mu'ayyad fi'l-Dīn*. See also Idrīs ʿImād al-Dīn b. al-Ḥasan, *ʿUyūn al-akhbār*, vol. 6, 329–359. For a modern study based on al-Mu'ayyad's *Sīra*, see Klemm, *Die Mission des fāṭimidischen Agenten*.

al-Basāsīrī, the Turkish military commander who briefly led the Fāṭimid cause in Iraq against the Seljuqs. Al-Mu'ayyad delivered the crucial material and financial support of the Fāṭimids to al-Basāsīrī who, in 450/1058, succeeded to seize Baghdad, where he had the *khuṭba* read for one full year in the name of al-Mustanṣir while the ʿAbbāsid caliph remained a captive in his own capital. In the same eventful year 450/1058, al-Mu'ayyad was appointed as the chief *dāʿī* (*dāʿī al-duʿāt*), the administrative head of the Fāṭimid *daʿwa* organization in Cairo, a post he held with the exception of one brief period until shortly before his death in 470/1078. Al-Mu'ayyad's principal work, the *Majālis al-Mu'ayyadiyya*, eight volumes containing a hundred "sessions" (*majālis*) each and representing the apogee of Ismāʿīlī thought, is based on the lectures he had delivered at the "sessions of wisdom" (*majālis al-ḥikma*) for the instruction of *dāʿī*s and other Ismāʿīlīs.[24]

Another prominent Iranian *dāʿī* of al-Mustanṣir's time was Nāṣir-i Khusraw. A learned theologian, a traveller, and a renowned poet of the Persian language, Nāṣir-i Khusraw was also the last major proponent of philosophical Ismāʿīlism in the Iranian lands. Nāṣir was born in 394/1004 near Balkh, which at the time was a part of the district of Marw in Khurāsān. In his youth, Nāṣir held administrative posts at Marw (now in Turkmenistan) under the Ghaznawids and their Seljuq successors. At the age of forty-two, however, Nāṣir experienced a spiritual upheaval which may have been connected to his conversion to Ismāʿīlism. Soon afterwards in 437/1045, he resigned from his post and set off on a long journey for the apparent reason of making the pilgrimage to Mecca. But this seven-year journey, described vividly in his *Safar-nāma* (*Travelogue*), took Nāṣir to the Fāṭimid capital where he arrived in 439/1047, the same year in which the *dāʿī* al-Mu'ayyad had arrived there. Nāṣir stayed in Cairo for three years and received intensive training as a *dāʿī*. During this period, he saw al-Mustanṣir and also established close relations with al-Mu'ayyad, who was to remain his mentor at the central headquarters of the Fāṭimid *daʿwa* and to whom he later dedicated several of his poems. In 444/1052 Nāṣir-i Khusraw returned to Balkh (near today's Mazār-i Sharīf in northern Afghanistan), and began his career

[24] For a list of al-Mu'ayyad's writings, see Poonawala, *Biobibliography*, 103–109. See also Halm, "The Oath of Allegiance (*ʿahd*)", in Daftary, ed., *Mediaeval Ismaʿili History*, especially 99–115.

as a Fāṭimid *dāʿī*, or according to himself as the *ḥujja* or chief *dāʿī* of Khurāsān.[25] At any rate, he established his secret headquarters at Balkh, from where he extended the *daʿwa* to Nīshāpūr and other districts of Khurāsān as well as to Ṭabaristān (Māzandarān) in northern Persia. By 452/1060, however, the hostility of the Sunnī *ʿulamāʾ* who denounced Nāṣir as a heretic (*mulḥid*) and an irreligious person (Persian, *bad-dīn*) and destroyed his house,[26] had obliged the *dāʿī* to flee to the valley of Yumgān, in the region of Badakhshān in the Pamirs. There, he sought refuge with his friend Abu'l-Maʿālī ʿAlī b. al-Asad, an autonomous Ismāʿīlī *amīr* of Badakhshān. This obscure Yumgān period in Nāṣir's life lasted until his death, sometime after 465/1072.

Like other Fāṭimid *dāʿī*s of the Iranian lands and elsewhere, Nāṣir-i Khusraw maintained his contacts with the *daʿwa* headquarters in Cairo, receiving books and his general instructions from there. Even in the remote Yumgān, Nāṣir had ready access to earlier Ismāʿīlī literature; and he was particularly influenced by al-Sijistānī, many of whose ideas are paraphrased in Nāṣir's writings. It was probably during this period of exile, if not earlier, that Nāṣir extended the *daʿwa* throughout Badakhshān (divided in modern times by the Oxus or Āmū Daryā between Afghanistan and Tajikistan). At any event, the Ismāʿīlīs of Badakhshān, and their offshoot community in the Hindukush region (now situated in Hunza and other northern areas of Pakistan) regard Nāṣir as the founder of their communities, and they still revere him under the name of Pīr or Shāh Sayyid Nāṣir. It was also in Yumgān that Nāṣir produced the bulk of his poetry and philosophico-theological works, including the *Zād al-musāfirīn* written in 453/1061 and the *Jāmiʿ al-ḥikmatayn*, his last known work completed in 462/1070 at the request of his Ismāʿīlī protector in Badakhshān.[27] The Ismāʿīlīs of Badakhshān have continued to preserve Nāṣir-i Khusraw's genuine and spurious works, all written in the Persian language. Nāṣir-i Khusraw's mausoleum is still in exis-

---

[25] See, for instance, Nāṣir-i Khusraw, *Zād al-musāfirīn*, 397, and his *Dīwān*, 8, 10, 17, 51, 56, 86, 92, 366, 416, 459, 490.

[26] Nāṣir-i Khusraw, *Zād al-musāfirīn*, 3, 402, and his *Dīwān*, 162, 234, 287, 436.

[27] Nāṣir-i Khusraw, *Kitāb jāmiʿ al-ḥikmatayn*, 16–17; French trans., *Le Livre réunissant les deux Sagesses*, 48. On Nāṣir-i Khusraw's life and writings, see Ivanow, *Problems in Nasir-i Khusraw's Biography*; Corbin, "Nāṣir-i Khusrau and Iranian Ismāʿīlism", 520–542; Bertel's, *Nasir-i Khosrov i ismailizm* 148–264; Persian trans., *Nāṣir-i Khusraw va Ismāʿīliyān*, 149–256, and Poonawala, *Biobibliography*, 111–125, 430–436.

tence on a hillock near the village of Jarm in the vicinity of Fayḍābād, the capital of Afghan Badakhshān.

By the early 460s/1070s, the Ismāʿīlīs of Persia in the Seljuq dominions had come to own the authority of a single chief *dāʿī*, ʿAbd al-Malik b. ʿAṭṭāsh, who had his secret headquarters at Iṣfahān, the main Seljuq capital. A learned *dāʿī*, Ibn ʿAṭṭāsh seems to have been the first *dāʿī* to have centrally organized the *daʿwa* and the various Ismāʿīlī communities of the Seljuq territories in Persia, from Kirmān to Ādharbāyjān. He may have been responsible for the *daʿwa* activities in Iraq as well; but his central supervision does not seem to have been extended to northern Khurāsān, Badakhshān and adjacent regions in Central Asia. Ibn ʿAṭṭāsh, who received his own instructions from Cairo, was also responsible for launching the career of Ḥasan-i Ṣabbāḥ, his successor and the future founder of the independent Nizārī Ismāʿīlī *daʿwa* and state centred at Alamūt.

Al-Mustanṣir died after a long reign in 487/1094. The dispute over his succession split the then unified Ismāʿīlī *daʿwa* and community into the rival Nizārī and Mustaʿlī branches. By that time, Ḥasan-i Ṣabbāḥ was already following an independent revolutionary policy as the leader of the Persian Ismāʿīlīs; and he did not hesitate to support the cause of Nizār, al-Mustanṣir's original heir-designate who had been deprived of his succession rights through the machinations of the all-powerful Fāṭimid vizier al-Afḍal. The vizier had swiftly installed Nizār's younger brother to the Fāṭimid caliphate with the title of al-Mustaʿlī. However, Ḥasan recognized Nizār as al-Mustanṣir's successor to the Ismāʿīlī imamate and severed his relations with the Fāṭimid *daʿwa* headquarters in Cairo, which had transferred their own allegiance to al-Mustaʿlī, recognizing him and, later, some of his descendants as their imams after al-Mustanṣir. Henceforth, the Ismāʿīlīs of the Iranian lands, who recognized the imamate of Nizār and his progeny and became known as the Nizāriyya, developed independently of the Ismāʿīlīs of Egypt and the communities in Yemen and Gujarāt dependent on the Fāṭimid regime; the latter communities comprised the Mustaʿliyya branch of Ismāʿīlism.

The Alamūt Period

During the Alamūt period of their history (483–654/1090–1256), the Ismāʿīlīs of Persia came to possess a state of their own, with a subsidiary in Syria. This state, with its central headquarters at the mountain fortress of Alamūt, was founded in the midst of the Seljuq sultanate by Ḥasan-i Ṣabbāḥ, and it lasted for some 166 years until it collapsed under the onslaught of the Mongol hordes in 654/1256. The Persian Ismāʿīlīs themselves produced official chronicles recording the events of their state, starting with the *Sargudhasht-i Sayyidnā* (*Biography of our Master*) which covered the life and career of Ḥasan-i Ṣabbāḥ as the first lord of Alamūt.[28] These chronicles, as well as the bulk of the meagre religious literature produced by the Nizārī Ismāʿīlīs of the Alamūt period, have not survived. However, the Nizārī chronicles were seen and utilized by three Persian historians of the Īlkhānid period, namely, Juwaynī (d. 681/1283), Rashīd al-Dīn Faḍl Allāh (d. 718/1318) and Abu'l-Qāsim Kāshānī (d. ca. 738/1337), who are our primary sources on the history of the Persian Ismāʿīlīs during the Alamūt period.[29]

Ḥasan-i Ṣabbāḥ was born in the mid-440s/1050s into a Twelver Shīʿī family in Qumm, a traditionally Shīʿī town in central Persia. Subsequently, the Ṣabbāḥ family moved to the nearby town of Rayy, another important centre of Shīʿī learning and an area of Ismāʿīlī activity. Soon after the age of seventeen, Ḥasan was introduced to Ismāʿīlī doctrines and was converted through the efforts of some local *dāʿīs*. In 464/1072, the newly initiated Ḥasan was brought to the attention of Ibn ʿAṭṭāsh, who was then staying in Rayy. Ibn ʿAṭṭāsh recognized Ḥasan's talents and appointed him to a post in the *daʿwa*, also instructing him to go to Cairo to further his Ismāʿīlī education. Ḥasan finally arrived in Fāṭimid Egypt in 471/1078, and spent some three years in Cairo and Alexandria. In Egypt, Ḥasan seems to have come into conflict with Badr al-Jamālī (d. 487/1094), the all-powerful Fāṭimid vizier and "commander of the armies", who had shortly earlier also succeeded al-Mu'ayyad al-Shīrāzī as the *dāʿī al-duʿāt*. At any rate, Ḥasan seems to have been banished under obscure circumstances from Egypt; he returned to the Persian *daʿwa* headquarters at Iṣfahān

---

[28] F. Daftary, "Persian Historiography", 91–97.

[29] Juwaynī, *Ta'rīkh-i jahān-gushāy*, vol. 3, 186–278; English trans., vol. 2, 666–725; Rashīd al-Dīn, *Jāmiʿ al-tawārīkh*, 97–195; Kāshānī, *Zubdat al-tawārīkh*, 133–233. For modern studies on the Persian Ismāʿīlīs and their state during the Alamūt period, see Hodgson, *Order*, 37–278, and his "The Ismāʿīlī State", 422–482; Lewis, *The Assassins*, 38–124; Daftary, *The Ismāʿīlīs*, 324–434, 669–699, and his "Ḥasan-i Ṣabbāḥ and the Origins of the Nizārī Ismaʿili Movement", in his *Mediaeval Ismaʿili History*, 181–204.

in 473/1081. He seems to have learned important lessons in Fāṭimid Egypt. Beset by numerous difficulties, the Fāṭimid regime was by then well embarked on its rapid decline. Ḥasan was now fully aware of the inability of the Fāṭimid state to support the Persian Ismāʿīlīs, taking this reality into account in his own subsequent revolutionary strategy.

In Persia, Ḥasan travelled for nine years in the service of the *daʿwa* to different localities, in Kirmān, Khūzistān, Qūmis, as well as the Caspian provinces in Daylam. It was during this period that Ḥasan formulated his revolutionary strategy against the Seljuqs, also evaluating Seljuq military strength in different parts of Persia. By 480/1087, he seems to have chosen the inaccessible mountain fortress of Alamūt, in the region of Rūdbār in Daylam, as a suitable site to establish his headquarters. Ḥasan, who was later appointed *dāʿī* of Daylam, now began to reinvigorate the *daʿwa* activities throughout Rūdbār. Ḥasan's activities were soon brought to the attention of Niẓām al-Mulk (d. 485/1092), who remained vizier for thirty years under the Great Seljuq Sultans Alp Arslān and Malik Shāh. However, Niẓām al-Mulk failed to capture Ḥasan, who in due time arrived in Rūdbār. In 483/1090, with his supporters infiltrating Alamūt and its surroundings, Ḥasan seized that impregnable fortress in the Alborz mountains according to a clever plan, signalling the open revolt of the Persian Ismāʿīlīs against the Seljuqs. The seizure of Alamūt also marked the foundation of what was to become the Nizārī Ismāʿīlī state in Persia. It is certain that Cairo had played no part in the organization or direction of this revolt, which was planned and carried out by Ḥasan on his own initiative.

Ḥasan-i Ṣabbāḥ seems to have had a complex set of religio-political motives for his revolt against the Seljuq Turks. As an Ismāʿīlī, he could not have tolerated the anti-Shīʿī policies of the Seljuqs, who as the new champions of Sunnī "orthodoxy" had sworn to uproot Fāṭimid Shīʿī rule from the Muslim world. Less conspicuously, Ḥasan's revolt was also an expression of Persian "national" sentiments, which accounts for its early popular appeal and success in Persia. By the opening decades of the 5th/11th century, a number of Turkish dynasties had established their rule over the Iranian lands, starting with the Ghaznawids and the Qarakhānids. A new alien age, with the Turks replacing the Arabs, in the Islamic history of the Iranian world was definitely initiated by the coming of the Seljuqs, who threatened the revival of Persian culture and national sentiments. This renaissance of a specifically Irano-Islamic culture had been based on the sentiments of the Islamicized Persians who had continued to be consciously aware of their Persian identity and cultural heritage during the centuries of Arab domination. This process, pioneered by the Ṣaffārids and maintained under the Sāmānids and the Būyids, had become quite irreversible by the time of the Turkish domination of the region.[30] At any rate, the Turkish Seljuqs were aliens in Persia and their rule was intensely detested by the Persians of different social classes. The anti-Turkish sentiments of the Persians were further aggravated due to the depredation caused in towns and villages by the Turks and their unruly soldiery, who were continuously attracted in new waves to Persia from the steppes of Central Asia by the successes of the Seljuqs. Ḥasan himself is reported to have expressed his resentment of the Turks and their rule over Persia.[31] It was, indeed, to the ultimate goal of uprooting Seljuq rule in Persia that Ḥasan dedicated himself and organized the Persian Ismāʿīlīs into a revolutionary force. In this connection, it is also significant to note that Ḥasan, as an expression of his Persian awareness and in spite of his uncompromising Islamic piety, substituted Persian for Arabic as the religious language of the Ismāʿīlīs of Persia. This was the first time that a major Muslim community had adopted Persian as its religious language; it also explains why the Ismāʿīlī literature of all the Persian-speaking (Nizārī) Ismāʿīlī communities of the Alamūt period and subsequent times was produced entirely in the Persian language.

After firmly establishing himself at Alamūt, Ḥasan-i Ṣabbāḥ extended his influence throughout Rūdbār and adjacent areas in Daylam, by winning converts and gaining possession of more strongholds which he fortified systematically for withstanding long sieges. There is evidence suggesting that Ḥasan also attracted at least some of the remnants of the Khurramiyya in Ādharbāyjān and elsewhere who, as an expression of their own Persian sentiments, referred to themselves

---

[30] Professor Bosworth has studied the Persian revival under Arab and Turkish rule in numerous studies; see, for instance, his "The Development of Persian Culture", 33–44, reprinted in his *The Medieval History*, article XVIII; "Interaction of Arabic and Persian Literature and Culture", 59–75, reprinted in his *Medieval Arabic Culture*, article VIII, and his *Saffarids*, 168–180. See also Stern, "Yaʿqūb the Coppersmith", 535–555.

[31] See Rashīd al-Dīn, 112, and the anonymous Nizārī treatise from the Alamūt period entitled *Haft bāb-i Bābā Sayyidnā*, 30; English trans., in Hodgson, *Order*, 314.

as Pārsiyan.[32] Soon, Alamūt came to be raided by the forces of the nearest Seljuq *amīr*, marking the initiation of an endless series of Seljuq-Ismāʿīlī military encounters in Persia. In 484/1091, Ḥasan sent the *dāʿī* Ḥusayn-i Qāʾinī to his native Quhistān to mobilize support there. This capable *dāʿī* met with immediate success in Quhistān, a barren region in southeastern Khurāsān, where the Ismāʿīlīs soon rose in open revolt against the Seljuqs and seized numerous castles as well as several major towns, including Tūn, Ṭabas, Qāʾin and Zūzan. As a result, Quhistān became the second major territory, after Rūdbār, for the activities of the Persian Ismāʿīlīs.

By 485/1092, Ḥasan had founded an independent territorial state for the Persian Ismāʿīlīs. Having become aware of the growing power of the Ismāʿīlīs, Sultan Malik Shāh had meanwhile sent major Seljuq expeditions against the Ismāʿīlīs of both Rūdbār and Quhistān. However, on Malik Shāh's death in 485/1092, the Seljuq forces dispersed, and the sultanate was thrown into civil war for more than a decade until 498/1105, when Muḥammad Tapar emerged victorious as the undisputed sultan while his brother Sanjar remained at Balkh as his viceroy in the East. During this period of strife in the Seljuq camp, Ḥasan-i Ṣabbāḥ readily consolidated and extended his power to other parts of Persia, including especially the medieval province of Qūmis where the Ismāʿīlīs seized Girdkūh and a number of other strongholds near Dāmghān. The Ismāʿīlīs also captured several fortresses in Arrajān, in the border region between the provinces of Khūzistān and Fārs. The Ismāʿīlī leader in Arrajān was the *dāʿī* Abū Ḥamza, who like Ḥasan, had spent some time in Egypt to further his Ismāʿīlī education. In Daylam itself the Ismāʿīlīs had repelled intermittent Seljuq offensives;[33] they had also acquired more strongholds in northern Persia, including the key fortress of Lamasar (or Lanbasar) to the west of Alamūt. Kiyā Buzurg-Ummīd, who had seized Lamasar by assault, stayed there as commander for more than twenty years until he was called to Alamūt to succeed Ḥasan-i Ṣabbāḥ. In addition, the Ismāʿīlīs were now spreading their activities to numerous towns throughout Persia, also directing their attention closer to the

[32] See Rashīd al-Dīn, 149–153; Kāshānī, 186–190, and Madelung, *Religious Trends*, 9–12. On the Khurramiyya, who were active in different parts of the Iranian world throughout the ʿAbbāsid times, and manifested anti-Arab, anti-Turkish or even anti-Islamic sentiments, see Madelung, "Khurramiyya", *EI*², vol. 5, 63–65.

[33] For a detailed analysis of these campaigns and the biased reports of the chroniclers favouring the Seljuqs, see Hillenbrand, "The Power Struggle", 205–220.

seat of Seljuq power, Iṣfahān. In this area, the Ismāʿīlīs under the leadership of Ibn ʿAṭṭāsh's son Aḥmad attained a major political success by seizing in 494/1100 the fortress of Shāhdiz, which guarded the main routes to the Seljuq capital. It is reported that the *dāʿī* Aḥmad succeeded in converting some 30,000 persons in the Iṣfahān area, where he also collected taxes in the districts around Shāhdiz. There is no evidence suggesting that the activities of Ḥasan and his immediate successors at Alamūt extended to Badakhshān and elsewhere in Transoxania. The remote and small Ismāʿīlī communities of these regions in Central Asia seem to have developed independently of Alamūt until sometime in the 7th/13th century. By the early years of the 6th/12th century, Ḥasan-i Ṣabbāḥ had also extended his activities into Syria by dispatching a number of Persian *dāʿīs* there. However, almost half a century of efforts were required before the Ismāʿīlīs could finally acquire a network of strongholds in Syria. Other than Ḥasan himself, the leading Persian Ismāʿīlī personalities of the early Alamūt period, such as Buzurg-Ummīd, Ḥusayn-i Qā'inī, and Ra'īs Muẓaffar, the governor of Girdkūh, were all capable commanders and military strategists suited to the task at hand, rather than learned theologians and philosophers like the earlier Iranian *dāʿīs* of the Fāṭimid times.

Soon, the anti-Seljuq revolt of the Persian Ismāʿīlīs acquired its distinctive pattern and methods of struggle, which were appropriate to the times. Ḥasan-i Ṣabbāḥ had recognized the decentralized nature of Seljuq rule as well as their vastly superior military power. As a result, he designed an appropriate strategy, aiming to subdue the Seljuqs locality by locality through acquiring a multiplicity of impregnable strongholds. He also resorted to the technique of assassinating prominent adversaries for attaining military and political objectives. In subsequent times, this policy became identified in a highly exaggerated manner with the Nizārī Ismāʿīlīs to the extent that almost any assassination of any significance in the central and eastern Islamic lands during the Alamūt period was attributed to the daggers of the Ismāʿīlī *fidā'īs*, the young self-sacrificing devotees who carried out the actual sectarian missions. And in time, a number of myths came to be fabricated and disseminated regarding the recruitment and training of these *fidā'īs*.[34] From early on, the assassinations led to the mas-

[34] For the origins and early development of these legends, which found their cul-

sacres of Ismāʿīlīs, and the massacres in turn provoked further assassinations of their instigators.

In the meantime, the Nizārī-Mustaʿlī schism of 487/1094 had split the Ismāʿīlīs into two rival factions. By that time, Ḥasan-i Ṣabbāḥ had emerged as the undisputed leader of the Persian Ismāʿīlīs, and perhaps of the Ismāʿīlīs of the entire Seljuq realm. He had already been following an independent revolutionary policy for several years, and now he supported Nizār's cause and broke off his relations with Cairo. Ḥasan had now in effect founded the independent Nizārī *daʿwa*. In this decision, he was supported by the entire Ismāʿīlī community of Persia, while the Ismāʿīlīs of Central Asia seem to have remained uninformed about this schism for quite some time. Nizār, who had led an abortive revolt in Egypt, was captured and executed by the Fāṭimid regime in 488/1095. Nizār did have male progeny, and some of them revolted against the later Fāṭimids. But Ḥasan-i Ṣabbāḥ did not divulge the name of Nizār's successor to the imamate. Numismatic evidence shows that Nizār's own name had continued to be mentioned on the coins minted at Alamūt for some seventy years after his death until the Nizārī Ismāʿīlī imams emerged at Alamūt and took charge of the affairs of their community and state.[35] In the absence of a manifest imam, Ḥasan continued to be obeyed as the supreme leader of the Nizārī Ismāʿīlī movement. Soon after 487/1094, Ḥasan was also acknowledged as the *ḥujja* or chief representative of the inaccessible imam, in the same manner that the central leaders of the early Ismāʿīlī movement had been recognized as the *ḥujjas* of the hidden imam.

It was under such circumstances that the outsiders from early on had acquired the impression that the movement of the (Nizārī) Ismāʿīlīs of Persia represented a "new preaching" (*al-daʿwa al-jadīda*), by contrast to the "old preaching" (*al-daʿwa al-qadīma*) of the Fāṭimid Ismāʿīlīs. Be that as it may, the "new preaching", expressed in the Persian language, was essentially the reformulation of an old Shīʿī doctrine of long standing among the Ismāʿīlīs, viz., the doctrine of *taʿlīm* or authoritative teaching by the imam. Ḥasan restated this doctrine vigorously in a treatise which has not survived, but it has been preserved fragmentarily by our Persian historians as well as the

mination in the tales recounted by Marco Polo, see Daftary, *The Assassin Legends*, especially 88–127.

[35] See, for instance, Miles, "Coins of the Assassins of Alamūt", 155–162.

contemporary theologian al-Shahrastānī (d. 548/1153) who may have been an Ismāʿīlī himself.[36] The doctrine of *taʿlīm*, emphasizing the autonomous guiding authority of each imam in his time, provided the foundation of the Nizārī teachings of the Alamūt period and subsequent times. The intellectual challenge posed by the doctrine of *taʿlīm*, which also refuted the legitimacy of ʿAbbāsid rule, called forth the official reaction of the Sunnī establishment, led by al-Ghazālī who attacked the Ismāʿīlīs in several polemical works.

Alarmed by the Nizārī successes, Sultan Barkiyāruq in western Persia and Sanjar in Khurāsān agreed in 494/1101 to deal more effectively, in their respective territories, with the Nizārī Ismāʿīlīs who were then posing a general threat to the Seljuqs. Despite new Seljuq offensives and massacres, however, the Nizārīs managed to retain all their strongholds. But the Nizārī fortunes began to be reversed with the accession of Muḥammad Tapar (498–511/1105–1118) to the sultanate, which marked the termination of dynastic disputes and factional rivalries among the Seljuqs. During his reign, the Persian Nizārīs lost most of their fortresses in the Zagros mountains; with the loss of Shāhdiz in 500/1107, the Nizārīs also lost their influence in the Iṣfahān region. Despite their superior military power and a prolonged war of attrition, the Seljuqs did not succeed in seizing Alamūt, where Ḥasan-i Ṣabbāḥ had continued to stay; and, the Persian Ismāʿīlīs by and large retained their regional positions in Rūdbār, Qūmis, and Quhistān. Nevertheless, by the time of Ḥasan's death in 518/1124, the armed revolt of the Persian Ismāʿīlīs against the Seljuqs had lost its effectiveness, much in the same way that Muḥammad Tapar's offensive against them had failed to realize its objectives. The Seljuq-Ismāʿīlī relations had now entered a new phase of "stalemate".

Kiyā Buzurg-Ummīd (518–532/1124–1138), the second lord of Alamūt, maintained the policies of his predecessor and further strengthened the Nizārī state, despite renewed Seljuq offensives against Rūdbār and Quhistān. Meanwhile, the Nizārī *daʿwa* was revived in southern Syria through the efforts of Bahrām (d. 522/1128) and other Persian *dāʿīs* sent from Alamūt, and by 527/1132, they began to acquire their permanent strongholds in central Syria. The scattered territo-

---

[36] Al-Shahrastānī, *Kitāb al-milal*, 150–152; partial English trans., 167–170; English trans. also in Hodgson, *Order*, 325–328. See also G. Monnot, "al-Shahrastānī", *EI*^{2}, vol. 9, 214–216.

ries of the Nizārī state now stretched from Syria to eastern Persia, and possibly parts of adjacent areas in Afghanistan, and yet this state maintained a remarkable cohesion and sense of unity amidst extremely hostile surroundings and despite suffering uninterrupted persecution. Indeed, the stability of this state and the unwavering obedience of the Nizārīs towards their leaders never ceased to amaze the Seljuqs and other Nizārī adversaries, including the European Crusaders. Comprised of mountain dwellers, villagers, and inhabitants of small towns, the Persian Nizārīs also maintained a sophisticated outlook and encouraged learning. They established impressive libraries at Alamūt and their other major strongholds in Persia, as well as Syria. In later Alamūt times, numerous Muslim scholars availed themselves of the Nizārī libraries and patronage of learning.

Buzurg-Ummīd was succeeded by his son Muḥammad (532–557/1138–1162). In his time, the Persian Nizārīs extended their activities to Georgia (Gurjistān). They also made a major effort through their *dāʿīs* to penetrate a new region, Ghūr, to the east of Quhistān, in present-day central Afghanistan. The Nizārī Ismāʿīlī *daʿwa* seems to have been established in that region around 550/1155 at the request of the Ghūrid ruler ʿAlāʾ al-Dīn Ḥusayn Jahānsūz. In Daylam, the Nizārīs had continued to confront the enmity of the Zaydīs as well as other local dynasties such as the Bāwandids of Ṭabaristān and Gīlān.

The fourth lord of Alamūt, Ḥasan II *ʿalāʾ dhikrihiʾl-salām* (557–561/1162–1166), proclaimed the *qiyāma* or the Great Resurrection, the long-awaited Last Day, in 559/1164 at special ceremonies held at Alamūt and Quhistān. Relying heavily on Ismāʿīlī *taʾwīl*, or esoteric exegesis, however, the *qiyāma* was interpreted spiritually to mean the manifestation of unveiled truth in the person of the Nizārī Ismāʿīlī imam. Accordingly, for the Nizārīs, who alone were capable of understanding the spiritual reality of the immutable religious truths (*ḥaqāʾiq*), hidden in the *bāṭin* of the positive laws, Paradise had now been actualized in this world. As a corollary, the outside world, comprised of non-Ismāʿīlīs, was relegated to the realm of spiritual non-existence. The declaration of the *qiyāma* was tantamount to the Nizārī declaration of independence from the "other". The Nizārīs of the *qiyāma* times did in fact practically ignore the outside world, refraining from any major campaign against their adversaries. As the person who had declared the *qiyāma*, Ḥasan II was also acknowledged by the Nizārī community as the *qāʾim* and the rightful imam from the progeny of

Nizār b. al-Mustanṣir. Ḥasan II's son and successor, Nūr al-Dīn Muḥammad II (561–607/1166–1210), devoted his own long reign to a systematic elaboration of the doctrine of the *qiyāma*.[37] This period also coincided with the career of Rāshid al-Dīn Sinān, the original "Old Man of the Mountain" of the Crusaders. Sinān had spent his youth at Alamūt, where he had furthered his Ismāʿīlī education before being sent by Ḥasan II to Syria soon after 557/1162. He led the Syrian Nizārīs for thirty years to the peak of their power and glory until his death in 589/1193.

Meanwhile, the Great Seljuq sultanate had been disintegrating in Persia and elsewhere after Sanjar's death in 552/1157. The Seljuqs were replaced by a number of Turkish dynasties in different regions. At the same time, a new power based on Khwārazm, the region on the lower Oxus, had emerged in the East. The hereditary rule of this region had passed earlier into the hands of a Turkish dynasty acting as vassals of the Seljuqs and carrying the region's traditional regnal title of Khwārazm Shāh. After Sanjār, the Khwārazm Shāhs began to assert their independence and expanded their territories into Khurāsān and other Iranian lands. Subsequently, the Khwārazm Shāhs expanded their empire westward across Persia, clearing away the remnants of Seljuq rule. As the successors of the Seljuqs, the Khwārazm Shāhs developed their own hostile relations with the Nizārīs of Rūdbār and elsewhere in Persia. In Quhistān, the Nizārīs had continued to have military encounters with the Ghūrids and the Maliks in the neighbouring Sīstān or Nīmrūz.[38] It was in the aftermath of the decline of the Seljuqs that the ʿAbbāsid caliph al-Nāṣir (575–622/1180–1225) found the long-awaited opportunity to revive the power and prestige of his dynasty. During this period, the next ruler of Alamūt, Jalāl al-Dīn Ḥasan III (607–618/1210–1221), attempted a daring rapprochement with the Sunnī establishment, ordering his followers to observe the *sharīʿa* in its Sunnī form. Later, this policy was explained as having represented a form of *taqiyya* or dissimulation to safeguard the survival of the community and improve

---

[37] The doctrine of the *qiyāma*, as elaborated under Muḥammad II, is expounded in the *Haft bāb-i Bābā Sayyidnā*, 4–42; English trans., with commentary, in Hodgson, *Order*, 279–324. For the best modern exposition of this doctrine, see Hodgson, *Order*, 162–180, while an interesting phenomenological account is contained in Jambet, *La grande résurrection*.

[38] See Bosworth, "The Ismaʿilis of Quhistān", in Daftary, ed., *Mediaeval Ismaʿili History*, 221–229, and his *Saffarids*, 387–410, 418 ff.

its relations with the rest of the Muslim society. At any rate, by contrast to the *qiyāma* times, the Nizārī Ismāʿīlī imam had now boldly accommodated his community to the outside world. The new Nizārī policy proved very successful; Jalāl al-Dīn Ḥasan was acknowledged by the caliph al-Nāṣir and other leading Sunnī rulers as an *amīr* in the Muslim world, and his rights to the Nizārī territories were officially recognized. Jalāl al-Dīn Ḥasan also participated in the caliph al-Nāṣir's intricate alliances. As a result of these developments, the Ghūrid attacks against the Nizārīs of Quhistān ceased, while the Nizārīs of Syria received timely help from the Ayyūbids in their conflicts with the Crusaders; and many Sunnīs, including scholars, who were then fleeing from the first Mongol invasions of Khurāsān, began to find refuge in the Nizārī towns and strongholds of Quhistān. Later in the 7th/13th century, the Nizārī *daʿwa* began to be actively propagated in Badakhshān where the Ismāʿīlīs had survived in small Pamiri communities. At the same time, Nizārī *dāʿīs*, later also called *pīrs*, were dispatched from Alamūt to spread the *daʿwa* in Multān and other areas of Sind.

The final decades of the Nizārī state in Persia, under ʿAlāʾ al-Dīn Muḥammad III (618–653/1221–1255), coincided with a most turbulent period in the history of the Iranian, and indeed Islamic, lands. By 617/1220, Chingiz Khan, ruler of the new Mongol empire, had captured Bukhārā and Samarqand. In the following year, he crossed the Oxus and seized Balkh. Then, the Mongols conquered Khurāsān, destroying Marw and Nīshāpūr. It was in the early years of ʿAlāʾ al-Dīn Muḥammad's reign that an increasing number of Muslims, both Sunnī and Shīʿī, found refuge among the Nizārīs of Quhistān who were still enjoying their stability and prosperity. The enviable contemporary conditions of the Quhistānī Nizārīs are described vividly by Minhāj-i Sirāj Jūzjānī, the Ghūrid historian and ambassador who visited Quhistān several times during 621–623/1224–1226 and met with the *muḥtasham* or chief of the Ismāʿīlīs there.[39]

The most prominent of the outside scholars who now availed themselves of the Nizārīs' patronage of learning was the Shīʿī philosopher, theologian and scientist Naṣīr al-Dīn al-Ṭūsī (597–672/1201–1274). It was around 624/1227 that al-Ṭūsī entered the service of Nāṣir al-Dīn ʿAbd al-Raḥīm b. Abī Manṣūr (d. 655/1257), the learned

[39] Jūzjānī, *Ṭabaqāt-i Nāṣirī*, 182–183; English trans., vol. 2, 1197–1205, 1212–1214.

muḥtasham of the Nizārīs of Quhistān. Al-Ṭūsī developed a close friendship with Nāṣir al-Dīn, to whom he dedicated his great work on ethics, the *Akhlāq-i Nāṣirī*. The period of his Ismāʿīlī connection, lasting some thirty years until 654/1256, was particularly productive for al-Ṭūsī, who also embraced Ismāʿīlism.[40] During this period, spent first in the Nizārī strongholds of Quhistān and later at Alamūt and Maymūndiz fortresses in Rūdbār, al-Ṭūsī also wrote a number of Ismāʿīlī works, including the *Rawḍat al-taslīm* (*Meadow of Submission*) which is the most comprehensive extant treatise on the Nizārī Ismāʿīlī teachings of the Alamūt period after the declaration of the *qiyāma*.[41]

With the demise of Jalāl al-Dīn Mingübirti (617–628/1220–1231), the last of the Khwārazm Shāhs who had also been engaged in war and diplomacy with Alamūt, the Nizārīs of Persia came to be confronted directly by the Mongols. The efforts of the Imam ʿAlāʾ al-Dīn Muḥammad to forge an alliance with the kings of France and England, in collaboration with the ʿAbbāsid caliph, against the Mongols proved futile; and all the Nizārī attempts to reach a peaceful accord with the Mongols themselves proved equally ineffective. At any event, when the Great Khan Möngke (649–657/1251–1259) decided to complete the Mongol conquest of western Asia, he assigned first priority to the destruction of the Nizārī state in Persia, entrusting the mission to his brother Hülegü.

The Mongol hordes had already started to exert constant pressures on the Nizārīs of Quhistān and Qūmis when ʿAlāʾ al-Dīn Muḥammad was succeeded by his youthful son, Rukn al-Dīn Khurshāh, in Shawwāl 653/December 1256; he would be the last lord of Alamūt. A few months later, in the spring of 654/1256, the main Mongol expedition led by Hülegü himself entered Persia through Khurāsān. In the final year of the Nizārī state, Khurshāh and Hülegü exchanged countless embassies and negotiated endlessly in vain.[42] Vacillating between resistance and surrender, Khurshāh seems to have hoped to save at least the major Nizārī strongholds of Persia from Mongol destruction, while Hülegü demanded nothing less than total Nizārī submission.

[40] On the controversy surrounding al-Ṭūsī's religious affiliation, see Dabashi, "The Philosopher/Vizier", 231–245, and also Madelung, "Naṣīr ad-Dīn Ṭūsī's Ethics", 85–101.

[41] Al-Ṭūsī, *Rawḍat al-taslīm*; French trans., *La Convocation d'Alamūt*. For al-Ṭūsī's Ismāʿīlī writings, see Poonawala, *Biobibliography*, 260–263.

[42] See Boyle, "The Ismāʿīlīs and the Mongol Invasion", 7–22; Daftary, *The Ismāʿīlīs*, 416–430, and his "Rukn al-Dīn Khurshāh", *EI*², vol. 8, 598–599.

Finally, Khurshāh surrendered on 29 Shawwāl 654/19 November 1256, after the main Mongol armies had converged on Maymūndiz, where the imam was then staying, and engaged the Nizārīs in fierce fighting. This marked the end of the Alamūt period in the Ismāʿīlī history of the Iranian lands. Alamūt itself was surrendered to the Mongols a month later, while Lamasar held out for another year, and Girdkūh, as the last Nizārī outpost in Persia, resisted its Mongol besiegers until 669/1270. Early in the following year, 655/1257, Möngke sanctioned a general massacre of the Nizārīs of Persia. Rukn al-Dīn Khurshāh's own tragic end came in the spring of 655/1257 when he was murdered by his Mongol guards somewhere in central Mongolia, whither he had gone in vain to see the Great Khan.

The Early Post-Alamūt Centuries

The collapse of the Nizārī state in 654/1256 marked the initiation of a new phase in the medieval history of the Iranian Ismāʿīlīs, who had now permanently lost their political prominence. Henceforth, the Ismāʿīlīs of the Iranian lands, all belonging to the Nizārī branch, survived as minority religious communities in Persia, Afghanistan and Central Asia. The first two centuries in the post-Alamūt history of these communities remain rather obscure. Only the major developments of this period have been recently clarified by modern scholarship on the basis of numerous regional histories and other primary sources as well as the oral traditions and the meagre writings of the Nizārīs themselves.[43]

In Persia, the Nizārīs were left in an utterly confused and devastated state in the aftermath of the Mongol catastrophe. Large numbers were put to the Mongol swords in Rūdbār and Quhistān; and in both regions the surviving groups were displaced from their traditional abodes, the mountain strongholds and their surrounding villages and a few towns. Many of the Nizārīs who had survived the Mongol massacres migrated to adjacent regions in Afghanistan and Badakhshān as well as Sind, while numerous groups, isolated in remote places or towns, soon began to disintegrate or gradually assimilated themselves into the religiously dominant communities of their surroundings. The Nizārīs were now also deprived of any form of central leadership,

[43] For the details and the relevant sources, see Daftary, *The Ismāʿīlīs*, 435–451.

provided earlier from Alamūt. It was under such circumstances that the highly disorganized and scattered Nizārī communities were once again obliged to observe *taqiyya* very strictly. For about two centuries after the fall of Alamūt, the Nizārī communities of Persia, Afghanistan and Badakhshān, and elsewhere in Syria and India, developed on a local basis and independently of one another under the local leadership of their own *dāʿīs*.

Meanwhile, a group of Nizārī dignitaries had managed to hide Rukn al-Dīn Khurshāh's minor son Shams al-Dīn Muḥammad, who had succeeded to the Nizārī imamate. He was evidently taken to Ādharbāyjān where he spent the rest of his life disguising himself as an embroiderer. These facts are attested by certain allusions in the unpublished versified *Safar-nāma* of Saʿd al-Dīn b. Shams al-Dīn Nizārī Quhistānī (d. 720/1320). A native of Bīrjand in Quhistān, and the first post-Alamūt Nizārī poet, Nizārī Quhistānī served for a while at the court of the Kart rulers of Harāt. Nizārī Quhistānī travelled widely, and he seems to have seen the Imam Shams al-Dīn Muḥammad around 678/1280 in Ādharbāyjān, possibly at Tabrīz. Practically nothing is known about the imams who succeeded Shams al-Dīn Muḥammad in Persia until the second half of the 9th/15th century.

Shams al-Dīn Muḥammad, the twenty-eighth Nizārī imam, died around 710/1310. An obscure dispute over his succession split the line of the Nizārī imams and their following into what became known as the Muḥammad-Shāhī and Qāsim-Shāhī branches. The Muḥammad-Shāhī line of Nizārī imams, who initially had numerous followers in Daylam and Badakhshān, was discontinued soon after 1201/1786. On the other hand, the Qāsim-Shāhī line has persisted to our times, and since the early decades of the 13th/19th century the imams of this line have become better known under their hereditary title of Aga Khan. At any rate, this schism provided another serious blow to the already devastated Nizārī *daʿwa* of the early post-Alamūt period.

Meanwhile, the Nizārīs had managed to regroup in Daylam, where they remained active throughout the Īlkhānid and Tīmūrid periods. At the time, Daylam was ruled by different local dynasties, and the political fragmentation of the region permitted the Nizārīs there to make periodic attempts to regain Alamūt and Lamasar, which had not been completely demolished by the Mongols. They also succeeded in winning several local rulers of northern Persia to their side. For instance, some of the Kushayjī *amīr*s, including Kiyā Sayf al-Dīn, who by 770/1368 controlled much of Daylam, adhered to Nizārī Ismāʿīlism.[44] A certain Nizārī leader known as Khudāwand Muḥammad, who may perhaps be identified with the Muḥammad-Shāhī Nizārī Imam Muḥammad b. Mu'min Shāh (d. 807/1404), had also appeared in Daylam, where he played an active part in local conflicts and alliances. Khudāwand Muḥammad established himself at Alamūt for a while, but was eventually obliged to seek refuge with Tīmūr who exiled him to Sulṭāniyya.[45] Later, the Banū Iskandar who ruled over parts of Māzandarān supported the Nizārī cause in Daylam.[46] The Nizārīs retained some importance in northern Persia until the end of the 10th/16th century, when the Caspian provinces were annexed to the Ṣafawid dominions. It is interesting to note that the Ṣafawids themselves used Alamūt as a royal prison for the rebellious members of their own household before the fortress was permanently abandoned.

The Nizārīs of Quhistān never really recovered from the Mongol onslaught, which left all of Khurāsān with its great cities in ruins. Subsequently, they survived in scattered villages around some of their former towns in Khurāsān, without acquiring any political prominence. The Nizārīs of Badakhshān, who were particularly devoted to Nāṣir-i Khusraw, had essentially remained outside of the confines of the Nizārī state. But, as noted, the Nizārī *daʿwa* had been propagated actively there during the later Alamūt period. According to the local tradition of the Nizārīs of Badakhshān, the Nizārī *daʿwa* was introduced to Shughnān by two *dāʿī*s sent from Alamūt. These *dāʿī*s, Sayyid Shāh Malang and Sayyid Shāh Khāmūsh, founded dynasties of *mīr*s and *pīr*s who ruled on a hereditary basis over Shughnān, Rūshān and adjacent districts of Badakhshān in the upper Oxus region.[47]

Subsequently, Badakhshān was fortunate to escape the Mongol debacle. The region was eventually annexed to the Tīmūrid empire in the middle of the 9th/15th century. Early in the 10th/16th century, Badakhshān was briefly conquered by the Özbegs, whose hegemony

---

[44] See Marʿashī, *Ta'rīkh-i Gīlān*, 66–68.

[45] Marʿashī, *Ta'rīkh-i Gīlān*, 52–66, 123–124.

[46] See Gīlānī, *Ta'rīkh-i Māzandarān*, 88–89, 100, and Fūmanī, *Ta'rīkh-i Gīlān*, ed. Dorn, 127–129, 192–195; ed. Sutūda, 164–166, 241–244.

[47] Badakhshī, *Ta'rīkh-i Badakhshān*, ed. Boldyrev, 227–253, and Semenov, "Shughnanskikh Ismailitov", 523–561.

was persistently resisted by different local rulers. It was under such chaotic conditions that Shāh Raḍī al-Dīn, a Muḥammad-Shāhī Nizārī imam, came from his original base of operations in Quhistān and Sīstān to Badakhshān, where he established his own rule with the help of the local Nizārīs. Shāh Raḍī al-Dīn was, however, killed in battle in 915/1509, and, subsequently, Mīrzā Khan, a local Tīmūrid *amīr* severely persecuted the Nizārīs of Badakhshān.

Meanwhile, the Nizārī imams of the Qāsim-Shāhī line had emerged at Anjudān, a large village in central Persia near Qumm and Maḥallāt, initiating the Anjudān revival in the post-Alamūt history of the Nizārī Ismāʿīlīs.[48] Imām Mustanṣir bi'llāh, who died in 885/1480, is the first imam of his line to have definitely established himself at Anjudān, where a Nizārī community already existed. By that time, Nizārī Ismāʿīlism had become infused in Persia with Sufi teachings and terminology, while Sufi *pīr*s themselves had begun to use ideas which had been more widely attributed to the Ismāʿīlīs. As a part of this coalescence between Nizārī Ismāʿīlism and Sufism in Persia, the Nizārīs had also adopted certain external features of the Sufi orders (*ṭarīqa*s), referring to their imams and themselves as *pīr*s (or *murshid*s) and *murīd*s. This disguise was partly adopted for the purposes of *taqiyya* to ensure the safety of the Nizārīs in predominantly Sunnī surroundings. However, the esoteric nature of the teachings of both communities, too, had made its own important contribution to bringing about this coalescence which left permanent imprints on the Nizārī community. This also explains why the Nizārīs of the Iranian lands, especially in Badakhshān, have continued to regard some of the great mystic poets of Persia, such as Farīd al-Dīn ʿAṭṭār and Jalāl al-Dīn Rūmī, as their co-religionists. Later in Ṣafawid times, the Persian Nizārīs also adopted the guise of Twelver Shīʿism, then the official religion of the Ṣafawid realm, as another *taqiyya* practice.

Anjudān served as the residence of the Qāsim-Shāhī Nizārī imams and the headquarters of their *daʿwa* for some two centuries, coinciding with the period of Ṣafawid rule over Persia. The tombs of the Imam Mustanṣir bi'llāh, who carried the Sufi name of Shāh Qalandar, and several of his successors are still preserved in Anjudān.[49] The Anjudān period ushered a revival in the *daʿwa* activities of the

---

[48] Daftary, *The Ismāʿīlīs*, 451–478.

[49] See Ivanow, "Tombs", 49–62, and Daftary, "Anjedān", *Encyclopaedia Iranica*, vol. 2, 77.

Nizārīs of the Iranian lands. This revival also resulted in the assertion of Anjudān's control over the various Nizārī communities which had hitherto developed on a local basis. The ground for the Anjudān revival had already been prepared by the spread of Shīʿī tendencies in Persia mainly through the activities of a number of Sufi orders; and this process eventually culminated in the adoption of Twelver Shīʿism as the religion of Ṣafawid Persia in 907/1501. The Ṣafawiyya themselves represented one of the most militant Sufi orders through which Shīʿī tendencies and ʿAlid loyalism had permeated Persia.

During the Anjudān period, the Qāsim-Shāhī Nizārī *daʿwa* was reorganized and reinvigorated under the direct leadership of the imams at Anjudān, not only to win new converts but also to gain the allegiance of those Iranian Nizārīs, especially in Badakhshān, who had hitherto supported the Muḥammad-Shāhī line of imams. By asserting their own leadership, the imams also succeeded in undermining the position of the hereditary dynasties of *dāʿīs*, *mīrs*, or *pīrs*, which had emerged in different Iranian Ismāʿīlī communities. The imams now began to appoint their own trusted representatives to administer the affairs of these communities, especially in Khurāsān, Afghanistan and Badakhshān. These agents visited Anjudān on a regular basis, to report on the affairs of their community and to deliver the much needed religious dues they had collected.

By the second half of the 11th/17th century, the Anjudān revival had led to significant achievements. Rapidly expanding and reorganized Nizārī communities had now emerged throughout the Iranian world, in central Persia, Kirmān, Khurāsān, Afghanistan, and Badakhshān. The Nizārī *daʿwa* directed from Anjudān had been particularly successful also in Sind, Gujarāt and other regions of the Indian subcontinent. At the same time, the bulk of the Muḥammad-Shāhī Nizārīs had switched their allegiance to the imams residing at Anjudān. The literary activities of the Iranian Nizārīs, too, were revived during the Anjudān period, starting with the writings of Abū Isḥāq Quhistānī, and Khayrkhwāh-i Harātī who died after 960/1553.[50] The Nizārīs of the Iranian lands, especially in Badakhshān, also preserved a substantial portion of the literary heritage of their community, produced in the Persian language during the Alamūt and post-Alamūt centuries.

---

[50] See Poonawala, *Biobibliography*, 268–277.

The Ismāʿīlīs of the Iranian lands were not destined to regain the prominence they had acquired during the Alamūt period of their history, a religio-political prominence that was abruptly ended by the all-conquering Mongols. Nevertheless, by the end of the Middle Ages the Anjudān revival had already started to compensate at least partially for the Mongol debacle, permitting the Nizārī Ismāʿīlīs to survive in Iran, Afghanistan and Central Asia, as well as in many other regions of the world, as peaceful and prosperous religious communities.

Bibliography

Āmulī, Awliyāʾ Allāh, *Taʾrīkh-i Rūyān*, ed. M. Sutūda, Tehran, 1348/1969.

Badakhshī, Mīrzā Sang Muḥammad, *Taʾrīkh-i Badakhshān*, ed. A.N. Boldyrev. Leningrad, 1959; ed. M. Sutūda, Tehran, 1367/1988.

Barthold, Vasilii V., *Turkestan down to the Mongol Invasion*, ed. C.E. Bosworth, 3rd ed., London, 1968.

Bertel's, Andrei E., *Nasir-i Khosrov i ismailizm*, Moscow, 1959. Persian trans. Y. Āriyanpūr, *Nāṣir-i Khusraw va Ismāʿīliyān*, Tehran, 1346/1967.

Bosworth, C. Edmund, *The Ghaznavids: Their Empire in Afghanistan and Eastern Iran, 994: 1040*, Edinburgh, 1963.

———, "The Development of Persian Culture under the Early Ghaznavids", *Iran* 6 (1968), 33–44, reprinted in his *The Medieval History of Iran, Afghanistan and Central Asia*, London, 1977, article XVIII.

———, "Interaction of Arabic and Persian Literature and Culture in the 10th and Early 11th Centuries", *al-Abḥāth*, 27 (1978–1979), 59–75, reprinted in his *Medieval Arabic Culture and Administration*, London, 1982, article VIII.

———, *The History of the Saffarids of Sistan and the Maliks of Nimruz (247/861 to 949/1542–3)*, Costa Mesa–New York, 1994.

———, *The New Islamic Dynasties*, Edinburgh, 1996.

———, "The Ismaʿilis of Quhistān and the Maliks of Nīmrūz or Sīstān", in Daftary, ed., *Mediaeval Ismaʿili History*, 221–229.

Boyle, John A., "The Ismāʿīlīs and the Mongol Invasion", in S.H. Nasr, ed., *Ismāʿīlī Contributions to Islamic Culture*, Tehran, 1977, 7–22.

al-Bundārī, al-Fatḥ b. ʿAlī, *Zubdat al-nuṣra*, ed. M.Th. Houtsma, Leiden, 1889.

Corbin, Henry, ed. and tr., *Trilogie ismaélienne*, Tehran–Paris, 1961.

———, "Nāṣir-i Khusrau and Iranian Ismāʿīlism", in *The Cambridge History of Iran*: Volume 4, *The Period from the Arab Invasion to the Saljuqs*, ed. R.N. Frye. Cambridge, 1975, 520–542.

———, *Cyclical Time and Ismaili Gnosis*, tr. R. Manheim and J.W Morris, London, 1983.

Dabashi, Hamid, "The Philosopher/Vizier: Khwāja Naṣīr al-Dīn al-Ṭūsī and the Ismaʿilis", in Daftary, ed., *Mediaeval Ismaʿili History*, 231–245.

Daftary, Farhad, *The Ismāʿīlīs: Their History and Doctrines*, Cambridge, 1990.

———, "The Earliest Ismāʿīlīs", *Arabica* 38 (1991), 214–245.

———, "Persian Historiography of the Early Nizārī Ismāʿīlīs", *Iran* 30 (1992), 91–97.

———, "A Major Schism in the Early Ismāʿīlī Movement", *Studia Islamica* 77 (1993) 123–139.

———, *The Assassin Legends: Myths of the Ismaʿilis*, London, 1994.
———, ed. *Mediaeval Ismaʿili History and Thought*, Cambridge, 1996.
———, "Ḥasan-i Ṣabbāḥ and the Origins of the Nizārī Ismaʿili Movement", in Daftary, ed., *Mediaeval Ismaʿili History*, 181–204.
———, "Carmatians", *Encyclopaedia Iranica*, vol. 4, 823–832.
al-Daylamī, Muḥammad b. al-Ḥasan, *Bayān madhhab al-Bāṭiniyya*, ed. R. Strothmann, Istanbul, 1939.
van Ess, Josef, "Bibliographische Notizen zur islamischen Theologie. I. Zur Chronologie der Werke des Ḥamīdaddīn al-Kirmānī", *Die Welt des Orients* 9 (1978), 255–261.
Fūmanī, ʿAbd al-Fattāḥ, *Taʾrīkh-i Gīlān*, ed. B. Dorn, St. Petersburg, 1858; ed. M. Sutūda, Tehran, 1349/1970.
Gardīzī, ʿAbd al-Ḥayy b. al-Ḍaḥḥāk, *Zayn al-akhbār*, ed. ʿA. Ḥabībī. Tehran, 1347/1968.
Gīlānī, Mullā Shaykh ʿAlī, *Taʾrīkh-i Māzandarān*, ed. M. Sutūda, Tehran, 1352/1973.
Haft bāb-i Bābā Sayyidnā, ed. W. Ivanow, in his *Two Early Ismaili Treatises*. Bombay, 1933, 4–44. English trans., in Hodgson, *Order of Assassins*, 279–324.
Halm, Heinz, *The Empire of the Mahdi: The Rise of the Fatimids*, tr. M. Bonner, Leiden, 1996.
———, "The Oath of Allegiance (*ʿahd*) and the 'Sessions of Wisdom' (*majālis al-ḥikma*) in Fatimid Times", in Daftary, ed., *Mediaeval Ismaʿili History*, 91–115.
———, *The Fatimids and their Traditions of Learning*, London, 1997.
Hamdani, Abbas, *The Beginnings of the Ismāʿīlī Daʿwa in Northern India*, Cairo, 1956.
Hillenbrand, Carole, "The Power Struggle between the Saljuqs and the Ismaʿilis of Alamūt, 487–518/1094–1124: The Saljuq Perspective", in Daftary, ed., *Mediaeval Ismaʿili History*, 205–220.
Hodgson, Marshall G.S., *The Order of Assassins*, The Hague, 1955.
———, "The Ismāʿīlī State", in *The Cambridge History of Iran*: Volume 5, *The Saljuq and Mongol Periods*, ed. J.A. Boyle. Cambridge, 1968, 422–482.
Ibn al-Athīr, ʿIzz al-Dīn ʿAlī b. Muḥammad, *al-Kāmil fiʾl-taʾrīkh*, ed. C.J. Tornberg, Leiden, 1851–1876.
Ibn Ḥawqal, Abuʾl-Qāsim ʿAlī, *Kitāb ṣurat al-arḍ*, ed. J.H. Kramers. 2nd ed., Leiden, 1938–1939.
Ibn Isfandiyār, Muḥammad b. al-Ḥasan, *Taʾrīkh-i Ṭabaristān*, ed. ʿA. Iqbāl. Tehran, 1320/1941.
Ibn al-Nadīm, Abuʾl-Faraj Muḥammad b. Isḥāq, *Kitāb al-fihrist*, ed., M.R. Tajaddud, Tehran, 1973. English trans. B. Dodge, *The Fihrist of al-Nadīm*, New York, 1970.
Ibn al-Qalānisī, Abū Yaʿlā Ḥamza b. Asad, *Dhayl taʾrīkh Dimashq*, ed. H.F. Amedroz. Leiden, 1908; ed. S. Zakkār. Damascus, 1983.
Idrīs ʿImād al-Dīn b. al-Ḥasan, *ʿUyūn al-akhbār wa-funūn al-āthār*, vol. 6, ed. M. Ghālib, Beirut, 1984.
Ivanow, Wladimir, "Tombs of Some Persian Ismaili Imams", *Journal of the Bombay Branch of the Royal Asiatic Society*, New Series 14 (1938), 49–62.
———, *Problems in Nasir-i Khusraw's Biography*, Bombay, 1956.
———, *Alamut and Lamasar: Two Mediaeval Ismaili Strongholds in Iran*, Tehran, 1960.
Jambet, Christian, *La grande résurrection d'Alamūt*, Lagrasse, 1990.
Juwaynī, ʿAlāʾ al-Dīn ʿAṭā Malik b. Muḥammad, *Taʾrīkh-i jahān-gushāy*, ed. M. Qazvīnī, Leiden–London, 1912–1937. English trans. John A. Boyle, *The History of the World-Conqueror*, Manchester, 1958.
Jūzjānī, Minhāj-i Sirāj, *Ṭabaqāt-i Nāṣirī*, ed. ʿA. Ḥabībī. 2nd ed., Kabul, 1342–1343/1963–1964. English trans. H.G. Raverty, *The Ṭabakāt-i-Nāṣirī: A General History of the Muhammadan Dynasties of Asia*, London, 1881–1899.
Kāshānī, Abuʾl-Qāsim ʿAbd Allāh b. ʿAlī, *Zubdat al-tawārīkh: bakhsh-i Fāṭimiyān va Nizāriyān*, ed. M.T. Dānishpazhūh, 2nd ed., Tehran, 1366/1987.

Khayrkhwāh-i Harātī, Muḥammad Riḍā b. Sulṭān Ḥusayn, *Taṣnīfāt*, ed. W. Ivanow, Tehran, 1961.
al-Kirmānī, Ḥamīd al-Dīn Aḥmad b. ʿAbd Allāh, *al-Aqwāl al-dhahabiyya*, ed. Ṣ. al-Sāwī, Tehran, 1977.
Klemm, Verena, *Die Mission des fāṭimidischen Agenten al-Muʾayyad fī d-dīn in Šīrāz*, Frankfurt, etc., 1989.
Lewis, Bernard, *The Assassins: A Radical Sect in Islam*, London, 1967.
Madelung, Wilferd, "Das Imamat in der frühen ismailitische Lehre", *Der Islam* 37 (1961), 43–135.
———, "Abū Isḥāq al-Ṣābī on the Alids of Ṭabaristān and Gīlān", *Journal of Near Eastern Studies* 26 (1967), 17–56, reprinted in his *Religious and Ethnic Movements in Medieval Islam*, Hampshire, 1992, article VII.
———, "The Minor Dynasties of Northern Iran", in *The Cambridge History of Iran*: Volume 4, *The Period from the Arab Invasion to the Saljuqs*, ed. R.N. Frye, Cambridge, 1975, 198–249.
———, "Aspects of Ismāʿīlī Theology: The Prophetic Chain and the God Beyond Being", in S.H. Nasr, ed., *Ismāʿīlī Contributions to Islamic Culture*, Tehran, 1977, 53–65, reprinted in his *Religious Schools and Sects in Medieval Islam*, London, 1985, article XVII.
———, "Naṣīr ad-Dīn Ṭūsī's Ethics Between Philosophy, Shiʿism and Sufism", in R.G. Hovannisian, ed., *Ethics in Islam*, Malibu, Calif., 1985, 85–101.
———, *Religious Trends in Early Islamic Iran*, Albany, N.Y., 1988.
———, "The Fatimids and the Qarmaṭīs of Baḥrayn", in Daftary, ed., *Mediaeval Ismaʿili History*, 21–73.
———, "Ḳarmaṭī", *EI*², vol. 4, 660–665.
al-Maqrīzī, Taqī al-Dīn Aḥmad, *Ittiʿāẓ al-ḥunafāʾ*, ed. J. al-Shayyāl and M.H.M. Aḥmad, Cairo, 1967–73.
Marʿashī, Ẓahīr al-Dīn, *Taʾrīkh-i Gīlān va Daylamistān*, ed. M. Sutūda, Tehran, 1347/1968.
———, *Taʾrīkh-i Ṭabaristān va Rūyān va Māzandarān*, ed. B. Dorn, St. Petersburg, 1850; ed. M. Ḥusayn Tasbīḥī, Tehran, 1345/1966.
Miles, George C., "Coins of the Assassins of Alamūt", *Orientalia Lovaniensia Periodica* 3 (1972), 155–162.
Minorsky, Vladimir, *Studies in Caucasian History*, London, 1953.
———, *History of Sharvān and Darband*, Cambridge, 1958.
Mīrkhwānd, Muḥammad b. Khwāndshāh, *Rawḍat al-ṣafāʾ*, Tehran, 1338–1339/1960.
Miskawayh, Abū ʿAlī Aḥmad b. Muḥammad, *Tajārib al-umam*, ed. and tr. H.F. Amedroz and D.S. Margoliouth under the title *The Eclipse of the ʿAbbasid Caliphate*, Oxford, 1920–1921.
al-Muʾayyad fiʾl-Dīn al-Shīrāzī, Abū Naṣr Hibat Allāh, *Sīrat al-Muʾayyad fiʾl-Dīn dāʿī al-duʿāt*, ed. M. Kāmil Ḥusayn, Cairo, 1949.
Nāṣir-i Khusraw, *Dīwān*, ed. M. Mīnuvī and M. Muḥaqqiq, Tehran, 1353/1974.
———, *Kitāb jāmiʿ al-ḥikmatayn*, ed. H. Corbin and M. Muʿin, Tehran–Paris, 1953. French trans. I. de Gastines, *Le Livre réunissant les deux Sagesses*, Paris, 1990.
———, *Zād al-musāfirīn*, ed. M. Badhl al-Raḥmān, Berlin, 1341/1923.
al-Nawbakhtī, al-Ḥasan b. Mūsā, *Kitāb firaq al-Shīʿa*, ed. H. Ritter, Istanbul, 1931.
Niẓām al-Mulk, Abū ʿAlī al-Ḥasan b. ʿAlī al-Ṭūsī, *Siyar al-mulūk* (*Siyāsat-nāma*), ed. H. Darke. 2nd ed., Tehran, 1347/1968. English trans. H. Darke, *The Book of Government or Rules for Kings*, 2nd ed., London, 1978.
Poonawala, Ismail K., *Biobibliography of Ismāʿīlī Literature*, Malibu, Calif., 1977.
al-Qummī, Saʿd b. ʿAbd Allāh, *Kitāb al-maqālāt waʾl-firaq*, ed. M.J. Mashkūr, Tehran, 1963.
Rabino, Hyacinth L., "Rulers of Gilan", *JRAS* (1920), 277–296.
———, "Les dynasties du Māzandarān", *Journal Asiatique* 228 (1936), 397–474.

Rashīd al-Dīn Faḍl Allāh, *Jāmiʿ al-tawārīkh: qismat-i Ismāʿīliyān va Fāṭimiyān va Nizāriyān va dāʿiyān va rafīqān*, ed. M.T. Dānishpazhūh and M. Mudarrisī Zanjānī, Tehran, 1338/1959.
al-Rāwandī, Muḥammad b. ʿAlī, *Rāḥat al-ṣudūr*, ed. M. Iqbāl, London, 1921.
Semenov, Aleksandr A., "Iz oblasti religioznuikh verovany Shughnanskikh Ismailitov", *Mir Islama* 1 (1912), 523–561.
al-Shahrastānī, Abu'l-Fatḥ Muḥammad b. ʿAbd al-Karīm, *Kitāb al-milal wa'l-niḥal*, ed. W. Cureton. London, 1842–1846. Partial English trans. A.K. Kazi and J.G. Flynn, *Muslim Sects and Divisions*, London, 1984.
Smet, Daniel De, *La Quiétude de l'Intellect: Néoplatonisme et gnose ismaélienne dans l'oeuvre de Ḥamīd ad-Dīn al-Kirmānī* (X^{e}/XIe s.), Louvain, 1995.
Stern, Samuel M., "Ismāʿīlī Propaganda and Fatimid Rule in Sind", *Islamic Culture* 23 (1949), 298–307.
———, "The Early Ismāʿīlī Missionaries in North-West Persia and in Khurāsān and Transoxania", *BSOAS* 23 (1960), 56–90.
———, "Yaʿqūb the Coppersmith and Persian National Sentiments", in C.E. Bosworth, ed., *Iran and Islam, in Memory of the Late Vladimir Minorsky*, Edinburgh, 1971, 535–555.
———, *Studies in Early Ismāʿīlism*, Jerusalem–Leiden, 1983.
Ta'rīkh-i Sīstān, ed. M.T. Bahār, Tehran, 1314/1935; ed. J. Mudarris Ṣādiqī, Tehran, 1373/1994. English trans. M. Gold, *The Tārikh-e Sistān*, Rome, 1976.
al-Ṭūsī, Naṣīr al-Dīn Muḥammad b. Muḥammad, *Rawḍat al-taslīm*, ed. and tr. W. Ivanow, Leiden, 1950. French trans. Ch. Jambet, *La Convocation d'Alamūt: Somme de philosophie ismaélienne*, Lagrasse, 1996.
Walker, Paul E., *Early Philosophical Shiism: The Ismaili Neoplatonism of Abū Yaʿqūb al-Sijistānī*, Cambridge, 1993.
———, "The Ismaili Daʿwa in the Reign of the Fatimid Caliph al-Ḥākim", *Journal of the American Research Center in Egypt* 30 (1993), 161–182.
———, *The Wellsprings of Wisdom: A Study of Abū Yaʿqūb al-Sijistānī's Kitāb al-Yanābīʿ*, Salt Lake City, 1994.
———, "Abū Tammām and his Kitāb al-Shajara: A New Ismaili Treatise from Tenth-Century Khurasan", *Journal of the American Oriental Society* 114 (1994), 343–352.
———, *Abū Yaʿqūb al-Sijistānī: Intellectual Missionary*, London, 1996.
———, "An Ismaʿili Version of the Heresiography of the Seventy-two Erring Sects", in Daftary, ed., *Mediaeval Ismaʿili History*, 161–177.
Ẓahīr al-Dīn Nīshāpūrī, *Saljūq-nāma*, Tehran, 1332/1953.

A PERSIAN POEM LAMENTING THE ARAB CONQUEST

François de Blois

The subject of this article[1] is a Zoroastrian text deploring the conquest of Persia by the Arabs and anticipating the arrival of the saviour from the East, Šāh-Bahrām-i Warjāwand, who will drive out the conquerors and restore the Good Religion. It is part of the miscellaneous collection of Pahlavi texts, some religious, some semi-secular in character, contained notably in a manuscript copied in the early part of the 14th century, and published by J.M. Jamasp-Asana in 1913.[2] English translations have previously been published by M.J. Jamasp Asa in 1914,[3] H.W. Bailey in 1943[4] and J.C. Tavadia in 1955,[5] the last with a transcription and a commentary which have contributed greatly to the comprehension of this document.

Although the text is written in Pahlavi script, its language, as we hope to demonstrate, is in reality a not particularly archaic Neo-Persian. This is disguised by the fact that the Persian words are represented either by the Aramaic and pseudo-Aramaic logograms or else by the archaic or quasi-archaic "phonetic" spellings (not really phonetic, but purely conventional already in Sasanian Middle Persian) that are characteristic of Pahlavi[6] orthography.

Moreover, though not divided into verses in the manuscripts, it is clearly a poem. The first to notice this was Muḥammad Taqī Bahār, in a short article published in Persian in 1937.[7] This contribution

---

[1] Transliteration of Oriental scripts is in Roman type; phonological transcriptions are in *italics*, following the system normally used by Iranists.

[2] *Pahlavi texts*, 160–1.

[3] Jamasp Asa, *Sir Jamsetjee Jejeebhoy Madressa jubilee volume*, 75–6. An English summary had previously been published by West, *Grundriss* ii, 114, and by Anklesaria, in *Pahlavi texts*, introduction, 52.

[4] Bailey, *Zoroastrian problems*, 195–6.

[5] Tavadia, *JRAS*, 1955, 29–36.

[6] To avoid any possible confusion we shall distinguish consistently between "Middle Persian" (language) and "Pahlavi" (script). As is known, "Pahlavi" actually means "Parthian" and, as a designation for Persian writing or language, is a misnomer, but this misnomer is so well established that it is now futile to protest against it.

[7] Bahār, *Mihr*, V/3, 217–8. A free translation of the whole poem in Persian

was overlooked by Bailey and Tavadia, but the latter came to the same conclusion, as it seems, independently. The poem consists, according to our count, of 26 lines all rhyming in *-ān*, but these group themselves, as both Bahār and Tavadia noticed, tolerably neatly into couplets. Each couplet, or double-verse, forms a discrete unit and in at least two cases (couplets 7 and 10) there is a clear enjambement between the two lines. The structure of the poem can thus be compared with that of Arabic poems in *rajaz* metre and with the rhyme-scheme known as *mašṭūr*, where the monorhyme recurs at the end of every half-verse (*miṣrāʿ*), and not merely at the end of each double-verse (*bayt*), as is the case with the other metres. Rhymes of this sort are extremely rare in classical Persian, though we do find them, for example, in three verses by the 10th-century poet Lawkarī,[8] or in two anonymous poems quoted in the 13th-century *Tuḥfat al-mulūk* of ʿAlī b. Abī Ḥafs Iṣfahānī, which have been studied by Lazard.[9] But while these scan more or less correctly as *hazaj* (in the case of Lawkarī's poem) or as *mutaqārib* (in that of the other two), our poem cannot be scanned according to any of the recognised Persian metres. However, virtually all of the lines do end with a uniform cadence (- - ∪ -) (*az hinduwān; dūδa-y kayān; ī xusrawān*; etc.), a cadence characteristic of *mutaqārib* and of many of the other Persian metres. It would seem thus that the poet has not only adopted the monorhyme of Neo-Persian poetry, but has even imitated, at the end of most lines, the cadence of Arabic and Persian quantitative metre, but without using quantitative metre throughout. On the whole, the poem seems to have an accentual metre with, probably, four stresses in each hemistich, and a variable number of unstressed syllables. In this it follows the same principles as Middle-Persian unrhymed poetry. But, with its couplets, its monorhyme and its fairly regular quantitative cadence, the poem already goes a good deal of the way towards the adoption of Arabic poetic norms.

The linguistic character of the text is revealed clearly by features of morphology, syntax and vocabulary. The most striking morphological trait is the consistent use of the specifically Neo-Persian form

---

quantitative metre, but retaining many of the original rhymes, is published in Bahār's *Dīwān* I, 548–9. It begins: *rūz-ī rasad ki āyad payg-ī zi Hinduwān * gūyad: dihīd mužda ki āmad xudāyagān.*

[8] ʿAwfī, *Lubāb* II, 15.

[9] Lazard, *Mémorial Jean de Menasce*, 433–40, with brief comments also on the poem discussed in this article.

of the past tense of transitive verbs, instead of the Middle-Persian ergative construction. Thus we have *bistaδand*, "they took" (in verses 6 and 7), and *nihāδand*, "they put", *bibaxtand* (or *bibaxšīδand*),[10] "they distributed" and *xwāstand* "they demanded" (all in vs. 8). In all cases these are represented graphically by the logograms for the MP past participles followed by the copula ḤWHd, e.g. for *staδand* we have YNSB̲WNt ḤWHd. In real MP this would stand for *stad hend*, "he took them", but here the meaning is clearly "they took", for which MP would require *-šān stad*. For this "ergative" construction there is no clear example in our text.[11] The NP form of the transitive past tense can be found here and there in late (i.e. post-Sasanian) Middle-Persian texts such as the *Kārnāma i Ardašīr*,[12] where it is used alongside the MP ergative construction. It is in fact quite clear that literate Zoroastrians of the early Islamic period were perfectly capable of writing more or less correct Middle Persian when they so desired, though they did sometimes let NP forms slip in. If our author uses only the NP past tense, then this is because he is not writing the dead language of religious discourse but the spoken idiom of his own time. Likewise, our text consistently uses the preposition PWN, i.e. *pa*(*δ*) or *ba*, both in locative and directional senses and has not a single occurrence of the preposition ʿL (i.e. *ō*),[13] one of the most frequent words in any MP text. Here too the language of the poem reveals itself as less archaic than that of the *Kārnāma*.

Our poem does use a number of words that are not attested in Muslim NP. Most of these are specifically Zoroastrian religious terms of the sort that can be found also in much later Zoroastrian writ-

[10] The stem is written ḤLKWNt, which in MP would stand for *baxt*. In NP the past stem of this verb is *baxšīδ*.

[11] In vs. 4 DP has LNH MH dyt, quasi *mā či dīδ*, "what we saw", but MK has Z̲NH MH dyt, "*īn či dīδ*", "what he saw".

[12] See, for example, *Kārnāma* (ed. Antia), Pahlavi section, 8, parag. 16–17, where we have twice *man kardam* (written: L klt ḤWHm), "I did it". Conversely, the MP ergative construction is still used sporadically in NP texts up until the 13th century, in the 3rd person singular fairly frequently (e.g. *guftaš*, "he said"), in the other persons only in conjunction with the modal particle *-ē* (e.g. *či kardimān-ē*, "what would we do?"; cf. Lazard, *Langue*, 257, 330–1).

[13] In Sasanian MP, *paδ* and *ō* are both used in the locative sense ("in, on, at") as well as in the directional sense ("towards, onto"). In late MP *ō* is increasingly replaced by *be ō* (literally "out towards"), and then simply by *be*, and all these are mostly restricted to the directional sense. At some point fairly early in the history of NP, *be* and *pa*(*δ*) merge as *ba*, but since early NP script rarely distinguishes between p and b it is very difficult to establish the chronology of this process. In the edition below we have, for simplicity, transcribed PWN by *pa*(*δ*) throughout.

ings in Arabic script; this is the case with *druj*, "demon" (vss. 9, 13), *warjāwand*, "having miraculous power", the standing epithet of Šāh-Bahrām (vs. 10), *uzdēzār*, "idol-temple" (vs. 12), *āwīn* (or however this is to be read), "lost?" or "invisible?"[14] (vs. 13) and *gušūδa*, "abortion, demonic offspring" (vs. 13). Linguistically more significant are two words without specifically religious connotations: *ōzaδ*, "killed" (vs. 5) and the particle *ā*-, "then" (vs. 12), neither of which seems ever to occur in Neo-Persian. Their use here must be as intentional archaisms, either on the part of the author, or that of a copyist. The same is presumably the case with the very first words of the poem, *kay bawāδ*, "when shall it be", where the old subjunctive with long thematic vowel is used for the future, as in MP, rather than as a precative, as always in NP. It is, however, also possible that YḤWWN'l is merely a scribal error for the indicative YḤWWNyt (*bawaδ*); the emendation would involve only the omission of a single tooth. Two further archaisms occur in the unrhymed sentence which follows vs. 6 (*bē*, "but, on the other hand",[15] and *riyahrī*, "mockery"), but this is evidently a scribal gloss in scholastic MP and is not part of the poem; see the commentary *ad loc.*

Whereas intentional MP writings even in the Islamic period assiduously avoid Arabic loan-words, our poem, like all NP texts, contains a fair number of borrowings from Arabic[16] and at least one semantic borrowing from the same language. The semantic borrowing is *xusrawān*, which is used twice (vss. 2, 6) in the meaning "Persian kings". Xusraw (Χοσρόης) is the personal name of two Sasanian monarchs, but as a general word for "king" it is restricted to NP, where it imitates the use of Arabic *kisrā* in the same meaning, notably in the set phrase *kisrā wa qayṣar*, "the Persian and the

[14] The word written 'wbyn' is widely taken to be an Aramaeogram ('WBDN'/ Ḥ(W)BAN) corresponding to Manichaean MP wny (*wany*), "lost, destroyed", but the evidence for this is circumstantial. 'wbyn, which Neryosangh transcribes as *avīn*, is used mainly in apocalyptic contexts, where it is a stock epithet for the defeated demons. I would suggest that it is a scholastic transcription of the first syllables of Gathic *ā vī.nə̄nāsā*, which it renders in *Yasna* 32,15; the Sanskrit translation has *anirīkṣaṇīya*-, "not to be seen", evidently analysing the Pahlavi wrongly as *a-wēn* (see Bartholomae, *AiWb*, col. 1055–6, s.v. [1]nas-), an analysis which seems also to underlie the very frequent hendiadyoin *āwīn ud a-paydāg*. For other views see Geiger, *WZKM* 40, (1933), 107; Henning, *Mitteliranisch* 99, n. 1; Tavadia's commentary on this verse; Nyberg, *Manual* II 37–8; Bailey, *Zor. Prob.*, new edition, xli.

[15] Early NP does use *bē ki* in this sense; see Lazard, *Langue*, 477.

[16] This was noted already in 1913 by Anklesaria, in *Pahlavi Texts*, introduction, 52, who recognised three Arabic words: *baṣīr, jizya* and *masjid.*

Byzantine king". Now the loan-words. bsyl (vs. 3), stands evidently for Arabic *baṣīr*, "perceptive" (hardly *bašīr*, "bearer of good news", as Bailey has it). tlgm'n, "interpreter", in the same verse, is an ancient cultural word in the Near East (Akkadian *targumānu*, Aramaic trgmn', twrgmn', Manichaean MP trkwm'n, Arabic *tarjumān, turjumān, tarjamān*) and it seems futile to seek to determine whether here it is an old borrowing from Aramaic or a recent borrowing from Arabic.[17] In the same verse we have also *laškar*, "army", but whether this is borrowed from Arabic *al-ʿaskar*, or the other way round, is again uncertain.[18] mzgt (vs. 12) could in principle stand either for Arabic *masjid* or for early NP *mazgit*; in either case the meaning is clearly "mosque".[19]

Two more Arabic words occur in the verse for which the manuscripts offer:

> gzyt (var. gzytk) QDM ḤNḤTWNt ḤWHd BR' ḤLKWNt ḤWHd QDM sl'n
> L'WḤL 'slyk BʿYḤWNst ḤWHd s'k̲ Y gl'n

[17] Bailey, *Zor. Prob.* 195, n. 2, quotes from Madan's edition of the *Dēnkard* tlgm'n (48.20) and twlgm'n (49.2). Here too a borrowing from Arabic is not out of the question.

[18] The Arabic philologists (e.g. Ibn Qutaybah, *Adab al-kuttāb*, 532) maintain that *al-ʿaskar* is a borrowing from Persian; this has its basis in the fact that the word is clearly not Arabic and that it resembles a Persian word. But none of the many Iranian etymologies proposed for *laškar* appears to be at all likely (see recently, Bailey, *Dictionary of Khotan Saka*, 24–5, where it is said "possibly" to be connected with Khot. *ālaṣka-*, "settlement, town", but Emmerick/Skjærvø, *Studies* I, 22–4, doubt the existence of this word), nor does it seem to occur in demonstrably pre-Islamic texts. It does occur, outside of Persian, as the Armenian loan-word *laškar* (only, I think, in late texts), as the nškr and nškyr of the Choresmian glosses to Zamakhsharī's *Muqaddimatu l-'adab* (343,4 and 504,8), and (as Professor Martin Schwartz has kindly informed me) as ..]škr[.. in an unpublished Sogdian Christian translation of the Psalter, apparently from the 9th century. Nöldeke proposed (apud Fraenkel, *Fremdwörter*, 239), but later retracted (*ZA* 23, 146) the suggestion that the Persian word is an early (non-literary) borrowing from Arabic *al-ʿaskar*, itself borrowed, via Aramaic and Greek, from Latin *exercitus*, with reversal of *-ks-* to *-sk-* (as in Arabic al-'Iskandar for Alexander) and with a "parasitic" *ʿayn* (as in other loan-words). This was accepted by Brockelmann, *Grundriss* i, 269–70, and by the present author in *EI*², s.v. "sīn and s̲h̲īn", and, as long as no plausible Iranian explanation is forthcoming, it still seems the most attractive etymology.

[19] Nöldeke, *Persische Studien* II, 37, derived Persian *mazgit* from Aramaic *masg(ə)δā*, itself the source of Arabic *masjid*, comparing for the *-z-* Mandaic m'zgd', alongside m'sgd'. This is possible, but hardly certain. The *-t* of Persian *mazgit* cannot be explained from Aramaic and points perhaps rather to a borrowing from Arabic: classical Persian has in post-vocalic position both *-δ* (in Persian and Arabic words) and *-d* (only in Arabic words), but it is possible that very early NP did not tolerate post-vocalic *-d*, and consequently borrowed Arabic *masjid* (older pronunciation: *mašgid*) as *mažgit* or *mazgit*.

The first word clearly belongs with Arabic *jizya*, early NP gzyt, late Syriac gzyt', all for some sort of tax. In which of the three languages the word actually originated is uncertain,[20] but in our text, at least, it is clear that it stands specifically for the "poll-tax" levied on the non-Muslim inhabitants of Islamic countries. We are told, namely, that the Muslims "imposed the *jizya* and apportioned it upon the heads (*bar sarān*)". This conforms with Islamic legal theory, according to which the *jizya* is a personal tax, imposed on "the heads" of the non-Muslims rather than on their property. For the point of view of the tax-payer one can compare the passage in the anonymous Syriac chronicle formerly attributed to Denys of Tellmaḥrē which complains of how the Umayyads imposed on the Syrian Christians a gzyt', "levied from the skulls of the men" (*meštaḳlā men ḳarḳafθē δ gaβrē*).[21]

Bailey translated the second half-verse as: "They have demanded again the principal, a heavy impost", reading the second word as Arabic *aṣlī*[22] and comparing NP *māl-i aṣlī*, "principal". This does not make particularly good sense. Tavadia proposed, tentatively, but no doubt rightly, that L'WḤL stands here not (as it should) for *abāz*

[20] Following Nöldeke (*Geschichte* 241, n. 1; *Persische Studien* II, 36), it has been widely accepted that both the Arabic and the Persian words were borrowed (independently) from Aramaic. The difficulty with this is that within Aramaic the word is attested only in Syriac authors of the Islamic period and there only with reference to the Muslim *jizya*. The word occurs already in the Qur'ān and has a good Arabic etymology ("payment, recompense") and the fact that it is not found in any of the numerous pre-Islamic Aramaic texts and documents relating to taxation does suggest that it is a specifically Arabic term. Thus, the Babylonian Talmud, reflecting Sasanian terminology, uses krg' (possibly from the MP ancestor of Arabic *xarāj*) for "poll-tax" and *ṭsk'* (= Greek τάξις, our "tax") for "land-tax" (see Nöldeke, *Geschichte*, loc. cit., with references). al-Khwārazmī, *Mafātīḥ* 59, claims that *jizya* is borrowed from "*gazyat*" (thus vocalised in the Leiden Ms., dated 556/1161), "which means tax (*xarāj*) in Persian". The vocalisation *gazyat* is also indicated, much later, in some of the Persian dictionaries, but the early poets (see the references in Wolff and Dihxudā) scan the first syllable as short. But it is possible that **gazyat* and *gazīt* (with *-ī-* from *-ya-*, as in NP *īzad* from *yazad*) were both used as Persianised adaptations of Arabic *jizyat*. In our text the reading gzyt (in Ms. DP) seems preferable; in MK it has apparently been "emended" to *guzīδa*, "chosen" (differently MacKenzie, *Dictionary*, 36, who reads the word for "poll-tax" as *gazīdag*). It is not, I think, otherwise attested in Pahlavi. [N. Sims-Williams has with customary generosity called my attention to an unpublished Bactrian text from the early Islamic period which refers to the payment of the ταζιαγγο γαζιτο, the "Arab *gazīt*". D.N. MacKenzie (letter dated 31/1/1997), among other comments on a draft of this paper) writes: "The entry *gazīdag* in CPD needs amending accordingly (to *gazēd*)".]

[21] Pseudo-Denys II, 154; translated in Palmer, *The seventh century*, 60.

[22] Jamasp Asa's translation "of low origin" evidently also assumes Arabic *aṣl*.

(NP *bāz*), "back, again", but is a misspelling for *bāz* (in NP more commonly *bāj, bāž*), "tax, tribute", comparing Pahlavi texts p. 115 (*Wizārišn ī čatrang*, par. 3), where, as here, *bāj* and *sāw* are mentioned together. In fact, the phrase *bāž (bāj) u sāw* is common also the *Šāhnāma*, and elsewhere in NP.[23] The next word is thus presumably an adjective qualifying *bāj*. Although various readings of the Pahlavi letters are possible, it would seem that *aṣlī* is most likely to be correct. I would connect it with a technical usage found in the 10th-century History of Qum by Ḥasan b. Muḥammad al-Qummī,[23a] which distinguishes between the "basic tax" (*ʾaṣl*, literally "root") and the "supplement" (*ʾiḍāfa*). In our text the "basic tax" is evidently called *bāj i aṣlī* and the supplementary duties *sāw*.[24]

We come now to the text of our poem. The transliteration of the Pahlavi is based on the edition and quotes all the variants from the two old manuscripts consulted by the editor: MK (which has colophons giving dates in the early 14th century)[25] and DP (undated), neither of which is copied from the other, but which both descend from a common source. The third manuscript collated by Jamasp-Asana, JJ, is an 18th-century transcript of MK and is cited in our footnotes only for those passages which were no longer legible in MK when the manuscripts were collated by the editor. Another version of what is fundamentally the same text was published and translated by Blochet[26] from a manuscript which he did not identify, but is presumably Paris supplément persan 1216.[27] Probably the same version

---

[23] See Wolff, s.v. *bāž*.

[23a] al-Qummī, *Tārīkh i Qum*, 122–3.

[24] Shaked, *Henning memorial volume*, 405, n. 37, retains *abāz*, and proposes that "one artificial Arabic word can be eliminated" by reading the second word as an apparently unattested *a-dilīg*, supposedly meaning "heartless", and by translating: "They have again demanded heartlessly a heavy impost". But for "heartless" one would expect **a-dil*, which, as a bahuvrihi, would already be an adjective and does not require the ending *-ī(g)*. NP *bē-dilī*, which Shaked compares, does not mean "heartless" but "heartlessness"; its ending thus goes back to MP *-īh*, not *-īg*.

[25] The dates in the Pahlavi and Sanskrit colophons are not without ambiguity and do not agree exactly with one another. The clearest chronological indication is the statement in the Sanskrit colophon that it was completed "at the time when Sulṭān Ghiyāth al-Dīn came to the throne". Ghiyāth al-Dīn Tughluq seized power in Delhi in Shaʿbān 720/1320; even if it might have taken some time for this news to reach the Parsees in Gujarat, the colophon can hardly have been written much later.

[26] Blochet, *RHR* 31, 1895, 241–3 and the lithographed pages 1–3 (text I).

[27] See Blochet, *Catalogue* no. 207/3.

was noted by Anklesaria in the Indian manuscript Ta.[28] The text published by Blochet is clearly derived from ours; more precisely, from the version of our text contained in manuscript DP. The author has transcribed a fair number of passages from the poem, replacing the Arabic words by Persian equivalents, and padded it out with material of his own invention. Since the author evidently used either DP, or a closely related manuscript, his version has no independent value for the establishment of the text.[29]

The transcription, without intending to prejudice the question of its date, indicates how the poem might have been read in about the 9th or 10th century. The particles *i* and *u* have been added where required; all other emendations are noted explicitly.

---

[28] See *Pahlavi Texts*, introduction, 13.

[29] The first half of the text published by Blochet runs as follows (the sections lifted from the poem are printed in italics): *kay bawāδ ki payg-ē āyaδ az hinduwān/ ki āyaδ ān Šāh-Bahrām az* Hinduwān (Paris catalogue: *dwtkʾn*, as in DP)/ *ki pīl hast hazār* bar *sarān u bar sar hast pilbān/ ki ārāsta dirafš dāraδ pa āyīn i šahyārān/ pēš i* sipah bar *barand* u andarūn purr *<sip>ahsālārān/ mard* i <. . .> *bāyaδ kardan* dānā u hōšmand *ki šawaδ bi ō hinduwān/ gōyaδ ki mā či* šahryārān, mā bā *tāziyān* u tūrī u rūm u činistān u dēwān i māzanigān kārzār bar burdand (read: burdēm) bar ēšān az sutōhī dīn i bih u wēža u parastiš i yazdān u amahraspandān u ātašān i surx i sōzā paδīruftand u az zamān i anōšēruwān Zardušt i Spitāmān dīn i wēža tā hazār sāl *rawēnīδ, u nūniz tāziyān i muš-xwar, ki xōy u xīm i mār dārand *čūn sag* xwarand *nān, bistaδand pāδšāhī az xusrawān na pa hunar u na pa mardī u* na pa zōr i xiraδ *bē pa afsōs u YYNSBNYN bistaδand*, etc. "(. . .) when he goes to the Indians he will say that we are princes, we have done battle with the Arabs, the Turanian, the Romans, China and the demons of Mazandaran, and, having been defeated, they accepted the pure Good Religion and worship of the Yazatas and the Amesha Spentas and the red, burning fires. From the time of the immortalised Spitama Zarathushtra the pure Religion held sway for a thousand years. But now the Arabs, those eaters of mice, who have the character and disposition of snakes and eat their bread like dogs, have seized royal power from the Chosroes, not by skill, not by bravery, not by the power of intellect, but have taken it by mockery", etc.

Transliteration

1 ’YMT YḤWWN’t ’MT pyk 1 Y’TWNyt MN ḥndwk’n
’MT mt ZK {Y} šḥw’ḥl’m MN dwt<k Y> ky’n[30]

2 ’MT pyl ’YT 1000 {QDM sl’n} QDM sl[31] ’YT pylp’n
’MT ’l’stk dlpš d’lyt PWN ’dwyt Y ḥwslwd’n

3 pyš lškl YB̲LWNd PWN sp’ḥsrd’l’n
GBR’ 1 bsyl ’p’yt krtn’ zylk’ tlgm’n

4 ’MT ‘ZLWNyt BR’ YMLLWNyt PWN ḥndwk’n
’MT Z̲NH[32] MH dyt MN dšt Y t’cyk’n

5 QDM ’ywk glwḥ dyn’ nz’l krt’ W BR’ Y̲KT<L>WNt MLK’n’[33]
LNH {W} MN ’yl ‘LHš’n cygwn ŠDY’’ < . . . >

6 W dyn’ YḤSNNd[34] cygwn KLB’ ‘ŠTHNd[35] LḤM’
BR’ YNSB̲WNt ḤWHd p’tḥšḥyḥ Y MN ḥwslwd’n

6a L’ PWN ḥwnl L’ PWN mltyḥ BR’ PWN ’psws {YNSB̲NYNN?} BR’
YNSB̲WNt ḤWHd ‘B̲YDWNd ’psws[36] W ly’ḥlyḥ

7 BR’ YNSB̲WNt ḤWHd[37] PWN stḥmb’ MN ’NŠWT’’n
NYŠH W ḥw’stkyḥ’ Y šylyn b’g bwst’n[38]

8 gzyt[39] QDM ḤNḤTWNt ḤWHd BR’ ḤLKWNt ḤWHd QDM sl’n
L’WḤL ’slyk B‘YḤWNst ḤWHd s’k̲ Y gl’n

9 BR’ nkyl ’MT cnd SLY’ LMYTWNt ZK dlwc PWN Z̲NH gyḥ’n
’MT L‘YT SLYtl MN ‘LH {w}wt’ gyḥ’n

10 MN LNH BR’ Y’TWNyt[40] ZK šḥw’ḥl’m
Y wlc’wnd MN dwtk ky’n

11 BR’ YḤYTYWNym kyn Y t’cyk’n[41]
cygwn lwtstḥm YḤYTYWNt 10 100 kyn Y gyḥ’n

12 ’š’n mzgtyḥ’ plwt ŠB̲KWNym BR’ nš’nym ’tḥš’n
’wzdstc’lyḥ’ BR’ ḤPLWNym W p’k ‘B̲YDWNym MN gyḥ’n

13 ‘D ’wbyn’ ‘ZLWNd dlwc gšwtk’n’
<. . .> MN Z̲NH gyḥ’n

---

[30] DP: k’n.

[31] MK omits the second QDM. QDM sl is a correction in the master copy for the preceding QDM sl’n.

[32] DP: LNH (i.e. *mā*)

[33] Thus DP and MK, in the latter followed by a lacuna. JJ has MLK’n’ Y MLK’Y, of which the last word is struck off.

[34] Thus DP. MK torn. JJ: YḤSNNy̲t̲.

[35] MK omits -N-.

[36] Thus DP. MK omits the words after the first ’psws up to and including the second ’psws, evidently by haplography. Its prototype must have had something similar here, for in the next line MK (but not DP) wrongly inserts ‘B̲YDWNd after BR’ YNSB̲WNt ḤWHd.

[37] MK inserts ‘B̲YDWNd; see the previous note.

[38] DP has the older spelling bwdst’n.

[39] MK: gzytk.

[40] MK: mt’, evidently under the influence of line 1.

[41] DP has kynyt’cyk’n as one word.

Transcription

1 kay bawāδ ki payg-ē āyaδ az hinduwān
ki <ā>maδ ān Šāh-Bahrām az dūδa i kayān
2 ki pīl hast hazār, bar sar hast pīlbān
ki ārāsta dirafš dāraδ pa āyīn i xusrawān
3 pēš i laškar barand pa sipāhsālārān
mard-ē baṣīr bāyaδ kardan zīrak tarjumān
4 ki šawaδ bigōyaδ pa hinduwān
k-īn či dīδ az dašt[42] i tāziyān
5 bar yak <bār> gurōh dēn nizār kard u biōzaδ šahān
mā azēr, ēšān čūn dēw <. . . -ān>[43]
6 u dīn <zabūn>[44] dārand u čūn sag xwarand nān
bistaδand pāδšāhī az xusrawān
6a [na pa hunar, na pa mardī,
bē pa afsōs bistaδand, kunand afsōs u riyahrī][45]
7 bistaδand pa sitam az mardumān
zan u xwāstahā i šīrīn u bāγ u bōstān
8 gazīt bar nihāδand, bibaxšīδand bar sarān
*bāj i aṣlī xwāstand u sāw i girān
9 bingar ki čand baδ afgand ān duruj paδ īn gihān
ki nēst battar az ōy baδ i gihān[46]
10 <pēš> az mā biāyaδ ān Šāh-Bahrām[47]
i warjāwand az dūδa i kayān
11 biāwarēm kīn i tāziyān
čūn Rustam āwurd dah saδ[48] kīn i gihān
12 ā-šān mazgitihā furōδ hilēm u binšānēm ātašān
uzdēzārihā bikanēm u pāk kunēm az gihān
13 tā āwīn šawand duruj-gušūδagān
<u bišawand> az īn gihān[49]

---

[42] Thus (dšt) in both MSS. Bailey's emendation (or misreading?) *dast* is not necessary.

[43] The line is clearly incomplete. Tavadia reads *ēmā hač ēr, avēšān čigōn dēv<ān>*, "we are from the Aryan (stock), they are like the Dēvs", which would presumably require *ēr<ān>*. Bailey omits everything from *mā* until *čūn sag* in the next line, evidently by inadvertence.

[44] "Some words signifying contempt, etc. are needed here to complete the sense" (T).

[45] This unrhymed period is a gloss on the preceding line, consisting, it seems, of two layers of commentary. First, a glossator explained that "they (the Arabs) seized it not by skill, nor by bravery, but by a spell (**afsūn*)", but someone miscopied ʾpswn as ʾpsws, "mockery". This now rather pointless sentence then receives a super-commentary: "they practice mockery and scorn".

[46] This is the least interventionist reading, ignoring only the first letter of wwtʾ; the rhyme-syllable is *-aδ*, followed by an imperfect *radīf: ī(n) gihān*. Or read: . . . <P>WN tn W *yʾn (*pa tan u jān*), "worse than whom is nothing in body and soul".

[47] Note the imperfect rhyme. The early MP form Warhrān (Avestan Vərəθraγna-) has no relevance for this text.

[48] Thus ("ten-hundred") in the text. Bailey's *gurz*, "club", is graphically possible, but *gurz i kīn i gihān* does not make very good sense.

[49] One can hardly feel happy about Tavadia's taking *az īn gihān* as a line on its own, nor does *āwīn šawand* go very well with *az* . . . It would seem rather that something has dropped out.

Translation

1 When shall it be that a courier comes from India saying: that Šāh-Bahrām from the family of the Kayanids has now come?
2 He has a thousand elephants and on the head of each one rides an elephant driver who holds unfurled a standard in the manner of the ancient kings.
3 They carry it before the army to the commanders. Then we shall have to make a clever man our wise interpreter.
4 When he goes to them he will say in India what he has seen come upon us from the desert of the Arabs.
5 At one blow that band has enfeebled the Religion and killed the princes. We are laid low and they <lord over us> like devils.
6 They hold the true religion <in contempt> and eat their bread like dogs[50] and have seized royal power from the Chosroes.
7 By force they have taken from men their wives, their private property,[51] their orchards and gardens.
8 They have imposed the poll-tax and apportioned it upon our heads. They have demanded the basic rent and a heavy impost as well.
9 Behold how much evil that demon has cast into this world. The most evil thing in the world is not worse than he.
10 But before us shall go that Šāh-Bahrām, the miracle-doer from the family of the Kayanids.
11 We shall let loose our hatred against the Arabs just as Rustam ten-hundred times let loose his hatred against the whole world.
12 Lo, we shall pull down their mosques and set up again the sacred fires. We shall destroy the idol-temples and purge them from the world,
13 so that the foul offspring of the demons shall become invisible and <vanish> from this world.

The poem obviously belongs to some time between the 7th century (the time of the Arab conquest) and the beginning of the 14th century (the date of manuscript MK), but it is difficult to be much more precise about the matter. The doubtless archaic features of language and versification, to which we have drawn attention, do not actually say very much about the date of a text which, like this one, lies outside the mainstream of Neo-Persian literature and which could, for all we know, be composed in some non-literary dialect, the historical development of which is unknown. The conventional Pahlavi orthography disguises totally the phonology of the piece, but also our own transcription of it as pre-classical Persian represents only

50 Zoroastrians, as is well known, are very particular about table etiquette.

51 *xwāstahā i šīrīn*, literally "sweet possessions". Compare NP *jān i šīrīn*, "one's own life".

one of several possible readings. Thus, it is not in principle impossible that the poem could be as late as the 13th century, but it could easily be several centuries older.

The content of the poem speaks largely for itself. The complaint about the iniquities of Muslim domination and the expectation that Zoroastrian rule will one day be restored, not through the efforts of the believers themselves, but at the hands of a traditional apocalyptic figure, can be found in much the same form in other works of post-Sasanian Zoroastrian apocalyptic[52] such as the Pahlavi *Zand i Bahrām-yašt* and *Jāmāsp-nāma*, the classical Neo-Persian *Zarātušt-nāma*, or similar writings contained in the Persian *Riwāyat*s. And sentiments of a similar sort are expressed also in Christian and Jewish apocalyptic texts from the Islamic period. And indeed even Muslim authors refer quite commonly to the fact that the *majūs* delude themselves into thinking that they will one day overthrow the dominion of Islam and restore the kingdom and religion of the Persians. In the light of such well-known stereotypes one must be wary of an overly romantic view of this text as if it were a highly seditious document, whispered at the dead of night by Zoroastrian conspirators. In fact, had this document fallen into the hands of a Muslim official and had he found someone who could read it to him, he is most unlikely to have been surprised or shocked by its contents; it is namely exactly the sort of thing that Muslims expected the *dhimmī*s to be saying. Unlike their modern counterparts, mediaeval polities did not imagine themselves to be borne by the will of the people; they derived their legitimacy from the will of God and did not need the consent of the governed, least of all of those who obstinently rejected the dominant religion. And in this sense mediaeval societies sometimes reveal themselves as more tolerant than modern ones as long as it is a question of purely verbal dissent. The poem that we have examined is doubtless a testimony of Zoroastrian discontent with Muslim domination, but the fact that it existed and has survived also testifies to the religious and cultural diversity which flourished during the classical period of Islamic civilisation.*

[52] Specifically for the figure of Bahrām i Warjāwand one can compare the rather speculative article by Czeglédy, "Bahrām Čōbīn and the Persian apocalyptic literature".

* A version of this paper was read at a conference in Zoroastrian House, London, in 1996. I am grateful for critical comments by I. Gershevich, M. Schwartz, N. Sims-Williams and especially D.N. MacKenzie. In the printed text of the transliteration

Bibliography

ʿAwfī (Sadīd al-Dīn Muḥammad b. Muḥammad), *Lubāb al-albāb*, ed. E.G. Browne and M. Qazvīnī, 2 volumes, London/Leyden, 1903–6.

Bahār, M.T., *Dīwān-i ashʿār*, I, Tehran, 1335 sh./1956.

———, "*Shiʿr dar Īrān 3*", Mihr V/3, (1316 sh./1937), 217–8.

Bailey, H.W., *Dictionary of Khotan Saka*, Cambridge, 1979.

———, *Zoroastrian problems in the ninth-century books*, Oxford, 1943. Reprinted with a new introduction, Oxford, 1971.

Bartholomae, Chr., *Altiranisches Wörterbuch*, Strassburg, 1904.

Blochet, E., *Catalogue des manuscrits persans de la Bibliothèque Nationale*. 4 vols. Paris, 1905–34.

———, "Textes religieux pehlvis", *Revue des l'histoire des religions* 31, (1895), 241–53 and the lithographed pages 1–10.

Brockelmann, C., *Grundriss der vergleichenden Grammatik der semitischen Sprachen*, 2 vols., Berlin, 1908–13.

Czeglédy, K., "Bahrām Čōbīn and the Persian apocalyptic literature", *Acta Orientalia Academiae Scientiarum Hungaricae* VIII, (1958), 21–43.

(Pseudo-)Denys of Tell-Maḥrē, *Chronicon anonymum Pseudo-Dionysianum vulgo dictum* I; *Incerti auctoris chronicon Pseudo-Dionysianum vulgo dictum* II (titles also in Syriac), ed. J.-B. Chabot, Paris, 1927, 1933 (= CSCO 91, 104; Scriptores Syri 43, 53).

Dihkhudā, *Lughat-nāma*, founded by ʿA.A. Dihkhudā, continued by M. Muʿīn *et al.*, Tehran, 1325–60 sh./1946–81.

Emmerick, R.E. and Skjærvø, P.O., *Studies in the vocabulary of Khotanese* I (= Sb. d. österr. Akad. d. Wiss., phil-hist. Kl., 401), Vienna, 1982.

Fraenkel, S., *Aramäische Fremdwörter im Arabischen*, Leiden, 1886.

Geiger, B., "Indo-Iranica", *WZKM* 40, (1933), 95–122.

Henning, W.B., "Mitteliranisch", in *Iranistik, erster Abschnitt, Linguistik* (= Handbuch der Orientalistik, I, iv, 1), Leiden/Cologne, 1958.

Ibn Qutayba (ʿAbdallāh b. Muslim al-Dīnawarī), *Adab al-kātib* [better: . . . *al-kuttāb*], ed. M. Grünert, Leiden, 1890.

Jamasp Asa, M.J., "Madam matan-î Shah Vahârâm-î Vârjavand", *Sir Jamsetjee Jejeebhoy Madressa jubilee volume*, ed. J.J. Modi, Bombay, 1914, 75–6.

Kārnāma = *Kârnâmak-i Artakhshîr Pâpakân. The original Pahlavi text, with transliteration in Avesta characters, translation into English and Gujarati, and selections from the Shâhnâmeh*, ed. E.K. Antia, Bombay, 1900.

al-Khwārazmī, *Mafātīḥ al-ʿulūm*, ed. G. van Vloten, Leiden, 1895.

Lazard, G., "Deux poèmes persans de tradition pehlevie", *Mémorial Jean de Menasce*, Louvain, 1974, 433–40.

———, *La langue des plus anciens monuments de la prose persane*, Paris, 1963.

MacKenzie, D.N., *A concise Pahlavi dictionary*, London, 1971.

Nöldeke, Th., *Geschichte der Perser und Araber zur Zeit der Sasaniden aus der arabischen Chronik des Tabari*, Leiden, 1879.

———, *Persische Studien II* (Sb. d. phil.-hist. Cl. d. k. Akad. d. Wiss., Bd. 126, XII), Vienna, 1892.

———, "Τάξις im Semitischen", *Zeitschrift für Assyrologie* 23, 1909, 144–8.

Nyberg, H.S., *A Manual of Pahlavi*, 2 vols., Wiesbaden, 1964–74.

Pahlavi texts (title in the second volume: *The Pahlavi texts contained in the codex MK . . .*),

the final "otiose stroke" is just about distinguishable from *aleph*. In reading the proofs I noticed that I had omitted the "otiose stroke" in four instances, but I have not reinserted it for fear of provoking more serious errors.

edited by J.M. Jamasp-Asana, with an introduction by B.T. Anklesaria, two volumes with continuous pagination, Bombay, 1897, 1913.

Palmer, A., *The seventh century in West-Syrian chronicles*, Liverpool, 1993.

al-Qummī, Ḥasan b. Muḥammad, *Tārīkh i Qumm*, Persian translation by Ḥasan b. ʿAlī Qummī from a lost original in Arabic, ed. J. Ṭihrānī, Tehran, 1943.

Shaked, S., "Specimens of Middle Persian verse", in *W.B. Henning memorial volume*, ed. M. Boyce and I. Gershevitch, London, 1970, 395–405.

Tavadia, J.C., "A rhymed ballad in Pahlavi", *JRAS*, (1955), 29–36.

West, E.W., "Pahlavi literature", in *Grundriss der iranischen Philologie*, ed. W. Geiger and E. Kuhn, II, Strassburg, 1896–1904, 75–129.

Wolff, F., *Glossar zu Firdosis Schahname*, Berlin, 1935.

al-Zamakhsharī (Jār Allāh Maḥmūd b. ʿUmar), *Horezmce tercümeli Muqaddimat al-Adab*, facs. ed. with an introduction by Zeki Velidi Togan, Istanbul, 1951.

DIE MAUSOLEENGRUPPE IN ADHERI, NW-PAKISTAN

Heinz Gaube

1. *Ausgangslage*

1988 erschien in den "*Memoirs of the Department of Archaeology, University of Peshawar*, No. 4" eine von der Universität Bonn 1987 angenommene Dissertation von Taj Ali: "Anonymous Tombs in the Gomal Valley, and the Beginning of Tomb Architecture in Pakistan".

In der Arbeit werden in NW-Pakistan gefundene Mausoleen aus dem an der Grenze zu Afghanistan, westlich des Indus liegenden "Dera Ismail Khan District" erstmals gründlich vorgestellt und kunstgeschichtlich interpretiert. Es handelt sich um eine Gruppe von elf Mausoleen, von denen nur noch vier in einem physischen Zustand sind, daß sie analysiert werden können sowie eine Reihe von Gräbern, die hier nicht behandelt werden sollen. Mausoleen, wie Gräber, sind zum Teil, sowohl im Rahmen der islamischen Dekorkunst des Indischen Subkontinents—wie der des weiteren ostiranischen Kunstraums—eigenartig verziert.

Sie liegen losgelöst von jeder archäologisch faßbaren Siedlung, finden heute von des Bevölkerung des Gebiets nur noch Beachtung als Steinbruch, und werden von ihr "Adhira/Adheri" (wohl: Adhīra/Adherī) genannt, das nach Taj Ali vom arabischen "Hazira" (Hazīra?) abgeleitet sei. Mit der Etymologie das Namens werde ich mich nicht auseinandersetzen. So viel nur: diese Herführung scheint mir zweifelhaft. Wichtiger ist in diesem Zusammenhang, daß sich offenbar keine lokalen Legenden um diesen Komplex weben, und daß er offenbar einer Zeit und einer Ethnie zugehört, zu denen die gegenwärtige Bevölkerung keine innere Beziehung hat.

Die Suche nach datierbarer Keramik im weiteren Umkreis der Bauten blieb für mich fruchtlos, auch Fragen nach Münzfunden in den umliegenden Dörfern waren ohne Erfolg. Da sich auch keine Inschriften an den Mausoleen und Gräbern finden, hilft nur eine Stilanalyse, ihren historischen Platz zu orten.

Wie schon der Titel seiner Arbeit zeigt, versucht Taj Ali die Eigenart der Konstruktionsmethoden und Dekorationen der Mausoleen an den Anfang einer islamischen Grabarchitektur in Pakistan zu stellen, und er bemüht kunstgeschichtliche Vergleiche aus dem weiteren iranischen Kulturkreis der Zeit vor ca. 1100 um seine Frühdatierungen zu untermauern, sieht aber nicht auf die Entwicklung in seiner Heimat. Schließlich kommt er dazu, daß diese Bauten und die sie umgebenden Gräber im Zuge der ghaznavidischen Eroberung von Teilen des Indischen Subkontinents entstanden sein dürften und damit Schlüsselmonumente für die islamische Grabarchitektur Pakistans seien.

Es wird eine gerade Entwicklungslinie vom "Samaniden"-Mausoleum in Bukhara über andere Grabbauten in Zentralasien und Iran konstruiert, die so nicht stimmen kann. Denn späte Formen und Motive lassen sich meist immer an frühen Bauten nachweisen. Nur sind damit spätere Bauten nicht früh. Es muß das Gesamte gesehen werden; und die Mischung von Bau- und Dekorformen macht unsere Bauten nicht so früh wie Taj Ali und andere sich das wünschen, stehen wir doch vor einem Konglomerat von Bau- und Dekorstilen. Und das kann nichts mit der ghaznavidischen Eroberung von Teilen des Indischen Subkontinents zu tun haben.

Der Hintergrund der Ghaznaviden war Zentralasien und Ostiran. Die von ihnen überlieferten Bauten spiegeln eine "internationale" oder interregionale Kunst wider, die Elemente aus dem Gebiet zwischen dem Zweistromland und Zentralasien aufnahm. Dies fehlt in den Bauten von Adheri. Sie atmen Provinz und Zwischenzeit, und sind sicher nicht aus der Zeit der Ghaznaviden, denen unser Jubilar so viel Zeit seines Lebens gewidmet hat.

Aber liest man Edmund Bosworth, bringt er uns auch hier wohl auf eine richtige Spur. In seinem Buch *The Later Ghaznavids: Splendor and Decay*[1] schreibt er, daß 1178 der Ghōride Muʿizz al-Dīn Muḥammad über den Gomal Pass zum Indus vorstieß. Der Weg über den Gomal Pass vom heutigen Afghanistan auf den Indischen Subkontinent war einer der von islamischen Heeren nach dort benutzten Wege; und steht man im Gomal Tal, erklärt sich das auch von der Topographie her. Nicht weit im Westen ragen die afghanischen Berge auf; und von diesen Bergen öffnet sich das Gomal Tal. Mit aus den afghanischen Bergen kommenden Eroberern, weder den Ghaznaviden und wohl auch nicht den Ghōriden, aber möglicherweise mit den afghanische Bergen verbunden gewesenen Rebellen müssen unsere Bauten in Beziehung gebracht werden. Sie sind eher postghōridisch.

[1] Edinburgh, 1997, 126.

Taj Ali veröffentlichte in seiner Arbeit Grundrisse und Schnitte der Bauten. Obgleich diese nicht den letzten Grad an Perfektion haben, spare ich mir hier die Publikation genauer gemessener Grundrisse. Sie bringen uns in unserer Fragestellung nicht weiter, da es sich um architektonisch recht einfache Gebäude handelt. Genauere Meßergebnisse gebe ich in den Baubeschreibungen. Man kann sich unseren Bauten nur über ihre Dekorationen nähern, die sich auf den schlechten Fototafeln in Taj Alis Arbeit nicht erschließen und für weitere Beschäftigung mit diesen unbrauchbar sind. Deshalb beschränke ich mich auf die Veröffentlichung einiger Fototafeln, so viel, wie sie der Rahmen dieser Publikation zuläßt, die eine weitere Diskussion möglich machen sollten.

2. *Die Bauten*

2.1. *Allgemeine Beschreibung*

Die hier behandelbaren Bauten liegen in einem Areal, das ca. 150 m Ost-West und ca. 110 m Nord-Süd mißt. Das östlichste Mausoleum ist das hier nach der Numerierung von Taj Ali Mausoleum Nr. 1 bezeichnete. Nr. 2 liegt ca. 60 m südsüdwestlich davon, Nr. 3 ca. 45 m westnordwestlich von Nr. 2, und Nr. 4, schließlich, findet sich ca. 50 m nördlich von Nr. 3.

Hier folgen nur kurze, allgemeine Baubeschreibungen. Mit den Wandgestaltungen und den Dekorationen werde ich mich im Anschluß an diese Übersicht Bauwerk für Bauwerk befassen. Alle vier Gebäude haben einen quadratischen Grundriß, und ihre Außenmauern konvergieren nach oben hin leicht. Zwei von ihnen (Nr. 1 und Nr. 2) verfügen über eingebundene Ecktürme. Nr. 1 ist das größte Gebäude (außen ca. 12,15 m einschließlich der Ecktürme, zwischen den Türmen: O: 9,10 m, N: 9,11 m, W: 9,10 m, S: 9.04 m; innen: O: 8,33 m, N: 8,25 m, W: 8,35 m, S. 8,24 m, Wandstärke ca. 1,20 m <ich gebe diese Maße, weil sie sowohl in den Plänen von Taj Ali, S. 26, 30, 34 und 38 wie auch in den Beschreibungen meist nicht korrekt sind>). Nr. 2 ist kleiner, es mißt außen mit Ecktürmen ca. 8,50 m × 8,50 m, zwischen den Türmen von Ost nach Süd (s.o.) 5,67 m, 5,80 m, 5,60 m und 5,60 m und innen (in derselben Folge) 5,35 m, 5,41 m, 5,34 m und 5,42 m, Wandstärke um 0,77 m. Bau Nr. 3 mißt außen zwischen 6,95 m und 7,09, innen zwischen 5,37 m und 5,40 m, Wandstärke ca. 0,75 m; und Nr. 4 mißt außen zwischen

8,25 m und 8,32 m, innen fast gleich auf allen Seiten 6,56 m. Die Gebäude stehen (bis zu den Kuppelansätzen) ca. 5,50 m (Nr. 1), ca. 4,70 m (Nr. 2), ca. 4,70 m (Nr. 3) und 4,70 m (Nr. 4) hoch an und sind auf quadratische Plattformen gebaut, die sich zwischen ca. 0,70 m und 1,00 m über dem sie umgebenden Grund erheben. Alle vier Bauten waren von parabolen Kuppeln überspannt, die mehr oder wenig stark eingestürzt sind. Die Überleitungszonen zwischen den quadratischen Baukörpern und den Kuppelansätzen bilden zum Innenraum hin durch Kielbögen abgeschlossene Trompen, in denen Ziegelmuster Stalaktiten imitieren sollen. Alle vier Bauten haben um ca. 0.80 m breite, niedrige Türen im Osten, Norden und Süden und im Westen der Innenseite je einen Miḥrāb.

2.2. *Mausoleum Nr. 1*

Auf diesen Bau und auf Bau Nr. 4 werde ich mehr Raum und Illustrationen verwenden als auf die übrigen zwei Mausoleen. Bau Nr. 1 scheint der älteste in dieser zeitlich eng zusammenliegenden Gruppe zu sein und nimmt vieles an Dekorformen voraus, das in den übrigen drei Gebäuden teils zitiert, teils weitergeführt wird.

Im Grundzug sind alle vier Fassaden des Bauwerks gleich gestaltet. In den Mitten der Ost-, Nord- und Süd-Seiten liegen reich dekorierte Portale, und die Außenwände sind durch horizontale Schmuckbänder aus türkiser Keramik und Terrakotta zwischen den Ecktürmen und den Portalen verziert (Pl. 1). Die Schmuckbänder der Fassaden setzen sich nicht in allen Registern in jenen der Ecktürme fort. Gleichfalls durch Keramik und Terrakotta verzierte Blendnischen mit abgestuften oberen Abschlüssen, acht im Osten, sechs im Süden und Norden sowie neun im Westen, gliedern die Fassaden. Hier (im Westen) ist eine zusätzliche breite Blendnische auf dem vorspringenden Miḥrāb angebracht (Pl. 1).

Betrachten wir die, von kleinen Abweichungen abgesehen, für alle vier Fassaden repräsentative Ostfassade (Pl. 1) genauer. Oben sind noch Reste eines Blendnischenfrieses aus von Ziegeln gerahmten undekorierten, türkisen Keramikplatten zu erkennen, der nur noch auf der Westseite (Pl. 1) teilweise erhalten ist. Hier (auf der Westseite) sehen wir, daß drei Ziegellagen über diesem Fries das Bauwerk ein glattes Band von zwei Lagen türkis glasierter Ziegel umlief. Zwei Ziegellagen darüber sind noch Reste eines Rhombenbandes aus Terrakotta vor türkis glasiertem Grund zu erkennen.

Doch zurück zur Ostfassade (Pl. 2), die einen etwas anderen und reicheren Aufbau als die Westseite hatte. Zwei Ziegelschichten unter dem Blendnischenfries folgt ein flaches Kettenband aus türkis glasierten Ziegel und unglasierten Halbkreisen. Drei Ziegelschichten darunter finden sich unglasierte, aus gleichseitigen Kreuzelementen zusammengesetzt Rhomben erhaben vor türkisem Grund. Wieder drei Schichten tiefer folgt ein von türkis glasierten Ziegeln gerahmtes und in Register unterteiltes Band von Terrakotta-Motiven (abgeleitet von Blüten?). Drei Schichten tiefer folgt ein weiteres Kettenband. Unter ihm, auf der Höhe des Eingangsbogens, markiert ein Blendnischenfries mit Rhomben-, Kreuz- und Kettenmustern aus glasiertem und unglasiertem Material die Fassade. Drei Schichten darunter sehen wir abermals ein Kettenband, vier Schichten darunter zwei Lagen türkis glasierter Ziegel, und fünf Schichten weiter unten schließen den Fassadenschmuck das schon bekannte (Blüten?)-Motiv, diesmal aber drei "Blüten" pro Register, kombiniert mit einem, gleichfalls von glasierten Ziegeln gefaßten Zick-Zack-Band aus Terrakotta ab. Zwei horizontale Nischenreihen und horizontale Schmuckbänder aus Terrakotta und türkis glasierten Kacheln bzw. Ziegeln gliedern also die Wände zwischen Portalen/Miḥrāb und Ecktürmen.

Da auf den Ecktürmen (Pl. 2) kein Platz für Blendnischen ist, unterscheiden sich deren Dekorationen von jenen der Fassaden. Neu sind hier gänzlich glasierte Kettenbänder und in Türkis gerahmte Terrakotta-Wellenbänder.

Anders die Portale: hier (Pl. 3) das am besten erhaltene Südportal; an den übrigen zwei Portalen wird mit den schon beschriebenen Schmuckelementen etwas anders umgegangen. Die engen und niedrigen Eingänge, die oben ein doppelter Kielbogen abschließt, liegen in einer flachen Nische, welche oben zwei Rhombenmuster (Ziegel mit eingelegten türkisen Keramikstücken), darüber das schon beschriebene "Blüten"-Band und ein aus um 45 Grad gedrehten Ziegeln gebildeter Zahnschnitt abschließt. Dies umgibt ein seitlich dreiteiliger, nach oben hin komplexerer Rahmen. Die beiden seitlichen Rahmen bestehen aus zwei äußeren Bändern auf Ziegelbasis mit Keramik oder Terrakottaeinlagen, die wir schon kennen (Rhomben, "Blüten"). Zwischen diesen liegt aber ein geometrisch aus Dreiergruppen gebildetes Keramik-Schmuckband (Pl. 3) von rechteckigen, türkis und weiß glasierten Stegen. Einer neuen Technik begegnen wir hier: die meisten der weißen Stege sind mit flüchtig hingeworfenen geometrischen, schwarz-türkisen Mustern in Glasurmalerei verziert.

Der "Sturz" des Portals (Pl. 3) ist durch reichere Dekoration herausgehoben. Über dem schon erwähnten Zahnschnitt der Eingangsnische sehen wir ein aus kleinen Terrakottarhomben gebildetes "Perl"-Band und direkt darüber ein Terrakotta-Kettenband, beide Türkis gefaßt. Über ihnen setzt sich der türkis-weiße Rahmen der Seiten fort, den ein weiter Zahnschnitt nach oben begrenzt. Abgeschlossen wird der "Sturz" durch Terrakottafelder vor türkisem Hintergrund, die wohl Zinnen darstellen sollen. Zwischen den "Zinnen" und über ihnen treffen wir auf die schon bekannten Rhombenmotive aus Terrakotta.

Das Innere des Bauwerks ist mit schon bekannten Motiven verziert. Der Miḥrāb (Pl. 4) wirkt formal wie eine Replik der Portale. Ein dreiteiliger Rahmen mit "Zinnen"-Abschluß oben faßt die Gebetsnische. Wie im ganzen Innenraum wird hier mit Dekorationen sparsamer umgegangen. Terrakottarhomben vor türkisem Grund dominieren. Die Kuppel umlaufen Zahnschnittbänder, Wellenbänder und Lagen glasierter Ziegel. Dasselbe Bild bietet sich auch in der Überleitungszone (Pl. 4). Hier zeigt sich, daß die Hauptlast der Überleitung hölzerne Balken und Ziegelbögen trugen, während die Trompen eher schmückende Funktion hatten.

2.3. *Mausoleum Nr. 2*

Bau Nr. 2 (Pl. 5) wirkt wie eine kleinere und einfachere Version von Bau Nr. 1. Deshalb kann er hier kurz behandelt werden. Lediglich in den Portalen (Pl. 6) begegnet uns im inneren und äußeren Rahmen ein neues U-förmiges Terrakotta-Motiv. Auch der Innenraum (Pl. 6) zeigt ganz nahe Verwandtschaft zu Bau Nr. 1 und bedarf keiner genaueren Beschreibung.

2.4. *Mausoleum Nr. 3*

Wie schon oben in der allgemeinen Beschreibung erwähnt, haben die Bauten Nr. 3 und Nr. 4 im Gegensatz zu den Bauten Nr. 1 und Nr. 2 keine Ecktürme. Trotzdem ist die nahe Verwandtschaft aller vier Bauten unverkennbar. Bei Bau Nr. 3 ist die Dekoration der Fassaden klar gegliedert aber weniger reich als bei Bau Nr. 1.

Die Fassaden sind fast identisch verziert, hier als Beispiel die Süd-Fassade (Pl. 7). Unter dem Kuppelansatz verläuft horizontal das schon von den ersten beiden Bauten bekannte Kettenband aus Terrakotta von türkisen Kacheln gefaßt. Darunter schließt sich ein Blendnischenfries an, wie er auch von den vorangegangenen Bauten belegt ist. Hinter einer vorderen Schicht von Ziegeln sind türkis glasierte Platten angebracht. Im Gegensatz zu den vorangegangenen Bauten, an denen diese Keramikplatten unverziert waren (obgleich Taj Ali, Pl. 44, an Bau Nr. 2 verzierte Kacheln gesehen haben will), sind hier aber einige der Keramikplatten vor der Glasur mit einfachen geometrischen Ritzdekorationen versehen worden.

Vier Ziegellagen unter dem Blendnischenfries liegt ein breites Rhombenband mit aus Terrakotta gebildeten, ineinander verwobenen Rhomben vor türkisem Grund. Ein zweites Blendnischenfries verläuft auf Höhe des Eingangsbogens, darunter folgen zweimal: je ein Band aus zwei Lagen glasierter Ziegel und je ein "Blüten"-Band.

Die Portale, hier als Beispiel das Süd-Portal (Pl. 7), sind wesentlich einfacher als bei den Bauten Nr. 1 und Nr. 2 gestaltet. Ihnen sind keine Rahmen vorgeblendet. Der Eingang ist flach eingenischt. Ein Rhombenband üblicher Art umläuft die Eingangsnische, der Eingang ist in einen einfachen Rahmen gefaßt, in dem sich die Wanddekorationen fortsetzen, und der Kielbogen des Eingangs ist spitzer als jene der vorangegangenen Bauten. Lediglich über dem Ost-Eingang (Pl. 8), dem Eingang, der auf den Miḥrāb führt, finden sich eigenartige Terrakotta-Dekorationen. Da sie sich an der Stelle befinden, an der bei "normalen" Mausoleen oft eine Inschrift steht, ist nicht auszuschließen, daß hier versucht wurde, ein arabische Inschrift zu imitieren. Es handelt sich um kleine rechteckige Terrakotta-Blöcke, in denen, oben von einem Halbkreis umgeben, in arabischer Schrift "M, F, Q̮" gesehen werden könnte. Dieses Zeichen ist mit einem weiteren Zeichen verbunden, das seitenverkehrt in arabischer Schrift "Ǧ, Ḥ, Ḫ" gelesen werde könnte. Fraglos handelt es sich hier um Bemühungen von Baumeistern und ihrer Schmuckgehilfen islamische Formen zu importieren oder anzuwenden, deren sie, zumindest was die Schrift angeht, noch nicht mächtig waren.

Innen (Pl. 8) hat das Bauwerk konstruktiv nahe Verwandtschaft mit den Mausoleen Nr. 1 und Nr. 2. Wir begegnen derselben Ecklösung, hier ohne Holz. Der Miḥrāb ist einfacher, vermittelt aber mit dem "Blüten"-Band die Formensprache der schon beschriebenen Bauten.

2.5. *Mausoleum Nr. 4*

Nahe verwandt dem Bau Nr. 3 wirkt dieses Mausoleum auf den ersten Blick. Wesentliche Unterschiede zeichnen sich aber ab, betrachten wir die Süd-Fassade (Pl. 9). Das gilt besonders für die äußere Gestaltung der Übergangszone und die zwei Blendnischen-Friese, deren oberen

Abschlüsse nicht abgestuft—sondern flach—sind. Ketten-, Rhomben- und "Blüten"-Bänder, die wir schon von den anderen Bauten kennen, zieren, neben den zwei Blendnischen-Friesen, die Fassade. Zu ihnen tritt ein türkis gerahmtes Band aus E-förmigen Terrakotta Blöcken und im unteren Teil der Fassade ein Band aus zwei Lagen türkis glasierter Ziegel.

Rahmen und Bogenform des S-Portals (Pl. 9) ähnelt jenem von Bau Nr. 3. Das Feld über dem Eingangsbogen und der innere Rahmen des Portals sind aber durch reliefierte Keramikplatten zusätzlich verziert. Rechts oberhalb des Eingangsbogens ist eine als pseudoepigraphisch deutbare Keramikplatte erhalten, rechts neben ihr, im inneren Rahmen des Portals, eine Keramikplatte mit einem zentralen Blütenmotiv.

Während bei den bisher vorgestellten Bauten die Kuppeln etwas ungeschickt direkt über den Ecktrompen ansetzten, findet sich hier (Pl. 10) eine reifere Lösung. Die Trompen leiten zu einer oktogonalen, durch Blendnischen verzierten Zwischenzone über, auf welche die Kuppel aufsetzt. Der Innenraum ist reicher als in Bau Nr. 3 verziert. Dasselbe gilt für den Miḥrāb (Pl. 10).

Was sich bei Bau Nr. 3 in den Dekorationen der Blendnischen an den Fassaden (s. Pl. 7) andeutet, hat an Bau Nr. 4 (für die lokalen Verhältnisse) seine Vollendung erfahren. Während bei Bau Nr. 3 auf manchen der die Blendnischen füllenden Keramikplatten flache geometrische Ritzdekorationen unter der Glasur angebracht waren, treten uns hier (meist) tief in den Grund geschnittenen (und nicht gemodelte) vegetabile und geometrische Muster entgegen (Pl. 11), die in solchem Kontext in der islamischen Kunst einzigartig sind. Sie weisen auf ein altes, u.a. aus dem Hellenismus abgeleitetes, bergbäuerliches Formkonzept, wie wir es von den Holzarbeiten aus Nuristan, den Swat-Tal und benachbarten Gebieten kennen.[2]

3. *Die Datierung*

Taj Ali schreibt:

> As already mentioned[3] I have suggested that the tombs in the Gomal valley were built in the 11th and early half of the 12th centuries.[4]

---

[2] Cf. Edleberg, "Nuristani house" and Kalter, *Arts and crafts*.
[3] Taj Ali, "Anonymous tombs", 92.
[4] Taj Ali, "Anonymous tombs", 94.

Schön wäre das für eine frühe islamische Kunst in Pakistan: Bukhara und Adheri gehörten damit zu einer Familie, die ganz am Anfang islamischer Mausoleen-Architektur stünden.

Hier irren Taj Ali und die Gutachter seiner Dissertation.

Es gab wohl eine Zwischenzeit, in der Kuppelbauten und flach gedeckte Bauten im Gebiet des heutigen Pakistan revalisierten und nebeneinander bestanden, wie ich das am Beispiel des Mausoleums des Yūsuf Gardīzī in Multan[5] zu zeigen versucht habe. Weitere Beispiele für dieses Nebeneinander von lokaler und importierter Grabarchitektur finden sich in Uchch.[6]

Zwar haben die Bauten Nr. 1 und 2 entfernte Ähnlichkeit mit dem sogenannten Samaniden-Mausoleum in Bukhara, das in das 10. Jh. datiert wird (ob an den Anfang oder eher gegen das Ende diese Jahrhunderts sei hinterfragt; Hillenbrand akzeptiert ein Datum vor 943),[7] sie beschränken sich aber auf die Ecksäulen, die in Bukhara jedoch eingebunden sind, die drei Eingänge und die in Bukhara offene Zwerkarkadenzone (im Gegensatz zu den Blendnischenzonen in Adheri) als oberer Abschluß der Fassade. Fraglos steht dieser Schlüsselbau der Mausoleumsarchitektur des östlichen iranischen Kulturkreises (womit nicht behauptet sei, daß es sich definitiv um ein Mausoleum handelt) auch hinter unseren Bauten, nur ist er Jahrhunderte früher.

Zu dem Ziel einer möglichen Datierung unserer Bauten halte ich die Analyse der Konstruktionsmethoden für einen falschen Weg. Sie sind provinziell und wohl Abklatsch von Bauten, die nicht mehr erhalten sind oder falsche Erinnerungen an Bauten, die in dieser Form nie bestanden haben, vielleicht auch Vereinfachungen von Gesehenem, nochmals: provinziell. Diese Feststellung, die in keiner Weise ein Qualitätsurteil ist, soll aber ihren Wert als baugeschichtliche und geschichtliche Zeugnisse in keiner Weise mindern; denn sonst brauchte man sich mit ihnen nicht zu beschäftigen.

Schlüssel für die Datierung der Mausoleen von Adheri und die Zuweisung ihrer möglichen Wurzeln sind für mich in erster Linie die Keramik-Dekorationen. Allgemein lassen sich grobe Eckdaten durch das Aufkommen der keramischen Verzierung von Bauwerken im iranischen Kulturkreis festlegen.

---

[5] Gaube, "Das Grab des Yusuf Gardizi".

[6] Cf. Khan, *Uchch*; Mufti, "Concept".

[7] Hillenbrand, "Turco-Iranian elements", 149.

Wilber[8] und Meinecke[9] (auf dessen Aufstellung ich mich hier beziehe) sehen das erste erhaltene mit Keramik verzierte Bauwerk in der Gonbad-e Sorkh in Marāgha (Nordwest-Iran). Das Bauwerk ist 1148 datiert. An ihm finden sich türkis glasierte, unverzierte Keramikeinlagen am Tympanon und in den Zwickelfeldern des Portals sowie in Mauerfugen.[10]

Damals war aber, wie der Denkmalsbestand zeigt, die Verwendung von Keramik als Baudekor erst leise auf dem Vormarsch, denn an einem 1162 datierten Mausoleum, der Gonbad-e Yūsuf b. Kutayyer, in Nakhidjawān findet sich noch keine Keramikdekoration. Dasselbe gilt für ein weiteres Bauwerk in Nakhidjawān die Gonbad-e Mu'mina Khātūn, von 1186, während ein anderes Bauwerk in Maghāra, der sogenannte "runde Turm" von 1168, wie das schon erwähnte Mausoleum am selben Ort, einfache Keramikdekorationen trägt. Gegen Ende des 12. Jh. ist somit—nach dem Ausweis der erhaltenen Denkmäler—der Beginn von Keramikdekorationen in der islamischen Architektur anzusetzen.

Daß der Nordwesten Irans dabei eine wegweisende Rolle gespielt hat, scheint wahrscheinlich; denn sehen wir auf den Osten, und gehen wir davon aus, daß die Keramikdekorationen der Maghōk-e ʿAṭṭārī-Moschee in Bukhara nicht in das 12. Jh. gehören,[11] so treffen wir bei den Prachtbauten der Ghōriden, dem Minaret von Djām (gebaut von Ghiyāth al-Dīn <1163 und 1202>)[12] den Mausoleen von Chisht[13] sowie dem Bogen von Bost[14] auf keine Verwendung von Keramik. Wie am "Samaniden-Mausoleum" von Bukhara sind bei diesen Bauten der gebrannte Ziegel, Terrakotta-Stege und Terrakotta-Felder einziges Dekorationsmaterial. Erst unter den späten Ghōriden, die noch von Ghazna aus herrschten, finden wir im ghōridischen Umbau des Palastes des Ghaznaviden Masʿūd III (1099–1114) und dem "Haus der Luster-Ware", die 1221 durch die Mongolen zerstört wurden, gemodelte, monochrome Keramikplatten,[15] die geometrisch, vegetabil oder figürlich verziert sind.

---

[8] Wilber, "Development", 35.
[9] Meinecke, *Fayencedekorationen*, I, 13.
[10] Literaturhinweise auch für die folgend erwähnten Bauten, bei Meinecke a.a.O.
[11] Das gegen Meinecke a.a.O, 15.
[12] Maricq-Wiet, *Le Minaret*, 16–67.
[13] Maricq-Wiet, *Le Minaret*, 69f.
[14] Schlumberger, *Lashkari Bazar*, Taf. 42–46.
[15] Scerrato, "Islamic glazed tiles".

Damit, der Zeit ab ca. 1220, wäre eine sinnvolle Frühdatierung unserer Bauten anzusetzen. Wir müssen sie aber auch im Kontext von Bauten im heutigen Pakistan sehen, namentlich den großen Mausoleen von Multan,[16] weniger jenen diese nach hinten zeitlich abrundenden in Uchch.[17] Der uns hier interessierende zeitliche Rahmen erstreckt sich über das wohl vor 1262 gebaute Mausoleum des Bahāʾ al-Dīn in Multan,[18] an dem sich ursprünglich mit größter Wahrscheinlichkeit keine keramische Dekoration fand, bis zum Mausoleum des Rokn-e ʿAlam,[19] das um oder nach 1335 errichtet wurde, und wohl ursprünglich mit keramischen Dekorationen ausgestattet war. Welcher Art diese keramischen Dekorationen waren, gehört hier nicht in meine Fragestellung. Was ich gesehen habe, und was mir in Restauratoren-Werkstätten deutlich wurde, ist reine Konfusion. Offenbar besteht schon eine recht alte Tradition, Hergekommenes und Hergenommenes zu vermischen.

Hillenbrand[20] hat diesem Bauwerk eine gründliche Studie gewidmet. Sie erstreckt sich im Wesentlichen auf die architektonische Form und ihre Ursprünge sowie auf Teile der Dekoration, wobei er wohl bewußt die Frage des bemalten Kacheldekors an diesem Bauwerk ausgrenzte: die Frage, was ist ursprünglich an diesem und ihm nahestehenden Bauwerken, nämlich jenen in Uchch? Das kann hier auch nicht behandelt werden, und meine Bedenken habe ich wenige Zeilen oben geäußert. Betrachte ich doch das frühe oder mittlere 14. Jh. als mögliches Datum für die Entstehung unserer Bauten; und da ist an bemalte Keramik, wie sie sich später in Multan entwickelte, noch nicht zu denken.

Wage ich eine solche Spätdatierung, gehe ich davon aus, daß die Bauherren unserer Mausoleen-Gruppe zu jenen nicht gerade erfolgreichen Eroberern oder Subherrschern des Gebietes von Multan gehörten, die aus den afghanischen Bergen (oder über die afghanischen Berge) kamen, ihr Glück im fruchtbaren Panjab suchten, aber letztlich sich nicht dort festsetzen konnten.

Dies würde die Vermischung ostiranisch-afghanischer Motive in den Dekorationen, namentlich jenen der Keramikplatten in den Blendnischen von Bau Nr. 4, die, wie ich schon oben erwähnte, für mich

[16] Khan, *Multan*, 189–296.
[17] Khan, *Uchch*; Mufti, "Concept".
[18] Khan, *Multan*, 189–193.
[19] Khan, *Multan*, 215–36.
[20] Hillenbrand, "Turco-Iranian elements".

aus der Holz-Kunst Nuristans, des Swat-Tales und ihrer Nachbargebiete verständlich sind—zumindest mit ihr in Beziehung gesetzt werden müssen, mit multanischen erklären. Ist es doch kaum denkbar, daß eines der Portale von Rukn-e ʿAlam in Multan[21] von unseren Bauten abgeleitet sein könnte. Wahrscheinlicher ist das Gegenteil. Letztlich sprechen auch für eine Spätdatierung in das 14. Jh. die ersten Versuche von bemalter Baukeramik an Bau Nr. 1 (Abb. 6).

Die Geschichte des Grenzgebietes zwischen dem Panjab und den Bergen des heutigen Afghanistan in der Zeit zwischen den Mongolen (sie erobern 1241 Lahor) und der Eroberung Delhis durch Timur (1398) ist noch so unzureichend erforscht, als daß wir unsere Bauwerke konkret mit einem bestimmten historischen Ereignis in Verbindung bringen könnten. Einen Eindruck von dem, was in der Mongolenzeit im Bergland vor sich ging, vermittelt Aubin.[22] Hier hörte die Geschichte mit den Ghōriden nicht auf; und mir scheint es nur zu wahrscheinlich, daß eine Reihe der Lehm-Befestigungsbauten[23] in den Bergen nicht notwendig ghōridisch sind, sondern in die mongolische Periode bzw. die postmongolische Periode gehören. In die Zeiten, in denen kleine oder größere "Tal"-Herren herrschten, die manchmal in den Panjab vorstießen und manchmal, wie das für Malik Šādū Lodī,[24] Gouverneur von Multan, der 1340 gegen Muḥammad b. Tughluq rebellierte, belegt ist, Aufständischen aus dem Panjab Zuflucht gewährten.

Aus diesen Überlegungen heraus schlage ich eine Datierung der Mausoleen von Adheri in die erste Hälfte oder die Mitte des 14. Jh. vor. Sie sind nur aus der Tughluq-Zeit verständlich; und da diese Periode der Geschichte des Indischen Subkontinents in der historischen Forschung, was die Regionalgeschichte angeht, noch viele weiße Flecken aufweist, wäre es wünschenswert, daß Forscher sich diesen weißen Flecken zuwenden, wie das E. Bosworth, neben anderem (man denke nur: "*The Mediaeval Islamic Underworld*"[25] und vieles mehr) für Sistan und Ostiran geleistet hat. Hier also ein Anstoß.

---

[21] Hillenbrand, "Turco-Iranian elements", fig. 21.
[22] Aubin, "L'Ethnogène".
[23] Z.B. Allchin-Hammond, *Archaeology*, fig. 6, 24, 25 und 30.
[24] Qureshi, "Muslim India", 17, mit Grundliteratur, 14f.
[25] Leiden, 1976.

Bibliography

Allchin, F.R. und N. Hammond, *The Archaeology of Afghanistan*, London, New York, San Francisco, 1978.
Aubin, J., "L'Ethnogène des Qaraunas", *Turcica* 1 (1969), 65–94.
Bosworth, C.E., *The Ghaznavids*. (2), Beirut, 1973.
———, *The Later Ghaznavids*. Edinburgh, 1977.
Edleberg, L., "The Nuristani House", in *Cultures of the Hindukush*, ed. K. Jettmar, Wiesbaden, 1974, 24–53.
Gaube, H., "Das Grab des Yūsuf Gardīzī in Multan", *Oriens* 34 (1994) 330–347.
Hillenbrand, R., "Turco-Iranian Elements in the Medieval Architecture of Pakistan. The Case of the Tomb of Rukn-i ʿAlam at Multan," *Muqarnas* 9 (1992), 148–174.
Kalter, J., *The Arts and Crafts of the Swat Valley*. London-New York, 1991.
Khan, A.N., *Multan. History and Architecture*, Islamabad, 1983.
———, *Uchch*. Islamabad, 1980.
Maricq, A. und G. Wiet, *Le Minaret de Djam*, Paris, 1959.
Meinecke, M. *Fayencedekorationen seldschukischer Sakralbauten in Kleinasien*, Tübingen, 1976.
Mufti, K. "Concept of Tomb Architecture at Uchch", in *Sultanate Period Architecture*, ed. S. Akbar, Lahore, 1991, 134–143.
Qureshi, I.H., "Muslim India before the Mughals", in *The Cambridge History of Islam*, 2., Cambridge 1970, 3–34.
Scerrato, U., "Islamic Glazed Tiles with Molded Decoration from Ghazni", *East and West* 11 (1962), 263–287.
Schlumberger, D., Lashkari Bazar, Paris, 1978.
Seherr-Thoss, H.C., *Design and Color in Islamic Architecture*, Washington, 1968.
Wilber, D.N., "The Development of Mosaic Faience in Islamic Architecture in Iran," *Ars Islamica* (6) 1939, 16–47.

Addendum

Beim Lesen der Korrekturen konsultierte ich nochmals die Literatur und stieß auf zwei Stellen, die im Zusammenhang mit den hier besprochenen Gräbern nicht unerwähnt bleiben dürfen, denn sie stützen überzeugend meine von der kunsthistorischen Evidenz her gewonnene Datierung. In dem Sammelband *Sultanate Period Architecture*, 78–86, schrieb M. Usman Hassan über: "Terra-cotta Plaque Decorated Tombs of Baluchistan". Die Fassaden dieser Mausoleen sind mit unglasierten Terracotta-Platten verziert, die teils figürliche Darstellungen tragen, teils aber geometrische Muster, nicht unähnlich den Keramikplatten an Bau 4. Diese Gräber sind wohl identisch mit den von G.P. Tate, *Sistan*, London 1910, 321f., beschriebenen Mausoleen, die dieser überzeugend mit den "Nikudar" in Zusammenhang bringt, die erstmals Ende des 13. Jh. in Khorasan auftauchten, dann nach Sistan-Makran weiterzogen und 1384 in Sistan von den Timur entscheidende geschlagen wurden.

COLOUR PLATES
1–11

Pl. 1 Bau 1: Ost-Fassade (oben) und West-Fassade (unten).

Pl. 2 Bau 1: Ost-Fassade, Detail (rechts) und Südost-Eckturm (links).

Pl. 5 Bau 2: Ost-Fassade (oben) und Ost-Fassade, Detail (unten).

Pl. 6 Bau 2: Ost-Portal (oben) und Miḥrāb (unten).

Pl. 7 Bau 3: Süd-Fassade (oben) und Süd-Portal (unten).

Pl. 8 Bau 3: Ost-Portal, Detail (oben) und Miḥrāb (unten).

Pl. 9 Bau 4: Süd-Fassade (oben) und Süd-Portal (unten).

Pl. 10 Bau 4: Innenraum nach Osten (oben) und Miḥrāb (unten).

Pl. 11 Bau 4: Keramikdekorationen.

A MID-FIFTEENTH CENTURY BYZANTINE AND OTTOMAN COIN HOARD FROM RUMELI: THE OTTOMAN COMPONENT (A PRELIMINARY REPORT)

Colin Heywood

I

The utility of coin hoards as a tool for the reconstruction of the history of late Seljuq Anatolia, when taken together with the abundant coinage of the period, has already been recognised.[1] For the history of the Ottoman state in the beylik period (i.e., prior to 1453), where the coinage is (relatively) so much less diverse, and the documentary and literary evidence (in comparison with late Seljuq Anatolia, at least) so much more extensive, coin hoards have tended to attract significantly less attention. This has been particularly the case for the crucial first century of Ottoman rule in Rumeli, from the conquest of Gallipoli in 1354 to the fall of Constantinople a century later. The Ottoman component of one such Rumelian hoard datable to the late beylik period, forms the subject of the present paper.[2]

In the early 1980s there appeared on the London market a large mixed hoard of Byzantine and Ottoman coins. The hoard, which was in two parcels, consisted of approximately 2000 Byzantine silver coins, mainly of the emperor John VIII Palaeologos (1421/25–48), but with smaller numbers from the reigns of John V (1341–91), John VII and Manuel II (1391–1425),[3] together with a slightly smaller number of

---

[1] Lowick, "A hoard of Seljuq dirhams"; Lindner, "Hordes and hoards in late Saljūq Anatolia".

[2] On the relationship between late Byzantine and early Ottoman coinage see Walther Hinz, "Hyperper und Asper", 79–89.

[3] Both the Byzantine and Ottoman components of the Çorlu hoard were subsequently dispersed in trade. I am profoundly grateful to Messrs A.H. Baldwin, and in particular to Mr Simon Bendall and Mr Beverley Curtis, for their many kindnesses and for their assistance in facilitating my study of the coins in question. In the interim, prior to its dispersal, the Byzantine component was studied by Mr Simon Bendall. On this component, beyond the brief notice in *Coin Hoards* referred to below (n. 4), see Simon Bendall's catalogue of his own collection, *A Private Collection of Palaeologan Coins*. The statistical breakdown by reign, denomination and sigla, of the Byzantine coins in the hoard is supplied in an Addendum (79–81) to Bendall's catalogue,

Ottoman silver akçes dating from the late fourteenth century to a slightly earlier terminal date, the end of the first reign (842/1421–848/1444) of the Ottoman sultan Murād II. The hoard was said to have been found at Çorlu, mid-way between Edirne and Istanbul, and although definitive proof of this assertion is, in the nature of things, lacking, it has already been accepted by Bendall and logged in *Coin Hoards*,[4] and will be maintained here as a working hypothesis. The Çorlu hoard's existence was duly made public,[5] but publication of the following preliminary report on the Ottoman component of the hoard has been inexcusably delayed. It is hoped that full publication of these coins will follow in due course.[6]

On the occasion of his seventieth birthday I offer the present summary description of the Ottoman component of the Çorlu hoard and a brief analysis of its historical significance in affectionate tribute to Edmund Bosworth. I hope he will be also willing to accept it as a token of our long friendship. This last, too, thanks to his great patience as editor of the *Encyclopaedia of Islam*, has managed to survive other equally maddening delays on the part of the author.

II

The Ottoman component of the Çorlu hoard consisted of 1851 identifiable coins, all Ottoman silver akçes dating (by year of issue)

---

which lists a total of 1899 coins. Bendall's figure of "approximately 2500" akçes would appear to be an over-estimate, and he now holds the view (conversation, January 1997) that the Ottoman coins studied here most probably represent the totality of Ottoman coins in the hoard.

It should be mentioned that in the hoard, and retained at the time of its dispersal by Mr Bendall, were a further two coins, one a Byzantine stavraton, and one an Ottoman akçe. Both of these coins had survived with fabric adhesions, which came presumably from the bag in which the hoard had been deposited at the time of its concealment. Mr Bendall kindly informs me that both coins were subsequently stolen (in the U.S.), but that an analysis of the adhesions undertaken at the time, which is also now lost, established without doubt that the Ottoman and Byzantine coins in both parcels all came from the same site.

[4] *Coin Hoards*, vii, # 371, 241–2 ("Gorlu" [sic]).

[5] In papers read at meetings of the Royal Numismatic Society on 21 January 1986 (Simon Bendall: "A mid-fifteenth century hoard from Thrace I: the Byzantine component") and 18 February 1986, by the present writer ("A fifteenth-century coin hoard II: the Ottoman component").

[6] The present report is based on two earlier, unpublished papers; (i) the RNS paper referred to above (n. 51), and (ii) a paper given at the 4th International Congress on Ottoman Economic and Social History, Munich, 1984.

from the late eighth/fourteenth century to the first third of the ninth/fifteenth, plus three unidentifiable coins of the same metal and similar fabric.[7] Classifying the coins by ruler, issue and, where applicable, by mint, the Ottoman coins from the hoard are of no fewer than 34 types (see Table I). All the issues of the three "recognised" Ottoman sultans of the period—Bāyezīd I (791/1389–805/1403), Meḥemmed I (816/1413–824/1421) and Murād II (first reign, 824/1421–848/1444) are represented, as are issues of certain of the sons of Bāyezīd I—Meḥemmed [I] Çelebi, Süleymān Çelebi, Mūsā Çelebi and the so-called "Düzme" ("False") Muṣṭafā—who were amongst the claimants of the Ottoman inheritance during the Ottoman "Time of Troubles", and who struck coins on various occasions during the years 805/1403–824/1421.[8]

The distribution of coins from the hoard amongst the various issuers is quite interesting; even, in one instance, surprising. With regard to the issues of the three "regular" sultans, Bāyezīd I, Meḥemmed I and Murād II, the distribution gradient is steep. As already implied, no aḳçes of Murād I (d. 791/1389) or his predecessors were found in the hoard. There were 37 aḳçes (2.02%) of the sole issue of Bāyezīd I (791/1389–805/1403), and 146 and 383 coins, respectively 7.97% and 20.92% of the total (1831) of identified Ottoman coins in the hoard, of the first (816/1413) and second (822/1419) issues of Meḥemmed I, a total for the reign of 529 coins (28.89%). The limited and scarce first issue of Murād II (824/1421), minted only at Bursa, is represented by only 26 coins (1.42%). By contrast, the hoard contained no fewer than 735 coins (40.14% of the Ottoman component), from six different mints, of Murād II's extensive second issue, first struck in 825 (26 Dec. 1421–14 Dec. 1422). This was replaced less than a decade later by Murād's third issue, dated 834, and thus first issued sometime between mid-September 1430 and early September 1431. Of this issue, the latest in date to be represented in the Çorlu hoard, 365 coins were found (19.93% of the Ottoman component). The total number of coins of Murād II, 1126 in all, represents 61.5% of the entire Ottoman component of the hoard.

To return, in order to fill the gaps between the end of Bāyezīd's reign and the beginning of Murād II's uncontested sultanate, i.e. the

[7] Plus one further aḳçe with fabric adhesions, now lost, referred to above (n. 3).

[8] A detailed and reliable overview of the complex political history of this period is provided by Colin Imber, *The Ottoman Empire*, 55–100.

years between 805/1403 and 825/1422. These years include the reign of Meḥemmed I as sole ruler (816/1413–824/1421), but they also encompass the first (805/1403–816/1413) and second (816/1413–825/1422) periods of the Ottoman "Time of Troubles", the years of struggle for succession to the sultanate between the sons and grandsons of Bāyezīd I.[9] The interesting—indeed, the most remarkable—feature of the Ottoman coins from this period in the Çorlu hoard is not the small number (3:0.16%) of Meḥemmed Çelebi's coins from this period, nor the single coin from each of Süleymān Çelebi's first and third issues (0.11%), but the appearance of no fewer than 139 (7.59%) of the aḳçes issued in Rumeli by the so-called Düzme (or "False") Muṣṭafā in the last stages of the Ottoman "Time of Troubles". Muṣṭafā was in fact a genuine son of Bāyezīd I, who had disappeared in the course of the battle of Ankara and reappeared a decade later in Rumeli.[10] The coins from his second attempt to establish a counter-sultanate, which followed on the death of Meḥemmed I in the summer of 1421, have been known hitherto in extremely limited numbers.[11] In the Çorlu hoard were found 10 of the undated aḳçes of "Düzme" Muṣṭafā struck at Serez, and hitherto attributed to his first attempt to seize the throne in 1415–6, together with 129 of his Edirne issue, dated 824 or "8224". All these coins, as I have demonstrated elsewhere, were minted during Muṣṭafā's counter-sultanate established at Edirne in the autumn and winter of 824–5/1421–2.[12]

To deal in a more systematic fashion with the distribution of mints represented in the hoard. The pattern is irregular and, to some extent, predictable (see Table I). The practice of placing the mint town on its coins was not one which the emergent Ottoman state continued from its Ilkhanid predecessors. No mints appear on the coins of Orhan, Murād I or Bāyezīd I, although it is reasonable to assume that the coins of the first-named ruler were minted at Bursa and of his two successors at both Bursa and (possibly) Edirne, after

[9] For a summary list of the Ottoman coinage struck in the years 805–22 see *EI*², s.v. "Meḥemmed I" (H. Inalcık), where, however, the 824/1421 coinage of "Düzme" Muṣṭafā is misdated to 822. The coinage of Murād II is ably discussed by Barbara Flemming, "The reign of Murad II: a survey (I)", 252–6.

[10] Cf. my "Muṣṭafā Čelebi. Düzme", *EI*², vii, 710–2.

[11] The British Museum, for example, does not possess any of the coins of "Düzme" Muṣṭafā.

[12] Cf. my preliminary study "824/'8224' = 1421: the 'False' (Düzme) Muṣṭafā and his ephemeral coinage", *Mélanges Sahillioglu*, Zaghouan, 1997, ii, 159–75; cf. Corrections to "824/'8224', *etc*", Wendover: privately printed, 1998.

the latter place passed definitively into Ottoman hands, most probably in 1378.[13] The first indication of mints (Bursa; Engüriye [i.e. Ankara] in 805; Amasya in 806) occur on the coins of Meḥemmed Çelebi issued during the "Time of Troubles"; possibly, since Meḥemmed coupled his name with that of his overlord, Tīmūr, they reflect Timurid practice. Similarly, both Mūsā Çelebi and Süleymān Çelebi struck coins at Edirne dated 813 (mid-1410–11). These were the first Ottoman coins to bear the Edirne mintmark and thus demonstrably struck in Rumeli. Serez (Sīrūz, Serrai, Serres) first appears as an Ottoman mint in the first issue of Meḥemmed I's sultanate (816/1413), as do Ḳaraḥiṣār, Ayaṣoluḳ (Agios Theologos) and Balaṭ (Palatia) in western Anatolia, and Temirḥiṣār (Byz. Siderokastron) in the hinterland of Thessaloniki. Finally, mention must be made of Üsküb (Skopje), in Macedonia, which appears as an Ottoman mint-town for the first time with the second (825/1422) issue of Murād II; and of "Nōvār", i.e. the medieval Serbian mining centre of Novo Brdo, represented in the coins from the third issue of Murād II which provides valuable evidence (discussed below) for a *terminus a quo* for the deposit of the Çorlu hoard.

Thus the Ottoman coins in the Çorlu hoard, disregarding those coins which show no mint-town, or on which, through careless striking, the mint legend is either off the flan or not struck up, comprise the products of ten attributable mints.[14] Preponderant, as one would expect for a Rumelian hoard, are the productions of Edirne (676; 41.81% of the 1617 coins so far identified by place of issue) and Serez (575; 35.56%). The largest number of coins from an Anatolian mint come, as might be expected, from Bursa (256; 15.83%). These three major mints together account for 1507 coins, or 93.2%, of the 1617 mint-identified coins. All the other mints which are represented in this hoard play a relatively insignificant role (110 coins; 6.8%) in its composition. From Anatolian mints other than Bursa we have 32 coins (1.98%) from Balaṭ; 28 (1.73%) from Ayaṣoluḳ, 26 (1.61%) from Amasya, and only three (0.185%) from the Bithynian mint of

[13] I disregard here the coin of the Ilkanid ruler Öljeitu which was struck possibly at Söğüt in 699/1299 and has been tentatively ascribed to ʿOsmān I (see Lindner, "Hordes and Hoards", 281).

[14] Most of the coins in the latter category can be attributed by stylistic analysis to a particular mint, a statistical refinement which I remit to the future full publication of the Ottoman component of the Çorlu hoard.

Ḳaraḥiṣār.[15] The secondary Ottoman mints in Rumeli are in the main equally poorly represented: five coins (0.31%) from the minor mint of Temirḥiṣār; and a solitary aḳçe (0.06%) from Üsküb. The exception is Nōvār (Novo Brdo), with 57 coins (3.525%) of Murād II's third (834/1430–1) issue.

It may be assumed that the surviving Ottoman coins from the Çorlu hoard give a true picture of the hoard as found (an assumption quite strongly based on the evidence, in that its obvious rarities, and in particular the "Düzme" Muṣṭafā coins, had manifestly not been "creamed off"). Missing from Ottoman issues of the period covered by the hoard are only the productions of Mūsā Çelebi issued at Edirne during his short régime (813/1411–816/1413) and the very rare coins of the so-called "Küçük" Muṣṭafā, the younger brother of Murād II, for whom coins were struck during his unsuccessful attempt in 825/1422–826/1423 to obtain the sultanate. In terms of both issues and mints, all the silver coins of Meḥemmed I are represented,[16] as, with three exceptions, one doubtful, are those of Murād II.[17]

III

An investigation of the reasons for the relatively plentiful supply of coins from Nōvār lead naturally into the important question of the

[15] There are a number of places named Ḳaraḥiṣār in central and western Anatolia. Ḳ-i şarkī (Şebīn Ḳ/Ḳoġonya/Colonia) was not taken until 878/1473; Ḳ-i Ṣāḥib, which belonged to Germiyān, was finally annexed in 1429; Ḳ-i Teke is also unlikely. The Ḳaraḥiṣār in question here, therefore, is most probably to be equated with "Ḳaraḥiṣār in the land of ʿOsmān" (Yāḳūt), i.e. Ḳaracaḥiṣār, near Inönü; located later in the *ḳażā* of Bilecik. This Ḳaracaḥiṣār was, of course, the site of the (possibly legendary) first conquest of ʿOsmān I (cf., for a discussion of the traditions which surround the event, cf. Rudi P. Lindner, *Nomads and Ottomans*, 20–1. Most significantly, in its vicinity there was a silver mine which was still in operation in the mid-sixteenth century (cf. Refik, *Osmanli devrinde Türkiye madenleri*, 1), and which was doubtless the site of the mint. Cf. *EI*², s.v. Ḳaraḥiṣār (J.H. Mordtmann/X. de Planhol), and E. Zachariadou, "Lauro Quirini", 241.

[16] Artuk, *Istanbul Kataloğu*, ii, 462, ff., nos. 1394–1403 (no coins from Balat, Timürḥiṣār, or Ḳaraḥiṣār).

[17] Artuk, nos. 1404, 1406–8, 1413–4, 1421–2. The exceptions are Murạd's aḳçes from Ankara (second issue) and Inebolu (third issue; cf. Schaendlinger, *Osmanische Numismatik*, 89–90), and some rare and untypical aḳçes with the mint name "Germiyan"; cf., for example Artuk, no. 1419. This coin was first published in Erel, *Nâdir bir kaç sikke*, no. 25. In view of its weight (0.60 gr = 3 ḳeyrāṭ), it should surely be classified as a half-aḳçe. For a discussion of the political and numismatic implications of this and other Germiyan coins in this period see Flemming, "Reign of Murad II", 253–4.

precise date of deposit of the Çorlu hoard. As Simon Bendall indicated in his study of the Byzantine component of the hoards, the Byzantine coins are not very helpful in this regard. The Byzantine emperor John VIII Palaeologus had a long reign, from 1425 to 1448. None of his coins are datable to a narrower period, and a single basic design did duty for the whole reign.[18] Nor, from the Byzantine side, does the extreme rarity of the coins of the last emperor Constantine IX allow us to state categorically that the hoard was concealed before the death of John VIII. The Ottoman coins, however, are of considerable assistance in this respect. As noted, the last issue to be represented, to the extent of 365 out of the 1851 identifiable Ottoman coins in the hoard, is the third issue of Murād II. Coins of this issue bear the *ḥicrī* date 834 (beg. 19 Sept. 1430). They continued to be issued, bearing the same date, until they were superseded by the first (and sole) issue of the first, brief reign of Meḥemmed II, which bears the accessional year 848 (beg. 20 April 1444). The first issue of Meḥemmed II, however, cannot have been made until after the abdication of Murād II. This took place in August 1444, during the false peace with Hungary and Serbia which followed the conclusion of the Treaty of Edirne. Soon after, Murād handed over the affairs of the sultanate to his young son Meḥemmed, and subsequently retired to Bursa.[19] Immediately thereafter, coins were struck in the name of Meḥemmed II, but at a reduced weight of 5 instead of 6 *ḳeyrāṭ*s (0.95–1.00 g instead of 1.15–1.20 g).[20] This was the first reduction in the weight of the aḳçe since its introduction in the fourteenth century; as a consequence, all the existing aḳçes in circulation were called in for recoining at the new lower weight, with consequent benefit to the Ottoman treasury.[21]

---

[18] Verbal communication from Mr Simon Bendall in his unpublished RNS paper, Jan. 1986.

[19] An agreement was made between Murād II and the king of Hungary, the despot of Serbia and the Hungarian magnate Janos Hunyady on 12 June at Edirne. Meḥemmed was placed on the throne as deputy (*ḳā'immaḳām*) for his father. In July Murād made a peace agreement with his old enemy the bey of Ḳaraman. He abdicated at Mihaliç, in the presence of his senior officials, in August 1444 (*Islâm Ansiklopedisi*, s.v. "Meḥemmed II" (H. Inalcık)). Cf. Professor Ménage's observation ("'Annals of Murād II'", 578, 582) that the "Annals of Murād II" place a laconic report of this series of occurrences as the first "event" of 848 (beg. 20.4.1444), whereas the Ottoman chroniclers, appending it to the events of 847, put it too early.

[20] Artuk, ii, 470.

[21] Ibid.; cf. below, n. 27. Barbara Flemming raises ("Reign of Murad II", 254)

We thus have a *terminus ad quem* of the summer of 1444 for the concealment of the hoard, and also a significant economic motive for its concealment at that time. At first sight the task of establishing a *terminus a quo* is less straightforward: 1425, apparently, from the Byzantine side (accession of John VIII), and 1430 (Murād II's third issue of 834) from the Ottoman. The wide spread of this fifteen-year period may be narrowed, however, by making reference to the 57 coins of Murād II's third issue minted at Nōvār. The coins of the third issue all bear the date 834 (19.9.1430–8.9.1431).[22] The coins bearing the mint-name Nōvār, however, could not have been struck until after the Ottoman conquest of Novo Brdo. It has generally been accepted that this occurred in the early summer of 1440, after the failure of Murād II's well-documented campaign in the summer of that year to wrest Belgrade from Hungarian occupation. The date of 845 offered by the corrupt chronology of the so-called "Annals of Murād II" has been corrected by Professor Ménage to 843, but in fact, as he points out, the "Annals" are wrong here: Novo Brdo, the last Serbian fortress to fall into Ottoman hands, capitu-

the problem of the aḳçes apparently struck by Murād II in 848 at the same weight and with the same fabric and basic design as the coins of Meḥemmed II's first issue of the same year, following Murād's abdication (reading [upwards] Murād b. Meḥemmed Ḫan rather than Meḥemmed b. Murād Ḫan). As she rightly points out, Novo Brdo having been relinquished by the treaty of Edirne, Murād would have had a desperate need of silver in that year of bitter warfare. The problems which the existence of these coins raise cannot be dealt with here; in any case, the extremely short period (from the signing of the Treaty of Edirne to Murād's abdication) in which they can have been issued does not affect the basic arguments for the dating of the Çorlu hoard.

[22] The Ottomans chronicles in general date this happening to 835 (Ménage, "'Annals of Murād II'", 582); the "Annals", however, provide the correct year as furnished by numismatic evidence. Attention should be drawn to Professor Ménage's emendation of the meaningless "īdī" in the "Annal's" text to *īrī* ("heavy"), as in one chronicle MS. tradition (cf. Ménage, 575, n. 29) and his observation (drawing on Akdağ, *Türkiye'nin iktisadî ve ictimaî tarihi*, i, 394, 422–5, cf. Flemming, "The reign of Murad II", when the same point is made) that "the issue of 834 represented a temporary return [sic] to the heavier aḳçe of 5 3/4 and even 6 1/4 ḳīrāṭ", which renders *īrī* "a tenable reading". But was this in fact the case? The aḳçe of Orhan weighed 6 ḳīrāṭ (one-quarter *mithḳāl*, 1.056 g), with 90% purity, which was maintained down to the reign of Murād II (*EI*², i, 317–8, s.v. "aḳče"), i.e., it was a one-third dīnār, exactly one-third in weight of the Ilkhạnid dīnār of the 2nd standard of Abū Sa'īd (1 dīnār = 18 ḳīrāṭ = 3.17 g), which was struck in precisely the years (729–1328 to 733/1332) when the long-lived initial standard for the Ottoman aḳçe was being established.

lated in June 1441.[23] What interval elapsed between the Ottoman conquest of Novo Brdo and their (re-)establishment of a mint there, is not known, but its initial life-span must have been, at the most, three years, before Novar and its surrounding districts were handed back to the reconstituted Serbian state in August 1444 by the Treaty of Edirne.[24]

Most of the 57 coins in the Çorlu hoard from Nōvār, like a large proportion of all the coins present of Murād II's third issue, show either very slight or no traces of wear. One or two, however, are slightly worn, an observation which would tend to suggest that within our now firmly established parameters—summer 1440 to summer 1444—for the concealment of the hoard, a date nearer to the end of the period is the more likely. Is it possible to control this hypothesis further by external evidence? My initial impulse was to suggest that we might settle on the bitter winter months of 1443–4. This was a time of great peril for the Ottoman state, when a powerful Christian army, under the direction of the Hungarian magnate Janos Hunyadi, penetrated the Balkans and advanced on Edirne. Its victorious progress was eventually halted in a standoff between the two armies at the Zlatitsa Pass (Ottoman: Izladı Derbendi) in the mountains between Sofia and the upper valley of the Maritsa river, the last physical obstacle to an invading army on the road to Edirne. Hunyadi and his forces halted and were obliged to retreat, and Edirne was saved, but the danger to Ottoman rule in Rumeli had been very great.[25] A second hypothesis, also based on external evidence, is to opt for a later date in 1444, after the abdication of Murād II, when a great panic broke out in Edirne and throughout Rumeli on receipt of the news that Ladislas II of Hungary had broken the

[23] Ménage, "Annals of Murād II", 582, sub anno "845" [sic]: *Murād Belgırāda varub, fetḥ olınmayub, andan gelüb, Nevābiri ḳalʿesine fetḥ etdi.* For the correct date see Jirecek, *Geschichte Serbiens*, ii, 178, cited by Ménage, and Fine, *The Later Medieval Balkans*, 531. At its fall Novo Brdo was the richest silver mine in the old Serbian lands, yielding an annual income of 12,000 ducats (Fine, 569).

[24] Inalcık, *Fatih devri*, i, 64, n. 46. Novo Brdo was reconquered by Meḥemmed II on 1 June 1455 (cf. Babinger, "Die Aufzeichnungen des Genuesen Iacopo de Promontorio—de Campis, 64 and n. 1). Cf., on Ottoman Nōvạr/Nevābir[d]e, Anhegger, *Beiträge zur Geschichte des Bergbaus*, 155–62. For the texts of the regulations of Meḥemmed II concerning the operation of the silver mines at Nōvār, see Anhegger and Inalcık, *Ḳānūnnāme-i sulṭānī*, 5–11.

[25] Cf. Imber, *Ottoman Empire*, 122 ff., for the events of this crisis.

Treaties of Edirne and Szeged, and was advancing down the Danube at the head of a large Christian army in the ill-fated military adventure known subsequently as the Crusade of Varna.[26] This second hypothesis, like the first, is equally unprovable, but is more open to criticism on the substantive grounds that the Çorlu hoard contains no aḳçes of Meḥemmed II, coins which must have been already in wide circulation from the Edirne mint by the advent of the Varna crusade. Let us therefore hedge our bets. I would suggest that the Ottoman evidence, economic and political, as well as numismatic, points to the concealment of the Çorlu hoard as occurring some time between the military crisis in the winter of 1443–4 and the Varna crisis almost a year later. It must have come about as a response to either of the military crises or to the intervening economic decision to recoin the aḳçe at a lower standard on or immediately following the first accession of Meḥemmed II.[27]

Thus either political or economic motives, or a combination of both, led, I suspect, to the concealment of the Çorlu hoard. The hearsay evidence that this hoard was indeed found at Çorlu is in itself inherently unverifiable. Nonetheless, it is an attractive proposition, both from the point of view of the hoard's contents, and for contemporary historical-topographic reasons. Ottoman Çorlu, formerly the Byzantine Tsurullon, lay on the great trading and military highway which since Roman times had linked Constantinople—still, in Murād II's time, in Byzantine hands—and the lands of the middle Danube.[28] By the latter part of Murād II's reign Çorlu had been in the possession of the Ottomans for perhaps three-quarters of a century,[29] occupying a strategic position in the Ottoman-Byzantine bor-

[26] The events in Edirne at this time are dealt with exhaustively by Inalcık, *Fātiḥ devri*, 35–8.

[27] For the implementation of this recoinage measure the sultan's executive officers were empowered to search houses, merchandise and caravanserais and to confiscate at its commercial value the silver money which they found (cf. the text of the "gümiş yasaġı" of Meḥemmed II in Anhegger and Inalcık, 4–5). Under its prescriptions the holding of silver beyond 200-dirhems' weight, not only the Ottoman coins of previous issues, but also the even weightier accumulation of Byzantine silver in the hoard would have attracted the unwelcome and confiscatory attentions of the Ottoman authorities.

[28] Jirecek, *Die Heerstrasse*.

[29] Çorlu was taken by the Ottomans early in the reign of Murạd I (cf. EI^2, i, 62, s.v. Čorlu (V.L. Ménage). Çorlu at this time was still close to the territories in Thrace east of a line Misivri-Bizye/Vize Heraclea/Eregli, i.e. at closest little more than 15 miles from Çorlu, which remained under Byzantine control until 1453, cf. A. Vakalopoulos, "Limites de l'empire byzantin", 56 ff.

derland, mid-way between Byzantine Constantinople and Ottoman Edirne. It is no difficult task to summon up the picture of some moderately well-to-do Muslim (or Christian, or Jewish) inhabitant of Edirne, caught up in the successive crises in Rumeli between the winter of 1443–4 and the autumn of 1444. Did our merchant or rich bourgeois, threatened with the confiscation of his accumulated wealth by the sultan's silver inspectors, and panicked still further by rumours of an impending attack on Edirne from the rear by the Byzantines, bury his accumulation of silver—the illegally held infidel coins of the Greeks and the equally illegal aḳçes of the old Ottoman régime—and, like so many others at the time, flee (possibly with his more portable gold and a supply of current *aḳçes*) either to Gallipoli or to some other small harbour on the northern shore of the Sea of Marmara, before taking ship and seeking sanctuary in Anatolia, or, depending on his religion, to the sanctuary of Byzantine Constantinople itself? En route, he buries his hoard at Çorlu (alternatively, perhaps, he resided there), and passes on his way, never to return to reclaim it.[30]

In conclusion, it may be observed that the Çorlu hoard, in all its aspects, provides valuable evidence for the nature of the monetary economy in south-eastern Europe in the decade preceding the fall of Constantinople: the existence of a mixed monetary economy in the Ottoman-controlled hinterland of Constantinople; the continuance of widespread circulation of Byzantine coinage at a very late date in the empire's history; the wide circulation area (western Anatolia to central Balkans) of aḳçes from specific Ottoman mints; and the long continuance in circulation of Ottoman aḳçes from Bāyezīd I's reign to the crisis of 1443–4. The Ottoman coins in the Çorlu hoard also offer the opportunity to open up other avenues of research: the ability to study in more depth the hitherto scarce coinage of "Düzme" Muṣṭafā, already in part realised, and, for example, to establish die linkages and issue totals for various issues and to analyse the metallic content of issues from various mints and perhaps thereby establish the sources of Ottoman silver in this period.

---

[30] It is impossible to enter further here into the phenomenology of the concealment of hoards. Cf. further (from amongst a rich literature) the discussions in Iliescu, "Un trésor d'aspres turcs"; MacKenzie, "Aḳçes of Mehemmed II"; Bivar, "A Mongol invasion hoard"; Lowick, "An early tenth-century hoard from Isfahan"; Album, "A hoard of silver coins"; Feary, Luther and Smith, "Two Ilkhanid hoards?".

TABLE I
SUMMARY TABLE OF THE DISTRIBUTION OF OTTOMAN COINS IN THE ÇORLU HOARD

All coins are *AR* akçes.

	No Mint	Edirne	Serez	Bursa	Ayaşoluḳ	Balat	Timür-ḥiṣār	Ḳara-ḥiṣār	Amasya	Üsküb	Nōvār	(missing from flan/not struck up)	issue totals	reign totals
BAYEZID I														
1st issue (792)	37												37	37
SÜLEYMAN ÇELEBI														
1st issue (806)	2												2	
3rd issue (813)		1											1	3
MUSA ÇELEBI														
1st issue (813)	2	11											13	13
MEHEMMED ÇELEBI														
1st issue (806)?	3												3	3
MEHEMMED I														
1st issue (816)		57	18	7	3	32	5	3				22[a]	147	
2nd issue (822)		141	97	119	21							5[b]	383	530
MUSTAFA ÇELEBI														
Sole issue (824)														
no date				10									10	
824		64										}		
"8224"		45										}20[c]	129	139
MURAD II														
1st issue (824)				26									26	
2nd issue (825)		250	268	77	4				24	1		113[d]	735	
3rd issue (834)		87	182	27					2		57	10[e]	365	1126
Mint Totals	44	656	575	256	28	32	5	3	26	1	57	170	1851	1851
Grand Total														1854[f]

[a] includes 4 brockages
[b] includes 2 brockages; 3 mints obscure
[c] includes 2 brockages
[d] includes 1 brockage; 1 adhesion; 4 mints not identified; 107 mints off flan or not struck up
[e] includes 3 brockages; 4 adhesions; 2 mints not identified
[f] includes 3 akçes not identified by ruler

Bibliography

Akdağ, M., *Türkiye'nin iktisadî ve ictimaî tarihi*, 2 vols., Ankara 1971.

Album, S., "A hoard of silver coins from the time of Iskandār Qara-Qoyunlu", *NC*, 7th ser., xvi (1976), 109–57.

Anhegger, R., *Beiträge zur Geschichte des Bergbaus im Osmanischen Reich*, i, Istanbul, 1943.

Anhegger, Robert and Inalcık, Halil, *Ḳānūnnāme-i sulṭānī ber mūceb-i ʿörf-i ʿosmānī*, Ankara, 1956.

Artuk, Ibrahim and Cevriye, *Istanbul Arkeoloji Müzeleri teşhirdeki Islâmî Sikkeler Kataloğu*, Istanbul, 2 vols. (with continuous pagination), 1974.

Babinger, Fr., "Die Aufzeichnungen des Genuesen Iacopo de Promontorio—de Campis über die Osmanenstaat um 1475", München, 1957, *Bayerische Akademie der Wissenschaften, Phil.-Hist. Klasse, Sitzungsberichte*, Jg. 1956, Heft 8, 000.

Bendall, Simon, "A mid-fifteenth century hoard from Thrace I: the Byzantine component". Unpublished paper read at a meeting of the Royal Numismatic Society on 21 January 1986.

Bivar, A.D.H., "A Mongol invasion hoard from eastern Afghanistan", *Afghanistan*, xxviii/1 (1975), 16–28; ibid., in *Near Eastern Numismatics. Studies in Honour of C.G. Miles*, Beirut, 1974, 369–81.

Coin Hoards, vii, London, *Royal Numismatic Society*, 1985.

Erel, Şerafeddin, *Nâdir bir kaç sikke*, Istanbul, 1963.

Feary, M.S., Luther, K.A., and Smith, J.M., Jr., "Two Ilkhanid hoards?", *Actes du 8e Congrès Internationale Numismatique, 1973*, 1976, 513–25.

Fine, John V.R., Jr., *The Later Medieval Balkans*, Ann Arbor, 198#.

Flemming, Barbara, "The reign of Murad II: a survey (I)" *Anatolica*, xx (1994), 249–67.

Heywood, Colin, "A mid-fifteenth century hoard II: the Ottoman component". Unpublished paper read at a meeting of the Royal Numismatic Society on 18 February 1986, *Corrections to "824/'8224' = 1421 (etc.)"*, Wandover, 1998 (privately printed).

———, "Muṣṭafā Čelebi. Düzme", *EI²*, vii, 710–2.

———, "824/'8224' = 1421: the 'False' (Düzme) Muṣṭafā and his ephemeral coinage", *Mélanges Sahillioglu*, Zaghouan [Tunisia], 1997, ii, 159–75.

Hinz, Walther, "Hyperper und Asper. Zur vorosmanischen Währungskunde", *Der Islam*, xxxix (1964), 79–89.

Iliescu, O., "Un trésor d'aspres turcs du XVe siècle trouvé probablement en Moldavie", *Studia et Acta Orientalia*, v–vi (1967), 267–85.

Imber, Colin, *The Ottoman Empire 1300–1481*, Istanbul, 1990.

Inalcık, Halil, *Fatih devri üzerinde tetkiler ve vesikalar*, i, Ankara, 1954.

Islâm Ansiklopedisi, 13 vols., Istanbul, 19##–86.

Jireček, C.J., *Die Heerstrasse zwischen Belgrad und Constantinopel*, Prague, 1877.

Lindner, Rudi Paul, "Hordes and hoards in late Saljūq Anatolia", in *The Art of the Saljūqs in Iran and Anatolia. Proceedings of a Symposium held in Edinburgh in 1982*, ed. R. Hillenbrand, Costa Mesa, 1994, 278–85.

———, *Nomads and Ottomans in medieval Anatolia*, Bloomington, Ind., 1983.

Lowick, Nicholas, "A hoard of Seljuq dirhams", *Spink's Numismatic Circular*, June 1970, 248–50, reprinted in idem, *Coinage and History of the Islamic World*, London: 1990, §VII, 1–6 (repaginated).

———, "An early tenth-century hoard from Isfahan", *NC*, 7th ser., xv (1975), 110–54, reprinted in idem, *Islamic Coins and Trade in the Medieval World*, London, 1990, §5.

———, *Coinage and History of the Islamic World*, London, 1990.

MacKenzie, K.M., "Akches of Mehemmed II (2nd reign): a hoard of the first issue dated 855", *Numismatic Circular*, lxxxiv (1976), 230–2.
Ménage, V.L., "The "Annals of Murād II'", *BSOAS*, xxxix/3 (1976), 570–84.
———, "Corlu", *EI*², i, 62.
Refik, Ahmed, *Osmanli devrinde Türkiye madenleri*, Istanbul, 1931.
Schaendlinger, Anton C., *Osmanische Numismatik von den Anfängen des Osmanischen Reiches bis zu seiner Auflösung 1922*, Braunschweig, 1973.
Vakalopoulos, A., "Les limites de l'empire byzantin depuis la fin du XIVᵉ siècle jusqu'à sa chute (1453)", *Byzantinische Zeitschrift*, lv (1962), 56–65.
Zachariadou, Elizabeth A., "Lauro Quirini and the Turkish sandjaks (ca. 1430)", in *Raiyyet Rüsûmu. Essays presented to Halil Inalcık*, 2 vols. (= *Journal of Turkish Studies*, x–xi), Harvard, 1986–7, ii, 239–47.

THE ARCHITECTURE OF THE GHAZNAVIDS AND GHURIDS*

Robert Hillenbrand

The achievement of the Ghaznavids and Ghurids is an unjustly neglected chapter in the history of medieval Iranian architecture. Several factors have conspired to bring this about. One is the widely dispersed distribution of the monuments themselves. The accidents of post-medieval history have parcelled out the surviving buildings of the once-monolithic Ghaznavid empire among no less than six modern sovereign states: Iran, Uzbekistan, Turkmenistan, Afghanistan, Pakistan and India.[1] Even within these countries the monuments are scattered far and wide. There is not a single cluster of them. No Ghaznavid or Ghurid equivalent of Merv, Jerusalem or Tlemcen, let alone Isfahan or Cairo, can be visited today. Thus the buildings have to be seen *seriatim*, and this militates against a successful conspectus of the whole school.

Moreover—and this is a second limiting factor—these buildings are more than just dispersed; even by Middle Eastern standards many of them are quite unusually remote, and it is a reasonable guess that no-one in the past century has seen more than two-thirds of the buildings mentioned in this article. Some have been destroyed or seriously damaged in recent times; others until the last decade have been accessible only to Soviet citizens; yet others, notably a series of mausolea in Sind and western Pakistan, have only very recently been brought to scholarly notice.[2] All this combines to create a somewhat insecure foundation for a survey of this important school of architecture, and it helps to explain why no serious attempt

---

* My warmest thanks go to Bernard O'Kane for giving me unlimited access to his photographic archives; all the black and white plates are from his negatives.

[1] For the general historical background, see Bosworth, *Ghaznavids*; Bosworth, *Later Ghaznavids*; Bosworth, "Ghurids", 1099–1104.

[2] For a treatment of one such group see Rahman, *Islamic Architecture of Pakistan*, 22 and pls. 5–9 and the article in this volume by Heinz Gaube entitled "Die Mausoleen-Gruppe in Adheri, NW-Pakistan". See also Edwards, *Genesis*, and a detailed study of Ghurid architecture in Pakistan currently being prepared by Dr F.B. Flood.

along these lines has yet been made. The vagaries of medieval politics also make it difficult to state positively that a given building on the fringes of Ghaznavid or Ghurid control was indeed produced under the patronage of either dynasty. For that reason the present article focuses on buildings in Afghanistan, even though contemporary buildings in Iran (such as Zuzan)[3] and Central Asia (such as Talkhatan Baba, Safid Buland, Uzgend and Mashhad-i Misriyan)[4] are sometimes very closely related to them. The justification for this reduction in scope is partly that this method best allows an accurate definition of the characteristic Ghaznavid and Ghurid style, and partly because the architecture of what is now Afghanistan—the area from which all the illustrations in this article are drawn—developed on the whole along slightly different lines, perhaps because of the pagan and Indian orientation of the area in the 11th to 13th centuries.

A third constraining factor lies in the nature of the scholarly attention that these buildings have received. By and large the published accounts of them are skimpy. General accounts have been limited on the whole to entries in encyclopaedias[5] or to review articles.[6] For many years Ghaznavid architecture was seriously misunderstood because the 12th-century tower or minaret of Bahramshah at Ghazna (colour pl. 1) was erroneously believed to date from the time of Mahmud, that is to say the early 11th century.[7] This led to its being regarded as a benchmark for baked brick decoration, a belief which seriously distorted the chronology of that type of decoration in the Iranian world. The information that is still missing, and is badly needed, includes serious architectural analyses of the minaret at Dawlatabad,[8] (colour pls. 2–3) the *madrasas* at Zuzan and Shah-i Mashhad,[9] the *iwan* at Pishvaran,[10] the great arch at Bust,[11] (colour pl. 4) the

---

[3] See Blair, "Zuzan", 75–91 and Godard, "Khorasan", 113–25. The site has now been comprehensively studied by Dr C. Adle.

[4] See respectively Pugachenkova, *Puti*, 248–56; Cohn-Wiener, "A Turanic Monument", 88–91; Cohn-Wiener, *Turan*, pls. X–XVI; and Pugachenkova, *Puti*, 260–6.

[5] For example, Bombaci, "Ghaznevid Art", 399–412; Sourdel-Thomine, "Ghaznavids", 1053–5.

[6] Sourdel-Thomine, "L'art ġuride", 273–80.

[7] This mistake was corrected by J. Sourdel-Thomine ("Deux minarets", 116).

[8] Meanwhile, see Sourdel-Thomine, "Deux minarets", 122–9.

[9] Casimir and Glatzer, "Šah-i Mašhad", 53–68; Barry, *Colour and Symbolism*, 32 and 48–9.

[10] Hill and Grabar, *Islamic Architecture*, pl. 608.

[11] Pope, "Qal'a-i-Bist", 7–11; Hill and Grabar, *Islamic Architecture*, pls. 152–4; Shokoohy, *Studies*, 93–5 and pls. 140–6 (pls. 144–6 show the arch under reconstruction);

buildings at Chisht (still seriously under-studied given their major importance, and their function has yet to be established; hence their identification here as mausolea is only tentative),[12] the so-called mausoleum of Khalid b. al-Walid near Multan,[13] perhaps a Ghaznavid *ribat*,[14] and the lesser mausolea of Rahimyar Khan, Adam Wahan and Muhammad b. Harun at Bela.[14] The shrines at Sar-i Pul are also still insufficiently known.[15] Detailed palaeographical analyses of the inscriptions found on most of these monuments (and especially of the minaret of Jam), including comparative tables of the Kufic alphabets used, are needed so that one of the distinctive achievements of this school of architecture can stand out in its full glory. The attention lavished on the excavations and indeed on the whole site of Ghazna[16] (fig. 1) and Lashkar-i Bazar[17] is no substitute for such studies, and indeed emphasises the uneven rate of publication of Ghaznavid and Ghurid architecture. The equally characteristic terracotta ornament displayed by so many of these monuments well deserves a separate monograph too.

To the disadvantages of inaccessibility and inadequate publication must be added a still more serious obstacle: the relative paucity of surviving monuments. Successive Mongol invasions devastated the area; sanguinary wars between the Ghaznavids and Ghurids wrecked the capital cities of both dynasties. The inhospitable mountainous terrain of Afghanistan meant that it never had more than a fraction of the arable land available in Iran, and that the area was therefore always rather thinly populated. So there would never have been the quantity of medieval monuments erected in Iran. The choice of

Sourdel-Thomine, *Lashkar-i Bazar*, 63–8; Schlumberger and Sourdel-Thomine, *Lashkar-i Bazar. Planches*, pls. 42d, e, 43–6; Allen, "Notes", 59–60, 67.

[12] Niedermayer and Diez, *Afghanistan*, 62 and pls. 182–4; Maricq and Wiet, *Djam*, 69–70, pls. VIII–IX; Hill and Grabar, *Islamic Architecture*, pls. 143–4; Melikian-Chirvani, "Herat", pl. 9; Samizay, *Islamic Architecture*, 16–19; Ball, *Gazetteer*, 76, with a detailed description by M. Le Berre and further references); Blair, "Zuzan", 81–2 and pls. 11–13, 15.

[13] Actually built by ʿAli b. Karmakh; see Edwards, "Ribat", 86.

[14] Khan, "Mausoleum", 276.

[15] Bivar, "Seljuqid *ziyarats*", 57–63; Shokoohy, *Studies*, 111–18; Shokoohy, "Shrine", 306–14.

[16] Bombaci, "Excavations at Ghazni", 3–22, Scerrato, "The first two excavation campaigns", 23–55.

[17] Schlumberger, *Lashkar-i Bazar* and Sourdel-Thomine, *Lashkar-i Bazar*, to be read in conjunction with Allen, "Notes on Bust", 55–68; "Notes on Bust (Continued)", 57–66; and "Notes 1990", 23–30.

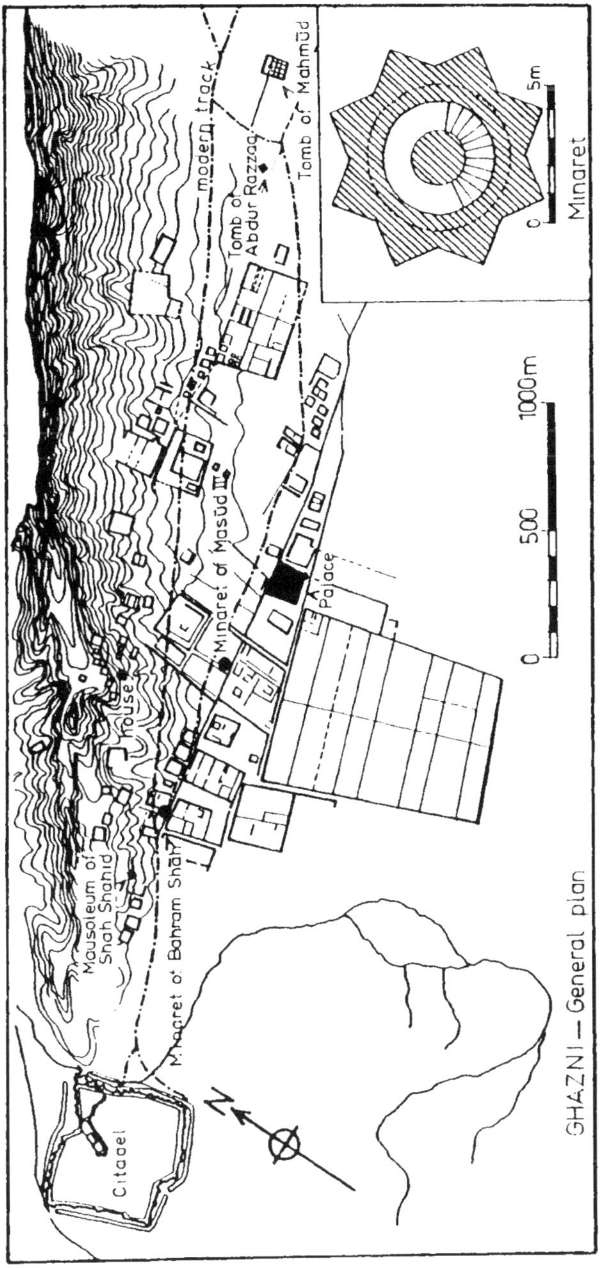

Fig. 1 Ghazna: site plan (after Ball)

Herat as the later Timurid capital must have condemned many an earlier building there to destruction. The very limited number of Ghaznavid and Ghurid buildings thus imparts to each of the survivals an evidential value which it ought not really to possess; as a group, these monuments cannot well support the weight of the generalisations they are made to bear.

Finally, and most seriously of all in practical terms, very little indeed of Ghaznavid and Ghurid architecture survives in a relatively good state of preservation. The fragments that do remain are a heartbreaking index of the phenomenal quality of that which has gone—and gone, moreover, in one genre after another, as in the Herat *jamiʿ*,[18] the Shah-i Mashhad *madrasa*, or the throne-rooms of Ghazna and Lashkar-i Bazar. The disappearance of adjoining buildings makes it hard fully to grasp the original physical context of the arch at Bust or the minarets of Jam,[19] Ghazna[20] and Dawlatabad—to say nothing of the closely related buildings put up by other dynasties, like those at Zuzan and Abivard.[21]

The rehearsal of these difficulties, however tedious, is indispensable in clearing the ground for a new survey of the material. In their essentials, Ghaznavid and Ghurid monuments must of course be viewed as an integral part of the architecture of the Iranian world in the continuum which stretched in time from the 10th to the early 13th century and in space from Iraq to the plains of Hindustan and the eastern steppes of Central Asia. The common denominator of this style was the use of baked brick as the medium of construction and of brick or terra cotta as the principal means of external decoration. For the sake of convenience this style is usually termed Saljuq, but that is really too crude a term. "Saljuq" might be construed to imply the inclusion of Syria and Anatolia, since these areas were under the political hegemony of the Saljuq dynasty; yet the building material in these areas was stone, and their monuments for that reason alone do not belong with those of the Iranian world. This is not the only reason why "Saljuq" is an inadequate term in

---

[18] Hill and Grabar, *Islamic Architecture*, pl. E; Melikian-Chirvani, "Herat", 322–7; Barry, *Colour and Symbolism*, 46–7.

[19] Maricq and Wiet, *Djam*, 15–29; Moline, "Minaret of Ǧam", 131–48.

[20] Sourdel-Thomine, "Deux minarets", 110–21; Hill and Grabar, *Islamic Architecture*, pl. 145 (a photograph of the minaret of Masʿud III when its upper cylindrical shaft was still standing); Pinder-Wilson, "Minaret", 89–102.

[21] Pugachenkova, *Puti*, 259–61.

this context; it is also misleading as a political label. In Iraq from the later 12th century power lay with the renascent ʿAbbasid caliphate; beyond the Oxus, and sometimes well to the south of it, lay the empire of the Khwarizmshahs; and the border between Ghaznavid and Ghurid territory and that of the Saljuqs was constantly changing. Smaller polities, such as that of the Qara Khitai in the Kirman region, also claimed independence. Moreover, within Iran itself the architectural style of the period can be subdivided into several architectural schools—those of Rayy, Qazvin, Azarbayjan, Kashan, Isfahan, the south-east, and Khurasan, to mention only the major groupings. Ghaznavid and Ghurid architecture, like that of Iraq or Central Asia, is best interpreted as one of these provincial schools—though like these two examples it had its own individual quality that set it apart from the Iranian schools. Yet this is no more than a matter of nuance. Even when it was translated into stone at Delhi,[22] Ajmir[23] and elsewhere, it retained the impress of Iranian modes with remarkable fidelity.

This distinct, individual quality of Ghaznavid and Ghurid architecture is less a matter of one or two trademarks than the cumulative effect of several characteristics which are relatively minor in themselves. They include new types of glazed tilework, an unequalled intensity in the use of terracotta, unusual arch profiles, a significant and unheralded emphasis on stone, especially marble, quantities of panegyric inscriptions, massive scale, and various experimental Kufic and cursive scripts whose ornateness consistently exceeds anything known in the rest of Iran in the Saljuq period. Taken all together, these features—many of them innovations at the time—mark Ghaznavid and Ghurid architecture as one of the two or three most progressive schools in the Iranian world in the 11th to 13th centuries, at least on a par with the regional styles of Isfahan and Khurasan. In some areas, notably terracotta and epigraphic ornament, this school was in the vanguard of change, bringing these types of architectural decoration to a pitch of technical mastery never to be excelled.

Although Ghaznavid and Ghurid monuments are few in number, enough of them survive to permit a definition of this school. There is some hope, too, that excavations and discoveries in the remoter reaches of Afghanistan will eventually allow further refinement of its

[22] Marshall, "Monuments", 575–9; Brown, *Indian Architecture*, 9–12.
[23] M.W. Meister, "Mosque", 57–63; Hillenbrand, "Political Symbolism", 105–17.

features. These may be summarised under the following heads: building types, structural forms, materials, epigraphy and decoration. It will emerge that the latter category offers the best hopes of defining the hallmarks of the architecture of Afghanistan between 1050 and 1250.

Building types In general the types correspond to those familiar in other parts of the contemporary eastern Islamic world. Nevertheless, the distribution of those types is decisively different, and some familiar genres—like caravansarais—are altogether absent. Most striking of all is the relative rarity of the two building types which are dominant to the west: mosques and mausolea. Some half-dozen important mosques[24] and the same number of major mausolea[25] are known to date. Among the mosques, the diminutive example of Larwand (fig. 6) is especially interesting on account of its pronounced Indian flavour (seen in its dressed stone construction and decorative motifs),[26]

---

[24] Others are known only from excavation (and, occasionally, literary sources too: cf. the celebrated mosque at Ghazni known as "the Bride of Heaven": Bombaci, "La 'Sposa del Cielo'", 21–34), or remain only in a very ruinous condition, such as the mosques at Shahr-i Ghulghula (figs. 2–3; cf. Ball, *Gazetteer*, 244 and 466).

[25] These are the two examples at Sar-i Pul, the Ghurid mausoleum at Herat, the mausolea of Salar Khalil/Baba Hatim, Shahzada Sarbarz at Bust, and those of Baba Rushnai (fig. 4) and Abu Huraira (fig. 5), near Balkh and Dawlatabad respectively (for these last two, see Pugachenkova, "Balkh area", 31–3 and figs. 1–5). To these might be added an anonymous structure whose *mihrab* has been published by Melikian-Chirvani, "Remarques", 82–3 and figure 24; the Imam Sahib *ziyarat* (Melikian-Chirvani, "Remarques", 80–2, figure 21). Other possibilities include the *ziyarat* known as Sultan Mas'ud at Ghazna (Galdieri, *Conservation*, 15–21, figs. 13–15 and pls. 5–7) and conceivably even the Ziyarat Hawja Laikwar, also at Ghazna (Galdieri, *Conservation*, 21–2, figs. 16–17 and pls. 12–14). The problem with these smaller mausolea in the area of Ghazna is that it is hard to distinguish Ghaznavid or Ghurid brickwork from archaising but simplified and considerably later versions of it. A good example of that archaising style, again in the Ghazna area, is the joint tomb of Ulugh Beg Miranshah and 'Abd al-Razzaq, datable (on grounds other than its brickwork) around 1500. For relevant examples of its brickwork, see Galdieri, *Conservation*, pls. 9 and 10; this issue is not dealt with in the articles on this building by J.D. Hoag: "The Tomb of Ulugh Begh and Abdu Razzaq at Ghazni, a model for the Taj Mahal", *Journal of the Society for Architectural Historians* 27 (1968), 234–48; "The Tomb of Ulugh Beg and Abdu Rassaq at Ghazni, a prototype for the Taj Mahal", in M.Y. Kiani and A. Tajvidi, *The Memorial Volume of the International Congress of Iranian Art & Archaeology. Tehran—Isfahan—Shiraz 11th–18th April 1968* II (Tehran, 1972), 102–7.

[26] For initial reports see Klimburg, "Afghanistan", 34; Klimburg, "Blick", 40–50; Klimburg, "Report", 16–19. The major publication is that by Scarcia and Taddei, "Masjid-i Sangi", 89–108.

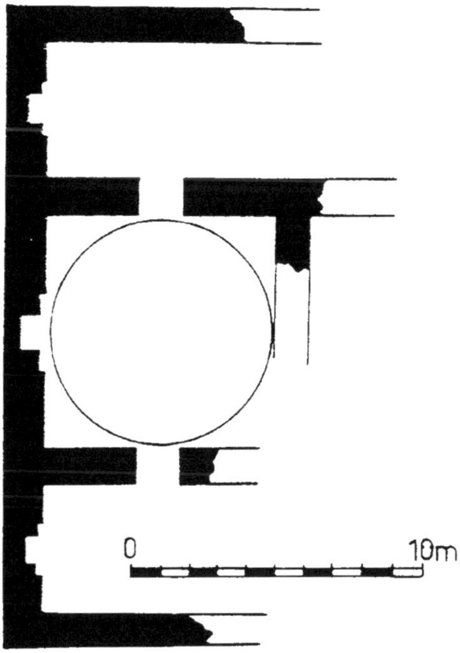

Fig. 2 Shahr-i Ghulghula, mosque: plan (after Ball)

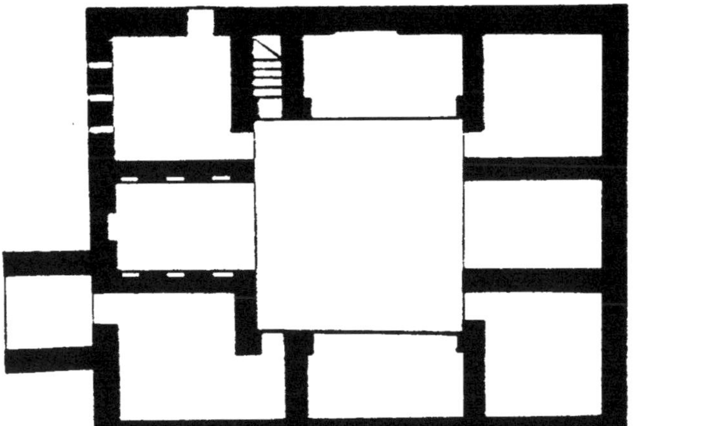

Fig. 3 Shahr-i Ghulghula, mosque: plan (after Ball)

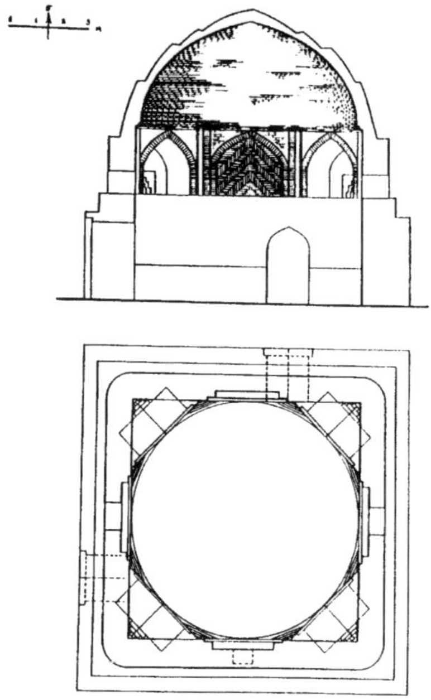

Fig. 4 Mausoleum of Baba Rushnai: plan and section (after Pugachenkova)

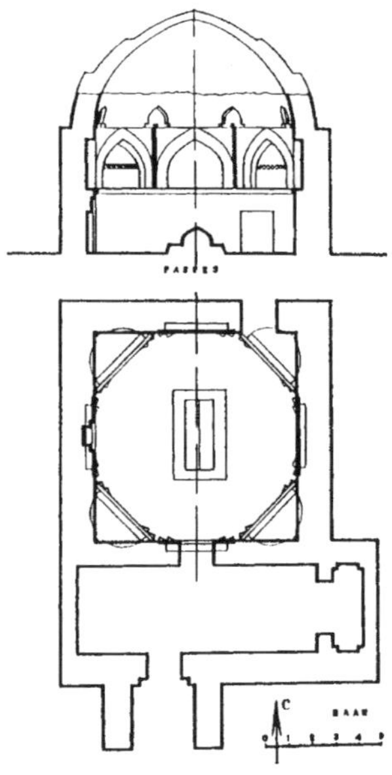

Fig. 5 Mausoleum of Abu Huraira: plan and section (after Pugachenkova)

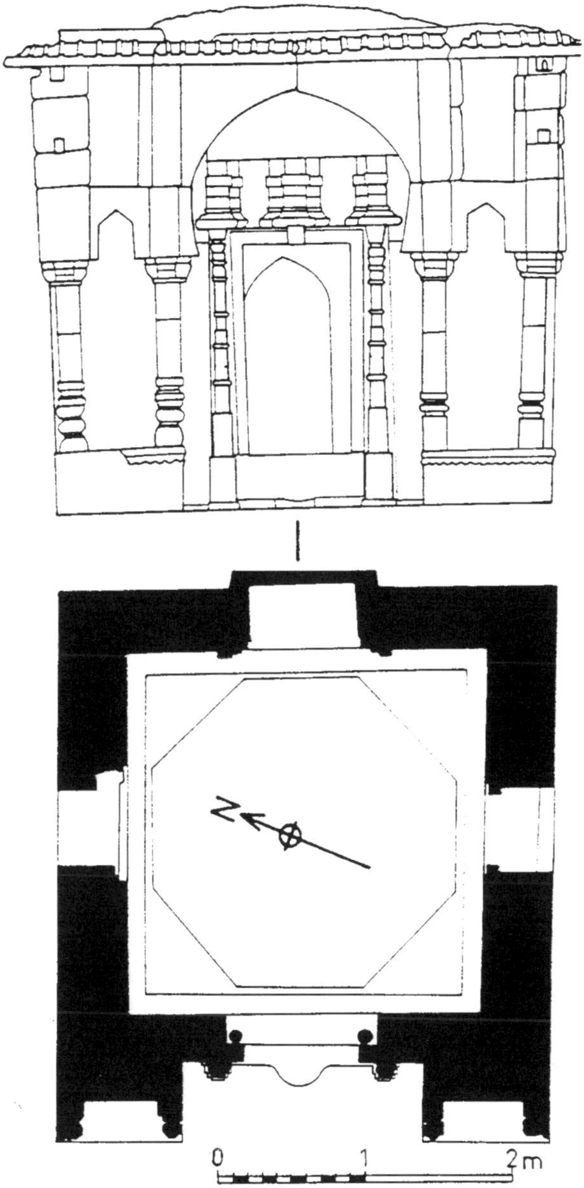

Fig. 6 Larwand, mosque: plan and elevation (after Ball)

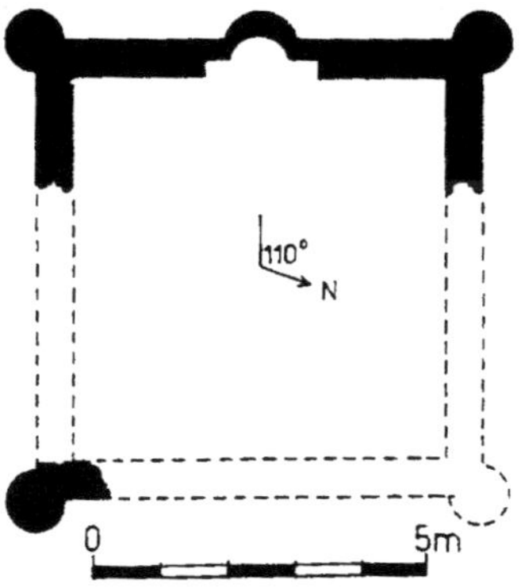

Fig. 7 Darra-yi Shakh: plan (after Ball)

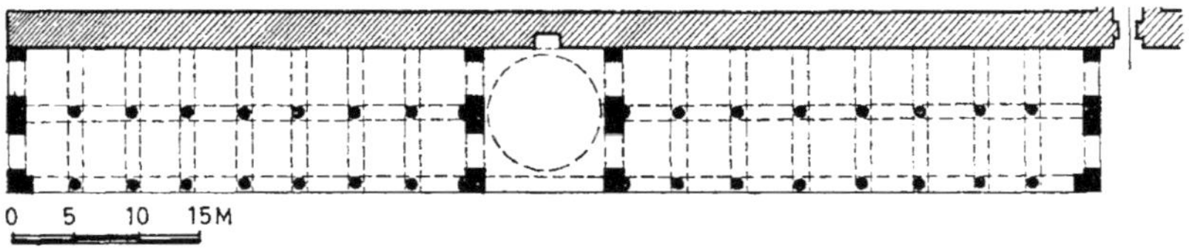

Fig. 8 Lashkar-i Bazar, palace mosque: plan (after Aslanapa)

that of Darra-yi Shakh[27] for its plan (fig. 7), fortified like a *ribat*, while the excavated mosque at Lashkar-i Bazar exhibits a novel combination of a domed chamber with an oblong multi-vaulted sanctuary and apparently no courtyard (fig. 8).[28] Pride of place, however, must go to the Friday Mosque at Herat,[29] whose fabric before its thorough-going restoration, which occurred in 1944 (fig. 9), included substantial areas of Ghurid work, with typically 12th-century four-centered arches carried on massive piers, often with a slight return at springing level. Before that reconstruction[30] (fig. 10) it had four *iwans*, aligned to the cardinal points, and 365 vaults—a circumstance which

[27] Pinder-Wilson, "Mihrab", 91.

[28] Schlumberger and Sourdel-Thomine, *Lashkar-i Bazar. Planches*, pl. 23; Schlumberger, *Lashkar-i Bazar*, 67–9. Professor Sourdel-Thomine believes this mosque to be Ghurid (*Lashkar-i Bazar*, 57).

[29] Klimburg ("Afghanistan", 32) calls this the only mosque in Afghanistan worth mentioning and seeing. The fullest account of its Ghurid parts is that of Melikian-Chirvani, "Herat", 322–7, which cites the major earlier discussions.

[30] Stuckert, "Baubestand", 3–5.

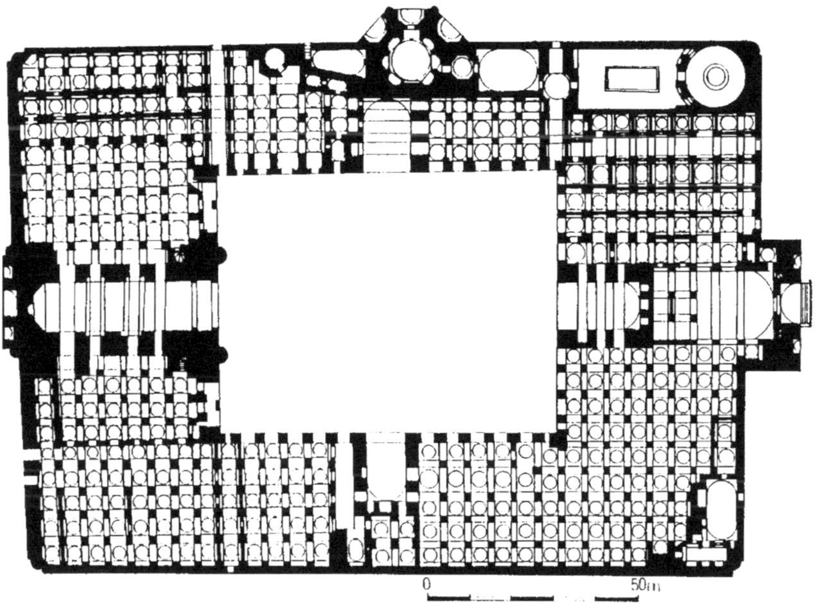

Fig. 9 Herat, Friday Mosque: plan after the 1944 reconstruction (after Ball)

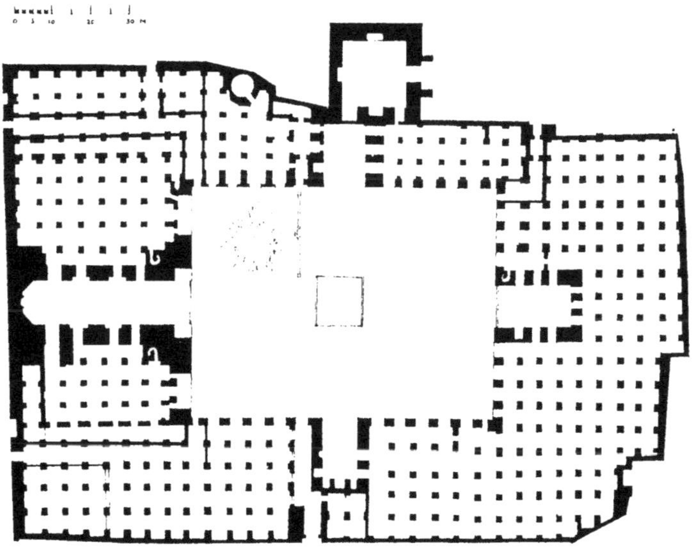

Fig. 10 Herat, Friday Mosque: plan before the 1944 reconstruction (after Stuckert)

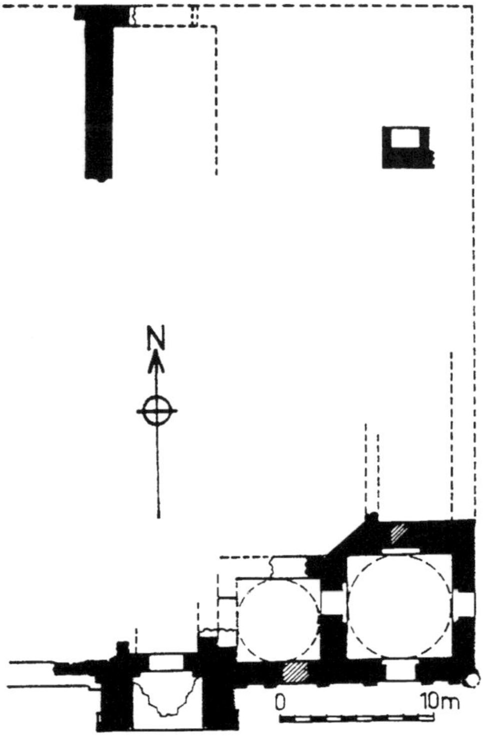

Fig. 11 Shah-i Mashhad, *madrasa*: plan (after Ball)

makes it tempting to suggest that the original figure was 360 and that a symbolic interpretation of time and space was intended here.

The principal and perhaps the only *madrasa* of the period in Afghanistan, that of Shah-i Mashhad, is beyond doubt the most splendid example in the Iranian world before the Timurid period (fig. 11).[31] Situated in Badghis (Gargistan) in north-western Afghanistan, on a site which was probably always remote, and built by an unnamed lady in 571/1175–6, it is of substantial size (44 × 41 m) and though the plan in its entirety has not been established by excavation it seems possible, judging by the surviving remains, that there was a substantial northern *iwan* as well as one to the south, which on the analogy of contemporary mosques and caravansarais in the Iranian world suggests that the layout might have followed the 4-*iwan* plan.

[31] See n. 9 above and Blair, "Zuzan", 81.

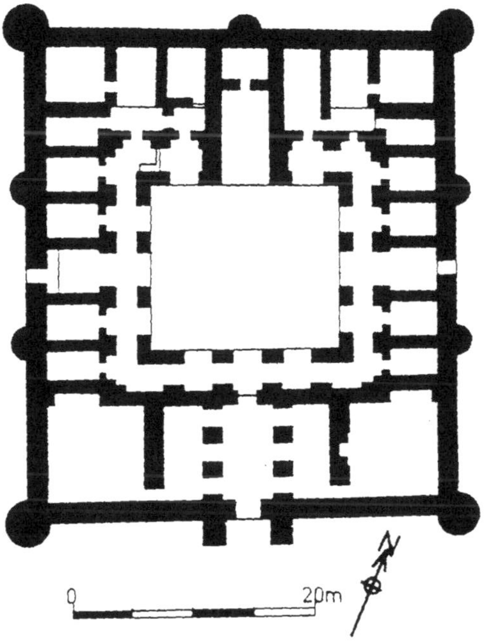

Fig. 12 Danistama: plan (after Ball)

Of special interest functionally is the pair of domed chambers in the south-east corner of the building, which seem to be precursors of the lecture room and *jamaʿat khana* found on either side of the main portal in later *madrasas* like Khargird.[32] Similarly, the bevelled exterior north-west corner of the larger domed chamber finds a ready parallel in Khargird, while the *qibla*-oriented niche on the east side of the main portal (presumably a *mihrab* for the use of travellers) recalls a similar feature at Ribat-i Sharaf.[33] Presumably rooms for students encircled the courtyard. The enigmatic building at Danistama,[34] whose environs include similar buildings though in a more ruined state,[35] might also be a *madrasa*; it too has the emphasis on major public rooms to the right and left of the entrance portal (fig. 12).

[32] O'Kane, "Khargird", 85–6 and fig. 1.
[33] Godard, "Khorasan", 26.
[34] Le Berre, "Danestama", 44–50.
[35] Le Berre, "Danestama", 44.

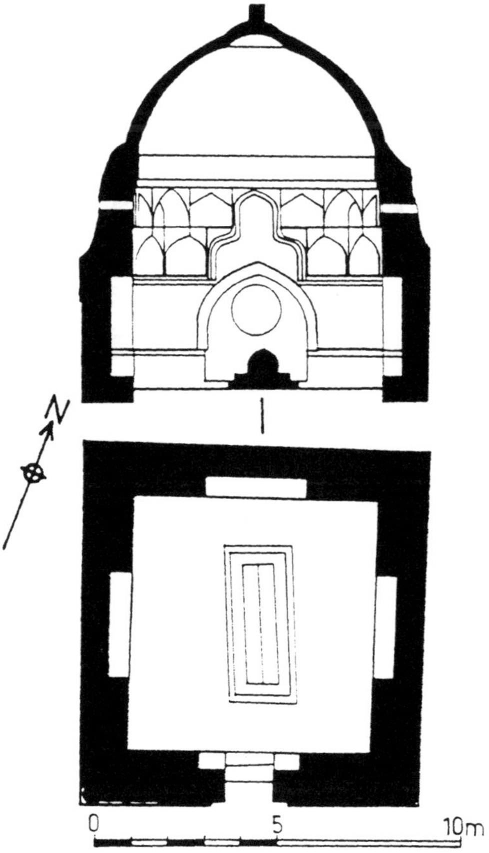

Fig. 13 Mausoleum of Salar Khalil (Baba Hatim): plan and section (after Ball)

Among mausolea the tomb of Salar Khalil, (fig. 13) known as Baba Hatim, is of a type standard in Central Asia (e.g. Safid Buland): a domed square with an exterior plain on three sides but highlighted on the fourth by a *pishtaq* framed by a magnificent Kufic inscription. The two mausolea at Chisht fall into the same general category, although their absolute height is greater and their proportions more slender and refined. One is dated, in Persian, to 562/1167[36] and the other is also probably of the later 12th century. More unusual is the

[36] Blair, "Zuzan", 81–2.

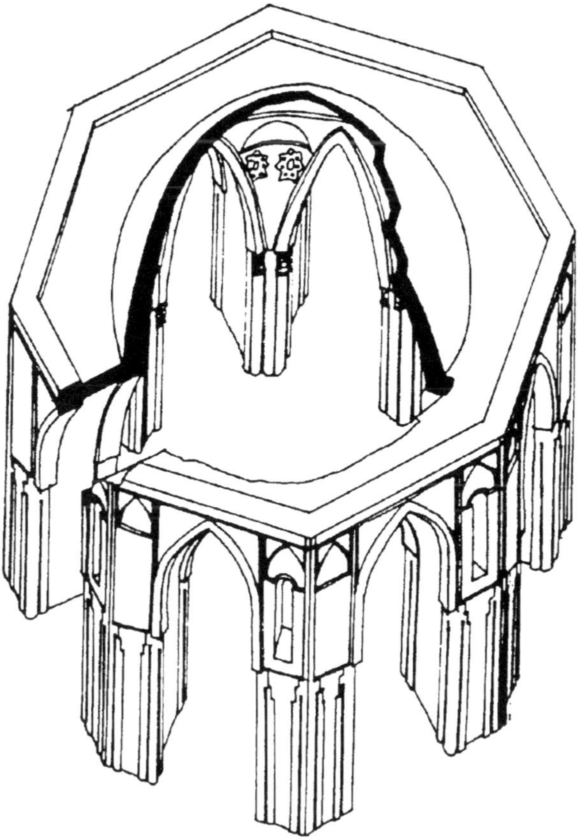

Fig. 14 Bust, mausoleum of Shahzada Sarbaz: three-dimensional view (after Hillenbrand)

undated mausoleum at Bust, known as Shahzada Sarbaz,[37] (fig. 14 and pl. 1) a curious squat open-plan octagon, essentially a canopy tomb—a rather rare type in Iranian lands, though parallels exist at Samiran, Qumm and elsewhere. The brickwork technique used on the interior of its dome (pl. 2) is very close to that of the minaret of Khwaja Siyah Push (see below). Especially notable in this tomb are the wedge-shaped piers which bear the dome: each has two faces

[37] Crane, "Anonymous tomb", 241–6; Hill and Grabar, Islamic Architecture, pls. 155–60; Shokoohy, *Studies*, 101–5.

Pl. 1. Bust, mausoleum of Shahzada Sarbaz: exterior.

Pl. 2. Bust, mausoleum of Shahzada Sarbaz: interior.

set at 45 degrees to each other, and these broaden dramatically to the exterior so that the pier seems spreadeagled (pl. 3). The lavish articulation of these piers, both externally and internally, by reveals and polygonal engaged columns (pls. 2 and 4) recalls the zone of transition in the Ghurid mausoleum at Herat (see below). The original form of the undated shrine of Imam-i Kalan at Sar-i Pul[38] (fig. 15) was probably a domed square with rounded buttresses at the corners and axial openings on three sides; the entasis of the walls and an arcaded gallery with corner finials made the link with the Samanid tomb at Bukhara still closer. The original southern portal probably exhibited a well-developed portal, now lost in the mass of the extra chamber added in a later building campaign.

Among the other building types recorded in this school special attention should be drawn to the great arch at Bust (colour pl. 4), a vastly enlarged version of the Du Baradar[39] near Ribat-i Sharaf; it seems to have had a ceremonial and indeed propaganda function, fronting as it did a vast empty *maidan* at the foot of the citadel which dominates the whole extensive medieval site, and may be ascribed to Ghurid patronage in the later 12th century. Its imposing span and height (pl. 5) would have made a comparison with Ctesiphon well-nigh mandatory, while the presence of decoration on both its front and rear sides clearly indicates that it was free-standing. Here, then, is an authentic Islamic reworking of the Roman triumphal arch theme. Apparently it was the third—and most splendid?—of the gates which led to the royal citadel (itself well preserved but neither planned nor described in detail),[40] so that it would have channelled traffic in such a way as to emphasise royal power. Rather less familiar is the *sardab* (sometimes rather confusingly called a well in the scholarly literature) in the citadel at Bust,[41] comprising not only a vaulted structure above ground but, much more significantly, a complex of vaulted underground chambers reaching down more than 20 metres underground and disposed along four levels, with provision ingeniously made for natural lighting and for ventilation (fig. 16). The largest

[38] Shokoohy, "Shrine", 310–12, figs. 4–8.
[39] Clevenger, "Minor monuments", 58 and pls. I–II.
[40] The best guide to date is Allen, "Notes", 55, 58–9 and pl. IV.
[41] Schlumberger, *Lashkar-i Bazar*, 99; Schlumberger and Sourdel-Thomine, *Lashkar-i Bazar. Planches*, pl. 118; Shokoohy, *Studies*, 95–101, pls. 147–61; Allen, "Notes", 59; Ball, *Gazetteer*, 63 (with further references) and 427.

Pl. 3. Bust, mausoleum of Shahzada Sarbaz: interior, spandrel.

Pl. 4. Bust, mausoleum of Shahzada Sarbaz: exterior, corner.

Pl. 5. Bust, arch: view showing base and soffit.

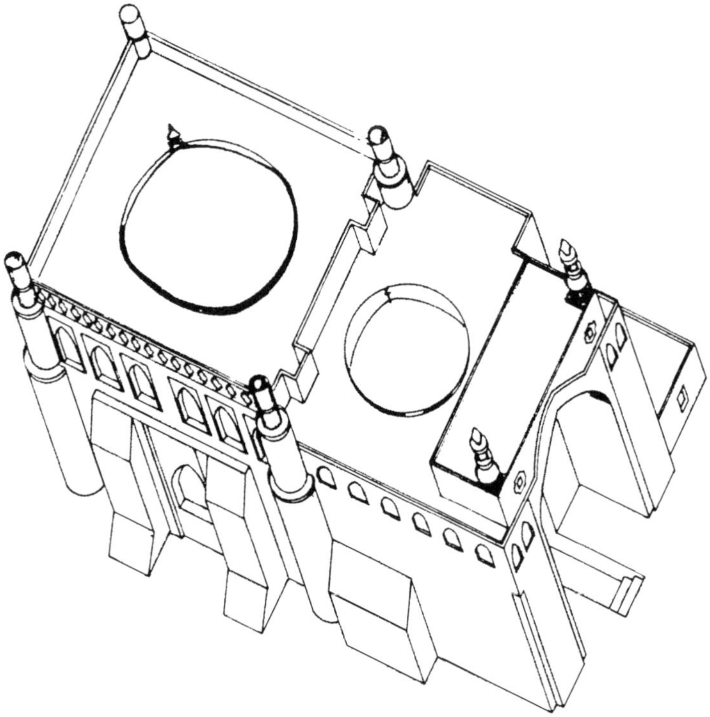

Fig. 15 Sar-i Pul, mausoleum of Imam-i Kalan: three-dimensional view (after Hillenbrand)

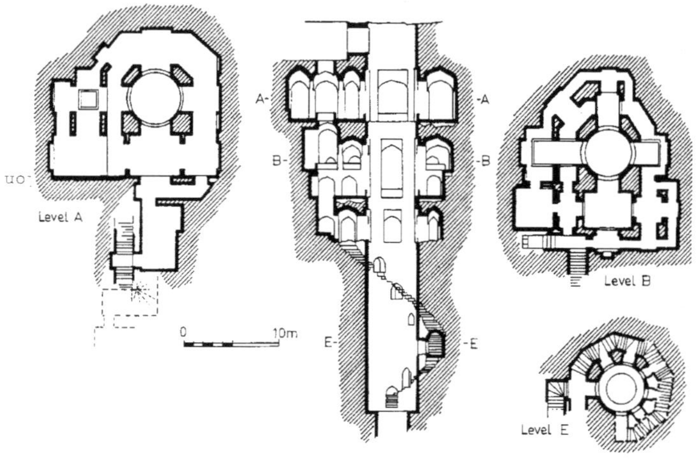

Fig. 16 Bust, *sardab* ("well"): plans and section (after Ball)

chamber on the second level was distinguished by carved stucco decoration, which lends weight to the suggestion that it might have served as a setting for social gatherings; there was no *mihrab* here.

Special importance attaches to the palaces of Lashkar-i Bazar, among which the South (or "Great") Palace, attributed to Mahmud of Ghazna (388–421/998–1030),[42] is outstanding for its scale, its rational organisation and its use of a riverside *iwan*-hall behind the *iwan*-cum-dome chamber combination on the principal axis of the building (fig. 17). It exhibits one of the very earliest developed 4-*iwan* plans in Islamic architecture, to say nothing of individual units within the plan which use 4-*iwan* or 2-*iwan* layouts. Its walls have a painted frieze of attendants, Qur'anic inscriptions (including one describing the enthroned Solomon receiving the Queen of Sheba),[43] and geometric ornament in brick and stucco. Seen as a whole, the South Palace is clearly in the Samarran tradition of a sprawling mud-brick city-palace, though its dimensions (170 × 90 m) are far more diminutive than those of many of its Mesopotamian forebears. Entirely different in concept was the Centre Palace,[44] an extremely compact rectangular structure divided into four equal units, each differently laid out from the next but each with its own courtyard. Axial passages quartered the building and met in a central courtyard. Largely blank walls and corner buttresses hid these subtleties from the exterior, except on the east side where a continuous arcade promised easy access to the interior. It is a marvel of compact planning, not least in the use of a central courtyard—reduced to a well of space in the manner of certain Central Asian *kushk*s—as the focus and pivot of the design (figs. 18–19). Finally, the North Palace[45] consists of at least three independent 4-*iwan* courtyard units squeezed

[42] Schlumberger, *Lashkar-i Bazar*, 19–67; for illustrative material, see Schlumberger and Sourdel-Thomine, *Lashkar-i Bazar. Planches*, pl. 4 (plan) and pls. 5–24, 49, 51–96. See also Allen, "Notes", 61 and "Notes on Bust (Continued)", 57, 59–60, in which he supports Schlumberger's dating to the early 11th century (Schlumberger, "Le palais ghaznevide", 252) as opposed to the Ghurid date proposed by Professor Sourdel-Thomine (*Lashkar-i Bazar*, 7–50). The three articles by Allen—"Notes on Bust", "Notes on Bust (Continued)" and "Notes 1990"—are required reading for any assessment of the sites of Bust and Lashkar-i Bazar, for they constitute a running commentary on the work of Schlumberger and Sourdel-Thomine.

[43] Sourdel-Thomine, *Lashkar-i Bazar*, 31.

[44] Schlumberger, *Lashkar-i Bazar*, 75–80; Schlumberger and Sourdel-Thomine, *Lashkar-i Bazar. Planches*, pls. 25–8; Allen, "Notes", 61–6.

[45] Schlumberger, *Lashkar-i Bazar*, 86; Schlumberger and Sourdel-Thomine, *Lashkar-i Bazar. Planches*, pls. 42–3.

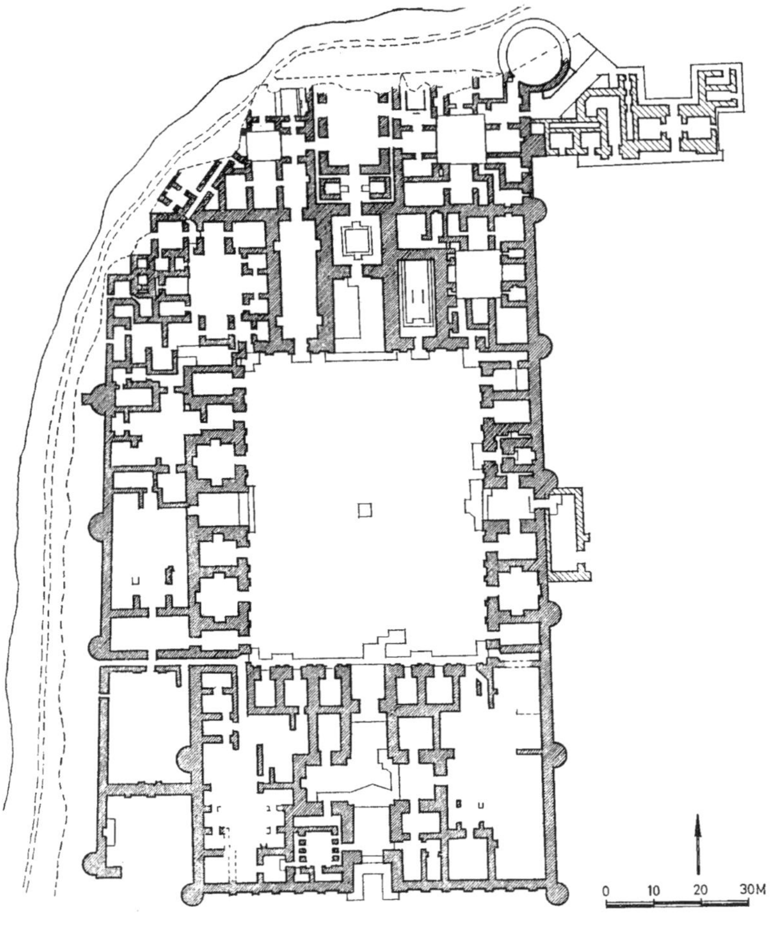

Fig. 17 Lashkar-i Bazar, south palace: plan (after Aslanapa)

Fig. 18 Lashkar-i Bazar, central palace: plan (after Schlumberger)

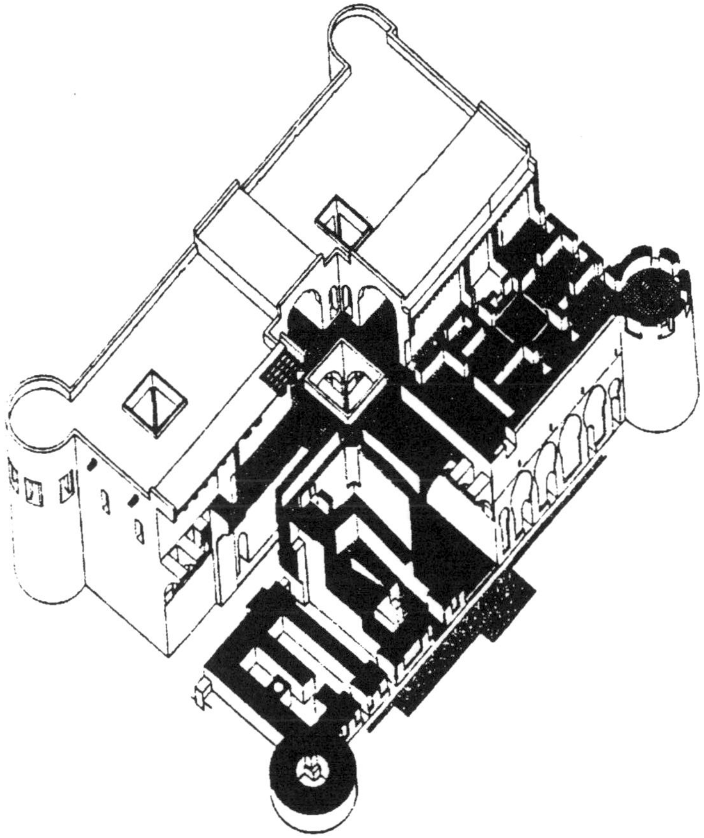

Fig. 19 Lashkar-i Bazar, central palace: three-dimensional view (after Schlumberger)

irregularly into a vast fortified square, with three empty enclosures taking up the remaining space (fig. 20). The emphasis on blind arcades is another reminiscence of Sasanian architecture.[46]

These three major palaces were set amidst gardens of which little but high enclosing walls remain. In addition to these major monuments a whole series of secondary palaces or residences of notables are scattered over the site of Lashkar-i Bazar[47] (fig. 21), some of them 3-storied. A frequently encountered type has rounded corner

[46] Klimburg, "Afghanistan", 33.

[47] Schlumberger, *Lashkar-i Bazar,* 89–94; Schlumberger and Sourdel-Thomine, *Lashkar-i Bazar. Planches,* pls. 111–4; Allen, "Notes 1990", 26–30, pls. IX–XI.

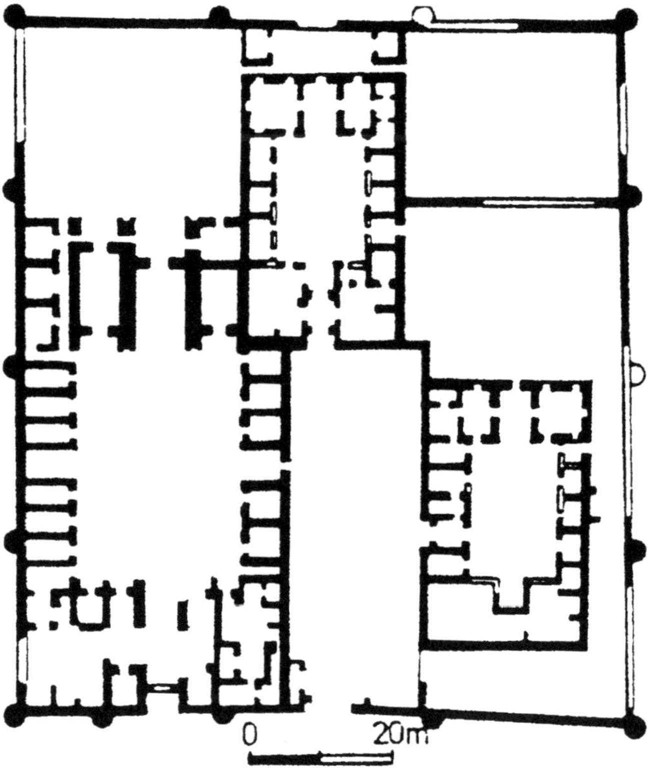

Fig. 20 Lashkar-i Bazar, north palace: plan (after Schlumberger)

bastions and semi-circular buttresses at intervals along the walls, and a 4-*iwan* plan within this rectangle. Others seem more akin to caravansarais in that they consist of a score or more rooms stacked side by side around a courtyard. One of the most elaborate of medieval baths has been found in the south palace,[48] while a pavilion in the great royal garden[49] is remarkably akin to the *dar al-imara* built by Abu Muslim at Merv around 745, as reconstructed by Creswell.[50]

[48] Schlumberger, *Lashkar-i Bazar*, 55–8; Schlumberger and Sourdel-Thomine, *Lashkar-i Bazar. Planches*, pls. 4, 21–2, 84c, 85–6.
[49] Schlumberger, *Lashkar-i Bazar*, 81–4; Schlumberger and Sourdel-Thomine, *Lashkar-i Bazar. Planches*, pls. 36, 104a, 105a, c–d, 106, 107a–d.
[50] Creswell, *Early Muslim Architecture*, 3–4.

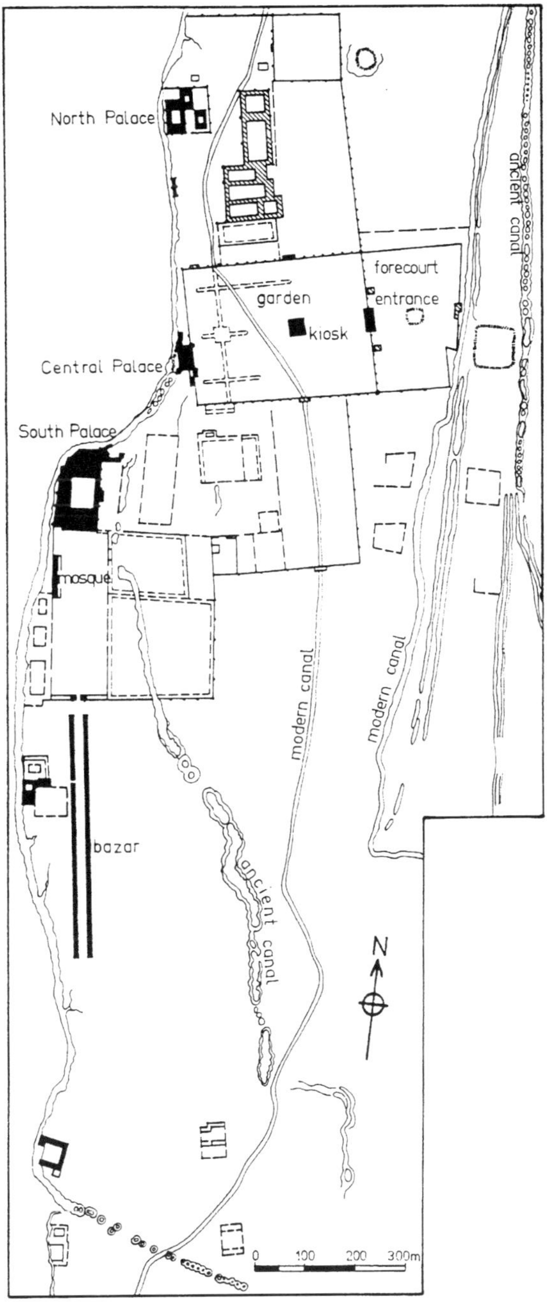

Fig. 21 Lashkar-i Bazar, site plan (after Ball)

All these buildings, like those of Bust, (fig. 22) are scattered over a very wide surface area.

Rather less ambitious than the palaces at Lashkar-i Bazar is the palace of Mas'ud III at Ghazna[51] (fig. 23). That city was the summer palace of the dynasty, as Lashkar-i Bazar was its winter capital. The Ghazna palace comprises an irregular quadrilateral of 158 × 127 m set on a platform and containing a large 4-*iwan* courtyard at the centre of the building entered by a long vestibule and leading at the end of this axis to a square throne room. A lesser but again 4-*iwan* courtyard adjoins it to the west, while an oratory opened off the main courtyard, also to the west. A bazar stretched the entire length of the palace some 25 m to the north of it—a similar feature occurs in front of the south palace at Lashkar-i Bazar, but at right angles rather than parallel to it. The Ghazna bazar stretches for over 500 metres, with the shops tucked away behind a continuous colonnade.

The single most important building type in Afghanistan from 1050 to 1250 (to judge by the rate of survival, perhaps an unreliable yard-stick—the last century has seen the collapse of a major example of the genre at Sirwan)[52] seems to have been the minaret. A remarkable variety of types survives. The most conventional is the example at Dawlatabad (dated 502/1108–9 according to one of its three historical inscriptions),[53] of cylindrical form and garnished by overall baked brick, stucco and terracotta decoration (colour pls. 2–3). Numerous parallels for this type exist in Iran proper.[54] Much more unusual is the undated minaret of Khwaja Siyah Push in Sistan, built of baked brick and with very simple geometric patterning in the same material, with bricks laid in wide bands of alternating horizontal and vertical bond. In form it is unique: its elevation and ground plan alike are alternately flanged and gadrooned.[55] Of related form was the minaret of Mas'ud III at Ghazna, (colour pl. 5 and pl. 6) datable by inscription (pl. 7) to the period 1089–1115; here a stellar lower elevation was crowned by a cylindrical shaft, most of it slightly gadrooned, with narrow vertical guard bands in high relief

[51] Bombaci, "Summary report", 3–22; Scerrato, "Excavation campaigns", 23–55.

[52] For a description of this flanged minaret, see N. de Khanikoff, *Memoire*, 370.

[53] Sourdel-Thomine, "Deux minarets", 123–4.

[54] For a convenient though not exhaustive list of those in the eastern Iranian world, see Sourdel-Thomine, "Deux minarets", 131–6.

[55] Fischer, "Archaeological studies", 95–6, figs. 2–5.

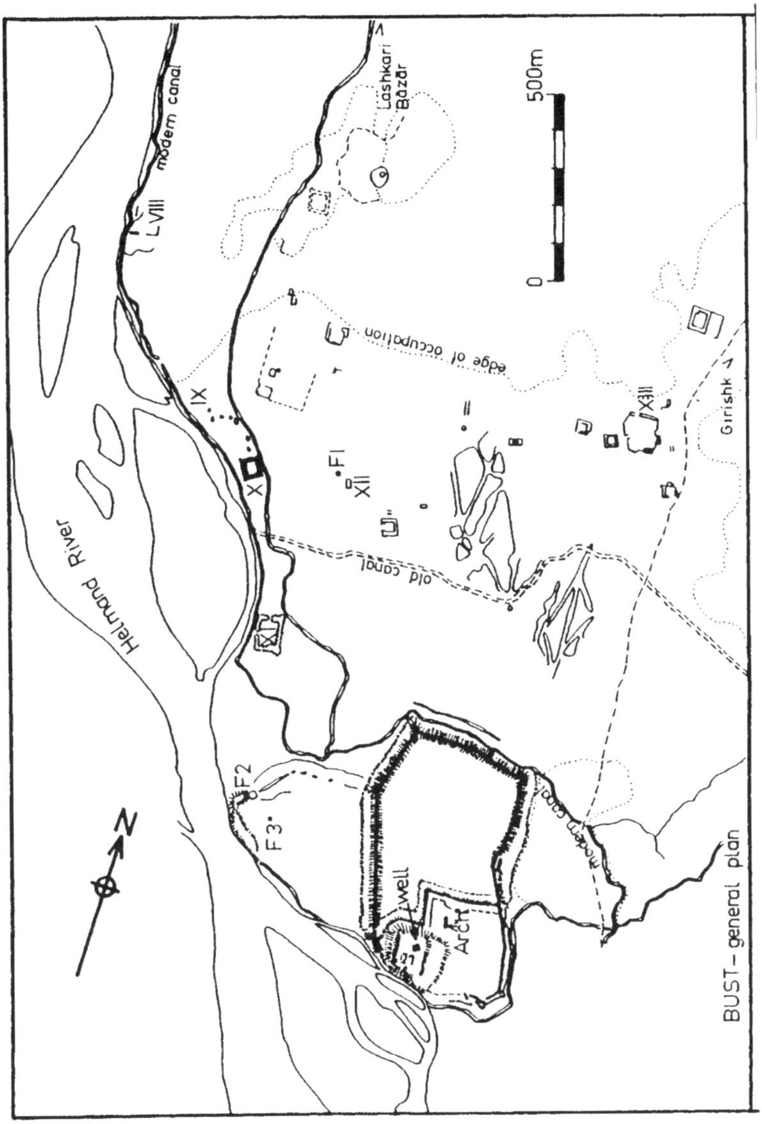

Fig. 22 Bust, site plan (after Ball)

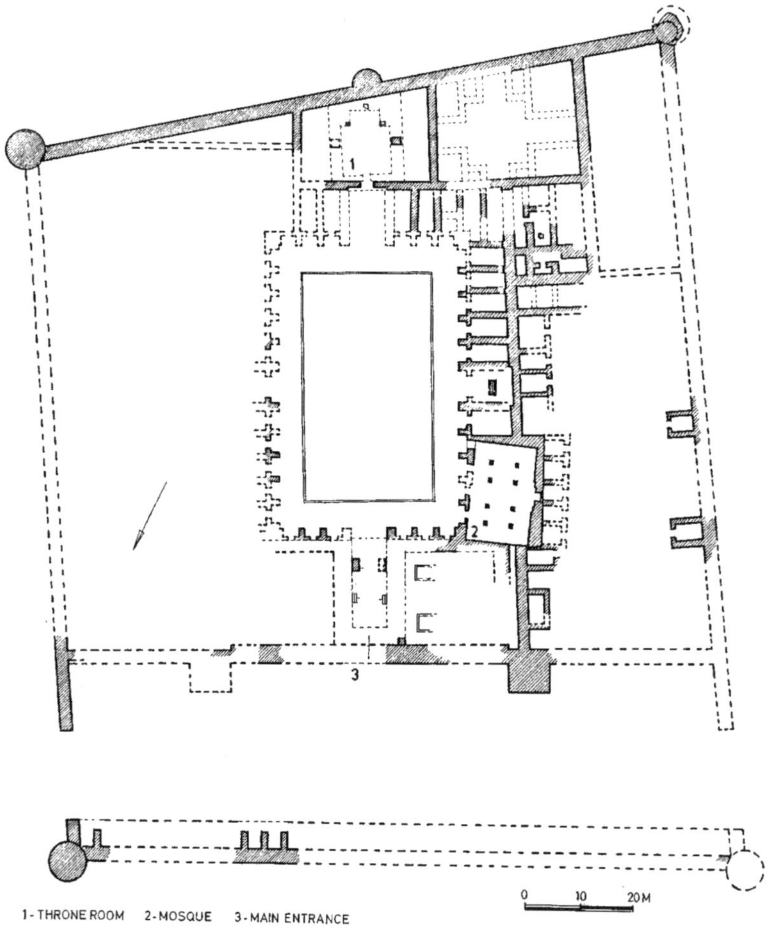

Fig. 23 Ghazna, palace of Masʿud III: plan (after Aslanapa)

separating each gadroon. Thus the motifs combined throughout at Khwaja Siyah Push (and found on the base only at the Zarand minaret in southeast Iran)[56] are here developed independently of each other. This was also done, though in reverse order, in the second and third stories of the Qutb Minar.[57] The total height was proba-

---

[56] Hutt, "Three minarets", 172–5.

[57] Page, *Memoir*; Husain, *Manara*, 27–49, 201–13; Koch, "Copies", 95–107, which demonstrates that the Qutb Minar is beyond question the most influential of all Ghurid buildings so far as later architecture is concerned.

Pl. 6. Ghazna, minaret of Masʿud III: exterior.

Pl. 7. Ghazna, minaret of Masʿud III: historical inscription at top of lower shaft.

bly c. 44 m. At least three inscription bands decorated the upper shaft, with a dwarf arcade below the main one, and the lower shaft had another three. One of these, executed in square Kufic and spread repetitively over all eight panels (colour pl. 6), gave Sultan Masʿud's name and titles, the first recorded use of this script for such a purpose (pl. 8). The neighbouring minaret of Bahramshah at Ghazna (erected between 511/1117 and 547/1153)[58] had the same form (colour pl. 1 and pl. 9).

The masterpiece among these buildings is of course the minaret of Jam, dated, as Pinder-Wilson has shown, 586/1190 and thus in the reign of Ghiyath al-Din Muhammad b. Sam (558–99/1163–1202) and set in a secluded valley ringed by mountains in central Afghanistan. In its time it was, so far as can be judged from surviving monuments, the loftiest minaret ever built—65 m subdivided into three diminishing tiers (fig. 24), the top one crowned by a domed open-plan aedicule of a kind formerly seen above one side of the entrance *iwan* of the Herat *jamiʿ*—a sign perhaps that this diminutive minaret too was Ghurid. At Jam a double spiral staircase ensures that those ascending do not meet those descending. In addition to actual windows the shaft, totally encased in terracotta ornament, bears several panels with transennae designs, giving the illusion of extra windows. Altogether the exuberance of the decoration is subordinate to an unflagging awareness of the grand design. Apart from the Shah-i Mashhad *madrasa*, this building has no rivals in the pre-Mongol Iranian world for the endless ingenuity and sustained panache of its decoration.

Structural forms Most of the structural forms employed by Ghaznavid and Ghurid builders were part and parcel of an inherited architectural tradition common to the entire Iranian world and—so far as brickwork techniques were concerned—well established by the tenth century if not earlier. Even so, certain features acquired a distinctive cachet under these dynasties. Among them is the decorated column—whether multi-ringed (Mosque of Quwwat al-Islam, Delhi[59] and two tombstones from Bust),[60] or painted, inscribed, (pls. 10–11) carved with a spiral design (pl. 12) or covered with arabesques (south

[58] See Sourdel-Thomine, "Deux minarets", 110–21.
[59] Edwards, "Ribat", pl. Xc.
[60] Sourdel-Thomine, "Steles", pl. VI.

Pl. 8. Ghazna, minaret of Masʿud III: panel with interlocking Kufic inscription.

Pl. 9. Ghazna, minaret of Bahramshah.

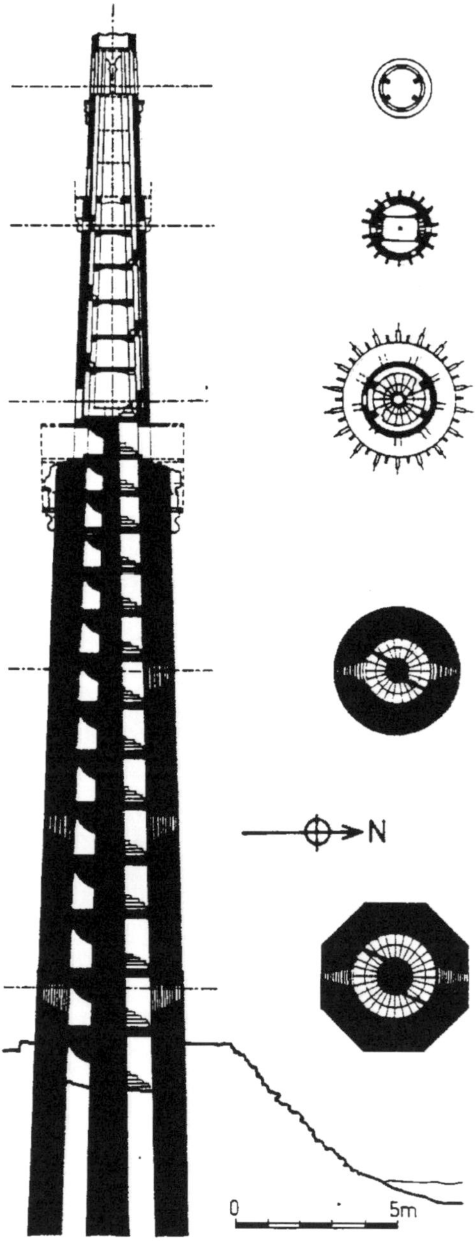

Fig. 24 Jam, minaret: plans and section (after Ball)

Pl. 10. Herat, Friday Mosque: Ghurid portal inscription.

Pl. 11. Bust, tombstone of 391/1195.

Pl. 12. Bust, tombstone of 595/1199.

palace, Lashkar-i Bazar).[61] On occasion the column may be metamorphosed into an inscription band[62] or an irregular oval (pl. 12).[63] Even more diagnostic is the lobed arch, whether trefoil[64] or, more commonly, 5- or 7-cusped, a form so popular[65] that it is found extensively even on contemporary gravestones[66] as well as travelling to India (Ajmir[67] and Delhi).[68] The trefoil arch sometimes takes a distinctively Indian form apparently derived from the *gavaksha* motif encountered in temple architecture (as in the "ribat" of Khalid b. Walid and the Quwwat al-Islam mosque in Delhi).[69] Most common of all is the horseshoe arch, distinguished from the type so familiar in Maghribi architecture by a tendency towards the pointed form at the apex. Such arches may be used singly (Pishvaran),[70] in pairs (Bust arch)[71] or in arcades (facade of south palace at Lashkar-i Bazar, and many areas within it).[72] Sometimes the two forms are combined (pl. 13);[73] and the field may be filled with carved stucco (south palace, Lashkar-i Bazar).[74] These varied forms co-exist with the four-centered and shouldered segmental arches (e.g. Ghurid mausoleum, Herat)[75] familiar in the rest of the Iranian world.

---

61 Schlumberger and Sourdel-Thomine, *Lashkar-i Bazar. Planches*, pls. 140D, 144a, c, d, g, i, k and 145.

62 At the "ribat" of ʿAli b. Karmakh: Edwards, "Ribat", pl. IX.

63 At the tomb of Mahmud of Ghazna: Auboyer, *Art*, pl. 109; cf. Kalter, *Linden Museum*, Abb. 2.

64 Sourdel-Thomine, "Steles", pl. VI; Flury, "Ghazna", pl. XXIV.

65 E.g. the *mihrab* in the palace of Masʿud III at Ghazna and the wooden *mihrab* at Charkh-i Lugar (Allchin and Hammond, *Archaeology*, figs. 6.9 and 6.17 respectively). Sometimes the lobes are much more numerous and closely-packed, as in a marble *mihrab* fragment probably from the palace mosque of Masʿud III at Ghazna, which has no less than seventeen lobes (Kalter, *Linden-Museum*, 36, Abb. 28).

66 Sourdel-Thomine, "Steles", pls. III, V and VI; Gaube, "Herat", Abb. 9.

67 Hillenbrand, "Ajmir", pls. IIa and IXb.

68 Fischer and Fischer, *Baukunst*, pl. II.

69 Edwards, "Ribat", 91 and 94, n. 77, and pl. Xa, c.

70 Hill and Grabar, *Islamic Architecture*, pl. 608.

71 Pope, "Qalʿa-i-Bist", figure 2 (this shows the original state of the then remaining arch in detail); Hill and Grabar, *Islamic Architecture*, pl. 152; Schlumberger and Sourdel-Thomine, *Lashkar-i Bazar. Planches*, pls. 42e and 43. These plates show clearly that one of the side arches is a modern reconstruction from start to finish; but it is hard to imagine any other solution for the matching side than a repetition of the same composition.

72 Schlumberger and Sourdel-Thomine, *Lashkar-i Bazar. Planches*, pls. 52, 56a and 57c; the list could be multiplied.

73 Schlumberger and Sourdel-Thomine, *Lashkar-i Bazar. Planches*, pl. 55e.

74 Schlumberger and Sourdel-Thomine, *Lashkar-i Bazar. Planches*, pl. 53a and 138d.

75 Wilber, *Architecture*, pl. 64.

Pl. 13. Ghazna, cenotaph of Sultan Mahmud: arch with Kufic inscription.

Some novel solutions were essayed to the perennial problem of the squinch form; indeed, given the relatively few surviving monuments, the variety of squinch forms is remarkable. At the Imam-i Khurd shrine, Sar-i Pul,[76] the squinches are of an unusual but rigorously logical form: a small semi-circular arch bridges the corner where the two walls meet and is enclosed by ten others, each one larger than the next, so as to fill up the zone of transition and create a powerful (and semi-illusionistic) sense of depth. The blind arches between the squinches are quite plain, which serves to underline the complexity of the arches themselves. In the south palace at Lashkar-i Bazar this same idea is expressed via a series of diminishing rectangles.[77] Squinches formed of a multiple stepped rectangle are also encountered at Lashkar-i Bazar,[78] but this site scarcely rivals Ribat-i Sharaf[79] for the number of variations on the squinch form which it contains. At Baba Hatim the form is an archaic trilobed arch, simplified into a more two-dimensional form in the adjoining blind arches but with a marked stilt in the upper lobe;[80] the whole arrangement is reminiscent of the squinch zone at Tim.[81]

Sometimes it is the entire zone of transition rather than the squinch itself which becomes a focus for experiment. In the smaller tomb at Chisht the squinches themselves, though of a markedly depressed profile, are not in themselves new, but the spaces between them are filled with a pair of "keyhole" arches—to borrow Dr Terry Allen's vivid term. This breaks the familiar convention that the blind arches in a zone of transition should echo the profile of the squinches on either side of them. Moreover, here the squinch zone itself has been crammed into a narrow and very compressed space, so that attention focusses instead on an intermediate zone between the squinches and the lower part of the square chamber. This zone, also square, is taken up by three blind keyhole arches: a large central arch flanked by two smaller ones. The effect of this radical innovation is to exag-

[76] Bivar, "Seljuqid *ziyarats*", pls. II and V. This type of squinch continued to be used in the following centuries, as at Kassan (Cohn-Wiener, *Turan*, pl. XXI).

[77] Schlumberger and Sourdel-Thomine, *Lashkar-i Bazar. Planches*, pls. 84b, 90f and 115d.

[78] Schlumberger and Sourdel-Thomine, *Lashkar-i Bazar. Planches*, pl. 115c. Cf. The tomb of Baba Rushnai (fig. 4): Pugachenkova, "Monuments", 31 and 32, fig. 2.

[79] Godard, "Khorasan", figs. 34, 40 and 43–4; this list is not exhaustive.

[80] Melikian-Chirvani, "Baba Hatem", 110, pl. 2 and 112, pl. 3.

[81] The most accessible illustration is in Grabar, "Visual Arts", pl. 9.

gerate the height of the chamber illusionistically, creating a deep well of space and a formidable vertical thrust. All this argues an unusually sophisticated apprehension of space (pl. 14). The larger mausoleum at Chisht, which has the same kind of depressed squinch (pl. 15), also breaks with custom in that the areas between the squinches in the zone of transition consist simply of flat oblong panels (pl. 16). This serves to highlight the squinch itself.

Special interest attaches to a treatment of the zone of transition first found at Shah-i Mashhad[82] and then refined in the Ghurid mausoleum at Herat.[83] In its essentials it comprises a trilobed squinch within a trilobed squinch, an arresting image of how the weight of the dome is rationally divided amongst its supporting members. The multiplicity of curvilinear and flanged forms here, executed on both a large and a small scale, imparts a unique vitality, indeed dynamism, to this zone. Only some two decades later, at Zuzan, the semi-dome of the northern *iwan* already contains a developed *muqarnas*,[84] and this was of course to be the standard solution in future centuries; but the late Ghurid form found at Herat and Shah-i Mashhad is perhaps the most elaborate realisation of the alternative collateral development of the trilobed motif known from the early 11th century. It is a clear reminder that the centre of gravity in Iranian architecture had moved decisively east of the Isfahan oasis, a fact reflected in the much greater number of surviving late Saljuq structures in the eastern as opposed to the western Iranian world. The implications of this shift have scarcely begun to be considered in the scholarly literature. In the realm of politics the long reign of Sultan Sanjar prepared the way for this trend, which was consolidated at his death by the rise first of the Ghurids and then of the Khwarizmshahs. The western Iranian world produced no countervailing polity of comparable power in the later 12th and early 13th century.

Although most Ghaznavid and Ghurid architecture was of baked brick, mud brick was also used on a scale not encountered for major public buildings in the rest of the Iranian world. Pishvaran,[85] the field of ruins around the minaret of Khwaja Siyah Push,[86] and many other sites in Sistan possibly of 11th–12th century date well illustrate

[82] Casimir and Glatzer, "Šah-i Mašhad", figs. 31–2.
[83] Wilber, *Architecture*, pl. 64; Glatzer, "Mausoleum", Abb. F and 11.
[84] Godard, "Khorasan", fig. 105.
[85] See in general Hackin *et al.*, *Recherches*.
[86] Fischer, "Field surveys", 135.

Pl. 14. Chisht, smaller mausoleum: interior.

Pl. 15. Chisht, larger mausoleum: interior.

Pl. 16. Chisht, larger mausoleum, interior: detail of squinch.

the popularity of this meanest but most accessible of building materials in south-west Afghanistan (and only in that part of the country) in medieval times.[87] But the principal site in this respect is Lashkar-i Bazar. Many of the royal or aristocratic buildings scattered over an area of 7 × 2 km are constructed of the basest of base materials, namely rammed earth, with mud brick, baked brick, stone and plaster used more sparingly in key locations.[88] The obvious parallel here is the ʿAbbasid royal capital of Samarra, also located on a riparian site and with royal or seigneurial buildings extending for many kilometres.[89] Here too the construction was of earth or mud brick decently masked by decoration in higher-grade materials, notably stucco.[90] Wood is used here and there in Ghaznavid buildings, both for structural purposes—as in the horizontal wooden frames in the minaret of Masʿud III at Ghazna (pl. 17)[91]—and for decoration, as in the wooden *mihrab* of the mosque of Charkh-i Lugar south of Kabul,[92] and of course the famous doors of the tomb of Sultan Mahmud of Ghazna, transported by the British to Agra in 1842.[93] Marble was widely used at Ghazna, and often bore figural designs of such strongly Indian character[94] that one is tempted to see in them the hand of the imported craftsman.[95] Marble, too, is the material used for the cenotaph of Sultan Mahmud, which remains at

[87] Fischer, "Preliminary remarks", 327–408; Fischer, "Rise", 301–55; Fischer, "Field surveys", 137–51; Fischer, "Archaeological Studies", 93–6. For an overall survey, see Fischer *et al.*, *Nimruz*.

[88] Schlumberger, *Lashkar-i Bazar*, 15–16. Allen, "Notes", 56 and 58.

[89] Creswell, *Early Muslim Architecture*, 227–42.

[90] Creswell, *Early Muslim Architecture*, 286–8.

[91] Galdieri, *Conservation*, 7–9, figs. 4–7 and 11–14.

[92] Klimburg, "Afghanistan", 34; Melikian-Chirvani, "Chef d'oeuvre inconnu"; Allchin and Hammond, *Archaeology*, fig. 6.17; Ball, *Gazetteer*, 69 (with further references); Bombaci, "Summary report", 16 and figs. 13–14; Rogers, "*Mashriq*", 249.

[93] Flury, "Schriftband", 215–9, 224–6, Taf. 4–5, 7; Hill and Grabar, *Islamic Architecture*, pl. 609. Rogers attributes them to an itinerant Fatimid craftsman working around 1100 ("*Mashriq*", 238–44). For the early 13th-century carved wooden door from Shahr-i Ghulghula, see Ball, *Gazetteer*, 244.

[94] Kalter, *Linden-Museum*, Abb. 54–55; Auboyer, *Art*, pls. 110–11; Bombaci, "Turcs", 69; Diez, *Persien*, pl. 70 (these sculptures are identified as being of stone). On the other hand, many elements of the marble decoration have no obvious Indian connections; see Hill and Grabar, *Islamic Architecture*, pls. 610–11 and Kalter Abb. 2, 28, 53 and 105.

[95] Despite the assertions to the contrary by Bombaci, "Turcs", 67; indeed, Bombaci himself notes that an Indian statue of Brahma, clearly a trophy, was found at Ghazna ("Turcs", 68).

Pl. 17. Ghazna, minaret of Masʿud III, exterior: central panel with Sura 48.

Ghazna (pl. 13).[96] It is worth remembering that there is a marble quarry only a few hundred metres from Ghazna.[97]

Epigraphy It is perhaps above all in the domain of epigraphy that the character of Ghaznavid and Ghurid art is most manifest.[98] This is moreover true of all aspects of monumental epigraphy:[99] style, variety, decoration, content and quantity. One building after another uses inscriptions on a prodigal scale. Even in its ruined state the Ghurid mausoleum at Herat had no less than eight inscriptions;[100] at Shah-i Mashhad fifteen survive, and that is in all probability only a quarter of the original total; the minaret of Masʿud III at Ghazna had at least six, while that of Jam had seven, among them the entire *sura* of Maryam with 98 verses. In several mausolea (Herat, both tombs at Chisht, Imam-i Khurd at Sar-i Pul) epigraphy dominates the decoration. The cenotaph of Sultan Mahmud is another case in point, but in a very different medium and context (pl. 18).

Aside from the sheer quantity of inscriptions, which makes these monuments huge billboards proclaiming various messages at those who enter them, is the question of content. This has been finely calculated. The Qurʾanic quotations are repeatedly taken from Sura 48, the *sura* of Victory (Shah-i Mashhad; Jam; oratory of the south palace at Lashkar-i Bazar; minaret of Masʿud III at Ghazna, where it is used in its entirety (colour pl. 6 and pl. 17). Both the shorter *shahada* (Baba Hatim; Jam; Imam-i Kalan at Sar-i Pul) and the longer one (Ghurid mausoleum at Herat) are given prominence, for example over the entrance (Baba Hatim)[101] or in the *mihrab* (Sar-i Pul).[102] Other Qurʾanic inscriptions evoke echoes of Solomon (south palace, Lashkar-i Bazar),[103] Abraham (Bust arch),[104] while the *sura* of Maryam

---

[96] Flury, "Schriftband", 221–2; Diez, *Persien*, pl. 70 (roundel); Flury, "Ghazna" 87–9 and pls. XVIII/1 and XXIII/1–2; Auboyer, *Art*, pls. 108–9; Sourdel-Thomine, "Cenotaphe", 127–35.

[97] Bombaci, "Turcs", 67. Elsewhere, Bombaci says it was three miles east of the modern centre of the city (*Kufic Inscription*, 6).

[98] The most accessible general discussion of this epigraphy to date is that by Blair, "Zuzan", 81–6.

[99] Coins are excluded from the present discussion, but it is worth noting that the mints at which Ghurid coins were struck stretched from Kirman in the west to Gwalior in the east (Ghafur, *Gorids*, 179).

[100] Glatzer, "Mausoleum", 16–18.

[101] Melikian-Chirvani, "Remarques", 84.

[102] Shokoohy, "Shrine", pls. VII and XIIb.

[103] Sourdel-Thomine, *Lashkar-i Bazar*, 31.

[104] Sourdel-Thomine, *Lashkar-i Bazar*, 65.

Pl. 18. Ghazna, cenotaph of Sultan Mahmud: main Kufic inscription.

inscribed at Jam[105] mentions more than a dozen Biblical prophets venerated in Islam, and others favoured by God—perhaps to lend a human touch to the transcendence of the Qur'an. The names of God are also part of the repertory (Shah-i Mashhad). Portals are decked out in lengthy historical inscriptions giving the titles of the ruler (south palace and mosque, Lashkar-i Bazar; Baba Hatim; Shah-i Mashhad), which are often enough repeated within the building (Herat *jami*ʿ; Ghurid mausoleum, Herat; and Chisht—see pl. 15). The pronounced geometric and decorative character of these bands is emphasised in an unexpected way by the occurrence of elaborate but anepigraphic portal frames where the absence of writing is not immediately apparent (Chisht: pl. 19).[106] Inscriptions with the ruler's titles are also common on minarets (Dawlatabad [colour pl. 3], both Ghazna minarets, Jam). This unusual emphasis on titulature,[107] for which there is ample supporting evidence in the literary record, makes Ghurid buildings in particular far more propagandist in tone than other contemporary Iranian buildings.

Naskhi script its repeatedly used for historical inscriptions (Pishvaran,[108] Dawlatabad,[109] Ghazna—both at the palace[110] and on the tomb of Sultan Mahmud [pl. 20][111]—and Chisht [pl. 15])[112] at a time when this was not so common a practice elsewhere in the Iranian world. On occasion terracotta letters of gigantic size were used standing out in high relief against a background of triangular indentations (Ghazna palace).[113] Epigraphy is by no means confined to long bands at key locations; it infiltrates every aspect of the decorative ensemble, being employed for example to decorate bricks (Bust),[114] as a minor border design, (Baba Hatim)[115] at the base of a soffit—for example, the word *al-sultan* at Chisht (pl. 21), for the decoration of columns (the

---

105 Maricq and Wiet, *Djam*, 25.
106 Blair, "Zuzan", 82 and pl. 11.
107 For a brief list of Ghurid regnal titles, with references to where they occur in the literary sources, see Ghafur, *Gorids*, 199; cf. Maricq and Wiet, *Djam*, 51–4.
108 Hackin *et al.*, *Recherches*, figs. 114–5.
109 Sourdel-Thomine, "Deux minarets", 123 and pl. XX.
110 For a colour plate of a detail, see Scerrato, *Islam*, 63.
111 Flury, "Ghazna", pl. XXIV.
112 Blair, "Zuzan", 82 and pl. 12.
113 Bombaci, *Kufic Inscription*, figs. 9 and 12.
114 Crane and Trousdale, "Inscribed bricks", 215–26.
115 Melikian-Chirvani, "Baba Hatem", 112, pl. 3.

Pl. 19. Chisht: general view showing both mausolea.

Pl. 20. Ghazna, cenotaph of Sultan Mahmud: cursive inscription.

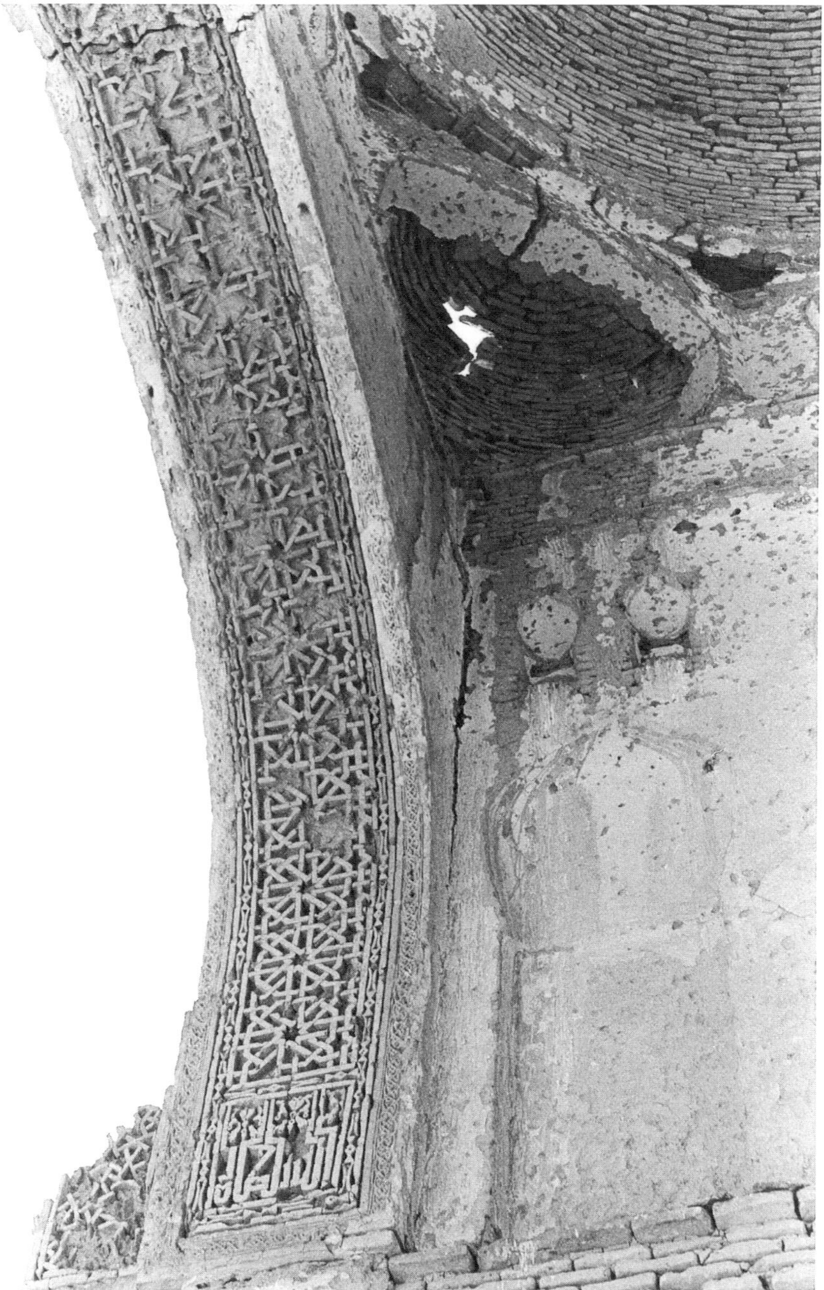

Pl. 21. Chisht, smaller mausoleum, interior: soffit.

south palace of Lashkar-i Bazar)[116]—a device also found at Nishapur[117] and one which has a long history in Islamic art[118]—or for the infill of small medallions (Dawlatabad [colour pl. 3],[119] the south palace of Lashkar-i Bazar,[120] and the arch at Bust [pl. 22]).[121] Interlocking Kufic script (known as "square" in the West, *muʿaqqali* locally)[122] spells out sacred names, as is common in Iran, but also the names and titles of the Ghaznavid and Ghurid sultans (minaret of Masʿud III at Ghazna: colour pls. 5–6 and pls. 6 and 8;[123] Ghurid mausoleum at Herat, where the inscription is in boustrophedon: *muʿizz al-islam wa'l-muslimin, sultan al-salatin al-sharq wa'l-gharb*),[124] and it also occurs on a 12th-century tombstone from the Jamiʿ-i Auliyaʾ at Ghazna.[125] Epigraphic roundels are also known (*shish Muhammad* at the mausoleum of Shahzada Sarbaz, Bust: pl. 23).[126]

Perhaps the most striking innovation so far as content was concerned was the Kufic inscription in Persian verses, a panegyric of Masʿud III, which at dado level encircled the courtyard preceding his throne room at Ghazna. Written partly in the metre of the *Shahnama* (*mutaqarib*), and heavily indebted to that poem for inspiration, it proclaims the achievements of the Ghaznavid dynasty both in championing the Islamic faith and in continuing the heroic traditions of pre-Islamic Iran.[127] The letters were painted in lapis blue against a red ground which was perhaps once gilded;[128] such a scheme might have been intended to imitate manuscript illumination.

Epigraphic *tours de force* abound: riddles (a huge panel endlessly

---

[116] Schlumberger and Sourdel-Thomine, *Lashkar-i Bazar. Planches*, pl. 144i, k and 145c, e, f.

[117] Wilkinson, *Nishapur*, 109, figure 1.96.

[118] Spuler and Sourdel-Thomine, *Kunst*, 162 and pl. 35c–d.

[119] Sourdel-Thomine, "Deux minarets", pls. XIX–XX; Hill and Grabar, *Islamic Architecture*, pl. 168.

[120] Schlumberger and Sourdel-Thomine, *Lashkar-i Bazar. Planches*, pl. 132.

[121] See pl. 22 One medallion has "Allah", another "*al-mulk*".

[122] Pinder-Wilson, "Minaret", 91.

[123] Godard, "Minaret de Masʿud III", 367–9; Pinder-Wilson, "Minaret", 90–1.

[124] Wilber, *Architecture*, pl. 63.

[125] Pinder-Wilson, "Minaret", pl. 4b. On this mosque, see Bombaci, *Kufic Inscription*, 8.

[126] Hill and Grabar, *Islamic Architecture*, pl. 159; one may note too the remains of an external Kufic inscription in fired brick (Hill and Grabar, *Islamic Architecture*, pl. 155).

[127] Bombaci, *Kufic Inscription*, 11–15, 33–42.

[128] Bombaci, *Kufic Inscription*, 8. He adds (p. 6) that the terracotta and stucco carving above the epigraphic dado was painted in yellow, red and blue.

Pl. 22. Bust, arch: soffit.

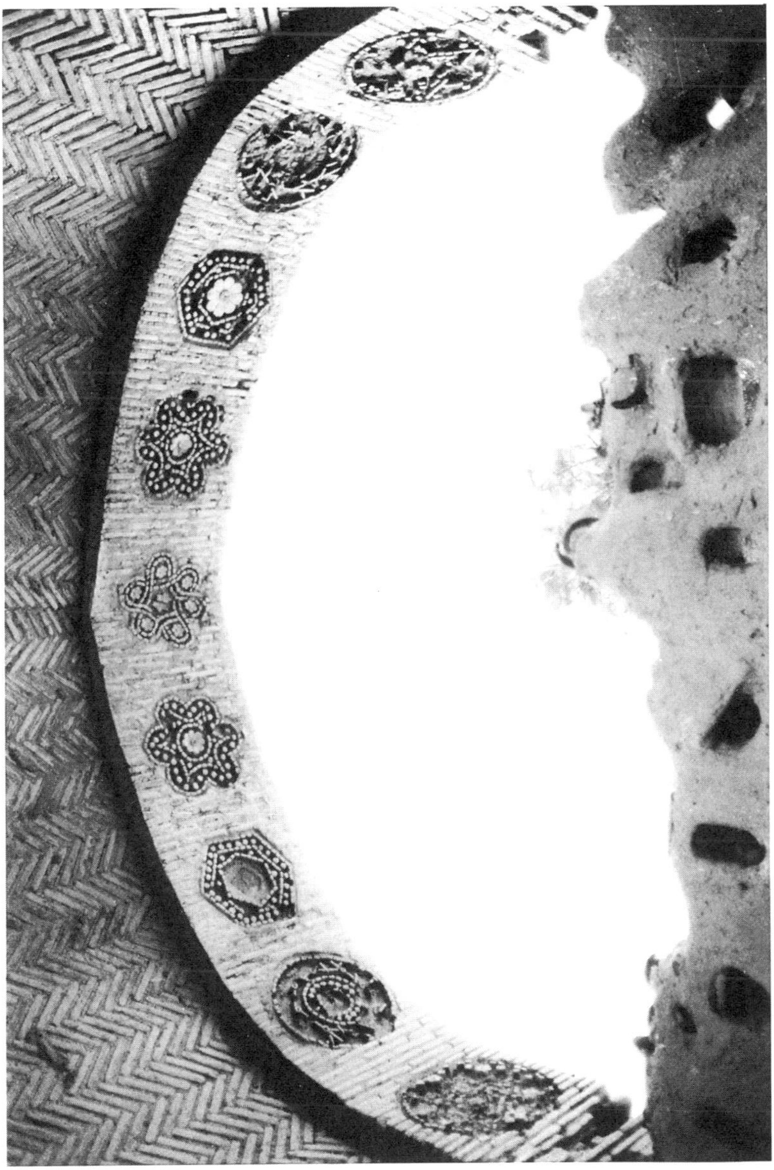

Pl. 23. Bust, mausoleum of Shahzada Sarbaz: soffit.

repeating the name ʿAli, at Shah-i Mashhad),[129] serrated *hastae* (Shah-i Mashhad),[130] and, in reverse, examples of ornament mimicking inscriptions (terracotta plugs on the portal of Shah-i Mashhad);[131] knotted forms unrelated to any particular letter but nevertheless incorporated into actual words as if they were (Bust arch: pl. 5);[132] the exalting of certain words like Allah, Muhammad or ʿAli b. Abi Talib by a sudden efflorescence of decoration in those specific letters (Shah-i Mashhad;[133] Dawlatabad minaret;[134] Imam-i Khurd, Sar-i Pul;[135] an artisan's signature divided into several cartouches interspersed amidst a longer historical inscription (Imam-i Khurd, Sar-i Pul).[136] Terracotta is used for *thulth* inscriptions full of compressed energy (Shah-i Mashhad;[137] Chisht [pls. 24–5]).[138] In both Kufic (pl. 26) and *naskhi* inscriptions the terminals are punctured with holes and strokes in such a way as to suggest zoomorphic forms (Ghurid mausoleum, Herat; Shah-i Mashhad; Pishvaran; Darra-yi Shakh).[139] At Chisht this device is developed with almost frenzied energy, so that not only the letters themselves but also the associated foliate are peppered with tiny holes (pl. 27).

Seen as a group, the inscriptions of Ghurid monuments (and even of some Ghaznavid ones) are notable for their reliance on knotted motifs to add extra decorative complexity to an inscription. This is not to deny the importance of other devices such as the double outlining of letters (*mihrab* in the oratory of Room I in the south palace

---

[129] Casimir and Glatzer, "Šah-i Mašhad", fig. 12.
[130] Casimir and Glatzer, "Šah-i Mašhad", figs. 22, 24 and 26.
[131] Casimir and Glatzer, "Šah-i Mašhad", fig. 21.
[132] Schlumberger and Sourdel-Thomine, *Lashkar-i Bazar. Planches*, pl. 127b.
[133] Casimir and Glatzer, "Šah-i Mašhad", figs. 17 and 22.
[134] Sourdel-Thomine, "Deux minarets", 127, fig. 3.
[135] Bivar, "Seljuqid *ziyarats*", pls. III (top left; cf. Kervran, *Structures Funeraires*, 58, fig. 72) and IV (top centre) though admittedly the words *Shaʿban* (pl. V, left; Kervran, *Structures Funeraires*, 58, fig. 75) and *wilaya* (pl. VII, centre) are also singled out for sudden outbursts of ornament.
[136] Bivar, "Seljuqid *ziyarats*", 60 and pl. I.
[137] Casimir and Glatzer, "Šah-i Mašhad", fig. 16.
[138] Maricq and Wiet, *Djam*, pl. VIII, 2–3.
[139] Melikian-Chirvani, "Herat", 325; for illustrations, see in general Glatzer, "Mausoleum", 18, and, in particular, Melikian-Chirvani, "Herat", pls. V–VI (Herat) and IX (Chisht); Casimir and Glatzer, "Šah-i Mašhad", figs. 33–4 (Shah-i Mashhad); Hackin *et al.*, *Diverses Recherches*, figs. 114–5 (Pishvaran) and Pinder-Wilson, "Mihrab", figure 14 (Darra-yi Shakh).

Pl. 24. Chisht, larger mausoleum, exterior: right-hand inscription.

Pl. 25. Chisht, larger mausoleum, exterior: left-hand inscription.

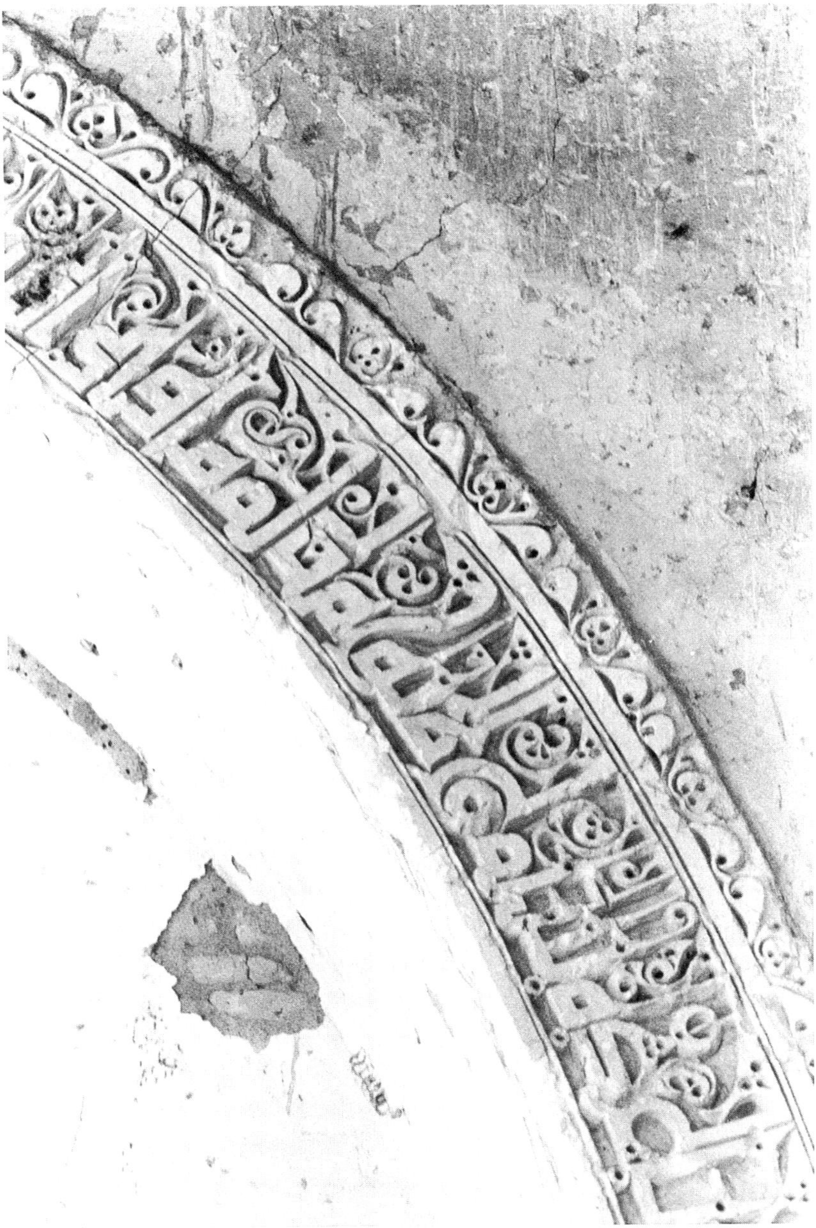

Pl. 26. Chisht, larger mausoleum, interior: Kufic inscription.

Pl. 27. Chisht, larger mausoleum, interior: cursive inscription.

of Lashkar-i Bazar [pl. 28],[140] Danistama[141] and the minaret of Jam;[142] a similar device is used on the minaret of Bahramshah at Ghazna [pl. 29]), or the deliberate elongation of *hastae* and compression of the letters themselves (Ghurid portal of Herat *jamiʿ*; pl. 10).[143] Yet it is the knotted motif which dominates. At Baba Hatim, for instance, the exterior portal inscription exhibits a series of adjoining knots, all different, rising to a climax of complexity in the passage over the doorway which identifies the building as the *mashhad* of one Salar Khalil.[144] Within the tomb, the Qurʾanic inscription displays knotted designs of only two kinds used in an *abab* rhythm.[145] The lowest inscription on the minaret of Jam employs four distinct knotted motifs, also in strict alternation: *abcdabcd.*[146] The Tirmidh minaret (423/1032) injects still more variety into this motif by changing not only the type of knot but also the level at which it occurs.[147] But nothing can rival the portal inscription of Shah-i Mashhad, whose knotted designs—never repeating themselves—take up most of the inscription band and reach new heights of elaboration.[148] The preference for terracotta rather than baked brick as the medium for such inscriptions made the work much more time-consuming but also permitted a degree of flexibility and curvilinearity simply not available to craftsmen using plain brick (cf. pl. 30 with pl. 31).

The prevailing religious tenor of this epigraphic material is striking. Perhaps it reflects that atmosphere of aggressive piety generated by the repeated campaigns of *jihad* mounted by Mahmud of Ghazna and his successors against India. The Ghurids of course continued this policy. Ghiyath al-Din Muhammad b. Sam, the principal patron of Ghurid architecture, took special pains to present himself in his

---

140 Schlumberger and Sourdel-Thomine, *Lashkar-i Bazar. Planches*, pl. 134a and 147a.

141 Le Berre, "Danestama", pl. VIa.

142 Moline, "Minaret of Ǧam", 134, figure 5. This is not the place to explore the comparative material from Iran proper, for example at Nishapur and Khargird.

143 Melikian-Chirvani, "Herat", pls. VII–VIII.

144 Melikian-Chirvani, "Remarques", 84, figure 1; for better close-up pictures of the two vertical parts of the inscription, see Sourdel-Thomine, "Baba Hatim", pls. XII–XIII. This mausoleum, as Bivar has shown ("Inscription", 148–9) was built by Salar Khalil for himself and his maternal grandmother.

145 Melikian-Chirvani, "Baba Hatem", pl. 5.

146 Maricq and Wiet, *Djam*, pl. VII/3.

147 Flury, *Islamische Schriftbander*, fig. 16 and pl. 20.

148 Barry, *Colour and Symbolism*, 48 (colour plate); Casimir and Glatzer, "Šah-i Mašhad", figs. 8–11.

Pl. 28. Lashkar-i Bazar, south palace, audience hall: Kufic inscription and stucco-work.

Pl. 29. Ghazna, minaret of Bahramshah: upper section.

Pl. 30. Lashkar-i Bazar, south palace, audience hall: Kūfic inscription and terracotta ornament.

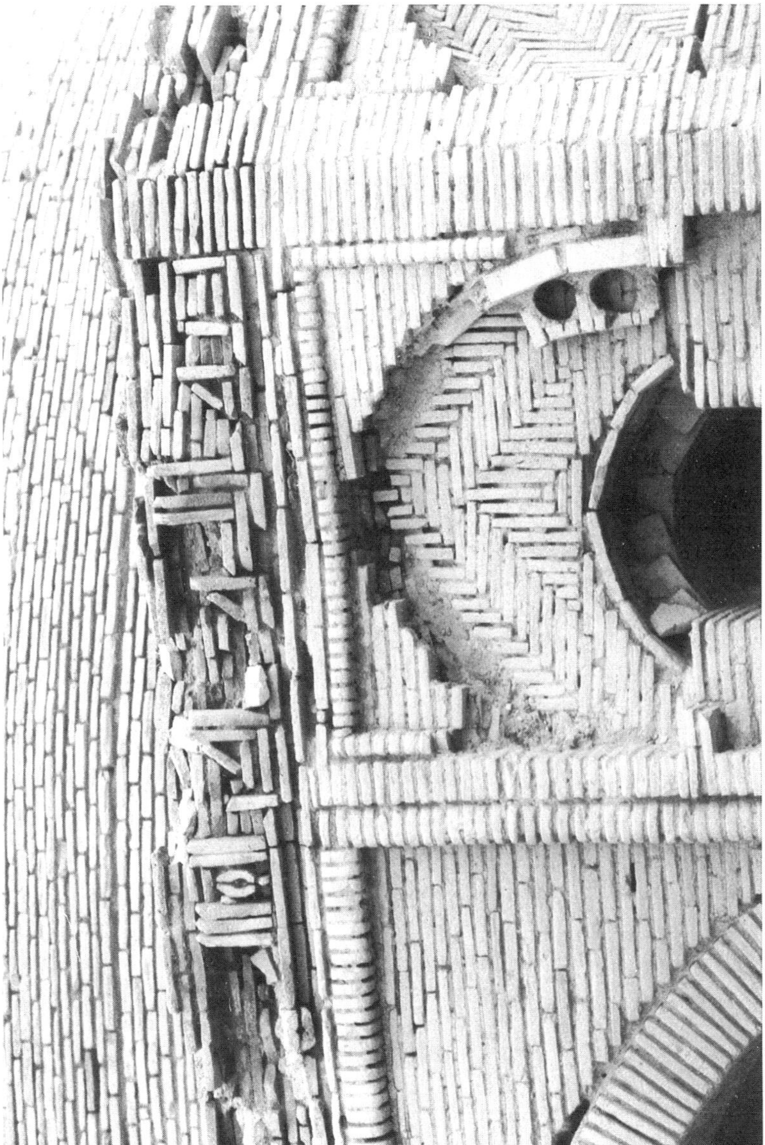

Pl. 31. Bust, mausoleum of Shahzada Sarbaz, exterior: brick Kufic inscription.

inscriptions as a champion of the faith. His titulature as attested in monumental epigraphy reveals a profusion of titles that harp on the theme of his role as a religious leader: "Shadow of God on earth [specifically a caliphal title and therefore dangerously close to *lèse majesté*], Support of [God's] slaves, Associate of the Commander of the Faithful, Guardian of God's lands, Helper of the world and of the faith, Exalter of Islam and of the Muslims, Sultan of God's earth, Helper of the Caliph".[149] His tomb was called a *mashhad* ("place of [Islamic] martyrdom") in its foundation inscription and his mosque in Herat was erected "in God's blessed month, Ramadan",[150] and was built, again according to its inscription, with his own money;[151] pious ejaculations (such as "God is most great" continuously repeated) ornament his tomb;[152] and his inscriptions often end with the pious wish that God will "perpetuate his rule and high rank", "exalt his dignity" and "illumine his proof".[153] In his most conspicuous building, the minaret of Jam, sited with a fine eye for dramatic effect in a remote valley at the very heart of his realm (perhaps intended as a visual statement that his empire rested on religious faith), the principal Qur'anic inscription is Sura 19, whose content is saturated with references to the Biblical prophets. This *sura* was famous as the one quoted by early Muslim refugees in front of infidels; the Prophet's cousin Ja'far b. Abi Talib had fled with a group of the faithful to the Negus of Abyssinia for asylum and quoted Sura 19 to that monarch as an illustration of what Muslims believed.[154] Sura 19 thus had a venerable connection with conversion to Islam. It is replete with promises of Paradise for the faithful and with warnings of the dreadful fate which awaits infidels. In the context of a countryside newly emerged from paganism[155] such words, allied to the domi-

[149] Maricq and Wiet, *Djam*, 27, 51–4; Melikian-Chirvani, "Herat", 323–4; Glatzer, "Mausoleum" 16–88. Cf. Combe *et al.*, *RCEA* IX, 116–7 (no. 3370), an inscription from the Dar al-Siyada in Mashhad dated 577/1181, where the titles closely fit those of Ghiyath al-Din but belong to the Ghurid sultan of Bamiyan, Muhammad b. Mas'ud (Maricq and Wiet, *Djam*, 53). This inscription and its background is discussed by Blair, "Zuzan", 82.

[150] Glatzer, "Mausoleum", 16.

[151] Melikian-Chirvani, "Herat", 323–4.

[152] Wilber, *Architecture*, pl. 63.

[153] For examples, see Melikian-Chirvani, "Herat", 323; Combe *et al.*, *RCEA* X, 14 (no. 3619); Glatzer, "Mausoleum", 15.

[154] Pickthall, *Meaning*, 307–8.

[155] Spuler, "Afghanistan", 356, citing the case of Ghurid soldiers who in 953 destroyed the mosque of a village in the neighbourhood of Herat.

nating visual splendour of the monument they decorate, would carry an extra weight of meaning, while the presence of a Jewish community nearby (attested by Judaeo-Persian inscriptions)[156] may be a further reason for the choice of a *sura* so full of echoes from the Old Testament. Thus while this minaret, far too high for the *adhan* to be audible from its summit, may indeed, as is often asserted, celebrate the victories of Muhammad b. Sam (indeed, the name of the Ghurid capital was Firuzkuh, "Mountain of Victory", and this is generally identified with Jam),[157] it is surely also a monument to his role as a religious leader. Like Shah-i Mashhad, another secluded religious monument of overwhelming magnificence, it may be seen too as an attempt to win converts by means of its grace, its beauty, its sense of contained power.

Decorative techniques A very wide range of decorative techniques characterises Ghurid architecture. All of them are known in Iran proper, but the emphasis is often subtly different. It may be summarised as a delight in terracotta rather than baked brick decoration. Baked brick is of course used, but—as Shah-i Mashhad or the Ghurid parts of the Herat *jami*ᶜ show—it is secondary to terracotta ornament. The minaret of Bahramshah at Ghazna (between 1117 and 1149; colour pl. 1 and pl. 9), that of Khwaja Siyah Push and the mausoleum at Bust are among the few structures to break this pattern in that they rely almost exclusively on brick for their ornament and thus look to Iran for inspiration. On the other hand, the two techniques are on occasion used side by side, as in the minaret of Masᶜud III at Ghazna,[158] one of the official rooms at Lashkar-i Bazar,[159] and the arch at Bust (pl. 5)[160]—where the spandrel design of stars and swastikas suggests brickwork from a distance but, on closer examination, reveals a surface covered with delicately carved arabesques (pl. 32). Similarly,

---

156 Bruno, "Notes", 206–8; Gnoli, *Iscrizioni*. These inscriptions testify that there was a Jewish community in the area of the minaret of Jam between 1149 and 1215.

157 For this much-disputed identification, see Kieffer, "Minaret", 27–41; Maricq and Wiet, *Djam*, Dawari, "Jam and Feroz-koh", 69–91; Habibi, "The city of Ferozkoh", 34–44; Herberg and Davary, "Topographische Feldarbeiten", 57–69; Leshnik, "Ghor", 36–49; Vercellin, "Firuz", 75–85 and "Identification of Firuzkuh", 337–40; "Firuzkuh", 319–28.

158 Pinder-Wilson, "Minaret", pls. 1, 2b, 3, 4a, 5, and 6a.

159 Schlumberger and Sourdel-Thomine, *Lashkar-i Bazar. Planches*, pl. 143a. The columns of the Great Mosque on the same site were also treated with *hazarbaf* ornament (Schlumberger and Sourdel-Thomine, *Lashkar-i Bazar. Planches*, pl. 94d–e).

160 Schlumberger and Sourdel-Thomine, *Lashkar-i Bazar. Planches*, pl. 42e.

Pl. 32. Bust, arch: spandrel.

detailed scrutiny of the minaret of Bahramshah discloses a sequence of elaborate terracotta designs employed to fill the thin strips which separate the major panels of brick ornament. Sometimes these strips use motifs derived from the vocabulary of epigraphic ornament (pl. 33). Moreover, *hazarbaf* designs as well as interlocking hexagons are used for the brick paving at the southern palace at Lashkar-i Bazar.[161] In the Iranian tradition too is the technique of animating a plastered wall by narrow slot-like vertical indentations (Imam-i Khurd shrine, Sar-i Pul;[162] Darra-yi Shakh[163]) like the finger-impressed joints popular in 11th-century Iran. But it was terracotta ornament which displayed the greatest finesse, for instance in small moulded spindle-shaped plugs, used side by side to form borders, a technique that readily lent itself to sudden changes in the design of such borders (Shah-i Mashhad).[164] Many parallels for this idea can be found in Central Asia (e.g. Maghak-i ʿAttari mosque, Bukhara,[165] and that of Talkhatan Baba near Merv[166]). Terracotta medallions in a variety of interlace patterns animate the spandrels, capitals and soffits of the mausoleum of Shahzada Sarbaz at Bust (pls. 23 and 34),[167] columns in the south palace at Lashkar-i Bazar,[168] the zone below the great historical inscription on the minaret of Jam,[169] and the sides of the entrance portal at Shah-i Mashhad.[170] The infill of the square, rectangular, polygonal, stellar, arcuated or otherwise curvilinear panels which parcel up the shafts of the minarets of Ghazna and Jam or the facade of Shah-i Mashhad are merely an enlarged version of this idea. The arresting resemblance of these designs to window grilles may be intended in an illusionistic sense. Another expression of the medallion idea (which is, incidentally, also to be found executed in

[161] Schlumberger and Sourdel-Thomine, *Lashkar-i Bazar. Planches*, pls. 56b, 59c, 60d, 61a and e, 63d and 101 (where a basket-work effect is secured by the alternation of groups of five stretchers at right angles to each other).

[162] Bivar, "Seljuqid *ziyarats*", pls. I–IX.

[163] Pinder-Wilson, "Mihrab", figs. 12 and 14.

[164] Casimir and Glatzer, "Šah-i Mašhad", figs. 23–7.

[165] Hill and Grabar, *Islamic Architecture*, pl. 7. Here this motif is used to break up the surface of engaged columns.

[166] Pugachenkova, *Puti*, figure on 253.

[167] Hill and Grabar, *Islamic Architecture*, pls. 158–60.

[168] Schlumberger and Sourdel-Thomine, *Lashkar-i Bazar. Planches*, pls. 144d, g, i, k and 145.

[169] Maricq and Wiet, *Djam*, pls. III–V; for colour plates see Barry, *Colour and Symbolism*, 54–5, and Auboyer, *Art*, pl. 119.

[170] Casimir and Glatzer, "Šah-i Mašhad", figs. 20 and 24.

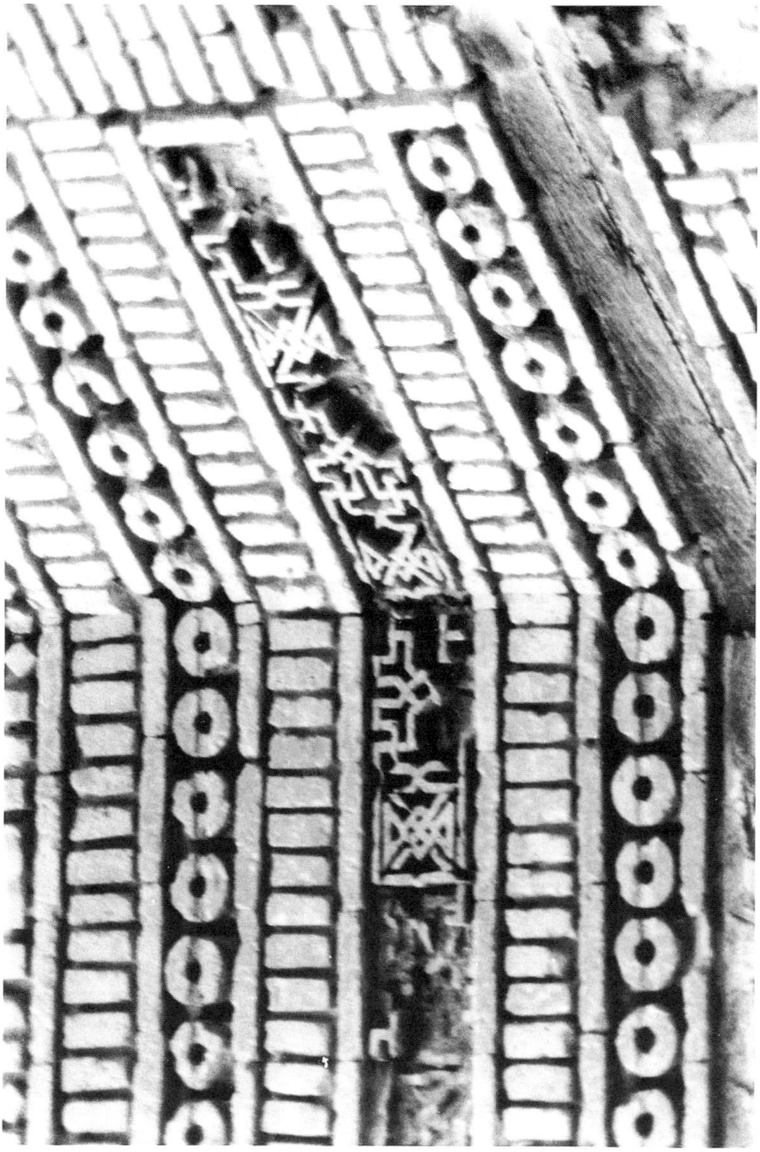

Pl. 33. Ghazna, minaret of Bahramshah: detail of guard-band.

Pl. 34. Bust, mausoleum of Shahzada Sarbaz: detail of soffit.

stucco at the shrines of Sar-i Pul,[171] at the mausoleum of Salar Khalil[172] and in the south palace at Lashkar-i Bazar[173]) is to be found in the overall angular geometric networks whose interstices contain regularly spaced, densely carved little cartouches. These panels, executed in terracotta or stucco, cover the walls of the oratory in the south palace at Lashkar-i Bazar (pls. 28 and 30),[174] the soffit of the

[171] Bivar, "Seljuqid *ziyarats*", pl. III; Shokoohy, "Shrine", pl. VIII.
[172] Sourdel-Thomine, "Mausolee", pls. XIV–XIX.
[173] Schlumberger and Sourdel-Thomine, *Lashkar-i Bazar. Planches*, pl. 138d.
[174] Schlumberger and Sourdel-Thomine, *Lashkar-i Bazar. Planches*, pls. 143a–c (terracotta) and 146, 147a–c, 149a and 150 (stucco).

arch at Bust (pl. 22),[175] the *mihrab*s at Danistama[176] and Darra-yi Shakh[177] and the minaret of Dawlatabad (colour pls. 2–3).[178] On the main shaft of the minaret of Jam the theme of vertically arranged interlaced panels is given new life by the constant change in the shape of the panels themselves.[179] Easily the most precocious of the monuments using terracotta decoration is the minaret of Masʿud III, but the scarcity of dated buildings makes it hard to evaluate its degree of originality.

Both examples of glazed inscription bands testify to a thorough understanding of the potential of this relatively new technique. The blue glazed Kufic inscription on the portal of the Herat *jamiʿ*[180] owes much of its breathtaking beauty to the deliberate austerity of its epigraphic style, in which knotting is rigidly confined to the centre of the band; to the high relief in which it is executed; and to the correspondingly flat, monochrome and lightly patterned background of half palmettes (the last feature found contemporaneously in the Ghurid mosque at Ajmir).[181] At Jam it is undoubtedly significant that the principal historical inscription with the ruler's titles, located at the centre of the minaret in the position of honour, is the one coated in blue glaze, which not only separates it visually from all the rest of the decoration but also makes it more legible (though its key phrase "Associate of the Commander of the Faithful", a particularly coveted title,[182] located on the west face where it would first meet the eye of anyone coming up the valley,[183] is interestingly enough executed on a smaller scale).[184] One technique not known elsewhere

[175] Schlumberger and Sourdel-Thomine, *Lashkar-i Bazar. Planches*, pls. 45 and 128.
[176] Le Berre, "Danestama", pls. III–IV.
[177] Pinder-Wilson, "Mihrab", fig. 13.
[178] Sourdel-Thomine, "Deux minarets", pls. XLX–XX.
[179] Maricq and Wiet, *Djam*, pls. I, II and IV.
[180] For colour plates see Frishman and Khan, *The Mosque*, 51; Barry, *Colour and Symbolism*, 47. Among the Iranian parallels which are particularly relevant because of their closeness to Ghurid territory but which there is not the space to discuss here, one may cite the glazed blue *naskhi* and Kufic inscriptions at Zuzan and the blue Kufic one at Nigar, as well as the light blue and dark blue insets at Sangan-i Pa'in, Sangan-i Bala and Farumad (Pickett, *Early Persian Tilework*, colour pls. 2, 4, 8, 15, 19 and 20).
[181] Hillenbrand, "Political Symbolism", pl. VIIIa.
[182] Maricq and Wiet, *Djam*, 52–4.
[183] Kieffer, "Firouzkoh", 43–4.
[184] Maricq and Wiet, *Djam*, pl. VII/1; see also Barry, *Colour and Symbolism*, 55, where the extreme close-up suggests that the word *mu'minin* has been incorrectly rendered—its final letter is the same as the terminal *kaf* of the phrase *khallada Allah mulkahu*.

is illustrated by a major find from the Ghazna palace: monochrome glazed floor tiles, square in shape and bearing single images of animals.[185] Known in a variety of colours—yellow, olive green, brick red, brown—their repertoire echoes that of some of the stone sculpture from the same site.[186] India would be an obvious source for this animal sculpture; the booty from the Indian campaigns of the Ghaznavids was legendary, and it is recorded that the mosque and citadel of Firuzkuh were decorated with Indian spoils.[187] Marble was used for arch frames and window transennae (one dated 505/1112) in the Ghazna palace,[188] and here again a tradition of stone-carving imported from India is the obvious explanation for its presence. Ghaznavid and Ghurid epigraphy betray much less influence from India; its riches, especially so far as examples on stone and marble are concerned, still await systematic investigation.[189]

Stucco is not only more rarely used than terracotta in these buildings; it is also noticeably more in line with contemporary work in Iran and Central Asia and does not seem to illustrate so marked a local style. Typical examples are the painted imitation of decorative brick bonding (south palace of Lashkar-i Bazar).[190] Some of the stucco panels at the Imam-i Kalan shrine,[191] like the work at Naʿin[192] and Nishapur[193] in Iran, have their roots in the Samarra tradition, while the stucco at Lashkar-i Bazar has numerous direct Iranian parallels

Kieffer suggests that this title was added after the main inscription ("Firouzkoh", 43); hence its smaller size. This feature is, however, found elsewhere in Ghaznavid epigraphy, as in the phrase *al-rahim* in the *bismillah* on the minaret of Masʿud III at Ghazna (pl. 35), or the two-tier composition of the words *islam* and *dawla*, which makes the letters in the upper tier look like afterthoughts (pl. 7).

185 Scerrato, "Islamic glazed tiles", 263–72, figs. 1–62. These have also entered various private and public collections (see, for example, Kalter, *Linden-museum*, 72, Abb. 66 and Grube, *World of Islam*, pl. 8). Scerrato dates these tiles between 1173 and 1221 ("Islamic glazed tiles", 267; cf. Rogers, "Mashriq", 249).

186 For example, Auboyer, *Art*, pl. 110; Barrett and Pinder-Wilson, pl. 15a. The Linden Museum in Stuttgart has several such pieces, still unpublished.

187 Kieffer, "Firouzkoh", 35, 40–1, 50–1 (quoting Juzjani, *Tabaqat-i Nasiri* I, 403–4, as does Wiet in Maricq and Wiet, *Djam*, 44).

188 Bombaci, *Kufic inscription*, 3 and pl. XXXVIII, fig. 133.

189 Such a study would need to take account of the many examples of Ghaznavid and Ghurid epigraphy in these materials which have passed through Western auction houses as a result of the Soviet-Afghan war.

190 Schlumberger and Sourdel-Thomine, *Lashkar-i Bazar. Planches*, pl. 151b.

191 Shokoohy, "Shrine", pls. VII, IX and XIIa–b.

192 Viollet and Flury, "Monument", figs. 1–7 and pls. XLII–XLV and Flury, "Mosquée", figs. 2–5, pls. VIII–XIII.

193 Wilkinson, *Nishapur*, 116–47, 192–202, 229–42.

Pl. 35. Ghazna, minaret of Masʿud III, upper inscription.

(Rasgat, Qurva, Takistan and Qazvin).[194] The primacy accorded to stucco inside the Imam-i Kalan shrine,[195] too, recalls Iranian interiors. Even when the stucco is thinly incised in square Kufic, in the Ghurid mausoleum at Herat,[196] so that the walls seem draped in textiles,[197] Iranian parallels such as the interior of the Sangbast mausoleum[198] are at hand. An especially popular motif also found in Iranian stucco is the proliferation of fat buds or blossoms attached to thin tendrils (Imam-i Kalan;[199] Darra-yi Shakh[200]); this, like some of the stucco at Shah-i Mashhad, presages Ilkhanid work at Bastam[201] and elsewhere.

The most celebrated frescoes from the period are the images of the royal bodyguard which encircled the throne room of the south palace at Lashkar-i Bazar, boldly painted in reds, whites and blues.[202] Literary sources record such ranks of bodyguards in courts as diverse as those of Mahmud of Ghazna[203] and Gagik of Vaspurakan;[204] their depiction here is presumably intended to suggest their protective presence even when they were physically absent. Central Asian parallels for these paintings, from sites as various as Afrasiyab, Varakhsha and Panjikent,[205] abound, while sartorial details such as the belt with

---

[194] Sourdel-Thomine, *Lashkar-i Bazar*, 20, 26–8, 45–6 and 68, discusses some of the Iranian parallels at length.

[195] Shokoohy, "Shrine", pls. VII–XII.

[196] Wilber, *Architecture*, pls. 63–4; Diez, *Persien*, pl. 73; for the best assemblage of documentation see Glatzer, "Mausoleum", figs. 11–12.

[197] For a discussion of this phenomenon in the specific context of Ghaznavid and Ghurid art, see Scerrato, "Islamic glazed tiles", 268–72.

[198] Diez, *Baudenkmaler*, 53, 55 and pls. 17 and 18/1 (these are the best visual record published so far); *Survey*, 1275–7, figure 460.

[199] Shokoohy, "Shrine", pls. VII and XII (a).

[200] Pinder-Wilson, "Mihrab", figs. 13–14.

[201] *Survey*, pl. 394; Wilber, *Architecture*, pl. 37.

[202] Schlumberger and Sourdel-Thomine, *Lashkar-i Bazar. Planches*, pl. 122.

[203] Schlumberger, "Palais", 264, notes 1–2, has assembled the relevant passages from the medieval sources for the Ghaznavids, the Delhi sultanate and the Samanids. For a lengthy account, translated from Baihaqi, of a court reception of Sultan Masʿud b. Mahmud, which also features a guard of honour, see Bosworth, *Ghaznavids*, 137.

[204] Thomas Artsruni, *History of the House of Artsrunik'*, tr. R.W. Thomson (Detroit, 1985), 357.

[205] For a general conspectus of the relevant material, see Schlumberger, "Palais", 265–7; Azarpay, *Sogdian Painting*, 97, fig. 43, 120, fig. 52, 122, 124 and 177. Cf. also the recurrence of this theme in marble carving at Ghazna, briefly discussed in Otto-Dorn, *Kunst*, 95–6.

pendant straps evoke the world of the Turco-Mongolian steppe.[206] A fragmentary column also from the south palace displays the painted head of a young man;[207] its stylistic idiom is close to that of Saljuq lustre pottery.

Conclusion What, then, are the hallmarks of the Ghaznavid and Ghurid style in architecture? Clearly, for all the variety of media employed, the characteristic strength of this style lay in its terracotta decoration. This featured multiple networks of adjoining polygonal compartments enclosing floral, geometric and epigraphic designs, transennae, decorated columns, facades conceived like picture galleries, with an implicit invitation to linger over individual panels (Jam, Shah-i Mashhad, minaret of Masʿud III), and an emphasis on angular rather than curvilinear geometry in the chosen designs. All this is executed with unrivalled mastery and panache, and a baroque exuberance for which the closest contemporary parallels are to be found at the other end of the Islamic world in such sites as Zaragoza, Fez and Marrakesh.[208] Many of these same qualities are recognisable in Ghaznavid and especially Ghurid epigraphy. The combination of terracotta ornament for the exterior and stucco for the interior is frequently encountered (Chisht, Baba Hatim, Ghurid mausoleum at Herat). Monuments with a religious function often face due west in defiance of a correct *qibla* orientation (Shah-i Mashhad, Herat *jamiʿ*, Chisht mausolea, oratory in south palace at Lashkar-i Bazar). The monuments themselves are few in number but of almost uniformly high quality. Some of them seem to be deliberately sited in remote areas difficult of access. Pride of place in Ghurid and Ghaznavid architecture must go to its monumental epigraphy. Quite apart from its remarkable aesthetic qualities, this has an emphasis on historical and propaganda content, and on Qur'anic verses carefully selected for their appropriateness (especially the Victory *sura*, which acquires a well-nigh talismanic quality), for which it is hard to find an equal in medieval Islam.

---

[206] Azarpay, *Sogdian Painting*, 120 (figure 52), 123–5; Otto-Dorn, "Bildgut", 8–18.

[207] Schlumberger and Sourdel-Thomine, *Lashkar-i Bazar. Planches*, pls. 121a and 124a; Otto-Dorn, *Kunst*, 97, Abb. 28 (colour). The very idea of using a column for figural painting of this kind indicates the constant readiness to experiment which characterises Ghaznavid and Ghurid art. It also, incidentally, betrays an indifference to the structural function of the column, for it treats the architectural form merely as a surface to be covered with decoration.

[208] Spuler and Sourdel-Thomine, *Kunst*, 181, 225–9 and colour pl. XXIII.

Bibliography

Allchin, F.R., and Hammond, N. (eds.), *The archaeology of Afghanistan from earliest times to the Timurid period* (London, 1978).

Allen, T., "Notes on Bust", *Iran* XXVI (1988), 55–68.

———, "Notes on Bust (Continued)", *Iran* XXVII (1989), 57–66.

———, "Notes on Bust (Continued)", *Iran* XXVIII (1990), 23–30.

Auboyer, J., tr. Kneebone, P., *The art of Afghanistan* (Feltham, 1968).

Azarpay, G., *Sogdian Painting. The Pictorial Epic in Oriental Art* (with contributions by Belenitskii, A.M., Marshak, B.I., and Dresden, M.J.) (Berkeley, Los Angeles and London, 1981).

Ball, W. (With the collaboration of J.-C. Gardin) *Archaeological Gazetteer of Afghanistan* (Paris, 1982).

Barrett, D., and Pinder-Wilson, R.H., *Ancient Art from Afghanistan* (Chatham, 1967).

Barry, M., *Colour and Symbolism in Islamic Architecture. Eight Centuries of the Tilemaker's Art* (London, 1996).

Bivar, A.D.H., "Seljuqid *ziyarats* of Sar-i Pul (Afghanistan)", *Bulletin of the School of Oriental and African Studies* XXIX/1 (1966), 57–63.

———, "The inscription of Salar Khalil in Afghanistan", *Journal of the Royal Asiatic Society* (1977), 145–9.

Blair, S.S., "The Madrasa at Zuzan: Islamic Architecture in Eastern Iran on the Eve of the Mongol Invasions", *Muqarnas* 3 (1985), 75–91.

Bombaci, A., *The Kufic Inscription in Persian Verses in the Court of the Royal Palace of Masʿud III at Ghazni* (Rome, 1966).

———, "Summary report on the Italian Archaeological Mission in Afghanistan. Introduction to the excavations at Ghazni", *East and West* 10 (1959), 3–22.

———, "Les Turcs et l'art ghaznevide", *First International Congress of Turkish Arts. Ankara 19th–24th October, 1959. Communications Presented to the Congress* (Ankara, 1961), 65–70.

———, "Ghaznevid Art", *Encyclopaedia of World Art* 6 (1962), 399–412.

———, "La 'Sposa del Cielo' ", *A Francesco Gabrieli; studi orientalistici offerti nel sessantesimo compleanno dai suoi colleghi o discepoli (Università di Roma, Studi orientali pubblicati a cura della Scuola Orientale, V)* (Rome, 1964), 21–34.

Bosworth, C.E., *The Ghaznavids. Their Empire in Afghanistan and Eastern Iran, 994–1040* (Edinburgh, 1963).

———, "Ghurids", *Encyclopaedia of Islam* (2nd ed.), II, 1099–1104.

———, *The Later Ghaznavids: Splendour and Decay. The Dynasty in Afghanistan and Northern India 1040–1186* (Edinburgh, 1977).

Bruno, A., "Notes on the discovery of Hebrew inscriptions in the vicinity of the Minaret of Jam", *East and West* 14 (1963), 206–8.

Casimir, M.J., and Glatzer, B., "Šah-i Mašhad, a Recently Discovered Madrasah of the Ghurid Period in Gargistan (Afghanistan)", *East and West* 21 (1971), 53–68.

Clevenger, W.M., "Some Minor Monuments in Khurasan", *Iran* VI (1968), 57–64.

Cohn-Wiener, E., *Turan. Islamische Baukunst in Mittelasien* (Berlin, 1930).

———, "A Turanic Monument of the Twelfth Century A.D.", *Ars Islamica* VI (1939), 88–91.

Crane, H., "Helmand-Sistan project. An anonymous tomb in Bust", *East and West* 29 (1979), 241–6.

Crane, H. and Trousdale, W., "Helmand-Sistan project. Carved decorative and inscribed bricks from Bust", *East and West* 22 (1972), 215–26.

Creswell, K.A.C., *Early Muslim Architecture* II (Oxford, 1940).

Dawari, G.J., "Jam and Feroz-koh: a new study", *Afghanistan* 30/iii (1977), 69–91.

Diez, E., *Churasanische Baudenkmäler* (Berlin, 1918).
Edwards, H., *The Genesis of Islamic Architecture in the Indus Valley* (unpublished Ph.D. thesis, New York University, 1990).
———, "The Ribat of ʿAli b. Karmakh", *Iran* XXIX (1991), 85–94.
Fischer, K., "Preliminary remarks on archaeological survey in Afghanistan", *Zentral-asiatische Studien* 3 (1969), 327–408.
———, Archaeological studies in Seistan and adjacent areas", *Afghanistan* 22/iii–iv (1969–70), 91–107.
———, "From the Rise of Islam to the Mongol Invasion", in *The Archaeology of Afghanistan*, eds. Allchin, F.R. and Hammond, N. London, 1978), 301–55.
———, "Archaeological Field Surveys in Afghan Seistan, 1969–70", in Hammond, N. (ed.), *South Asian Archaeology* (London, 1973), 131–55.
———, Morgenstern, D. and Thewalt, V. (eds.), *Nimruz. Gelandebehegungen in Sistan 1933–1973 und die Aufnahme von Dewal-i Khodaydad 1970*, 3 vols. (Bonn, 1974–6).
Fischer, K. and Fischer, C.-M.F., *Indische Baukunst islamischer Zeit* (Baden-Baden, 1976).
Flury, S., "Das Schriftband an der Türe des Mahmud von Ghazna", *Der Islam* VIII (1918), 214–27.
———, "Le décoration épigraphique des monuments de Ghazna", *Syria* 6 (1925), 61–90.
———, "La mosquée de Nayin", *Syria XI* (1930), 43–58.
———, *Islamische Schriftbänder. Amida-Diarbekr XI Jahrhundert. Anhang: Kairuan, Mayyafariqin, Tirmidh* (Basel, 1920).
Frishman, M., and Khan, H., *The Mosque. History, Architectural Development & Regional Diversity* (London, 1994).
Galdieri, E. *A few conservation problems concerning several Islamic monuments in Ghazni (Afghanistan): technical report and notes on a plan of action* (Rome, 1978).
Gaube, H., "Herat und sein näheres Umland im 15. Jahrhundert nach literarischen und archäologischen Quellen", 203–13.
Ghafur, M.A., *The Gorids. History, culture and administration 543–612/1148–1215–16* (Ph.D., Hamburg, 1960).
Glatzer, B., "Das Mausoleum und die Moschee des Ghoriden Ghiyath ud-Din in Herat", *Afghanistan Journal* 7/1 (1980), 6–22.
Gnoli, G., *Le Iscrizioni Giudeo-Persiane del Ghur* (*Afghanistan*) (Rome, 1964).
Godard, A., "Ghazni", *Syria* 6 (1925), 58–60.
———, "Khorasan", *Athar-e Iran* IV/1 (1949), 7–150.
Godard, Y., "L'inscription de Masʿud III à Ghazna", *Athar-e Iran* I/2 (1936), 367–9
Grube, E.J., *The World of Islam* (Feltham, 1967).
Habibi, A.H., "The city of Ferozkoh, where was it?", *Afghanistan* 33/i (1980), 34–44.
Hackin, J., Carl, J., and Meunie, J., *Diverses Recherches Archeologiques en Afghanistan (1933–40) Mémoires de la Délégation Archéologique Française en Afghanistan VIII* (Paris, 1959).
Herberg, W. and Davary, Djelani, "Topographische Feldarbeiten in Ghor: Bericht über Forschungsarbeiten zum Problem Jam-Ferozkoh", *Afghanistan Journal* 3 (1976), 57–69.
Hill, D., and Grabar, O., *Islamic Architecture and its Decoration* (2nd ed., London, 1967).
Hillenbrand, R., "Political Symbolism in Early Indo-Islamic Mosque Architecture: the Case of Ajmir", *Iran* XXVI (1988), 105–18.
Husain. A.B.M., *The Manara in Indo-Muslim Architecture* (Dacca, 1970).
Hutt, A.M., "Three minarets in the Kirman region", *Journal of the Royal Asiatic Society* (1970), 172–80.
Kalter, J., *Linden-Museum Stuttgart. Abteilungsführer islamischer Orient* (Stuttgart, 1987).
Kervran, M., *Les structures funéraires et commémoratives en Iran et en Asie Centrale du 9ème au 12ème siècle* (These d'Universite de Paris Sorbonne [Paris IV], 1987, 493 pp.).
Khan, A.N., "Mausoleum of Shaikh Baha' al-Din Zakariya at Multan and the Introduction of Central Asian Traditions in South Asian Subcontinent", *Rivista degli Studi Orientali* 59 (1987).

Khanikoff, N. de, *Mémoire sur la partie méridionale de l'Asie Centrale* (Paris, 1864).
Kieffer, C., "Le Minaret de Ghiyath al-Din à Firouzkoh. (Minaret de Djam)", *Afghanistan* 1960, no. 4, 16–60.
Klimburg, M., "Die islamische Kunst in Afghanistan", *Bustan* (1963, *Heft* 3), 32–5.
———, "Blick auf Ghor", *du* 231 (June 1960), 40–50.
———, "Short preliminary report on our expedition to the Ghorat in October 1958", *Afghanistan* 1958, no. 4–1959, no. 1, 16–19.
Koch, E., "The Copies of the Qutb Minar", *Iran* XXIX (1991), 95–108.
Le Berre, M., "Le monument de Danestama en Afghanistan", *Revue des Etudes Islamiques* XXXVIII (1970), 43–53.
Leshnik, L.S., "Ghor, Firuzkuh and the Minar-i Jam", *Central Asiatic Journal* 12 (1968), 36–49.
Maricq, A., and Wiet, G., *Le minaret de Djam. La découverte de la capitale des sultans ghorides (XIIe–XIIIe siècles)* (Paris, 1959).
Marshall, J.H., "The Monuments of Muslim India", in *The Cambridge History of India. III. Turks and Afghans* (London, 1928), 568–640, 659–63.
Meister, M.W., "The 'Two-and-a-half-day' Mosque", *Oriental Art* N.S., XVIII/1 (1972), 57–63.
Melikian-Chirvani, "Remarques préliminaires sur un mausolée ghaznévide", *Arts Asiatiques* XVII (1968), 59–92.
Melikian-Chirvani, A.S., "Eastern Iranian architecture: apropos of the Ghurid parts of the Great Mosque of Harat", *Bulletin of the School of Oriental and African Studies* XXXIII/2 (1970), 322–7.
———, Baba Hatem. Un chef d'oeuvre inconnu d'époque ghaznévide en Afghanistan", *Memorial Volume of the Vth International Congress of Iranian Art and Archaeology* II (Teheran, 1972), 108–24.
———, "Un chef d'oeuvre inconnu dans une vallée afghane", *Connaissance des Arts* CCCVIII (October 1977).
Moline, J., "The Minaret of Ǧam (Afghanistan)", *Kunst des Orients* 9 (1973–4), 131–48.
Niedermayer, O. Von and Diez, E., *Afghanistan* (Leipzig, 1924).
O'Kane, B., "The Madrasa al-Ghiyasiyya at Khargird", *Iran* XIV (1976), 79–92.
Otto-Dorn, K., "Türkisch-islamisches Bildgut auf den Figurenreliefs von Achthamar", *Anatolia* 6 (1961–2), 1–69.
———, *Die Kunst des Islam* (repr. Baden-Baden, 1980).
Page, J.A., *An Historical Memoir on the Qutb, Delhi, Memoirs of the Archaeological Survey of India* XXII (Delhi, 1926).
Pickett, D., *Early Persian Tilework. The Medieval Flowering of Kashi* (Mississauga, Ontario, 1997).
Pickthall, M., *The Meaning of the Glorious Koran. An Explanatory Translation* (London, 1957).
Pinder-Wilson, R.H., "The minaret of Masʿud III at Ghazni", in Pinder-Wilson, R.H., *Studies in Islamic Art* (London, 1985), 89–102.
———, "Le Mihrab décoré de Darra-i-Shakh, Gorzivan", in Grenet, F., Lee, J., and Pinder-Wilson, R.H., "Les monuments anciens du Gorzivan (Afghanistan du Nord-ouest)", *Studia Iranica* 9 (1980), 69–98.
Pope, A.U., "The Mosque at Qalʿa-i-Bist", *Bulletin of the American Institute for Iranian Art and Archaeology* IV (1935), 7–11.
Pope, A.U., and Ackerman, P. (eds.), *A Survey of Persian Art from Prehistoric Times to the Present* (London and New York, 1939).
Pugachenkova, G.A., *Puti Razvitiya Arkhitekturi Yuzhnogo Turkmenistana Pori Rabovladeniya i Feodalizma* (Moscow, 1958).
———, "Little known monuments of the Balkh area", *Art and Archaeology Research Papers* 13 (1978), 31–40.
Rahman, A., *Islamic Architecture of Pakistan, An Introduction* (Peshawar, n.d., c. 1980).
Rogers, J.M., "The 11th Century—A Turning Point in the Mashriq?", in D.S. Richards (ed.), *Islamic Civilisation* 950–1150 (Oxford, 1973), 211–49.

Samizay, R., *Islamic architecture in Herat: a study towards conservation* (Kabul, 1981).
Scarcia, G., and Taddei, M., "The Masjid-i Sangi of Larvand", *East and West* 23 (1973), 89–108.
Scerrato, U., "Summary report an the Italian Archaeological Mission in Afghanistan. The first two excavation campaigns at Ghazni, 1957–1958", *East and West* 10 (1959), 23–55.
———, "Islamic glazed tiles with moulded decoration from Ghazni", *East and West* 13 (1962), 263–87.
Schlumberger, D., "Le Palais ghaznévide de Lashkari Bazar", *Syria* XXIX (1952), 251–70.
Schlumberger, D., *et al., Lashkari Bazar. Une résidence royale ghaznévide et ghoride. L'architecture* (Paris, 1978).
Schlumberger, D., and Sourdel-Thomine, J., *et al., Lashkari Bazar. Une résidence royale ghaznévide et ghoride. Planches* (Paris, 1978).
Shokoohy, M., *Studies in the Early Mediaeval Architecture of Iran and Afghanistan* (unpublished Ph.D. thesis, Heriot-Watt University, Edinburgh, 1978).
———, "The shrine of Imam-i Kalan in Sar-i Pul, Afghanistan", *Bulletin of the School of Oriental and African Studies* LII/2 (1989), 306–14.
Sourdel-Thomine, J., *et al., Lashkari Bazar. Une résidence royale ghaznévide et ghoride. La décoration figuratif et les inscriptions* (Paris, 1978).
Sourdel-Thomine, J., "Deux minarets d'époque seljoukide en Afghanistan", *Syria* XXX (1953), 108–36.
———, "L'art ġuride d'Afghanistan d'après un livre recent", *Arabica* 7 (1960), 273–80.
———, "Le mausolée dit de Baba Hatim en Afghanistan", *Revue des Etudes Islamiques* XXXIX/2 (1971), 293–320.
———, "Les décors de stuc dans l'est iranien à l'époque salǧuqide", *Akten des Vierundzwanzigsten Internationalen Orientalisten-Kongresses* (Wiesbaden, 1959), 342–44.
———, "Stèles arabes de Bust (Afghanistan)", *Arabica* III (1956), 295–306.
———, "Ghaznavids. Art and Monuments", *Encyclopaedia of Islam* (2nd ed.), II, 1053–5.
———, "A Propos du Cenotaphe de Mahmud à Ghazna", in Daneshvari, A., (ed.), *Essays in Islamic Art and Architecture In Honor of Katharina Ottto-Dorn* (Malibu, 1981), 127–35, pls. 1–4.
Spuler, B., "Afghanistans Geschichte und Verwaltung in früh-islamischer Zeit", in *Festschrift Werner Caskel zum siebzigsten Geburtstag 5. Marz 1966 gewidmet von Freunden und Schülern*, ed. E. Graf (Leiden, 1968), 350–9.
Spuler, B., and Sourdel-Thomine, J., *Die Kunst des Islam* (Berlin, 1973).
Stuckert, R., "Der Baubestand der Masjid-al-Jami in Herat 1942/43", *Afghanistan Journal* 7/1 (1980), 3–5.
Vercellin, G., "Firuz, Firuzkuh, Firuzkuhi", *Annali Ca' Foscari* 15/iii (1976) (Ser. Or. 7), 75–85.
———, "The identification of Firuzkuh: a conclusive proof", *East and West* 26 (1976), 337–40.
———, "Sulla voce 'Firuzkuh' in *E.I.*", *Rivista degli Studi Orientali* 50 (1976), 319–28.
Viollet, H., and Flury, S., "Un monument des premiers siècles de l'Hégire en Perse", *Syria* II (1921), 226–34 and 305–16.
Wilber, D.N., *The Architecture of Islamic Iran. The Il Khanid Period* (Princeton, 1955).

Addendum

This essay is affectionately dedicated to Edmund Bosworth, in the hope that it will remind him of his travels in happier times to a Muslim country that is especially close to his heart.

COLOUR PLATES
1–6

Pl. 1 Ghazna, minaret of Bahramshah.

Pls. 2–3 Dawlatabad, minaret (left)and Dawlatabad, minaret: detail (right).

Pl. 4 Bust, arch.

Pl. 5 Ghazna, minaret of Masʿud III.

Pl. 6 Ghazna, minaret of Masʿud III: detail.

THE FALL OF THE GHURID DYNASTY

Peter Jackson

Introduction and early history

During the latter half of the 6th/12th century the Shansabanid rulers of Ghūr (more commonly known as the Ghurids) in present-day Afghanistan emerged as a major power in the Islamic world.[1] From fairly modest beginnings as petty lords (*maliks*) of Mandēsh, one of the districts into which this mountainous region was divided, they had come to dominate the entire region of Ghūr, reducing the other local rulers to subordinate status. The various branches of the dynasty, descended from the sons of ʿIzz al-Dīn Ḥusayn (d. in *c.* 1140), ruled at centres such as Warshād, Istiya, Sanga, Mādīn and Jurmās (Jurwās); but the empire was essentially a family confederacy under the senior prince at Fīrūzkūh, the new capital built in the 1140s and identified by André Maricq in 1957 with ruins at Jām on the Harī Rūd.[2] Tributaries at first of the Ghaznawids and then of the Seljuqs, the Ghurids profited from the upheavals that accompanied the arrival of the Ghuzz (Oghuz), Turkish tribesmen who had been dislodged from Central Asia by the heathen Qara-Khitan. The Ghurid ʿAlāʾ al-Dīn Ḥusayn b. Ḥusayn (d. 556/1161), who had already earned himself the sobriquet of *Jahānsūz* ("World-burner") by sacking Ghazna in *c.* 545/1150, was able to establish his autonomy and to assume the style of sultan.[3]

Following the brief reign of his son Sayf al-Dīn Muḥammad (d. 558/1163), the throne of Fīrūzkūh passed to the branch of the family

---

[1] Maricq and Wiet, *Le minaret*, 31–44, for a survey of the dynasty's history down to 1206; *ibid.*, 61–4, for remarks on the earlier history of Ghūr. For the whole period, see Bosworth, "Ghūrids"; the section on the Ghurids' last years in Kieffer, "Les Ghôrides", part II, 40–4, is superficial.

[2] Maricq and Wiet, *Le minaret*, 55–60; Kieffer, "Le minaret". For a revival of the older view that Fīrūzkūh lay well to the south, in the vicinity of Taywāra, see Leshnik, "Ghor". But Maricq's identification is supported by the fact that Jūzjānī says that Pul-i Āhangarān was close by, *TN*, 1:127 (tr. 1047), and that he gives the distance from Fīrūzkūh to the town of Zamīndāwar as forty *farsakhs* (approximately 200 km.), *ibid.*, 1:364 (tr. 386).

[3] For the struggle with the Ghaznawids, see Bosworth, *The later Ghaznavids*, 111–31.

ruling at Sanga, in the person of a cousin, Ghiyāth al-Dīn Muḥammad b. Sām (d. 599/1203).[4] Throughout his reign Ghiyāth al-Dīn acted in more or less close collaboration with his brother Muʿizz al-Dīn (formerly Shihāb al-Dīn) Muḥammad. Muʿizz al-Dīn, installed at Ghazna when Ghiyāth al-Dīn had wrested it from the Ghuzz in 569/1173–4, spent much of his time in campaigns further east, where the truncated Ghaznawid principality at Lahore was extinguished (582/1186) and much of the north Gangetic plain was conquered from its Hindu rulers. But he was also called upon to support his brother in Khurāsān, where Ghiyāth al-Dīn was in conflict with the Turkish Khwārazmshāhs.[5] The Khwārazmshāhs, who like the Ghurids were former tributaries of the Seljuqs, suffered from two handicaps that did not afflict their rivals: the overlordship of the heathen Qara-Khitan to their rear and the hostility of the ʿAbbasid Caliph al-Nāṣir (575–622/1180–1225). Incited by a series of caliphal embassies, Ghiyāth al-Dīn and his brother made war on the Khwārazmshāhs Tekish (d. 595/1200) and his son ʿAlāʾ al-Dīn Muḥammad (595–618/1200–1221). After Ghiyāth al-Dīn's death (599/1203), Muʿizz al-Dīn mounted an invasion of Khwārazm, only to suffer a major defeat at Andkhūd (601/1204) by the Qara-Khitan, to whom the shah had appealed for assistance. He was preparing for another campaign against the Qara-Khitan when he was murdered at Dumyak,[6] on his way back from India, on 1 Shaʿbān 602/13 March 1206. During the next few years the Ghurid empire disintegrated. While his kinsmen struggled for control of Fīrūzkūh and Ghūr, Ghazna and the Indian provinces passed into the hands of his Turkish slave lieutenants. Only one power benefited from these conflicts: the Ghurids' great rival, the Khwārazmshāh Muḥammad, who by 612/1215–16 had asserted his control not merely over the dynasty's conquests in Khurāsān but also over its core territories. His triumph was short-lived, however, since within a few years Muḥammad and his empire were overwhelmed by the Mongols of Chinggis Khan, who estab-

[4] Sanga, the capital (*dār al-mulk*) of Mandēsh, had been the seat of his father Bahāʾ al-Dīn Sām b. Ḥusayn: *TN*, 1:336, 337 (tr. 340, 341). IA, 11:109/166, confirms that Ghiyāth al-Dīn Muḥammad and his brother held Sanga (SNJH) early in their career.

[5] For the conflict with the Khwārazmshāhs, see Bosworth, "Political and dynastic history", 159–66.

[6] The spelling of this name, which normally appears in secondary works as "Damyak", is suggested by the form DWMYK found in Fakhr-i Mudabbir, *Shajara*, 72.

lished their rule over the erstwhile Ghurid dominions west of the Indus.

This paper is concerned with events following Muʿizz al-Dīn's death. It relies principally upon the great Iraqi chronicler Ibn al-Athīr (d. 630/1232), whose information is often very full, though his sources are obscure;[7] and Minhāj-i Sirāj Jūzjānī, whose general history, *Ṭabaqāt-i Nāṣirī*, written at Delhi in 658/1260, is in some measure a chronicle of the Ghurid dynasty in particular.[8] The history of the Khwārazmshāhs found in the *Taʾrīkh-i Jahān-gushā* of Juwaynī (d. 682/1283) yields a more skeletal account of the Khwarazmian advance in Khurāsān: Juwaynī's version is naturally slanted towards the glorification of the Khwārazmshāhs in the same way that Jūzjānī favours the Ghurids. Nasawī's biography of the last Khwārazmshāh, Muḥammad's son Jalāl al-Dīn *Mingbarnī (d. 628/1231),[9] yields some detail on the later activities of Ghūrīs in Khwarazmian service at the time of the Mongol invasion.

The succession to Muʿizz al-Dīn

Despite the reverse at Andkhūd, the empire at the time of Muʿizz al-Dīn's assassination was still extensive. To the west, Herat and certain other towns in Khurāsān were in the hands of Ghurid lieutenants. To the south the Ghurids ruled over Zamindāwar, Jarūm, Tigīnābād and Bust.[10] To the north-east, ʿAlāʾ al-Dīn had established at Bāmiyān another brother, Fakhr al-Dīn Masʿūd. This branch of the dynasty had extended its control over Shughnān, Ṭukhāristān as far as Dārkōt, and Bolor, regions that were richly endowed with mines of silver and gold and precious stones.[11] It too was drawn into the war against the Khwārazmshāh. Shams al-Dīn Muḥammad b. Masʿūd seconded his cousins' efforts, receiving from them in return

[7] Richards, "Ibn al-Athīr", 88.

[8] A critical edition of this work is very much a *desideratum*: I have checked Ḥabībī's printed text against the early 14th-century B.L. ms. Add. 26,189.

[9] The form Mingīrnī (Turkish *ming*, "thousand", and *eren*, "men"), proposed by Jackson, "Jalāl al-Dīn", 51 n. 1 must be discarded (unpublished paper by Mr. W. Spengler).

[10] *TN*, 1:348–9, 357 (tr. 362–3, 376). The precise location of Tigīnābād is unknown: for the argument that it must have lain close to Qandahār and may even have been identical with it, see Bosworth, *The later Ghaznavids*, 149–51.

[11] *TN*, 1:385, 387 (tr. 422–4, 426); for mineral wealth, see 1:384 (tr. 421).

in 587/1191 the style of sultan;[12] in 594/1198 his son and successor, Bahā᾽ al-Dīn Sām, seized Balkh from the Qara-Khitan, while in 601/1205 his governor at Balkh took Tirmid from them also.[13] The succession to Muʿizz al-Dīn's territories was a matter of some moment, given the wealth at stake. Ghazna was a valuable prize in view of the booty from India amassed there by Muʿizz al-Dīn, including (or so Jūzjānī was told by the late sultan's treasurer) 1,500 *manns* of jewels, and the late monarch had not touched his brother's hoard at Fīrūzkūh.[14]

The dynasty had come to rely for its military forces and high-ranking officers not only on the tribesmen of Ghūr itself, but also upon other groups: "Tājīk" elements from the new conquests in Khurāsān; the Khalaj, inhabiting the warm tracts, or *garmsīr*, of present-day southern Afghanistan, who have long been classed as Turks, although their ethnicity is by no means certain;[15] Ghuzz tribesmen; and elite Turkish slave (*ghulām, banda*) troops of the kind recruited by Muslim rulers since as early as the 2nd/8th century. Ghiyāth al-Dīn Muḥammad is known to have maintained Turkish slaves (*turkān-i khāṣṣ*) early in his reign; and Jūzjānī expressly tells us that Muʿizz al-Dīn purchased a great number of them.[16] Ghurid conquests in the eastern Panjāb were largely the work of his Turkish slave lieutenants, notably Quṭb al-Dīn Aybeg, who occupied Delhi in 589/1193 and made it his headquarters. Professor Irfan Habib has recently suggested that Muʿizz al-Dīn was careful to promote *ghulām*s in particular to administrative and military office in his own territories of Ghazna and India, in contrast with the older Ghurid lands.[17]

Jūzjānī alleges that Muʿizz al-Dīn, who left no son, intended his dominions to pass to his slaves after his death, and Ghazna in par-

---

[12] *Ibid.*, 1:303, 359, 387 (tr. 249, 379, 427).

[13] IA, 12:88/134, 135/206.

[14] *TN*, 1:375 (tr. 405), for Fīrūzkūh (400 camel-loads of pure gold, etc.); 1:404 (tr. 487–8), for Ghazna; see also the share carried away by Jalāl al-Dīn ʿAlī of Bāmiyān in 602/1206, allegedly totalling 250 camel-loads of gold ingots, vessels of gold and silver, and articles encrusted with jewels, *ibid.*, 1:390, 408 (tr. 433, 494).

[15] Bosworth, "Khaladj"; Minorsky, "The Turkish dialect"; Bosworth and Clauson, "Al-Xwārazmī", 6, 8–9; and cf. Habib, "Formation", 3, n. 12.

[16] *TN*, 1:410 (tr. 497), for Muʿizz al-Dīn's purchase of Turkish slaves; 1:354–5 (tr. 371), for Turks at Ghiyāth al-Dīn's court.

[17] Habib, "Formation", 4–7. For the Indian conquests, see Habibullah, chap. 3, "The initial conquest"; K.A. Nizami, in Habib and Nizami, *The Delhi Sultanat*, 156–90.

ticular to Tāj al-Dīn Yildiz, who is described as the senior or chief among them[18] and who held the *iqṭāʿ* of Kurramān. Muʿizz al-Dīn is also credited with a prediction that his slaves would take over his inheritance.[19] Jūzjānī, of course, writing in the Delhi Sultanate, clearly saw it as his duty to portray its monarchs as Muʿizz al-Dīn's true heirs within his Indian territories.[20] Here he was confronted by a major stumbling-block, since the proclamation of Quṭb al-Dīn Aybeg as ruler at Lahore in 602/1206 and of Aybeg's own *ghulam* Iltutmish at Delhi in 607/1210–11 constituted a disjunction from what had gone before. Jūzjānī therefore had to fashion some kind of continuity with the Ghurid regime, in just the same way as Fakhr-i Mudabbir earlier in the century had sought to depict his patron Aybeg as Muʿizz al-Dīn's designated successor.[21] But modern writers have accepted and even refined upon Jūzjānī's testimony. In the view of Professor M. ʿAziz Ahmad, for instance, Muʿizz al-Dīn's Indian conquests were his *peculium* which therefore passed by right to his slaves rather than to his heirs by blood.[22] This is, to say the least, a highly dubious proposition. In Islamic law it is the master who inherits the slave's property and has some claim to that of his freedman.[23]

What arrangements, if any, Muʿizz al-Dīn had actually made for his extensive dominions, we cannot know. Although there appear to have been no recognized rules for the succession, considerable weight was given to seniority. Early in Ghiyāth al-Dīn Muḥammad's reign, his surviving uncle, Fakhr al-Dīn Masʿūd of Bāmiyān, had made an abortive bid for the throne of Fīrūzkūh. Jūzjānī states that even after his defeat the sultans and *maliks* of Ghūr attended his court (*ūrā khidmat kardandī*), suggesting that the paramountcy of Ghiyāth al-Dīn and his brother may have dated only from Fakhr al-Dīn's death.[24] By 602/1206 there were a number of plausible senior candidates. ʿAlāʾ

[18] For Yildiz's rank, see IA, 12:141/215; *TN*, 1:411 (tr. 498). According to a later tradition, he was Muʿizz al-Dīn's son-in-law: Baranī, *Taʾrīkh*, 550. His name is Turkish *yulduz/yildiz*, "star": Clauson, *An etymological dictionary*, 922–3.

[19] For Muʿizz al-Dīn's alleged intentions, see generally *TN*, 1:410–11 (tr. 497); regarding Yildiz, 1:393, 412 (tr. 438, 500).

[20] *Ibid.*, 1:323, 411, 415 (tr. 310, 497–8, 508–12).

[21] Fakhr-i Mudabbir, *Shajara*, 28, 32–3. On this, see Nizami's comments, in Habib and Nizami, *The Delhi Sultanat*, 197–8.

[22] ʿAzīz Ahmad, *Political history*, 99; see also 118, 146, 149.

[23] Crone, *Roman, provincial and Islamic law*, 36–8. Forand, "The relation", 61.

[24] *TN*, 1:355, 386 (tr. 371–2, 425).

al-Dīn Atsiz, for instance, the son of "Jahānsūz", had earlier been in Muʿizz al-Dīn's service at Ghazna, but had been dismissed from court when Ghūrī amirs began to view him as their future sovereign. The representative of a line that had forfeited the sovereignty in 558/1163, he seems to have enjoyed an exalted status among the Ghurids.[25] Another senior prince was ʿAlāʾ al-Dīn (formerly Ḍiyāʾ al-Dīn) Muḥammad b. Abī ʿAlī, of the branch that ruled at Jurmās, who was married to a daughter of Ghiyāth al-Dīn Muḥammad and who, we are expressly told, was older than his cousins the sultans. On his brother's death in 599/1203, Muʿizz al-Dīn had transferred ʿAlāʾ al-Dīn Muḥammad from Bust to Fīrūzkūh and bestowed on him the territories of Ghūr, Gharchistān and Zamindāwar. ʿAlāʾ al-Dīn Muḥammad was an experienced campaigner who had recently fought against the Ismāʿīlīs in Qūhistān and earlier, in 596/1200, had served as governor of Nīshāpūr during the brief Ghurid occupation.[26] That he is the only Shansabanid prince known to have accompanied Muʿizz al-Dīn on campaign in India[27] may possibly indicate that he was being groomed for the succession to the headship of the empire. But whatever the case, Muʿizz al-Dīn had kinsmen enough to whom he might bequeath his territories, either in their entirety or piecemeal, without being obliged to fall back upon his *ghulams*: that savours rather too much of *ex post facto* justification.[28]

These kinsmen, moreover, had plans of their own. Muʿizz al-Dīn's action in 599/1203 had bypassed the late sultan's son, his nephew Ghiyāth al-Dīn Maḥmūd, whom he deemed unsuitable and who was compensated with an appanage comprising Bust, Isfizār and Farāh.[29] The most powerful member of the dynasty was the sultan of Bāmiyān, Bahāʾ al-Dīn Sām, a cousin of Ghiyāth al-Dīn and Muʿizz al-Dīn and also their sister's son, who had formed the design of taking over the Ghurid dominions in succession to his uncles. He had accordingly made a pact with the disgruntled Ghiyāth al-Dīn Maḥmūd for

---

[25] *Ibid.*, 1:379–80 (tr. 413–14).

[26] IA, 12:124/189, and *TN*, 1:370–1 (tr. 393), for Qūhistān; for Nīshāpūr, see *TN*, 1:360, 370 (tr. 381, 393), and Juwaynī, *Taʾrīkh*, 2:49 (tr. 316). For his marriage, see *TN*, 1:360, 369, 373 (tr. 381, 391–2, 397); and for his ancestry and age, *ibid.*, 1:340, 369 (tr. 345–6, 391). Jurmās (or Jurwās) lay "in the heart of Ghūr": *ibid.*, 1:381 (tr. 416); for its probable location, see Maricq and Wiet, *Le minaret*, 61–3.

[27] *TN*, 1:370 (tr. 393).

[28] See also the comments of Nizami, in Habib and Nizami, *The Delhi Sultanat*, 198–9.

[29] IA, 12:118/181. *TN*, 1:370, 372–3, 401 (tr. 392, 393, 396–7, 472).

the partition of the empire on Muʿizz al-Dīn's death: Maḥmūd was to receive his father's territories, Ghūr and Fīrūzkūh, while Bahāʾ al-Dīn would take Ghazna and India. Now, on the news of the assassination at Dumyak, Bahāʾ al-Dīn wrote to Ghiyāth al-Dīn Maḥmūd, to ʿAlāʾ al-Dīn Muḥammad b. Abī ʿAlī, and to the Ghurid governor of Herat, ordering them to make the *khuṭba* in his name. But as he moved on Ghazna, he died, a mere nineteen days after the late sultan. His final instructions to his two sons, ʿAlāʾ al-Dīn Muḥammad and Jalāl al-Dīn ʿAlī, were to continue the march and to reach an accommodation with Ghiyāth al-Dīn Maḥmūd.[30]

The rise of Ghiyāth al-Dīn Maḥmūd and the failure of the Bāmiyān princes

Following Muʿizz al-Dīn's death, Fīrūzkūh only briefly remained under the rule of ʿAlāʾ al-Dīn Muḥammad b. Abī ʿAlī, who had extracted oaths from the leading amirs that they would assist him against the Khwārazmshāh or against Bahāʾ al-Dīn Sām; Ibn al-Athīr notes that Ghiyāth al-Dīn Maḥmūd's name was omitted out of contempt. Maḥmūd himself, at Bust, initially made no move and waited to see what Bahāʾ al-Dīn Sām would do; but on learning of the death of his powerful relative, he had the *khuṭba* read in his own name and advanced on Fīrūzkūh. The Ghūrī amirs were induced to abandon the army sent against him under ʿAlāʾ al-Dīn's son, who withdrew. ʿAlāʾ al-Dīn himself, fleeing from Fīrūzkūh, was pursued, brought back and imprisoned in the fortress of Ashiyār in Gharchistān.[31] A year later his son Rukn al-Dīn Maḥmūd Īrān Shāh made an attempt on Fīrūzkūh which was beaten off.[32]

At Ghazna the situation was more balanced. Here, although the populace looked to Ghiyāth al-Dīn Maḥmūd, Bahāʾ al-Dīn's sons could count on significant support. Their father had been popular with the Ghūrīs in Ghazna: Ghūrī amirs had brought him the news of Muʿizz al-Dīn's murder, and the justiciar (*amīr-i dād*), who acted as governor (*wālī*) of the citadel, had written urging him to make

[30] IA, 12:142–3/217–18, 147/223. For his death, see also *TN*, 1:389 (tr. 431–2).

[31] IA, 12:146–8/223–4. *TN*, 1:371, 373 (tr. 394, 397–8), furnishes a briefer account, but specifies Ashiyār.

[32] *Ibid.*, 1:371, 374 (tr. 395, 399): the attack is said to have occurred when Ghiyāth al-Dīn Maḥmūd had been on the throne for one year, i.e. in 603/1206–7.

haste.[33] This was Sulaymān b. Shīsh, who according to Jūzjānī had held that office under Muʿizz al-Dīn: the same author names Sulaymān and the *sipāhsālār* Kharvash (or Kharfash) as the two leading Ghūrī amirs in Ghazna who summoned Bahāʾ al-Dīn.[34] They may have been among the "amirs of Ghūr" whom Muʿizz al-Dīn had brought from Fīrūzkūh and installed at Ghazna following his brother's death in 599/1203, in preparation for the invasion of Khwārazm.[35]

That Bahāʾ al-Dīn's sons were nevertheless unable to establish themselves at Ghazna was due primarily to the actions of Muʿizz al-Dīn's wazir, Muʾayyad al-Mulk Muḥammad b. ʿAbd Allāh Sajzī,[36] and the late sultan's Turkish slave elite. Already, as Muʾayyad al-Mulk, together with troops of the Indian army (*lashgar-i Hindūstān*), conveyed Muʿizz al-Dīn's bier from Dumyak, tensions had arisen among them between the Ghūrīs and the Turks,[37] the former upholding the claims of Bahāʾ al-Dīn Sām whereas the Turks supported Ghiyāth al-Dīn Maḥmūd. Jūzjānī has the Turks securing a decisive advantage when they took possession not only of Muʿizz al-Dīn's bier but also of his treasure.[38] Ibn al-Athīr, however, shows that this occurred in two distinct stages. First Muʾayyad al-Mulk and the Turks induced the Ghūrīs to follow an alternative route via Nangrahār, while they themselves made for *Shinqurān and Kurramān. Here they were met by Tāj al-Dīn Yildiz, who prevailed upon the wazir to surrender Muʿizz al-Dīn's treasure. Yildiz then accompanied them to Ghazna, where they arrived on 22 Shaʿbān/3 April 1206 and buried their late master.[39] Ibn al-Athīr's more circumstantial account

33 IA, 12:142–3/217.

34 *TN*, 1:390, 408 (tr. 433, 493–4); for Sulaymān as *amīr-i dād*, see *ibid.*, 1:406 (to be corrected from B.L. ms. Add, 26,189, fol. 163b; cf. also tr., 491).

35 *Ibid.*, 1:401 (tr. 473); Habib, "Formation", 7.

36 Muʾayyad al-Mulk's *nisba* generally appears as "Sanjarī" in Ḥabībī's edition of *TN* and is so transcribed by Raverty, but the "Sijistān" of IA, 12:140/213, and the "Sīstānī" of *TN*, 1:380 (tr. 415), are conclusive.

37 For Jūzjānī, the word "Turk" seems generally to signify "Turkish *ghulām*". Note in this context the contrasting juxtaposition of "Turks and free men" (*atrāk-u aḥrār*) in the account of the last Ghaznawid Sultan: *ibid.*, 1:243 (Raverty's trans., 114, fails to bring out the full significance).

38 IA, 12:140–1/213–15. *TN*, 1:390, 408 (tr. 432, 492).

39 IA, 12:141/214–15 (but reading NNKRHAR for the MKRHAN of the text). Nangrahār lay on the middle Kabul river and is the present-day Jalalabad region: see C.E. Bosworth, "Nangrahār, Ningrahār", *EI*². Shinqurān, often mentioned with Kurramān, was identified by Raverty (498–9 n. 7 of his trans. of *TN*) with Shalūzān, and may also be connected with the Shinwārī tribe of Afghans (Bosworth, *The later*

is preferable to that of Jūzjānī, who alleges that Mu'ayyad al-Mulk and the Turkish amirs made contact with Yildiz, inviting him to come and oust the princes of Bāmiyān, only when the army reached Ghazna.[40]

ʿAlāʾ al-Dīn Muḥammad b. Sām and his brother arrived at Ghazna on 1 Ramaḍān 602/11 April 1206. Yildiz had evidently returned to Kurramān, and at first the Turks acquiesced reluctantly in the welcome given to ʿAlāʾ al-Dīn and Jalāl al-Dīn by the Ghūrīs. By distributing largesse among the Turks, the Bāmiyān princes secured an oath of loyalty, but only saving the rights of Ghiyāth al-Dīn Maḥmūd. At this juncture Yildiz advanced on Ghazna at the head of an army of Turks, Khalaj, Ghuzz and others, spurning an offer from the Bāmiyān princes of a larger *iqṭāʿ* in return for his allegiance. When he arrived outside the city, ʿAlāʾ al-Dīn Muḥammad b. Sām sent troops against him, but among them were a number of Turks, headed by Yildiz's brother-in-law Sevinch, who deserted to Yildiz and massacred the Ghūrīs. Jalāl al-Dīn ʿAlī fled, and after a short investment of the citadel ʿAlāʾ al-Dīn was compelled to surrender and to withdraw to Bāmiyān. Yildiz took up residence at Ghazna on 10 Ramaḍān/20 April 1206.[41] In mid Ramaḍān/at the end of April 1206, he was able to act against the pro-Bāmiyān party in the city, arresting the *amir-i dād*. A feeble riposte by Ghūrīs in the service of Bāmiyān, who plundered Kurramān and *Shinqurān, was soundly checked by Yildiz's forces under Sevinch.[42]

At the beginning of Dhu'l-Qaʿda/in the second week of June 1206, the brothers ʿAlāʾ al-Dīn Muḥammad and Jalāl al-Dīn ʿAlī occupied Ghazna a second time, defeating Yildiz, who fled to Kurramān, only to be dislodged from here in turn by the Bāmiyān forces. Deflected from plundering Ghazna by Sulaymān b. Shīsh, the rulers of Bāmiyān compensated their troops from the treasure that Yildiz had earlier extracted from Mu'ayyad al-Mulk and which had now fallen into their hands. But the brothers shortly fell out over Mu'ayyad al-Mulk, whom each wished to appoint as his vizier and who was arrested

Ghaznavids, 125): it lay astride one of the routes from Peshawar to Ghazna (IA, 12:140/214), on which see Bivar, "Naghar".

[40] *TN*, 1:408–9 (tr. 494).

[41] IA, 12:143–5/218–20; for the dates of this, his second stay at Ghazna, see 12:153/231–2.

[42] *Ibid.*, 12:145–6/221–2 (with SWRAN); see also his brief résumé of Yildiz's takeover in Ghazna at 12:153/231–2.

and imprisoned by ʿAlāʾ al-Dīn in a fit of pique, while Jalāl al-Dīn left. From Ibn al-Athīr's account of this incident, it appears to have lost the princes of Bāmiyān much of their support among the people of Ghazna.[43] Yildiz was thus encouraged to make another bid to take over the city. The Ghūrī force in Kurramān was eliminated by a detachment under Aytegin, a former ghulām of Muʿizz al-Dīn, and towards the end of Dhu'l-Ḥijja/early in August 1206 Yildiz himself appeared before Ghazna and besieged ʿAlāʾ al-Dīn Muḥammad b. Sām in the citadel. When Jalāl al-Dīn ʿAlī came to his brother's assistance, he was routed and taken prisoner. After a four-month investment, ʿAlāʾ al-Dīn was obliged to surrender by Yildiz's threat to massacre his captives. Most of his Ghūrī troops had already abandoned him and gone off to join Ghiyāth al-Dīn Maḥmūd at Fīrūzkūh: one of the more distinguished among them was Sulaymān b. Shīsh, whose son had fallen in the encounter with Yildiz's forces in Kurramān; in Ṣafar 603/September-October 1206 he was appointed *amīr-i dād* at Fīrūzkūh.[44] Yildiz released ʿAlāʾ al-Dīn Muḥammad and his brother and allowed them to return to Bāmiyān; but they soon quarrelled, and ʿAlāʾ al-Dīn left for Khwārazm, in a vain attempt to obtain the shah's intervention on his behalf.[45] For the time being, Yildiz's control of Ghazna was undisputed.

Our sources afford sporadic insights into the reasons why the various contenders won or lost support. It is possible that the stance initially taken by Sulaymān b. Shīsh at Ghazna echoes a feud that had developed between the Ghurid Sultans and the Shishanids some decades previously. Sulaymān's brother Abu'l-ʿAbbās had avenged the murder of a third brother by slaying Sultan Sayf al-Dīn Muḥammad in 558/1163, and had then been instrumental in Ghiyāth al-Dīn Muḥammad's succession. But Ghiyāth al-Dīn and Muʿizz al-Dīn had in turn encompassed the death of Abu'l-ʿAbbās.[46] Sulaymān had no cause, therefore, to love the late sultans, and his partisanship of Bahāʾ al-Dīn Sām could perhaps be seen as a more subtle form of revenge on them.

[43] *Ibid.*, 12:153–4/232–4.
[44] *Ibid.*, 12:155–6/234–6. There are briefer references to Yildiz's second seizure of Ghazna in *TN*, 1:390, 409 (tr. 433–4, 495), of which the latter gives the duration of the siege.
[45] *Ibid.*, 1:409–10 (tr. 495–6).
[46] *Ibid.*, 1:351–2, 354–5 (tr. 366–7, 369–71).

For Ibn al-Athīr the choice at Fīrūzkūh was all a matter of religious affiliation. In 595/1198–9 the court and military establishment there had been torn by a dispute between the Karāmī sect and the orthodox Shāfiʿī and Ḥanafī schools, as a result of which Ghiyāth al-Dīn Muḥammad had abandoned the Karāmiyya for the Shāfiʿiyya.[47] ʿAlāʾ al-Dīn Muḥammad b. Abī ʿAlī had championed the Karāmiyya on that occasion, and we are told that the people of Fīrūzkūh in 602/1206 rejected him partly because he was a Karāmī and they were Shāfiʿīs: indeed, after his fall and imprisonment some of his amirs, also described as Karāmīs, were executed.[48] The leading antagonist of the Karāmiyya at Fīrūzkūh had been the scholar Fakhr al-Dīn Rāzī, who had meanwhile taken up residence at Muʿizz al-Dīn's court at Ghazna. He was now falsely accused of the sultan's murder by certain "mischief-makers" (*mufsidūn*) in that city, but escaped thanks to the protection of the vizier Muʾayyad al-Mulk.[49] This suggests that similar religious considerations may have underlain the struggle for Ghazna, where the people were predominantly Ḥanafīs.[50] According to Ibn al-Athīr, Rāzī had arrived at Ghiyāth al-Dīn Muḥammad's court after leaving the service of Bahāʾ al-Dīn Sām,[51] and it is possible that the court at Bāmiyān, like most of the Ghūrīs, inclined towards the Karāmiyya. But this must remain a matter of conjecture.

Even taking into account these sectarian conflicts, however, the widespread popularity of Ghiyāth al-Dīn Maḥmūd is striking and is not easily explained. When he advanced on Fīrūzkūh, Maḥmūd, according to Jūzjānī, was joined by the Khalaj amirs of the Garmsīr with a numerous following. Their leader was doubtless the chief called Ismāʿīl al-Khaljī, who according to Ibn al-Athīr won over a number of Ghūrī amirs.[52] It was a Ghūrī, the *sipahsālār* Ḥasan-i ʿAbd al-Malik *sar-i zarrād*, who commanded the squadron that brought back the fugitive ʿAlāʾ al-Dīn Muḥammad b. Abī ʿAlī.[53] One prominent element among the Ghūrīs was the Marghanī family, who had

---

[47] IA, 12:99–100/151–2, 101/154. On this episode, see Bosworth, "The early Islamic history", 129–32.
[48] IA, 12:147/223, 148/224; for his Karāmī sympathies, see also 12:99/151.
[49] *Ibid.*, 12:140/214. This episode is omitted in Anawati, "Fakhr al-Dīn al-Rāzī".
[50] *TN*, 1:362 (tr. 384).
[51] IA, 12:99/151.
[52] *TN*, 1:373 (tr. 397). IA, 12:147–8/224.
[53] *TN*, 1:371 (tr. 394).

transferred to the Ghurids' service after the death of their previous master, Sulṭān Shāh, brother to the Khwārazmshāh Tekish, in 587/1191–2.[54] Muḥammad al-Marghanī and his brother, together with Muḥammad b. ʿUthmān al-Marghanī, are named among the amirs of Fīrūzkūh whom ʿAlāʾ al-Dīn Muḥammad b. Abī ʿAlī ordered to submit in 602/1206 but who within a few weeks went over to Ghiyāth al-Dīn Maḥmūd.[55] Ibn al-Athīr also names Sevinch the *amīr-i shikār*, Zangī b. Kharjūm and Ḥusayn al-Ghūrī, lord of Tigīnābād, among those who rallied to Maḥmūd's banner.[56] The list is significant, suggesting as it does that Maḥmūd could count on the allegiance of representatives of each of three distinct groupings in the Ghurid dominions: the Khalaj troops, Turkish *ghulāms*, and the Ghūrīs. There is a striking contrast with Maḥmūd's later opponent, ʿAlāʾ al-Dīn Muḥammad's son Rukn al-Dīn Maḥmūd Īrān Shāh, whose support was drawn mainly from the Kashī tribe, a recalcitrant people on the fringes of Ghūrī society, as it were, and ever ready to back dissident princes.[57]

In some measure Maḥmūd clearly benefited from the loyalty of many of the Ghurids' subjects to the son of their old sultan, Ghiyāth al-Dīn Muḥammad; one of his first actions had been to appoint to the vizierate ʿAbd al-Jabbār b. Muḥammad al-Kīdānī, who had been his father's vizier.[58] Perhaps also his character played a part. He gained a reputation as a convivial, pleasure-loving prince, much given to acts of generosity. He is also accused of lethargy and irresponsibility.[59] But there may have been more to Maḥmūd's character. Some energy and military skill can possibly be discerned behind Jūzjānī's laconic reference to his campaign against Marw in 601/1204.[60] Later he personally led the armies that defeated successive attempts on

---

[54] IA, 12:115/176. ʿUmar al-Marghanī, governor of Herat for Ghiyāth al-Dīn Muḥammad, had defended the city against the Khwārazmshāh in 598/1202: *ibid.*, 11:252/384 and 12:108/164, 115–16/176; Juwaynī, 2:50–1 (tr. 318–19), giving him the *laqab* ʿIzz al-Dīn. His daughter married the king of Sīstān: *TN*, 1:280 (tr. 193). His brother Ḥusayn fell fighting against the Khwarazmians at Qara-su in 600/1204: IA, 12:121–2/185–6.

[55] *Ibid.*, 12:147–8/223–4.

[56] *Ibid.*, 12:147/223, 224.

[57] *TN*, 1:371 (tr. 395). For the insubordinate character of the Kashīs, see also 1:348, 350 (tr. 361–2, 364).

[58] IA, 12:147/223; for the vizier, 12:148/224.

[59] *TN*, 1:372, 375–6 (tr. 396, 404–6). Juwaynī, 2:62 (tr. 328).

[60] *TN*, 1:373 (tr. 397).

Fīrūzkūh by Rukn al-Dīn Maḥmūd Īrān Shāh and by ʿAlāʾ al-Dīn Atsiz (below, p. 223).[61] This testifies, perhaps, to Maḥmūd's capacity in the field.

The vicissitudes of Ghiyāth al-Dīn Maḥmūd

The task confronting Ghiyāth al-Dīn Maḥmūd, that of asserting his authority over the rest of his father's and his uncle's empire, was a daunting one. Jūzjānī alleges not only that "the outlying parts (*aṭrāf*) of the kingdom of Ghūr, namely Gharchistān, Ṭāliqān, Gurzuwān, the territory of Qādis, and the Garmsīr", came under the control of his servitors, but that the *khuṭba* was made for him "throughout Ghūr, Ghazna and Hindūstān".[62] This is an overstatement. In India, it is true, his authority was in theory recognized by Muʿizz al-Dīn's *ghulām* lieutenant and commander of the Hindūstān forces, Quṭb al-Dīn Aybeg. Troopers who held *iqṭāʿs* from Aybeg, and who were with Muʿizz al-Dīn's army at the time of his assassination, were duly sent back to India by Muʾayyad al-Mulk when he conveyed the sultan's bier to Ghazna,[63] so that Aybeg may have benefited from an increase in his military strength at this juncture. At any rate, he advanced from Delhi to Lahore and on 17 Dhu'l-Qaʿda/25 June 1206 set himself up as ruler there.[64] He seems to have been careful to act in Maḥmūd's name from the outset.[65]

At Ghazna it was a different matter. The regime of Bahāʾ al-Dīn Sām's sons was hostile, as might be expected. Jūzjānī's account suggests that Rukn al-Dīn Maḥmūd Īrān Shāh enjoyed the support of the Bāmiyān princes for his attempt on Fīrūzkūh, since he came from Ghazna and withdrew there on his defeat.[66] Another rival claimant who enjoyed the hospitality of the Bāmiyān rulers was the son of Jahānsūz, ʿAlāʾ al-Dīn Atsiz, whose daughter was married to ʿAlāʾ al-Dīn Muḥammad b. Sām and who at some point (probably

[61] *Ibid.*, 1:371, 374, 380 (tr. 395, 399–400, 414).
[62] *Ibid.*, 1:373 (tr. 398–9: at 398 Raverty reads "his slaves, such as . . . Yalduz . . .", which is misleading).
[63] IA, 12:140/214.
[64] The date is in Fakhr-i Mudabbir, *Shajara*, 32–3. *TN*, 1:417, has the 18th (but cf. tr. 525–6).
[65] IA, 12:165/249.
[66] *TN*, 1:371, 374 (tr. 395, 399).

in the wake of the *débâcle* at Ghazna) left for Khwārazm to seek assistance in a bid for the throne of Fīrūzkūh.[67]

Yet if Ghazna under ʿAlāʾ al-Dīn Muḥammad b. Sām was a haven for his enemies, Maḥmūd nevertheless failed to derive any substantial benefit from the transfer of the city to Yildiz. For a short time Yildiz affected to be representing Maḥmūd, from whom, he had assured Muʾayyad al-Mulk and the Turks at the outset, he had received authorization to act as his lieutenant (*nāʾib*) in Ghazna.[68] Significantly, however, he had the *khuṭba* made there not for Mahmūd but simply for the ʿAbbasid Caliph al-Nāṣir. And on 16 Ramaḍān/26 April 1206, after moving against the pro-Bāmiyān party in the city, he showed his hand by proclaiming his own sovereignty at Ghazna in an assembly comprising the military commanders, the jurists, the *qāḍīs*, and the caliphal envoy Ibn al-Rabīʿ.[69] The Turks who supported Ghiyāth al-Dīn Maḥmūd were chagrined, but they were quietened by a judicious distribution of *iqṭāʿ*s and gifts of money. Muʾayyad al-Mulk agreed reluctantly to act as Yildiz's vizier. Various Ghūrī amirs obtained Yildiz's permission to leave, and made their way either to Ghiyāth al-Dīn Maḥmūd at Fīrūzkūh or to Bāmiyān.[70]

According to Ibn al-Athīr, Maḥmūd had written to Yildiz thanking him for dislodging the Bāmiyān princes from Ghazna on the first occasion, sent him a robe of honour, and requested him to strike coins and make the *khuṭba* in his name. Yildiz declined, and sought manumission, the style of "Malik", and a marriage alliance with the dynasty; this demand in turn was rejected by Maḥmūd.[71] Following his second victory over the rulers of Bāmiyān, Yildiz again wrote to Maḥmūd, forwarding their standards and some of his captives;[72] but he was clearly unprepared to acknowledge him as his sovereign. His response to Maḥmūd's renewed demand that he be mentioned in

[67] *Ibid.*, 1:374, 380 (tr. 399, 414).

[68] IA, 12:141/215, 144/219. Echoes of this specious claim are found in *TN*, 1:412 (tr. 501–2).

[69] The qadi Majd al-Dīn Abū ʿAlī Yaḥyā b. al-Rabīʿ b. Sulaymān al-Wāsiṭī, twice caliphal ambassador to the Ghurids. He had left Baghdad for Ghazna in Muḥarram 601/Sept. 1204 and was to die on 27 Dhu'l-Qaʿda 606/23 May 1210: Ibn al-Sāʿī, *al-Jāmiʿ*, 9:143, 297–9. For his embassies to the Ghurids, see also *TN*, 1:301–2 (tr. 243). The obituary in IA, 12:190/288, ignores them and dates his death in Shawwāl 606/March-April 1210.

[70] *Ibid.*, 12:145–6/221–2.

[71] *Ibid.*

[72] *Ibid.*, 12:156/236.

the *khuṭba* was to have the prayers read in his own name and to boast to the Ghurid Sultan of having won Ghazna by his own efforts.[73] At length, it seems, Maḥmūd decided to make the best of the situation. His despatch of a ceremonial parasol (*chatr*) and a deed of investiture (*mithāl*) entitling Yildiz to take possession of the Ghazna region, as reported by Jūzjānī, must have occurred immediately after this. Such appears to be the implication of Ibn al-Athīr, who adds that Maḥmūd now manumitted Yildiz and that the latter sent back the parasol.[74]

Ghiyāth al-Dīn Maḥmūd's main problem, however, was Herat, whose governor, ʿIzz al-Dīn Ḥusayn b. Kharmīl, had a history of duplicity. At the battle of Andkhūd in 601/1204 he had deserted Muʿizz al-Dīn and had been prevented from fleeing to Khwārazm only by the grant of the office of *amīr-ḥājib*.[75] When he learned of Muʿizz al-Dīn's assassination, he was reluctant to submit to the authority of Ghiyāth al-Dīn Maḥmūd and tried to extract oaths of allegiance from the populace against possible enemies, though they stipulated that Maḥmūd be excepted. While Ibn Kharmīl therefore played for time by corresponding with Maḥmūd, he appealed to the Khwārazmshāh, and Khwarazmian forces based at Nīshāpūr and other towns in Khurāsān were ordered to move to his assistance. Although warned of Ibn Kharmīl's double game by Ḥusām al-Dīn ʿAlī b. Abī ʿAlī, lord of Kālyūn, Maḥmūd was dissuaded from moving against Herat by some of his amirs, who counselled waiting on events.[76] When Ibn Kharmīl welcomed Khwarazmian troops into Herat, Maḥmūd retaliated by confiscating his *iqṭāʿ* of Gurzuwān.[77] But the army he sent against Herat was betrayed by Amīrān b. Qayṣar, who had been deprived of his *iqṭāʿ* of Ṭāliqān by Maḥmūd only to be then unaccountably placed in command of the van. Maḥmūd's forces were consequently ambushed and defeated by Ibn Kharmīl: the capture of the Khalaj chief Ismāʿīl may well have dealt the sultan a severe

---

[73] *Ibid.*, 12:163–4/247. Yildiz's coins bear the name of the late sultan Muʿizz al-Dīn as well as his own: Sourdel, *Inventaire*, 129–32.

[74] *TN*, 1:373 (tr. 398). IA, 12:164/248.

[75] *Ibid.*, 12:122/187. For his desertion, see also *TN*, 1:402 (tr. 474–5).

[76] IA, 12:148–9/224–6. This is presumably the person called Ḥusām al-Dīn Muḥammad b. Abī ʿAlī, lord of Fīwār and Kālyūn, by Jūzjānī: *TN*, 1:378, 379 (tr. 409, 412).

[77] IA, 12:149–50/226–7. *TN*, 1:402 (tr. 474–5), earlier refers to him as one of the maliks of "Juzurwān".

blow.[78] Maḥmūd would have advanced on Herat in person, but the news that ʿAlāʾ al-Dīn Muḥammad b. Sām had recovered Ghazna led him to adopt a cautious posture.[79]

In the meantime the Khwārazmshāh's first move, on learning of Muʿizz al-Dīn's murder, had been against Balkh. Here again the role played by the simultaneous conflict over Ghazna further south was crucial. At first Balkh put up a strenuous resistance under its governor, the amir ʿImād al-Dīn ʿUmar b. al-Ḥusayn al-Fīwārī, who represented the rulers of Bāmiyān. When his brother ʿAlī Shāh failed to secure the submission of the city, the Khwārazmshāh in person arrived before Balkh in Dhu'l-Qaʿda/June-July 1206. The reinforcements ʿImād al-Dīn had expected from Bāmiyān did not materialize. Jalāl al-Dīn, who had been preparing to go to his aid, was diverted to Ghazna by his brother's appeal; and on the news that the Bāmiyān princes had been taken prisoner by Yildiz, ʿImād al-Dīn surrendered at the end of Rabīʿ I 603/beginning of October 1206.[80] Over the next few months, the Khwārazmshāh took Gurzuwān from Ḥusām al-Dīn ʿAlī b. Abī ʿAlī and Tirmid from ʿImād al-Dīn's son. At the same time ʿImād al-Dīn was arrested and sent to Khwārazm, and Balkh was conferred on Badr al-Dīn Chaghir.[81] From Tirmid the Khwārazmshāh moved to Maymana and Andkhūd and reduced Ṭāliqān, which was held by Maḥmūd's *amīr-i shikār* Sevinch. A bid to secure the submission of Ḥusām al-Dīn ʿAlī b. Abī ʿAlī at Kālyūn, however, failed, and the Khwārazmshāh retired to Herat in Jumādā I 603/December 1206.[82] Ibn Kharmīl had meanwhile obtained the surrender of Isfizār in Rabīʿ I/October-November, and had induced the *malik* of Sīstān to make the *khuṭba* in the name of the Khwārazmshāh.[83]

The Khwarazmian advance must have been a bitter blow to the

---

[78] IA, 12:149–51/226–8.

[79] *Ibid.*, 12:151/229. There is a brief account of the Khwarazmian takeover of Herat in Juwaynī, 2:62 (tr. 328–9).

[80] IA, 12:151–2/229–30; cf. also 12:156/235. For a less detailed account of the submission of ʿImād al-Dīn, called "the chief amir of Bāmiyān", see Juwaynī, 2:63–4 (tr. 329–30).

[81] IA, 12:152–3/230–1. Juwaynī, 2:64 (tr. 330–1). The Khwarazmian commander's name *is çaqir* ("blue", "blue-grey"): Clauson, *An etymological dictionary*, 409.

[82] IA, 12:162/245–6. For Ṭāliqān, see also Juwaynī, 2:64–5 (tr. 331).

[83] IA, 12:163/246. Juwaynī, 2:65 (tr. 331), says that the *malik* attended the Khwārazmshāh's court.

successor of the two men who had devoted their last years to checking it. But Ghiyāth al-Dīn Maḥmūd was prepared to turn the situation to good account. When the Khwārazmshāh wrote to propose a marriage alliance and offered to help him wrest Ghazna from Yildiz in return for a share of its revenues, he agreed. Whether the offer was sincere is unclear; but in any case no aid was forthcoming, since the Khwārazmshāh was distracted by the need to intervene in a succession struggle in Māzandarān.[84] At some point in the year 604/1207–8 he was to make peace with Ghiyāth al-Dīn Maḥmūd on the basis of their existing territorial possessions in Khurāsān, in order to concentrate on his war against the Qara-Khitan. Maḥmūd then finally recognized Khwarazmian overlordship and acquiesced, presumably, in Ibn Kharmīl's position as the shah's viceroy in Herat.[85] It was presumably prior to this settlement that Ghiyāth al-Dīn Maḥmūd was called upon to repulse an attempt by ʿAlāʾ al-Dīn Atsiz b. Ḥusayn to take Fīrūzkūh with Khwarazmian assistance;[86] though we cannot discount the possibility that the episode represented a breach of the treaty by the shah.

Ibn Kharmīl did not long enjoy the fruits of his treachery towards the Ghurids. While the Khwārazmshāh was preparing for his attack on the Qara-Khitan, his officers encountered opposition from Ibn Kharmīl, who wrote to him to complain about the treatment of the peasants of Herat by Khwarazmian troops. A force was sent to Herat under ʿIzz al-Dīn *Childeg b. Toghril. Ibn Kharmīl was treacherously arrested, and executed when his vizier thereupon barricaded the city against the Khwarazmians. But despite the arrival of reinforcements, *Childeg was unable to take Herat; and when news arrived from Transoxiana that the Khwārazmshāh had been defeated and captured by the Qara-Khitan, the besieging army scattered. It was not until the Khwārazmshāh's release and his appearance in Khurāsān in person in 605/1208–9 that the campaign was resumed

[84] IA, 12:164/248; for the death of the ruler of Māzandarān, and subsequent developments, in 603/1206–7, see 12:166/251. The more contemporary Ibn Isfandiyār, *Taʾrīkh-i Ṭabaristān*, 2:171, dates the death of the ruler, Ḥusām al-Dīn Ardashīr, in 602/1205–6.

[85] IA, 12:172/260. Juwaynī, 2:65–6 (tr. 332), dating the Shah's return to Khwārazm in Jumādā II of an unspecified year: in 604, this month would have begun on 23 Dec. 1207.

[86] *TN*, 1:374 (tr. 399): the invasion is dated two and a half years into Maḥmūd's reign, i.e. at the turn of 604–5/in the summer of 1208.

and after an eleven-month investment Herat finally passed under his direct government.[87]

The second struggle for Ghazna

The news of possible military cooperation between Maḥmūd and the formidable Khwārazmshāh had alarmed Yildiz, who occupied Tigīnābād and Bust and had the *khuṭba* for Maḥmūd there discontinued. At the same time he wrote to both Ibn Kharmīl and the malik of Sīstān, ordering them also to end the *khuṭba* for Mahmūd and threatening to attack them.[88] That he had already invaded Sīstān once we know from the indigenous chronicle tradition, which briefly describes Yildiz's devastation of the country *sub anno* 602/1206.[89] Jūzjānī, who omits any mention of Yildiz's recalcitrance towards the sultan at Fīrūzkūh, believed—or intended his readers to believe—that these operations were mounted on behalf of Ghiyāth al-Dīn Maḥmūd.[90]

At this juncture, however, Yildiz found his power jeopardized by a major coalition of his enemies. Following his second capture of Ghazna, he had sent off Jalāl al-Dīn ʿAlī b. Sām to recover his throne, which had been usurped during his captivity by an uncle or a cousin;[91] Jalāl al-Dīn was escorted by a force under Aytegin, Yildiz's

[87] IA, 12:172–6/260–6. The Khwarazmian commander's name, spelled JLDK by IA, seems to be *çildeg*, "an ulcer which forms on the chest of a horse": Clauson, *An etymological dictionary*, 419. For the duration of the siege, see *TN*, 1:307, and 2:121 (tr. 259, 1038); though Jūzjānī confuses this campaign with the Khwārazmshāh's earlier expedition to Herat at Ibn Kharmīl's invitation, and hence follows it with the attack on Balkh (above). The chronology in Juwaynī, 2:66 (tr. 333), is also confused here, since he has Ibn Kharmīl (who was already dead) intriguing with the Ghurid Maḥmūd in the wake of rumours of the Khwārazmshāh's capture. But at 2:70–1 (tr. 337), he dates the Khwārazmshāh's arrival at Shadyākh, on his way to Herat, on 11 Ramaḍān 604/30 March 1208, which would place the city's fall squarely in 605/1208–9. For Ibn Kharmīl's execution and the subsequent resistance of his vizier, see *ibid.*, 2:67–9 (tr. 334–6). The date 604, which is also given in the anonymous *Taʾrīkh-i Sīstān*, 392 (tr. 366), is accepted by Barthold, *Turkestan*, 359, 361–2.

[88] IA, 12:164/248–9.

[89] Anonymous, *Taʾrīkh-i Sīstān*, 392 (tr. 366). *TN*, 1:413 (tr. 503–4). Bosworth, *The history of the Saffarids*, 401–2.

[90] *TN*, 1:412–13 (tr. 503).

[91] Both IA, 12:161–2/244–5, and *TN*, 1:390–2 (tr. 434, 435–7), speak of the seizure of Bāmiyān by an uncle. The former calls him ʿAbbās (saying earlier, 12:142/217, that he had briefly occupied the throne on the death of Shams al-Dīn

*muqṭa*ʿ of Kābul, who was under orders to assist him. But Aytegin left the prince and made for Kābul. Here he entered into correspondence with Quṭb al-Dīn Aybeg, whom Maḥmūd had manumitted at the same time as Yildiz and who had occupied Peshawar, evidently in preparation for hostilities with Yildiz.[92] Aybeg urged Aytegin to attack Ghazna, and also wrote to Ghiyāth al-Dīn Maḥmūd, advising him to accept the Khwārazmshāh's demands for the present until the problem of Yildiz had been dealt with. Yildiz himself had been forewarned, however, and had sent word to his lieutenants, so that when Aytegin reached Ghazna on 1 Rajab 603/1 February 1207 the citadel held out and he was able to do no more than plunder the city and make the *khuṭba* for Maḥmūd. Yildiz, covering himself by the reinstatement of Maḥmūd's name in the prayers at Tigīnābād, now hurried back to Ghazna, and Aytegin withdrew to Tamurān in Ghūr, whence he sent Ghiyāth al-Dīn Maḥmūd a portion of the treasure he had looted. In return Maḥmūd manumitted him and conferred upon him the style of chief amir (*malik al-umarā*ʾ). Reinforcements were sent to Aytegin, and Maḥmūd himself reoccupied Bust and the neighbouring region.[93]

The outcome of this struggle is unknown. It is evidently to be distinguished from a subsequent clash between Yildiz and Aybeg, which is referred to by Jūzjānī. His description of this conflict as originating over Lahore suggests that Yildiz claimed authority over Muʿizz al-Dīn's territories east of the Indus as well as Ghazna, and that he endeavoured to enforce his claim by invading Aybeg's principality. The engagement was fought somewhere near the Panjāb: Yildiz was defeated, and Aybeg was able to advance on Ghazna and occupy the city. But after a period of forty days devoted, if we are to believe Jūzjānī, exclusively to revelry, he was obliged to retire when Yildiz was invited back by "the Turks of Ghaznīn and the Muʿizzī *malik*s".[94] This episode seems to belong to 605/1208–9, for Jūzjānī

Muḥammad, but had been displaced by Ghiyāth al-Dīn and Muʿizz al-Dīn in favour of their nephew Bahāʾ al-Dīn Sām); Jūzjānī names him as ʿAlāʾ al-Dīn Masʿūd. But since IA, 12:165/249, says that Yildiz gave Jalāl al-Dīn ʿAlī aid against a cousin (*ibn ʿamm*), we appear to be dealing with two separate episodes.

[92] IA, 12:164/248. Aytegin's name is spelled ʾYDKZ in error throughout, but is clearly *ay*, "moon", and *tegin*, "prince": Sauvaget, "Noms et surnoms", 40 (no. 41). Ḥasan-i Niẓāmī, *Tāj al-Maʾāthir*, fol. 210b, confirms that Aybeg's authority was acknowledged at Peshawar after Yildiz's defeat (*baʿd az inhizām-i malik tāj al-dīn*).

[93] IA, 12:164–6/249–51.

[94] *TN*, 1:412, 413–4, 417 (tr. 503, 506, 526–8).

speaks elsewhere of Aybeg's advance to Ghazna and his despatch of a certain Niẓām al-Dīn Muḥammad as envoy to Fīrūzkūh in that year: Ghiyāth al-Dīn Maḥmūd responded by sending a scarlet *chatr* and a diploma investing Aybeg with the government of India.[95] Two years later, in 607/1210–11, Aybeg died in an accident while playing polo (*chawgān*) at Lahore. The lack of any evidence for campaigns against the independent Hindu powers during his four-year reign[96] may well indicate either residual designs on Ghazna or a continuing reluctance to expose his capital to incursions by Yildiz. After Aybeg's death Yildiz no longer had to fear any attempt on Ghazna from the east. He and Nāṣir al-Dīn Qubacha, another former slave of Muʿizz al-Dīn who controlled the lower and middle Indus valley, disputed Lahore;[97] while Aybeg's own *ghulam* Iltutmish, who now set himself up as ruler at Delhi, was ready to acknowledge Yildiz's authority and accepted from him a *chatr* and a *dūrbāsh*.[98]

The Khwarazmian conquest of Ghūr and Ghazna

The year in which Aybeg died also saw the death of Ghiyāth al-Dīn Maḥmūd. He had for some months been host to the fugitive Khwarazmian prince ʿAlī Shāh, whose activities during the Khwārazmshāh's captivity in Transoxiana had aroused his brother's anger.[99] The account of what followed as given by Ibn al-Athīr lacks detail: he says simply that the Khwarazmian general Amīn Malik was sent against Fīrūzkūh, that Maḥmūd asked for quarter, and that he and ʿAlī Shāh were arrested and put to death on the Khwārazmshāh's orders.[100] Since this appears both to telescope events that transpired over several months and to confuse Maḥmūd with his son and successor, Jūzjānī's version is to be preferred. According to that author, ʿAlī Shāh arrived at Fīrūzkūh four years after Ghiyāth al-Dīn Maḥmūd's

95 *Ibid.*, 1:373 (tr. 398). The printed text has "Ghūr, Ghaznīn and Hindūstān", but B.L. ms. Add. 26,189, fol. 152a, reads simply *bi-ḍabṭ-i mamālik-i Hind*.

96 Hardy, "Dihlī Sultanate", 260. Jackson, "Ḳuṭb al-Dīn Aybak".

97 *TN*, 1:418, 419 (tr. 530, 532).

98 *Ibid.*, 1:444 (tr. 607). For his name, see Digby, "Iletmish". For the *dūrbāsh*, "the mace or club used as an emblem of military dignity", see Burton-Page, "Dūrbāsh", where it is stated in error, however, that the earliest mention of it in Muslim India is found in Amīr Khusraw's *Nuh Sipihr* (718/1318); also Hodivala, *Studies*, 1:375.

99 IA, 12:174–6/263–5.

100 *Ibid.*, 12:176/266–7.

accession (i.e. in 606/1209–10), only to be imprisoned at the Khwārazmshāh's instigation.[101] ʿAlī Shāh's followers, frustrated that their pleas for his release were ignored, assassinated Maḥmūd in his palace (*qaṣr*) on the night of Tuesday 7 Ṣafar 607/31 July 1210.[102] Not long into the brief reign of Maḥmūd's young son Bahāʾ al-Dīn Sām, the Khwarazmian army appeared before Fīrūzkūh in a second bid to instal ʿAlāʾ al-Dīn Atsiz. ʿAlī Shāh was therefore set free by the Ghūrīs and took charge of the defence of Fīrūzkūh, which fell, however, on Friday 15 Jumādā I/4 Nov. 1210. ʿAlāʾ al-Dīn Atsiz was enthroned as sultan, while ʿAlī Shāh escaped and made for Ghazna.[103]

With the establishment of a pro-Khwarazmian regime in Fīrūzkūh, Ghazna became the main focus of opposition to the Khwārazmshāh. Yildiz had already begun to secure allies for himself. When releasing the rulers of Bāmiyān, he had made a compact with them (*har dū-rā ʿahd dād*); and it was in fact Jalāl al-Dīn ʿAlī b. Sām who alerted him to Aytegin's projected revolt.[104] ʿAlī Shāh was doubtless welcome at Ghazna as a counterweight to the Khwārazmshāh's pretensions, and is said to have remained there some time, until induced to leave Ghazna by overtures from his brother: he thereupon rejoined the Khwarazmian forces, but was treacherously put to death at Tigīnābād in 609/1212–13.[105] From Ghazna Yildiz also engaged in hostilities with the puppet regime at Fīrūzkūh headed by ʿAlāʾ al-Dīn Atsiz. His first efforts were attended by failure, when his vizier Mu'ayyad al-Mulk Sajzī, moving against Fīrūzkūh with an army, was defeated in the region of Kīdān and Margh-i Nūla.[106] Then in 610/1213–14 Yildiz sent another army, under the command of his *amīr-i shikār*, Naṣīr al-Dīn Ḥusayn. Atsiz was killed and the Ghazna forces were able to occupy Fīrūzkūh.[107] Initially a Ghūrī *malik* Ḥusām

[101] *TN*, 1:305, 374–5 (tr. 253, 400, 402–3). Juwaynī, 2:85 (tr. 352), says that he arrived during the Khwārazmshāh's campaign against the Qara-Khitan, i.e. early in 607, *ibid.*, 2:76 (tr. 344).

[102] *TN*, 1:376–7 (tr. 406–7). IA dates Maḥmūd's death in 605, which is too early; Juwaynī, 2:85 (tr. 352), in 609, which is too late. In the B.L. ms Add. 26,189 of *TN*, fols 153b etc., as in the printed edition, the year appears consistently as 607.

[103] *TN*, 1:378–9 (tr. 409–11); this episode is abridged in ʿAlī Shāh's biography at 1:305–6 (tr. 253).

[104] *Ibid.*, 1:409 (tr. 495), for the compact. IA, 12:165/250, for Jalāl al-Dīn ʿAlī's warning to Yildiz.

[105] *TN*, 1:306 (tr. 253).

[106] *Ibid.*, 1:380–1 (tr. 415).

[107] *Ibid.*, 1:381, 382 (tr. 415–16, 417): at 1:382 the printed text gives as the year "610 or 611", but B.L. ms. Add. 26,189, fol. 155a, has simply 610.

al-Dīn Ḥasan b. ʿAbd al-Malik *sar-i zarrād*, was put in control, but not long afterwards Yildiz reinstated as ruler at Fīrūzkūh ʿAlāʾ al-Dīn Muḥammad b. Abī ʿAlī, whom his troops had freed from confinement in Ashiyār and sent to Ghazna.[108]

If the new ruler was intended to act as a bulwark against Khwarazmian expansion, the expedient was a failure, for ʿAlāʾ al-Dīn Muḥammad held the throne for little more than a year before surrendering Fīrūzkūh to the Khwārazmshāh in 612/1215–16.[109] During this period, Khwarazmian pressure on the Ghurids had mounted steadily. In *c.* 610/1213–14 the Khwārazmshāh annexed Bāmiyān and put to death Jalāl al-Dīn ʿAlī b. Sām.[110] Parts of Gharchistān were held for a time after the death of Atsiz by his two elder sons, who were put to death by the Khwārazmshāh's agents at the instigation of the governor of Herat, Amīn Malik; but at what point we are not told.[111] The shah was now free to turn his attention towards Ghazna. According to Ibn al-Athīr, he was treacherously invited into the city during Yildiz's absence by one of the latter's officers, a former *ghulam* of Muʿizz al-Dīn named Qutlughtegin, whose only reward was execution. Jūzjānī says nothing of this, but his briefer account does suggest that Yildiz was currently away on campaign in India. Bereft of his capital, Yildiz moved into the Panjāb, where he wrested Lahore from Qubacha; but as he pushed east he was defeated on 3 Shawwāl 612/25 January 1216 by his erstwhile subordinate, Iltutmish, the ruler of Delhi, imprisoned and later put to death.[112] His tomb at Badāʾūn became a place of pilgrimage according to Jūzjānī, who does not explain why;[113] but it is possible that Yildiz was remembered as the Khwārazmshāh's principal opponent in the region.

ʿAlāʾ al-Dīn Muḥammad b. Abī ʿAlī was treated with honour in Khwārazm, where he died some years later.[114] A number of the last Ghurids remained in captivity there until the Mongol onslaught.

---

[108] *Ibid.*, 1:382 (tr. 417–18).
[109] *Ibid.*, 1:382–3 (tr. 418–19).
[110] *Ibid.*, 1:309, 391 (tr. 266–7, 434). Jalāl al-Dīn is credited with a reign of seven years at Bāmiyān, i.e. presumably dating from 603 when he and his brother were released by Yildiz and he wrested Bāmiyān from his uncle (above and n. 91).
[111] *TN*, 1:381–2, to be corrected from B.L. ms Add. 26,189, fol. 155a (see also tr., 416–17).
[112] *Ibid.*, 1:309, 413, 445 (tr. 267, 505–6, 608). IA, 12:202–3/309–12. The account given by Juwaynī, 2:85 (tr. 353), appears garbled.
[113] *TN*, 1:413 (tr. 506).
[114] *Ibid.*, 1:383 (tr. 419).

Jūzjānī implies that ʿAlāʾ al-Dīn Muḥammad b. Sām died following the capture of Bāmiyān,[115] but according to Nasawī he was put to death later, on the orders of the Khwārazmshāh's mother Terken Khātūn when she evacuated Ürgench and fled before the Mongols in 616/1219–20. The same fate befell the sons of Ghiyāth al-Dīn Maḥmūd, Bahāʾ al-Dīn Sām, who as a boy had briefly reigned at Fīrūzkūh in 607/1210, and his brother Shams al-Dīn Muḥammad.[116] The Shansabanid prince of Mādīn, Shihāb al-Dīn ʿAlī b. Sūrī b. Muḥammad, had been put to death by the Khwarazmians when they took Fīrūzkūh, where he was at that time imprisoned.[117] But at least one member of the dynasty, his brother Nāṣir al-Dīn Abū Bakr b. Sūrī, is known to have survived and obtained asylum in Delhi.[118]

The downfall of the dynasty: an assessment

In assessing the reasons for the collapse of the Ghurid empire, some credit should be given to the Khwārazmshāh's diplomatic acumen. Even during the lifetime of Muʿizz al-Dīn he had made an agreement with Ghiyāth al-Dīn Maḥmūd that each would regard the other's enemies as his own,[119] and at the fall of Nīshāpūr in 596/1199–1200 had extracted an oath from ʿAlāʾ al-Dīn Muḥammad b. Abī ʿAlī not to take up arms against him at any time.[120] These mortgages were each called in at a critical juncture, securing first the incarceration of his brother ʿAlī Shāh and then the surrender of Fīrūzkūh itself in 612/1215–16. It may be no accident, either, that the shah's final moves against the Ghurids occurred only after he

[115] *Ibid.*, 1:410 (tr. 496).

[116] *Ibid.*, 1:379 (tr. 412); for the brother's name, see 1:377 (tr. 408). For the deaths of all the Ghurid princes held captive in Khwārazm, see also Nasawī, Pers. tr., 57; Houdas' Arabic text, 39 (tr. 66), here omits the sons of Ghiyāth al-Dīn Maḥmūd, though their captivity is mentioned earlier (21, tr. 37).

[117] He is known to have been imprisoned there following the murder of Ghiyāth al-Dīn Maḥmūd: *TN*, 1:377 (tr. 408). *Ibid.*, 1:339 (tr. 344), Jūzjānī speaks of his death "at the hands of the Turks of Khwārazm at the time of their conquest", which could well refer to the point at which ʿAlāʾ al-Dīn Atsiz and his allies took over Fīrūzkūh in 607/1210.

[118] *TN*, 1:340 (tr. 345): he is listed among the *malik*s of Sultan Iltutmish at 1:451 (tr. 626).

[119] *Ibid.*, 1:374 (tr. 400–2).

[120] *Ibid.*, 1:382 (tr. 418); for the surrender of Nīshāpūr, see 1:370 (tr. 393).

had repudiated the overlordship of the heathen Qara-Khitan and could thus pose as an exponent of the *jihād*.[121]

But the Ghurid polity was intrinsically vulnerable. It was easy for an external rival to profit from the disputes among Muʿizz al-Dīn's kinsmen and his *ghulām*s, so that the kingdom of Sīstān, for instance, was soon detached from the Ghurid sphere of influence and providing troops instead for the Khwārazmshāh.[122] In his operations, the shāh was sometimes able to capitalize on events elsewhere in the Ghurid dominions, for instance the embarrassments of the rulers of Bāmiyān. We are told that in 603/1206–7 he had actually abandoned the siege of Balkh and was withdrawing when he learned of their capture by Yildiz, of which he duly, and with some relish, notified their lieutenant ʿImād al-Dīn. Again, Ghiyāth al-Dīn Maḥmūd would have advanced on Herat late in 602/in mid 1206 had it not been for the recovery of Ghazna by his Bāmiyān rivals.[123] We should also not forget the notoriously refractory character of the Ghūrī clans: Jūzjānī remarks that every year one district or another would rebel and withhold revenue, right down to the end of the Ghurid regime.[124] This may have cost the government at Fīrūzkūh resources which were vital for its capacity to mount an effective resistance.

The conflicts among the Ghurids' supporters did not necessarily pit Ghūrī and Tājīk against Turk. At Fīrūzkūh, as we have seen (pp. 217–18), Ghiyāth al-Dīn Maḥmūd won the support of both groups. By the time Rukn al-Dīn Maḥmūd Īrān Shāh attacked Fīrūzkūh, Ghiyāth al-Dīn Maḥmūd may well have taken steps to reduce his dependence on the Ghūrīs, since Jūzjānī seems to draw a distinction between his forces and the vanquished "Ghūrīs" led by his opponent.[125] In this connection, the fact that Maḥmūd purchased and promoted numerous Turkish slaves, as his uncle Muʿizz al-Dīn had done, is surely significant.[126] Yet after his death Jūzjānī depicts "the Ghūrī and Turkish amirs" as gathering in unison around the throne of his infant son; though the *ghulām*s were a turbulent group and put to death or imprisoned a number of Ghurid princes (includ-

[121] See Barthold, *Turkestan*, 353 ff.
[122] Bosworth, *The history of the Saffarids*, 401–2.
[123] IA, 12:151–2/229–30.
[124] *TN*, 1:333 (tr. 334).
[125] *Ibid.*, 1:371 (tr. 395); cf. also 1:374 (tr. 399).
[126] *Ibid.*, 1:375–6 (tr. 405).

ing Rukn al-Dīn Maḥmūd Īrān Shāh himself) whom they saw as a danger to their new master.[127]

On the other hand, Ghūrī amirs are found supporting the Khwarazmians and their clients, and there is strong evidence that many of them accepted the shah's rule. He employed a leading Ghūrī amir, Muḥammad b. ʿAlī b. Bashīr, to win over the Ghurids' adherents at Balkh by peaceful means and later to oversee the murder of ʿAlī Shāh.[128] When Fīrūzkūh fell to Atsiz and his Khwarazmian allies in 607/1210, Jūzjānī indicates that those who commanded the hill-tops at Fīrūzkūh were left unharmed. This must include ʿUthmān al-Marghanī the *sar-i jāndār* and Quṭb al-Dīn Ḥasan b. ʿAlī b. Abī ʿAlī, a member of another distinguished Ghūrī clan, the "Bāʿalīs", since these amirs are named among the defenders.[129] Both are shortly found in the service of Atsiz, commanding the right wing in the battle with the Ghazna forces in 611/1214–15.[130] Later, the Khwārazmshāh deputed a group of Ghūrī amirs to serve under his son Rukn al-Dīn "Ghūrīshānastī" in newly conquered Iraq,[131] and at the time of the Mongol onslaught he relied considerably on Ghūrīs in arranging for the defence both of Ghūr itself and of Transoxiana. The amirs commissioned by the Khwārazmshāh with the task of garrisoning and setting in order the fortresses of Ghūr were Quṭb al-Dīn Ḥasan "Bāʿalī" and the Ḥasan-i ʿAbd al-Malik *sar-i zarrād* who had earlier served Ghiyāth al-Dīn Maḥmūd (p. 217).[132] Ghūrī amirs and their troops are mentioned among the garrison of Samarqand in Muḥarram 617/March-April 1220: they included Zangī b. Kharjūm, who had rallied to Ghiyāth al-Dīn Maḥmūd in 602/1206.[133] Even Ikhtiyār al-Dīn Muḥammad b. ʿAlī Kharpūst, who had held out

[127] *Ibid.*, 1:371–2, 377 (tr. 395–6, 408).

[128] IA, 12:151/229. Juwaynī, 2:85 (tr. 353).

[129] *TN*, 1:378 (tr. 410), for the amirs named; 1:379 for their survival (tr., 412, "escaped in safety", for *ba-salāmat bimāndand*, is slightly misleading). Quṭb al-Dīn's name is given as Ḥusayn in the printed text and by Raverty, but appears consistently throughout B.L. ms. Add. 26,189 as Ḥasan. He later served the Delhi Sultans. Jūzjānī employs the *nisba* "Baʿalī" for his cousin ʿImād al-Dīn Zangī: *TN*, 2:132 (tr. 1056). Raverty read it as "Baʿlamī", but the mss. give clearly BʿLY. There is a parallel formation, "Bāhalīm", from "Bū Hālīm": *ibid.*, 1:241–2 (tr. 110); Bosworth, *The later Ghaznavids*, 102.

[130] *TN*, 1:381 (tr. 416).

[131] *Ibid.*, 1:309, 314 (tr. 266, 282).

[132] *Ibid.*, 2:110–11, 135 (tr. 1002–3, 1063).

[133] *Ibid.*, 1:312, and 2:107 (tr. 274, 979–80). Nasawī, Arabic text, ed. Houdas, 36 (tr. 62–3; tr. Buniiatov, 81, incorrectly punctuated), and Persian trans., ed. Mīnuwī, 54, including among them "the son of ʿIzz al-Dīn K.t.": regrettably there

against the Khwarazmian forces for ten years in a fortress near Ṭāliqān, was subsequently appointed to the *iqṭā*ʿ of Peshawar and is found in the service of the shah's son Jalāl al-Dīn at the time of the Mongol invasion.[134] We are left with the impression that powerful elements in Ghūr knew when to change sides and that the shah was ready to recruit them.

Such a pattern of fickle allegiances may have been repeated a decade after the fall of the Ghurid dynasty. When the Khwarazmian empire was reeling from the Mongol invasion, the activities of Ghūrī elements may have served further to undermine it. Ikhtiyār al-Dīn Kharpūst now seized control of Ghazna, an action seen at the time as the prelude to a Ghūrī revolt against the Khwārazmshāh.[135] Shortly afterwards, Ghazna was occupied by another group of Ghūrīs headed by Aʿẓam Malik, allegedly the son of the one-time ruler of Balkh, ʿImād al-Dīn, although they made a timely submission to prince Jalāl al-Dīn on his arrival.[136] One particular Ghūrī clan was to carve out a distinguished path for itself on the ruins of the Ghurid and Khwarazmian empires. This was a branch of the Marghanī family, which we have already encountered. In 622–3/1225–6 Jūzjānī travelled on a series of missions for Rukn al-Dīn Muḥammad b. ʿUthmān al-Marghanī, the commander of Khaysār,[137] who at this late date can only have held the fortress on behalf of the Mongols. He was in all probability the amir listed among Ghiyāth al-Dīn Maḥmūd's supporters in 602/1206 and the son of the above-mentioned *sar-i jāndār* ʿUthmān. There is good reason to believe that he was also the father of Shams al-Dīn Muḥammad, founder of the Kartid dynasty which reigned at Herat from the 1240s until its destruction by Temür in

is a lacuna in the B.L. ms. Or. 5,662 (between fols 15 and 16) at this point, but the name looks suspiciously like "Kart" (see below and n. 138). IA, 12:147/223, for Zangī b. Kharjūm's joining Maḥmūd.

[134] *TN*, 2:110, 116 (tr. 1002, 1013); for the grant see *ibid.*, 1:315 (tr. 285–6).

[135] Juwaynī, 2:192–3 (tr. 460–1). Nasawī, ed. Houdas, Arabic text, 79 (tr. 132; tr. Buniiatov, 123). The account in *TN*, 2:116 (tr. 1012–13), is briefer. Barthold, *Turkestan*, 440, thought the charge groundless.

[136] Juwaynī, 2:195 (tr. 462–3). *TN*, 2:117 (tr. 1015–16). There is evidently some confusion regarding this Aʿẓam Malik, whom Nasawī, ed. Houdas, Arabic text, 21, 80 (tr. 37, 134; tr. Buniiatov, 65, 124), twice refers to among the captive princes in Khwārazm (though on the first occasion calling him the son of "Tāj al-Dīn"). It is therefore conceivable that we are here dealing with a different person.

[137] *TN*, 1:285, 297, and 2:122, 135, 183–5 (tr. 201, 233, 1039, 1061–2, 1198–1205); cf. also 2:104 (tr. 967).

791/1389. Shams al-Dīn's genealogy varies in the sources;[138] but this possibility, first suggested by Raverty, finds corroboration in a source of which he was unaware. According to Waṣṣāf, writing towards the end of the 7th/13th century, Shams al-Dīn alleged in a petition to the Mongol *qaghan* Möngke that his family had governed Khaysār and Ghūr by virtue of a diploma (*yarligh*) from Chinggis Khan.[139] That Rukn al-Dīn Muḥammad and his father 'Uthmān may thus have served three different regimes in turn—the last of them heathen and Islam's deadly enemy—should not perhaps surprise us. In the first quarter or so of the 7th/13th century the loyalties of these Ghūrī chiefs were in a constant state of flux.

Abbreviations Used

B.L.	British Library
CAJ	*Central Asiatic Journal*
*EI*²	*Encyclopaedia of Islam*, new ed. (Brill: Leiden, 1954–in progress)
IA	Ibn al-Athīr, *al-Kāmil fi'l-Ta'rīkh*
TN	Jūzjānī, *Ṭabaqāt-i Nāṣirī*

Bibliography

Anawati, G.C., "Fakhr al-Dīn al-Rāzī", *EI*².
Anonymous, *Ta'rīkh-i Sīstān*, ed. Malik al-Shu'arā' Bahār, Tehran, 1332/1914; tr. L.P. Smirnova, *Istoriia Sistana*, Pamiatniki pis' mennosti vostoka, 42, Moscow, 1974.
'Aziz Ahmad, Muhammad, *Political history and institutions of the early Turkish empire of Delhi (1206–1290 A.D.)*, Lahore, 1949; repr.: New Delhi, 1972.
Baranī, Ḍiyā' al-Dīn, *Ta'rīkh-i Fīrūzshāhī*, ed. S.A. Khán, Calcutta, 1861–2.

[138] For the dynasty, see Haig and Spuler, "Kart". Their ancestry is discussed in a note to Ḥabībī's edition of the *TN* (1:280) and in a long and confused note to Raverty's translation (1198–1200 n. 8). The earliest extant chronicler of Herat, Sayfī, 140–1, makes Shams al-Dīn the son of Rukn al-Dīn Abū Bakr b. 'Izz al-Dīn 'Umar, but also mentions, 144–5, a Rukn al-Dīn Muḥammad b. Tāj al-Dīn 'Uthmān. Abū Bakr was surely the Abū Bakr Marghanī (? Marjaqī in the text) who was installed alongside the Mongols' own representative following their first capture of Herat in 1220 (*ibid.*, 71, 72–6), and the son of the 'Izz al-Dīn 'Umar who had governed the city at an earlier date (above, n. 54). For yet another genealogy, which makes Shams al-Dīn's father Rukn al-Dīn Abū Bakr the son of a certain Sanjar and the maternal grandson of 'Uthmān Marghanī, see Faṣīḥ-i Khwāfī, *Mujmal*, 3:102.

[139] Waṣṣāf, lithograph ed., 81/ed. and tr. Hammer-Purgstall, 1:163 (tr. 154). This section of Waṣṣāf's work forms part of the first book, which was completed in 698/1298–9: lithograph ed., 25/ed. Hammer-Purgstall, 1:50 (tr. 48–9).

Barthold, W., *Turkestan down to the Mongol invasion*, 3rd ed. by C.E. Bosworth, London, 1968.

Bivar, A.D.H., "Naghar and Īryāb: two little known Islamic sites of the north-west frontier of Afghanistan and Pakistan", *Iran* 24 (1986), 131–8.

Bosworth, C.E., "The early Islamic history of Ghur", *CAJ* 6 (1961), 116–33; reprinted in his *The medieval history of Iran, Afghanistan and Central Asia*, London, 1977.

———, "Ghūrids", *EI*².

———, *The history of the Saffarids of Sistan and the Maliks of Nimruz (247/861–949/1542–3)*, Costa Mesa, California, and New York, 1994.

———, "Khaladj, i. History", *EI*².

———, *The later Ghaznavids: splendour and decay. The dynasty in Afghanistan and northern India 1040–1186*, Edinburgh, 1977.

———, "Nangrahār, Ningrahār", *EI*².

———, "Political and dynastic history of the Iranian world (A.D. 1000–1217)", in J.A. Boyle (ed.), *The Cambridge History of Iran*, v. *The Saljuq and Mongol periods*, Cambridge, 1968.

———, and Clauson, Sir Gerard, "Al-Xwārazmī on the peoples of Central Asia", *Journal of the Royal Asiatic Society* (1965), 2–12; repr. in Bosworth C.E., *The medieval history of Iran, Afghanistan and Central Asia*, London, 1977.

Burton-Page, J., "Dūrbāsh", *EI*².

Clauson, Sir Gerard, *An etymological dictionary of pre-thirteenth-century Turkish*, Oxford, 1972.

Crone, Patricia, *Roman, provincial and Islamic law*, Cambridge, 1987.

Digby, Simon, "Iletmish or Iltutmish? A reconsideration of the name of the Dehlī Sultan", *Iran* 8 (1970), 57–64.

Fakhr-i Mudabbir, *Shajarat al-Ansāb*, partial ed. Sir E. Denison Ross, *Ta'ríkh* [sic]-i *Fakhru'd-dín Mubáraksh※áh*, London, 1927.

Faṣīḥ-i Khwāfī, *Mujmal-i Faṣīḥī*, ed. Maḥmūd Farrukh, 3 vols., Tehran, 1339–41 Sh./1960–2.

Forand, P.G., "The relation of the slave and the client to the master or patron in medieval Islam", *International Journal of Middle East Studies* 2 (1971): 59–66.

Habib, Irfan, "Formation of the Sultanate ruling class of the thirteenth century", in Habib I. (ed.), *Medieval India 1: researches in the history of India 1200–1750*, Oxford and Delhi, 1992, 1–21.

Habib, Mohammad, and Nizami, Khaliq Ahmad (eds.), *The Delhi Sultanat (A.D. 1206–1526)*, A comprehensive history of India, v, New Delhi, 1970.

Habibullah, A.B.M., *The foundation of Muslim rule in India*, 2nd ed. Allahabad, 1961.

Haig, T.W., and Spuler, B., "Kart", *EI*².

Hardy, P., "Dihlī Sultanate", *EI*².

Ḥasan-i Niẓāmī al-Nīshāpūrī, *Tāj al-Ma'āthir*, India Office Library ms. 15 (Ethé, no. 210).

Hodivala, S.H., *Studies in Indo-Muslim history*, 2 vols., Bombay, 1939–57.

Ibn al-Athīr, *al-Kāmil fi'l-Ta'rīkh*, ed. C.J. Tornberg, Leiden, 1851–63; repr. Beirut, 1385–6/1965–6, with different pagination [references are given to both printings, in that order].

Ibn al-Sā'ī, *al-Jāmi' al-Mukhtaṣar*, vol. 9 ed. Muṣṭafā Jawād and Anastase Marie de St. Élie, Baghdad, 1353/1934.

Ibn Isfandiyār, *Ta'rīkh-i Ṭabaristān*, ed. 'Abbās Iqbāl, Tehran, n.d.

Jackson, Peter, "Jalāl al-Dīn, the Mongols and the Khwarazmian conquest of the Panjāb and Sind", *Iran* 28 (1990), 45–54.

———, "Ḳuṭb al-Dīn Aybak", *EI*².

Juwaynī, 'Alā' al-Dīn Aṭā Malik, *Ta'rīkh-i Jahān-gushā*, ed. Mīrzā Muḥammad Qazwīnī, 3 vols., Leiden and London, 1912–37; tr. J.A. Boyle, *The history of the World-conqueror*, 2 vols. with continuous pagination, Manchester, 1958.

Jūzjānī, Minhāj-i Sirāj, *Ṭabaqāt-i Nāṣirī*, 2nd ed. ʿAbd al-Ḥaiy Ḥabībī, 2 vols., Kabul, 1342–3 Sh./1963–4); tr. H.G. Raverty, *Ṭabaḳāt-i Nāṣirī*, Calcutta, 1873–81; B.L. ms. Add. 26,189.

Kieffer, Ch., "Les Ghôrides, une grande dynastie nationale, IIIe partie: le déclin et le démembrement de l'empire ghôride", *Afghanistan* 16 (1961), part IV, 37–50, and 17 (1962), part II, 40–56.

———, "Le minaret de Ghiyath al-Din à Firouzkoh (minaret de Djam)", *Afghanistan* 16 (1960), part IV, 16–60.

Leshnik, Lorenz S., "Ghor, Firuzkoh and the Minar-i Jam", *CAJ* 12 (1968), 36–49.

Maricq, André, and Wiet, Gaston, *Le minaret de Djam. La découverte de la capitale des sultans Ghorides (XIIe–XIIIe siècles)*, Mémoires de la délégation archéologique française en Afghanistan, 16, Paris, 1959.

Minorsky, V., "The Turkish dialect of the Khalaj", *BSOAS* 10 (1940), 417–37; repr. in his *The Turks, Iran and the Caucasus in the Middle Ages*, London, 1978.

Nasawī, Muḥammad b. Aḥmad, *Sīrat al-Sulṭān Jalāl al-Dīn*, Arabic text ed. and tr. O. Houdas, *Histoire du Sultan Djélal ed-Din Mankubirti*, 2 vols. Paris, 1891–5; also tr. Z.M. Buniiatov, *Dzhizneopisanie Sultana Dzhalal ad-dina Mankburny*, Baku, 1973; 13th-century Persian translation ed. Mujtabā Mīnuwī, Persian Texts series, 19, Tehran, 1344 Sh./1965.

Richards, D.S., "Ibn al-Athīr and the later parts of the Kāmil: a study of aims and methods", in *Medieval historical writing in the Christian and Islamic worlds*, ed. D.O. Morgan, London, 1982, 76–108.

Sauvaget, Jean, "Noms et surnoms de Mamelouks", *Journal Asiatique* 238 (1950), 31–58.

Sayfī (Sayf b. Muḥammad b. Yaʿqūb al-Harawī), *Ta'rīkh-Nāma-yi Harāt*, ed. M.Z. aṣ-Ṣiddíqí, Calcutta, 1944.

Sourdel, Dominique, *Inventaire des monnaies musulmanes anciennes du Musée de Cabul*, Damascus 1953.

Waṣṣāf, *Tajziyat al-Amṣār wa-Tazjiyat al-Aʿṣār*, lithograph ed. Bombay, 1269/1853; ed. and tr. J. von Hammer-Purgstall, *Geschichte Wassafs*, vol. i, Vienna, 1856; all published.

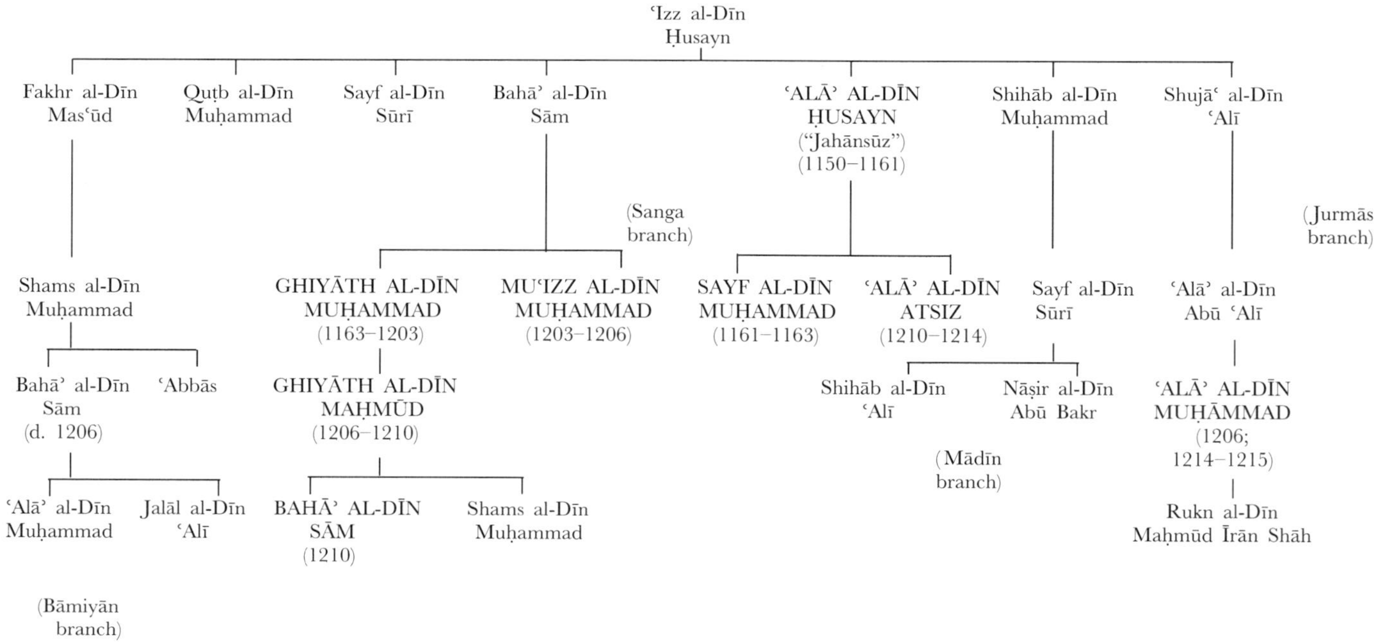

ʿIzz al-Dīn Ḥusayn
Fakhr al-Dīn Masʿūd
Quṭb al-Dīn Muḥammad
Sayf al-Dīn Sūrī
Bahāʾ al-Dīn Sām
ʿALĀʾ AL-DĪN ḤUSAYN (“Jahānsūz”) (1150–1161)
Shihāb al-Dīn Muḥammad
Shujāʿ al-Dīn ʿAlī
(Sanga branch)
(Jurmās branch)
Shams al-Dīn Muḥammad
GHIYĀTH AL-DĪN MUḤAMMAD (1163–1203)
MUʿIZZ AL-DĪN MUḤAMMAD (1203–1206)
SAYF AL-DĪN MUḤAMMAD (1161–1163)
ʿALĀʾ AL-DĪN ATSIZ (1210–1214)
Sayf al-Dīn Sūrī
ʿAlāʾ al-Dīn Abū ʿAlī
Bahāʾ al-Dīn Sām (d. 1206)
ʿAbbās
GHIYĀTH AL-DĪN MAḤMŪD (1206–1210)
Shihāb al-Dīn ʿAlī
Nāṣir al-Dīn Abū Bakr
ʿALĀʾ AL-DĪN MUḤĀMMAD (1206; 1214–1215)
(Mādīn branch)
ʿAlāʾ al-Dīn Muḥammad
Jalāl al-Dīn ʿAlī
BAHĀʾ AL-DĪN SĀM (1210)
Shams al-Dīn Muḥammad
Rukn al-Dīn Maḥmūd Īrān Shāh
(Bāmiyān branch)

THE GHURIDS

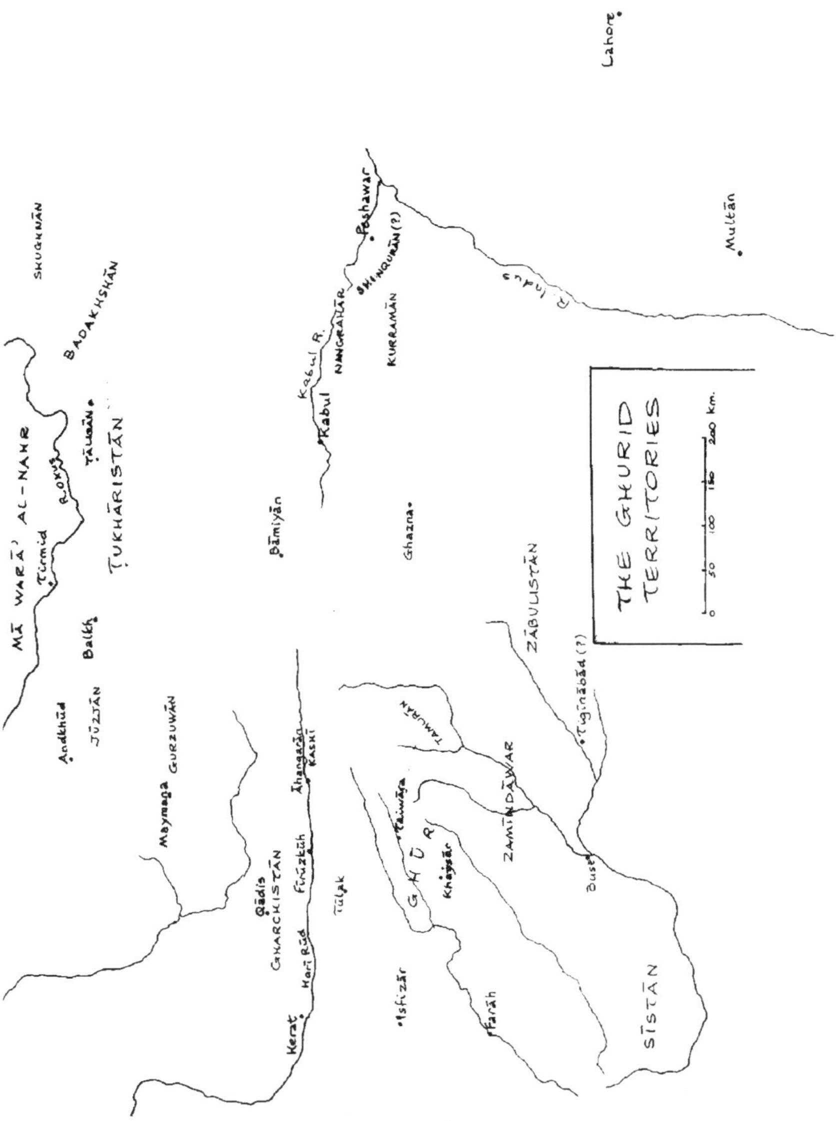

THE GHURID TERRITORIES

POEMS FROM THE TURKISH

TRANSLATED BY BERNARD LEWIS

Since there is no permanence in this world of ruin
a thousand years, a single moment, count the same.

Rose time has come, the world is fresh and young again.
Feast and roister while you are young.

Sufi! Don't deny the goodness of wine—
The Master of wisdom ordained it so in a book . . .

There is no choice but to come, moaning, to your door.
By God, sir, in this respect I am not at fault.

Baki, seeing the cupbearer's cheek reflected in the winecup,
thinks it is the flaming sun at dawn.

Baki (1526–1600)

Cupbearer! The wine-glass makes a beautiful rose—
he who takes it in his hand becomes a nightingale.

Whoever sees the fresh wound in my breast
will admire a beautiful red carnation.

The pale breath of my sigh of longing for your lovelock
becomes a slender blue hyacinth.

Whoever explores the locks of the beloved
becomes enmeshed and bound in her tresses.

If the waters of attainment do not save Baki
he will burn to a cinder in the fire of separation.

Baki

Your cheek is like fresh water
your chin like a bubble

The sunbeams of your cheek strike my heart
like moonlight on the water.

By your skilled penmanship, the page of my heart
is like an illuminated book.

At the feast of sorrow my bloodshot eyes
are like two winecups.

Love for that moon grips the whole world
like the light of the sun.

O Baki the perfumed mole of the beloved
is like pure musk, scented and black.

Baki

My stock is Albanian
all my race live by the sword.
What if this lion-quelling people,
like falcons, make their home in the rocks.
This is the merit of the Albanian—
He is like a jewel in stone.

Yahya of Tashlica (d. 1575)

My tipsy darling, what magic made you so bold,
made you taller than a cypress?

Your tender flesh is more fragrant than perfume, more limpid
than color
as if a particolored rose had nourished you at its breast—

You wear a rose-patterned brocade, and I fear for you my dar-
ling,
a scratch from the shade of the thorn of the rose on that
brocade—

You came with a rose in one hand, a cup in the other,
which should I take, the rose, the cup, or you?

Nedim (?–1730)

Were I your treasure, you would squander me;
were I your mirror, you would dazzle me.

From the arrow of the eye to the scar of the heart,
look on what sights you will see.

Cupbearer, inspiration is either with you or with me:
you are making the sea the guest of bubbles.

With passionate looks, O eye,
you have made fire and water the same.

O pious man, that moonlike beauty is such a light,
you can not call it an idol; you may even believe.

Words are less than the sound of an empty drum.
Galib! You lament in vain.

Respond to the music of the spheres; be a Mevlevi,
and you will meditate and you will turn.

Şeyh Galib (1755–1799)

However tenacious the tyrant
we shall shatter the pillars of his tyranny.
Though we be cast into the bowels of the earth
we shall split the earthly globe and break free.

Namık Kemal (1840–1888)

We were a thousand horsemen, merry as boys on our raids;
A thousand horsemen, that day we conquered a giant army.
The silver-helmeted Beylerbey shouted "forward!"
On a summer day we crossed the Danube with our caravans
Like lightning we struck at a land, in seven columns,
Like lightning, where the Turkish heroes had once passed.
One day, riding our horses at full gallop
We rose in flight from earth to seventh heaven
Even today, when we see the roses bloom in paradise
That crimson memory quivers in our eyes.
We were a thousand horsemen, merry as boys on our raids,
A thousand horsemen, that day we conquered a giant army.

Yahya Kemal Beyatlı (1885–1958)

THE IRANIAN NATIONALISTS IN ISTANBUL DURING WORLD WAR I

J.P. Luft

Organising diverse political groups and individuals in exile into an effective front with a coherent political strategy is a major task for every opposition. Besides the various different notions about aims, strategy and tactics for changing the political system at home, or at least some kind of reform of its existing order, various other interests influence the fortunes of these groups. The support which they enjoy from their host governments depends to a large part upon their usefulness. Foreign policy issues and the intricate web of international relations play an important role in the success or failure of their endeavours. In times of war or similar international crisis situations these groups can offer opportunities which do not exist under normal conditions, or are not properly recognised as such. Undoubtedly the polarisation of political forces and the clearcut divisions between the interests and aims of states at war allow oppositional forces in exile to gain definite political or even financial support for their cause from their host nation if they have decided to throw their lot behind it.

Iran's political émigrés in the pre World War I period were neither particularly well organised nor concentrated in one political group, although the majority belonged to more radical deputies of the second *Majlis* where they formed an influential wing later called the Democratic caucus. During the difficult and eventful years of 1909–1912 which first witnessed the downfall of Muhammad ʿAlî Shâh, and then what seemed to be the final destruction of the constitutional assembly in Iran, a number of the radical politicians went into exile to Turkey or further away to Europe, most prominent among them the member of parliament from Tabriz, Sayyid Hasan Taqîzâda. He who had been the leader of the Social Democrats in the *Majlis* was forced to leave Iran twice. In 1908 during the Lesser Despotism, he and a number of leading constitutionalists, among them former cabinet minister and *Majlis* deputies had to flee the country. Some of them settled in Paris, others in London.[1] Taqîzâda had gone into exile to England, though only for a short period. Here he became much involved in the formation of a pressure group, the Persian Committee, which was founded on October 30, 1908. E.G. Browne and H.F.B. Lynch were then the driving force in organising the various oppositional voices inside and outside the Parliament against what was considered the disastrous course of British foreign policy under Sir Edward Grey, in particular its close alliance with the Czarist Government.[2] However, by 1913, the Persian Committee had lost its political momentum.

Also participating in the fight against Muhammad ʿAlî Shâh was another member of the first *Majlis* Abu'l-Hasan Pirnîyâ Muʿazzad al-Dawla from Nâ'în. He did not stay on in London but went to Paris where at the same time other leading figures of the Constitutional Movement, among them Sardâr-i Asʿad, Mukhbir al-Saltana and ʿAlî Akbar Dihkhudâ had moved too after the closing of the *Majlis* in June 1908. There a similar society, the *Anjuman-i Frankpersan* (Union Franco-Persane) was established with support of the French Ministry of Foreign Affairs. Members included the editors of major French newspapers. The only other European member was E.G. Browne. The Iranian envoy in France, ʿAbd al-Samad Khân Mumtâz al-Saltana was its honorary president, although the affairs were mainly directed by the French parliamentarian Jules Roches.[3]

The problems which the Iranian government and the *Majlis* had been facing since the middle of 1910 led to increased tensions between the two major powers, Great Britain and Russia, but also to near financial collapse of the central government and the breakdown of law and order in the provinces. By that time Taqîzâda was no longer a main player in Iran itself, his parliamentary party, the Democrats (*firqa-yi Dimûkrât*) were fighting with their opponents of moderate members of parliament (*firqa-yi Iʿtidâl*) for control over the government, and in July 1910 gained for a couple of months a dominat-

[1] See Bayat, *Iran's first revolution*, 245.

[2] Browne, *The Persian Revolution of 1905–1909*, 264–65; for an assessment of this committee see McLean, "A professor extraordinary", 399–408 and its wider political context "English radicals", 338–52; s.a. Gurney, "E.G. Browne", 164–5.

[3] *Welt des Islam*, III (1915), 161. Its usefulness for serious political work has been sometimes doubted. E.g. Ibrâhîm Safâ, *Rahbarân-i*, I, 633 claims that they were mainly squabbling, not pursuing the cause of fighting for freedom. Undoubtedly Dihkhudâ's radical newspaper *Sûr-i Isrâfîl* supported by Muʿazzad al-Dawla was the spearhead of the attack against the autocratic regime in Iran.

ing position. Although a more liberal government had been formed under the Qajar politician Mustawfî al-Mamâlik, the chronic financial situation remained serious. This and other seemingly insoluble problems were exacerbated by the showdown with the hard core of the revolutionary movement, the *mujâhidîn*, supported by the radical Social Democrats. The militant wing of the party, increasingly left out of the mainstream parliamentary activities, finally lost out when police forces loyal to the moderate regime cracked down on the unruly *fidâ'î* and *mujâhidîn* groups in August 1910. In the autumn of 1911, as a consequence of the deteriorating relations with Czarist Russia, the independence of the country was further threatened by the intervention of Russian troops in various parts of northern Iran. The position of the nationalist forces was finally undermined in the Morgan Shuster affair, which ended with the suspension of the constitution and the closing down of the *Majlis* on 24th December by order of the regent Nâsir al-Mulk.[4]

The bleak situation in Iran created a feeling of resignation about the future of the country leading to demoralisation, particularly among the Social Democrats. Still the majority of their members in the second *Majlis*, and many of their activists stayed on in Iran. More radical elements like Taqîzâda, Haydar Khân Amû Oghlû and Rasûlzâda, however, had already been forced to emigrate. Other more prominent members of the Democrats like Husayn Qulî Khân Navvâb, the former Minister for Foreign Affairs, and Vahîd al-Mulk, a leading member of the second *Majlis*, finally went into exile to Europe, Navvâb to Switzerland, Vahîd al-Mulk to Paris from where he seems to have returned to Iran in 1913. A much harder fate befell the *mujâhidîn* from Azarbayjan and Tehran. Persecuted and hunted down, quite a number of them had to move to Istanbul, where they suffered severe economic hardship. Nûrullâh Yakânî describes how they tried to survive as peddlers and in other menial jobs. Several of them succeeded in gaining admission to the Police Academy in Istanbul with the support of the Ottoman government; but as Iranian nationals they could not find employment. About 150 *mujâhidîn* from Azarbayjan served in the Ottoman army during the Balkan wars and received as a reward for their valuable services two villages abandoned by their Bulgarian owners in the wars.[5] In the case of

[4] McDaniel, *The Shuster mission*, 198.
[5] Kasravî, *Târîkh-i hîjdah sâl*, 594–5.

Taqîzâda, it was probably not so much his political radicalism which made him *persona non grata* for Russia and Great Britain, but the opposition raised against him in the ranks of the *ʿulamâʾ* as well as conservative political circles.[6] Taqîzâda continued his political activities abroad, frequently travelling between Istanbul, London and Paris until 1913. Although elected to the 3rd *Majlis* in 1914, he did not dare return to Iran. Finally he moved to the United States of America where he remained until the outbreak of World War I.[7]

For a number of reasons Istanbul had been the first place where political activists went if they had to leave their country in these difficult years. During the preceding decades, the Ottoman capital had been serving as a focal point for all shades of opponents against the autocratic regime in Qajar Iran. It was acting as a clearing house for various activities of a wide political nature embedded in the well-established community of merchants mainly from Azarbayjan. The American financial adviser to the Iranian government Morgan Shuster who on his way to Tehran spent five days in Istanbul, writes in his memoirs that a large colony of Persians (in the widest sense) were in residence there:

> The Turkish capital is always in close touch with Tehran, and there we met many Persians who had but recently come from their own country. Some were in political exile, like the famous Constitutionalist deputy from Tabriz, Taqî-zâde, who called on me and talked for an hour of the troubles in Persia. Others whom we met had taken prominent parts in the nationalist movement, among them being merchants, priests, foreign-office officials and diplomats.[8]

The Iranians who in their majority were from the north of Iran, in particular Azarbaijan, had organised themselves into a number of societies and clubs. They published newspapers and pursued a range of political and non-political activities. After the coup d'etat of Muḥammad ʿAlî Shâh the émigrés had made a major impact on the political

---

[6] Safâ, *Rahbarân*, II, 248; Vatandoust, *Sayyid Hasan Taqîzâdeh*, 15, following Safâ, *Rahbarân*. Taqîzâda had originally asked the *Majlis* for three months leave of absence. Cf. *Muzakirât-i Majlis*, Dawra-yi duvvum, Jalasa 111, 24. Jum. II, 1328.

[7] Sayyid Hasan Taqîzâda describes in his memoirs the difficulties in earning his living through occasional work in the United States of America and how the German Consul in New York invited him to come to Germany; see his *Zindigî-yi tûfânî*, 174–81. It seems likely that Taqîzâda met already in the USA a number of Indian revolutionaries who at that time lived mainly in California.

[8] Shuster, *The Strangling of Persia*, 36.

awareness and the organisations of the Iranians living there and had exerted a major influence on their organisations. As in the western European capitals, a society, the *Anjuman-i Saʿâdat*, was founded to support the efforts of the constitutionalists to gain the upper hand in their fight against the Shah of Iran. This society became a centre and political rallying point which was active in communicating information to Persian émigrés and their friends in Great Britain and elsewhere.[9] It was influential in raising support for the revolutionary cause in Iran through its agents in various Iranian cities, particularly in the south. The close contacts between these expatriate associations and a network of *anjûmans* in Iran were an important factor for the political struggle in the country. A more radical *anjuman*, called *Jamʿîyat-i Ittihâd va Taraqî-yi Irânîyân-i Istanbul*, was founded, probably with the help of Taqîzâda, in spring 1909.[10] This society played an influential role in raising support for the revolutionary cause in Iran through their agents in various Iranian cities. These radical activists among the newcomers, many of them from Azarbayjan, did not always find support in the more conservative merchant circles in Istanbul. On the other hand, members of the Turkish constitutional movement, their natural allies, seem to have co-operated with them closely. The activists often stayed only a short period in the Ottoman capital, and after the lifting of the siege of Tabriz in May 1909 most of them returned to Iran. In Rabîʿ al-Avval 1329/ March 1911 another society in support of the national struggle in Iran, the *Jamʿîyat-i muʿavinat-i millîyya*, developed activities with the

[9] The society had been founded after the attack on the *Majlis* in June 1908, s. Gurney, E.G. Browne, 165–66; Djoudaki, "*L'Anjoman-e Saʿdat*", 87 refers to the year 1326, quoted in Kasravî, *Târîkh-i Mashrûtîyat*, 278; Iraj Afshâr mentions in his edition of the *Khâtirât va asnâd-i Mustashâr al-Dawla*, vol. II: *Asnâd-i Mashrûta, 1325–1330*, the year 1324/1906 (!). The society played an even more important role in the coordination of the various activities of the revolutionary *anjumans* in Iran during the siege of Tabriz by royalist forces leading finally to the deposition of Muhammad ʿAlî Shâh in July 1909, in particular the provincial *anjuman* of Azarbayjan. In addition to Istanbul other Iranian political associations existed in Baghdad: *Anjuman-i Ukhuvvat-e Irânîyân-i Baghdad*, Tiflis: *Kûmîta-yi Azâdî-khvâhân-i Qafqâz*, London: *Persian Committee* and Paris: *Anjuman-i Ittihâd va Taraqqî*, Djoudaki, *L'Anjoman-e Saʿdat*, 85.

[10] See a letter of the *Jamʿîyat-i Ittihâd va Taraqqî-yi Irânîyân-i Istanbul* to E.G. Browne dated 31 May 1909, Browne Papers, Cambridge University Library, Box 9/9.—Members of the *Anjuman-i (Jamʿîyat) Ittihâd va Taraqqî* informed the constitutional forces in Gilan under Yiprîm Khân and the Bakhtîyâr leader Sardâr-i Asad about the machinations of Muhammad ʿAlî Shâh. See Kasravî, *Târîkh-i hîjdah sâla*, 34.

aim of strengthening the defence of the constitutional government and providing financial help.[11]

In the years before World War I, Iran's external and internal affairs were both increasingly influenced and manipulated, if not dictated, much further away in European capitals, above all London and St. Petersburg. This clearly influenced the constitutionalists in their search for centralising and modernising Iran. Models of European governmental structures and social control mechanisms served as blueprints for a number of reformers who, hazy as their vision often might have been, were fighting continuously for changes in Iran. These reform-minded politicians in and outside Iran were also keen to establish contacts with liberal circles in western countries interested in supporting changes in Iran and what was considered the just cause. Two main protagonists of these circles were Sayyid Hasan Taqîzâda and the former Minister for Foreign Affairs Mîrzâ Husayn Qulî Khân Navvâb. Although hard hit by the intervention of Czarist Russia, the constitutional movement remained alive and finally forced the government and the regent Nâsir al-Mulk to hold general elections for a new National Assembly in autumn 1914. However, the British and Russian governments did not allow the newly constituted *Majlis* to convene until November 1914.[12] The Democrats won 31 seats and emerged as the strongest faction followed by the Moderates (*I'tidâliyyûn*) with 29. The *Hay'at-e 'ilmiyya* got 14 seats and there were also 20 independent deputies who quite often sided with the Democrats.[13] Sulaymân Mîrzâ became the leader of the Democrat members of parliament, making a return of Taqîzâda to the front seat less likely for some time to come.

With the outbreak of war, the situation in Iran seemed to become

---

[11] See a copy of a letter to the Ministry of Interior in Tehran published in *Mustashâr al-Dawla*, vol. II, 332.

[12] 16 Muharram 1333/5 December 1914, Sipihr, *Irân dar jang-e buzurg*, 101; Olson, *Anglo-Iranian relations*, 68.

[13] 98 out of 116 elected members were finally accepted. See *Asâmî-yi namâyandigân-i Majlis-i Shûrâ-yi Millî*, 28–33; see also Nûrî, *Hizb-i dimûkrât-i Irân*, 196–7. Originally the Democrats did not gain a seat in Tehran, but after the opening of the *Majlis* in a second round they won the majority of seven vacated seats (ministers) representing the capital. Sipihr, *Târîkh*, 102–4 lists only 23 I'tidâlîyûn members. Bahâr, *Târîkh-i mukhtasar*, 13–14 maintains that the moderates originally won the majority in the new parliament. However, Mansûra Ittihâdîya (Nizâm Mâfî), *Ihzâb-i sîyâsî* table VIII, provides an interesting list of the distribution of seats in the 3rd *Majlis* which gives the Democrats 31, the *I'tidâlîyûn* 22, the religious groups (*'ilmiyya*) 16 and independent members 20 seats.

more open again. The formation of a new government under Mustawfî al-Mamâlik on 25 Ramazân 1332/16 August 1914, and the opening of the *Majlis* revived the political activities of the nationalist forces among whom the Democrats played an important role. They still commanded a well distributed network of cells and local groups in all major Iranian cities. Although considerably weakened and shaken by the events of the last four years, their presence in the *Majlis*, the administration, high government offices, and at the local level what was left of the once powerful *anjûmans* provided them with an opportunity to fight for the liberation of their country as did the involvement of Czarist Russia and Great Britain. Even the badly mauled radical elements of the *mujâhidîn*, who were no longer properly linked to the Democrats in Tehran or in other major Iranian cities outside Azarbayjan, were brought back into the political arena, mostly allying themselves to the Turkish forces and their Kurdish supporters when they were invading the north-west of Iran.

However, the war presented a new and major threat to the still intact, but fragile independence of Iran, since neither the Entente nor the Central powers were actually prepared to pay much attention to the declaration of neutrality by the Iranian government.[14] Mustawfî al-Mamâlik and all subsequent governments were in fact not in a position to overcome any of the problems forced upon Iran from outside. On the other hand, in such a difficult and dangerous situation a better understanding and political co-operation developed between the different factions inside and outside Iran, something that had not been seen for some time. Among the various candidates for the Premiership who supposedly represented different parties, or the interests of one of the powers, a certain kind of collusion existed in search of a line of policy favourable to Iran.[15]

With the war progressing, increasingly little room was left for manoeuvring. Already at an early stage the Democrats, driven by their strong anti-Russian feelings, hoped to secure the support of the German Reich. They nourished the hope that through this political move they would be able to exert enough pressure on the British

[14] The Iranian Government declared its neutrality in two notes to the British and Russian Ministers on 3 October which was reiterated in a *farmân* of Ahmad Shâh on 12 Zû'l-hijja 1332/1 November 1914. Texts s. Litten, *Wer hat die persische Neutralität verletzt*, Document 5 & 41; Gehrke, *Persien in der deutschen Orientpolitik*, vol. I, 29–30 & vol. II, document No. 1; s.a. Vogel, *Die Persien- und Afghanistanexpedition*, 43/1.

[15] Olson, *Anglo-Iranian relations*, 66.

Government to restrain Russia's military expansion in the north of Iran. Similar help was expected from the German diplomats and politicians to prevent the advance of the Ottoman army into Azarbayjan in order to fight the Russian troops on Iranian soil. In 1915 the leaders of the Democrats in Tehran, Sulaymân Mîrzâ and Vahîd al-Mulk Shaybânî, met regularly with the German Chargé d'Affaires to discuss the necessary steps.[16] In the long run, in the event of a victory for the Central powers, they expected to win back Iran's independence. The Auswärtige Amt and the German High Command were for strategically reasons quite keen to develop a policy of their own, independent from the Ottoman government, but they did not have the means of gaining access to Iran and Afghanistan without some support from the Ottoman government. Expectations were running high but with little success. Throughout the whole period of World War I the Ottoman Government preserved to some extent an independent eastern policy vis-a-vis its allies. The German military High Command and the Auswärtige Amt on the other hand (and here the Ottoman military was without doubt hard pushed to support such efforts), tried to establish a physical presence in Iran through a number of commandos and to stir up anti-Entente forces in Iran and Afghanistan in order to create concern among British politicians.[17]

As one of the prominent exiled politicians, Taqîzâda had been elected as a representative to the 3rd *Majlis* in 1914. However, political events prevented him taking up his seat and instead he accepted an offer by the German government to create a committee which

---

16 Olson, *Anglo-Iranian relations*, 68. Hâjjî Mîrzâ 'Abd al-Husayn Khân Vahîd al-Mulk Shaybânî Kâshânî was educated in an English school in Bombay. He became later a lector in Persian for E.G. Browne in Cambridge, from where he returned to Tehran, in order to teach law at the Dâr al-Funûn only to be dismissed in 1908. In 1909 he was elected as a member of the 2nd *Majlis* where he joined the democrats. After the Shuster affair he was arrested in May 1912 and, like Navvâb, exiled. He returned to Iran before the outbreak of World War I and was again elected a member of the *Majlis* for the 3rd legislature period. He moved with the *muhâjirîn* to Kirmânshâh but fell out with the leader of the Democrats, Sulaymân Mîrzâ. See Gehrke, *Persien*, vol. II, 280/223.

17 The failure to agree about a coordinated policy hampered decisively the efforts of the Germans and the Turks to achieve more permanent results in Iran and Afghanistan. Whereas German diplomacy hoped for change by influencing the political establishment in Tehran, the Ottomans were relying on their military operations and the mobilisation of tribal forces. The campaign of Rauf Bey and his expeditionary force in west Iran during 1915 clearly indicated the differences in approach. About Rauf Bey's expedition s. Gehrke, *Persien*, vol. I, 72–76.

was supposed to organise the political activities of Iranians living in Europe or temporarily out of the country with the aim of rescuing Iran. "Rescue from the Russian and British slavery" and "the unity of the nation" became magic words for mobilising the disparate and dispersed anti-Entente forces. For the German government the establishment of a political centre for Iranian opposition politicians in Berlin, similar to the previously founded Indian National Committee, provided a useful channel for propagating and pursuing its interests in an area from which it had been largely excluded during the preceding decades. It was also a helpful tool for contesting the Ottoman government which claimed to be the sole protector of the Islamic people beyond its eastern borders.[18]

At first glance the Ottoman capital appeared to be the ideal point for rallying the political activists from Iran, as there already existed a large community of Iranians with strong links to most parts of Iran. What seemed to count even more in its favour and made it a more natural base was the fact that it was the capital of a Muslim state whose ruler, the Sultan, was considered by most Muslims as their caliph. From the beginning, the Ottoman Government had been quite eager to use this claim in order to mobilise sympathy for its policies, in particular among the Muslims on the Indian subcontinent. Ten days after breaking off diplomatic relations with Russia, on 10th November 1914, the Turkish Sultan Mehmed Resat Han V, proclaimed *jihâd* against the powers of the Entente, which was confirmed by a *fatwâ* of the Shaykh al-Islam two days later. It is somewhat ironic that one part of the *Dâr al-harb* was quite naturally not only excluded from the Holy War but that the powers of the Entente were threatened with heavy punishment in the event of their attacking the German Reich or Austria-Hungary. If that weapon in defence of the Islamic world was already creating some confusion among the believers, even less convincing were the actions taken by Shî'î 'ulamâ' in the shrine cities of Iraq, the *'atabât*.

As expected, the call for the defence of Islamic countries against the infidel Russians and British received the full support of the leading

[18] This clear decision of Taqîzâda to side with the German Reich in the Great War has not prevented Iranian academics and journalists from accusing him of having been a *tarafdâr-e sîyâsat-e Inglîstân dar Irân*. See e.g. the defence of Taqîzâda by Jamâlzâdah, "Man Jamâlzâda", 39. They completely overlook the fact that Taqîzâda had a cordial relationship with Germany and the Germans between 1915 and 1922.

mujtahids in the *ʿatabât*, who issued *fatâvî* following the same line as their Sunni brethren in Istanbul. However, as the Iranian government upheld for quite obvious reasons its declaration of strict neutrality, the *fatâvî* made no real impact upon the people and stirred up more emotional feelings in places like Mashhad where the bombing of the Holy Shrine in 1912 was still fresh in people's memory. In Tehran such an action was seen as potentially undermining the efforts of the government to keep Iran out of the war. A similar position seemed also to have been taken by Hâjjî Mîrzâ Hasan Aqâ, the leading mujtahid in Azarbaijan, who did seem to have approved the *fatâvî* issued by his colleagues in the *ʿatabât* but was more inclined to back the Iranian government.[19] However, that senior mujtahids in the *ʿatabât* continued to endorse their position is indicated by their visits to the front, where they inspired Turkish soldiers to *jihâd*. But under these circumstances, the whole issue of *jihâd* should not be seen as a purely religious matter, but as a political stratagem as well, to the extent that nationalist factors took precedence. In any case the moral high ground of defending the nation had already been taken by radical nationalist forces whose influence stretched much further than the boundaries of their party. The preservation of some kind of sovereignty, and the need to survive in a country which was partially occupied by imperialist military forces had become such important, pressing issues that stronger defences seem to be needed than *fatâvî* of some religious leaders.[20] Only help from outside might just do that.

The claim by the Ottoman Government that it would look after the interests of Iran and its people was flawed for this and other reasons, not the least that the idea of Islamic unity was seen by many Iranians, especially those in the northern provinces as another pretext for an imperialistic aggrandisement of the Ottoman empire. Relations between Iran and the Ottoman empire had been rather

---

[19] Gehrke, *Persien*, vol. II, 22, notes 64–67; Ende, "Iraq in World War I", 58, 65. The leading mujtahids in the *ʿatabât* had already issued a *fatvâ* in support of the Young Turks in December 1914. Even the anti-constitutionalist *marjaʿ al-taqlîd* of Najaf, Muhammad Kâzim Yazdî, supported the call for *jihâd*, although only after some hesitation.

[20] An example of a close and effective cooperation between a religious leader and tribal opposition against the British in Iran is Sayyid ʿAbd al-Husayn Lârî from Fârs who supported the Qashqâ'î under Saulat al-Dawla with a *hukm-i jihâd* at the beginning of the war. See Âdamîyat, *Fârs va jang*, 356. The exact date of the *fatvâ* is not mentioned.

complicated for some time. This was quite obvious in another sphere, namely solving the long protracted boundary problems which, despite the negotiations of the international boundary commission in 1913/14, still had not found a satisfactory solution. But also in the legal field (e.g. private law) discrepancies had been created through discrimination in the case of marriages between Shiʿi and Sunni on Ottoman soil. In addition, it had soon become obvious to Iranian politicians that in the alliance of the Central Powers the Ottoman government was undoubtedly both the weaker and the junior partner, dependent on the military and financial aid of the German Reich. If the Iranian nationalists wanted to break the hold of Russia and Great Britain, only a power like the Reich appeared to be able to create an effective counterweight. The impressive record in modernising its economy and administration, and its military successes since the 1860s, had not failed to impress Taqîzâda and his circle, even if propaganda and war efforts might have distorted the reality. The chance for the leader of the Democrats to regain some control over affairs in Iran with German help were all too obvious.

Although this point was not lost on Taqîzâda, his reasons for siding with the Germans were probably not merely political. A committee in Berlin undoubtedly gave him a welcome opportunity to influence policy-making vis-a-vis Iran from the centre of one of the politically, industrially and technically advanced countries in the western world. Although Germany was more autocratic than Great Britain, the differences in the socio-political structure between the two countries appeared to Taqîzâda only, if at all, as marginal. In pre-war western Europe the behaviour patterns of the ruling political elites, the industrial structure and social organisation were similar in most countries and often presented to non-Europeans an impression of striking, if not baffling likeness. The only difference which was marked and therefore really mattered for a secularised, radical Iranian politician like Taqîzâda were the policies pursued by their governments towards his homeland. This became increasingly a rather crude division between goodies and baddies—those who had occupied Iran, and those who had not. Taqîzâda's decision to move to Berlin was probably also influenced by his own precarious and uncertain situation in the years before the outbreak of World War I. As he did not have a private income like many other political leaders in Iran, his independence seemed always to be much more vulnerable, exposed to pressures from the outside, although his political position was less influenced by it than might at first have been seen to be the case.[21]

To act politically with the support of the establishment in Germany and the authorities representing the government of the Reich from outside Iran provided Taqîzâda with the opportunity to become the architect, organising and reuniting various opposition groups and individuals inside and outside Iran under the umbrella of a national defence committee. It also meant the establishment, or re-establishment, of a network of cells in Iran, the possibility of influencing decision-making in Berlin, something never previously granted any Iranian politician, and of setting up an independent base in Istanbul where a number of his former comrades and friends had moved deliberately or had taken refuge. Istanbul became therefore an important springboard for any future action. Although the German diplomats and military were generally considered as wielding much influence in the Ottoman capital, their position was less powerful in the provinces. It was therefore necessary to have a well-organised committee in Istanbul as well, and if possible in other eastern provincial capitals of the Ottoman Empire, and not just to rely on co-operation with the Young Turk government. Istanbul with its sizeable community of Iranians was not only an important bridge to Iran, the centre of the Islamic world, and Iran's neighbour with a long border. The Holy Shrines of several Twelver Shiʿi Imams were on Ottoman soil, something which was seen as another useful channel through which politics in Iran could be influenced.

Taqîzâda arrived in Berlin from New York on 13 January 1915. Previously no pro-German community of Iranians in a proper sense had existed; only a certain Asadallâh Hidâyat who was engaged in writing pamphlets, and the former secretary of the Iranian embassy in Brussels, Husayn Akhtar Khân, were known to the Auswärtige Amt in Berlin. Now that all changed. With the full support of foreign office officials and military officers, Taqîzâda brought together as many Iranians as possible residing in Europe. It is interesting that at first the German authorities did not consider him as the obvious

[21] E.G. Browne with whom he had maintained a good relationship since he first left Iran, helped him to get some cataloguing work of a private manuscript collection in the USA. But that seemed to have come to an end after some while. See Jamâlzâda, "Kûmîta-yi millîyûn", 44. Taqïzâda himself describes in his autobiography *Zindigî-yi tûfânî*, 177–80, how he survived by doing occasional jobs as a translator and bibliographer (e.g. for Prof. Jackson).

leader, but tried to attract one of the other prominent figures of the Democratic party. However, none of them was living in Europe except Husayn Qulî Khân Navvâb, who resided in Paris but was ill. The Persian Minister in Berlin, Hovhannis Khân Musâ'id al-Saltana, an Armenian, was in the eyes of the Democrats, unlike his colleagues Mîrzâ Mustafâ Khân in Vienna and Mîrzâ Mahmûd Khân Ihtishâm al-Saltana in Istanbul, not trustworthy. He was later recalled and replaced by Husayn Qulî Khân Navvâb. Therefore the Iranian representative in Vienna, Mîrzâ Mustafâ Khân Safâ al-Mamâlik, was entrusted with the task of establishing the committee.[22] However, he soon had to return to his diplomatic post and therefore Taqîzâda became its main leader. During the next weeks and months, a number of young Iranians, mainly students, like Ghulâm Rizâ Khân, a grandson of Nâsir al-Mulk, arrived from Brussels, Husayn Kâzimzâda, Lector in Persian from Oxford, Nasrullâh Khân, Mîrzâ Mahmûd Ashrafzâda and Sayyid Muhammad 'Alî Jamâlzâda from Switzerland, joined the newly established committee.[23] None of them belonged to the circle of senior Iranian politicians and officials at that time. But their dedication to the nationalist cause, their clear political acumen, and their intelligent use of the facilities available under the leadership of the seasoned politician and parliamentarian Taqîzâda soon created an effective political instrument in the fight for the independence of Iran.[24] The publication of the journal *Kâva*, from 1916 onwards, with its important political and cultural articles, underpinned the central position of the group in Berlin in guiding and co-ordinating the various political and military activities. The committee relied for its success to a large part on the effective network which it had established right from the beginning of the war. Still it was

[22] Taqîzâda was described to the AA as a socialist-republican, probably by Husayn Khân Akhtar, who belonged to the monarchical-nationalist camp. Auswärtiges Amt Bonn, *Archiv* (further as *AA*) Wesendonk WK11e/7 A4276.

[23] Jamâlzâda, "Man, Jamâlzâda", 39; *AA* WK11e/7 4920, 4953, 5134, s.a. Gehrke, *Persien*, vol. II, 70. It was originally planned to ask the old fighters and Taqîzâda's long-standing Azarbayjani colleagues Mîrzâ Ismâ'îl Nawbarî, Mîrzâ Ismâ'îl Khân Yakânî, Mîrzâ Aqâ Nâlih Millat, Hâj Ismâ'îl Amîr Khîzî and Mîrzâ Rizâ Khân Tarbîyat, the brother of Taqîzâda's brother-in-law, who were in Istanbul and came to Berlin, to join the Committee in Berlin, but this idea was shelved, when the mission in Istanbul, Baghdad and in Iran started to work, *AA* WK11e/8 A7481, 7817.

[24] Taqîzâda had been elected as a member of the Democrats for Tabriz in the 3rd *Majlis*. In May 1915 his colleagues in Tehran asked him to return to Iran. The official opening of the Parliament was on 17 Muh. 1333/6 Dec 1914. *AA* Reuss to AA 4 May 1915 WK11e/7 15696; s.a. Gehrke, *Persien*, vol. I, 134.

an uneven battle, as Great Britain and Russia were increasingly able to expand their military control in Iran during the eventful years of 1915–16 and to strengthen their ties with the majority of the Qajar establishment which after the upheavals and years of struggle during the Constitutional Revolution yearned for a respite, even under the shadow of foreign occupational forces. In the years that followed until the end of the war, the committee was led by Taqîzâda, who was recognised as its sole representative. It was his creation. The organisation and control of its finances, provided by the Auswärtige Amt, were in his hands.

On 7 March 1915 he submitted a memorandum in the name of the newly founded Persian Committee, *Kûmîta-yi millîyûn va vatankhvâhân-i millî-yi Irân* or *La Ligue des patriotes persans*, to the Auswärtige Amt. It called for the creation of a general union of the Persians, comprising all patriotic forces (La création de l'union générale) who were striving for a united and strong Persia by means of propaganda and the establishment of clubs all over the country. It endeavoured to rally all legal political forces (e.g. the Shah, the *Majlis* and the government), in order to secure the necessary means from the Central Powers to strengthen the military forces in Iran and to liberate the country with their help from England and Russia, the historical enemies of Persia, Islam, and its friends.[25] With the establishment of similar national committees in Istanbul, Baghdad, Tehran and Shiraz through its representative, not only could the people in Iran be won over to the cause of the national forces and a strong pro-German sentiment created, but it was quite obvious that Taqîzâda hoped to gain major influence on political decision making in the two capitals.[26] Undoubtedly these activities depended completely on the financial

---

[25] *AA* WK11e/8 A8322. See the first four points of the document in Gehrke, *Persien*, Vol. II, Annex, 313–4. The programme which was considered by the German authorities as an ideal plan contained among other things a catalogue of 12 steps or initiatives which the government in Tehran should take, action plans for the individual committees and a budget. In this context it is interesting to note the idea that Iran should be strengthened militarily with the help of Germany and Turkey by augmenting the gendarmerie up to 20,000 men, mobilising tribal groups and using guerrilla forces. Mustawfî al-Mamâlik had made a similar suggestion to the British and Russian Governments about raising a military force of up to 20,000 for the crown prince in order to return to Azarbayjan. See Olson, *Anglo-Iranian relations*, 39.

[26] Gehrke, *Persien*, vol. I, 89 considers it mainly as an action to support the interest of the German Reich in Iran, ultimately directed towards Afghanistan and India.

support provided by the German treasury. In 1915 the estimates to finance the committee in Berlin and the other centres for the period of six months were 1 million Reichsmark. Nadolny, the senior official in charge of Middle Eastern Affairs in the German High Command, considered the sum as a useful investment for propaganda purposes. The bulk of the money was earmarked for actions in Iraq and Iran.[27] In December 1915 he demanded in a memo submitted to the Auswärtige Amt that a provisional government should be formed with the aim of liberating the Shah and the country from the Russians and British by military means. However, at that point German foreign policy was against such a radical step, since they still hoped to move the Iranian premier Mustawfî al-Mamâlik to a more friendly position.

The Istanbul Committee stood out among the rest as an important centre of emigrant activities and as a relay-station for Taqîzâda. If he and his group wanted to win influence outside the German Reich, Istanbul was the right place. Such a committee could become an effective weapon in the confrontation with the British and Russian forces, but for that it was necessary to overcome the opposition to Taqîzâda among a considerable part of the exiled Iranians living there. One of the first activities of the Berlin Committee was to establish contact with the Istanbul-based Persian newspaper *Khâvar*, edited by Sayyid Muhammad Tawfîq, who was one of Taqîzâda's main opponents in the Ottoman capital.[28] The differences between these

[27] Committee Berlin 30.000 RM; missions in Tehran 503.600 RM, in Baghdad 186.900 RM, in Shiraz 76.400 and in Constantinople [Istanbul] 39.800 DM. In addition 64.400 RM should be paid in Berlin for the activities of the four missions abroad. See Memo Taqîzâda, *AA* WK11e/A8322. By the end of the war, the Committee in Berlin alone required more than 300.000 RM.—In March 1915 Nadolny had come to the conclusion that Germany had to move onto the offensive in Iran, otherwise Russia and Britain would stabilise their position there. He thought of "setting on fire the whole area from the Caucasus to Calcutta". See Gehrke, *Persien*, vol. I, 99ff.

[28] According to Gehrke, *Persien*, vol. II, 125/170 the representatives of the Indian National Committee in Istanbul [or Baghdad ?] had turned to the Auswärtige Amt in Berlin for support and proposed Tawfîq Beg as organiser of a local committee on 10 March 1915. As the 'ulamâ' and the tribal chiefs were the main aim of the propaganda activities, Tawfîq Beg and the committee were considered to be the better choice. See *AA* WK11e/12 A10239. It is interesting that Mustafâ Khân Safâ al-Mamâlik planned to travel with the help of the AA to Istanbul already at the beginning of March 1915—according to a report from the German Embassy in Vienna, *AA* WK11e/9 A 8014.—The German ambassador in Constantinople, von Wangenheim, was quite critical about the infighting between the different groups of Persians. But a months later he reported to the German Chancellor Bethman-

two men were, however, soon patched up. Already on 21 March 1915 a local committee was formed which wrote in its programme:

> We declare ourselves all agreed and united in our sincere desire and wish to carry out all that is necessary and required for the liberation of our country and the good of mankind. We promise to carry out the plan of work of the Persian Committee in Berlin as faithfully and quickly as possible on receiving it, altering it only as far as local conditions necessitate it. We have forgotten all old parties and have now settled to work in harmony for the great cause.[29]

The founding members were Muhammad Tawfîq, Hasan Beg Khâvar, Mîrzâ Muhammad Ghanîzâda, Mîrzâ Rizâ Khân Tarbîyat, Hâjjî Hasan Qulî Aqâ, Asadullâh Ahmadzâda and Mîrzâ Ismâ'îl Khân 'Asâ al-Vuzarâ, most of whom soon moved to their new destinations in Iraq and Iran.[30] The Istanbul Committee could not expect ever to be able to pursue its own ways, as the purse strings were obviously in the hands of the German ambassador and his staff. Jamâlzâda had been sent to guide its first moves. Taqîzâda also exercised some controlling influence through Mîrzâ Rizâ Khân Tarbîyat, the brother of his brother-in-law, who became the main representative of the Berlin committee.[31] But he needed that support.

Hollweg that the Committee had declared "we have forgotten all old parties and have now settled to work in harmony for the great cause". See letter Wangenheim to Bethman-Hollweg, 3 April 1915, *AA* WK11e/12 A12288.

[29] Wangenheim to AA, 21 March 1915, *AA* WK11e/10 A10239. The committee asked to send Kâzimzâda but as he was supposed to work in Iran Jamâlzada went in his place. See Gehrke, *Persien*, vol. II, 125/170.

[30] Wangenheim to AA, 21 March 1915, *AA* WK11e/10 A11104. See also Gehrke, *Persien*, vol. II, 125/170. It soon became apparent to the organisers that it was important to have a strong contingent of Democrats working for the cause from inside the Ottoman empire. See for example notes of 28 February 1915, *AA* WK11e/8 A 7481 & 7817. In another report by Wangenheim Nawbarî, Amîr Khîzî, Pur-i Dâvud, Ashrafzâda, Sa'dullâh Khân Na'ala who had been asked to work with the missions in Baghdad and Shiraz are also mentioned as members of the Committee. According to a report by the Berlin Committee (21 May 1915) about the activities of the other missions it becomes clear that Nawbarî, Amîr Khîzî, Pûr-i Dâvud and Mîrzâ Rizâ Khân arrived in Baghdad in the middle of May 1915. Nawbarî was supposed to win over Sayyid Kâzim Yazdî, one of the leading 'ulamâ' in Najaf, but returned later to the Ottoman capital. Jamâlzâda took over from Kâzimzâda who moved on to Tehran establishing the Istanbul committee. Sayyid Hasan (Taqîzâda) *AA* WK11e/13 A13567; s.a. 12 A 10239 & 11104.

[31] Rizâ Khân Tarbîyat was forced to leave Azarbayjan in 1912 and had lived for the last three years in Istanbul. Gehrke, *Persien*, vol. II, 125/172. Taqîzâda received from his confidants in the other committees or missions fairly regular progress reports, the main contents of which he sent to the Auswärtige Amt. The

> He has opponents inside and outside Persia who on account of specific reasons which it is impossible to put down here, refuse to have anything to do with him . . . the members of the Persian Committee are more or less selected from his own party and his influence will be confined in great part to Azarbayjan and north Persia,

wrote an Indian member of the military group operating from Baghdad to the National Indian Committee in March 1915.[32] However, Tawfîq Beg who was considered to be a bitter opponent of Taqîzâda, promised to co-operate with him and his men, among them also one of the leading defenders of Tabriz in 1908/9, Mîrzâ Ismâʿîl Nawbarî. The establishment of the other missions, mainly run by his *muhâjirîn* supporters and his closest collaborators in Germany, left Taqîzâda vulnerable to political manoeuvring of his opponents in the Ottoman capital. That became more obvious when the Kirmanshah government collapsed in 1916 and leading politicians moved to Istanbul.

The Committee in Istanbul was also supposed to fulfil another important function. All the activities proposed and agreed to between the Persian Committee in Berlin and the German authorities in Iran and in Baghdad had to be financed through merchants who had major business interests in Iran or through trustworthy Iranian merchants trading in Istanbul. The Persian Committee submitted a number of names, among them Hâjjî Abû al-Qâsim and Aqâ ʿAbd al-Jaʿfar. But not only Persian but also Azarbayjani and Greek merchants became involved as financial agents; even Castelle, a European trading house is among them.[33]

During the following twelve months, members of the Berlin and the Istanbul Committees became heavily involved in propagating the aims of German foreign policy in Tehran and other major towns in western Iran. The centre of preparing their activities was Baghdad where Jamâlzâda, Nawbarî, Ismâʿîl Amîr Khîzî, Ibrâhîm Pûr-i Dâvud and Vâʿiz established a mission which published in August 1915 the first issue of the newspaper "Rastakhîz", only to be closed down by the Ottoman censor at Baghdad in the spring of 1916. At the same

---

German officials secretly checked and translated most of the correspondence exchanged between the different Iranian groups.

[32] Wangenheim to AA n.D, *AA* WK11e/12 A10239.

[33] See Persian Committee to AA, *AA* WK11e/10 A9464. In *AA* WK11e/10 A10365 Hâjjî Bâbâ Ganjaʾî, Rasûl Sadâqîyânî, Ibrâhîm Antîqîchî and Leon Askenâsî are mentioned.

time another group to which Kâzimzâda, Husayn Akhtâr Khân, Mîrzâ Ismâʿîl Khân Yakânî belonged (and, briefly, also Jamâlzâda) operated in Tehran for the liberation of Iran.[34]

In October 1915 a major crisis developed. The German Reich tried to win over the government of Mustawfî al-Mamâlik with a treaty of friendship and assistance; with it the last vestiges of Iran's already invalid notion of neutrality were endangered. When this action failed and the Entente powers issued an ultimatum that Russian troops would march towards Tehran, Ahmad Shâh, the government and the *Majlis* considered transferring the capital temporarily to Isfahan. On the 15th and 16th of November, however, the more cautious elderly statesmen like ʿAyn al-Dawla, Saʿd al-Dawla, Samsam al-Saltana, Farmânfarmâ and Sipahsâlâr pressurised Ahmad Shâh into staying.[35] In the end only 33 member of the *Majlis* and their followers, together with a number of foreign diplomats, took up residence in Qum. There they formed a national defence committee (*kûmîta-yi difâʿ-i millî*), a move which changed the political fortunes of the Democrats for some time to come. An important fact was, however, that a number of senior members of the *Iʿtidalîyûn*, among them their leader and vice-president of the *Majlis*, Mîrzâ Muhammad Sâdiq Tabâtabâʾî,[36] as well as a leading member of the group of ʿulamâʾ in the *Majlis*, Aqâ Sayyid Hasan Mudarris, followed the emigrants (*muhâjirîn*).[37] When in January 1916 the retreating opposition forces finally formed a provisional government in Kirmânshâh under the elderly Qajar

[34] *AA* WK11e/A12211, 12657, 13565. See also Gehrke, *Persien*, vol. I, 134.

[35] *Operations in Persia, 1914–1919*, introduced by Dr. G.M. Bayliss, 119–23, 125.

[36] Mîrzâ Muhammad Sâdiq Tabâtabâʾî, son of Âqâ Mîr Sayyid Muhammad Tabâtabâʾî, editor of the newspaper *Majlis*, was one of the leading mujtahids in the Constitutional Revolution. Member of parliament in the 2nd (for Mashad) and 3rd (for Tehran) period he became its vicepresident in the 3nd *Majlis* and leader of the *Iʿtidâlîyûn*. Originally a supporter of strict neutrality he moved his position in 1915 and followed the *muhâjirûn* to Qum where he together with other members of *Majlis*, above all the Democrats, founded the *Kûmîta-yi difâʿi millî*. He played an important role in the exile government of Nizâm al-Saltana together with Sayyid Hasan Mudarris, in particular for the relations with the Ottoman authorities. S. Mihdî Bâmdâd, *Târîkh-i rijâl-i Irân*, 2, 409–10; Safâʾî, *Rahbarân*, vol. II, 571–600; Gehrke, *Persien*, vol. II, 280–81.

[37] Still no comprehensive study exists about the *muhâjirîn*. The recent article *Muhâjirat* by ʿAbd al-Rizâ Salâr Bihzâdî in *Âyanda* Sal-i 19 (1372), 609–37 is a useful start for discussing the issue but it is mainly concerned with the policy surrounding the exit from Tehran. It is mainly based on the collection of documents from the Ministry of the Interior in Tehran, edited by Kâva Bayât, *Jang-i jahânî-yi avval*, 1369 and Sipihr's work about World War I.

grandee Nizâm al-Saltana, the governor of Lûristân, the Democrats under Sulaymân Mîrzâ were weakened. The old controversies between the moderates and the radical-democratic forces, which had been already simmering under the surface, now broke out into the open again. The situation became more complicated when some 'ulamâ' called for a policy based on "*Ittihâd-i Islâm*". The further away from the Iranian capital the *muhâjirîn* were operating, the less influential Sulaymân Mîrzâ became. Most of the Committee members in Iran as well Baghdâd supported him and other Democrat politicians, but the de facto power of Nizâm al-Saltana in western Iran left little room for political discussion.

With the collapse of an independent policy of the German Reich, the Ottoman government took full control of all political and military activities on its eastern border. But this did not mean the end of the co-operation between the Allies. On 19 August 1916 the military commands of the two countries agreed to act together in their future campaigns against the British and Russians. Always resenting their dependence on German political, military and financial support the emphasis of the Ottoman Government shifted back to the notion of the Caliph as a defender of the Muslim people based on the strength of the Turkish military, who played the main role in the actions.[38] How much the *muhâjirîn* feared the expansionist ideas directed towards Iran nourished by the Turkish War Minister, Enver Pasha, and most of the Turkish officials and military officers becomes clear in the letters which members of the Committee in Istanbul wrote to Taqîzâda. Their fear was not completely baseless. Already during the Qum interlude, the Turkish military attaché in Tehran, who had followed the *muhâjirîn* to the holy city, had speculated as to his possible appointment as War Minister in a future government, probably with the intention of rekindling the idea of a holy war.[39]

Although political decision-making remained very much dependent

[38] The military agreement was followed by a political one two days later. See the texts in Gehrke, *Persien*, vol. II, D. 31 & 32. These agreements were after the event as the XIII army corps of the VI Turkish army under 'Alî Ihsan Pasha had already invaded Iran in summer 1916 and occupied first Kirmânshâh and then Hamadân 13 August 1916. In this crisis situation the British reached a financial moratorium with the government of Sipahdâr in return for considering some form of a defensive alliance with the Entente powers. Olson, *Anglo-Iranian relations*, 116 remarks: "Thus the long-feared coup at the capital was an Allied one."

[39] Gehrke, *Persien*, vol. II, 238.

upon the actual military situation which the Ottoman army was facing in Iraq during 1916, Enver Pasha had been pursuing long-term plans for a closer alliance between Iran, Turkey and Afghanistan.[40] In May 1916 he signed an agreement with Nizâm al-Saltana in Baghdâd in which Iran's territorial integrity was guaranteed while at the same time the leadership of Ottoman Turkey became more directly involved in the political affairs of the eastern countries. The members of the Committees in Berlin and Istanbul but even more those of the Committee of exiled Iranians in Kirmânshâh, viewed this development with horror. The prospect that they would be squeezed out by this unholy alliance of the leading Turkish military officer and a representative of the old Qajar order dismayed them greatly. The Democrats in Kirmânshâh began to show signs of cracking, and as a consequence a number of their prominent members like Vahîd al-Mulk, Mîrzâ Muhammad ʿAlî Klûb, Adîb al-Saltana and Mîrzâ Ahmad Khân changed sides and went over into the camp of Nizâm al-Saltana. Sulaymân Mîrzâ, who was a member of the executive council in Kirmânshâh and responsible for internal affairs, was excluded from all negotiations with the Turkish representatives.

The closing down of the Baghdâd mission in which Kâzimzâda had played such an important role as Taqîzâda's trusted contact did, however, not really affect the work of the Committee in Berlin. The position of Taqîzâda, who had shown considerable skill in negotiating between the various groups of exiled Iranians, remained untouched by the events, although his direct influence upon internal affairs in Iran seems to have been diminished. His position in the nationalist camp, however, was not really weakened as the calls for his return to Tehran after World War I and the elections for the fourth *Majlis* showed.

In July 1916 Nizâm al-Saltana formed a short-lived government-in-exile with Turkish support (Fewzi Bey) in Kirmânshâh, leaving out the Democrats Sulaymân Mîrzâ, Sayyid Muhammad Rizâ Musavat, Kâzimzâdah, Amîr Khîzî and Yakânî who had stayed in Baghdad for some while. He wanted from Germany the recognition of his provisional government, a declaration to respect Iran's territorial integrity and various kinds of support. Vahîd al-Mulk and Tabâtabâ'î, who at the end of June 1916 had gone as Nizâm al-Saltana's rep-

[40] Gehrke is probably right that Enver Pasha was already harbouring pan-Turanian plans.

resentatives in a first step to Istanbul in order to gain the agreement of the Ottoman government, were disappointed not to be invited to Germany. The Auswärtige Amt was not prepared to accept such a major decision. In September 1916 Vahîd al-Mulk still travelled alone to Berlin but failed to achieve his aims and to establish himself as a separate mission, although he found some support among the members of the National Committee in Berlin. It appears that in the tussle between Nadolny (who had become the German Chargé d'Affaires in Kirmânshâh) and Nizâm al-Saltana, the former won the upper hand, as he was able to obstruct successfully the recognition of a second, separate representative in Berlin.[41] This, however, did not hinder Nizâm al-Saltana from continuing to undermine the position of the Democrats and radical nationalists. In December 1916 Kâzimzâda, Yakânî and Sayyid Jalîl were imprisoned, accused of planning an attempt on Nizâm's life.[42] Interestingly, Vahîd al-Mulk did not return to Kirmânshâh or Baghdâd but stayed in Istanbul, as did one of the other leaders of the *I'tidalîyûn* emigrants, Mîrzâ Muhammad Sâdiq, son of the *mujtahid* Aqâ Mîr Sayyid Muhammad. The member of *Majlis* Tabâtabâ'î remained a major figure in the political scenery at the Ottoman capital, and seems to have been recognised as the representative of the *hukûmat-i millî* by the Ottoman authorities, who considered him as their guest, much to the annoyance of the accredited ambassador Mahmûd Khân Ihtishâm al-Saltana.[43] But the latter continued to have the backing of the majority of the Iranians living there.[44]

The collapse of Nizâm al-Saltana's government as a consequence of the defeat of the Ottoman army in Iraq during the spring of 1917—Baghdad had fallen into British hands on 11 March—displayed again the dilemma of the Iranian opposition, which was caught

[41] About the visit of Vahîd al-Mulk s. Gehrke, *Persien*, vol. I, 277–283; s.a. Vahîd al-Mulk, 'Abd al-Husayn Shaybânî, *Khâtirât-i muhâjarat*, 127–29. Vahîd al-Mulk was not successful in his negotiations with the Auswärtige Amt in Berlin in gaining clear recognition for the temporary government of Nizâm al-Saltana in Kirmânshâh and an underwriting of Iran's independence. At that moment in history the Foreign Minister, Zimmermann, did not unequivocally want to commit the German Reich to such a step. In the diary of Vahîd al-Mulk there is no indication that he wanted to sideline Husayn Qulî Khân Navvâb or intended to establish himself in a commanding position among the Persian nationalists in Berlin. See in particular 210ff.

[42] Gehrke, *Persien*, vol. II, 292.

[43] Safâ, *Rahbarân*, vol. II, 571–60.

[44] Tarbîyat to Taqîzâdah (only extracts), October 1917, *AA* Pers 23/11 35657.

between the German anvil and the Ottoman hammer. The hope to achieve a major breakthrough with the help of the Ottoman army had failed in the south and west of Iran. The efforts of the nationalist forces to change the government in Tehran was on the other hand boosted by the February Revolution in Russia. The activities of the Democrats concentrated therefore on taking a more dynamic role in Iran's internal politics. By autumn a number of the political activists had returned to Tehran. Others tried to consolidate their positions in Berlin or Istanbul. As a result of these changes the emigrants in the Ottoman capital seem to be able to exert again some influence on the events in Iran. After the resignation of Vusûq al-Dawla on 27 May and his replacement by ʿAlâʾ al-Saltana a more independent line was pursued. Several members in the new cabinet were considered as pro-German. The Bolshevik October Revolution and the Brest-Litowsk armistice of 5 December 1917 presented the Democrats with a further chance, as both Bolshevik Russia and Ottoman Turkey had given the undertaking in article VIII of the peace treaty of Brest Litowsk to respect the political and economic independence of Iran. The elections for the fourth *Majlis* in November 1917, although mainly confined to Tehran, confirmed the consolidated position of the nationalist forces among the Iranian electorate. Taqîzâda, Sulaymân Mîrzâ, Navvâb, Musâvat, Tunakâbunî, from among the Iranian living abroad, were all elected. A considerable weakness of the nationalists, and in particular the Democrats, was however the fact that they were geographical separated but also that their main leaders were residing abroad. Factionalism lead to the split into the *Tashkîlîyûn* and Non-*Tashkîlîyûn* in Tehran. The former wanted immediate action whereas the supporters of the latter demanded to wait until their party leaders had returned from aboad.[45]

[45] Malik al-Shuʿrâ Bahâr, who was one of the organisers of the *Taskîlîyûn* faction, maintains that the Democrats lost the elections for the 4th *Majlis* due to that dissent. Bahâr, *Târîkh-i ahzâb*, vol. 1, 28. Bahâr's group published several influential newspapers, *Irân, Irân-i naw* and *Zabân-i âzâd*. The oppositional forces gathered around Muhammad Kumârâhî, supported by the newpaper *Sitâra-yi Irân*. The divisions between these two groups were not clearcut at all. Before Bahâr and his brother had taken over the editorship of *Irân* Sayyid Husayn Ardabîlî, one of Taqîzâda's supporters, was in charge. See Sadr-Hâshimî, *Târîkh-i jarâʾid*, vol. 1, Isfahan: Kamâl, 1363, 313.—In a letter by Taqîzâda to Muhammad ʿAlî Tarbîyat in *AA* Pers 19/4 A 37019, s.a. a telegram from AA to Pera No. 966 Pers 19/4 A39117, are a list of candidates for the elections which appears to indicate that leading figures like Taqîzâda and Sulaymân Mîrzâ were considered to be candidates for both groups.

Whereas Taqîzâda and his Berlin committee sprang into action in order to make contact with the new Russian leadership, the Iranian community in Istanbul was troubled by the re-emerging divisions between the Democrats and the Moderates. The followers of Nizâm were led by Tabâtabâ'î and those of Ihtishâm al-Saltana by Shaykh Asadullâh Ahmadzâda.[46] Invited by the Ottoman Sultan, Nizâm al-Saltana moved to Istanbul, where he tried to obtain recognition as the sole representative of the shah. However, Mahmûd Khân again resisted energetically any attempt to have another centre of Iranian politicians emerging in the Ottoman capital.[47] Taqîzâda became the main mediator between the two different groups. He tried in particular to re-establish good relations with Adîb al-Saltana, Klûb, Mîrzâ Ahmad Khân Qazvîni and Ardabîlî who had previously joined Nizâm's camp.[48] The Democrats among the *muhâjirîn* who were partly living in the capital but had also stayed behind in Aleppo and Mosul were much dependent on the material support of the German Government.

The different groups were trying to consolidate their positions in either Berlin or Istanbul. A third group, which included Musâvât, followed Sulaymân Mîrzâ. Khalkhâlî, Husayn Tihrânî, Tunâkabunî and Shâhrûdî, however, decided to stay in Mosul where the Iranians had retreated from Bâghdâd for the time being but planned to return to Iran at the first possible opportunity. Taqîzâda too advised the *muhâjirîn* Democrats, including Sulaymân Mîrzâ, to return to Iran, in order to continue their political mission there and to re-establish contact with the more moderate political forces in Tehran instead of joining the ranks of other activists in Berlin and Istanbul. However, von Blücher, one of the German diplomats who resided in Mosul, considered such a move at that point as premature and dangerous. The Ottoman government, who did not want any interference in their own dealings with the Iranian affairs, invited Sulaymân Mîrzâ and Musâvât to Istanbul.[49] But both declined. In September 1917

[46] Tarbîyat to Taqîzâdah (only extracts), n.D, *AA* Pers 23/11/A25246.

[47] Sâsânî quotes in his *Yâdbûdhâ-yi sifârat-i Istânbûl*, 34-36 a letter of loyality from 46 *muhâjirîn* for the Iranian ambassador, dated 23 Rabî' I 1336, emphasising that the temporary leadership of the national forces by Nizâm al-Saltana is now null and void.

[48] S. Letter des Taqîzâda to Muhammad Tarbîyat, dated 20/10/1917, *AA* Pers 23/13 A 35290.

[49] Sulaymân Mîrzâ had informed Blücher (Mosul) that he wanted to leave Mosul for Qasr Shîrîn with trusted elements, but without the other Iranians from Aleppo and Istanbul. The German diplomat expressed his doubts about the usefulness of

Sulaymân Mîrzâ finally left with his brother for Iran to establish contacts with Mustawfî al-Mamâlik at a time when the position of the Democrats seemed to improve. The Bolshevik Commissaries under the leadership of Lenin announced the withdrawal of Russian troops from Iranian soil on 3 January 1918, followed by Trotsky's decree of 29 January about the abrogation of the 1907 agreement. On the other hand, the British Government circles had wavered about the best policy vis a vis the nationalist camp since summer 1917. But Sulaymân Mîrzâ never arrived in Tehran, as he was arrested by tribal forces in Kirmânshâh who handed him over to the British authorities in Iran.[50] The Democrats lost with him one of their experienced politicians. Several other senior party members like Vahîd al-Mulk tried to establish links with other socialist groups, in particular the Bolsheviks, from neutral European countries.

During the following months, the Committee in Istanbul lost even more of its former position. Many of the followers and friends of Taqîzâda made their way to Berlin where the national Committee tried to organise support for them and their repatriation to Iran. The forthcoming elections for the *Majlis* promised some kind of new beginning, but under the tutelage of Great Britain. Taqîzâda, although duly elected, still did not return for some time to come. He wanted to continue the fight for a new Iran from outside, less on political than on ideological grounds. The physical presence of the British in Iran and their opposition to the return of the former supporters of the German Reich, did not make the task easier.

Several Azarbayjânî members from the committee in Istanbul moved backed to Tabriz after the October Revolution. Ismâʿîl Nawbarî who had been forced to leave Iran in 1911 was together with Shaykh

his returning to Iran. See Blücher to Sommer, 25/71917, *AA* Pers 23/11/27822; see also a letter by Blücher to Sommer, 17/11/1917, *AA* Pers 23/11/A41618 about the imminent departure of Shâhrûdî, Tunakâbunî and Khalkhâlî to Tehran.

[50] According to *Who's who in Persia 1918*, published by General Staff of India, Simla, he was arrested by members of the British Force D in February 1918. It appears that the British Consul of Kirmânshâh, Kennion, had him detained when he came to a meeting in the consulate. Zürrer, *Persien zwischen England und Rußland*, 40. The Tehran committee of the Democrats protested vehemently against the violation of Iran's independence and organised with other political groups a demonstration in the capital, but to no avail. See Sipihr, *Irân dar jang*, 491. For the discussions about the future approach of the government in London and in particular the wavering position of Marling, the British Minister in Tehran, see Olson, *Anglo-Iranian relations*, 180–85.

Khiyâbânî the main driving force behind the political comeback of the democrats in Tabrîz during 1918. In collaboration with the governor general, Muhtasham al-Saltana, they prevented major chaos emerging in the wake of the collapse of the czarist forces in northwest Iran. Whereas more turcophile local politicians like Mîrzâ Aqâ Bulûrî supported the invading Ottoman troops when they re-occupied western Azarbayjan for a short period in May 1918, Nawbarî opposed the Turkish solution to the "Persian question".[51] Together with Shaykh Khiyâbânî and another member of the Democratic camp he was arrested by the retreating Ottoman forces and taken to Kârs where he was released only several weeks later. But as one of the ardent opponents of the government under Vusûq al-Dawla he was forced into internal exile to Hamadan soon after his return to Tabrîz.[52]

The various committees and missions established abroad by members of Iranian nationalists in the years before and during World War I did not achieve the liberation of their homeland, but their activities helped in considerably raising awareness about the necessity for major changes in the political system in Iran. After the war, however, they had a greater influence in the ideological sphere than in the political arena. In the final clash between the representatives of the old Qajar elite and the radical westernising forces led by the ruthless Rizâ Khân (Rizâ Shâh) only a few of the activists found a place in the emerging "New Order".

Bibliography

Unpublished sources:

Auswärtiges Amt Bonn, Archiv (AA) WK11e; Pers 19 & 23.
Browne, E.G., *Papers*, Cambridge University Library, Box 9.
Public Record Office Kew, Foreign Office (FO) 248.

Book and articles:

Muhammad Husayn Ruknzâda Âdamîyat, *Fârs va jang-i bayn al-millal*, Tehran, 1349.
Asâmî-yi namâyandigân-i Majlis-i Shûrâ-yi Millî az aghâz-i Mashrûtîyat tâ dawra-yi 24 qânûn-guzârî, ed. 'Atâ'ullâh Farhang Qahrimânî, Tehran, n.d.

[51] British representatives in western Iran considered him wrongly as an ardent pro-Turkish politician who changed only into the anti-Turkish camp after he had broken with Bulûrî in June 1918. See Coffey to Tehran 17/11/1918, Public Record Office Kew *FO* 248/1216.

[52] Cheikh Mohammad Khiabani, *Iranshahr* 14. Berlin-Wilmersdorf, 1926, 29–31.

Malik al-Shuʿarâ Bahâr, *Târîkh-i mukhtasar-i ahzâb-i sîyâsî-yi Irân*, Tehran, 1371.
Mihdî Bâmdâd, *Târîkh-i rijâl-i Irân dar qarn-i 12 va 13 va 14 hijri*, Tehran, 1347.
Kâva Bayât, *Jang-i jahânî-yi avval. Asnâd-i vizârat-e dâkhilî*, Tehran, 1369.
Bayat, M., *Iran's first revolution*, Oxford, 1991.
Browne, E.G., *The Persian Revolution of 1905–1909*, London, 1966.
Cheikh Mohammad Khiabani, *Iranshahr* 14, Berlin-Wilmersdorf, 1926.
Djoudaki, H., "L'Anjoman-e Saʿdat", In: *Les Iraniens d'Istanbul*, ed. Th. Zarcone & F. Zarinebaf, Paris–Tehran–Istanbul, 1993, 185–93.
Ende, W., "Iraq in World War I: the Turks, the Germans and the Shiʿite mujtahids' call for jihad", in: *Proceedings of the 9th Congress of the Union Européene des Arabisants et Islamisants, Amsterdam, 1st to 7th September 1978*, ed. R. Peters, Leiden, 1981, 57–71.
Gehrke, U., *Persien in der deutschen Orientpolitik während des Ersten Weltkrieges*, 2 vols., Stuttgart, 1960.
Gholamreza Vatandoust, *Sayyid Hasan Taqîzâdeh and "Kâveh"*, Ph.D. University of Washington, 1977.
Gurney, J.D., "E.G. Browne and the Iranian community in Istanbul", in: *Les Iraniens d'Istanbul*, ed. Th. Zarcone & F. Zarinebaf, 143–75, Paris–Tehran–Istanbul, 1993.
Mansûra Ittihâdîya (Nizâm Mâfî), *Ihzâb-i sîyâsî dar Majlis-i sivvum, 1333–34 h.q.*, Tehran, 1371.
Muhammad ʿAlî Jamâlzâda, "Man, Jamâlzâda dar bâra-yi Taqîzâda shihâdat mîdaham", in *Yâdnâma-yi Taqîzâda*, ed. H. Yaghmâ'î, Tehran, 1349, 39–48.
Ahmad Kasravî, *Târîkh-i hijdah sâl-i Azarbâyjân*, Tehran, 1340.
Litten, W., *Wer hat die persische Neutralität verletzt*, Berlin, 1920.
McDaniel, R.A., *The Shuster mission and the Persian Constitutional Revolution*, Minneapolis, 1971.
McLean, D., "A Professor extraordinary: E.G. Browne and his Persian campaign, 1908–1913", *The Historical Journal* 21 (1978), 399–408.
———, "English radicals, Russia and the fate of Persia, 1907–13", *The English Historical Review* 43 (1978), 338–52.
Mustashâr al-Dawla, *Khâtirât va asnâd*, vol. II: *Asnâd-i Mashrûta, 1325–1330*, ed. I. Afshar, Tehran: Kâviyân 1362.
Muvârrikh al-Dawla Sipihr, *Irân dar jang-e buzurg*, Tehran, 1372.
Muzakirât-i Majlis, Tehran, Dawra-yi duvvum.
ʿAlî Gharavî Nûrî, *Hizb-i dimûkrât-i Irân dar dawra-yi duvvum-i Majlis-i Shawrâ-yi Millî*, Tehran, 1352.
Olson, Wm.J., *Anglo-Iranian relations during World War I*, London, 1984.
Operations in Persia, 1914–1919, introd. by Dr. G.M. Bayliss, London, 1987.
Muhammad Sadr-Hâshimî, *Târîkh-i jarâ'id va majâlât-i Irân*, 2 vols., Isfahan, 1363.
Ibrahim Safâ, *Rahbarân-i mashrûta*, 2 vols., Tehran, 1344.
Khân Malil Sâsânî, *Yâdbûdhâ-yi sifârat-i Istânbûl*, Tehran, 1345.
Shuster, M., *The Strangling of Persia*, New York, 1968.
Sayyid Hasan Taqîzâda, *Zindigî-yi tûfânî. Khâtirât-i Sayyid Hasan Taqîzâda*, ed. I. Afshâr, Tehran, 1372.
Vahîd al-Mulk, ʿAbd al-Husayn Shaybânî, *Khâtirât-i muhâjarat. Az dawlat-i muvaghghat-i Kirmânshâh tâ kumîta-yi milliyun-i Birlan*, ed. I. Afshâr & Kâva Bayât, Tehran, 1378.
Vogel, R., *Die Persien- und Afghanistanexpedition Oskar Ritter von Niedermayers, 1915–16*, Osnabrück, 1976.
Welt des Islam, Vol. III (1915).
Who's who in Persia 1918, Simla, 1918.
Zürrer, W., *Persien zwischen England und Rußland, 1918–1926*, Bern–Frankfurt am Main, 1978.

THE TRIAL OF THE BĀB: SHI'ITE ORTHODOXY CONFRONTS ITS MIRROR IMAGE

Denis MacEoin

Trials of religious heretics have always assumed a central importance in religious history, and have frequently been the subject of close scrutiny in the modern period. The trials of Jesus Christ,[1] al-Ḥallāj,[2] Galileo,[3] Giordano Bruno,[4] Joan of Arc,[5] Michael Servetus,[6] and others have drawn the attention of scholars for a wide variety of reasons. More broadly, and for similar reasons, we have seen studies of the Inquisition,[7] witchcraft trials (often linked to the inquisition),[8] the Albigensians,[9] the persecution of heresy in general,[10] and, for the

---

[1] The literature on this subject is, not surprisingly, large. The following should be noted: Bammel, *The Trial*; Blinzler, *Der Prozess Jesu*; Brandon, *The Trial of Jesus*; Burkill, "The Trial of Jesus"; Buss, *The Trial of Jesus*; Catchpole, *The Trial of Jesus*; Carmichael, *The Death of Jesus*, Cohn, *The Trial and Death of Jesus*; Duncan Derrett, *An Oriental Lawyer*; Di Miscio, *Il Processo di Cristo*; Isorin, *Le vrai proces de Jésus*; Kartelge, *Der Prozess gegen Jesus*; Kilpatrick, *The Trial of Jesus*; Knowlton, *The Trial of Jesus*; Koch, *Zum Prozess Jesu*; Lietzmann, *Der Prozess Jesus*; Nordi, *Il processo di Gesu*; Rimmer, *Outlines for Study*; Rosadi, *The Trial of Jesus*; Stalker, *The Trial*; Strobel, *Die Stunde der Wahrheit*; Winter, *On the Trial of Jesus*.

[2] See Louis Massignon, *La Passion de Husayn Ibn Mansūr Hallāj*, Eng. trans. Mason. The section covering the trials constitutes chapter VI of volume 1.

[3] See Blackwell, *Galileo, Bellarmine, and the Bible*; Feldhay, *Galileo and the Church*; Finocchio, *The Galileo Affair*; De Santillana, *The crime of Galileo*; Westfall, *Essays on the Trial of Galileo*; H. Vedrine, *Censure et pouvoir*.

[4] See Mercati, *Il sommario*; Aquilecchia, *Giordano Bruno*; Boulting, *Giordano Bruno*.

[5] See *The Trial of Joan of Arc*; Morice, *Joan of Arc*; Pernoud, *The retrial*; Scott, *The Trial of Joan of Arc*; Quicherat, *Proces*; Sullivan, *Inquiry and Inquisition*.

[6] See Bainton, *Hunted Heretic*; Friedman, *Michael Servetus*.

[7] See Dondaine, *Les hérésies*; Gorham, *The Medieval Inquisition*; Hamilton, *The Medieval Inquisition*; Kamen, *The Spanish Inquisition*; Henningsen, *Inquisition*; Lea, *The Inquisition*; Monter, *Frontiers of Heresy*; Netanyahu, *The Origins*; Roth, *The Spanish Inquisition*; Sabatini, *Torquemada; Domenico Scandella*; Seidel Manchi, *Erasmus*; Shannon, *The Medieval Inquisition*; Symposium Internacional, *The Spanish Inquisition*; Tedeschi, *The Prosecution of Heresy*; Turberville, *Medieval Heresy*; Wakefield, *Heresy*.

[8] See Association of Social Anthropologists, *Witchcraft Confessions*; Boguet, *An Examen of Witches*; Ewen, *Witch Hunting*; Hansen, *Zauberwahn*; Henningsen, *The Witches' Advocate*; Martin, *Witchcraft*.

[9] See Oldenbourg, *Massacre at Montsegu*; Strayer, *The Albigensian Crusades*; Hamilton, *The Albigensian Crusade*; Warner, *The Albigensian Heresy*.

[10] See Peters, *Heresy and Authority*; Tanner, *Heresy Trials*; Kieckhefer, *Repression of Heresy*.

modern West, the Scopes "Monkey trial",[11] and the activities of anti-cult organizations and "de-programmers".[12] The treatment of heretics, both religious and secular,[13] is central to the self-identification of all orthodoxies, and to study how any given establishment seeks to define and control heresy is a crucial task for the understanding of any dominant belief system. The heresy trial is clearly the showpiece within which self-definition takes place, the moment when orthodoxy maps out the perimeters of belief and unbelief, and for this reason the content of actual trials is of immense importance, not just at the theological level, but also at the social and political.[14]

In the modern period, Islamic heresy trials have achieved a large degree of notoriety in the Western media, the best known being the semi-formal condemnation and demonization of Salman Rushdie. Other widely-reported cases include the trials in Bangladesh of the writer Taslima Nasreen, in Egypt of the writer ʿAlā Ḥāmid and others, and in Saudi Arabia of the surviving participants in the 1979 seizure of the Great Mosque in Mecca. Less publicized in the West have been numerous trials or *fatwā*s concerning Aḥmadīs and Bahāʾīs.[15]

Even if the modern period has seen more than its fair share of such trials, they have not been uncommon in the past. The *takfīr* formula has been used repeatedly by both Sunni and Shiʿi *ʿulamāʾ* to condemn those—very often Sufis—whose beliefs or actions were deemed injurious to the Sharīʿa.

---

[11] See *Monkey trial*; Sprague De Camp, *The Great Monkey Trial*; Halliburton, *The Scopes "Monkey Trial"*; Olasky, *When world views collide*; McGowen, *The great monkey trial*; Bledsoe, "*Scopes 'Monkey' trial*"; Harrison, *The Scopes "monkey trial", revisited.*

[12] See Shupe Jr. and Bromley, *The New Vigilantes*; Rabbino, *Cults*; Bromley and Richardson, *Brainwashing*; Kelley, "Deprogramming; Biermans, *The Odyssey.*

[13] Though insufficiently studied, the definition of heresy within science (particularly medicine) is of immense importance. Thomas Kuhn's study of paradigm shifts (*The Structure of Scientific Revolutions*) and Harry Collins's work on replication (*Changing Order*) both indicate the broad context within which such studies can shed light on the creation and maintenance of scientific orthodoxy. Thomas Szasz's controversial but lucid studies of the links between psychiatry and the law are equally illuminating (*Law, Liberty, and Psychiatry; The Therapeutic State; The Manufacture of Madness*). See also Wallis, *On the Margins of Science*; Wallis and Morley, *Marginal Medicine.*

[14] For an examination of the links between social normalization, punishment, tutelage, torture, and the political and social realms, see Rejali, *Torture and Modernity.*

[15] The Aḥmadī/Qādiyānī issue is mainly restricted to Pakistan, although *ʿulamāʾ* and newspapers in other Muslim countries do issue condemnations from time to time. Trials of Bahāʾīs in Iran are well known, but there have been several important judgements in cases throughout the Islamic world, including Morocco (1962), Egypt (1985), and even Turkey (1928, 1933). The literature on this subject is immense. I intend to publish a bibliography of Arabic and Persian material shortly.

Surprisingly, however, there are not many cases of heresiarchs being formally arraigned before tribunals, whether religious or civil (or both combined). Though condemned by *fatwā* and sermon, almost none of the major leaders of heretical or semi-heretical movements in modern Islam—Muḥammad Ibn ʿAbd al-Wahhāb, Aḥmad al-Tijānī, Mīrzā Ghulām Aḥmad Qādiānī, Muḥammad Aḥmad al-Sayyid ʿAbd Allāh the Sudanese Mahdī, Shaykh Aḥmad al-Aḥsāʾī, and Mīrzā Ḥusayn ʿAlī Bahāʾ Allāh—was publicly tried on account of what they had personally written or preached.[16]

The Trial of Sayyid ʿAlī Muḥammad Shīrāzī

In general, the condemnation of heresy has tended to remain an informal matter, dependent very much on the whims of individual *ʿulamāʾ*. There are, however, two important exceptions to this, both of them related. In January 1845, Mullā ʿAlī Basṭāmī, one of the first converts to Babism, and the sect's first exponent in Iraq, was tried before a combined panel of Sunni and Shiʿi *ʿulamāʾ*, whose verdict was issued in an unusual *fatwā* signed by clerics of both communities. This *fatwā* and the circumstances surrounding Basṭāmī's trial have been well studied by Momen and Amanat.[17]

A few years later, in Shaʿbān 1264/July 1848,[18] the Bāb himself (Sayyid ʿAlī Muḥammad Shīrāzī) was brought before a consistory

---

[16] There were some inquisitions of leaders of the Niʿmat Allāhī Ṣūfī revival in late eighteenth-century and early nineteenth-century Iran (Royce, "Mir Maʿsum ʿAli Shah", 173). We have details of the inquisition of Maʿṣūm ʿAlī Shāh, but only in an anti-Ṣūfī treatise by the ʿālim who organized the trial and issued the death sentence, Mullā Muḥammad ʿAlī Bihbihānī (see ibid., 170, cited Bihbihānī's *Risāla-yi Khayrātiyya* as cited in other works). Sayyid Kāẓim Rashtī, al-Aḥsāʾī's successor as head of the Shaykhī school, was summoned to more than one inquisitorial gathering; but these seem to have been more in the nature of debates than formal trials (see MacEoin, *"From Shaykhism to Babism"*, 106, 108–109). Our record of these meetings is extremely limited.

Bahāʾ Allāh was briefly detained and interrogated by the civil authorities during his exile to Acre, following the murder of three Azalī Bābīs by seven of his followers. This interrogation was part of the investigation of the crime and does not seem to have touched on his religious claims or beliefs (see Balyuzi, *Bahá'u'lláh*, 326–30).

[17] Momen, "The Trial of Mullā ʿAlī Basṭāmī", 113–43; Amanat, *Resurrection and Renewal*, 220–238.

[18] The *Nāsikh al-tawārīkh* mistakenly places this event under the year 1263.

(variously described as a *majlis, majlis-i muḥāvarat, majlis-i khāṣṣ-i valī-ahd, majlis-i guftugū, jalasa-yi guft u shunūd, munāẓara, maḥẓar, hayʾat*, and *majmaʿ*, but seldom as *maḥkama, bar-rasī*, etc.)[19] of *ʿulamāʾ* and state officials, presided over by the Crown Prince, Nāṣir al-Dīn Mīrzā.[20] The tribunal was held in the provincial capital Tabriz, then the seat of the heir to the throne. Most sources indicate that the gathering was held on the direct instructions of Muḥammad Shāh.[21] In its course, the Bāb was questioned and given the opportunity to reply and, if he wished, recant. A *fatwā* condemning him was written by two *ʿulamāʾ*, Abu ʾl-Qāsim al-Ḥasanī al-Ḥusaynī and ʿAlī Aṣghar al-Ḥasanī al-Ḥusaynī, two leading Shaykhī *ʿulamāʾ* of the city.[22] A separate report of the trial, described by some authors[23] as having been penned by Nāṣir al-Dīn Mīrzā, but in the text ascribed to his uncle, Amīr Aṣlān Khān, was written and almost certainly sent to the king, Muḥammad Shāh.[24] We also possess a document, supposedly written shortly after this arraignment, and apparently in the Bāb's handwriting, in which the young prophet recants any claim to a divine mission.[25]

Two days later, the Bāb was bastinadoed in the presence of the Shaykh al-Islām. It was after this that he was treated for his wounds by the British doctor, William Cormick, who left a brief account of their meetings over a few days.[26]

---

[19] Māzandarānī uses, among others, the terms *majlis-i mukālima, bāz-khwāst*, and *muḥākama*. Mazandarani, *Kitāb-i ẓuhūr al-ḥaqq*, vol. 3, Tehran, n.d., 14.

[20] Zaʿīm al-Dawla describes it as *hayʾatī az ʿulamāʾ va fuqahāʾ va fuḍalāʾ va umarāʾ va shakhṣiyyathāyi buzurg az aʿyān va sarān-i shahr, bi-riyāsat-i khudash* [i.e. The Crown Prince] (Mīrzā Mahdī Khān Zaʿīm al-Dawla), *Miftāḥ Bāb al-abwāb*, 137.

[21] It is not impossible that the idea of confronting the Bāb with a tribunal made up chiefly of clerics came from the prophet himself. In one of his letters to Muḥammad Shāh, dated 1264, he writes: "Why do you not summon the *ʿulamāʾ* of the land and then summon me, so that I may confound them just as I did with others before them, from among the deniers?" (*Muntakhabātī az āyāt az āthār-i Ḥaḍrat-i Nuqṭa-yi Ulā*, 11).

[22] A facsimile, text, and translation of this *fatwā* were published by Browne (Browne, *Materials*, 258–59). Browne suggests that ʿAlī Aṣghar was Mīrzā ʿAlī Aṣghar Shaykh al-Islām, but is unable to identify Abu ʾl-Qāsim. The latter was, in all probability, the Shaykh al-Islām's son, Shaykh Abu ʾl-Qāsim. Curiously enough, it is likely that neither of these men was actually present at the tribunal. Abu ʾl-Qāsim later wrote an attack on the Bāb entitled *Qalʿ al-Bāb*, which has not been published. Amanat (p. 388) describes him as ʿAlī Aṣghar's "nephew" and finds references to him in Zarandī and Muʿīn al-Salṭana which are not there.

[23] See, for example, Māzandarānī, *Ẓuhūr al-ḥaqq*, 15; Navāʾī, *Fitna-yi Bāb*, 127.

[24] For facsimile, text, and translation, see Browne, *Materials*, 248–55.

[25] For facsimile, text, and translation, see ibid., 256–58.

[26] See ibid., 260–62.

Although the *fatwā* recommended the sentence of death (unless the Bāb could be found to be mad), the prisoner was returned to prison in Chihrīq, where he remained for almost exactly two years. In July 1850, he was again brought to Tabriz, briefly re-examined by individual *ʿulamāʾ*, and executed.

The 1848 trial is important, not least because it was conducted by a court which included, not only regionally-prominent clergy, but also nationally-eminent men of state, and presided over by the future king. The event, though short in duration, was clearly accorded more than ordinary significance, for reasons that are obvious, given the very real threat to public order posed by the Bāb's growing popularity.

The Sources

The problem for the historian is how to disentangle the numerous contradictory accounts of the trial itself. There are about nine of these, although several may originate in a single, earlier source. Six are by Muslim writers: Riḍā Qulī Khān Hidāyat's *Rawḍat al-ṣafā-yi Nāṣirī*;[27] Lisān al-Mulk Sipihr's *Nāsikh al-tawārīkh*;[28] ʿAlī Qulī Khān Iʿtiḍād al-Salṭana's *al-Mutanabbīʾīn*;[29] Mīrzā Mahdī Khān Zaʿīm al-Dawla's *Miftāḥ Bāb al-abwāb*; Mīrzā Muḥammad Taqī Māmaqānī's *Nāmūs-i Nāṣirī*; and the above-mentioned report of Amīr Aṣlān Khān. The other three are the work of Bābī or Bahāʾī historians: Mullā Muḥammad Taqī Hashtrūdī's *Abwāb al-hudā*, quoted in the much later historical narrative of Muʿīn al-Salṭana Tabrīzī; Mīrzā Muḥammad Nabīl Zarandī's narrative;[30] and Mīrzā Jānī Kāshānī's *Nuqṭat al-Kāf*.[31]

Browne, Amanat, and others have treated Mīrzā Muḥammad

---

[27] Hidāyat, *Tārīkh*, vol. 10, 423–28. A translation of this account, with additions and adjustments, is provided by Browne in *A Traveller's Narrative*, 277–90. Volume 10 of the *Rawḍat al-ṣafā* was first published in 1274/1857.

[28] Sipihr, *Nāsikh al-tawārīkh*, vol. 3, 126–30. Sipihr finished the Qājār volumes of his history in 1274/1857–58, and the first edition was probably a continuation of the 1273 edition of the entire history.

[29] Published as *Fitna-yi Bāb*, 20–28. An earlier edition is recorded in the Russian version of Storey: vol. 1, ed. Qāsim Rāḍī, Tehran, 1343/1964. Navāʾī is coy about the manuscript which forms the basis of his text. There appears to be a manuscript in the Majlis library.

[30] So far published only in English translation, or in translations based on it: Zarandī, *The Dawn-Breakers*, 314–19. For comments on this source, see MacEoin, *Sources*, 166–69.

[31] Kāshānī, *Kitáb-i-Nuqtatu'l-Káf*, 133–36. For details of this source, see MacEoin, *Sources*, 134–52.

Tunakābunī's *Qiṣaṣ al-ʿulamā'* as a separate source, but I prefer not to do so, on the grounds that it is almost a verbatim (but unattributed) transcription of the text in *Rawḍat al-ṣafā*. Either Tunukābunī copied his account directly from Hidāyat or also made use of the report by Niẓām al-ʿUlamā'. In either case, he provides no significant variants.

Most commentators have remarked on the noticeable differences between these texts, drawing the conclusion that it is hard to place much reliance on any of them. Certainly, we possess no single account which commands our unreserved respect. But that is not to say that something useful cannot be done to reconstruct some of the main features of the trial and from there to analyse the chief concerns of those involved. If there are striking differences between the narratives, there are also significant resemblances, some substantial, some trivial, and it seems likely that the surviving accounts reflect with varying degrees of distortion the general content of the questions and (much less dependably) the Bāb's answers to them.

The relationship between the Muslim accounts can be roughly estimated on the basis of their chronological order. The earliest must, by any reckoning, be Amīr Aṣlān Khān's "official report", probably written to Muḥammad Shāh soon after the trial, and certainly before the king's death on 6 Shawwāl/4 September.

Māmaqānī[32] refers to an account of the trial in the hand of Ḥājī Mullā Maḥmūd Tabrīzī, Niẓām al-ʿUlamā', the crown prince's tutor, and the leading cleric present at the trial, whose questions form the bulk of the inquisitorial text in most versions. Riḍā Qulī Khān states that his version of the trial is a direct transcript from Niẓām al-ʿUlamā''s autograph.[33] It is possible that, in terms of content, this account also formed the basis for the versions in *Nāsikh al-tawārīkh*, *al-Mutanabbi'īn*, and the *Qiṣaṣ al-ʿulamā'*. It is, however, more likely that the *Nāsikh al-tawārīkh* account is built around that of the *Rawḍat al-ṣafā*,[34] and that both the *al-Mutanabbi'īn* and *Qiṣaṣ al-ʿulamā'* narratives are lifted straight from it.

[32] Māmaqānī, *Nāmūs-i Nāṣirī*, 26.

[33] Hidāyat, *Tārīkh*, vol. 10, Qum, 1339 sh./1961. Navā'ī (*Fitna*, 127) states that Niẓām al-ʿUlamā's son compiled a file (*daftar*) from which Hidāyat and Sipihr took their accounts.

[34] This is difficult to establish. Both books were finished and published around 1273/1274, but it does seem to be the case that Sipihr borrowed from his contemporary.

Māmaqānī's account was written for Nāṣir al-Dīn Shāh in Ramaḍān-Shawwāl 1306/June–July 1889, and is described by the author as a corrective to the versions given in the *Nāsikh al-tawārīkh* and *Rawḍat al-ṣafā*. For all that, there are numerous parallels between the three accounts. Māmaqānī argues that Niẓām al-ʿUlamā''s account was written when the author was getting on in years and growing forgetful, and that his own account, based on his father's eye-witness rendition, is a much closer approximation to the truth. His father, Mullā Muḥammad Māmaqānī[35] took a leading part in the trial and was later one of the *ʿulamā'* who signed *fatwā*s for the Bāb's execution in 1850.

Iʿtiḍād al-Salṭana's history of the Bābī insurrections, which forms part of a longer work entitled *al-Mutanabbi'īn*, is rather odd. Most of it constitutes a verbatim re-write, either of the *Rawḍāt al-ṣafā* or the account by Niẓām al-ʿUlamā', but at one point the text breaks off, leaving out material which is introduced in very different form before the quoted material begins (and without any indication of what comes from where). One very odd thing about this is that, where Hidāyat clearly attributes the quotation of a verse to Nāṣir al-Dīn Mīrzā, Iʿtiḍād al-Salṭana (who has been following that account very closely to this point) only says it was spoken by "one of those present". Quite what one is to make of this jumble is not yet clear. Did Iʿtiḍād al-Salṭana have a different source, or did something just go wrong with his transcription?

Mīrzā Mahdī Khān Zaʿīm al-Dawla published his book on the Bābīs and Bahā'īs in Cairo in 1321/1903–4, which makes it by far the latest of the Muslim accounts. Its claim to accuracy rests on the fact that the author's, father, Mīrzā Taqī Tabrīzī, and grandfather, Muḥammad Jaʿfar, were both present at the trial and supplied him with details of it. It does, however, have numerous exact parallels with and some verbal resemblances[36] to the *Rawḍat al-Ṣafā* and *Nāsikh al-tawārīkh*, and it is hard to believe that Zaʿīm al-Dawla did not make use of them.

The Bābi/Bahā'i accounts are much less detailed, although that of Hashtrūdī lays claim to some degree of first-handedness, and does contain small details that suggest the presence of an eye-witness. It

[35] Or Mamaqānī.

[36] These are more difficult to be sure of. The original text was published in Arabic, and the Persian version is a translation.

is, for example, the only account to note that lamps were lit and tea served mid-way through the proceedings. I have not been able to establish a date for the writing of the *Abwāb al-hudā* (which apparently is no longer extant); but Muʿīn al-Salṭanā's history, which quotes from it, was completed around 1340/1921–22.[37]

The *Nuqṭat al-Kāf* is a much earlier text, possibly written in the early 1850s in Baghdad,[38] but it has no particular claim to authenticity in respect of the trial. There are, however, enough similarities between it and other reports to suggest, if not a common source, a reliable informant. Kāshānī's account has enough parallels to the main Muslim reports that it seems likely he had access to one of these. If not, his description of the trial provides strong corroboration for many of the details found in those texts.

The brief account in Zarandī's narrative has fewer resemblances to other descriptions of the trial, but is recorded as being based on the evidence of Shaykh Ḥasan Zunūzī, who was one of a number of people outside the hall where the arraignment was held, but who claimed that he could follow the conversation inside. This, again, is a late composition, having been written between 1888 and 1890.

Taking all these texts together, it is difficult (and intriguing) to see that no simple pattern of plagiarism emerges. Some texts are very closely linked, but in other cases questions and statements occur in different places with no discernible system (as will be demonstrated below). In many ways this is encouraging to the historian, since it suggests a definite core of information which has managed to survive in spite of the forgetfulness or bias of any one source or group of sources. It will require a lot of work to piece the jigsaw together properly, but the following attempt provides a starting-point.

The Questions

A proper attempt to restructure the trial is beyond the resources of this article, and should await the publication of the complete texts of all the accounts, along with translations. In the meantime, it will be worth trying to tabulate the main themes pursued in the interrogation

[37] See MacEoin, *Sources*, 175. My text for the section dealing with the trial of the Bāb (201 ff.) is a photocopy of poor quality, which adds to the difficulties posed by bad handwriting. Access to the original manuscript is presently impossible.

[38] See MacEoin, *Sources*, 151.

and how far these occur in the different versions. The attached tables show the occurrence of questions and answers across the sources. Since we are obviously dealing with attempts to reconstruct statements from memory, in some cases long after the event, I have created simplified versions of questions and answers that cover as many different wordings as seems justifiable. In some cases it might have made sense to conflate even more: for example, it seems clear that at some point the Bāb said he would "reveal a verse" concerning his staff, or that he responded to a request to do so: our variants might very well be subsumed into a single heading "recites verses concerning his staff". The same is true for several other entries.

In order to give a more coherent sense of the proceedings, however, I also append a translation of Māmaqānī's account in the *Nāmūs-i Nāṣirī*, which can be read in conjunction with the versions given by Browne.

Of the sixty-two questions listed, eighteen occur in only one source, fifteen in two, eight in three, five in four, thirteen in five, and three in six. Of the thirty-five answers (omitting numerous citations of "yes" and "he did not answer"), ten occur in one source, eight in two, six in three, three in four, two in five, five in six, and one—quite outstandingly—in all nine.

Mere numerical frequency is a poor indicator of reliability, bearing in mind the interdependence of the five main Muslim sources, which together account for the bulk of all the information we possess. The really interesting questions and answers are those which occur across unlikely combinations, particularly, of course, Babi and Muslim accounts.

One of the most significant of these is question number one, "Are these your writings?", which occurs in all the Muslim texts and also in the *Nuqṭat al-kāf*. It seems immediately apparent from this and from other references to writings of the Bāb shown or referred to in the course of the hearing, that the tribunal had not been hastily assembled, and that some effort had been made to assemble writings of the heresiarch and to use them as the basis for some of the questioning. The *Rawḍat al-ṣafā*, indicates that Niẓām al-ʿUlamā showed these documents to the Bāb and asked him to admit to their authorship.

Further evidence that works of the Bāb were referred to occurs in a number of passages in which questions are framed around pericopes selected for their heretical content. These questions are mostly put to the Bāb by Ḥājī Murtaḍā-Qulī Marandī ʿAlam al-Hudā, a wealthy mujtahid who seems to have taken the trouble to study some of the texts in question. With two exceptions, these questions (numbers 20, 22, 23, 26, 27, 34, 36, 37) occur in one source only, the *Nāmūs-i Nāṣirī*; but precisely because they can in theory be cross-checked against known writings of the Bāb,[39] they are more open to external authentication than most of the trial material.

Three of the questions (26, 34 and 36) have definite analogues in the Bāb's writings. The first, which quotes the Bāb as saying "The first to believe in me (*awwal man āmana bī*) was Muḥammad ibn ʿAbd Allāh" (or "The first to believe in me was the Light of Muḥammad, and ʿAlī"), which parallels a couple of passages in late letters of the Bāb.[40] The second is put by ʿAlam al-Hudā as follows: "In your book you have said that you dreamed that they had killed the Prince of Martyrs (Ḥusayn), and that you drank a few drops of his blood and that the gates of heavenly grace were thereupon opened to you". This is close to a statement in the early *Ṣaḥīfa-yi ʿadliyya*,[41] where the Bāb describes a vision of the head of Ḥusayn and his drinking seven drops of blood from it, and that, as a result, his breast was filled with "convincing verses and mighty prayers".

The third asserts that "In your book, you have said that if jinn and men were to assemble together, they could not produce the like of half a word from your book". This is close, in spirit, if not precisely in wording, to two pericopes from the *Qayyūm al-asmāʾ*: "O assembly of jinn and men. If you are able, bring forth a book like this"[42] and "O people of the earth. Even if you were to gather together to produce a word like a single word of my knowledge, you would be unable to do so."[43]

I am less sure about the authenticity of another pericope cited by ʿAlam al-Hudā, who states that, in his "Qurʾān", the Bāb had indicated that one-third of any booty was to be given to "the Remembrance" (i.e. the Bāb). It should be relatively easy to find such a

[39] For a comprehensive review of these, see D. MacEoin, *The Sources*.

[40] See [Sayyid ʿAlī Muḥammad the Bāb] and [Sayyid Ḥusayn Kātib-i Yazdī], *Qismatī*, 13 (*awwal man bāyaʿa bi Muḥammad Rasūl Allāh, thumma ʿAlī*) and 17 (*awwal man bāyaʿa bi ʾl-Qāʾim Muḥammad Rasūl Allāh*). The first of the Bāb's disciples, Mullā Muḥammad Ḥusayn Bushrūʾī, is often referred to in Bābī texts as *Awwal man āmana*. For a little more on this theme, see MacEoin, "Hierarchy", 105–.

[41] [Tehran], n.d., 14. See also Zarandī, *Dawn-Breakers*, 253.

[42] *Qayyūm al-asmāʾ*, Cambridge University Library, Browne Or. Ms. F. 11. f. 66b.

[43] Ibid., f. 99a.

statement. The reference to "the Remembrance" (*al-Dhikr*) would date this as coming from an early work of the Bāb's, while the description of the book as the Bāb's "Qur'ān" makes it tempting to identify it as a passage from the *Qayyūm al-asmā'*, the prophet's first major work, which is described in its own text as "this Qur'ān",[44] and was referred to at the trial of Mullā 'Alī Basṭāmī in the same terms.[45] The temptation is greater because the *Qayyūm al-asmā'* is the main source for the Bāb's thoughts about *jihād* in the earliest period;[46] but there really does not seem to be a verse alluding to the division of booty anywhere there or, as far as I know, in other early works. References to booty in later works such as the Persian *Bayān* are quite different.

Another passage that has a strong air of authenticity is one in which Nāṣir al-Dīn Mīrzā confronts the Bāb with a sphere of the heavens and asks him to explain the circles and figures on it, which the Bāb says he is unable or unwilling to do. It occurs in the *Nāmūs-i Nāṣirī* and two Bābī texts, the *Nuqṭat al-kāf* and *Abwāb al-hudā*, an unlikely conjunction. Its presence in the *Namūs* is compelling, in that the work was submitted to Nāṣir al-Dīn Shāh in person. One must assume that Māmāqānī would not have risked fabricating an incident that the king could so easily have said never happened. But quite why the other sources omit such a vivid sequence is hard to explain.

The Answers

As noted above, one of the Bāb's answers (number 6: "I am that person you have been awaiting for one thousand years") occurs in some form in all nine sources, and I think we must conclude that it is the most authentic statement recorded from the trial. It seems highly plausible that he should have made such an egregious claim at this point. In 1263/1847, while in prison in Mākū, the Bāb had made an open claim to Mahdihood, a claim which he was now developing in his writings while in Chihrīq.[47]

---

[44] Ibid., f. 65a. Cf. ff. 35a, 67b, 72b, 75a, 141b, 167b.

[45] A copy of the *Qayyūm al-asmā'* was used in that trial as a point of reference for the charges against the Bāb's emissary.

[46] See D. MacEoin, "The Bābī Concept", 93–129.

[47] See Amanat, *Resurrection*, 375 ff. On the development of the Bāb's claims and other Bābī theophanic ideas, see MacEoin, "Hierarchy", 97–113.

There are three other passages which have analogues in the Bāb's writings, although (with two exceptions) they occur in a form which does not imply quotation. One ("question" 5) occurs in two sources, in the first as a question ("In these books of yours, have you not called yourself the Tree of Sinai [*shajara-yi Ṭūr*]?",[48] in the second as a statement ("What you mean when you say 'My words are from God' is that your tongue is like the Tree on Sinai").[49] In our other sources (see answer 4), the Bāb himself states that his writings are "like the revelation of words from the Tree on Sinai". Question 61 is put by Māmaqānī: "You have said in your books that the light that shone on Moses out of the Burning Bush was your light: is that correct?" Answer 35 attributes the statement directly to the Bāb. The *Qayyūm al-asmā'* contains several short passages which parallel this, and which may have been the basis for the questions.[50]

Passing from the terse to the prolix, we can be reasonably sure that the passage cited by Hashtrūdī, listing grammatical inaccuracies in the text of the Qur'ān, apart from being off the mark more than once, is highly unlikely to be genuine. The likelihood of the Bāb being allowed to expatiate on the grammatical inadequacies of holy writ is very small indeed.

In four sources, the Bāb claims to be able to write 1,000 (or 2,000, or 10,000) verses in a single day. A similar claim appears in several passages of the Bāb's writings,[51] and several histories give details of incidents when a public demonstration was made of the prophet's ability to reveal verses of speed, which, it is said, had the effect of convincing onlookers of his divine power.[52] In fact, this is exactly what several sources say happened during the trial, and there is every reason to regard those descriptions as broadly accurate, certainly in respect of the Bāb's own insistence on providing proof of his claims by these means.

In general, however, the Bāb's answers are much more difficult

---

48 *Miftāḥ*, 138.

49 *Rawḍat al-ṣafā*, 424.

50 *Qayyūm al-asmā'* ff. 40a, 89b, 133a ("I am he who spoke from the fire"), 147b ("I am the fire that spoke on Mount Ṭūr").

51 See *Bayān-i Fārsī*, 2:1, 13 and 17 (1,000 verses in 5 hours); *Tafsīr Sūrat al-kawthar*, CUL, Browne Or. Ms. F. 10, f. 5a (1,000 verses in 6 hours); letter to Manūchihr Khān, Browne Or. Ms. F. 2w1, 91 (ditto); *Risāla-yi dhahabiyya II*, Iran National Baha'i Manuscript Collection 53, 164 (a complete *ṣaḥīfa* in 1 hour).

52 Zarandī, *Dawn-Breakers*, 61, 202; *Nuqṭat al-kāf*, 108, 121.

to evaluate than the questions attributed to his accusers. Not unsurprisingly, the Muslim accounts do not portray the villain of their piece in a very favourable light. But so unintelligent are the answers they do attribute to him that it is very hard to believe he was ever capable of making a favourable impression on anyone, let alone the many *ʿulamāʾ* who became his followers.

This is particularly noticeable in the jibes directed at the young prophet's Arabic. No-one who has read his books and letters in that language will deny that the Bāb's Arabic was idiosyncratic; nonetheless, they are very far from being the products of someone who could not decline *qāla* (or even says *qāla*? What *qāla*?) or vocalizes *al-samawāti* as *al-samawāta*. The Bāb had a relatively sophisticated grasp of Arabic, and it is hard to imagine him mumbling and stumbling his way through a series of easy questions on grammar.

But it is equally easy to see that we are, in fact, witnessing the acting-out of a sort of unrehearsed play, or the playing of an elaborate game. The Bāb's behaviour, even as reported by the hostile accounts, may have been deliberately designed to convey a range of symbolic meanings. Here, for example, is someone claiming to be the Mahdī, yet his opponents insist on his declining Arabic verbs or answering questions about veterinary medicine. A dignified silence, or perhaps a statement to the effect that he had studied some grammar as a child but since forgotten it might well be seen as responses designed to point up the inappropriateness of the line of questioning being taken. And we should not forget that the Bāb himself, taking his cue from popular notions of the Prophet Muḥammad's illiteracy, made a point of saying he was a merchant by training, not a divine.[53] Hence the difficulty of interpreting almost anything the Bāb is reported to have said and done during this session.

Finally, it is worth remarking on the presence of several incidental features that lend some of the narratives a degree of credibility just by being there. Hashtrūdī's references to the time of day, the lighting of lamps and candles, and the serving of tea and *qalyāns* all suggest an eye-witness account, even if the bulk of his narrative is sparse. Zarandī's description of the throng gathered outside the assembly hall and the statement that they remained there, listening through the doors again has the smell of first-hand knowledge on

---

[53] See, for example, his letter to Muḥammad Shāh in *Muntakhabāt-i āyāt*, 14.

the part of his informant, Shaykh ʿAlī Zunūzī. Similarly, more than one source (and, tellingly, his son's in particular) refers to Mullā Muḥammad Māmaqānī growing angry at repeated intervals. By contrast, Niẓām al-ʿUlamāʾ is reputed to have possessed a sense of humour, and this comes through in more than one remark attributed to him. Small details like these may tell us very little in themselves, but they do tend to suggest genuine knowledge of what went on during the trial.

In one instance, however, there is a serious discrepancy between our sources. According to some (*Rawḍat al-ṣafāʾ*, *Miftāḥ*), the Bāb was seated in a place of honour near the Walī-ʿAhd; Māmaqānī says he was placed to one side; two Bābī accounts (Hashtrūdī and the *Nuqṭat al-kāf*) say he was not offered a seat and had to sit in a corner; and the other Bābī source (Zarandī) says he actually took the seat that had been reserved for the Crown Prince.

Conclusions

There is no space here for a full analysis of the trial and its wider significance. Amanat's account is perceptive, drawing particular attention to the conflicting aims of the government (who wanted to humiliate the Bāb, but to avoid a death sentence that might have aroused resentment among the populace at a time when the prophet was enjoying considerable popularity) and the *ʿulamāʾ* (many of whom wanted to put the apostate to death).

The affair is undeniably peculiar. Although the questioning is conducted in the main by *ʿulamāʾ*, state officials are not only present, but take part in the interrogation. Most of the city's *ʿulamāʾ* are absent, leaving the questioning almost wholly in the hands of Shaykhīs such as Niẓām al-ʿUlamāʾ and Māmaqānī. A *fatwā* for the Bāb's death (subject to his being found sane) is issued after the event by two *ʿulamāʾ* (Shaykh ʿAlī Aṣghar Shaykh al-Islām and Shaykh Abu 'l-Qāsim) who were not present at the trial. That is outmanoeuvred by presenting the Bāb to Dr. William Cormick, a British physician, who naturally complies with a letter recommending clemency.

The questioning itself has an almost Weberian quality (Lloyd, not Max). The innocent prophet, assailed by the forces of church and state, faced with a barrage of at times ridiculous questions which have little or no bearing on his claims, offers an almost classic contrast to his sarcastic, pedantic, irritable interlocutors. One senses almost that the *ʿulamāʾ* fell into an avoidable trap. A modern PR agent would have torn his hair out in despair.

But perhaps that is too facile a reading of events. Granted that human nature butts its head in repeatedly, there is still plenty of evidence that the basic line of questioning had been pre-meditated and adhered to with some degree of rigour. We have to remember that the Shīʿī *ʿulamāʾ* (and this includes the Shaykhīs, particularly those of Ādharbāyjān, as much as the regular Uṣūlīs) during this period were consolidating their authority within the developing Qājār state.[54] That authority was, as much as anything, built on the claim of the *ʿulamāʾ* to superior learning, particularly in areas like *fiqh*; but it also rested increasingly on the routinized charisma of senior mujtahids and, above all, *marājiʿ al-taqlīd*.[55] As the 19th century progressed, there was a growing tendency to focus the charismatic pole of religious authority within an increasingly tiny number of individuals or a single individual.

The problem with charismatic authority is, of course, its instability. The Uṣūlī establishment had already fought off a major challenge in the form of revived Niʿmat Allāhī Sufism in the late 18th century and (ironically, given the allegiance of the Bāb's accusers) Shaykhism in the 1830s and early 1840s. Other challenges of a less pressing nature hovered about on the periphery of religious life,[56] but none had the same resonance as Bābism, which demonstrated an ability to attract not only the masses, but also substantial numbers of *ʿulamāʾ*.

At the heart of the original Bābī summons to repentance and expectation of the millennium lay an insistence on the superiority of intuition over learning, the heart over the mind, the divinely aroused over the book-laden. It was hardly an original theme, but it is certainly marked in the accounts of the Bāb's trial. By parading their knowledge of grammar, jurisprudence, astronomy, mathematics, and all the rest before the representatives of the state, the *ʿulamāʾ* were

---

[54] For general accounts of state-*ʿulamāʾ* relations in this period, consult. Algar, *Religion and State*; Arjomand, *The Shadow of God*, Part Three.

[55] On this theme in general, see MacEoin, "From Shaykhism to Babism", chapter 1.

[56] For a very good account of some of these alternatives to orthodoxy, see Amanat, *Resurrection*, chapter 2.

not only trying to face down the Bāb, but to stake their claim to whole areas of public life.

The real implications of what was going on here can best be seen in the development of Babism after about 1850, when the Bāb was executed in Tabriz. Prior to that date, with the exception of the Bāb himself, leadership of the movement lay exclusively in the hands of young *ʿulamāʾ* like Mullā Ḥusayn Bushrūʾī and Muḥammad ʿAlī Bārfurūshī. After the virtual eradication of that leadership in the Bābī-state struggles of 1848–50, a new cadre emerged from among the lay following. Both Azalī and Bahāʾī Babism produced inspired claimants to divine authority, and an entirely fresh interpretation of the criteria for hierarchy.[57]

The trial of the Bāb may, therefore, be seen as something of a watershed, a moment when the representatives of knowledge-based hierarchy confronted the representative of what was coming. This was, in many ways, precisely what the clergy had awaited for over one thousand years: an unlearned man capable of subverting the very basis of their authority. Azali Babism produced secular reformers like Aqā Khān Kirmānī and Shaykh Aḥmad Rūḥī. Not quite what the Bāb had in mind, perhaps, but part of the vanguard of an army of educated challengers who came close to sweeping the old hierarchy away entirely.

[57] For details, see MacEoin, "Divisions and Authority Claims, 93–129.

(42 ff.)
Then the late Niẓām al-'Ulamā' said to my father [Mullā Muḥammad Māmaqānī]: "Before we move on to a discussion of scholarly matters, I have some questions I'd like to put to him, with your permission."

Then he faced the Bāb and asked: "These writings, some of which are in the style of the Qur'ān, and others in the style of sermons and prayers, and which have been distributed among the people by your followers—are they yours, or have they just been attributed to you?"

Bāb: "They are from God."

NU: "Be that as it may, did you write them?"

Bāb: "Yes, like the revelation of words from the Tree on Sinai."

NU: "Now, here's something I don't understand. Who gave you this title of 'Bāb'?"

Bāb: "God."

NU: "That's very presumptious of you. Exactly when did God bestow this 'Goodnight' on you?"

The Bāb grew angry and said: "You're making fun of me."

NU: "Well, let's leave it there. What are you the Gate of?"

Bāb: " 'I am the City of Knowledge and 'Ali is its Gate.' "

NU: "You are the Gate of the City of Knowledge?"

Bāb: "Yes. 'And pass through the Gate, prostrating yourselves.' "

NU: "Are you also the Bāb of prostration?"

Bāb: "Yes."

NU: "Since you are the Gate of the City of Knowledge, will you answer any question people may put to you?"

Bāb: "Yes. You do not recognize me. I am that very person you have been awaiting for over one thousand years."

Whereupon my father said: "Sayyid—you started by claiming to be the Gate of the Imām. Have you now become the hidden Lord of the Command in person?"

Bāb: "Yes. I am he for whom you have been waiting since the very beginning of the Islamic revelation."

My father grew very angry at these vain words, and said: "Sayyid, why aren't you ashamed of yourself? What sort of foolishness is this you're mouthing? If we're waiting, we're waiting for that Imām whose father was Imām Ḥasan al-'Askarī, and whose mother was Narjis the daughter of Yashūʿā, son of the king of Byzantium, who was born of his mother in the year 256 in Samarra, and who will appear in Mecca with the sword. Since when have we ever waited for Sayyid ʿAli Muḥammad, the son of Sayyid Riḍā the Shirazi grocer, who only left his mother's womb yesterday? In any case, when the Lord of the Age appears, he will bring with him all the inheritance of the prophets, from Adam to the Seal. Why don't you produce one of those heirlooms so we can see it?"

Bāb: "I am not permitted to at this moment."

My father grew angry and said: "If you didn't get permission, you made a big mistake coming here and nailing your head to the wall. Off you go and get permission, then you can come back. A Lord of the Command who comes without permission is jumping the gun. In any case, the Lord of Command can perform miracles. In the name of God, turn your staff into a dragon so we will all believe."

Bāb: "I shall cause a verse to descend upon this staff."

The onlookers laughed loudly and said: "What verse will you reveal?"

With his hand placed behind his ear like a singer, he chanted in a singing voice: "Praise be to God Who created this staff and made it a sign among His signs, that you may fear Him."

They said, "Is this your verse?"

Bāb: "Yes."

The late Amīr Aṣlān Khān Majd al-Dawla, who was present, said: "If your being an Imām can be established by such a verse, I can reveal a better one than you. 'Praise be to God Who created this staff and made the morning and the evening that you may give Him thanks.' What is there to choose between your verse and mine?"

The sayyid could not come up with an answer. Then he faced my late father and said: "Indeed, you have the right to reject me. It has come down in the traditions that when the Lord of the Age, may God hasten his advent, appears, forty thousand clerics will issue *fatwā*s for his death."

My late father said: "Sayyid, why do you invent traditions, and why do you talk nonsense? To begin with, it would be a miracle if forty thousand muftis gathered together at a single time. Secondly, the Lord of the Command won't come as such a miserable creature as you, that anyone would dare issue a sentence for his death. The sword Dhu 'l-Fiqār will be in his hand, and if anybody resists him he will strike his neck like a dog. Tell me the truth, in which book did you find this tradition, and from which Imām did it come?"

Bāb: "It may not be forty thousand, but the forty that are here."

The onlookers laughed loudly at this exaggeration and its sudden playing down.

Māmaqānī: "That isn't even a tradition. What book is it in, which Imām is it from?"

Bāb: "Well, it's certainly written that some of the *ʿulamāʾ* will turn against him."

Māmaqānī: "Nor is that a tradition. It's something that was said by Muḥyī 'l-Dīn ibn ʿArabī—that when the promised Mahdi comes, the majority of those who reject him will be the outwardly learned (*ʿulamā-yi ẓāhira*). Since you are so seriously ill-informed about the texts and traditions, you lay claim to the Imamate with idle talk, and say you are the Gate of the City of Knowledge. *He who disbelieves speaks slander.*"

Then the late Niẓām al-ʿUlamā said: "Yes, your statements in regard to this tradition are exactly the same as those which an unlettered man asked of a learned one: 'Which Imām was it who was eaten by a jackal in Baṣra?' He meant his holiness Joseph. [The scholar] replied: 'He wasn't an Imām, he was a prophet; it wasn't Baṣra, it was Egypt; it wasn't a jackal, it was a wolf; and it didn't eat him.'"

The onlookers laughed loudly.

Then Niẓām al-ʿUlamāʾ said: "Since you lay claim to the Imamate, we won't ask you to perform another miracle. Our king is suffering from gout. Please pray for his ailment to be healed. If it is, we shall all believe in you."

His Excellency the Shadow of God[1] said: "Why travel so far? Let him restore you to youth in this very assembly, and we shall all believe."

There was no response. Then the Bāb turned to my late father and said: "You consider the *Ṣaḥīfa-yi Sajjādiyya* to be among the miracles of his holiness (Imām) Sajjād, and to be a proof of his Imamate. I have written ten times that number of prayers. Are they not sufficient as a miracle for me?"

Māmaqānī: "'Praise be to Thee, this is a great calumny.' In the first place, when did we ever say that the *Ṣaḥīfa-yi Sajjādiyya* is one

[1] I.e. Nāṣir al-Dīn Mīrzā.

of the miracles of his holiness? Why do you have to make things up? The most we say is that those prayers stand among the words of human kind in the highest degree of eloquence and elegance. In the second place, what relationship can there be between your words, which are filled with mistakes from beginning to end, and the *Ṣaḥīfa-yi Sajjādiyya*? What link is there between the earth and the pure world (*ʿālam-i pāk*)? And how can incorrect and stumbling words be considered miraculous?"

NU: "Jināb-i Āqā! One of the prayers from the *Ṣaḥīfa* reads: 'O Thou through Whom the knot of the deceiver is untied.' Do you write a prayer like it and we shall believe in you."

There was no reply.

Māmaqānī: "In His Book, God says in respect of Jesus, using the words of his followers: 'They said, "How can we speak with one who is in his cradle, a babe?"' Such a distancing and expression of amazement is perfectly understandable, since conversing with a baby while still in the cradle would be a miracle. Now, you put yourself on a level with this verse in your own book. You say: 'How can one speak the words of God when he is in truth only twenty-five years old?' Leaving aside the mistakes in the words themselves, what would be a cause for bewilderment and surprise in a twenty-five-year-old man speaking on behalf of God that you should take the trouble to defend yourself against it? What fool would say such a thing for you to feel it necessary to refute him? You who have still to learn how to put a few words together. *He who disbelieves slanders.*"

Then the late ʿAlam al-Hudā said: "Sir, God has said in His Book: 'Know that whenever you have taken booty, a fifth of it belongs to God.' Has the decree laid down in this verse been abrogated, or does it still stand?"

Bāb: "It still stands."

A.H.: "In that case, on what grounds do you in your book say: 'Know that whenever you have taken booty, a third of it belongs to the Remembrance'? Doesn't this decree abrogate the Word of God?"

Bāb: "Well, the share of the Imām belongs to me."

A.H.: "The Imām's share is one half of a fifth, and half a fifth is a tenth, not a third."

Bāb: "No, it is a third."

All the onlookers laughed. In the end, ʿAlam al-Hudā, with a thousand perhapses and maybes and calculations on the finger showed him that half a fifth is a tenth. Once he had been convinced, he said: "It was a slip."

Then my late father said: "You who possess such skill in counting, will you tell me how many fractions there are in arithmetic?"

Bāb: "I have never studied arithmetic."

Then ʿAlam al-Hudā said: "Jināb-i Sayyid. It is an essential tenet of our faith that the gate of original revelation has been closed since the days of the Prophet. Even Gabriel said at the time when the Prophet died that this was his final descent to the earth. What he meant was his coming down to bring an original revelation."

Bāb: "Yes, that is the case."

ʿAlam al-Hudā: "But then you say in your book: 'Truly, we have sent a revelation down to you even as we sent it down to Muḥammad before you.' What is the meaning of this? Especially since, in your style of writing, a likeness is identical to what it is likened to."

Bāb: "It was closed then, and now it has been opened again. What's the harm in that?"

ʿAlam al-Hudā: "No harm, but it does mean that the Prophet [Muḥammad] is not the Seal of the Prophets, and that the words: 'There shall be no prophet after me' are a lie."

There was no reply. Then ʿAlam al-Hudā said: "In your book you have said: 'We have caused you to be raised up above a station, or to a nearer place'. Is that so?"

Bāb: "Yes."

ʿAlam al-Hudā: "To begin with, what's the purpose in using the transitive in the verb *'arfaʿnāka'* [We have caused you to be raised up]?, bearing in mind that God, when He says concerning Idris in His Book, 'And We raised him up to a high place' does not use the transitive. Secondly, the furthest limit travelled to by the Prophet during his ascension to heaven was the station of 'or nearer', for there is nothing higher than that world in the realm of creation. You who have gone five stops beyond Mecca and placed your foot above the station of prophethood [reading *nubuwwat* for *nawbat*], where do you plan to go now? On this basis, your rank must be higher than that of the Prophet. *He who has disbelieved slanders.*"

Then my late father said: "You have said in your books that the light that shone on Moses out of the Burning Bush was your light: is that correct?"

Bāb: "Yes."

Māmaqānī: "What's your proof for that?"

Bāb: "Well, there is a tradition that the light which shone forth upon Moses was the light of one of the followers (Shīʿīān) of the Prince of Believers. Isn't that so?"

His excellency the Shadow of God, who was at that time seventeen years old, asked out of his understanding and sagacity: "What makes you think that's you? How does that prove your claim? The Prince of Believers has plenty of followers."

My late father said: "The criticism is correct. Apart from that, 'You have remembered something, and you have forgotten many things'. You have heard something, but you haven't understood its meaning in the least. The light of one person does not shine on another, when they are separated by a distance of isolation (*nūr-i dīgarī bi-dīgarī ka mīān-i ānhā baynūnat-i ʿuzlatīst, tajallī namī-kunad*). Rather, it shone for it and upon it (*tajallā la-hā bi-hā*) and through it it was kept apart from it; this meaning is perfectly clear in the philosophy of the Imāms. The meaning of this light is the light of the reality of Moses himself, who is one of the followers of the Prince of the Believers; for the Imām has made this clear in another tradition, in which the transmitter asked his holiness about the cherubim. His holiness declared 'They are a people from among the followers of the Prince of Believers, from the first creation, [dwelling] behind the throne; if the light of any one of them were to be split up among all the people of the earth, there would be enough to go round. When his holiness Moses asked his God what he asked Him, God commanded one of those cherubim, *And he shone forth upon the mountain, and laid it level with the earth, and Moses fainted away*.'[2] The transmitter asked 'What are their names?' He answered: 'Noah, Abraham, Moses, and Jesus.' The transmitter asked: 'Whose light was it that shone forth on Moses?' He said: 'The light of Moses.'"

"You, you poor wretch, who know nothing about the traditions and possess no insight into the rules governing philosophy, what sort of ridiculous claims are you making?"

Then he said: "Let's leave these abstruse questions, and let me ask you a question concerning religious law. Tell me, in our law, how many types of divorce are there? Which type constitutes 'innovative divorce'? Which one is 'legitimate divorce'? And within legitimate divorce, which is irrevocable, which revocable, and which healthy (?*ʿadhā*)?"

---

[2] The Quranic part-verse (7:143) quoted here is not cited accurately.

He said: "I have not studied religious law."

After this, my late father asked a question regarding medicine, which I do not remember.

He said: "I have not studied medicine."

Then he (Māmaqānī) said: "In a letter you wrote to me, in which you invited me to join you, [you have written]: 'The first to believe in me was Muḥammad ibn ʿAbd Allāh'. Was this letter written by you?"

Bāb: "Yes."

Māmaqānī: "Well, in that case your rank is above that of the Prophet, since it is the follower who believes in him whom he follows, and not the other way round."

There was no reply from that Gate of the City.

Then the late ʿAlam al-Hudā asked: "You have referred to yourself as 'Lord'? Why is that?"

Bāb: "Well, my name is numerically equivalent to the word 'Lord'."

My late father said: "Your name isn't unique to you. On the strength of what you say, shouldn't anybody called ʿAlī Muḥammad or Muḥammad ʿAlī be considered a Lord apart from God?"

No reply could be heard. Then he put his hand to his ear and said: "Listen. I shall reveal a verse: 'Praise be to God Who created the heavens and the earth'", putting the vowel "a" at the end of the word "heavens" (*samawāt*).[3]

His majesty said: "You don't even know the rules of Arabic grammar. 'Whatever takes its plural in *tā'* and *alif* is vocalized with "i" in both accusative and genitive'."

Bāb: "Listen: 'And he made the sun and the moon'", vocalizing the *shīn* of *shams* [the sun] with "i".

The onlookers exclaimed: "You've made a mistake. Why do you put the vowel 'i' where you should have 'a'?"

Bāb: "Now, listen. . . ."

My late father grew angry and said: "Who wants to listen to words with mistakes in them?"

His (the Bāb's?) breath was cut short. By chance there happened to be a sphere of the heavens in the room. His excellency the Shadow of God said: "Bring that sphere over and show us the figures and circles on it."

Bāb: "I have not studied astrology (*nujūm*)."

---

[3] Thus, *al-samawāt*[a] instead of *al-samawāt*[i].

My late father grew angry and said: "You donkey! This isn't astrology, it's astronomy!"

Niẓām al-ʿUlamāʾ said: "You, sir—what's the meaning of these words of ʿAllāma:[4] 'If a man should have intercourse with a hermaphrodite, or a hermaphrodite with a woman, ablutions are obligatory for the hermaphrodite, but not for either the man or the woman'. Explain the mode of this ruling, and what was ʿAllāma's thinking."

Bāb: "I've already said that I have not studied religious law."

Niẓām al-ʿUlamāʾ: "Ma'mūn asked his holiness Riḍāʾ the following: 'Where is your proof for the caliphate of your grandfather [ʿAlī]?' His holiness replied: 'The Quranic verse "Ourselves"'. Ma'mūn said: 'But for our wives'. His holiness made the rejoinder: 'But for our sons'. What is the character of the proof cited by the Imām, and the nature of Maʾmūn's objection, and the sense of Riḍā's response to it in this tradition?"

Bāb: "Is it really a tradition?"

Niẓām al-ʿUlamāʾ: "Yes."

Bāb: "I can't think of anything."

Nizam al-ʿUlamāʾ: "God says: 'He it is Who causes you to behold the lightning, for fear and for hope'.[5] How are the phrases 'for fear' and 'for hope' construed according to the rules of grammar?"

Bāb: "I haven't studied grammar."

Niẓām: "Tell me the meaning of this tradition: *May God curse the eyes, for they have behaved unjustly towards the one eye.*"

He hesitated for a moment, then said: "I don't know."

Then the late ʿAlam al-Hudā said: "Sir! In your book, you have said that if jinn and men were to assemble together, they could not produce the like of half a word from your book. Is this true?"

Bāb: "Yes."

ʿAlam al-Hudā: "In His Book, God has challenged men to (produce) a single sura, saying: 'Produce a sura like it'. How did your book come to be elevated above the Book of God? Secondly, half a word cannot be pronounced, in order for this to be a permissible challenge. To impose what is impossible is reprehensible. Secondly [sic], fine speech and eloquence are attributes of words and combined

[4] ʿAllāma Jamāl al-Dīn Abū Manṣūr Ḥasan al-Ḥillī, Ibn al-Muṭahhar (648/1250–726/1325).

[5] Qurʾān 13:12; cf. 30:24

letters; in the case of separate letters, both eloquent and ineloquent are reduced to the same level. Look—if I were to utter an *alif*, how would it differ from an *alif* in your book? If you should say that the *alif* in your book is divine (*lāhūtī*) and my *alif* earthly (*nāsūtī*), it seems to me that I could turn the whole thing round the other way. For what I say and what you say are both claims unsubstantiated by any proof. What is the point in this sort of challenge?"

His excellency the Bāb remained astonished, and said nothing. But after that he showed no shame, and said: "This Qur'ān that I have brought—no-one else could produce one like it. This proof is sufficient as testimony to the truth of my claims."

My father grew angry and said: "Sayyid, how long will you keep singing this nonsense? Your book is full of mistakes from beginning to end, and all it says is foolishness. We consider ourselves more dignified than to descend to competing with your nonsense. And unlike you we are not lacking in shame, first of all to desecrate God's Qur'ān, and then to make remarks about how it has been put together and make ourselves fit to be reviled. If you insist on this matter, here is one of our *'ulamā'*. His name is Mīrzā Ḥasan, and he is one of the *'ulamā'* of Khūy. For the sake of proving the point to you, he will compose a few pages in the style of your writings, and if you like they will be brought to you so you can see that in respect of accuracy, eloquence, and refinement of style his words will not bear the slightest resemblance to these jumbled scribblings of yours."

The sayyid remained silent, and did not reply. Then the Niẓām al-'Ulamā' said: "It has been reported with respect to the revelation of the Sura of Kawthar that his holiness the Prophet was walking through an alleyway, when 'Ās the father of 'Amr said: 'This man has no children. He'll soon die, leaving no descendants.' His holiness the Prophet grew sad, and to comfort him the sura in question was revealed. In what way did it comfort him?"

Bāb: "Was the occasion for the revelation of the sura really as you have said?"

Niẓām: "Yes."

He thought for a bit, then said: "Nothing springs to mind."

Then the late 'Alam al-Hudā said: "Sir! In your book you have said that you dreamed that they had killed the Prince of Martyrs (Ḥusayn), and that you drank a few drops of his blood and that the gates of heavenly grace were thereupon opened to you. Is that correct?"

Bāb: "Yes."

My late father said: "Sayyid, what enmity do you hold for the Prince of Martyrs, that you should eat him after they put him to death?"

Niẓām al-ʿUlamāʾ said in jest: "Well, after all, Hind was a liver-eater."

There was no reply from the Bāb. Then, my late father, having been angered, indeed incensed by these nonsensical words, said: "Very well, you Shirazi rascal, what sort of hypocrisy and and double-dealing is this? When the followers of the Shaykh-i Aḥsāʾī ask you, you write: 'Aḥmad and Kāẓim, may God bless them both'. But what about Sayyid Yaḥyā, the son of Sayyid Jaʿfar Dārābī? The father disagrees with the opinions of the late Shaykh-i Aḥsāʾī about the resurrection. But when the son asks you, you write in reply that the shaykh was wrong about the resurrection, and you openly declare him a heretic, and you write: 'In truth, Sayyid Jaʿfar Dārābī was correct in what he wrote concerning the words: "His lightning flashed forth, encompassing the eastern and western horizons"'. So what was all that 'may God bless them' of yours about? And what's this condemnation and excommunication? If you're an honest man, why can't you just stick to one position?"

The sayyid hung his head and made no reply. The late Niẓām al-ʿUlamāʾ said: "Let's leave these questions. If a man should be uncertain [in the ritual prayer] between two and three, how should he begin?"

Bāb: "He should begin with two."

My late father grew angry, and the sayyid immediately said, "No, I made a mistake. He should begin with three."

The onlookers laughed. My father said: "Since it wasn't two, it had to be three."

Niẓām al-ʿUlamāʾ: "You wretch! If you'd stuck to your first remark and not said anything about having made a mistake, it would have been better for you, since that position used to be held by some in the past. You could at least have maintained that it was your legal ruling, since engaging in an indubitable duty demands fulfillment of that indubitable duty.[6] But why didn't you ask whether the doubt was in the case of ritual prayer of two, three, or four prostrations?

[6] This last phrase taken from Browne's translation of *Rawḍat al-ṣafāʾ* (*Traveller's Narrative*, 286).

Or whether it was before or after the two prostrations? Or before or after completion?"

The Bāb hung his head down and said nothing.

NU: "Since you don't know the answer to any of these questions, let me ask you a simple question. What tense is the verb *qulnā*[7] in, and how does its weak letter mutate?

Bāb: "I haven't studied syntax."

My late father grew angry again and said: "You donkey! This is morphology, not syntax. And you lay claim to the Imāmate with an intelligence like yours."

Then the late Niẓām al-ʿUlamāʾ saw that the Bāb wasn't up to a learned debate, so he started to deride him, saying: "You, sir! When did I send you as an Imām? Why did you come talking such nonsense?"

Bāb: "Are you claiming to be God?"

NU: "Yes. An Imām like you deserves a God like me."

When the discussion reached this point, and the degrees of the Bāb's ignorance and dullness were made obvious to everyone, there was no need to proceed further. His Excellence the Shadow of God spoke to the Farrāshbāshī, saying: "This idiot isn't fit to debate with the *ʿulamāʾ*. Take him away."

They took him away from that place swiftly and placed him in the house of Kāẓim Khān the Farrāshbāshī. And so the meeting came to an end. *Take heed, ye that have eyes to see.*

[7] Ar. "We said."

From Muʿīn al-Salṭana 201 ff.

There is also the account of ʿĀlim-i Hashtrūdī, who was in Tabriz at that time; and the narratives of some others from the early period, both believers and non-believers, agree with Hashtrudi's account. . . .

Hashtrūdī says: It was near sunset when they brought the Bāb, who had just emerged from the public bath, to that assembly of misery. When he entered, the *ʿulamāʾ*, who had arrived early, had already occupied the main seats, sitting to the left and right of the heir to the throne, and there was no room left for anyone to sit. His holiness entered the assembly and greeted those present, but no-one returned his greeting, nor did they show him a place to sit. For a moment, the Bāb remained standing, like someone who awaits a welcome and expects to be shown a seat by the owner of the house or his host, but no-one paid any heed. But on the faces of those present could be clearly seen the signs of imposture and meanness, of hatred and enmity, of obstinacy and opposition.

So his holiness went to a corner, with that polite and dignified manner which he always possessed, and removing his hands from his sleeves, sat down in the posture of oneness. The *ʿulamāʾ* had been conversing a little together in private, and had asked the heir to the throne about the health of the king and his wife, and he had answered them. And they had uttered prayers and murmured "Amen" in the most abjectly flattering manner.

When they turned their attention to his holiness the Bāb, they asked: "What is this affair of yours, and what is the truth of the matter, and what is the nature of your claim?"

His holiness the exalted, without the least change in his manner, and with the utmost firmness and dignity, declared: "I am the Qāʾim for whom you have been waiting" (*Anā 'l-Qāʾim alladhī kuntum bihi muntaẓirūn*).

No sooner had they heard these words, it was as if an earthquake had struck and had cast the inhabitants of the place into a state of fear and confusion. A strange murmuring passed among those present at the assembly. One said: "I ask God's forgiveness, and repent to Him. What audacity has this man shown!" Another said: "There is no god but God." Another said from the bottom of his heart: "May God protect us from it. Amen." [Another] said: "No strength or power is there save in God, the Exalted, the Great. Why hasn't the ground opened up and why haven't the heavens fallen?"

At that time, the *'ulamā'* and clerics of the Muslims and the judges of the holy law considered themselves to be God's representatives and the pillars of heaven and earth, inasmuch as the *'ulamā'* interfered greatly through their legal rulings and their sentencing in the affairs of the nation and the important matters of state. The dominance of the *'ulamā'* of those days cannot be compared to what it is today. . . .

After a great murmuring and much talking, they demanded evidence, and started to ask academic questions. First of all, the heir to the throne took a silver ball on which had been drawn circles and lines [showing] the form of the heavens, corresponding to the heavenly bodies of Ptolemy, and which the astronomers and astrologers call a globe. Nāṣir al-Dīn Mīrzā held it in his hand, then rolled it in the direction of his holiness, asking a question concerning the stars and planets. His holiness replied: "I have not studied astronomy or astrology, and am unlettered and bereft in the acquisition of such sciences."[1]

The *fuqahā'* and *'ulamā'* said: "What is the proof of the truth and the evidence for the rightness of your claim?"[2] His holiness the Most Mighty Gate replied, saying: "The verses of God [possess?] a divine spirit, inasmuch as they descended upon a beloved and honoured servant [illegible]. [Illegible] is a [confirmation?] of this, inasmuch as he has said: 'He shall appear with verses like the Qur'ān'. [Such verses] descend upon and flow from my tongue and pen. The lasting proof is the verses of God."

They said: [illegible]

Without hesitation, his holiness the most exalted began to recite verses, and continued to do so for a little time. The *'ulamā'* criticized the verses of his holiness on the grounds of [illegible], and said: "They do not comply with the rules of grammar and syntax, and are replete with errors."

[Text reverts abruptly to Mu'in al-Salṭana here.] But none of the historians, including 'Ālim-i Hashtrūdī himself, who is the narrator of this account and the author of the *Abwāb al-hudā*, have recorded the verses that were revealed at that time. I myself have taken much

---

[1] Reading end of sentence as: *va az taḥṣīl-i īn qabīl 'ulūm bī bahr va ummī hastam.*

[2] Reading this section as: *fuqahā' wa 'ulamā' guftand* [illegible] *dalīl-i ḥaqīqat wa burhān-i ṣidq-i id'ā-yi shumā chīst?*

trouble and asked both believers and non-believers, but have never obtained a text of those verses. I would also hesitate to square this with the text[3] of the verses cited by Nāṣir al-Dīn Mīrzā in his letter,[4] as I shall soon explain in my account of my own opinion.

[Returning to Hashtrūdī's narrative?] Then his holiness the most exalted [said?]: "I am unlettered [*man ummī hastam*] and have studied none of your sciences. These verses flow forth upon my tongue and mind, but you divines, who hold the rules of grammar and syntax in such high esteem, will you please tell me which rules of grammar does the following passage, which was revealed in the noble Qur'ān, conform to? *And a word from Him, his name is the Messiah.*[5] 'A word' [*kalima*], which is [grammatically] feminine is referred to by a masculine pronoun. He should have said 'from it'.[6] And [in the case of] the words *It is only a reminder to men,*[7] which were revealed in respect of the Qur'ān itself, the [masculine form] *huwa* should have been used, since the pronoun refers back to the Qur'ān or the Book of God, which is masculine, not feminine.[8] And [in the case of] the verse: *It is one of the greatest things, as a warning to men,*[9] which refers to the Prophet himself,[10] it should have read 'He', since the Prophet is not feminine. And [in the case of] this noble verse, where He has said *These two men are sorcerers,*[11] the scholars of grammar say that (the particle) *in* [illegible] is a 'word resembling the verb', whose noun should be in the accusative. The accusative case is indicated by the letter *ya'* [?], so it should read: *These two men are indeed sorcerers*".[12]

---

[3] Reading *matn*.

[4] This is presumably a reference to the letter (now in the Majlis Library) assumed to be by Nāṣir al-Dīn Mīrzā, but which Browne believed to have been written by Amīr Aṣlān Khān (see Browne *Materials*, 248–255 for notes with the text and translation of this letter, and a reproduction of the original.)

[5] The passage is quoted incorrectly and incompletely here, reading *wa kalimatun minhu ismuhu 'l-Masīḥ*. The correct quotation reads [Qur'ān 3:45] *(inna 'llāha yubashshiruki) bi-kalimatin minhu ismuhu 'l-Masīḥu ('Īsā ibn Maryama)*.

[6] The argument presented here is confused. The problematic pronoun in this passage is not the *hu* in *minhu*, but the *hu* in *ismuhu* (which is in fact not problematic, since it refers forward to Jesus, not back to the word *kalima*.

[7] Qur'ān 74:31.

[8] The original reads: *wa mā hiya illā dhikrā li 'l-bashar*. The pronoun *hiya* must be assumed to take its gender from the word *dhikrā*, which is feminine. "It" is generally taken to refer to the Qur'ān.

[9] Qur'ān 74:35–36.

[10] This is by no means an obvious reading of the text.

[11] Qur'ān 20:63. The Arabic reads: *In hādhāni la-sāḥirāni*.

[12] The emendation in Arabic reads: *Inna hādhayni la-sāḥirayni*. This is strictly

"Similarly you *ʿulamāʾ* say that nunation is a form peculiar to the noun, and is never used for a verb, yet in the noble Qurʾān He has said: *We shall drag him by the forelock.*[13] 'We shall drag' is an imperfect verb in the first person (plural) which has been altered [? *maʿa 'l-ghayr*] and given nunation. Likewise, in the Qurʾān the feminine has been mentioned in the masculine form: *Some women in the city said.*[14] This should have read: '[they (fem.)] said [*qālat*]. Likewise, He has mentioned the pronoun before the [noun?], when He says: *Say, He is God, One.*'"[15]

When the speech reached this point, the *ʿulamāʾ* were unable to give a reply. Whereupon, Mīrzā Aḥmad[16] the Imām-Jumʿa, who was recognized as the leading mujtahid of Tabriz, said to his holiness the exalted: "You say you have studied no branches of learning, so where did you pick up all this?" His holiness the Herald said in reply: "These things flow forth upon my tongue just like those verses. I have not studied them."

At this point, Ḥājī Mullā Maḥmūd, Niẓām al-ʿUlamāʾ, the teacher and Mullābāshī of the Walī-ʿAhd, asked his holiness: "Will you reveal a verse suitable to the circumstances and appropriate to this gathering?" But just then the sun had gone down and night had started to fall, and the servants had lit magnificent lamps such as various kinds of candelabra (*chil-chirāgh, jār, mirdanakī*?), and gold and silver and crystal candlesticks, such as were fit for a king's court, and the gathering was lit up anew by pure [reading *sāda*] light and illumination.

In accordance with the request of Niẓām al-ʿUlamāʾ, verses resembling the Light Verse[17] were revealed, but neither Hashtrūdī nor any other historian has recorded the precise words of these verses. So,

---

incorrect, since the last word should still read *la-sāḥirān*. In fact, the argument put forward here misses the point. Where the particle *in* is used as the 'lightened' form (*al-mukhaffafa min al-thaqīla*) of *inna*, it requires a following *la*, which is provided in the Qurʾānic text. (See W. Wright, *A Grammar of the Arabic Language*, 3rd ed., Cambridge, CUP, 1971, vol. 2, 81 D).

[13] Qurʾān 96:15. The original reads: *la-nasfaʿan bi 'l-nāṣiyya*, where the verb is written, not with the suffixed *nūn* of the energetic, but with a *fatḥa* and *tanwīn*. This affects only the written form, not the spoken.

[14] Qurʾān 12:30. The original reads: *wa qāla niswa fī 'l-madīna.*

[15] Qurʾān 112:1. The original reads: *Qul: huwa 'llāhu aḥadun*. Presumably, the argument that would have followed here is that this passage should have read: *Allāhu, huwa aḥadun.*

[16] Amanat argues that Hashtrūdī is in error in including Mīrzā Aḥmad among the participants (*Resurrection and Renewal*, 388, f.n. 64).

[17] Qurʾān 24:35.

just as I have written, they too have written that verses like the Light Verse of the Qur᾽ān were sent down. Although I have searched hard, I have not been able to obtain an accurate record of those verses.

In the end, Ḥājjī Mullā Maḥmūd wrote down those revealed verses, and kept them for himself. At this point, the Walī-ʿAhd asked for tea to be served. The servants and butlers served to those present. After the tea and hookahs had been served, Niẓām al-ʿUlamā᾽ said to the Bāb that he wanted him to reveal the same verses a second time. The Bāb began to write down the verses and [*several words illegible* Niẓām al-ʿUlamā᾽?] also wrote down [*illegible* these verses?].

The text of these new verses differed slightly from that of the first. [Ḥājjī?] Mullā Maḥmūd turned to those present and said: "[word unclear] Look, these [two?] (sets of) verses are different [*illegible*—from one another?]."

[A digression follows concerning thoughts expressed in a Baha'i gathering "fifty years ago" about this incident.]

After these discussions and remarks, Ḥājjī Mīrzā ʿAlī, the son of Mīrzā Masʿūd, the Foreign Minister,[18] who [*illegible*] was someone well-versed in Arabic, and who had been accounted among the invitees in order to help distinguish between truth and falsehood, asked the Bāb: "What grammatical form [*ṣīgha*] does the phrase *qawluhu*[19] take?" His holiness the exalted did not reply. He got up and left the gathering. The oppressors returned the Bāb to his prison in the Citadel.

[18] Ḥājj Mīrzā Masʿūd Anṣārī Ishlīqī Garmrūdī became Foreign Minister in 1251/1835-36. His eldest son, Ḥājj Mīrzā ʿAlī, was a calligrapher and poet.

[19] Ar. "His word".

Questions, rebukes, statements etc. made during the interrogation of the Bāb

	Question etc.	Source									
		NN	RS	NT	MBA	FB	AKh	NK	AH	DB	Total
1	"Are these your writings?"	√	√	√	√	√		√			6
2	"Who gave you the title Bāb?"	√	√	√	√	√		√			6
3	"When did God bestow this title?"	√	√[1]			√[2]					3
4	"What are you the gate of?"	√	√[3]			√					3
5	"Did you call yourself/your tongue is like Tree of Sinai?"[4]		√		√						2
6	Quotes "Ask me before I am gone. . . ."			√	√						2
7	"Are you the hidden Imām in person?"	√	√[5]	√[6]	√[7]	√					5
8	"The Imām we await is so-and-so. You are someone else."	√	√	√	√	√					5
9	"Why did you not bring the heirlooms of the Prophet?"	√					√				2

[1] "Where?"
[2] "Where?"
[3] "What is the meaning of 'Bāb'?"
[4] Some other sources have the reference to the Tree on Sinai as a statement of the Bāb's.
[5] "In person or in type?" (*shakhsī yā nawʿī*)
[6] "In person or in type?" (*nawʿī būdaʾī yā shakhṣī mībāshī*)
[7] "In person or in type?"

10	"Go and get permission (to bring heirlooms)"	√					√		2
11	"Turn your staff into a dragon"	√							1
12	"Do you have a verse for your staff?"	√				√		√	3
13	"I can reveal a better verse than that" (Aṣlān Khān)	√				√	√	√	4
14	"It is not a tradition, but from Ibn al-'Arabī"	√							1
15	"A jackal in Baṣra"	√							1
16	"Pray for Muḥammad Shāh's health"	√	√	√	√	√			5
17	"Restore Niẓām al-'Ulamā' to youth"	√	√	√	√	√			5
18	"O Thou through Whom the knot of the deceiver is untied"	√							1
19	"How can we speak with one in his cradle?"[8]	√							1
20	"Does the Quranic decree on booty still stand?"	√	√	√	√[9]	√			5
21	"How many fractions are there in arithmetic?"[10]	√							1
22	"We have sent a revelation to you as to Muḥammad"[11]	√							1
23	"We have caused you to be raised up a station . . ."[12]	√							1

[8] Asked by Māmaqānī.

[9] This is the only source to attribute this question to a certain Mīrzā 'Abd al-Karīm Mullābāshī. The others say it was asked by 'Alam al-Hudā.

[10] Asked by Māmaqānī.

[11] Asked by 'Alam al-Hudā.

[12] Asked by 'Alam al-Hudā.

	Question etc.	Source									
		NN	RS	NT	MBA	FB	AKh	NK	AH	DB	Total
24	"How many kinds of divorce are there in *fiqh*?"	√									1
25	"A question on medicine"	√[13]	√[14]	√[15]	√[16]	√[17]					5
26	"Queries claim that first to believe in Bāb was Muḥammad"	√	√[18]	√[19]	√[20]	√					5
27	"You refer to yourself as 'Lord'. Why?"	√									1
28	"Whatever takes its plural in *ta*ʾ and *alif*. . . ."[21]	√	√	√	√	√[22]					5
29	"Explain the figures on this sphere of the heavens"[23]	√						√	√		3
30	Quotes ʿAllāma al-Ḥillī on hermaphrodite.	√	√	√	√	√					5
31	Quotes question of Maʾmūn to Imām Riḍā	√	√	√	√	√	√				6
32	"He it is Who causes you to behold the lightning. . . ."	√	√	√	√	√					5
33	"May God curse the eyes. . . ."	√	√	√	√	√					5
34	"You claim that men and jinn cannot produce a word . . ."[24]	√									1

[13] Asked by Māmaqānī. Māmaqānī's son did not remember what this was.
[14] Asked by Niẓām al-ʿUlamāʾ.
[15] Asked by Niẓām al-ʿUlamāʾ.
[16] Asked by Niẓām al-ʿUlamāʾ.
[17] Asked by Niẓām al-ʿUlamāʾ.
[18] "The Light of Muḥammad".
[19] "The Light of Muḥammad".
[20] "The Light of Muḥammad".
[21] Quoted by Nāṣir al-Dīn Mīrzā.
[22] Attributed to "one of those present".
[23] Said by Nāṣir al-Dīn Mīrzā.
[24] Said by ʿAlam al-Hudā.

35	On remark of ʿĀṣ the father of ʿAmr	√	√	√	√	√				5
36	Claim to have drunk drops of blood of Ḥusayn[25]	√								1
37	Bāb's hypocrisy regarding al-Aḥsāʾī and Rashtī	√								1
38	"If a man is uncertain between two and three (*rakʿas*)"	√	√			√	√	√		5
39	"What tense is *qulnā*?/Decline *qāla*"	√	√[26]			√				3
40	"When did I send you as an Imām?"	√	√			√				3
41	Quotes "If it is allowed for a tree to say 'I am the Truth'"		√			√	√			3
42	"Are you content with this name?"		√							2
43	"Are you the Gate of the City of Knowledge?"		√			√				2
44	"I have waited 40 years to meet one of the *abwāb*"		√			√				2
45	"I shall give this throne to you"[27]		√	√	√	√				4
46	"Are knowledge, hearing etc. of the Essence?"		√			√				2
47	"Religious sciences depend on *ṣarf* etc."		√	√	√	√				4
48	"Show the mutation of the defective letter in *qāla*"		√			√				2
49	"What is the grammatical form of *qawluhu*?"							√	√	2

[25] Said by ʿAlam al-Hudā.
[26] The Bāb is asked to decline *qāla* and cannot. Niẓām al-ʿUlamāʾ declines as far as *qulnā* and asks him to finish.
[27] Said by Nāṣir al-Dīn Mīrzā.

	Question etc.	Source									
		NN	RS	NT	MBA	FB	AKh	NK	AH	DB	Total
50	"*Iʿjāz*, *faṣāḥa*, and *balāgha*"		√	√	√	√					4
51	"Engaging in an indubitable duty. . . ."	√	√[28]								2
52	"What are the fractions of nine?"		√			√					2
53	Quotes "How long these words . . .?"		√			√					2
54	"Show me a miracle"		√	√	√	√					4
55	"What needs improving in Islam? How do you improve it?"				√[29]						1
56	"On the true nature of Christ"s ascension to heaven."				√[30]						1
57	"Be quiet, be quiet"[31]				√						1
58	"What were the names of your father and mother . . .?"				√						1
59	Trouble in Khurasan etc. on account of writings			√	√						2
60	"What is this affair . . . truth of matter . . . nature of claim?"								√		2
61	"Light from Burning Bush was your light—is that so?"	√									1
62	"Why should that Shīʿī be you?"	√[32]				√[33]	√[34]				3

[28] This comment is dropped in the text of *al-Mutanabbiʾīn*.
[29] Asked by Zaʿīm al-Dawla's grandfather.
[30] Ditto.
[31] Said by Nāṣir al-Dīn Mīrzā.
[32] Atrributed to Nāṣir al-Dīn Mīrzā.
[33] Attributed to unnamed individual(s).
[34] Attributed to Amīr Aṣlān Khān.

Key to sources:
NN: *Nāmūs-i Nāṣirī* (Māmaqānī)
RS: *Rawḍat al-ṣafā-yi Nāṣirī* (Hidāyat)
NT: *Nāsikh al-tawārīkh* (Sipihr)
MBA: *Miftāḥ bāb al-abwāb* (Zaʿīm al-Dawla)
FB: *Fitna-yi Bāb/al-Mutanabbiʾīn* (Iʿtiḍād al-Salṭana)
AKh: *Letter of Mīrzā Aṣlān Khān*
NK: *Nuqṭat al-kāf* (Kāshānī)
AH: *Abwāb al-hudā* (Hashtrūdī in Muʿīn al-Salṭana)
DB: Nabīl's Narrative/*Dawnbreakers* (Zarandī)

Answers given during the interrogation of the Bāb

	Answer	Source									
		NN	RS	NT	MBA	FB	AKh	NK	AH	DB	Total
1	"God [gave me this title]"	√	√	√	√	√					5
2	"These verses are from God"	√	√	√	√	√		√			6
3	"They are my writings"	√	√	√	√	√		√			6
4	"Like the revelation of words from the Tree on Sinai"	√	√	√	√[1]	√[2]	√[3]				6
5	Quotes "I am the City of Knowledge, 'Alī is its Gate"	√	√	√	√[4]	√		√			6
6	"I am that person you have awaited for 1000 years"	√	√	√	√	√	√	√	√[5]	√	9
7	"I am not permitted [to produce heirlooms]"	√					√				2
8	"I am the Gate of adoration"	√					√				2
9	"I shall cause a verse to descend on this staff"	√									1
10	Verse about staff	√				√	√				3

[1] Appears as a question (see questions table).
[2] Said by Bāb and Niẓām al-ʿUlamāʾ.
[3] Differs.
[4] *Bāb al-ʿilm.*
[5] In Arabic as: *Anā ʾl-Qāʾim alladhī kuntum bihi muntaẓirūn.*

11	"40,000 *ʿulamāʾ* will reject him"	√					√			2
12	"Or 4,000"	√					√			2
13	"Light from Burning Bush that of one of Shīʿa"	√				√	√			3
14	"I have not studied *fiqh*"	√								1
15	"I have not studied medicine"	√	√	√	√	√				5
16	"My name is numerically equivalent to *rabb*"	√	√			√				3
17	"Praise be to God. . . ." (with *fatḥa* on *samawāt*)	√	√	√	√	√[6]	√[7]			6
18	"And he made the sun and moon" (with *kasra* on *shīn*)	√								1
19	"I have not studied astrology"	√						√	√	3
20	"I have not studied grammar"	√								1
21	"I studied grammar as a child but have forgotten it"		√	√	√	√				4
22	"He should begin with two (*rakʿas*)"	√								1
23	"I have not studied *naḥw*"	√								1
24	"I have written ten times the bulk of the *Ṣaḥīfa* . . ."	√								1

[6] Differs.
[7] Differs.

	Answer	Source									
		NN	RS	NT	MBA	FB	AKh	NK	AH	DB	Total
25	"I can write 1,000/2,000/10,000 verses per day"		√	√	√	√				√[8]	5
26	"Blessings be upon you"[9]		√		√	√					3
27	"You are Ḥājī Mullā Maḥmūd"		√			√					2
28	"Identical with the Essence"		√			√					2
29	"I have not studied *ḥikmat*"		√			√					2
30	"One third is half of a fifth"	√[10]	√		√	√					4
31	"I have not studied arithmetic"	√									1
32	"My name is ʿAlī Muḥammad etc."[11]		√	√	√						3
33	"To reply to such questions needs another time & place"				√						1
34	"You are well informed about different religions"[12]				√						1
35	"Light on Sinai was my light"					√	√				2

[8] Expressed as "Within the space of two days and two nights, I declare Myself able to reveal verses of such magnitiude as will equal the whole of the Qurʾān" (317).

[9] To Niẓām al-ʿUlamāʾ.

[10] Different wording.

[11] The Bāb's age as given in this passage is 35, which is about six years out. This passage is omitted in *al-Mutanabbiʾīn*.

[12] To the grandfather of Zaʿīm al-Dawla.

Key to sources:

NN: *Nāmūs-i Nāṣirī* (Māmaqānī)
RS: *Rawḍat al-ṣafā-yi Nāṣirī* (Hidāyat)
NT: *Nāsikh al-tawārīkh* (Sipihr)
MBA: *Miftāḥ bāb al-abwāb* (Zaʿīm al-Dawla)
FB: *Fitna-yi Bāb/al-Mutanabbiyyīn* (Iʿtiḍād al-Salṭana)
AKh: *Letter of Mīrzā Aṣlān Khān*
NK: *Nuqṭat al-kāf* (Kāshānī)
AH: *Abwāb al-hudā* (Hashtrūdī in Muʿīn al-Salṭana)
DB: Nabīl's Narrative/*Dawnbreakers* (Zarandī)

Bibliography

Algar, H., *Religion and State in Iran 1785–1906*, Berkeley/Los Angeles, 1969.
Amanat, A., *Resurrection and Renewal: The Making of the Babi Movement in Iran, 1844–1850*, Ithaca and London, 1989.
Aquilecchia, G., *Giordano Bruno*, Rome, 1971.
Arjomand, S.A. *The Shadow of God and the Hidden Imām*, Chicago, 1984, Part Three.
Association of Social Anthropologists of the Commonwealth, *Witchcraft Confessions and Accusations*, London & New York, 1970.
Bāb, Sayyid 'Alī Muḥammad Shīrāzī, *Muntakhabātī az āyāt az āthār-i Ḥaḍrat-i Nuqṭa-yi Ūlā*, [Tehran], 134 badī'/1977–8.
———, *Qayyūm al-asmā'*, Cambridge University Library, Browne Or. Ms. F. 11.
———, *Risāla-yi dhahabiyya II*, Iran National Baha'i Manuscript Collection 53.
———, *Tafsīr Sūrat al-kawthar*, CUL, Browne Or. Ms. F. 10.
Bainton, R.H., *Hunted Heretic: The Life and Death of Michael Servetus, 1511–1553*, Boston, 1953.
Balyuzi, H.M., *Bahá'u'lláh The King of Glory*, Oxford, 1980.
Bammel, E., (ed.), *The Trial of Jesus: Cambridge Studies in Honour of C.F.D. Moule*, London, 1970.
Biermans, J.T., *The Odyssey of New Religious Movements: A Case Study of the Unification Church*, Lewsiton, NY, 1986.
Blackwell, R., *Galileo, Bellarmine, and the Bible*, Notre Dame, 1991.
Bledsoe, W.C., "Scopes 'Monkey' trial", in *Tennessee's role in U.S. constitutional development: a series of essays*, Murfreesboro, TN, 1991.
Blinzler, J., *Der Prozess Jesu*, rev. ed., 1969; Eng. trans. of 1st. ed. as *The Trial of Jesus*, Cork, 1959.
Boguet, H., *An Examen of Witches Drawn from Various Trials of Many of this Sect in the District of Saint Oyen de Joux Commonly known as Sainte Claude in . . . Burgundy*, trans. E.A. Ashwin, ed. M. Summers, London, 1929.
Boulting, W., *Giordano Bruno: His Life, Thought and Martyrdom*, London, 1914.
Brandon, S.G.F., *The Trial of Jesus of Nazareth*, London, 1968.
Bromley, D. and Richardson, J. (eds.), *The Brainwashing/Deprogramming Controversy: Sociological, Psychological, Legal, and Historical Perspectives*, New York, 1993.
Browne, E.G., *A Traveller's Narrative Written to Illustrate the History of the Bāb*, Cambridge, 1891.
———, *Materials for the Study of the Bábí Religion*, Cambridge, 1918.
Burkill, T.A., "The Trial of Jesus", *Vigiliae Christianae*, XII (1958).
Buss, S., *The Trial of Jesus, Illustrated from Talmud and Roman Law*, 1906.
Carmichael, J., *The Death of Jesus*, London, 1962.
Catchpole, D., *The Trial of Jesus: a study in the Gospels and Jewish historiography from 1770 to the present day*, Leiden, 1971.
Cohn, H., *The Trial and Death of Jesus*, New York, 1967.
Collins, H., *Changing Order: Replication and Induction in Scientific Practice*, London, 1985.
De Santillana, G., *The crime of Galileo*, New York, 1953.
Di Miscio, G., *Il Processo di Cristo*, Milan, 1967.
Domenico Scandella known as Menocchio: His Trials before the Inquisition (1583–1599), Binghampton, N.Y., 1996.
Dondaine, A., *Les heresies et l'Inquisition Xii^e–Xiii^e siècles: documents et etudes*, London, 1990.
Duncan Derrett, J., *An Oriental Lawyer Looks at the Trial of Jesus and the Doctrine of Redemption*, London, 1966.
Ewen, C.H.L., *Witch Hunting and Witch Trials: the Indictments for Witchcraft from the Records of 1373 assizes held for the Home Circuits AD 1559–1736*, London, 1929.

Feldhay, R., *Galileo and the Church: political inquisition or critical dialogue?*, Cambridge, 1995.
Finocchio, M.A., (ed. and trans.), *The Galileo Affair: A Documentary History*, 1989.
Friedman, J., *Michael Servetus: A Case Study in Total Heresy*, Geneva, 1978.
Gorham, C.T., *The Medieval Inquisition: A Study in Religious Persecution*, London, 1918.
Halliburton, R., *The Scopes "Monkey Trial" and its thirty-fifth anniversary celebration*, n.p., 1964, Reprinted from the Proceedings of the Oklahoma Academy of Science, vol. 44, 1964.
Hamilton, B., *The Albigensian Crusade*, 1974.
———, *The Medieval Inquisition*, London, 1981.
Hansen, J., *Zauberwahn, Inquisition und Hexenprozess im Mittelalter, und die Entstehung der grossen Hexenverfolgung*, 1964.
Harrison, S.L., *The Scopes "monkey trial", revisited: Mencken and the editorial art of Edmund Duffy*, USA, 1993.
Henningsen, G., *The Witches' Advocate: Basque Witchcraft and the Spanish Inquisition, 1609–1614*, 1980.
———, *Inquisition and Interdisciplinary History: Report from an International Symposium on the Medieval and Modern Inquisition*, Copenhagen, 1979.
Hidāyat, Riḍā Qulī Khān *Tārīkh-i Rawḍat al-ṣafā-yi Nāṣirī*, vol. 10, Qum, 1339 sh./1961.
Isorin, J., *Le vrai proces de Jésus*, Paris, 1967.
Kamen, H., *The Spanish Inquisition*, New York, 1956.
Kartelge, K. (ed.), *Der Prozess gegen Jesus: Historische Rückfrage und theologische Deutung*, Freiberg, 1989.
Kāshānī, Ḥājī Mīrzā Jānī, *Kitáb-i-Nuqtatu'l-Káf*, ed. E.G. Browne, London & Leiden, 1910.
Kelley, D.M., "Deprogramming and Religious Liberty", *The Civil Liberties Review*, July/August 1977, 23–33.
Kieckhefer, R., *Repression of Heresy in Medieval Germany*, Ph.D., University of Texas at Austin, 1972.
Kilpatrick, G.D., *The Trial of Jesus*, London, 1953.
Knowlton, J., *The Trial of Jesus: A Study in Jewish Jurisprudence*, Washington, D.C., 1900.
Koch, W. (ed.), *Zum Prozess Jesu*, Leiden, 1967.
Kuhn, T. *"The Structure of Scientific Revolutions"*, 2nd. ed., Chicago, 1970.
Lea, H.C., *The Inquisition of the Middle Ages: Its Organization and Operation*, New York, 1900.
Lietzmann, H., *Der Prozess Jesu*, repr. in *Kleine Schriften II: Studien zum Neuen Testament*, Berlin, 1958, 251–63.
MacEoin, D., "Divisions and Authority Claims in the Bābī Community, 1850–1866", *Studia Iranica*, 18 (1989), 93–129.
———, "Hierarchy, Authority, and Eschatology in Early Babi Thought", in P. Smith, ed., *In Iran: Studies in Babi and Baha'i History 3*, Los Angeles, 1986, 105–.
———, "The Bābī Concept of Holy War", *Religion* 12 (1982), 93–129.
———, *From Shaykhism to Babism*, Ph.D., University of Cambridge, 1979.
———, *The Sources for Early Bābī Doctrine and History: A Survey*, Leiden, 1992.
Martin, R., *Witchcraft and the Inquisition in Venice 1550–1650*, Oxford, 1989.
Massignon, L., *La Passion de Husayn Ibn Mansūr Hallāj: martyre mystique de l'Islam executé a Baghdad le 26 mars 922: étude d'histoire religieuse*, 2 vols., Paris, 1922; new ed., Paris, 1975. Eng. trans. by H. Mason as *The Passion of al-Hallāj, Mystic and Martyr of Islam*, 4 vols., Bollingen Series XCVIII, Princeton, 1982.
Māmaqānī, Mīrzā Muḥammad Taqī, *Nāmūs-i Nāṣirī*, published as *Guft-u-shunūd-i Sayyid 'Alī Muḥammad Bāb bā rawḥānīyūn-i Tabrīz*, ed. Ḥasan Mursilvand, Tehran, 1374 sh./1996.

Māzandarānī, Mīrzā Asad Allāh Fāḍil-ī, *Kitāb-i ẓuhūr al-ḥaqq*, vol. 3, Tehran, n.d.
McGowen, T., *The great monkey trial: science versus fundamentalism in America*, New York, 1990.
Mercati, A., *Il sommario del processo di Giordano Bruno, con appendice di documenti sull' eresia e l'inquisizione a Modena nel secolo 16*, Vatican City, 1942.
Momen, M., "The Trial of Mullā 'Alī Basṭāmī: A Combined Sunnī-Shī'ī *Fatwā* against the Bāb", *Iran* 20 (1982), 113–43.
Monkey trial: the State of Tennessee vs. John Thomas Scopes, Boston, 1960.
Monter, W., *Frontiers of Heresy: the Spanish Inquisition from the Basque Lands to Sicily*, Cambridge, 1990.
Morice, L., *Joan of Arc: a Recreation of her 1431 trial for treason*, Lakeside, Ca., 1991.
Navā'ī, 'Abd al-Ḥusayn (ed.), *Fitna-yi Bāb*, 2nd. printing, Tehran, 1351/1973.
Netanyahu, B., *The Origins of the Inquisition in Fifteenth Century Spain*, New York, 1995.
Nordi, C., *Il processo di Gesu, re dei Guidei*, Bari, 1966.
Olasky, M.N., *When world views collide: journalists and the great monkey trial: paper presented at the annual meeting of the Association for Education in Journalism and Mass Communication* (69th, Normou, OK, August 3–6, 1986), Alexandria, VA., 1986.
Oldenbourg, Z., *Massacre at Montsegur: A History of the Albigensian Crusade*, New York, 1961.
Pernoud, R., *The retrial of Joan of Arc: the evidence at the trial for her rehabilitation, 1450–1456*, London, 1955.
Peters, E., *Heresy and Authority in Medieval Europe*, London, 1980.
Quicherat, J., *Proces de condamnation et de réhabilitation de Jeanne d'Arc*, New York, 1960.
Rabbino, T., *Cults, Culture, and the Law*, Chico, Ca., 1985.
Rejali, D.M., *Torture and Modernity: Self, Society, and State in Modern Iran*, Boulder, San Francisco, Oxford, 1994.
Rimmer, H., *Outlines for Study in the Trial and Death of Jesus*, Los Angeles, 1928.
Rosadi, G., *The Trial of Jesus*, 3rd. ed., 1905.
Roth, C., *The Spanish Inquisition*, 1964.
Royce, W., *Mir-Ma'sum 'Ali Shah and the Ni'mat Allahi Revival 1776–77 to 1796–97*, Ph.D., Princeton University, 1979.
Sabatini, R., *Torquemada and the Spanish Inquisition*, rev. ed., Boston 1930.
Sayyid, 'Alī Muḥammad [the Bāb] and [Sayyid Ḥusayn Kātib-i Yazdī], *Qismatī az alwāḥ-i khaṭṭ-i Nuqṭa-yi Ulā wa Sayyid Ḥusayn-i Kātib*, Tehran, n.d.
Scott, W.S., The *Trial of Joan of Arc*, 1968.
Seidel Manchi, S., *Erasmus als Ketzer: Reformation und Inquisition im Italien des 16 Jahrhunderts*, Leiden, New York, 1993.
Shannon, A.C., *The Medieval Inquisition*, Washington, D.C., 1983.
Shupe, A.D. Jr. and Bromley, D.G. *The New Vigilantes: Deprogrammers, Anti-Cultists and the New Religions*, Beverley Hills, London, 1980.
Sipihr, Mīrzā Muḥammad Taqī Lisān al-Mulk *Nāsikh al-tawārīkh: Salāṭīn-i Qājār*, Tehran, 1385/1965, 4 vols. in 2.
Sprague De Camp, L., *The Great Monkey Trial*, New York, 1967.
Stalker, J. *The Trial and Death of Jesus Christ*, 1897.
Strayer, J.R., *The Albigensian Crusades*, Ann Arbor, 1971.
Strobel, A., *Die Stunde der Wahrheit: Untersuchungen zum Strafverfahren gegen Jesus*, Tübingen, 1980.
Sullivan, K., *Inquiry and Inquisition in Late Medieval Culture: the Questioning of Joan of Arc and Christine de Pisan*, Ph.D., University of California, 1993.
Symposium Internacional sobre la Inquisizion Espanola, *The Spanish Inquisition and the Inquisitorial Mind*, Boulder, Colo., 1987,
Szasz, T., *Law, Liberty, and Psychiatry*, London, 1974.
———, *The Manufacture of Madness: A Comparative Study of the Inquisition and the Mental Health Movement*, New York, 1970.

———, *The Therapeutic State*, Buffalo, NY, 1984.
Tanner, N.P. (ed.), *Heresy Trials in the Diocese of Norwich, 1428–31*, London, 1977.
Tedeschi, J., *The Prosecution of Heresy: Collected Studies on the Inquisition in Early Modern Italy*, Binghampton, NY, 1991.
The Trial of Joan of Arc: Being the Verbatim Report of the Proceedings from the Orleans Manuscript, Westport, Conn., 1956.
Turberville, A.S., *Medieval Heresy and the Inquisition*, London, 1920.
Vedrine, H., *Censure et pouvoir: trois proces: Savonarole, Bruno, Galilée*, Paris, 1976.
Wakefield, W.C., *Heresy, Crusade and Inquisition in Southern France 1100–1250*, London, 1974.
Wallis, R. (ed.), *On the Margins of Science: The Social Construction of Rejected Knowledge*, Keele, 1979.
Wallis, R. and Morley, P. (eds.) *Marginal Medicine*, London, 1976.
Warner, H.T., *The Albigensian Heresy*, London & New York, 2 vols., 1922.
Westfall, R.S., *Essays on the Trial of Galileo*, Notre Dame, 1989.
Winter, P., *On the Trial of Jesus*, Berlin, 1961.
Za'īm al-Dawla, Mīrzā Mahdī Khān *Miftāḥ Bāb al-abwāb yā tārīkh-i Bāb va Bahā*, Persian trans. Ḥājj Shaykh Ḥasan Farīd-i Gulpāygānī, 3rd. ed., Tehran, 1328 sh./1968.
Zarandī, Mullā Muḥammad Nabīl *The Dawn-Breakers: Nabíl's Narrative of the Early Days of the Bahá'í Revelation*, ed. and trans. Shoghi Effendi, Wilmette, Ill., 1932.

ABU L-MUʿĪN AL-NASAFĪ AND ASHʿARĪ THEOLOGY

Wilferd Madelung

Abu l-Muʿīn Maymūn b. Muḥammad al-Nasafī (d. 508/1114) was the most eminent theologian of the *kalām* school of the Ḥanafī scholars of Samarqand after its founder Abū Manṣūr al-Māturīdī (d. 333/944).[1] In his *Tabṣirat al-adilla*, a massive sum of *kalām* recently published in a good critical edition by Claude Salamé,[2] he set out to elaborate the major proofs on which the shaykhs of the *Ahl al-sunna wa l-jamāʿa* had relied in supporting their doctrines in the credal questions of Islam and in refuting the doctrines of their opponents.[3] The shaykhs of the *Ahl al-sunna wa l-jamāʿa* were for him primarily the Ḥanafī scholars of Samarqand and, most authoritative among them, the Imam Abu l-Manṣūr al-Māturīdī. Abu l-Muʿīn quotes al-Māturīdī most frequently and only rarely deviates from his teaching. Given the linguistic obscurity of al-Māturīdī's own writings, Abu l-Muʿīn's work, written in a lucid if somewhat prolix style, became the most influential and authoritative exposition of Māturīdī doctrine for the later adherents of the school.

Al-Māturīdī had developed and expounded his teaching mainly in opposition to the Muʿtazila, the major *kalām* school in his time. If he was aware of the new *kalām* taught in Baghdad by his contemporary Abu l-Ḥasan al-Ashʿarī—also in the name of the *Ahl al-sunna wa l-jamāʿa* but understood as meaning Ḥanbalī traditionalism—, he did not consider it as significant enough to respond to it. By the time of Abu l-Muʿīn, the school of al-Ashʿarī had fully emerged and, spreading quickly from Baghdad, had established itself in particular in Nishapur, where its most famous representatives taught during the 5th/11th century. The Muʿtazila were now, a century after the Qāḍi l-quḍāt ʿAbd al-Jabbār (d. 415/1024), in full retreat within Sunnī Islam, though certainly still active. The school of Samarqand could

[1] On the teaching of al-Māturīdī and his place in the Ḥanafī school of Samarqand see now especially Rudolph, *Al-Māturīdī*. The school name Māturīdiyya is late and was not known in the time of Abu l-Muʿīn. It is used here merely for convenience.

[2] *Tabṣirat al-adilla*.

[3] *Tabṣirat al-adilla*, 3.

not ignore the triumphant rise of the rival Ashʿarī school, and Abu l-Muʿīn's older contemporaries Abū Shakūr al-Sālimī and Abu l-Yusr al-Bazdawī (d. 493/1099) had taken Ashʿarī school doctrine fully into account in their theological writings. Abu l-Muʿīn was thoroughly familiar with the teaching of the major Ashʿarī theologians after the founder, al-Bāqillānī Abū Bakr b. Fūrak, ʿAbd al-Qāhir al-Baghdādī, and Abū Isḥāq al-Isfarāyīnī and frequently refers to them. He also quotes some Ashʿarī opponents, who criticized Māturīdī teaching, without identifying them, and mentions that he debated with one of them.[4] Abu l-Muʿīn was, on the other hand, also familiar with the teaching of the prominent representatives of late Muʿtazilism, ʿAbd al-Jabbār and Abu l-Ḥusayn al-Baṣrī (d. 436/1044), the founder of the last school among the Muʿtazila, but does not mention that he ever had any debate with any of their followers.

Abu l-Muʿīn thus faced the task of defining and defending the doctrine of the school of Samarqand, not only against the old adversary, the Muʿtazila, but also against the new rival, the Ashʿariyya. He does indeed frequently distance himself from the views of al-Ashʿarī and his followers. Yet his attitude to the two *kalām* schools clearly differs. His criticism of the Muʿtazila is invariably strident, polemical, and vituperative. He magnifies differences between Māturīdī and Muʿtazilī doctrine, ascribes sinister motives to the Muʿtazila, and seeks to conceal agreement.

A typical example is his treatment of the dispute about the meaning of the word *shayʾ*, thing. The later Muʿtazila defined *shayʾ* as *maʿlūm*, known or knowable, while the Māturīdiyya and Ashʿariyya identified *shayʾ* and *mawjūd*, existent. In common Arabic usage *shayʾ* had at first meant a corporeal object. This concept of *shayʾ* was reflected in the early *kalām* discussions of the 2nd/8th century, as the "corporealists" argued that God, in order to be an eternally existent *shayʾ*, must be a material body (*jism*).[5] Anti-anthropomorphist theologians were forced to admit that *shayʾ* could refer to incorporeal existents. Other incorporeal existents such as accidents in bodies were then also accepted

---

[4] 364–5.

[5] This concept is reflected in the formulation ascribed to Hishām b. al-Ḥakam that God is a body unlike bodies (*jism lā ka'l-ajsām*). It was in his view merely a logical parallel to the formula that He is "a thing unlike things" (*shayʾ lā ka'l-ashyāʾ*) accepted by most *kalām* theologians (al-Ashʿarī, *Maqālāt* 32, 208, 521). The Jahmiyya, on the other hand, denied that God was a *shayʾ* (al-Ashʿarī, *Maqālāt*, 181, 280, 518).

as being *ashyāʾ*. The problem of the meaning of *shayʾ* came up also in the question of God's attribute of knowledge. Some early theologians such as Jahm b. Ṣafwān and several Shīʿīs maintained that God's omniscience was not eternal or that He did not know things before He created them. The Shīʿī Zurāra b. Aʿyan is quoted as arguing that

> whoever asserts that God knows the thing (*shayʾ*) before bringing it into being, while it does not yet exist, asserts that God knows nothing (*zaʿama annahū yaʿlamu lā shayʾ*).[6]

Such arguments evidently induced the Muʿtazila to redefine *shayʾ* as what is knowable and thus as contained in the eternal omniscience of God. The Ashʿariyya and Māturīdiyya retained the modified earlier meaning as existent, though not necessarily material.[7]

In line with common anti-Muʿtazilī polemics, Abu l-Muʿīn accuses the Muʿtazila of lending support to the materialists (*dahriyya*) who taught the eternity of the world. The Muʿtazila, he argues, assert that all things are eternal and claim that the Creator could not produce anything out of nothing. They merely try to conceal the implications of their doctrine out of fear of the disgrace of being punished with the sword (*khāfū maʿarrat al-sayf*).[8] A purely terminological disagreement, initially without any theological or ontological significance, was by such polemics distorted into an issue of heresy and unbelief. Yet the polemics were effective in the long term, and some modern scholars have expressed the opinion that the Muʿtazila, influenced by Greek philosophy, really believed in the eternity of the world.[9]

Abu l-Muʿīn's attitude towards the Ashʿariyya, whom he counts among the *kalām* theologians of the Traditionists (*mutakallimū ahl al-ḥadīth*), is mostly positive and respectful. When he expresses disagreement with their views, his criticism is usually measured. Substantial differences are minimized, concealed, or reduced to verbal issues.

---

[6] See the heresiography quoted in Abū Tammām, *Kitāb al-Shajara*, Arabic text, 73.

[7] The distinction drawn by the *falāsifa* between existence in the mind (*dhihn*) and external existence (*biʾl-khārij*) was not known in *kalām*. Existence thus meant existence in the external world.

[8] 74–5.

[9] Even Gimaret states that the Muʿtazilī concept of *shayʾ* "implies, in a certain fashion, the eternity of the world." *Théories*, 184. Yet in Ashʿarī and Māturīdī doctrine the non-existent, though not called *shayʾ*, is equally contained in God's eternal knowledge and will. The world is thus eternal in exactly the same fashion in Sunnī belief.

Most significant in this respect is Abu l-Muʿīn's treatment of the Ashʿarī doctrine concerning God's justice, determinism and human free will. The differences between al-Māturīdī and al-Ashʿarī were here deep and irreconcilable.[10] For al-Māturīdī, just as for the Muʿtazila, good and evil were objective values inherent in the created world and recognizable by the human mind. For al-Ashʿarī, they were arbitrary rules laid down by God's command and prohibition and could be known only through revelation. For al-Māturīdī, the acts of man, although created by God, were freely chosen between alternatives by man; capacity for any act was equally valid for its opposite.[11] For al-Ashʿarī, God was the sole agent in the world, and the "acts of man" were merely acquired, but not acted, by man. Man's "choice" was in fact preordained by God's choice; there was no alternative. Man was, as Fakhr al-Din al-Rāzī was to formulate it, consistently "compelled in the guise of a freely choosing agent."[12]

Transoxanian Ḥanafī creeds and treatises had recognized the fundamental conflict between the two positions and had not hesitated to qualify the Ashʿariyya as heretical compulsionists (*jabariyya, mujbira*), while describing their own doctrine as intermediate between the Qadariyya and Jabariyya.[13] Abu l-Muʿīn, in contrast, reserves the term Jabariyya to Jahm b. Ṣafwān and his followers, and merely observes that al-Ashʿarī, unlike all other groups of the Community, would not call man an agent (*fāʿil*) since the real agent, in his view, was only God.[14] The Ashʿariyya, Abu l-Muʿīn explains,

---

[10] See Watt, *Free Will*, 150–60; Gimaret, *Théories*, esp. 172–95.

[11] Māturīdī doctrine on this latter question was not definite. It was generally admitted that Abū Ḥanīfa had taught that capacity was potentially valid for opposite acts. According to Abu l-Muʿīn, al-Māturīdī himself described both this view and the view that capacity was valid only for a specific act without trying to refute either one and without stating a preference. Most of al-Māturīdī's discussion, however, indicated that he inclined to the view that capacity was not valid for opposites (544–5). The Transoxanian Ḥanafī *Sharḥ al-fiqh al-akbar*, on the other hand, supports the doctrine of Abū Ḥanīfa that "the power by which man performs the sinful act is essentially able to effect the act of obedience." (Watt, *Free Will*, 135). Abu l-Muʿīn follows al-Māturīdī in refraining from expressing a preference. The chapter heading added by the editor: (*fī anna l-istiṭāʿata taṣluḥu li l-ḍiddayn*), is misleading. The matter was not really vital in Māturīdī doctrine since it admitted, in contrast to the predestinarian position of the Ashʿariyya, the freedom of choice of alternatives. God gave the capacity to act in accordance with the free choice of man.

[12] Gimaret, *Théories*, 147; Madelung, "The Late Muʿtazila", I, 245.

[13] Watt, *Free Will*, 154–160.

[14] 539.

> even though they agree with us in the reality of the doctrine, claim that whatever is subject to the capability of man is called acquisition but may not be called action (*fiʿl*), just as it may not be called creation.

They thus refrain from employing the verb used by God in the Qurʾanic command (22:77): "do (*ifʿalū*) what is good", and elsewhere, and used by all speakers of the Arabic language. Moreover, al-Ashʿarī and his followers, like other *kalām* theologians, call this chapter of theology the Chapter of the Creation of men's acts (*bāb khalq afʿāl al-ʿibād*). Their doctrine was thus contradictory. Al-Ashʿarī, according to Abu l-Muʿīn, here adopted the view from the Najjārī theologian Abū ʿĪsā Muḥammad b. ʿĪsā Burghūth.[15] In reality, however, the disagreement was merely in expression (*ʿibāra*), not in the substance of the doctrine.[16]

In discussing the question of whether God may impose on man obligations that are beyond his power, Abu l-Muʿīn quotes the *Kitāb al-Nawādir* of al-Ashʿarī where the latter had stated that the imposition of what is beyond power is admissible and, if God were to order His servant to combine contraries, this would be neither folly (*safah*) nor absurd. Abu l-Muʿīn comments that this was consistent with al-Ashʿarī's principles. It was among his principles that if God were to torment mankind for ever and ever in hell fire without any offence on their part, this would be an act of wisdom and sound judgment and should be described as good (*yūṣafu . . . bi'l-ḥusn*). If He were to forgive the infidels and to place them in paradise, this would likewise be an act of wisdom and sound judgment; for He may dispose in His kingdom and property however He wishes. The imposition of something impossible was, according to al-Ashʿarī's view, evil on earth only because no one who is subject to religious obligation (*mukallaf*) disposes of his own property. He is, moreover, under order in this world to seek benefit and to ward off harm to himself, and that is not feasible with the imposition of impossible duties. The Creator, however, is exalted above seeking benefit and warding off harm. Man does not deserve paradise or hell fire by his acts. His obedience or disobedience were rather mere signs indicating that God will torment this one in hell fire and will place that one in par-

[15] See on his views Watt, *Free Will*, 110–15.
[16] 596.

adise. It would therefore be reasonable for God to impose on His servant duties beyond his capacity and to make this a sign of his future punishment.[17] According to Abu l-Muʿīn, the Ashʿarī theologian Abū Isḥāq al-Isfarāyīnī held that the imposition of duties beyond man's capacity by God was impossible because it was at variance with the very concept of imposing obligation, not because it was evil or folly in itself. The concept of the imposition of obligations required that the one obliged should deserve some punishment for any failure to comply.[18]

This theological monstrosity, which destroyed the concept of God's justice at its root, does not evoke any protest on the part of Abu l-Muʿīn. Rather he goes on to argue polemically that it was the Muʿtazila who upheld God's imposing obligations beyond man's capability since their doctrine that capability precedes the act meant that the act occurred independently of man's capability.[19]

Abu l-Muʿīn's own solution rests on the distinction that he, following al-Māturīdī,[20] recognized between the "capability of the means and tools" (*istiṭāʿat al-asbāb wa'l-ālāt*), which exists before the act, and the "real capability" (*ḥaqīqat al-qudra*), which is simultaneous with the act and is its cause (*ʿilla*).[21] The Ashʿariyya and the Jabariyya, he explains, do not stipulate the presence of either of these two capabilities for the imposition to be sound, while the Muʿtazila combine the real capability with the capability of means as a condition for the imposition. The true view upheld by the school of Samarqand, however, was that only the capability of the means and tools was a condition for the soundness of the imposition, not the real capability. In the presence of the means and tools, the real capability could be lost by the agent through voluntary neglect and disregard of the obligation.[22]

The argument was reasonable on the basis of Māturīdī doctrine which allowed a free choice between alternatives. The act, though willed and created by God and caused by the simultaneous capability provided by Him, was nevertheless the result of man's free choice. Abu l-Muʿīn does not note that this solution would not work

[17] 586.
[18] 586–7.
[19] 587.
[20] Rudolph, *Al-Māturīdī*, 341.
[21] 541.
[22] 588–90.

on the basis of the Ashʿarī view according to which man's choice itself was predetermined by God's arbitrary will.

Quite different is Abu l-Muʿīn's attitude to the Ashʿariyya in his chapter on the divine attribute of existentiation (*takwīn*). Here he counts them, together with the other *kalām* schools of the Traditionists, among the people of falsehood (*ahl al-bāṭil*) and sects of error (*firaq al-ḍalāl*).[23] The chapter is the largest one in his book, and he apologizes at the end of it for the prolixity of his discussion, noting that his companions stood alone in this question and that, after the demise of their investigative scholars, their opponents had started a campaign of false clamour and slander against them.[24] Abu l-Muʿīn here evidently has the Ashʿariyya in particular in mind, for the major part of the chapter is devoted to the refutation of the arguments of Ashʿarī opponents, particularly the attacks of an unnamed Ashʿarī slanderer (*mushanniʿ*) on the Māturīdī position. This Ashʿarī scholar had written a book about the tenets of the upholders of the eternity of the world in which he described the doctrine of Proclus that the reason for the creation of the universe was the generosity (*jūd*) of God and that, since God's generosity was eternal, the world must equally be eternal. He had gone on stating that the doctrine of an unnamed group (*ṭāʾifa*) of Muslims was close to that of Proclus and then described the position of the school of Samarqand as that doctrine.[25] In his description of Māturīdī doctrine, the slanderer had mostly copied from the book entitled *al-Muqniʿ* of another Ashʿarī scholar, Abū Manṣūr b. Ayyūb, without acknowledging his source.[26] This Abū Manṣūr b. Ayyūb is most likely identical with Abū Manṣūr al-Ayyūbī al-Naysābūrī, whose full name is given by Ibn ʿAsākir, quoting the historian of Nishapur Abu l-Ḥasan ʿAbd al-Ghāfir b. Ismāʿīl, as Muḥammad b. Abī Ayyūb. He was a pupil and son-in-law of Abū Bakr b. Fūrak and died in Dhuʾ l-Ḥijja 421/1030 in Nishapur. ʿAbd al-Ghāfir describes him as the most perspicacious scholar of the Ashʿarī school in his time and as "more penetrating and bolder (*anfadh wa-ashjaʿ*)" than his teacher.[27] He may well have been the first one to launch the Ashʿarī assault on the Transoxanian

---

23 306, 345.
24 372.
25 315.
26 315, 333.
27 Ibn ʿAsākir, *Tabyīn*, 249.

kalām school. Given the intense rivalry between the Shāfiʿīs and Ḥanafīs in Khurāsān at the time, it is not surprising that the conflict should have been started by the Shāfiʿī Ashʿarīyya in Nishapur rather than in Baghdad.

Aside from the charge that the Māturīdī doctrine on *takwīn* implied the eternity of the world, Abu l-Muʿīn was particularly incensed by the claim of the Ashʿariyya opponents than it had not been held by any of the pious ancestors and was in fact invented after the 4th/10th century. One of them had claimed that this doctrine was invented by a sect called al-Zābrāshiyāʾiyya, the followers of a certain Abū ʿĀṣim al-Zabrāshāʾī, emerging after the year 400/1009 in Marw.[28]

The question of a divine attribute of *takwīn* could appear as new to *kalām* theologians outside Transoxania since they were not familiar with the use of this term, although the subject matter itself was certainly discussed in early *kalām*. Abu l-Muʿīn explains that *takwīn* was synonymous with creation (*takhlīq, khalq*), bringing into existence (*ījād*), origination (*iḥdāth*), invention (*ikhtirāʿ*), and similar terms. In employing the term *takwīn* he was merely following the practice of his predecessors (*aslāf*), evidently meaning the authorities of the school of Samarqand.

The subject was grounded in the wider problem of the relationship of an eternal God to a world created and evolving in time. The mainstream of *kalām* theologians had early on adopted the principle that God's essence must be eternally immutable and unaffected by the temporal changeability of His creation. Views of some early theologians that the changes in the world somehow had to affect the knowledge of God were soon hereticized and discarded. Among the later *kalām* schools, only the Karrāmiyya, vigorously and scornfully condemned by the other schools, admitted that temporals, accidents could arise in the eternal essence of God. The Muʿtazila had come to distinguish between eternal, unchangeable attributes of God's essence and temporal attributes of His acts that were extrinsic to His essence. They held, Abu l-Muʿīn explains, that whatever attribute was constant and could not be negated under any circumstance was an attribute of essence and whatever was subject to God's eternal discretionary power (*qudra*) was an attribute of act.[29]

---

[28] 310, 355–6.
[29] 309, 367.

This definition could be found objectionable in that it asserted the temporal and non-essential nature of some of the names and attributes widely used by the pious in glorifying God, such as His being the creator and His possessing the only effective will (*mashīʾa, irāda*) in the universe. Abu l-Muʿīn quotes the creed (*K. al-ʿaqāʾid*) of the Egyptian Ḥanafī scholar al-Ṭaḥāwī (d. 321/933) as affirming that God

> was continuously with His attributes before His creatures and He did not, through their existence, acquire any attribute that was not with Him before them . . . The meaning of Lordship belonged to Him when there was nothing ruled and the meaning of creatorship when there was nothing created.[30]

The statement was clearly formulated to counter the notion of divine attributes of act arising in time.[31]

The Ashʿariyya retained the distinction between eternal attributes of the divine essence and temporal attributes of act. According to Abu l-Muʿīn, they and the other theologians of the Traditionists redefined the concept of attributes of essence as meaning all those whose negation would imply a deficiency in God.[32] Thus they added to the five attributes of essence generally recognized by the Muʿtazila two more, that of will and that of speech (*kalām*). By turning the divine will into an eternal attribute of essence, they highlighted their dogma that everything in the universe occurs according to the will of God, against the Muʿtazilī doctrine that the evil acts of men and unbelief were not willed by God. Recognition of speech as an attribute of the divine essence reflected their support of the dogma of the Traditionists of the uncreated and eternal nature of the Qurʾān. They argued that a temporary lack of speech on the part of God would imply defect, incapacity and dumbness.[33]

Creation or, in Abu l-Muʿīn's preferred term, existentiation was no attribute of the divine essence in the view of al-Ashʿarī and his followers. Like most *kalām* theologians, the Ashʿariyya held that the assertion of such an eternal attribute must necessarily lead to the

---

[30] 355.

[31] Al-Ṭaḥāwī's creed is presented by himself and by Abu l-Muʿīn as based on the statements of Abū Ḥanīfa, Abū Yūsuf and al-Shaybānī. It is unlikely that the formulation goes back to Abū Ḥanīfa since the concept of temporal divine attributes of act probably originated after his death.

[32] 309–10.

[33] 310.

affirmation of the eternity of the world. Although they certainly did not deny that God could be described as the creator of everything, they, like most of the Muʿtazila and the Najjāriyya, maintained that there was no attribute of *khalq* or *takwīn* at all, arguing that these terms had no other meaning than what is created (*makhlūq*) or existentiated (*mukawwan*).[34] An attribute of creation was indeed superfluous, for it could only mean the power (*qudra*) to create. God would thus have two attributes of power, since all-power was already recognized by all theologians as an eternal attribute of God.[35]

Abu l-Muʿīn had no difficulty in disposing of the former argument. The act of creating was surely distinct from what was created, the *takwīn* was logically distinct from the *mukawwan*. Although the term *khalq*, in parallel to other verbal nouns, was often used, in the Qurʾān and ordinary speech, to denote the object of creation, its basic meaning was the act of creation. Abu l-Muʿīn could convincingly demonstrate that it must mean the act, not the created beings, in some passages of the Qurʾān.[36]

More problematical was Abu l-Muʿīn's attempt to refute the second point and to prove that God must have an eternal attribute of existentiation. He was certainly able here, too, to score some points against his Ashʿarī opponents. One of his Māturīdī companions had pointed out that God describes himself in Qurʾān 59:24 as the creator and had argued that, since God's speech was eternal, this must be understood as a title of glory belonging to Him in eternity. An Ashʿarī scholar had countered that the verse was merely informatory like God's word that Ibrāhīm was gentle (*ḥalīm*)[37] and that Muḥammad was the Messenger of God and did not mean that the information applied to God eternally. Abu l-Muʿīn replied that, while this was true in respect to Ibrāhīm and Muḥammad, God existed eternally and the verse was unquestionably said in self-praise.[38] In accordance with the principle upheld by the Ashʿariyya that every title of glory whose absence would imply a defect must be counted as an attribute of the divine essence, creation thus must be one of

[34] 306.
[35] 314.
[36] 312–13, 320–1. Abu l-Muʿīn refers to Qurʾān 2:164, 3:190, and 40:57.
[37] Qurʾān 11:75
[38] 370–1, 353–4.

God's eternal attributes, in parallel to His attributes of hearing, seeing, and speech.[39]

Al-Ashʿarī and all his followers moreover tied God's creation to His command "be" (*kun*) in accordance with the Qur'anic verse (16:40):

> Our word to anything when We want it is only that We say to it: "be", and it is.

They thus confirmed that existentiation was not identical with the existentiated and required more than just divine all-power. Abu l-Muʿīn's Māturīdī companions held that the divine attribute of *takwīn* was expressed in this verse by the creative imperative *kun* and interpreted the whole verse as describing the quickness and ease of God's bringing everything into being.[40]

In Ashʿarī doctrine the creative imperative *kun* as part of God's speech (*kalām*) was eternal. Abu l-Muʿīn reminds his Ashʿarī opponents that they and his Māturīdī companions were united in maintaining that God's speech, in order to be His own speech, must necessarily subsist in His essence and in charging the Muʿtazila with ignorance in their claim that speech created by God outside Himself in the world could be truly His speech. He argues that likewise, if existentiation were no attribute of the divine essence, the created world would not be God's creation. The Ashʿariyya, by claiming that creation does not subsist in the creator, were deviating from their own principle and contradicting themselves.[41]

Abu l-Muʿīn, however, gets into trouble in trying to refute the claim of the opponents that an eternal attribute of existentiation in God would necessitate the eternity of the world. He again refers the Ashʿariyya to their doctrine that God created by His creative imperative *kun*, which was eternal, while the created beings were temporal.[42] Yet it was he, not the Ashʿarī opponents, who identified the creative imperative with an attribute of existentiation. The possibility of a pre-eternal command for something to come into existence at a certain time could be argued, just as a command made to apply in the future to those not yet in existence was reasonable.[43] Abu

[39] See 314.
[40] 316–7, 344.
[41] 327–8.
[42] 363.
[43] 364–5.

l-Muʿīn also refers to God's will (*irāda*), an attribute of the divine essence according to Ashʿarī and Māturīdī doctrine, which did not necessitate the eternity of what was willed (*murād*).[44] A will attaching to a matter or event in the distant future presented no conceptual difficulty. A pre-eternal act of existentiation that would bring something into being in the distant future was a different matter. Abu l-Muʿīn was unable to invalidate the charge of the Ashʿarī critic—it must be Abū Manṣūr b. Ayyūb—that for creation to be an eternal attribute of essence it would have to mean the power to create and thus would duplicate God's eternal attribute of power which was power to create.

If God must indeed have an essential attribute of *takwīn* enabling Him to create in time, as Abu l-Muʿīn argues, why should He need an additional attribute of power? Abu l-Muʿīn explains in general that power is necessary for the agent to be freely choosing (*mukhtār*), not constrained, in his act, and will was necessary for the effects of the act to come about in proper succession (*tartīb*) and order.[45] This was consistent with Muʿtazilī teaching. Later, however, he argues in respect to God that His act (*fiʿl*) is not subject to His will and His power, against Muʿtazilī doctrine; rather only the effect of His act (*mafʿūluh*) is affected by both of these attributes.[46] Power here obviously cannot imply freedom of choice but must mean, as in Ashʿarī usage, simply capacity to perform the act. This different significance of the term power reflects the fact, nowhere discussed as such by Abu l-Muʿīn, that, with the affirmation in Ashʿarī and Māturīdī dogma of an eternal, immutable, and invariably effective divine will, God had ceased to be a freely choosing agent. God's action was eternally determined by His coeternal will. His power could and must effect only what His will had determined; there never could have been any choice.

The insistence of the *kalām* schools on the timeless immutability of God and His attributes had progressively removed their concept from the God acting and reacting freely in space and time envisaged by the Qurʾān and popular piety. This is well illustrated in their interpretation of the Qurʾanic description of God's creative activity:

---

[44] 364.
[45] 343.
[46] 367.

> Our word to anything when We will it is only that We say to it: "be", and it is.

The Muʿtazila, distinguishing between attributes of essence and of act, were able to preserve the temporality expressed in the verse. God created in time through temporal will acts and the command "be." Since will for them was an attribute of act outside God's essence, they were forced to assume that the divine will act was an accident without a substrate. The Ashʿariyya moved both will and speech into God's essence as eternal and immutable attributes and then tied creation to an eternal command, explaining away the temporality implied in the words: "when We will." The school of Samarqand and Abu l-Muʿīn interpreted the verse as a metaphorical expression for the speed of God's creation which consisted in a single timeless attribute and act of *takwīn* producing innumerable effects in time.

Bibliography

Al-Ashʿarī, *Maqālāt al-islāmiyyīn*, ed. H. Ritter, Istanbul 1929–33.

Al-Nasafī, Abu l-Muʿīn Maymūn b. Muḥammad, *Tabṣirat al-adilla fī uṣūl al-dīn ʿalā ṭarīqat al-imām Abī Manṣūr al-Māturīdī*, ed. Klūd Salāma, 2 vols., Damascus 1990–93.

Gimaret, D., *Théories de l'acte humain en théologie musulmane*, Paris 1980.

Ibn ʿAsākir, *Tabyīn kadhib al-muftarī*, Damascus 1347/[1928–9].

Madelung, W., "The Late Muʿtazila and Determinism: The Philosophers Trap", in *Yād-nama in Memoria di Alessandro Bausani*, ed. B.S. Amoretti and L. Rostagno, Rome 1991, 245–57.

Madelung, W. and Walker, P.E., *An Ismaili Heresiography: The "Bāb al-shayṭān" from Abū Tammām's Kitāb al-shajara*, Leiden 1998.

Rudolph, U., *Al-Māturīdī und die sunnitische Theologie in Samarqand*, Leiden 1997.

Watt, W.M., *Free Will and Predestination in Early Islam*, London 1948.

BAHRAM GŪR'S SPECTACULAR MARKSMANSHIP AND THE ART OF ILLUSTRATION IN QĀJĀR LITHOGRAPHED BOOKS

Ulrich Marzolph

Bahrām Gūr, ruler of Persia from 420 to 438, in Persian legend, literature, and folklore is remembered as a pleasure-loving hero, famed most of all for his spectacular hunting feats. The stereotype attribute of legendary marksman is aptly illustrated by the anecdote about Bahrām Gūr and his favourite slave girl, who challenges him to shoot the foot and the ear of an onager with a single arrow. Bahrām succeeds in doing so by first hitting the animal with a pebble, making the onager scratch its ear with its hind leg. At that very moment, he shoots an arrow penetrating both leg and ear.[1]

The basic content of this anecdote in variant readings is recorded in Arabic and Persian sources from the late ninth century.[2] The earliest known version, given in Ibn Qutayba's (died 276/889) *ʿUyūn al-akhbār*, is a prose text of a few lines. Other versions which are more or less elaborated testify to the lasting prominence of the anecdote at least until the 16th century: in Arabic sources it is mentioned or alluded to by various authors of geographical, historical, and *adab*-literature, such as Ibn al-Faqīh, al-Thaʿālibī, al-Rāghib al-Iṣfahānī, Yāqūt, al-Zamakhsharī, al-Qazwīnī, al-Damīri, Ibn Iyās, and al-Ibshīhī. Yet the versions most influential insofar as a popular repercussion and spread of tradition are concerned are those in Persian poetry incorporated in Firdausī's (died probably 411/1020) *Shāhnāma* and Niẓāmī's (died 605/1209) *Haft paikar*, the latter being imitated numerous times in such widely appreciated versions as the ones by Amīr Khusrau Dihlavī (died 725/1325),[3] Mīr ʿAlī Shīr Navāʾī (died 906/1501),[4] or ʿAbdallāh Hātifī (died 927/1521).[5] Through the

---

[1] Khaleghi-Motlagh, "Āzāda"; Hanaway, "Bahrām Gōr".

[2] References for the following are given by Fontana, *La leggenda di Bahrām Gūr*, 103–120; Marzolph, *Arabia ridens*, vol. 2, no. 135.

[3] Amīr Khusrau Dihlavī, *Hasht Bihist*, 47–70; Aliev, *Temy i sjuzhety Nizami*, 45–58.

[4] *Ibid.*, 151–161.

[5] Bernardini, "La caccia di Bahrām Gūr"; Hâtefi, *I sette scenari*, 127–141, 291–297, verses 252–461; Aliev, *Temy i sjuzhety Nizami*, 244–248.

intermediary of Jacques de Vitry, bishop of Palestinian Acre from 1216 to 1226, the anecdote also passed into Western literature where it eventually became a well known tall tale.[6] Meanwhile, in Near Eastern literatures, notably in Persian literature, it continued to constitute a romanticized, though serious element of mythical history. Considering the exemplary character of Bahrām Gūr's spectacular marksmanship, it is not surprising to see this particular anecdote belonging to the most often illustrated scenes in Persian art.[7] In addition to numerous representations on seals, ceramic objects, tiles, and metalwork, dating as far back as Sasanian times, it is represented on modern carpets[8] and on contemporary popular paintings,[9] besides constituting part of the standard corpus of scenes represented in miniature illustrations of Firdausī's *Shāh-nāma*[10] and Niẓāmī's *Khamsa*.[11]

The illustrations of both works have been published and studied many times, yet almost exclusively manuscript tradition with its beautifully inspired coloured illuminations has been taken into consideration.[12] However, there is no obvious reason why illustrations in printed books should be neglected. It may be true that illuminated manuscripts are often of a high artistic standard, appealing to Western taste, but there is no reason to justify why researchers were lured into supposing that the art of illustration in printed books ceased to

[6] Wesselski, *Märchen des Mittelalters*, 107, no. 38; Spies, "Drei arabische Lügengeschichten", 587–590; Thompson, *Motif Index*, N 621.

[7] Numerous references in Simpson, "Narrative Allusion and Metaphor"; Fontana, *La leggenda di Bahrām Gūr*.

[8] Fontana, *La leggenda di Bahrām Gūr*, fig. 44; Taghyjeva, *Nizami obrazlary khalchalarda*, no. 36, 49.

[9] Painting by Fatḥallāh Qūllar Āqāsī reproduced in Fontana, *La leggenda di Bahrām Gūr*, fig. 45, Maison de l'Iran, *Les Peintres populaires*, no. 30, cf. also nos. 29 (detail), 31 (by ʿAbbās Bulūkfar); Saif, *Naqqāshī-yi qahva-khāna*, no. 18, 48.

[10] Norgren and Davis, *Shah-Nameh Illustrations*, list 32 representations of the scene "Bahram Gur hunts in the company of Azadeh"; another seventeen illustrations depict the subsequent scene "Bahram Gur's Mount Tramples Azadeh".

[11] Dodkhudoeva, *Poemy Nezami*, 212–214, no. 178, lists 40 representations of the scene "Bahrām and Fitna hunting" in manuscripts of the 14th through 17th centuries.

[12] The literature concerning illuminated Persian manuscripts is vast, and many illustrated monograph publications probably contain one or more reproductions of the particular illustration discussed here, see e.g. Binyon, *The Poems*, plate 16; Stchoukine, *Manuscrits tîmûrides*, plate 47; idem, *Manuscrits safavis*, plate 69; idem, *Manuscrits de Shāh ʿAbbās*, plate 5; Robinson, *Bodleian Library*, no. 1292; idem, *India Office Library*, nos. 108, 287, 1140; idem, *John Rylands Library*, no. 628; Nizami Gänjävi, plates 88, 89; Duda, *Persische Handschriften*, plate 126; Titley, *Persian Miniature Painting*, fig. 37; eadem, *Miniatures from Persian Manuscripts*, subject index s.v. Āzādeh, Bahrām Gūr, Dilārām, Fitneh.

be of an attractive quality. The introduction of printing to Iran in the first decades of the nineteenth century eventually resulted in the superseding of the manuscript tradition. On the other hand, it also resulted in a new genre of books, whose illustrations are not devoid of a similar, even though admittedly more humble charm, to those in illuminated manuscripts. In some ways, these illustrations are comparable to woodcuts in European incunabula, with which they share the aspect of experimenting with a new technique, yet they are much more refined. The artists who produced them could, on the one hand, profit from many centuries of experience and expertise in splendid book illumination and drawing; on the other hand they were facing a new medium of drawing, unfamilar and strange at first, which they then explored, and soon mastered to produce a number of beautiful books. These stand up in their own right in comparison to illustrated books of any other style, period, or region.

Unfortunately, the history of printing in Iran is a highly underrepresented area of research, though a number of short surveys[13] and at least one detailed publication exist. The latter is an extensive study by the Russian Persianist O.P. Shcheglova, which has been neglected in previous research.[14] It is based mainly on her catalogue of the extensive holdings in the Oriental Department of the St. Petersburg (formerly Leningrad) Branch of the Russian (formerly Soviet) Academy of Sciences.[15] It should be pointed out that publishing in Iran for about a century (from 1840 to 1940) was mainly achieved by lithograph printing. Printing in moveable types was known and practiced more than two decades earlier than the process of lithograph printing, a printing press having been established in Tabriz as early as 1227/1812,[16] but books printed with lead characters were not very successful and therefore this mode of production was largely abandoned after the middle of the nineteenth century until it made another more successful appearance in the first decades of the twentieth century. Besides the fact that the crude shape of

[13] Afshār, *Sair-i kitāb*; Maḥbūbi Ardakāni, *Tārikh-e mu'assasāt*, 209 ff. See also the recent series of articles by Gulpāygānī, "Tārikh-i chāp".

[14] Shcheglova's publications are not mentioned in the two recent encyclopedic surveys Floor, "Čāp", 762 f., and idem, "Maṭbaʿa".

[15] Shcheglova, *Katalog litografirovannykh knig*; idem, *Iranskaya litografirovannaya kniga*.

[16] With this summary statement I do not intend to participate in the discussion on when the first book in Iran ever was printed, for which see Floor, "First Printing-Press".

lead characters did not appeal to the Iranian aesthetic sentiment, the main reason for the failure of printing in moveable type in the nineteenth century is most probably to be seen in the strong aversion of the writers' guilds defending their position against the threat of the new technique. Lithograph printing, on the other hand, achieved a smooth continuation of previous modes of book production both for its aesthetic standards as well as for the artists involved, calligraphers and illustrators alike, and only later led to new developments.

Another advantage of lithograph printing was the possibility of incorporating illustrations into any given text without major organizational restraints. There was no need for separate cliches, woodcuts, metal engravings or the like—the artist would draw the illustration onto the very same surface the calligrapher had been writing on.[17] Obviously, it took Persian publishers a while to grasp and put into practice this combination. Evidence for this assumption is supplied by the fact that early lithographed copies of books later published in standard illustrated editions are still devoid of illustrations. The copy of *Alf laila wa laila* printed in 1261/1845 (written by ʿAlī Khᵛushnavīs) does not contain any illustrations, neither do the 1257/1841 or 1264/1847 editions of Saʿdī's *Kulliyāt*; and the 1261/1845 de luxe edition of Niẓāmī's *Khamsa* (written by Naṣrallāh Tafrishī) contains free spaces for illustrations to be included, yet the illustrations are not executed[18]—the most plausible reason for this lack appears to be the publisher's inability (or maybe only impatience?) to hire a competent artist in the early years of lithograph book illustration. Besides, publishers kept experimenting with other combinations to produce illustrated books. The 1261/1845 edition of the *Rauẓat al-mujāhidīn* (commonly known as *Mukhtār-nāma*) is printed with lead characters and contains eight illustrations executed as metal

[17] There are various pieces of evidence for determining the sequence in which different artists worked. At first, lines would be drawn to fix the size of the page and shape of the layout—this was most probably done by a person of minor rank other than the calligrapher. In the case of illuminated headings, triangles (on the margins) or other decorative illuminations, this step might already have involved the artist, who would either fit his illustrations later in designated areas left free or draw first, leaving it up to the calligrapher to cover any additional space by stretching the calligraphy (which often was done by writing lines diagonally).

[18] The edition is termed "de luxe" because of its lavishly decorated binding. The illustrations are not executed in all of several different copies examined, in libraries in Munich (Staatsbibliothek), Paris (École des langues orientales), and Tehran (National library).

engravings,[19] while the 1272/1856 folio edition of the *Ṭūfān al-bukā'* contains eight full page lithographed illustrations incorporated into a book otherwise printed with lead characters.

The first Persian illustrated lithographed book ever produced, according to the pioneer studies by Sa'īd Nafīsī,[20] is a 1259/1847 edition of Maktabī's *Lailī va Majnūn*. It contains four illustrations which in their crude execution document the fact that artists still had to familiarize themselves with the new technique.[21] Ten years later, the calligrapher of the 1267–8 edition of Sa'dī's *Kulliyāt*, Muṣṭafā-Qulī b. Muḥammad Hādī "Sulṭān Kajūrī", in a personal note added in the margins of the introduction, asked the reader's forgiveness for any mistakes he might have produced due to the unfamiliar handling with viscid ink he was forced to use for writing on the special paper employed for lithographic printing. Yet, as the rapidly growing range of production shows, obviously customers were fond of the new genre of illustrated books. Items produced at first were of small size and popular content, evidently requiring minimal investment and promising large readership—such as the popular romances *Nūsh-Āfarīn Gouhartāj*, *Salīm-i Javāhirī*, *Chihil Ṭūṭī*, or *Dalla-yi Mukhtār*, all of which were printed in 1263/1847.[22] These ventures must have met with approval and success, since only a few years after the first publications a large number of illustrated books were available and publishers even dared to risk large investments in the time-consuming production of voluminous works. The production of the illustrated edition of Firdausī's *Shāh-nāma* (written by the above mentioned Muṣṭafā-Qulī b. Muḥammad Hādī "Sulṭān Kajūrī" and containing 57 large illustrations by 'Alī-Qulī Khū'ī) eventually published in 1267/1850 lasted for almost two years,[23] and Mīr Khᵛānd's *Raużat*

[19] See Gulpyāygānī, "Tārīkh-i grāvūr-sāzī".

[20] Nafīsī, "Ṣan'at-i chāp"; idem, "Nakhustīn chāphā".

[21] Some of the illustrations of this book are also reproduced by Afshār, *Sair-e ketāb*, and Gulpāygānī, "Tārīkh-i grāvūr-sāzī".

[22] On Persian popular romances see Marzolph, *Dāstānhā-ye širīn*; on specific compilations see idem, *Die vierzig Papageien*, and idem, "Social values".

[23] Ṣafī-Nizhād, "Shāh-nāmahā", 30, has drawn up a table comparing the respective book (chapter), number of pages, amount of illustrations and illuminated chapter headings in correspondence with the year of completion. It is interesting to note that books 1–4 of the *Shāh-nāma* were first produced consecutively from 1265 to 1267 (1265: 309 pages; 1266: 490 pages; 1267: 349 pages), while the introductory *Hajv-nāma* and the preface (*dībācha*) are signed in 1266 and 1267 respectively, and thus were probably written only when production of the book was almost achieved.

aṣ-ṣafā took the calligrapher ʿAlī Aṣġar Tafreshī almost five years to complete (1270–74/1853–57).

Books published in illustrated editions were almost exclusively of a narrative (and thus predominantly fictional) character. In the first place they comprised such Persian classics as Firdausī's *Shāh-nāma*, Niẓāmī's *Khamsa*, the *Kulliyāt* by Saʿdī, or Hablarūdī's popular book on proverbs and their tales, *Jāmiʿ at-tamṯīl*; next in number came religious narratives about the tragic events of Kerbela, of which the *Ḥamla-yi Ḥaidarīya* by Mullā Bamūn-ʿAlī, the *Asrār al-shahāda* by Ismāʿīl Burūjirdī and the *Ṭūfān al-bukāʾ* by Jauharī were the most widely appreciated. Besides, imaginative narrative compilations such as the Persian translation of *Alf laila*, the Persian version of *Kalīla va Dimna* (*Anvār-i Suhailī*) or the prose epics *Iskandar-nāma* and *Ḥamza-nāma* were produced, plus a large and ever growing number of less extensive popular works.[24] Masterpieces of lithograph book illustration include the 1264/1848 edition of Niẓāmī's *Khamsa* illustrated by ʿAlī-Qulī Khūʾī;[25] the profusely illustrated 1267/1851 edition of a collection of religious legends in poetry, *Akhbār-nāma*, prepared by an unknown artist, probably the same ʿAlī-Qulī; the 1275/1859 edition of *Alf laila*, illustrated by Mīrzā Ḥasan; and the 1280/1863 edition of *Tuḥfat aẕ-ẕākirīn* by Mīrzā Muḥammad b. ʿAlī-Muḥammad Chelābī "Bīdil", containing more than one hundred full page illustrations executed by Bahrām Kirmānshāhānī. However, until now neither the titles nor the overall amount of lithographed Persian books produced in the nineteenth century are known, nor is the number of various editions of specific works. More than two hundred illustrated books in sometimes up to about a dozen different editions might have been produced, but the few definite answers available as to modes of production, artists involved, distribution, and readership are outnumbered by a large amount of unsolved questions, most of which have not even been considered yet.

Thus, though it appears fairly easy to supply a rough sketch of the development of Persian lithographed books, it is extremely difficult to judge whether such a sketch will retain its apparent reliability when more data become known. As for the present situation, and this statement will increase in relevance in the future, Persian lithographed books ought to be treated with the same respect and care

[24] See Bertel's, "Persidskaja 'lubochnaja' literatura".
[25] Robinson, "The Tehran Nizami".

as manuscripts. Many of the books which were probably printed in some 300 or 400 copies might well survive in only a single copy in some unknown private collection, and though the plain text of many a book compiled may be preserved in other editions, each lithograph edition contains a specific layout, and, if illustrated, a number of at times highly individual illustrations. Printed books in Iran until very recently were treated with little respect, and public awareness of their value is only just emerging at a time when huge amounts of books have already decayed. Fortunately for research, considerable collections of nineteenth century Persian lithographed books besides those in Tehran are available in the specialized public libraries of St. Petersburg,[26] London,[27] and Paris.[28] About half a dozen serious studies have been published,[29] indicative of the fact that the actual importance of the thousands of lithographed drawings available for understanding the historical development of drawing and narrative illustration in the Qājār period remains greatly underestimated, if not totally neglected.[30] Above all, these illustrations constitute a prime source of information for specific questions concerning a wide range of topics, including iconography and symbolism, costume, music, manners, technical development and numerous other aspects of everyday life in the Qājār period.

Among the different ways to analyze the data available, the following presentation proposes to discuss a number of lithographed illustrations of the anecdote about Bahrām Gūr's spectacular marksmanship quoted above, in order to point out some questions of more general concern. The plates reproduce altogether sixteen illustrations of the same scene, taken from various editions of Firdausī's *Shāh-nāma* and Niẓāmī's *Khamsa* published in a period covering the complete range of Persian lithograph illustration (1840–1940). The publication details are as follows:[31]

---

[26] See Shcheglova, *Katalog litografirovannykh knig*; eadem, *Iranskaya litografirovannaya kniga.*

[27] See the list given by Robinson, "The Tehran Nizami"; to be supplemented by a thorough check of Edwards, *Persian Printed Books.*

[28] Massé, "L'Imagerie populaire".

[29] In addition to those already quoted see Afshār, "Shāh-nāma"; Ṣafī-Nizhād, "Shāh-nāmahā-ye chāp-i sangi". The ongoing series by ʿAnāṣurī, "Muʿarrifī-yi kutub-i chāp-i sangī", is a predominantly superficial presentation of one item per issue.

[30] Cf. e.g. the blunt final statement by Swietochowski, "Drawing", 547 that "artists of the 19th and 20th centuries continued to draw subjects evolved in the 15–17th centuries".

[31] Not all of the books considered could be inspected with care in public libraries,

1) Niẓāmī, *Khamsa*, Tehran, 1264/1847–8; written by ʿAlī Aṣghar Tafrishī; no. 24 out of a total of 38 illustrations, four of which are signed by ʿAlī-Qulī Khūʾī; original size appr. 11,9 × 8,3 cm;[32]

2) Firdausī, *Shāh-nāma*, Bombay, 1264/1949; written by Sayyid Riżā b. Aḥmad al-Ḥusainī al-Shīrāzī; no. 46 out of a total of 57 illustrations; original size appr. 13,8 × 12 cm;[33]

3) Niẓāmī, *Khamsa*, Tehran, 1269/1852–3; written by ʿAlī Aṣghar Tafrishī; no. 23 out of a total of 37 illustrations, two of which are signed by ʿAlī-Qulī Khūʾī;

4) Niẓāmī, *Khamsa*, Tehran, 1270/1853–4; no. 28 out of a total of 44 illustrations, three of which are signed by ʿAlī-Qulī Khūʾī; 14,5 × 9,8 cm;

5) Firdausī, *Shāh-nāma*, Bombay, 1272/1855–6; written by Muḥammad Ḥusain Khān "Auliyāʾ Samīʿ"; no. 44 out of a total of 58 illustrations; original size appr. 13,6 × 11,8 cm;[34]

6) Niẓāmī, *Khamsa*, Tehran, 1276/1859–60; written by ʿAbd al-Ḥusain Farīdanī; no. 24 out of a total of 41 illustrations; original size appr. 11 × 7,3 cm;

7) Firdausī, *Shāh-nāma*, Bombay, 1276/1859–60; written by Muḥammad Ḥusain Khān "Auliyāʾ Samīʿ"; no. 35 out of a total of 47 illustrations, one of which is signed by Sayyid Muḥammad b. [. . .] Mīrzā Kāẓim al-Ḥusainī al-Shīrāzī; original size appr. 16 × 11,1 cm;[35]

---

and for some of those in private possession which I had the opportunity to examine, I neither had the leisure to write down all the important details, nor was there the possibility to arrange for a copy of more than the actual illustrations. Thus, I apologize for any lacuna in detailed bibliographical documentation. The data supplied should, however, suffice to facilitate exact identification.

[32] On this edition see Robinson, "The Tehran Nizami", 61–67. It is interesting to see that the copy in the Tehran National Library differs in its first part, the *Makhzan al-asrār*, from the copy in Robinson's possession; though the rest of the book is exactly the same in both copies, obviously the plates for the first part were produced twice in their entirety. The most obvious change occurs in the first illustration (Nūshīrvān and the owls in the ruined village), which in the Tehran copy does not bear the artist's signature.

[33] This is probably the second illustrated lithographed *Shāh-nāma* produced, the first one according to Ṣafī-nizhād being published in Bombay, 1262/1846, written by the same calligrapher, who signed as Sayyid Riżā al-Ḥusainī al-Shīrāzī; see Ṣafī-Nizhād, "Shāh-nāmahā", 27–28; Shcheglova, *Katalog litografirovannykh knig*, vol. 2, 405, no. 1012; Edwards, *Persian Printed Books*, 249, this edition, 248.

[34] On this edition see Afshār, "Shāh-nāma", 32–3, this illustration reproduced ibid., 23.

[35] This edition referred to by Afshār, "Shāh-nāma", 33 as being produced 1276 shamsī/1897 (?).

8) Firdausī, *Shāh-nāma*, Bombay, 1276/1859–60; written by Āqā Mīrzā Muḥammad Ḥusain Shīrāzī; no. 46 out of a total of 58 illustrations; original size appr. 16 × 11,5 cm;

9) Niẓāmī, *Khamsa*, Tehran, 1286/1869–70; written by Mīrzā Āqā Kamra'ī; no. 28 out of a total of 43 illustrations; original size appr. 12,8 × 8,6 cm;

10) Niẓāmī, *Khamsa*, Tehran, 1299–1300/1881–3; no. 32 out of a total of 50 illustrations, this one signed "ʿamal-i Muṣṭafā 1300"; original size appr. 10,2 × 7,2 cm;

11) Firdausī, *Shāh-nāma*, 1306–8/1888–11; written by Sayyid Nāẓim Ḥusain Riżavī; no. 42 out of a total of 54 illustrations; original size appr. 17,5 × 11,4 cm;

12) Firdausī, *Shāh-nāma*, Tehran 1307/1889–90; written by Muḥammad Riżā Ṣafā, nicknamed "Sulṭān al-kuttāb"; no. 45 out of a total of 60 illustrations, this one signed "Muṣṭafā 1307"; original size appr. 16 × 12,2 cm;[36]

13) Firdausī, *Shāh-nāma*, Bombay, 1308–15/1890–8; (partly) written by Murtażā al-Ḥusainī Mīr Barẕaqānī; no. 44 out of a total of 56 illustrations; original size appr. 18 × 15,8 cm;[37]

14) Niẓāmī, *Khamsa*, Tehran, 1316/1898–9; written by Zain al-ʿĀbidīn b. Mīrzā Sharīf Qazvīnī; no. 32 out of a total of 49 illustrations, this one signed "rāqima-yi Javād 1316"; original size appr. 11,1 × 7,5 cm;

15) Niẓāmī, *Khamsa*, Bombay, 1328/1910–1; written by Mīrzā ʿAlī-Khān Shīrāzī; no. 30 out of a total of 49 illustrations, this one signed "rāqima-yi ʿAli Akbar naqqāsh zargar-i shirāzī"; original size appr. 13,5 × 9 cm;

16) Niẓāmī, *Khamsa*, Shīrāz, 1312 shamsī/1933–4; written by Muḥammad Ibrāhīm "Mishkīn-qalam" Shīrāzī; no. 32 out of a total of 52 illustrations; original size appr. 12,9 × 8,2 cm.[38]

A combination of the above bibliographical data, even though they are scarce, with a careful iconographical analysis of the illustrations, leads to a number of interesting results. It should be kept in mind

[36] Shcheglova, *Katalog litofgrafirovannykh knig* 2, 407, no. 1017.
[37] Ibid., vol. 2, 407, no. 1019.
[38] This is the copy concerning which Saʿīd Nafīsī in an inimitably sarcastic tone remarked that "it were better had it never been produced"; see Nafīsī, "Ṣanʿat-e chāp", 35.

that the above listing is not complete, and does not aim to be.[39] However, care has been taken to choose representative examples within the range of editions available for close inspection, and at least for Niẓāmī's *Khamsa* the listing is close to being comprehensive.[40]

It is a slightly frustrating situation that most of the artists remain anonymous. While calligraphers would normally mention their name in the colophon of the book, or in the colophons at the bottom of each chapter, artists rarely cared to sign their illustrations. Moreover, when they did, we know only rarely of other works they illustrated.[41]

The most prominent illustrator of the early years of lithographed illustration, as has rightly been pointed out by Basil Robinson, appears to have been ʿAlī-Qulī Khūʾī. Robinson based his evaluation predominantly on the magnificent copy of Niẓāmī's *Khamsa* of 1264. Yet, ʿAlī-Qulī was not only a brilliant and inventive but also a most prolific and productive illustrator, who signed some 28 works in the decade between 1263/1847 and 1272/1856;[42] besides, many illustrations in other works dating from the same period might also be his work, although there is no possibility of ascertaining this. It was by no means unusual that an artist would illustrate the same book more than once. ʿAlī-Qulī himself illustrated twice Saʿdī's *Kulliyāt* (1267–8/1850–1 and 1268/1251) and Jauharī's *Ṭūfān al-bukāʾ* (1269?/1852 and 1272/1855), and of Niẓāmī's *Khamsa* even three different editions bear illustrations signed by him. And yet again it is extremely difficult to be sure whether all of the illustrations in a book containing illustrations bearing his signature were prepared by the same artist. Faithful copying of earlier illustrations was the common rule to such an extent that almost identical replicas were (re)produced. This mode of production in many cases makes it almost impossible to judge the authorship of illustrations from stylistic criteria, since not only the motif of a given illustration would be copied,

[39] The present author is conducting a large scale research project indexing and cataloguing Persian lithographed illustrations which has resulted so far (1999) in more than 10,000 items filmed or copied, scanned and ready for reproduction and analysis by electronic device.

[40] To compare with the listing of lithograph editions of the *Khamsa* as given in Rādfarr, *Kitābshināsī-yi Niẓāmī Ganjavī*, 34–5.

[41] See the relevant entries in Karīmzāda Tabrīzī, *Aḥvāl va āsār*, most of which for the lesser known artists concerned here, besides a limited number of additional items, do not even contain basic information.

[42] Meanwhile, an extensive study on ʿAlī-Qulī has been prepared by the present author, containing updated and additional data; see Marzolph, "Mirzâ ʿAli-Qoli Xuʾi".

but also the style of the copy would be made to resemble the original as closely as possible.

Besides, it was by no means unusual that a book was illustrated by different artists. A beautiful example of this kind of cooperation is the 1272/1855 edition of *Alf laila*, jointly illustrated by ʿAlī-Qulī (who, judging from his mature style, was the senior artist), Mīrzā Ḥasan and Mīrzā Riżā-yi Tabrīzī. Fortunately, in this case most of the illustrations are either signed or can clearly be attributed to ʿAlī Qolī by means of stylistic peculiarities. But even then, the attribution of two illustrations which do not bear a signature remains uncertain, and the perspective is much less clear in the numerous cases of books where none of the illustrations included is signed at all.

The situation is further complicated by the fact that some owners of the copies preserved today, besides using the illustrations as a convenient inspiration for crude sketches executed on the margin, obviously took pleasure in adding to the original illustration a caption or signature not originally intended. For instance, illustration no. 31 (Bahrām Gūr and the shepherd who hanged his dog) in the 1269 copy of Niẓāmī's *Khamsa* in the Tehran National Library bears a signature reading "ʿamal-e Mīrzā ʿAlīqulī Khū'ī", executed in thin dotted lines, which is not present in the copy of the same edition in the possession of the New York Public Library. Considering the crude and atypical execution of the signature, it was most probably added at a later date by a person other than the original artist.

Given these considerations, it remains mysterious whether all of the illustrations in the 1269 edition of Niẓāmī's *Khamsa* (no. 3) were produced by ʿAlī-Qulī. As for this particular illustration, it gives the impression of a slightly careless and crude copy of the previous illustration in the 1264 edition (no. 1). Moreover, it appears strange that just one year later, in 1270 (no. 4), the same artists should illustrate the same scene in a completely different style.

The illustration in the 1270 edition of Niẓāmī's *Khamsa* (no. 4) shows a number of significant differences in details, most of all in costume: the earlier illustrations show Bahrām Gūr wearing a crown, which—alluding to the reign of Muḥammad-Shāh (1250/1834–1264/1848)—is commonly known as Tāj-e Muḥammadī. While this symbol of royal representation is retained in the Indian style illustrations (nos. 5, 6, 8, 11, 13), in illustrations of books produced in Iran during the reign of Nāṣir al-Dīn Shāh (1264/1848–1313/1896) it became fashionable to portray important characters of the narratives in the likeness of the present ruler Nāṣir al-Dīn himself, wearing a uniform and the typical high felt hat. This remained the standard (nos. 7, 9) until Muṣṭafā introduced a flat hat as head cover in 1299 (no. 10), which in subsequent years, in accordance with the growing awareness of the historical crowns of the Sasanian kings, was further modified by Javād (no. 14) and those who copied him (no. 15). Besides, Javād introduced the iconographical peculiarity known as "angusht-i taḥayyur", namely the slave-girl putting the index finger to her lips in bewilderment (taḥayyur), admiration and surprise.

A general disparity in the various illustrations is concerned with the dress and habit of the spectating slave girl (and her companions). While in the early illustrations by ʿAlī-Qulī (nos. 1, 3) she has partly covered her face and discreetly watches from behind a hill, in most later illustrations she has been moved to the foreground close to participating in the action. In the Indian illustrations her head at most is covered by a thin scarf, while in the Iranian illustrations her veil is thrown back, uncovering her face (nos 4, 7, 9) or she wears a scarf casually arranged around her shoulders.

Compared to the large variety of landscapes and scenic representations encountered in manuscript illuminations of the scene, the scope of variation in the lithographed illustrations of Bahrām Gūr's spectacular shot is restricted. In all cases but one (no. 7) the arrow has hit the animal, which in most cases is portrayed as an onager/gazelle, only sporadically in the Persian tradition (nos. 1, 10, 14, 15) rendered with horns. The animal is always heading for the far end of the picture, either left or right, yet the rider is pictured in three out of four possible positions: (a) either heading towards the left and shooting to the right (nos. 1, 3, 4, 7, 9), or (b) heading towards left and shooting to the left (nos. 1, 5, 13), or (c) heading towards the right and shooting to the right (nos. 6, 8, 10, 11, 12, 14, 15, 16); a possible representation (d) heading to the right and shooting to the left is nowhere to be found. This detail is not as superficial and insignificant as it may seem at first glance, since an analysis underlines the identification of the different strands of tradition as well as the various origins that contributed to the formation of the later hybrid forms. All the different ways of representation ultimately derive from the two earliest known lithograph illustrations, while (a) is encountered exclusively in the Persian tradition as well as only in illustrations of Niẓāmī's *Khamsa*; (b) is specific to illustrations of the *Shāh-nāma* first encountered in the Indian strand of tradition; and (c) in this rendering is the faithful mirror image of (b) which, though originating as an illustration of the *Shāh-nāma*, later—probably by the intermediary of Muṣṭafā, who is the only artist known to have illustrated the scene concerned in both the *Shāh-nāma* and the *Khamsa*[43]—also replaced the earlier version of illustrations in Niẓāmī's *Khamsa*.

The most obvious point, however, in the range of illustrations representing the historical development of lithograph illustration over a period of roughly a century, is the appalling decline in artistic quality. Besides the early illustrations (nos. 1, 2, 4) only those prepared by Muṣṭafā (and, to a lesser degree, Javād, who imitates Muṣṭafā in his own peculiar way) can claim to result from original inspiration. All other illustrations, though some of them are executed in a careful manner, are copies (or rather, to a Western understanding, plagiarized versions) of earlier illustrations. This may sound a rash conclusion, since it appears to be based on the analysis of only one topic, but in any case it is evident that both inventiveness and care degenerated, in India as well as in Iran.

The illustration of Bahrām Gūr's spectacular marksmanship is but one example of how to employ Persian lithographed illustrations for decoding aspects of cultural and art history in the golden age of the Qājār period. Much remains to be done, and in fact the enterprise has not yet started. Libraries in Iran are just about to acknowledge the precious value of lithographed books by arranging specialized sections (similar to those for manuscripts), by preparing catalogues or initiating relevant studies. Yet even basic questions have not even been considered, such as the definition of Iranian incunabula.[44] On the other hand, the major work on the history of printing in Iran has passed almost unnoticed by scholarship, Western and Iranian alike,[45] and—most important of all—no comprehensive collections of Persian lithographed books exist. Yet, though some cultural treasures

[43] ʿAlī-Qulī also illustrated a *Shāh-nāma* (Tehran, 1265–7/1848–50), but it does not contain the illustration under consideration.

[44] For India cf. Priolkar, "Indian Incunabula", proposing to fix the time limit for Indian incunabula at 1867, the year in which the 25th Press Act was passed. Priolkar mentions that from "this year onwards quarterly lists of all publications in India have been published, but no comparable record is available of the books published prior to that year" (133). If one were to apply similar considerations to Iran, this would encompass a major part of the period of lithograph production, since regular lists of publications only started to be published in the Pahlavī era (1924–1979).

[45] Shcheglova, *Iranskaya litografirovannaya kniga*.

are only acknowledged once they have been lost for good, it may not be a vain hope that there is still time for an adequate evaluation of Persian lithographed illustrations.

Bibliography

Afshār, Ī., *Sair-e kitāb dar Irān*, Tehran, 1344/1965.

———, "Shāh-nāma, az khaṭṭi tā chāpi", *Hunar va mardum* XIV, 162 (2535/1976), 17–45.

Aliev, G.Ju., *Temy i sjuzhety Nizami v literaturakh narodov vostoka*, Moscow, 1985.

Amīr Khusrau Dihlavī, *Hasht bihist*, Moscow, 1972.

ʿAnāṣorī, J., "Muʿarrifi-yi kutub i chap-i sangī", *Ṣanʿat-i chāp*, issue 112 (1370/1991) ff.

Bernardini, M., "La caccia di Bahrām Gūr e della sua ancella nella versione di ʿAbdallāh Hātifī (1492)", *Yād-nāma in memoria di Alessandro Bausani*, vol. 2, Rome, 1991, 275–294.

Bertel's, E.E., "Persidskaja 'lubochnaja' literatura", *Sergeju Fedorovichu Ol'denburgu k pjatidesjatiletiju nauchno-obshchestvennoi dejatel'nosti 1882–1932*, Leningrad, 1934, 83–94.

Binyon, L. *The Poems of Nizāmī*, London, 1928.

Dodkhudoeva, L.N., *Poemy Nezami srednovekovoi miniaturnoi zhivopisi*, Moscow, 1985.

Duda, D., *Die illuminierten Handschriften der österreichischen Nationalbibliothek, Islamische Handschriften 1. Persische Handschriften. Tafelband*, Wien, 1983.

Edwards, E., *A Catalogue of the Persian Printed Books in the British Museum*, London, 1922.

Floor, W., "Čāp", *Encyclopædia Iranica IV* (1990), 760–764.

———, "Maṭbaʿa, 3. In Persia" *EI*² VI, 803–804.

Floor, W.M., "The First Printing-Press in Iran", *Zeitschrift der Deutschen Morgenländischen Gesellschaft* CXXX (1980), 369–371.

Fontana, M.V., *Le leggenda di Bahrām Gūr e Āzāda, Materiale per la storia di una tipologia figurativa dalle origini al XIV secolo*, Naples, 1986.

Gulpāygānī, Ḥ., "Tārikh-i chāp va chāpkhāna dar Īrān", *Ṣanʿat-i chāp*, issue 109 (1370/1991) ff.

———, "Tārikh-i grāvūr-sāzī dar Īrān", *Ṣanʿat-i chāp*, issue 127 (1372/1994) 58–59.

Hanaway, W.L., "Bahrām Gōr in Persian Legend and Literature", *Encyclopædia Iranica* III (1989), 519.

Hâtefi, ʿAbdallâh, *I sette scenari*, ed. M. Bernardini, Naples, 1995.

Karīmzāda Tabrīzī, M.ʿA., *Aḥvāl va ās̱ār-i naqqāshān-i qadīm-i Īrān*, vols. I–III, London, 1985–91.

Khaleghi-Motlagh, Dj., "Āzāda", *Encyclopædia Iranica* III (1989), 519.

Maḥbūbī Ardakānī, H., *Tārikh-i muʾassasāt-i tamaddunī-yi jadīd dar Īrān*, vol. 1, Tehran 1354/1975.

Maison de l'Iran, *Les Peintres populaires de la legende persane/Popular Paintings and the Persian Legend*, Paris, 1974.

Marzolph, U., *Die Vierzig Papageien, Das persische Volksbuch "Čehel Ṭuṭi"*, Walldorf, 1979.

———, *Dāstānhā-ye širin. Fünfzig persische Volksbüchlein aus der zweiten Hälfte des zwanzigsten Jahrhunderts*, Stuttgart, 1994.

———, *Arabia ridens, Die humoristische Kurzprosa der frühen adab-Literatur im internationalen Traditionsgeflecht*, vol. 1–2, Francfort, 1992.

———, "Social Values in the Persian Popular Romance 'Salīm-i Javāhirī' ", *Edebiyât*, New Series V (1994), 77–98.

———, "Mirzâ ʿAli-Qoli Xu'i: Master of Persian Lithograph Illustration", *Annali* (in print).
Massé, H., "L'Imagerie populaire de l'Iran", *Arts asiatiques* VII (1960), 163–78.
Nafīsī, S., "Ṣanʿat-i chāp-i muṣavvar dar Īrān", *Payām-i nau* II, 5 (1324–25/1945–46), 22–35.
———, "Nakhustīn chāphā-yi muṣavvar dar Īrān", *Rāhnamā-yi kitāb* I, 3 (1337/1958), 232–40.
Nizami Gänjävi, *Khämsä miniaturlär*, Baky, 1983.
Norgren, J., and E. Davis, *Preliminary Index of Shah-Nameh Illustrations*, Ann Arbor, 1969.
Priolkar, A.K., "Indian Incunabula", *Comparative Librarianship, Essays in Honour of D.N. Marshall*, ed. N.N. Gidwani (Delhi etc. 1973), 129–135.
Rādfarr, A., *Kitābshināsī-yi Niẓāmī Ganjavī*, Tehran, 1371/1992.
Robinson, B.W., "The Teheran Nizami of 1848 & other Qajar Lithographed Books", *Islam in the Balkans/Persian Art and Culture in the 18th and 19th Centuries*, ed. J.M. Scarce, Edinburgh, 1979, 61–74, (also in idem, *Studies in Persian Art*, vol. 1, London, 1993, 328–341).
———, "Persian Painting under the Zand and Qājār Dynasties", *The Cambridge History of Iran, 7: From Nadir Shah to the Islamic Republic*, ed. P. Avery and Ch. Melville, Cambridge etc., 1991, 870–889.
———, *A Descriptive Catalogue of the Persian Paintings in the Bodleian Library*, Oxford, 1958.
———, *Persian Paintings in the India Office Library*, London, 1976.
———, *Persian Paintings in the John Ryland Library*, London, 1980.
Ṣafi-Nizhād, J., "Shāh-nāmahā-yi chāp-i sangi", *Mirāṣ-i Jarhangī* XIV (1374/1996), 24–30.
Saif, H., *Naqqāshī-yi qahva-khāna*, Teheran, 1369/1990.
Shcheglova, O.P., *Katalog litografirovannykh knig na persidskom jazyke v sobranii Leningradskogo otdeleniya Instituta vostokovedeniya AN SSR*, vol. 1–2, Moscow, 1975.
———, O.P., *Iranskaya litografirovannaya kniga*, Moscow, 1979.
Simpson, M.S., "Narrative Allusion and Metaphor in the Decoration of Medieval Islamic Objects", *Pictorial Narrative in Antiquity and the Middle Ages*, ed. H.L. Kessler, M.S. Simpson, Washington, 1985, 131–149.
Spies, O., "Drei arabische Lügengeschichten", *Die islamische Welt zwischen Mittelalter und Neuzeit, Festschrift Hans Robert Roemer*, ed. U. Haarmann, P. Bachmann, Beirut, 1979, 583–590.
Stchoukine, I., *Les peintures des manuscrits tîmûrides*, Paris, 1954.
———, *Les peintures des manuscrits du Shāh ʿAbbās Ier à la fin des Ṣafavīs*, Paris, 1964.
———, *Les peintures des manuscrits safavis*, Paris, 1959.
Swietochowski, M.L., "Drawing", *Encyclopædia Iranica* VII, 5 (1995), 537–547.
Taghyjeva, R., *Nizami obrazlary khalchalarda*, Baky, 1991.
Thompson, S., *Motif Index of Folk Literature*, vols. 1–6, Copenhagen, 1955–8.
Titley, N.M., *Miniatures from Persian Manuscripts*, London, 1977.
———, *Persian Miniature Painting and Its Influence on the Arts of Turkey and India*, London, 1983.
Wesselski, A., *Märchen des Mittelalters*, Berlin, 1925.

ill. 1

ill. 2

ill. 3

ill. 4

ill. 5

ill. 6

ill. 7

ill. 8

ill. 9

ill. 10

ill. 11

ill. 12

ill. 13

ill. 14

ill. 15

ill. 16

WHY WRITE HISTORY IN PERSIAN? HISTORICAL WRITING IN THE SAMANID PERIOD

Julie Scott Meisami

One of the most indefatigable and productive researchers on local Iranian dynasties from the 4th/10th to the 6th/12th centuries (and beyond) has without doubt been Edmund Bosworth. His studies of the Ghaznavids and the "Kings of Nimruz", his investigations into the political and cultural milieux of various of the local houses, and his articles on a wide variety of matters relating to medieval Iran are too well known, and too numerous, to be mentioned here, though they will be referred to frequently in this essay. It is in recognition of his invaluable contributions that I offer this discussion of another aspect of medieval Iranian culture: the writing of the first historical works in Persian.

The first histories written in New Persian appeared in the 4th/10th century in Khurasan and Transoxania, then ruled by the Samanids. The circumstances surrounding both the sudden emergence and the early stages of Persian historical writing have received little attention from students of Islamic historiography, which for most equals history written in Arabic, Arabic being the language of "serious" scholarship, and Arabic historians having been located, for the most part, in the central Islamic lands. Scholars have often been dismissive of Persian historiography, especially that of the pre-Mongol period; Bertold Spuler wrote that before this time:

> hardly any work written in Persian exists which deals with the history of Persia. . . . Works on the first centuries of islamized Persia . . . must be based on sources in foreign languages, in the first place Arabic.[1]

This begs several questions (how "foreign" was Arabic to those scholars, many of Persian origin, who wrote the histories of the early centuries? what "native-language" sources, written or oral, might they have had access to, and have preserved in translation?); it reflects the view of the scholar who sees historical texts solely as sources of

[1] Spuler, "The Evolution of Persian Historiography," 126.

data concerning events in the past. Different enterprises entirely are the study of historiography and of intellectual and cultural history. For both, historical works are invaluable, as they provide revealing insights about attitudes towards the past in the political and intellectual milieux in which they were written.[2]

Those scholars who *have* addressed themselves to Persian histories (and especially to the earliest texts) have generally confined themselves to philological rather than historiographical problems, or have dealt with historical writing in the broader context of the rise of Persian prose during the so-called "Persian Renaissance" of the Samanid period, or have attempted to identify the sources used by Persian historians.[3] Few have concerned themselves with the hows, whys and wherefores of Persian historiography: with the motives for writing history in Persian rather than in Arabic (or, for that matter, for writing history at all), with the perceived utility of history, with questions of method and of style, with problems of patronage and of audience.

Thus there is a clear need to put early Persian historical writing back on the map of Islamic historiography; to examine its distinctive or characteristic features; to address questions that have seldom been asked, and for which answers may not readily be found. Much of what I will have to say here will be speculative, as far more work remains to be done before we can have a fuller picture of Persian historiography than we do now, and we can scarcely hope to arrive at a complete one. Nor can Persian historiography be considered in isolation from Arabic; for if the two traditions ultimately diverge,[4] early Persian historians were well aware of their Arabic counterparts. The 4th/10th century saw important developments in Arabic historiography; and if scholarly discussions about the nature and uses of history took place largely in Arabic, they nonetheless affected Persian

---

[2] Cf. Rosenthal, *History of Muslim Historiography*, 6; Luther, "Chancery Writing," 1; idem, "Bayhaqi and the Later Saljuq Historians," 18–20; idem, "Islamic Rhetoric". Waldman, *Towards a Theory of Historical Narrative*, is critical of scholars who "use historical narratives almost exclusively as unstructured, uninterpretive mines of factual information," and neglect "the relevance of the whole source to the history of ideas" (1).

[3] For philological studies see e.g. Lazard, *La langue des plus anciens monuments du prose persane*; idem, "The Rise of the New Persian Language"; on Persian prose in the context of the "Persian literary Renaissance" see especially Richter-Bernburg, "Linguistic Shuʿūbīya"; on source studies see e.g. Cahen, "The Historiography of the Seljuqid Period".

[4] See e.g. Cahen, "Historiography, 75; Gibb, "Tarikh", 125.

writers. The views expressed in these discussions, moreover, support the argument to be made here: that medieval historians were less concerned with the recording of historical "facts" than with the presentation of the past in such a manner as to make it relevant to, and usable by, the present—that is to say, by *their* present.

Why, then, in a particular place, and at a particular time, begin writing history in Persian? One might argue that this development was inevitable; but this does not explain why it happened when, where, and in the manner in which it did.[5] John O. Ward observes:

> An age characterized by a rich variety of historical writing will be an age in which a significant number of persons endowed with literacy find themselves in problematical or challenging social or political circumstances.[6]

That the Samanid period was such an age becomes clear as we consider the circumstances surrounding the appearance of historical writing in Persian.

* * *

What assumptions might Persian writers have brought to the writing of history? Franz Rosenthal has argued that in medieval Islamicate societies history was not a recognized "science" with a specific object and methodology (as for example was the "science" of *Ḥadīth*), that it held no special place in classifications of the sciences, and that it did not form part of the educational curriculum of the mosque or the *madrasa*.[7] The first two assumptions are open to question, as will be suggested in what follows; and if history was not taught formally in mosque or *madrasa*, it was an important component of elementary education, as Rosenthal himself has shown, and was considered indispensable in the education of princes, as in that of those who served them: military leaders, viziers, secretaries, and royal boon-companions.[8] It is however generally true that, as Nancy Partner observes for the classical period in the West,

---

[5] Cf. Daniel, "The Samanid 'Translations' of Ṭabarī", [5]. I am grateful to the author for providing me with a copy of this paper prior to its publication.

[6] Ward, "Some Principles of Rhetorical Historiography," 103.

[7] Cf. Rosenthal, *Muslim Historiography*, 30 ff., 42–43; Ahmad, "Some Notes on Arabic Historiography", esp. 96.

[8] Rosenthal, *Muslim Historiography*, 49, 51–53.

There were no historians who were not something else first and more importantly.[9]

Those who wrote history came from many different walks of life; they included *Ḥadīth* scholars and *ʿulamāʾ*, court secretaries and officials, judges, physicians, and the occasional free-lance, each of whom brought to his task his own professional concerns and methods.

By the 4th/10th century, Persian writers had a variety of models of historical writing available to draw upon. One was the "universal", or more properly "general", history, represented most famously by Ṭabarī, whose *Taʾrīkh al-rusul wa-al-mulūk* was "translated" into Persian in 353/963 by the vizier Abū ʿAlī Balʿamī for the Samanid ruler Manṣūr ibn Nūḥ (r. 350–365/961–976). Despite their pretensions to generality, the chief focus of such works is on Islamic history—especially that of the caliphate—to which the accounts of past nations serve as prelude; thus they are arguably related to dynastic history (see further below). Moreover, the annalistic structure elaborated by Ṭabarī and employed by many later Arabic historians, which had already been modified by writers like Madāʾinī and Dīnawarī, was rarely adopted by Persian writers.[10]

Another model was local history, often seen by modern scholars as reflecting a sense of local or regional pride.[11] The term is slightly misleading, as many such works, both in Arabic and later in Persian, while they may indeed devote much space to description of their respective regions, are also concerned with the history of the rulers of those regions. Moreover, Persian seems to lack early representatives of the Arabic "local histories" whose chief focus is on biography, primarily of scholars; such works as Sallāmī's (lost) history of the governors of Khurasan (ca. 340/950), or the histories of Bukhara, Nishapur, Jurjan, Isfahan and so on, were written in Arabic. Later works, such as ʿAlī ibn Zayd al-Bayhaqī's Persian history of Bayhaq (*Tārikh-i Bayhaq*), written in the mid 6th/12th century, combine local history with topography and biography.[12]

---

[9] Partner, "The New Cornuficius", 11.

[10] For types of Arabic history see Khalidi, *Arabic Historical Thought in the Classical Period*; Rosenthal, *Muslim Historiography*.

[11] Cf. Rosenthal, *Muslim Historiography*, 150; Bulliet, *Islam: the View from the Edge*, 103–05.

[12] On regional and "biographical" histories see Rosenthal, *Muslim Historiography*, 160–66; see also Bulliet, *Islam*. On Sallāmī, who was used extensively by later historians, Treadwell comments that "loyalty to his Muḥtājid patrons and their Sāmānid sovereigns resulted . . . in a rather partisan account of Samanid history," e.g., in his

The pre-Islamic Iranian historical tradition, which had been preserved in Arabic histories and which, in Gibb's view, had exerted an "unfavorable" influence on Arabic historiography,[13] was revived in the Samanid period, and I shall have more to say about this later. Another important model, which was to have a lasting influence on Persian historiography, was currently in the making: contemporary dynastic history, represented by the lengthy section of Miskawayh's *Tajārib al-umam* devoted to the history of the Buyids up to the year 369/980 and by other works dealing with that dynasty. These were followed in the mid-5th/11th century by Persian histories of the Ghaznavids and Saffarids, and in the late 6th/12th century of the Seljuqs.

Some scholars have seen the rise of dynastic history as evidence of the decline of a once-noble discipline. Gibb lamented that with its appearance

> The old theological conception which had given breadth and dignity to history was discarded, and annalistic [history] tended to concentrate more and more upon the activities of the ruler and the court.[14]

Dynastic history was written by court officials and secretaries, who brought to its writing the rhetorically sophisticated chancery style (*kitābat al-inshā'*) which characterized their professional compositions, and who also elaborated an important, if not exactly new, conceptual model for history. For the very term for "dynasty", *dawla*, was, as Rosenthal notes, "connected . . . with a theory of recurrent cycles of political power;" and the rise and fall of states was to become, in the words of Aziz Al-Azmeh, the "essential paradigm of human history."[15]

---

treatment of Abū 'Alī Chāghānī's revolt (see further below) and his failure to mention "the Qarmaṭī scandal at Naṣr ibn Aḥmad's court" (which is passed over by most historians) (*The Political History of the Sāmānid State*, 8, and see 7–9).

[13] "As soon as history passed outside the Islamic field the old difficulty of distinguishing between legendary, semi-legendary and historical elements reappeared, and with it the tendency to take on trust whatever materials were available" (Gibb, "Tarikh", 117). This is precisely the sort of criticism levelled at histories written in the *Shāhnāma* tradition by later writers such as Bayhaqī. The question of the influence of Sasanian historical traditions on Arabic, and later on Persian, historiography are beyond the scope of this discussion. See e.g. Lewis & Holt, *Historians of the Middle East*, 9; Rosenthal, *Muslim Historiography*, 49; Gibb, "Tarikh", 118; Daryaee, "National History or Keyanid History".

[14] Gibb, "Tarikh", 120.

[15] Rosenthal, *Muslim Historiography*, 89; and see Al-Azmeh, *Ibn Khaldun*, 11–46.

Dynastic history is an important representative in the Islamic world of what Western scholars have termed ethical-rhetorical historiography, which has been widely studied with respect to pre-modern Europe but has received less attention from students of Islamic history.[16] Two points deserve mention here. The first is that the use of history to point moral lessons—so disparaged by Gibb[17] and by von Grunebaum[18]—constitutes the rule rather than the exception for pre-modern historiography. As Rosenthal observes:

> All Muslims shared in the firm conviction that all politics was the work of individuals and understandable in the light of their personal qualities and experiences.

History was a mine of ethical examples (positive and negative) of both the great men and the great villains of the past.[19]

In ethical historiography, rhetorical strategies pertaining to both structure and embellishment play an important role in conveying the historian's message. This was not truly grasped by the likes of Gibb, von Grunebaum, or Rosenthal, who saw in the application of rhetoric to history yet another symptom of decline. For von Grunebaum, one result of the "upsurge of the educational ideal of the *kātib*, the civil official or the clerk" was "a gossipy and clever historiography," in which

> Style came to be cultivated for its own sake . . . and the substance of what the author had set out to convey almost evaporated in a fireworks of rhetoric.[20]

---

[16] For representative studies see e.g. Paul Plass, *Wit and the Writing of History*; Donald Lateiner, *The Historical Method of Herodotus*; Ernest Breisach (ed.), *Classical Rhetoric and Medieval Historiography*; Richard A. Lanham, *The Motives of Eloquence: Literary Rhetoric in the Renaissance.*

[17] "In place of [history's] earlier theological justification, the historians now pleaded the moral value of its study; history perpetuates the record of virtuous and evil actions and offers them as examples for the edification of future generations" ("Tarikh", 121). The emphasis by historians on the rise and fall of states as part of the divine plan should be noted here.

[18] "The weakness of Arabic historiography is its concentration on personalities and on military incidents and court cabals. . . . For the most part happenings are explained as results of intrigues and ambitions of kings, generals, or politicians. . . . The public came to be interested in the lesson history taught. But the lesson learned was *merely* one of morality, insight into human character, and the vagaries of fate" (*Medieval Islam*, 282–83; emphasis added).

[19] Rosenthal, *Muslim Historiography*, 101.

[20] Von Grunebaum, *Medieval Islam*, 227; cf. Rosenthal, *Muslim Historiography*, 173, 176 ff. Gibb speculates that the rise of this "new fashion" of historical writing

But for the historians in question message and style are inseparable, and the rhetorical style is not merely the inevitable result of history being written by, and for, courtiers. As the late Allin Luther pointed out,

> the modern researcher cannot use these histories simply by "extracting the facts". The nature of the whole work is important if we are to understand the entirety of the author's message. We must be aware of the writer's purpose and of the way in which he arranged and ornamented his work to serve that purpose.[21]

Luther was speaking specifically of Seljuq histories; but the principle is more broadly applicable.

* * *

On the map of Persian historical writing (which may be far from accurate, due both to the loss of many works and to the practice by later historians of incorporating often large portions of earlier works into their own) we see a number of peaks and valleys. The first peak is in the mid-4th/10th century, in the Samanid domains. The second comes a decade or so after the Seljuq defeat of the Ghaznavids in 431/1040, in what remained of the Ghaznavid empire in the east. The third begins in the late 6th/12th century, around the time of the accession of the last Great Seljuq sultan Ṭughrïl III ibn Arslān (571–590/1176–1194), and culminates around the turn of the century. Then come the Mongols, whose impact on historical writing is beyond the scope of this discussion. There are a few blips here and there along this undulating curve; but in the main they represent works which are peripheral to the main currents of Persian historical writing, and which are in any case outside the scope of this discussion.[22]

"may . . . be connected with the revival of Persian and of the Persian historical tradition in the east, and may even have been influenced by the Persian epic poetry which was simultaneously coming into existence" ("Tarikh", 123–24). This seems unlikely; the use of elaborate rhetorical artifice, and in particular of *saj'*, which characterizes earlier Arabic histories such as that of 'Utbī, is not seen in Persian until the 6th/12th century.

[21] Luther, "Islamic Rhetoric and the Persian Historians", 96–97.

[22] These include such works as the *Tārīkh-i Sīstān* (c. 448/1056); Ibn al-Balkhī's *Fārsnāma* and the anonymous *Mujmal al-tavārīkh va-al-qiṣaṣ* (early 6th/12th c.); and Ibn Isfandiyār's *Tārīkh-i Ṭabaristān* (early 7th/13th c.).

In general the curves of historical writing do not duplicate those of dynastic florescence, but follow them by about a couple of decades. The Samanid period is an exception; but by the time Firdawsī completed his *Shāhnāma* and dedicated it to Maḥmūd of Ghazna the Samanids were themselves history. Moreover, they produced no dynastic histories, either contemporary or retrospective. Although Abū Naṣr ʿUtbī's Arabic history of the Ghaznavids was written at the height of Maḥmūd's reign, Ghaznavid history was not written in Persian until after the collapse of most of Maḥmūd's empire. The history of the Seljuqs was not written at all until they were well into decline; the first Arabic histories appear around the same time as do the Persian, in the last quarter of the 6th/12th century.[23]

In what follows I shall be chiefly concerned with the first peak on the map of Persian historical writing: its emergence in the Samanid period.[24] The last half-century of Samanid rule witnessed a variety of tensions and conflicts, both cultural and political, which not only encouraged the writing of history but were expressed (if indirectly) in its pages, and it is some of these tensions and conflicts that I propose to examine here.

* * *

Why did the first historical works in Persian appear in the Samanid period, and in their domains? Lutz Richter-Bernburg has argued that early Persian prose works (both translations and original compositions) represented a "linguistic Shuʿūbiyya" meant to legitimize the use of Persian in fields hitherto dominated by Arabic.[25] While this argument has its attractions, it oversimplies a complex phenomenon; and the fact is that Persian never *replaced* Arabic as a scholarly language. The same patrons supported "scholarly" writing

[23] See Cahen, "Historiography", 68–69.

[24] I wish to express my indebtedness to Professor Elton Daniel, for whose willingness to exchange views on this subject and for whose comments on earlier drafts of this essay I am deeply grateful.

[25] Richter-Bernburg puts the question thus: "Was Islam to remain a monolingual religion and civilization or could other languages become Muslim tongues of equal rank?" ("Linguistic Shuʿūbīya", 55). This is overstated, as the only "other language" seriously at issue in this early period was Persian. As S.M. Stern pointed out, "Of all the peoples incorporated into the Islamic empire the Persians possessed the strongest national identity"; this identity was not merely religious but secular, and included an ancient historical tradition (Stern, "Yaʿqūb the Coppersmith", 536–37).

in Arabic, and other types of writing in Persian (notably poetry, which falls outside the scope of Richter-Burnberg's discussion but is relevant to ours) which were clearly aimed at different audiences. Even if Bīrūnī's much later remark, that the Persian language "is fit only for the accounts of (Persian) kings and for entertaining stories told at nightly gatherings," is interpreted as dismissive of Persian as a scholarly language, we should beware of taking it too generally.[26] There was indeed a division of functions between the two languages, a division which was perhaps beginning to break down, but which never did so completely, as Persian came to be acknowledged as the chief language of communication within the Samanid domains, and Persian letters were enthusiastically patronized from the reign of Naṣr ibn Aḥmad (r. 301–331/914–943) onwards.[27] The *ʿulamāʾ* who produced the *fatwā* authorizing the translation into Persian of Ṭabarī's other great work, his Koranic *Tafsīr*, declared:

> Here, in this region, the language is Persian, and the kings of this realm are Persian kings.[28]

And since the rise to prominence of Persian as a literary medium went hand in hand with a renewal of interest in the Iranian past and in the revival of Iranian customs and traditions, it cannot be seen as merely a literary-linguistic phenomenon.[29]

Elton Daniel argues convincingly that the

> decision to "translate" Ṭabarī . . . almost certainly constituted an effort to propagate a state-sanctioned, 'official' ideology of Islamic history and dogma, presumably in defence of the Samanid regime,

---

[26] As Daniel notes, Bīrūnī's native tongue was Khwarazmian, and for him, as for speakers of other dialects, Arabic "would have levelled the playing field" ("The Samanid 'Translations' ", [17] n. 46). Bīrūnī's comment (which reflects the "Islamic" attitude to the Persian historical tradition discussed infra) was made in his *Kitāb al-ṣaydana*, written for the Ghaznavid Mawdūd (r. 432–440/1041–1048–9), and is preceded by this remark: "However much some vassals [*tawābiʿ*]—and especially the Jīlīs and Daylamīs among them—strove to clothe the government [*dawla*] in the robes of barbarism [*ʿujma*, which may, or may not, mean 'Persian'], they did not succeed in their aim" (*Book on Pharmacy*, 15; the editor's comments, introduction, 29, are completely off the mark).

[27] See the discussions by Daniel, "The Samanid 'Translations'", [5] and notes; Treadwell, *Political History*, 180.

[28] *Tarjuma-i Tafsīr-i Ṭabarī*, vol. 1, 5.

[29] See Daniel, "The Samanid 'Translations'"; Treadwell, *Political History*.

and was a part of a broader legitimating project.[30] The latter argument is strengthened by the inclusion in the History of extensive materials on Bahrām Chūbīn, the Samanids' putative ancestor, not found in Ṭabarī.[31] That this project was bound up with the desire to propagate an "official" and "correct" Islamic ideology is also convincing in view of the vigorous activities of Ismāʿīlī missionaries in the Samanid domains and the frequency of sectarian strife, especially in Khurasan, where the Karrāmiyya sect flourished.[32] The conversion of Naṣr ibn Aḥmad and various members of his court to Ismāʿīlism, and the appearance in Nūḥ ibn Naṣr's reign of a "false prophet" from Chaghaniyan who called himself the Mahdī, were matters both of recent history and of on-going concern; and if we are to credit Niẓām al-Mulk's account in the *Siyar al-mulūk* (the dating of which Daniel has convincingly corrected), Ismāʿīlī activities were again strong in the period just prior to Manṣūr ibn Nūḥ's accession.[33]

This period also saw the revival of the Iranian *Shāhnāma* tradition, represented by the prose *Shāhnāma* of Abū Manṣūr Maʿmarī compiled in 346/957, in the reign of ʿAbd al-Malik ibn Nūḥ (r. 343–350/954–961), for Abū Manṣūr Muḥammad ibn ʿAbd al-Razzāq Ṭūsī the governor of Nishapur (and later *sipahsālār* of Khurasan), by the unfinished metrical *Shāhnāma* begun by Daqīqī (d. ca. 366/977) at the behest of Nūḥ ibn Manṣūr, and culminating in Firdawsī's

---

[30] Daniel, "Manuscripts and Editions", 286; see also idem, "The Samanid 'Translations'", and Meisami, "The Past in Service of the Present".

[31] Precisely when the Samanids began to assert this genealogical claim is not known; but other newly arising dynasties made similar efforts, among them the Buyids (cf. Bīrūnī, *Chronology*, 44–51). See in general Bosworth, "The Heritage of Rulership"; Meisami, "The Past in Service of the Present", 249–51. I intend to discuss issues relating to the Samanid claim elsewhere.

[32] See Daniel, "The Samanid 'Translations' "; on the Karrāmiyya see Madelung, *Religious Trends*, 39–46; Bosworth, "The Rise of the Karāmiyyah".

[33] On this "false prophet", who attracted a large following and who was finally seized and executed by Abū ʿAlī Chaghānī on the orders of Nūḥ ibn Naṣr, see Gardīzī, *Zayn al-akhbār*, 87, 158; on Ismāʿīlī activities in the Samanid period see Niẓām al-Mulk, *Book of Government*, 212–218, 220–226; on the correction of Niẓām al-Mulk's dating see Daniel. "The Samanid 'Translations' " [7–8]; Treadwell, *Political History*, 202. To Niẓām al-Mulk's accounts may be added that of al-Baghdādī, who reports that after the death of the Buyid ʿAḍud al-Dawla in 373/983, the Fatimid caliph (al-ʿAzīz) approached various eastern princes attempting to gain their allegiance; he was generally rebuffed, and Nūḥ ibn Manṣūr had his missionaries executed. Al-Baghdādī also attributes Abū ʿAlī Sīmjūrī's revolt against Nūḥ in the 380s/990s to the Simjurid's "Ismāʿīlī sympathies" (*Moslem Schisms*, 129–30).

poem, begun in the last decades of Samanid rule.[34] The coexistence of two major, and to some extent mutually exclusive, authoritative historical narratives, one Iranian, one Islamic, suggests that despite their common language these different narratives were aimed at different audiences. But both undoubtedly lent support to the Samanids' (and others') legitimizing enterprise.

The Samanids ruled over a heterogenous population amongst whose constituent groups there was often considerable friction. One important group was the aristocratic *dihqān* class of Transoxania and Khurasan, from which the Samanids themselves had sprung, and who were, as the prose *Shāhnāma* affirms, the guardians of the Iranian historical tradition. Another was a mixed group made up largely of Arabs, descendants of the military conquerors and emigrants to the towns of Khurasan and Transoxania, and of Iranian converts to Islam associated with the Arabs as clients, whose culture was highly Arabized. A third consisted of the large numbers of Turks brought into the Samanid realm as slaves, many of whom rose to prominence and power in the Samanid court and military—so much so that from the reign of ʿAbd al-Malik ibn Nūḥ onwards, Turkish governors controlled both Transoxania and Khurasan. This period also saw mass conversions among the Turks of Transoxania.[35] All these groups (and other, smaller ones as well) were potential targets for various versions of history.

It should also be noted that, for those who wrote it, history had other ends, and that pragmatic concerns were accompanied by more general ethical ones. The interest in the ethics of kingship and government and in the lessons of history, seen in such Arabic historians as Masʿūdī and Miskawayh, was shared by their Persian counterparts, whatever type of history they wrote. What broader purposes history might serve was expressed by Miskawayh in the preface to his *Tajārib al-umam*, "The Experiences of the Nations":

> When I perused the accounts of peoples and the lives of kings, and read the histories of (diverse) lands . . . I found therein material which

[34] On this tradition, which includes earlier (now lost) works, by Masʿūdī Marvazī and others, whose precise dates are uncertain, see Hanaway, "The Iranian Epics"; Rosenthal, *Muslim Historiography*, 179–80; on its relation to Samanid legitimation see von Grunebaum, "Firdausi's Concept of History", 168–69.

[35] On the friction between various groups at the Samanid court see Daniel, "The Samanid 'Translations' ", [5–7]; on the conversions, see ibid., [6]; Treadwell, *Political History*, 233–36, and the references cited there.

> furnished an experience of matters whose like continues to be repeated, and whose similitudes and likenesses may be expected to recur: such as mention of the origins of states and the growth of kingdoms; of the intrusion of some flaw thereafter; of the efforts of those who repaired and put (this flaw) to rights . . . and of the negligence of those who ignored and rejected (such flaws) until they led to destruction and ruin. . . . For the world's affairs are similar, and its conditions resemble one another; and all that a man observes of this sort of (events) becomes as if it were his own experience.[36]

Miskawayh's observations bring us back to contemporary discussions on history mentioned earlier, discussions in which the classification of history among the sciences was indeed an issue, as history was seen as pertaining not merely to simple accounts of the past (*akhbār*) but to wisdom and to ethical philosophy.[37] Among those concerned with the status and the uses of history was a certain Ibn Farīghūn, a student of Abū Zayd al-Balkhī (d. 332/934) and (as Minorsky suggested) possibly a member of the Farighunid family who ruled the province of Juzjanan under the Samanids.[38] Ibn Farīghūn's short encyclopedia (or rather, manual for secretaries), the *Jawāmiʿ al-ʿulūm*, was written (in Arabic) in the very period, and in the very region, in which the first Persian histories appeared.[39] It was dedicated to the Muhtajid ruler of Chaghaniyan, Abū ʿAlī Aḥmad ibn Muḥammad ibn al-Muẓaffar, who had succeeded his father as governor of Khurasan for the Samanids in 329/940, rebelled against the Samanid ruler Nūḥ ibn Naṣr in the 330s/940s, and finally defected to the Buyids and died in Rayy in 344/955.[40] Abū Manṣūr ibn ʿAbd al-Razzāq Ṭūsī (who commissioned the prose *Shāhnāma*) ruled Nishapur on behalf of Abū ʿAlī Chaghānī around 334/945, and joined his rebellion; he, too, defected to the Buyids (twice), and met a sticky end in 350/962. Credited by the author of the prose *Shāhnāma* with the

---

[36] Miskawayh, *The Tajarib al-umam*, 1–2; on Miskawayh see Rosenthal, *Muslim Historiography*, 141–42; Arkoun, "Éthique et histoire".

[37] Cf. Arkoun. "Éthique et histoire".

[38] Minorsky, "Ibn Farīghūn", 191, and see 193–94 n. 3.

[39] I am grateful to Hans Hinrich Biesterfeldt for making available to me his *Habilitationsschrift*, *Die Zweige des Wissens*, which comprises an edition and study of Ibn Farīghūn's *Jawāmiʿ al-ʿulūm*, and to which the folio references refer.

[40] On Abū ʿAlī Chaghānī's revolt see Treadwell, *Political History*, 212–20; and see in general Bosworth, "The Rulers of Chaghāniyān", 4–10. As noted above (n. 1), the historian Sallāmī was a protégé of the Muhtajids.

recapture of Tus, traditionally ruled by his ancestors, Abū Manṣur Ṭūsī was also known to, and eulogized by, Firdawsī.[41]

Ibn Farīghūn stresses the importance of historical knowledge for court secretaries (who must "know the histories of the three nations", i.e., of the Persians and "the caliphs", presumably both Umayyad and Abbasid [f.18b]). Under the general rubric of "the science of wisdom" (*ʿilm al-ḥikma*) and the specific category (*jins*) of "knowledge of causes" (*ʿilm al-ʿilla*) he devotes a chapter to history (*ʿilm al-taʾrīkhāt* [f.68a]), a "species" (*nawʿ*) of such knowledge and one that is indispensable. History comprises

> the mention of famous events which occurred in past times or over extensive periods, such as a ruinous deluge, a destructive earthquake, epidemics, or famines which annihilate nations; the names of famous rulers in (the various) regions, their number, days, and the length of their reigns; and the transfer (of power) from one (house) to another [*intiqāl duwalihim*]; knowledge of the beginning of creation and its return (to its origins; i.e., the events surrounding the End of Days); and the physical and intellectual conditions of previous ages. But this (knowledge) may be contaminated by falsification because of remoteness in time. . . . Only that should be accepted (from informants) which is spoken of in books or in reliable accounts.

History also includes

> accounts of the Prophet's birth, his mission, his battles and his circumstances up to the time of his death, which are useful for political matters and warfare against enemies; knowledge of the lives of the caliphs of Quraysh, their conquests, administration, the revolts [*fitan*] that took place between those contending for leadership from among the Khawārij and from the time of the transfer of rule from the Umayyads to the Hashimites, so that these may provide object lessons [*ʿibar*] of the vicissitudes of time.

Knowledge of the battle days of the Arabs and of tribal matters, "in which may be found eloquent language and poetry," and of "the Persian books and biographies," is also of use in matters of politics and government and in dealing with the grievances of the populace. Accounts of famous rulers and their wise sayings, of "persons of

---

[41] On Abū Manṣūr's death see Minorsky, "Older Preface", 164–65; on his recapture of Tus see ibid., 179; on Firdawsī, see ibid., 166; and cf. *Shāhnāma*, vol. 1, 23–24.

noble birth, scholars, secretaries, poets, eloquent men," and in general of those who possess outstanding virtues, are also instructive.[42]

Ibn Farīghūn's statements reveal a concern for both the pragmatic and the ethical functions of history; while his reference to the transfer of rule as providing "object lessons of the vicissitudes of time" invokes the historical paradigm of the rise and fall of states. His discussion of history in a work meant to instruct functionaries of the Muhtajid court testifies (as does Sallāmī's *Taʾrīkh wulāt Khurāsān*) to the growing concern with the nature and function of historical writing in the Samanid domains. It was not long before that concern was translated (both literally and figuratively) into the writing of history in Persian.

The intertwined themes of the transfer of power and the ethics of kingship inform Persian histories regardless of whether they are based on the Iranian or on the Islamic narrative. Abū Manṣūr Maʿmarī states in the preface to the prose *Shāhnāma* (all that survives of that work),

> Four times kingship disappeared from Iran [and] strangers would come and seize the kingdom with humiliations. . . . Thus it was in the time of Ǧamshīd, at that of Naudhar, at that of Iskandar and so on.[43]

The pattern of recurrent dynastic cycles provides the unifying framework of Firdawsī's *Shāhnāma*: the Pīshdādīs give way to the Kayānids, the Ashkanians (dismissed in a scant twenty-odd lines) to the Sasanians. Each dynasty rises, prospers, and falls into decline, linked to the moral decline of the ruler; each Iranian ruler is replaced by a foreign one: Jamshīd by the evil Arab Zaḥḥāk, Darius by his half-brother the Greek Alexander, and the last Sasanian Yazdigird III by the Arabs and Islam.[44] In all but this final instance, legitimate Iranian rule is ultimately restored. But rather than seeing the end of Iranian sovereignty as the tragic end of Iranian history, it is not unlikely that Firdawsī envisioned a final cycle in which Islamic and Iranian sovereignty would be combined, as is suggested by the panegyrics to

---

[42] Biesterfeldt, *Die Zweige des Wissens*, vol. 2, 43–44 [= f.68a]. Compare Rosenthal, *Muslim Historiography*, 34–36, whose summary of this passage presents slight differences due to his use of different manuscripts (see ibid., 34–35 n. 5; Biesterfeldt, *Zweige*, vol. 1, 60–65.)

[43] Minorsky, "The Older Preface", 174–75.

[44] The decline of the Sasanians is linked not to Yazdigird, who attempted to revive the dynasty's fortunes, but to Khusraw II Parvīz, who turned to injustice and was murdered by his son, Shīruya.

Maḥmūd of Ghazna which punctuate the poem at crucial points.[45]

Bound up with the transfer of power is that of knowledge, linked to the memorializing function of discourse. Abū Manṣūr Maʿmarī states,

> As long as the world has existed, people have sought knowledge, held speech great, and considered it the greatest memorial.[46]

He recounts an apocryphal story concerning the caliph Maʾmūn, who, on the advice of his secretary Ibn al-Muqaffaʿ [sic!], was moved to emulate the example of Khusraw Anūshīrvān—who, by commanding that the book of *Kalīla wa-Dimna* be translated from "Indian" into Pahlavī, ensured himself a lasting memorial—by ordering that same work translated into Arabic. Maʾmūn's example, in turn, inspired the Samanid Naṣr ibn Aḥmad to have the work translated into Persian prose by his vizier Abū al-Fażl Balʿamī (the father of Abū ʿAlī) and then versified by Rūdakī. It was Naṣr ibn Aḥmad's example that led Ibn ʿAbd al-Razzāq Ṭūsī to order the compilation of the prose *Shāhnāma*,

> so that men of knowledge may look into it and find in it all about the wisdom of the kings, noblemen and sages, the royal arrangements, nature and behaviour, good institutions, justice and judicial norms, decisions and administration, the military organisation in battles, storming of cities, punitive expeditions and night attacks, as well as about marriages and respecting honour.[47]

---

[45] On the panegyrics see further Meisami, "The Past in Service of the Present", 258–61. The pattern of just rule—moral decline—rule by foreigners—restoration recapitulates that of both Zoroastrian and Islamic apocalypses; see infra.

[46] Minorsky, "The Older Preface", 167.

[47] Minorsky, "The Older Preface", 169. Maʾmūn plays an important role in the legitimating myth of the Samanids, as it was he who was said to have favored Asad ibn Sāmānkhudā and his four sons (cf. Gardīzī, *Ẓayn al-akhbār*, 146). Ibn al-Muqaffaʿ (who was, of course, long dead by Maʾmūn's reign) also serves as a legitimatory figure in connection with the original transfer of Persian learning into Arabic. The story recurs (without the anachronistic reference to Ibn al-Muqaffaʿ) in Firdawsī's *Shāhnāma*, where Maʾmūn—said to possess "the heart of a *mawbad* and the judgement of the Kayānids"—is again credited with having commissioned the translation of the *Kalīla wa-Dimna* (vol. 8, 254). Treadwell comments, "It can be no coincidence that an anthology of wisdom literature . . . was translated before Ṭabarī's works and the Ḥanafī creed [the *Sawād al-aʿẓam*]" (*Political History*, 183); but we should note both Naṣr ibn Aḥmad's extreme youth at his accession, and the fact that the *Kalīla wa-Dimna* was considered a work of advice to princes. Firdawsī attributes Khusraw II Parvīz's increased anxiety concerning Bahrām Chūbīn to his discovery that Bahrām has been reading the *Kalīla wa-Dimna* (*Shāhnāma*, vol. 9, 15–16).

Firdawsī reiterates these themes in a passage addressed to Maḥmūd:

> I shall make a memorial to him in this world that will never be hidden so long as men live. In this tale of kings of old, of great men and mounted warriors of the past, there are battles and feasts, good counsels and (wise) speech, that occurred in ancient times. That same wisdom, faith, virtue and judgement; that same guidance to the Hereafter; those things that they approved: all are of benefit today. They are the memorial of those great ones, the solace of their lives.[48]

Both the *Kalīla wa-Dimna* and the *Shāhnāma*, in their different ways, are works of instruction in the ways of kingship. Both represent Iranian traditions that passed through Arabic back into Persian; and both have clear implications with respect to an anticipated transfer of power to the east. The political implications of the transfer of knowledge are equally clear in the case of Balʿamī's Persian version of Ṭabarī, written at a time when relations between the Samanids and the Buyid-controlled caliphate had deteriorated to the point where the damage had become irreparable.[49] If, as Tarif Khalidi suggests, Ṭabarī's History presented the Islamic *umma* as "the prophetic heir of the Biblical tradition and the temporal heir of Persian dominion,"[50] Ṭabarī himself had relatively little to say about the Persians. But just as temporal power had passed from the Persians to the Muslims, so had their learning, as it was translated into Arabic. Now that learning was being re-translated into Persian; and what better way for the Samanids to symbolize their own appropriation of temporal power in the East than by the appropriation of Ṭabarī's authoritative work, "Persianized" with respect to both its perspective and its form? Indeed, in Balʿamī's comment (which is not in Ṭabarī) that after his destruction of the Barmakids Hārūn al-Rashīd lost respect and was, without those able *Persian* administrators, unable to govern his domains, we sense a foreshadowing of the decline of Abbasid power.[51]

Who were the audiences for these early histories in Persian, both of which, though they transmit different narratives, constitute (in the

---

[48] Firdawsī, *Shāhnāma*, vol. 6, 323, ll. 21–26.

[49] See Daniel, "The Samanid 'Translations'" 5–6; Treadwell, *Political History*, 216–17. I intend to discuss elsewhere the particular importance of Rayy, one of the most vigorously contested zones in the military conflicts between the Buyids and Samanids.

[50] Khalidi, *Arabic Historical Thought*, 79.

[51] Balʿamī, *Tārīkhnāma-i Ṭabarī*, vol. 2, 1199–2000; see also Meisami, "Masʿūdī on Love and the Fall of the Barmakids," 260–61.

loosest and most medieval sense of the word) translations?[52] Certainly not scholars who could read history in Arabic, or well-educated *ʿulamāʾ* and members of the secretarial class, who were schooled in both languages. It is more likely that they were targeted at other groups among the various political and ethnic constituencies ruled by the Samanids: in the case of Balʿamī's Ṭabarī, at those who did not know, had little interest in, or were not encouraged to learn, Arabic, except for such knowledge as was necessary for religious observance; in the case of works in the *Shāhnāma* tradition, at others who sought an alternative to the Islamic historical narrative. It is clearly significant that at the time the first histories appeared, Samanid sovereignty itself was being seriously challenged internally, both by aristocratic *dihqān*s such as Abū ʿAlī Chaghānī and Ibn ʿAbd al-Razzāq Ṭūsī, and by Turkish commanders such as the Simjurids. The prominence of the Turkish element in Samanid politics undoubtedly influenced the historical works in a variety of ways.

The Samanid rulers espoused differing cultural policies. Aḥmad ibn Ismāʿīl (295–302/907–914) was partial to Arabic and to the *ʿulamāʾ*; his murder by his Turkish slave-soldiers has been seen by some historians as a negative reaction to these policies.[53] Naṣr ibn Aḥmad favored Persian (and Ismāʿīlism); ʿAbd al-Malik ibn Nūḥ, Manṣūr's predecessor, cultivated Ibn ʿAbd al-Razzāq Ṭūsī (whom Niẓām al-Mulk accused of Ismāʿīlī leanings) and alienated the Turkish elements in the army.[54] History clearly played a prominent part in the cultural and political battles of the period. Rebellious *dihqān*s like Abū Manṣūr Ṭūsī and Abū ʿAlī Chaghānī, and Persianizing Samanid princes like Naṣr ibn Aḥmad and ʿAbd al-Malik ibn Nūḥ, may well have sought to legitimate their claims to rule in the east through promoting Persian historical traditions, as well as Persian letters. The genealogy constructed for Abū Manṣūr Ṭūsī in the prose *Shāhnāma* was certainly meant both to bolster his claims to the rule

[52] This is perhaps less true of Firdawsī's poem than of Balʿamī's Ṭabarī; yet it could be argued that the versification of prose accounts drawn from various sources (quite probably in different languages) constitutes a type of *translatio* in the sense both of transfer of knowledge and of translation.

[53] See Treadwell, *Political History*, 142, citing the opinion of Ḥamd Allāh Qazvīnī.

[54] See Daniel, "The Samanid 'Translations'", [17], n. 47. The possible links between Ismāʿīlī leanings and the propagation of Persian cultural and historical traditions lie beyond the scope of this essay, but I intend to pursue this line of inquiry elsewhere.

of Tus (and, possibly, of Khurasan) and to counter those of his Simjurid rivals.[55]

The issue of Turkish ethnicity has often been raised in connection with Maḥmūd of Ghazna's cool reception of Firdawsī's *Shāhnāma*. This coolness is however shared by the court poets of the Ghaznavids and early Seljuqs, as well as by the Ghaznavid historian Bayhaqī, and it is likely that the real reasons lie elsewhere.[56] There is no reason to think that Maḥmūd's Turkish *ghulāms* would not have enjoyed tales of the heroic deeds of warriors both Iranian and Turanian.[57] But Firdawsī's work was conceived under the Samanids, at a time both of intense rivalry between Persian and Turkish elements in the Samanid court and of attempts at *rapprochement* between them, at the forefront of which was the vizier Abū ʿAlī Balʿamī.

Balʿamī, "Persophile in culture" but with close connections with the Turkish generals, and a staunch foe of heterodoxy, was probably the real motivating force behind the translation of both Ṭabarī's History and his *Tafsīr*, works so closely related that they must be considered as forming a single project.[58] That the commission for both was delivered via Manṣūr ibn Nūḥ's powerful chamberlain Fāʾiq al-Khāṣṣa lends strength to the argument that both were designed to unite heterogeneous elements under the banner of Persian Islam. Balʿamī's unified narrative of Islamic history (and of non-Islamic prehistory), in which he did away with Ṭabarī's *isnād*s and restructured

[55] For this genealogy, which traces Abū Manṣur's descent to a commander of Khusraw II Parvīz (and ultimately to Kayūmars), see Minorsky, "Older Preface", 176–79. Bīrūnī views both this claim and that of the Buyids (to descent from Bahrām V Gūr) as forgeries (*Chronology*, 45–46).

[56] See Meisami, "The Past in Service of the Present", 261–64. Ibn al-Athīr states that when (in 420/1029) Maḥmūd took Rayy from the Buyid Majd al-Dawla (who had sought Maḥmud's help against his rebellious army), he summoned that prince and asked him, "Have you not read the *Shāhnāma*, which is the history of the Persians, and Ṭabarī's History, which is that of the Muslims?" When Majd al-Dawla replied in the affirmative, Maḥmūd responded, "Your situation is not that of one who has read them" (i.e., who has understood their lesson) (*al-Kāmil*, vol. 9, 371–72). Even if the report is apocryphal it points both to the importance of history in the education of princes and to the perception of the existence of two distinct historical traditions.

[57] Cf. Mélikoff, *Abū Muslim*, 30–31. The Turkic Qarakhānids—rivals both of the Samanids and of their Ghaznavid successors—traced *their* descent to Afrāsiyāb, the Turkish ruler and enemy of the Kayānids, and an important figure in the *Shāhnāma*. The earliest version of the *Abū Muslim Nāma* was attributed to one Abū Ṭāhir Ṭūsi, "a storyteller in the entourage of sultan Maḥmūd of Ghazna" (ibid., 31, and see 31–36).

[58] See Daniel, "The Samanid 'Translations'", [6–8].

his discrete accounts, omitting some, correcting others, and adding yet others, leads directly, if implicitly, to the Samanids.[59] His style is simple, straightforward, and entertaining, rather than scholarly, and thus accessible to a broad and relatively unsophisticated audience. This audience might have included Turkish members of the court and military; Turkish *ghulāms* being trained up to hold important and sensitive positions; and recent or potential Turkish converts. All would have been presented with an inspiring, as well as ideologically correct, version of the past.

Daniel argues that the translations were designed

> to reshape [Ṭabarī's] texts and in effect to discourage the reading of the Arabic originals. In that sense, [they] constituted a virtual declaration of political and cultural autonomy conceived as part of a futile effort to save the Samanid polity.[60]

He further suggests that this effort must have seemed especially crucial at a time when apocalyptic prophecies of the imminent end of the world (and, presumably, of the Samanids) were rife,[61] by insisting that "no one, not even the Prophet Muḥammad himself, actually possessed . . . knowledge" of the date of the end of the world or of the planetary arrangements that would signal it, the Ṭabarī translations served both

> to discredit the Ismāʿīlī cosmological schemes being developed at this time and to reassure readers that the end of the world, and thus the collapse of Samanid authority, was not imminent.[62]

In sum, they

> provided standardized, officially approved, and carefully designed religious texts which could be used to instruct unsophisticated believers in a uniform way and avoid the dangers of ad hoc responses to

[59] Not only does Balʿamī not mention the Samanids, but he omits Ṭabarī's few references to them, including—signally—mention of early Samanid victories over the steppe Turks (see Daniel, "The Samanid 'Translations'", [2]).

[60] Daniel, "The Samanid 'Translations'", [5, 11].

[61] See Daniel, "The Samanid 'Translations'", [11]; Treadwell, *Political History*, 207–08.

[62] Daniel, "The Samanid 'Translations'", [11]. A passage in the *Tafsīr* translation (vol. 1, 197; attributed to Ṭabarī, presumably without basis) refers to the then-current *ḥadīth* that the signs of the Hour will appear 400 years after the Prophet's death. The approach of the year 400/1009–10 is also alluded to by Firdawsī (see n. 65 below).

heterodoxy by local religious leaders. At the same time, they served as important tools for the further Persianization of frontier areas and the acculturation of the new Turkish military elite, and this contribution to the forging of Turko-Persian culture may well be their greatest legacy.[63]

If the Persian versions of Ṭabarī were meant to defuse (or to modify) apocalyptic prophecies in circulation at the time, they did so with a clear eye on the content of these prophecies, which included not only mention of the signs of the End of Days but of the events which would precede them. Zoroastrian apocalypses predicted the coming of a "king from the east", at the end of the fourth Zoroastrian millennium, who would restore justice (along with Persian religion and Persian rule) to the earth; Ismāʿīlīs preached the advent of the Mahdī.[64] Such predictions were clearly suited to serve both Buyid and Samanid claims, as well as those of rebellious vassals, *dihqān*s and Turkish governors alike.[65]

Thus both historical narratives, Iranian and Islamic, played a part in the "eschatological politics" of the Samanids, as they strove both for autonomy in the east and against Buyid claims which, too, drew on Iranian traditions.[66] But if works in the *Shāhnāma* tradition were

---

[63] Daniel, "The Samanid 'Translations"', [12].

[64] See e.g. Māshā'allāh, *Astrological History*, 113–14, 121–22 (as edited and expanded by Ibn Hibinta, writing at the court of the Buyid ʿAḍud al-Dawla); Ibn al-Nadīm, *Fihrist*, vol. 1, 469 (in his discussion of the Ismāʿīlīs).

[65] This is to oversimplify a complex issue which I intend to treat in more detail elsewhere. Among the figures identified as the "king from the east" are Abū Muslim and Bahrām Chūbīn, who are often conflated; Abū Muslim, moreover, was said to be in concealment along with the Mahdī (see Destrée, "Quelques reflexions"; on Bahrām Chūbīn see *EIr*, art. "Bahrām Čōbīn"). According to Treadwell, the Qāḍī ʿAbd al-Jabbār states that Muḥammad ibn Aḥmad Nasafī, the Ismāʿīlī *dāʿī* who converted Naṣr ibn Aḥmad and various of his courtiers, "told Naṣr about the appearance in the *maghrib* of the *mahdī* who could bring the dead to life" (implying a reference to the Fatimid al-Qā'im; see *Political History*, 205–06; cf. Ibn al-Nadīm, Fihrist, vol. 1, 467–68). Since Nasafī (initially at least) did not support Fatimid claims (see Daftary, *The Ismāʿīlīs*, 235–41), this probably represents anti-Fatimid propaganda. Firdawsī refers to the approach of the year 400/1009–10 in recounting Daqīqī's prophecy of great triumphs for a future "ruler of the East", identified by Firdawsī with Maḥmūd (*Shāhnāma*, vol. 6, 65, ll. 6–7). An important source for the prophecy of Rustam Farrukhzād in the *Shāhnāma* is the *Zarātusht-nāma*, a New Persian Zoroastrian apocalypse in verse by one Kay-Kā'ūs of Rayy, which François de Blois suggests may have been written in 347 Y./978 (*Persian Literature*, 173).

[66] Early in their rule the Buyids adopted Iranian imperial customs and titulature (cf. Madelung, "The Assumption"). Later, local Buyid princes sponsored various works based on Iranian historical traditions (as did other local princes as well; cf. Hanaway, "The Iranian Epics".

meant to bolster the aspirations of Persianizing Samanid princes (who might also see a way thereby of diminishing the pretensions of their Turkish commanders), as well as of *dihqāns* seeking to carve out for themselves independent enclaves of power in remote regions like Chaghaniyan, or even in Khurasan, the very heart of Īrānshahr[67] (and there are indications in Firdawsī's poem that such hopes once flourished), these aspirations were ultimately frustrated with the fall of the Samanids and the transfer of rule to the Ghaznavids.[68] This was to have a momentous effect on subsequent historical writing, as Maḥmūd, the *sulṭān-i ghāzī*, was celebrated by poets and historians alike as the Islamic ruler *par excellence*.[69]

* * *

In the end, it was the Islamic narrative which triumphed; for despite the incorporation of Iranian history into more general histories, the main focus of subsequent historiography in the pre-Mongol period is dynastic history. Historians, first of the Ghaznavids and later of the Seljuqs, as well as of regional rulers (e.g. of Sistan, Kirman, Tabaristan) addressed themselves increasingly to the theme of the transfer of power between Islamic dynasties, seen in Islamic terms. Abū Naṣr ʿUtbī's Arabic history of the Ghaznavids up to

---

[67] See the vision of Īrānshahr presented in the preface to the prose *Shāhnāma* (*Minorsky*, "Older Preface", 171–72).

[68] The historians invariably treat this transfer of power as legitimate. The Samanid realms were in chaos, and they themselves unable to produce a viable candidate for rule (the last three Samanid rulers came to the throne as minors, and were the tools either of their viziers or of their Turkish commanders); Maḥmūd is thus celebrated as having restored order to these troubled domains. ʿUtbī claims it was the *dihqāns* themselves who, dissatisfied with a series of ineffectual Samanid rulers, felt it was time for a change of *dawla* and approached both Maḥmūd and the Qarakhanid ruler Bughrā Khān for assistance (see *al-Taʾrīkh al-Yamīnī*, vol. 1, 163–64; Treadwell, *Political History*, 249–50).

[69] Maḥmūd appears not to have been interested in presenting himself as an *Iranian* sovereign in the old tradition, perhaps because such an image had little relevance in his home territories of Ghazna, and none to his self-presentation as the loyal vassal of the caliph (see Bosworth, "Maḥmūd of Ghazna", 87–89). Interest in Iranian history seems to have declined at this time; an exception is Thaʿālibī's *Ghurar akhbār mulūk al-Furs* (a general history of which only the section on pre-Islamic Iranian monarchy survives), which exhibits many parallels with materials in the *Shāhnāma*, but breaks with the *Shāhnāma* tradition stylistically by being written in the "secretarial style" (*Histoire des rois des perses*, l). It was composed at the behest of Maḥmūd's brother Abū al-Muẓaffar Naṣr, governor of Khurasan, suggesting that there perhaps Iranian traditions of kingship still aroused sympathetic responses.

411/1020 (translated into Persian around the beginning of the 7th/13th century) begins with the onset of the decline of the Samanids in the late 360s/970s and the rise to power of Sabuktigīn, which sets the stage for the transfer of power to the Ghaznavids.[70] While ʿAbd al-Ḥayy Gardīzī's *Zayn al-akhbār* (ca. 444/1053) is ostensibly a "general" history, Gardīzī's true interest is in the Ghaznavids, to whom all previous history leads, and in presenting Maḥmūd's reign as the shining pinnacle of all that preceded.[71] Abū al-Fażl Bayhaqī's history of the Ghaznavids (of which only those volumes treating the reign of Masʿūd I survive, but which was widely used by later writers) intended to provide benefit and instruction to "kings and other than kings" and to serve as an admonition to the wise[72]—is particularly concerned with the transfer of power: how it came to the Ghaznavids, as well as how it was lost by Masʿūd. Bayhaqī's view of history is resolutely Islamic: the achievements of such rulers as Alexander and Ardashīr pale in comparison to those of the Ghaznavids, who have "surpassed both in all things," and "were the greatest on the face of the earth."[73] Their rise to power was a sign of God's favor to "the just prince Sabuktigīn", whom He guided "from unbelief to faith", and "elevated him so that from the root of that blessed tree branches sprang forth much stronger than the root. With those branches He adorned Islam, and bound to them the power of the caliphs of the Prophet of Islam."[74]

Like Miskawayh (whose influence is clear), Bayhaqī is convinced of the ethical value of history; and like his predecessor he is a partisan of "serious" history.[75] The Iranian historical tradition plays virtually no part in his work.[76]

---

[70] See ʿUtbī, *al-Tārīkh al-Yamīnī*, vol. 1, 102. Treadwell suggests that ʿUtbī, writing in Arabic and (as he himself states) "for the people of Iraq", intended his work as anti-Buyid propaganda aimed at the caliphal court in Baghdad (*Political History*, 10).

[71] Written for Maḥmūd's sole surviving son, ʿAbd al-Rashīd (r. 441–444/1050–1053), who had recently come to power, Gardīzī clearly sought both to legitimate his rule and to encourage his emulation of Maḥmūd's achievements. On ʿAbd al-Rashīd see Bosworth, *The Later Ghaznavids*, 41–47. Gardīzī's history breaks off in the reign of Mawdūd, suggesting that intervening events in ʿAbd al-Rashīd's reign prevented its completion.

[72] Cf. Bayhaqī, *Tārīkh*, 118; 212; 451.

[73] Bayhaqī, *Tārīkh*, 112, 114.

[74] Bayhaqī, *Tārīkh*, 116.

[75] See Bayhaqī, *Tārīkh*, 903–06; and cf. Miskawayh, *Tajarib*, 5.

[76] When it does, it is often to provide negative examples; see e.g. the story of Anūshīrvān's imprisonment and subsequent execution of his vizier Buzurgmihr (which does not figure in the *Shāhnāma*) (*Tārīkh*, 425–28).

For the Turkish Seljuqs, historical continuity was never a major legitimatory topos; they could claim neither genealogical links with the past, as did the Samanids and Buyids, nor the assumption of the mantle of power from a burnt-out dynasty, as did the Ghaznavids. They were, more or less, *sui generis*, and had no connection with either the Iranian or the Islamic past. Their primary means of legitimation was religious, expressed through their patronage of *ʿulamāʾ*, seen perhaps most substantially and to most long lasting effect in the institutionalization of the *madrasa* system by the vizier Niẓām al-Mulk. This is evident in the two major histories of the dynasty, Ẓahīr al-Dīn Nīshāpūrī's *Saljūqnāma* and Muḥammad ibn ʿAlī Rāvandī's *Rāḥat al-ṣudūr wa-āyat al-surūr* (largely based on Nīshāpūrī). Nīshāpūrī's history ends with the accession of Ṭughrïl ibn Arslān, a minor "transferred from the cradle to the throne;"[77] Rāvandī's continues up to the death of Ṭughrïl and the fall of the Great Seljuqs.[78] While different in style and method—Nīshāpūrī's is a concise, unadorned account of events, although it is not devoid of comments on their significance;[79] Rāvandī's style is highly rhetorical and marked by an abundance of interpolations drawn from a variety of sources (among them, notably, the *Shāhnāma*)—both share common concerns.

Both Nīshāpūrī and Rāvandī attribute the Seljuqs' rise to power and initial prosperity to piety, religious patronage and good works, and their downfall to the spread of irreligion and heresy, the declining repute of the *ʿulamāʾ*, and the injustice, immorality and corruption of officials and military commanders. Rāvandī's overriding ethical concerns are emphasized by his rhetorical style and his use of interpolations, in particular those drawn from the *Shāhnāma*, which he clearly viewed as a source of perennial wisdom on matters of kingship and ethics. But he is uninterested in the poem's narrative content; his achievement is to reintegrate the *Shāhnāma* tradition into historiography, not as narrative, but as wisdom literature. His

---

[77] Nīshāpūrī, *Saljūqnāma*, 83.

[78] On the circumstances of the work's composition see Rāvandī, *Rāḥat al-ṣudūr*, 57–63; it is described by its author as a compilation of edifying prose and verse (Rāvandī apparently intended to write a separate history of the Saljuqs; ibid., 44). On this work see further Meisami, "Rāvandī's *Rāḥat al-ṣudūr*".

[79] See for example his observations on the series of military clashes and deaths of important personages which preceded the death of sultan Arslān ibn Ṭughrïl and which, for him, clearly signalled the decline of the dynasty (*Saljūqnāma*, 81–82).

political motives are also clear, as he laments the fate of his patron Ṭughrïl and the widespread suffering in Iraq and Fars at the hands of the Khwārazmian invaders and exhorts the book's dedicatee, the Seljuq ruler of Konya Kaykhusraw ibn Qïlïj Arslān, to restore the fortunes of the Seljuqs and drive out the invaders.[80]

* * *

Successive generations of Persian historians wrestled with the question of how to create a "usable past" (or pasts)—Iranian, Islamic, dynastic, or universal. Their answers were different; the differences have much to do with the purposes for which, and the audiences for whom, they wrote. The purposes ranged from the politically and ideologically pragmatic to the ethically edifying and the rhetorically impressive, and often combined elements of all of these; the audiences changed over time, so that by the end of the Seljuq period history was being written primarily by bureaucrats for other bureaucrats, as continued to be the case in the post-Mongol period.[81]

The ultimate purpose of writing history, as our authors never tire of stating, is to memorialize, and the ultimate audience, posterity. For while historical works were written in the light of present, often pressing, concerns, they were also intended as monuments both to the rulers they commemorate and to their authors. It thus seems appropriate to conclude with Firdawsī's words to Maḥmūd of Ghazna:

> O prince, I have performed a service which will remain my memorial in this world. Prosperous buildings become ruined by rain and the heat of the sun; but I have laid in verse the foundation of a lofty palace which will not be harmed by wind and rain. Years will pass over this book, and it will be read continually by all who possess wisdom, and who will praise the world-ruling monarch. . . .[82]

[80] Rāvandī, *Rāḥat al-ṣudūr*, 403.
[81] Cf. Luther, "Islamic Rhetoric".
[82] *Shāhnāmah*, vol. 5, 338–39, ll. 63–67.

Bibliography

Ahmad, M. Hilmy M., "Some Notes on Arabic Historiography During the Zengid and Ayyubid Periods (521/1127–648/1250)." In *Historians of the Middle East*, eds. Bernard Lewis and P.M. Holt, 79–97, London, 1962.

Al-Azmeh, Aziz, *Ibn Khaldun*, London, 1990 [1982].

Arkoun, Mohammed, "Éthique et histoire d'après les *Tajarib al-Umam*," in *Atti del Terzo Congresso di Studi Arabici e Islamici, Ravello 1966*, Naples, 1967, 83–112.

al-Baghdādī, ʿAbd al-Qāhir ibn Ṭāhir, *Moslem Schisms and Sects* (*Al-Fark Bain Al-Firak*. part 2, trans. Abraham S. Halkin, Tel Aviv, 1935.

Balʿamī, Abū ʿAlī, *Tārīkhnāma-i Ṭabarī, bakhsh-i chāp-nāshuda*, ed. Muḥammad Rawshan, 3 vols., Tehran, 1366/1987.

Bayhaqī, Abu'l-Fażl, *Tārīkh-i Bayhaqī*, ed. ʿAlī Akbar Fayyāẓ, Mashhad, 1971.

Biesterfeldt, Hans Hinrich, *Die Zwiege Des Wissens: Theorie und Klassifikation der Wissenschaften im Mittelalterlichen Islam in der Darstellung Des Ibn Farīgūn*, Habilitationsschrift, Bochum, n.p., n.d.

al-Bīrūnī, Abū Rayḥān, *Al-Biruni's Book on Pharmacy and Materia Medica*, ed. and trans. Hakim Muhammad Said, Karachi, 1973.

———, *The Chronology of Ancient Nations*, trans. C.E. Sachau, London, 1879.

Bosworth, C.E., "The Heritage of Rulership in Early Islamic Iran and the Search for Dynastic Connections with the Past. *Iran* 9 (1973), 51–62.

———, *The Later Ghaznavids: Splendour and Decay; the Dynasty in Afghanistan and Northern India, 1040–1186*, New York, 1977.

———, "Mahmud of Ghazna in Contemporary Eyes and in Later Persian Literature," *Iran* 4 (1966), 85–92.

———, "The Rise of the Karāmiyyah in Khurasan." *The Muslim World* 50 (1960), [6]–14.

———, "The Rulers of Chaghāniyān in Early Islamic Times," *Iran* 19 (1981), 1–20.

Breisach, Ernest, ed. *Classical Rhetoric and Medieval Historiography*, Studies in Medieval Culture, vol. 19, Kalamazoo, 1985.

Bulliet, Richard W., *Islam: The View from the Edge*, New York, 1994.

Cahen, Claude, "The Historiography of the Seljuqid Period." In *Historians of the Middle East*, eds. Bernard Lewis and P.M. Holt, London, 1962, 59–78.

Daftary, Farhad, *The Ismāʿīlīs: Their History and Doctrines*, Cambridge, 1992 [1990].

Daniel, Elton L., "Manuscripts and Editions of Balʿamī's *Tarjamah-i Tārīkh-i Ṭabarī*." *JRAS* 00 (1990), 282–321.

———, "The Samanid 'Translations' of Ṭabarī." Unpublished conference paper, University of St. Andrews, 1995.

Daryaee, Touraj, "National History or Keyanid History? the Nature of Sasanid Zoroastrian Historiography," *Iranian Studies* 28 (1995), 129–41.

de Blois, François, *Persian Literature: A Bio-Bibliographical Survey*, Vol. 5 part 1: *Poetry to Ca. A.D. 1100*, London, 1992.

Destrée, Annette, "Quelques reflexions sur le héros des récits apocalyptiques persans et sur le mythe de la Ville de cuivre," in *La Persia nel Medioevo* (= *Quaderno dell'Accademia Nazionale dei Lincei* 160 (1971)), 639–54.

Firdawsī, Abū al-Qāsim, *Shāhnāma*, edited by E. Bertels', 9 vols., Moscow, 1962–71.

Gardīzī, ʿAbd al-Ḥayy, *Zayn al-akhbār*, ed. ʿAbd al-Ḥayy Ḥabībī, Tehran, 1968.

Gibb, H.A.R. "Tarikh," in *Studies on the Civilization of Islam*, eds. Stanford J. Shaw and William R. Polk, Princeton, 1982 [1962], 108–37.

Hanaway, William L., "The Iranian Epics," in *Heroic Epic and Saga*, ed. Felix J. Oinas, Bloomington and London, 1978, 76–98.

Ibn al-Athīr, ʿIzz al-Dīn, *al-Kāmil fī al-taʾrīkh*, ed. C.J. Tornberg, 12 vols., Beirut, 1965–7 [Leiden, 1851–1876].

Ibn al-Nadīm. *The Fihrist of Al-Nadīm; a Tenth-century Survey of Muslim Culture*, ed. and trans. Bayard Dodge, 2 vols., New York, 1970.
Khalidi, Tarif, *Arabic Historical Thought in the Classical Period*, Cambridge, 1994.
Lanham, Richard A., *The Motives of Eloquence: Literary Rhetoric in the Renaissance*, New Haven, 1976.
Lateiner, Donald, *The Historical Method of Herodotus*, Toronto, 1989.
Lazard, Gilbert, *La Langue des plus anciens monuments de la prose persane, Études linguistiques*, 2. Paris, 1963.
———, "The Rise of the New Persian Language." In *The Cambridge History of Iran*, Vol. 4: *From the Arab Invasion to the Saljuqs*, ed. Richard N. Frye, Cambridge, 1975, 595–632.
Lewis, Bernard, and P.M. Holt, eds., *Historians of the Middle East*, London, 1962.
Luther, K. Allin, "Bayhaqi and the Later Seljuq Historians: Some Comparative Remarks," in *Yādnāma-i Abū al-Fażl Bayhaqi*, Mashhad, 1971, 14–33.
———, "Chancery Writing as a Source of Constraints on History Writing in the Sixth and Seventh Centuries of the Hijra." Unpublished Paper, University of Michigan, 1977.
———, "Islamic Rhetoric and the Persian Historians, 1000–1300 A.D.," in *Studies in Near Eastern Culture and History in Memory of Ernest T. Abdel-Massih*, Ann Arbor, 1990, 96–98.
Madelung, Wilfred, "The Assumption of the Title Shāhanshāh by the Būyids and 'The Reign of the Daylam (*Dawlat Al-Daylam*)'", reprinted from *Journal of Near Eastern Studies* 28 (1969), 84–108, 168–183, in *Religious and Ethnic Movements in Medieval Islam*, London, 1992.
———, *Religious Trends in Early Islamic Iran*, Columbia Lectures on Iranian Studies, no. 4, Albany, 1988.
Māshā'allāh, *The Astrological History of Māshā'allāh*, eds. E.S. Kennedy and David Pingree, Cambridge, Mass., 1971.
Mélikoff, Irène, *Abū Muslim le "porte-hache" du Khorasan dans la tradition épique Turco-iranienne*, Paris, 1962.
Meisami, Julie Scott, "Mas'ūdī on Love and the Fall of the Barmakids," *JRAS* (1989), 252–77.
———, "The Past in Service of the Present: Two Views of History in Medieval Persia," *Poetics Today* 14 (1993), 247–75.
———, "Rāvandī's *Rāḥat al-ṣudūr*: History or Hybrid?" *Edebiyat* n.s. 5 (1994), 181–215.
Minorsky, Vladimir, "Ibn Farīghūn and the *Ḥudud al-'ālam*" in *A Locust's Leg: Studies in Honour of S.H. Taqizadeh*, London, 1962, 189–96.
———, "The Older Preface to the *Shāh-nāma*," in *Studi Orientalistici in Onore de Giorgio Levi Della Vida*, vol. 2, Rome 1956, 159–79.
Miskawayh, The *Tajarib al-umam. Vol. 1, to A.H. 37*, ed. Leone Caetani, Leiden and London, 1909.
Nīshāpūrī, Ẓahīr al-Dīn, *Sāljūqnāma*, ed. Ismā'īl Afshār, Tehran, 1953.
Niẓām al-Mulk, *The Book of Government or Rules for Kings*, trans. Hubert Darke, London, 1978 [1960].
Partner, Nancy F., "The New Cornuficius: Medieval History and the Artifice of Words", in *Classical Rhetoric and Medieval Historiography*, ed. Ernst Breisach, Studies in Medieval Culture, vol. 19, Kalamazoo 1985, 5–59.
Plass, Paul, *Wit and the Writing of History; the Rhetoric of Historiography in Imperial Rome*, Madison, 1985.
Rāvandī, Muḥammad ibn 'Alī, *The Ráḥat-uṣ-ṣudúr wa áyat-as-surúr*, ed. Muhammad Iqbal, Leiden and London, 1921.
Richter-Bernburg, Lutz, "Linguistic Shu'ūbīya and Early Neo-Persian Prose," *JAOS* 94 (1974), 55–64.

Rosenthal, Franz, *A History of Muslim Historiography*, 2nd revised ed., Leiden, 1968 [1952].
Spuler, Bertold, "The Evolution of Persian Historiography", in *Historians of the Middle East*, eds. Bernard Lewis and P.M. Holt, London, 1962, 126–32.
Stern, S.M., "Yaʿqūb the Coppersmith and Persian National Sentiment," in *Iran and Islam: in Memory of the Late Vladimir Minorsky*, ed. C.E. Bosworth, Edinburgh, 1971, 535–55.
Tarjuma-i Tafsīr-i Tabarī, ed. Ḥabīb Yaghmāʾī, 3d ed., 7 vols., Tehran, 1367/1978.
al-Thaʿālibī, Abū Manṣūr, *Histoire des rois des perses*, ed. and trans. H. Zotenberg, Paris, 1900.
Treadwell, W.L., *The Political History of the Sāmānid State*, D. Phil., University of Oxford, 1991.
al-ʿUtbī, Abū Naṣr, *al-Taʾrīkh al-Yamīnī*, with the commentary of Shaykh Aḥmad al-Manīnī, 2 vols., Cairo 1286/1869.
von Grunebaum, G.E., "Firdausi's Concept of History", in *Islam: The Making of a Cultural Tradition*, London, 1955, 168–84.
———, *Medieval Islam*, 2nd ed., Chicago, 1962.
Waldman, Marilyn Robinson, *Toward a Theory of Historical Narrative: A Case Study in Perso-Islamicate Historiography*, Columbus, 1980.
Ward, John O., "Some Principles of Rhetorical Historiography in the Twelfth Century", in *Classical Rhetoric and Medieval Historiography*, ed. Ernest Breisach, Studies in Medieval Culture, vol. 19, Kalamazoo, 1965, 103–65.

REFLECTIONS ON MONGOL COMMUNICATIONS IN THE ILKHANATE

David Morgan

The governmental and administrative institutions of the Mongol empire have received a good deal of attention in recent years. While at one time it may have seemed reasonable to regard that empire as a polity the government of which the Mongols, with their limited experience of sedentary societies, left largely in the hands of non-Mongol bureaucrats—Khitans, Uighurs, Chinese, Persians—it is now beginning to be realised that the Mongols have been underrated. Admittedly they got off to a somewhat unpromising start, establishing a record in terms of wanton massacre and destruction which stood unchallenged for some time—at any rate until the era of Tīmūr, even if it no longer seems so impressive by twentieth century standards. But few historians would now maintain that the Mongol phenomenon is simply one of military achievement, barbarity and general vandalism. It seems merely implausible to suppose that the Mongols could not only have conquered the enormous swathe of territory from Korea to Hungary, but have retained and ruled it for at least a century, and in parts for very much longer, if they were totally uninterested in the actual practice of government and administration. The notion of the Mongols as a people who concerned themselves exclusively with hunting, herding, warfare and the other traditional activities of the steppe peoples, while leaving the business of government, and especially tax collection, to their Persian or Chinese bureaucrats, has perhaps had its day.

That this is so is partly due to a greater appreciation of the nature and limitations of the source material available to the historian of the Mongol Empire. Put simply, the problem is that we know next to nothing about the Mongols from the Mongols themselves. Most of our principal sources are the work of non-Mongols—whether from conquered or enemy peoples—and in the former case, mainly from the pens of bureaucrats. There is a conspicuous exception: the *Secret History of the Mongols*. If this remarkable and strange document had not chanced to survive, we should have had very little direct evidence of the Mongol perspective on their world. But the *Secret History*, invaluable though it is, reaches no further in time than the latter part of the reign of the Great Khan Ögedei (d. 1241). From that point we are dependent, for good and ill, on what non-Mongols tell us.

Although Mongol institutions have been much more intensively studied than used to be the case, it is curious that what seems, by common consent, to have been their most unqualified institutional success has been largely ignored. This is the communications network, generally referred to in the Persian sources as the *Yām* (Mongolian: *jam*). Most general studies of the Mongol Empire have some discussion of it,[1] but I know of only one detailed monograph on the subject: it remains useful, but it was written over forty years ago, and it is concerned only with China.[2] It is perhaps hardly necessary to point out that since the Mongols ruled the most extensive land empire in the history of the world, an efficient system of communications, and indeed some way of obtaining speedy intelligence, was an absolute necessity if that empire was to have any prospect of being held together. Even the origins of the *Yām* system remain shrouded in obscurity, and although the Chinese end of the empire has been studied, little has been written about how the system operated in other parts of the Mongol realm such as the Ilkhanate.

It has been customary to say that we have no certain knowledge of what communications arrangements Chinggis Khan himself may have made (though he must presumably have had some, even if only *ad hoc*, arrangements), in that the date we are given for the beginnings of the *Yām* system is 1234, well into the reign of the second Great Khan, Ögedei.[3] The authority for this is twofold: the *Secret History of the Mongols* and the *Jāmiʿ al-tawārīkh* of Rashīd al-Dīn. That authority is certainly weighty, given the status of the *Secret History* and the fact that Rashīd al-Dīn is presumably here drawing on the now lost Mongolian sources to which we know he had access. His account of the beginnings of the *Yām* system occurs in a part of the *Jāmiʿ al-tawārīkh* in which he is content for the most part to follow

[1] See e.g. J.J. Saunders, *The History of the Mongol Conquests*, 65; D.O. Morgan, *The Mongols*, 103–7; R. Marshall, *Storm from the East*, 67–8. There is also, rather unexpectedly, a chapter on the *Yām* in F. Dvornik, *Origins of Intelligence Services*, 262–99.

[2] P. Olbricht, *Das Postwesen in China unter der Mongolenherrschaft im 13. und 14. Jahrhundert.*

[3] See e.g. Morgan, *The Mongols*, 104.

the earlier historian Juwaynī; but this passage has no parallel in Juwaynī's work.

According to the *Secret History*, what Ögedei proposed was this:

> We shall settle the matter once and for all by providing post-station masters (*jamuchin*) and post-horse keepers (*ula'achin*) from the various chiliarchies of different areas, by setting up a post-station (*jam*) at every stage, by not allowing the couriers to move freely among the population unless on urgent business, but *instead* by having them ride in haste through the post-stations.[4]

The idea was enthusiastically taken up by other members of the Mongol imperial family, notably Ögedei's formidable elder brother Chaghatai. It was agreed that the courier networks in the various parts of the Mongol Empire should be linked together. This sheds interesting light on Ögedei's standing as Great Khan, and on the limits of his power. Ögedei was clearly no autocrat. Matters of general imperial policy were decided on a consultative basis. According to the evidence we have, Chinggis Khan chose Ögedei to be his successor, with the agreement of his brothers, because of his generally recognised amenability and amiability. Under Ögedei, whatever may have been the case before and after him, the Mongol Empire seems to have been run as a kind of family firm, not as the kingdom of an absolute ruler. I have suggested elsewhere that this might be taken as showing "the old steppe notion of family sovereignty at work",[5] though this particular steppe principle is not, in general, as conspicuously operative under the Mongols as it had been during the Seljuq period, or as it was arguably to be again during the Timurid century (is it possible that family sovereignty was in reality more a Turkish than a general steppe principle?)

Rashīd al-Dīn's account is very similar to the *Secret History*'s, though it contains more detail (such as an explicit statement to the effect that Chinggis Khan's youngest son, Tolui, was involved in the setting up of the network, and, in a later passage, material concerning the establishment of a *Yām* route between Qaraqorum and north

[4] *Secret History*, para 279: translation by I. de Rachewiltz, "The Secret History of the Mongols, chapter twelve", 39. For another translation see U. Onon, *The History and the Life of Chinggis Khan*, 170. The parallel passages in Rashīd al-Dīn's history are in *Jāmiʿ al-tawārīkh*, II/i, ed. A.A. Alizade, 121–2; 143–4; translated (from the earlier edition by E. Blochet) by J.A. Boyle, *The Successors of Genghis Khan*, 55–6; 62–3.

[5] Morgan, *The Mongols*, 104.

China). One might have supposed that Juwaynī, writing half a century before Rashīd al-Dīn, would have been in a better position than the later historian to have ascertained the facts about the early history of the *Yām* system. He certainly regarded it as of great importance, since he included a discussion of its establishment in his crucial chapter on Chinggis Khan's regulations and *yāsās*.[6] But in fact Juwaynī attributes the inauguration of the communications network to no single individual ruler, and he offers no precise date for its inauguration. He tells us that after the foundation of the Mongol Empire it was necessary to transport goods from west to east and vice versa, and for the rulers to be able to receive information about what their enemies were about. The Mongols therefore established *yām*s, for which the necessary men, animals and provisions were to be supplied by the army (the soldiers presumably obtaining these necessities from the subject population, since the burden was to be distributed in accordance with the census returns, and an annual inspection was to ensure that the peasantry replaced anything that was missing or lost).

Despite the lack of firm dating in Juwaynī's account, what he says does broadly confirm the details to be found in the *Secret History* and Rashīd al-Dīn. But it does seem to me that it is possible to interpret this evidence as not quite implying the *foundation* of a communications network by Ögedei in 1234.[7] What we have here is in fact, it appears, the first of several attempts at a reform of an already existing system. This is made clear enough in the *Secret History*: the reason for Ögedei's measures is (allegedly in the Great Khan's own words), that

> when the couriers ride in haste, We allow them to ride, moving freely among the population and, *as a result*, the pace of *these* riding couriers is slow and they are an affliction on the people.[8]

Similarly Rashīd al-Dīn gives the coming and going of *īlchī*s, envoys or messengers, as the reason for the setting up of *yām* stations. I think, therefore, that we can say something about what arrangements for communications during Chinggis Khan's time are likely to have been. It would seem that *īlchī*s did travel the empire on official business (as indeed they must have done), and that they exacted what

[6] Juwaynī, *Tārīkh-i Jahān Gushā*, I, 160–25; tr. J.A. Boyle, *The History of the World Conqueror*, I, 23–34.
[7] This was suggested to me by Gisele Cocchi.
[8] Tr. de Rachewiltz, 39.

they needed by way of mounts and other supplies as they went. What was lacking was permanent, established machinery for facilitating these journeys; and that is what Ögedei's changes were designed to supply. More, then, a reform than an innovation: and the similarities between what Ögedei brought in and the communications system formerly operated by the Khitans in north China are too striking to be easily dismissed as coincidental[9]—the more so when one takes into account the strong influence exercised by Khitan officials on the early administrative structure of the Mongol Empire.

If it is likely that the *Yām* system's ultimate origins were Chinese, it is perhaps not surprising that more is knowable about how it worked in China than in other parts of the empire. It is not just that Olbricht's monograph happens to exist: the sources are also much fuller than for other areas. Even for those who cannot read Chinese, there is the account of the *Yām* in Marco Polo's *Travels*.[10] This is a very detailed and exceedingly well-informed discussion. In this respect the account is one of many reasons for remaining sceptical about claims that Marco Polo may have travelled no nearer to China than the Levant or the Black Sea.[11] If Marco Polo's is second-hand knowledge gained at a distance, it is even more remarkable than if he had acquired it in China itself.

The impression our sources give us of the *Yām* system in China is that of a strikingly efficient and flourishing institution. As Olbricht puts it,

> unter ihrem (the Mongols') Einfluss erlebte das Postwesen in China eine Blüte.[12]

This may of course be no less than the truth. But by contrast, what we hear most about in the sources which tell us about the operations of the *Yām* in the western parts of the Mongol Empire is what went wrong. I strongly suspect that the contrast was not as stark as this might lead us to suppose—even though it is not difficult to believe that Yüan administration in China was a good deal more efficient than what went on in the Ilkhanate. The difference is in all probability due simply to the fact that the sources for the Ilkhanate

[9] Morgan, *The Mongols*, 107.
[10] *The Travels of Marco Polo*, ed. A. Ricci, 152–7.
[11] F. Wood, *Did Marco Polo go to China?*. See further D.O. Morgan, "Marco Polo in China—or not".
[12] Olbricht, *Das Postwesen*, 39.

discuss the *Yām* mainly when there is an attempt to reform it: hence a concentration on maladministration and abuses is inevitable.

I have argued above that the first information we have about the *Yām* system is about an early attempt, by the Great Khan Ögedei, to reform its operations so as to make it more efficient and less oppressive. In the Persian sources we hear of it again from Juwaynī: he refers to it briefly in connection with the administrative reforms introduced by the Great Khan Möngke after the coup d'état which brought him to power in 1251:

> As for the more important *elchis*, they should not make use of more than fourteen *ulaghs* (post horses); they should proceed from *yām* to *yām* and should enter no village or town in which they had no specific business; and they should take no more provisions (*ʿulūfa*) than each man could eat.[13]

Rashīd al-Dīn, who follows Juwaynī here, adds a mention of another very prevalent abuse:

> In the reign of Qā'ān (i.e. Ögedei) it had been the custom for merchants to come to Mughūlistān (i.e. Mongolia) on post-horses. He (Möngke) denounced this practice, saying: "Merchants journey to and fro for the sake of gain. What is the point in their riding *ūlāgh*?" And he commanded them to travel on their own animals.[14]

Even Geikhatu, generally regarded as among the least effective of the Īlkhāns, is said to have made an attempt at reforming the *Yām*: according to Ḥamd Allāh Mustawfī Qazwīnī, in 1295 Geikhatu's minister Ṣadr al-Dīn organised the *yāms* in such a way as to remove the current fear of *īlchīs*' requisitioning post-horses other than from the official post stations.[15]

Our main body of evidence regarding the *Yām* in the Ilkhanate is also concerned with a reform, one about which we are told a great deal more, by both Rashīd al-Dīn and his contemporary Waṣṣāf: the communications network was one of the institutions to which the Īlkhān Ghazan (reg. A.D. 1295–1304) turned his attention as part of his ambitious attempt to undo the damage of the previous

---

[13] Juwaynī, *Tārīkh*, III, 76–7: tr. Boyle, *The History*, II, 599. I have modified the translation.

[14] Rashīd al-Dīn, II, ed. Blochet, 312: tr. Boyle, *Successors*, 219.

[15] *Tārīkh-i Guzīda*, 603. This is repeated by the later historian Muʿīn al-Dīn Naṭanzī, *Muntakhab*, 139.

seven decades of Mongol rule. In accordance with his usual practice, Rashīd al-Dīn prefaces his account of Ghazan's reform in this area of administration with a series of lurid stories about how appalling the situation was before Ghazan put things right.

He tells us that the numbers of *īlchīs* travelling about the country had become so vast that

> even if five thousand mounts had been stationed at each *yām*, they would not have been enough for them. Inevitably they took as mounts all the herds of the Mongols that were in the summer and winter pastures. And they compelled to dismount all (those travelling in) caravans and travellers who were coming from the direction of Khitai and Hindūstān and other quarters far and near—amīrs, *bāsqāq*s, *malik*s, *bītikchī*s, *qāḍī*s, *sayyid*s, *imām*s and plaintiffs who were coming to the (royal) camp (*ūrdū*)—they took their horses and would leave them on the road, and some in dreadful places, with their baggage. So many *īlchī*s behaved in this way that affairs reached such a state that thieves and robbers masqueraded as *īlchī*s, blocked the road, saying, "we are *īlchī*s", and having taken their (the travellers') horses as *ūlāgh*, they would suddenly seize them, tie them up and plunder their baggage.

Eventually "affairs reached the point that whoever had more weapons and greater power took the post-horses of the other". Since, as we have seen, "the herds of the Mongols" were requisitioned as mounts, it was apparently not only the subject Persian population that suffered. But the situation was particularly bleak for villagers who had the misfortune to live within easy reach of the main roads:

> Whatever they (the *īlchī*s) found in the villages they tyrannically took, and if in one day they came to ten villages and post-houses (*khayl-khāna*), they would take from all those places provisions (*ʿalafa*) double what the custom was. And since it would be more than they needed for their food, they would sell it.[16]

One result of these troubles was that all *īlchī*s came to be tarred with the same brush, so that if from time to time it was really necessary for an *īlchī* to travel on some important state business, he would be much hindered by the ill-repute of *īlchī*s as a class. He would find that no horses were available, or only thin ones. His journey would consequently take two or three times longer than expected. This dearth of suitable horses is hardly surprising: if Rashīd al-Dīn is to

[16] Rashīd al-Dīn, III, 480–1.

be believed, in the period before Ghazan's accession *īlchīs* tended to travel with anything from two or three hundred to five hundred or a thousand attendant cavalry, all of whom had to be mounted and fed even if they did not otherwise misbehave.[17]

All this, Rashīd al-Dīn tells us, was dealt with by Ghazan. *Yāms* were to be at intervals of three, or according to Waṣṣāf four, *farsakhs* on the major roads. If we take Yāqūt's word for it that "the *farsakh* is three miles",[18] then what is implied is a rather short stage of nine to twelve miles on the main routes. This compares with Marco Polo's assertion that post-stations were established, in the parts of the Mongol Empire through which he travelled, every twenty-five or thirty miles, or every thirty-five or forty in uninhabited or roadless areas.[19] A supply of horses was to be held in readiness: there should be fifteen head of fat horses (*asp-i farba*, i.e. horses in good condition) at each station. This seems so small a number as to be wholly credible: it compares with Marco Polo's two or four hundred, and Rashīd al-Dīn's assertion that in the days before Ghazan, post-stations had five hundred head of horses—which might well have been necessary if *īlchīs* really did travel with the numbers of attendants he claims (though it may be that his figure is not intended to be taken literally, as he goes on to say that even with such large numbers, there would not remain even two *asp-i farba*).

Each *yām*, according to Ghazan's reform was entrusted to a great amīr. Funds for maintenance were allotted which were more than sufficient, so that there could be no excuse for irregularities. The officials in charge of the stations were to ensure that no one made use of the post-horses whose documents were not properly authorised with the appropriate seals—*nishān* and *āltūn tamghā*. Provision was made for messengers on missions of special urgency. *Īlchīs* were only to be sent on official government business, and their animals' fodder was to be provided by the Treasury.[20] Waṣṣāf adds some interesting details. He says that at each stage, the time of a messenger's departure was to be noted at the top of his documents, and this should be verified at the next stage. If he arrived on time, a circle with a vertical line across it was to be inscribed under the

[17] Rashīd al-Dīn, III, 482–3.
[18] *The Introductory Chapters of Yāqūt's Muʿjam al-Buldān*, 55.
[19] Marco Polo, 153.
[20] Rashīd al-Dīn, III, 483–5.

green *tamghā* which was on the cover of the messenger's documents. If there had been any delay, the circle was to have a horizontal line across it. Salaries were to be allotted to all the officials involved, so that no burden should fall on the peasants or anyone else.[21]

Both Rashīd al-Dīn and Waṣṣāf have something to say about Ghazan's regulations regarding runners, called *payk* by Rashīd al-Dīn: Waṣṣāf uses several other terms. According to the former, each post-station was to have two *paykān*, who, running from messenger to messenger (*ūlām bi-ūlām*, i.e. passing on the message as a sequence of relay runners), could between them cover thirty *farsakhs* in twenty-four hours (Waṣṣāf suggests forty *farsakhs*).[22] Marco Polo also speaks of runners: according to him they were positioned in villages at intervals of three miles between post-stations: they wore a belt of bells so that they might be heard at the next station, where the next runner would make himself ready to take over. Marco Polo would have us believe that the runners were used for the transport not only of messages to the Great Khan, but also of fresh fruit.[23]

This all sounds distinctly impressive. Are we to take it at face value? As ever, the question tends to boil down to whether or not we choose to believe Rashīd al-Dīn when he is talking about the splendours of Ghazan's reforms and how appalling things were before that time. Certainly he was in a position to know a great deal about the workings of the *Yām* system in the Ilkhanate. Not only was he for many years one of the two chief ministers, but according to Waṣṣāf, the administration of the *yāms* was among the specific responsibilities entrusted by Ghazan to Rashīd al-Dīn when he was appointed *nā'ib* and vizier.[24] My own view is that we should be wise to remain a little sceptical. It is all too easy to assume that, because Rashīd al-Dīn's stories of the dreadful goings-on in the days before Ghazan are so detailed and circumstantial, they must therefore be true. But in reality no such assumption is warranted: Rashīd al-Dīn, as the great reformer's chief minister, has far too obvious an axe to grind; and the same caveat must apply to his account of the reforms themselves. We do not really know how successful they were: whether or not Ghazan's excellent measures for regularising the operations

---

[21] Waṣṣāf, 387.
[22] Rashīd al-Dīn, III, 484; Waṣṣāf, 387.
[23] Marco Polo, 154.
[24] Waṣṣāf, 347.

of the *Yām* system were actually implemented, or if they were, how widely and for how long, is not something which our sources can tell us.

That said, however, the *Yām* system ought not to be underestimated. There can be no doubt that for the Mongol World-Empire it was a crucial institution, without which the empire could hardly have operated except as a series of very small fragments. Those who wish to conquer and rule most of Asia have to have an effective system of communications; and while Khitan and other Chinese precedents may well have been helpful in terms of machinery and organisation, I doubt if the Mongols needed anyone to put the basic idea that communications were necessary into their heads: it is simply too obvious. Perhaps the system did work better in China than elsewhere. Certainly it survived the expulsion of the Yüan dynasty, as the Timurid Shāh Rukh's ambassadors to the Ming court discovered.[25] And it remained an important institution for the Mongol Empire as a whole, even after that empire had to a great extent broken up into virtually independent and often mutually hostile khanates. In 1305 the Īlkhān Öljeitü, writing to King Philip the Fair of France, observed that

> Heaven has inspired us with the thought that We, Temür Khāqān (of China), Chabar and Togha (Khans in Central Asia), and We other descendants of Chinggiz Khāqān should put an end to the vituperation which had been going on for forty-five years up to now, and now, thanks to Heaven, all of us brothers get on well together and, moreover, from the land of the Chinese where the sun rises, to the Talu Sea, we have joined Our mail lines (*jamud-iyan*) together, in order to connect the states.[26]

For the Īlkhāns, then, as for other Mongol rulers, the *Yām* was important; and the fact that we tend to know of it chiefly in connection with attempts to reform abuses, while that may well not tell us that the abuses were effectively dealt with, does at least assure us that the Mongol rulers had some conception both of what was wrong and of what needed to be done about it. They evidently did not regard the *Yām* as something which could safely be left in chaos.

---

[25] See Ḥāfiẓ Abrū, *A Persian Embassy to China*.

[26] Spuler, *History of the Mongols*, 143: see also Mostaert and Cleaves, *Les Lettres des ilkhan*, 55–6.

Bibliography

Dvornik, F., *Origins of Intelligence Services*, New Brunswick, 1974.
Ḥāfiẓ Abrū, *A Persian Embassy to China*, ed. and tr. K.M. Maitra, Lahore, 1934.
Juwaynī, *Tārīkh-i Jahān Gushā*, ed. M.M. Qazwīnī, 3 vols, Leiden and London, 1912, 1916, 1937; tr. J.A. Boyle, *The History of the World Conqueror*, 2 vols., Manchester, 1958.
Marshall, R., *Storm from the East*, London, 1993.
Morgan, D.O., *The Mongols*, Oxford, 1986.
———, "Marco Polo in China—or not", *JRAS*, 3rd series, 6 (1996), 221–5.
Mostaert, A., and Cleaves, F.W., *Les Lettres de 1289 et 1305 des ilkhan Arghun et Öljeitü à Philippe le Bel*, Cambridge, MA, 1962.
Naṭanzī, Muʿīn al-Dīn, *Muntakhab al-tawārīkh-i Muʿīnī*, ed. J. Aubin, Tehran, 1957.
Olbricht, P., *Das Postwesen in China unter der Mongolenherrschaft im 13. und 14. Jahrhundert*, Wiesbaden, 1954.
Onon, U., *The History and the Life of Chinggis Khan*, Leiden, 1990.
Polo, Marco, *The Travels*, tr. A. Ricci, London, 1931.
Qazwīnī, Ḥamd Allāh Mustawfī, *Tārīkh-i Guzīda*, ed. ʿA. Nawāʾī, Tehran, 1958–61.
Rachewiltz, I. de, "The Secret History of the Mongols, chapter twelve", *Papers in Far Eastern History*, 31 (March 1985), 21–93.
Rashīd al-Dīn, *Jāmiʿ al-tawārīkh*, II/i, ed. A.A. Alizade, Moscow, 1980; II, ed. E. Blochet, Leiden and London, 1911; tr. J.A. Boyle, *The Successors of Genghis Khan*, New York and London, 1971; III, ed. A.A. Alizade, Baku, 1957.
Saunders, J.J., *The History of the Mongol Conquests*, London, 1971.
Spuler, B. (tr.), *History of the Mongols*, London, 1972.
Wood, F., *Did Marco Polo go to China?*, London, 1995.
Yāqūt, *The Introductory Chapters of Yāqūt's Muʿjam al-Buldān*, tr. W. Jwaideh, Leiden, 1959.

THE OTTOMAN MERCHANT MARINE

S. Soucek

John H. Pryor writes in his book *Geography, technology, and war: Studies in the maritime history of the Mediterranean 649–1571*:

> It . . . is significant that a historian of his stature [i.e., F. Braudel] believes that the Ottoman merchant marine was easily the largest in the Mediterranean by the end of the 16th century . . . This flowed directly from the superior quality of the strategic bases acquired for the Ottoman navy and from the logistical advantages held by the Ottoman navy and corsairs in an age when maritime traffic continued to ply the age-old coastal trunk routes of the sea and when the main strike weapon at sea was still the oared galley.[1]

Let us compare this statement with what Ronald C. Jennings writes in his book *Christians and Muslims in Ottoman Cyprus and the Mediterranean World, 1571–1640*:

> Cyprus has an ideal location for a naval base [and] for long distance trade, for smuggling, and for piracy. Had the Ottomans chosen to do so, they could have made . . . Magosa [= Famagusta] the kind of international trading emporium that . . . Izmir became in the 17th century . . . Magosa had first-class fortifications . . . Not even English or Dutch ships would have threatened Magosa. If the Ottomans had tried to use Magosa commercially, . . . foreign merchants might once again have been encouraged to settle there . . . Magosa had great possibilities even for fleets of ships. The presence of Ottoman and foreign merchants would have stimulated the production of luxury goods . . .[2]

The Ottomans' conquest of Cyprus was a costly one—the defeat at Lepanto was part of the price—but exploiting all the assets of the island should have justified that investment. So if Braudel and Pryor are right, and the Turks had the largest merchant marine in the Mediterranean by the end of the 16th century, why *did they not* turn Magosa into a thriving emporium? Moreover, the Ottoman navy should have been able to protect the empire's commercial shipping

---

[1] Cambridge, 1988, 191–92.
[2] New York, 1993, 345–50.

with its mighty fleet, the Battle of Lepanto notwithstanding: even well into the 17th century, "the sultans maintained a formidable naval presence in the Mediterranean" (S. Faroqhi, in the *Social and Economic History of the Ottoman Empire*).[3]

Here is Jennings's explanation:

> Disaster eventually came to the Ottoman navy in the Mediterranean only because it continued so long to rely on galleys . . . From 1595 English ships dominated not just the long-distance trade of the Levant but also the local carrying trade. Soon a strong Dutch presence also was felt. Goods which once had been carried on Venetian or Ottoman commercial vessels then preferred English ships, which provided security from pirates . . . Ships of Atlantic origin took up virtually all the burden of transportation to the Latin Mediterranean and beyond. . . . Ultimately, Magosa was virtually ignored as a port . . . The problems arising from dealing with pirates and the failure to develop a fleet of sailing ships were the greatest obstacles that the Ottomans found in the Levant.

Contrary to Jennings's assertions, Ottoman commercial shipping did not collapse so suddenly. Evliya Çelebi gives a vivid account of what he witnessed half a century later, although it is not Magosa but Istanbul that he writes about. Among the "Esnaf-i Tüccar-i Misr ve Savahil-i Bahr-i Sefid" ("Merchants of Egypt and the Mediterranean coasts"), who thrived in his time, there were shippers who owned 10 *kalyons* each, and their wealth amounted up to forty or fifty thousand *keses*. These merchants had many business partners in India, Yemen, Arabia, Persia, and Europe.[4]

"Kalyon" had by then acquired the connotation of a large sailing ship and was the Ottoman version of its Western cousins, the carack and the galleon. Evliya Çelebi tells us that it was armed with cannon, and like its foreign kinsmen, it could serve the double purpose of a freighter and a man-of-war. This function was most dramatically demonstrated by the Portuguese in the Indian Ocean, but they had no monopoly on it; the principle asserted itself on all seas and

---

[3] Cambridge, 1995, 188 89. Faroqhi's statement needs a qualification. The Turks had the *potential* for a formidable naval presence, but after the 16th century they ceased availing themselves of it. The conquest of Crete (1645–69) proved so laborious because the navy of Venice, despite the republic's dwindling resources, repeatedly gained control of the Aegean and even blocked the Ottoman fleet in the Dardanelles.

[4] *Seyahatname*, vol. 1, 553.

among all mariners, once they or their governments chose to apply it. The corsairs of Algiers did so in the very first years of the 17th century, and the shipowners of Istanbul did not stay far behind.

Evliya Çelebi does not go into further details, but we know that this traffic that he mentions must have persisted along the vital axis linking Istanbul with Egypt and other ports of the Eastern Mediterranean on the one hand, and Caffa and other ports of the Black Sea on the other; and that much of it consisted of sailing ships. Jennings's explanation of why the Ottomans neglected Magosa may therefore not be satisfactory. It is helpful, however, in one special sense, for it resembles the efforts to explain the slightly earlier Ottoman failure to successfully confront the Portuguese in the Indian Ocean.

The Turks could not oust the intruders because their galleys were the wrong ships with which to fight the Portuguese caracks—we are told by Braudel and as a result by a host of other historians. First of all, this is inaccurate: the Ottomans did include sailing ships equipped with cannon in their major campaigns (Hadim Süleyman Paşa in 1538, Piri Reis in 1552), and they had the resources to increase their number had they chosen to do so.[5] Their total withdrawal from the Indian Ocean, no less than their partial withdrawal from the Mediterranean, had, in my opinion, different and more profound causes.

The main cause—or perhaps still only a symptom—was, I would suggest, the fact that the Ottomans never sufficiently encouraged a merchant marine in the true sense of the word: a fleet built and operated with the overriding purpose of acquiring wealth for its owners, whether private or public. Such a fleet would have included increasing numbers of sailing ships, just as the fleets of Venice, Genoa, Catalonia and Ragusa did. In fact, the very symbol of 16th century European mastery of the Indian Ocean, the carack, had first been developed in Genoa, and became a common sight in Turkish waters when it ferried alum from Foça to Italy.[6] But the Turks did not have to go to the *Dār al-Ḥarb* for inspiration or for the acquisition of such ships. Their own vassal Ragusa (now better known as Dubrovnik) possessed one of the greatest merchant fleets of the 15th and 16th centuries. Ragusa's version of the carack, which became known in English as the argosy, plied the waters between Istanbul,

[5] Soucek, "Ottoman naval policy," 144–45.
[6] Lane, *Venetian ships*, 42.

Beirut and Alexandria at one end and London and Antwerp at the other. Success did not come easily to the Ragusans; they first had to shake off the stifling suzerainty of Venice, and then to withstand the fierce competition from this erstwhile overlord and from other seafaring traders of the Mediterranean and Atlantic, such as the Genoese and the Iberians.[7]

It is of course true that comparing Ragusa, Venice or Genoa with Turkey could be misleading or perhaps somewhat insulting to the mighty Islamic state. Overseas maritime trade constituted the wealth of the three republics, whereas it remained negligible in the case of the Ottoman Empire. The merchants and shipowners of Istanbul, Evliya Çelebi's "anka bezirgânları" ("very rich merchants") may have accumulated wealth from trade that spanned the empire's Black Sea-Red Sea axis, but we would search in vain for their fleets calling at other ports, and even in their home waters, those of the eastern Mediterranean, they made no real attempt to compete with visitors from the world at large—as the case of 17th century Izmir illustrates. (The Black Sea was a special case, for the geographical configuration of the straits of the Dardanelles and the Bosphorus, both fortified at strategic points, made it possible to declare that sea "off limits" to foreign shipping until Russia entered the scene in the course of the 18th century.)

Why was this so? A partial answer has already been suggested. Investing in overseas trade and then practising it required a genuine motivation and tenacity on the part of an influential segment of society, a segment that had either its government's backing or, better still, participation. This involvement of the government—so vital in the case of Europe's dynamic trading nations of the late Middle Ages and early modern period—was absent in the Ottoman empire. But again, why? There were several reasons, such as the very self-sufficiency of the empire and the success of its caravan trade. On the waterfront the sultans allowed the merchants to come to knock on their doors, but did not feel any need to venture into uncharted waters in search of some future gain. In the rare instances when they broke this rule, they did so for political rather than economic reasons, and quickly withdrew at the first signs of difficulties, in sharp contrast to the relentless tenacity of the Europeans. A dramatic illustration of this difference was the gigantic contest for the Indian Ocean, or

[7] Krekić, "Ragusa (Dubrovnik) e il mare", 137.

perhaps for the oceans of the Orient and their trade, that was played out in the 16th and 17th centuries.

The conquest of Egypt in 1517 gave the Ottomans control over Suez, where the Mamluks had recently developed a respectable naval base, and over Jedda, the terminus—or doorstep—of merchant ships calling from India and China. Moreover, the time was right, although somewhat overdue: the Portuguese were terrorizing Muslim shipping anywhere between Sofala in East Africa and Malacca in Malaysia, and had just seized Hormuz in 1515, but they had failed before Aden in 1513. This famous emporium and potential naval base was, as it were, beckoning to Selim I, and soon to his son Suleyman, to come and take it, and then drive out the infidel from the eminently Muslim ocean. The Ottomans did take Aden, but they waited two decades to do so (1538), and they did not rid the Indian Ocean of the Portuguese. The events of 1538 are revealing. The seizure of Aden—not from the infidels, but from a local Arab chieftain—occurred in the course of an Ottoman expedition whose aim was to wrest the Indian fort of Diu from the Portuguese. The siege of this base dragged on, and when Hadîm Süleyman Paşa heard that a Portuguese relief fleet was approaching, he raised the siege and sailed back. The Turkish fleet's mission was not a total failure, for on its return trip it anchored at the South Arabian port of Shihr whose ruler declared himself a vassal of the sultan. More significant, however, is the fact that no further attempt was ever made to acquire a naval and commercial base on the Indian subcontinent.

Again, why? We hear the standard explanation: The Ottoman galleys, built for the Mediterranean. . . . I have already alluded to the fallacy of this thesis. The causes, I think, are deeper, and not surprisingly they have the same roots as those of the empire's withdrawal from the competition in the Mediterranean. The Ottoman sultan was not a merchant king; his empire was so vast and rich ("une économie-monde," according to Braudel) that setting his sights beyond the maritime horizons had no appeal to him. And for some reason, none of the Muslim merchants and shipowners from among his subjects had either the drive or the means of persuasion to receive state backing for embarking on ventures comparable to those of the Europeans.

Admittedly, this statement contradicts the other perennial (and contradictory) refrain found in historiography: the Ottomans understood the importance of the spice trade as well as the Portuguese did, and it was because of their intervention in the Indian Ocean that this trade, initially captured by the Atlantic invaders and deflected to Lisbon and Antwerp, eventually reverted to its traditional route through the Red Sea and Alexandria. This is only partly true, and is valid only for the 16th century. In order to fully throttle the flow of trade through the Red Sea, the Portuguese would have had to conquer Jedda and Suez, and this remained beyond their means, although they tried to do so at Jedda in 1517 and at Suez in 1541.[8] They had to overcome formidable odds inherent in such an enterprise. Navigation between Jedda and Suez was so treacherous that local pilots were indispensable; the defenders were entrenched in fortified home bases; the invaders, themselves members of a small nation whose human resources had been stretched to the limits, had to endure a voyage from the Indian coast before even entering the Red Sea; and after the initial shock, Muslim traders of the Indian Ocean, such as the Gujaratis and Achinese, displayed a splendid resilience and fighting spirit with which they broke the Portuguse stranglehold.[9]

So if it is true that Ottoman mastery of the Red Sea saved it from becoming a Portuguese lake, the motivation of the Turkish intervention is not as clear-cut. The prestige of being the "Protector of the two holy cities, [Mecca and Medina]," a title which adorned the Ottoman sultan's attributes, certainly played a role. On the economic level, the government was delighted to draw revenue from customs raised on pepper entering the empire or transiting it on the way to Europe, and issued *kanunnames* on this taxation, but that is a far cry from fitting out fleets to cross the ocean and capture the trade itself. Had Sultan Süleyman shared the Portuguese king Dom Manuel's mentality, he too would have fitted out caracks in Suez or Aden and sent them to India and Indonesia in search of spices or, better still, with the mission of establishing Ottoman naval and commercial bases there. Moreover, some of the very odds facing the Portuguese would have been assets for the Turks: not only were the seafaring populations in India and Indonesia mostly Muslim, but they repeatedly invited Süleyman to come and deliver them from

[8] Orhonlu, *Osmanlî Imparatorluğu'nun güney siyaseti*, 7, 20; Bacqué-Grammont & Kroell, *Mamlouks, Ottomans et Portugais en Mer Rouge*; and numerous studies by S. Özbaran, now collected in *The Ottoman response to European expansion.*

[9] Orhonlu, *Osmanlî Imparatorluğu'nun güney siyaseti*, 9.

the infidels; the distances to cover were not only much shorter, but their ships did not have to face the dangers of the stormy southern latitudes around the Cape of Good Hope. The potential of the Ottomans to become the dominant maritime power in the Indian Ocean was further enhanced by the possession of Basra and penetration into the Persian Gulf. Once again, they failed to seize this opportunity. For that goal it would have been useful—though not indispensable—to capture Hormuz, held by the Portuguese since 1515. In fact, even in its own right, the island fortress was worth a determined effort. Let me quote two authors who left characteristic statements on this subject. First, the Ottoman mariner and cartographer Piri Reis (1526):

> . . . Know that [Hormuz] is an island. Many merchants visit it. . . . But now, O friend, the Portuguese have come there and built a stronghold on its cape. They control the place and collect the customs—you see into what condition that province has sunk! The Portuguese have prevailed over the natives, and their own merchants crowd the warehouses there. Whatever the season, trading cannot now happen without the Portuguese . . .[10]

Here is the Englishman Joseph Selbanck (1609):

> . . . From there [= from Masqat], I was conueied in chaines to Ormus, crossing the mouth of the Persian Gulfe. Ormus is an Island in circuit about thirtie miles; and it is the driest Iland in all the world, for there is nothing growing in it but salt: for their Water, Wood, Victualls, and other necessaries come out of Persia, which is about twelue miles from thence. The Portugals have a strong Castle here, which standeth near unto the Sea, where there is a Captaine sent by the King of Spaine, hauing under him a conuenient number of souldiers, wherof some part remaine in the Castle, and some in the Towne. In this Towne are Marchants of many Nations, and many Moores and Gentiles. Here is very great trade of all sorts of Spices, Drugs, Silkes, cloth of Silke, fine Tapistries of Persia, great store of Pearles, as also Horses of Persia, which serue for all India . . . From Ormus they sent me prisoner to Goa . . .[11]

[10] Piri Reis, *Kitabı Bahriye*, 65–66.

[11] *Purchas His Pilgrimes*, part 3, ch. 9, par. 4 (238). This account is included in a letter written by Selbanck "unto Sir Thomas Smith" in 1609. It also reflects the rivalry between England and Portugal, which eventually led to British support of Abbas I of Iran in his successful effort to recover Hormuz (1625); Boxer, "A Note on Portuguese Reactions", 415–28, and repr. in his *Portuguese Conquest and Commerce*.

The fact that the Ottomans tried only once to take Hormuz (Piri Reis in 1552) speaks for itself, especially when we remember that similar efforts by the Portuguese at Hormuz, Diu, and Malacca had failed at their first attempts. But let us return to the broader theme of the spice trade in the Indian Ocean, the irruption of the Portuguese, and the claim that the Ottomans deliberately and effectively intervened to redress the situation. As I have suggested, the evidence points to only a marginal interest in this struggle, and shows a few half-hearted and insufficiently supported naval expeditions in those waters. The gigantic campaigns repeatedly undertaken by Süleyman and his predecessors, successors, and subjects on land and in the Mediterranean dwarf anything launched from Suez. These campaigns, however, were not of the economic and commercial kind typifying those of the Christian powers. They aimed at conquering territory, expanding the *Dār al-Islām*, and curbing the Habsburg infidel or the Shia heretic. The navy played a supporting role in these campaigns, and acquisition of commercially lucrative sites was only incidental to the main goal. Magosa in Cyprus is a case in point; the conquest of other places, mostly captured from Venice, could be added to this list. There were Turkish merchants among the various Ottoman subjects sailing from such ports to a few places in Italy such as Venice and Ancona, but they did so in Ragusan or Venetian or Genoese or Pisan ships, just as the "Rumi" merchants sailed to India or Indonesia in Gujarati ships. In all these cases, Turkish Muslim merchants remained marginal and gradually withdrew from the scene.

Furthermore, the marginality of Ottoman interest in the spice trade and in the affairs of the Indian Ocean is underscored by the nonchalance with which the Porte witnessed—or perhaps barely noticed—the collapse of the spice trade route through its domains, that is, the Red Sea, Egypt, and Syria in the 17th century. As if to make the picture clearer, history repeated itself a century after the Portuguese irruption—with an important difference: this time the Dutch and the English bore in with a vengeance and a firepower that pushed the Portuguese to the sidelines and definitively deflected the spice trade to the all-maritime route, besides establishing the foundations of their colonial empires. Preferring to look the other way, the Ottomans withdrew from Aden in 1630, and in the Red Sea they contented themselves with controlling only the navigation of its northern half between Suez and Jedda. The Dutch and English hegemony of course did not mean a cessation of seafaring in the Indian Ocean, and the goods carried to Europe around the Cape were far surpassed in volume by the merchandise traded among the peoples of the area. This traffic remained primarily indigenous, and the shippers were Muslim Gujaratis, Arabs, Persians, East Africans and others, but not the subjects of the Ottoman sultan. The Ottoman merchant marine, such as it was, operated along a longitudinal axis represented by Caffa in the Crimea and Jedda in the Red Sea. Even the new substitute for spices, coffee grown in the Yemen, ended up making the first leg of its journey to the Turkish consumer in foreign bottoms—ships of Gujarati merchants who had a colony in Mocha and carried the harvest to Jedda.[12] It was at about this time that an anonymous Ottoman observer wrote the following comment on the margin of a page in the book called *Tarih-i Hind-i Garbi*:

> They (the Europeans) set out in the Atlantic and, coasting western Africa, they head south; subsequently they turn east and face all the adversities involved in passing by the sources of the Nile and beyond the Mountains of the Moon. Then they sail by the shores of the Red Sea and cross over to those of India. [The newcomers,] by means of good alliances and clever measures, have subjugated most ports of India, and for a number of years they have been barring the route to Muslim merchants from those countries . . . It is indeed a strange fact and an odd affair that a group of unclean unbelievers have become strong to the point of voyaging from the west to the east, braving the violence of the wind and calamities of the sea, whereas the Ottoman Empire, which is situated at half the distance in comparison with them, has not made any attempt to conquer [India]: this despite the fact that voyages there yield countless benefits, bringing back desirable objects and articles of luxury whose description exceeds the bounds of the describable and explicable . . .[13]

An Ottoman merchant marine? There was one, but on the scale of a global overseas trade that crossed political or ideological frontiers, it remained marginal. Its primary function was to keep the imperial capital well supplied with all the necessities, and to assure the links between Istanbul, Anatolia, and Egypt, and between Suez and Jedda. Considerations of expanding their merchant marine beyond these limits hardly ever entered the policies of the Ottoman government.

---

[12] Tuscherer, "Activité des Turcs," 321–64.
[13] Goodrich, *The Ottoman Turks*, 84–85.

Quite to the contrary: in the course of the 17th and 18th centuries, a period which witnessed a considerable degree of administrative consolidation and economic resilience within the confines of the empire, even the carrying trade serving Ottoman ports and passenger traffic (including pilgrims to Mecca) increasingly relied on foreign, especially French ships.[14]

Ottoman naval strength could not but be affected by the absence of a merchant marine. First of all, a fleet is an expensive proposition. If it was not built and used for purposes that were directly or indirectly economic, its maintenance became much too onerous, and its fighting capabilities and effectives declined. Without the economic returns, none of the seafaring nations, whether Portuguese, Spanish, English, Dutch, or French could have afforded the grandiose ventures they undertook. This applies even to the smaller-scale Mediterranean navigation. Diminutive Venice could face the navy of the mighty Ottoman Empire century after century because its fleet was a money-making proposition, whereas that of the Turks was not.

The absence of a full-fledged Ottoman merchant marine or of a navy maintained for the purpose of supporting a mercantile strategy, however, was up to a point compensated or camouflaged by the phenomenal exploits of Turkish maritime *gazis* (warriors for Islam). They performed for the empire some of the functions that other nations accomplished by aggressive commercial expansion. Like the traders, the *gazis* paid their way, not only costing little or nothing to the imperial exchequer but even sharing with the state some of the spoils of their lucrative *gaza*; moreover, they constituted a special kind of naval academy, training first-class officers and admirals for the Ottoman navy. Without the Barbarossa brothers, it is unlikely that North Africa would have become Ottoman; without Kemal Reis and Hayreddin Paşa, the confrontations with the Christians might have had different outcomes; and even later, in the days of multiplying woes, captains from the Maghrib came to rescue the Ottoman navy on more than one occasion—notably Mezemorta Hüseyin Paşa in the 1680s and 1690s,[15] and Cezayirli Hasan Paşa in the 1770s

---

[14] Sadok, *La régence de Tunis*, 97–101; Panzac, *Commerce et navigation dans l'empire ottoman au XVIIIe siècle*, Istanbul, *ISIS*, 1996, passim.

[15] Orhonlu, "Husayn Pasha, Mezzomorto," *Encyclopaedia of Islam*, 2nd ed., vol. 3, 629–30.

and 1780s.[16] Nevertheless, the "Barbary corsairs," however successful, remained marginal and parasitic. Had the central government changed its attitude and entered the arena of economic expansion that included maritime trade and a mercantile use of overseas bases, these mariners might have played an invaluable role. But this was not the case, and in the end the corsair states of North Africa had to surrender their ships, ports and even sovereignty to an expanding Europe, while the core of the Ottoman Empire was saved by rivalry between such imperial powers as Britain and Russia.

Bibliography

Bacqué-Grammont, L. and Kroell, A., *Mamlouks, Ottomans et Portugais en Mer Rouge: L'affaire de Djedda en 1517*, Cairo, 1974.

Boxer, C.R., "A note on Portuguese reactions to the revival of the Red Sea spice trade and the rise of the Atcheh, 1540–1600", *Journal of South-East Asian History*, 10 (1969), 415–28.

———, *Portuguese conquest and commerce in southern Asia 1500–1750*, London, 1985.

Evliya, Çelebi, *Seyahatname*, Istanbul, 1324.

———, *Social and economic history of the Ottoman empire*, ed. H. İnalcık and B. Quataert, Cambridge, 1995.

Goodrich, T.D., *The Ottoman Turks and the New World*, Wiesbaden, 1990.

Jennings, R.C., *Christians and Muslims in Ottoman Cyprus and the Mediterranean world, 1571–1640*, New York, 1993.

Krekić, B., "Ragusa (Dubrovnik) e il mare: aspetti e problemi (XIV–XVII secolo)" in *Ragusa e il Mediterraneo*, ed. A. Di Vittorio, Bari, 1990.

Lane, F.C., *Venetian ships and shipbuilders of the Renaissance*, Baltimore, 1934.

Orhonlu, C., *Osmanlî Imparatorluğu'nun güney siyaseti: habeş eyaleti*, Istanbul, 1974.

Özbaran, S., *The Ottoman response to European expansion: studies on Ottoman Portuguese relations in the Indian Ocean and Ottoman administration in the Arab lands during the sixteenth century*, Istanbul, 1994.

Panzac, D., *Commerce et navigation dans l'empire ottoman au XVIIIe siècle*, Istanbul, 1996.

Piri, Reis, *Kitabi Bahriye*, ed. F. Kurtoğlu and H. Alpagut, Ankara, 1935.

Pryor, J.H., *Geography, technology and war: Studies in the maritime history of the Mediterranean, 649–1571*, Cambridge, 1988.

Sadok, B., *La régence de Tunis au XVIIe siècle: ses relations commerciales avec les ports de l'Europe méditerranéene, Marseille et Livourne*, Zaghouan, Ceroma, 1987.

Selbanck, J., *Purchas his pilgrimes*, London 1625.

Soucek, S., "Ottoman naval policy in the Indian Ocean", *Proceedings of X Türk Tarih Kongresi*, Ankara, 1993.

Tusherer, M., "Activité des Turcs dans le commerce de la Mer Rouge au XVIIIème Siècle, in *Les villes dans l'empire ottoman: activités et sociétés*, ed. D. Panzac, Paris, 1991, I, 321–64.

[16] Mordtmann-Kuran, "Djeza'irli Ghazi Hasan Pasha," *Encyclopaedia of Islam*, 2nd ed., vol. 2, 533–34.

IBN ẒĀFIR AL-AZDĪ'S ACCOUNT OF THE MURDER OF AḤMAD B. ISMĀʿĪL AL-SĀMĀNĪ AND THE SUCCESSION OF HIS SON NAṢR

Luke Treadwell

The manuscript

The Ambrosiana manuscript of Ibn Ẓāfir al-Azdī's (d. 613 A.H.) *Akhbār al-duwal al-munqaṭiʿa* which contains the following extract was identified by W. Madelung.[1] It is written in a clear *naskhī* hand, with diacritical points supplied for most words, but very sparse vocalisation and no *hamza*s. In the following edition, *hamza*s and such vocalisation and punctuation as are required to elucidate ambiguous passages have been supplied.

Edition of the text

(ا١١٩) و كان سبب مقتل أحمد بنِ إسمعيل أن ابن قارن صاحب جبل دنباوند قد استأمن إليه فأقام ببابه أياما كثيرة لم يُوصل إليه. فشكا ذلك إلى كنداتكين بن كنداجور الديلمي، أحد قواد أحمد. فقال له هل حملت إلى مشايخ الباب شيئا (٢)؟ فقال لا. قال هو السبب في عدم إيصالك . قال فما أصنع ؟ فقال كنداتكين أنا أدخل إلى أبي الحسن الكاتب و أتعرف منه كيف السبب إلى الوِصول . ومضى فدخل عليه وسأله عن ذلك . فقال الكاتب يحتاج إلى ستة ألف دينار تُرضى بها مشايخ الباب. فمضى الديلمي إلى ابن قارن وأخبره . فاقترض من التجار ستة ألف دينار. وسلمها له فأخذها (ب١١٩) كنداتكين(٣) و أوصلها إلى أبي الحسن . فأخذها وأوصل ابن قارن إلى أحمد في اليوم الثالث . فأكرمه أحمد وقربه وأنزله وسر بمقدمه. ثم قال لأبي الحسن تعرّف منه هل عوده إلى بلاده أحب إليه أم بقاؤه بحضرتنا؟ فسأله أبو الحسن عن ذلك فاختار العود إلى بلاده. فخلع عليه أحمد خلعا تصلح للملوك وحمل بين يديه عشر بدر وقاد بين يديه عشرة أفراس بمراكب حلى ورده إلى بلده ووكل عليه حتى يخرج من أعمال أحمد . وكتب إلى أمراء (٤) الأعمال بإنزاله وإكرامه وصرفه شاكرا.

---

[1] Madelung, "Yemenite historical manuscripts," 175–180. My thanks are due to Professor Madelung, Chase Robinson, Donald Richards and Julia Ashtiany-Bray for their comments on this paper.

٢ MS. شيا.

٣ MS. كنداكين.

٤ MS. امرا .

فلما وصل مرو، وكان واليها محمد بن علي المعروف بصعلوك المقدم الذكر في هذا الكتاب، أنزله عنده. وسأله صعلوك كيف رأيت الأمير السيد؟ قال أما رؤيته فاشتريتها بستة ألف دينار. قال ممن؟ قال من أبي الحسن الكاتب. فكتب صاحبِ الخبر بذلك لوقته وابن قارن لا يشعر. فلما ورد الكتِاب علي أحمد، كتب من ساعته ان يُرد ابن قارن حيث ما أدرك وأن يترك كل ما معه و يُمضى الى بلاده، و يرجع مع خمسة غلمان.
ثم ركب أحمد بعد ذلك لصيد سبع كان يؤذي الناس على شاطيء جيحون.

فأدرك الرسول ابن قارن بمرو فرجع به إلى أحمد بن إسمعيل، وهو في الصيد . فلما لقيه، قال له أحمد يابا منصور، رددناك وشغلنا قلبك . ثم قال ضع يدك على رأسي ، فوضعها. فقال أقسم بها كم غرمت على بابي. فقال ستة ألف دينار، ولو وصلت إليك بأولادي ، كانت قليلا . فقال ومن أخذها منك ؟ فقال أبو الحسن الكاتب . فجدد له (١٢٠ا) أحمد صلة أخرى.(٥) واستدعى أبا الحسن وقال له رجل غريب ترك نعمته من غير خوف ولا لنا في بلاده طمع، جاء(٦)إلينا بنفسه وأهدى لنا الهدايا الخطيرة، يُفعل معه ما فعلت، كأنك ما تذكر مجيئك (٧) إلي ودراعتك ما تساوي ستة دراهم. أنالك بهذه إذا عدنا إلى بخارا.

ثم اتفق صيد السبع الذي كان خرج لأجله على ضيعة يقال لها فربر فبات بها. فعلم أبو الحسن أنه إن أصبح ودخل بخارا، أناله بعقوبة. فعمل على قتله وأجابه إلى ذلك الغلمان بعد أن وعدهم وحلف لهم أنه يبايع لإسحق بن أحمد، عم أحمد بن إسمعيل، ويزيدهم في أرزاقهم ويصير كل واحد من قوادهم أميرا على بلد. وأمر الخازن وصاحب الكسوة بقتله وضمن لهما مالا جزيلا . فدخلا عليه في قبته وذبحاه فيها.

ذكر الوزير أبو القاسم (٨) المغربي في كتاب أخبار خراسان أنه كان لأحمد أسدان داجنان يربضان على باب البيت الذي فيه مبيته كل ليلة ، فلا يتمكن أحد أن يلم به ، و أنه تغافل تلك الليلة، فلم يربضهما على باب القبة فقتل . وكان قتله في سنة إحدى وثلثمائة.(٩) فكانت مدة مملكته سبع سنين. وكان من أجمل الناس صورة وأحسنهم سيرة. ولما قتل لقب بالشهيد . أولاده الأكبر أبو العباس الفضل وأبو الحسن نصر وأبو زكريا يحيى وأبو إسحق إبرهيم وأبو صالح منصور.(١٠)

أبُو الحَسن نصْر بن احْمَد بن إسمَعيل (١١)

(ب١٢٠) لقبه أصحابه فى حياته (المؤ)يد (١٢) و بعد وفاته السعيد. ذكر ذلك غرس النعمة في تأريخه.

---

٥ MS. اخرى.
٦ MS. جا ?
٧ MS. محيك.
٨ MS. القسم .
٩ MS. ثلثمايه.
١٠ This sentence is transcribed as it appears in the manuscript, although one might have expected it to have begun: .... وله أولاد.
١١ This chapter heading is vocalised in the manuscript.
١٢ The first part of this word is illegible.

ولما فرغ الغلمان من قتل أحمد بادروا إلى أبي الحسن وأعلموه فجاء(١٣) وقبض على الخزانة وأعطى الغلمان الكبار والذين (١٤) باشروا قتل أحمد ما كان قرر لهم. وأمرهم بالركوب والمسير إلى بخارا. وقال لهم إسرعوا واسبقوا الخبر واملكوا القهندز ودار الإمارة وبيوت الأموال لئلا (١٥) يبلغ الخبر إلى محمد بن أحمد (١٦) ، يعني نائب أحمد بن إسمعيل على مدينة بخارا، فلا يعلم ما يكون منه. فساروا مسرعين وأحمد محمولا في عمارية مع الأثقال. فتقدم الغلمان الصغار الذين لم يكونوا في البيعة وأجمعوا على إنفاذ رسول إلى والدة أحمد بن إسمعيل يخبرها. فبعثوا رسولا منهم فأخبرها الخبر. فبعثته إلى محمد بن أحمد وساكن الخادم الرومي، و كان من الناصحين لمواليه. فلما وقف محمد بن أحمد على الخبر بادر بالركوب وجاء (١٧) إلى باب القهندز واستوثق منه واستركب المطوعة ووكل منهم ألف رجل بدار الإمارة وبيت المال. وأمر العيارين بلبس السلاح وأخرج البنود وخرج بهم فوقف في مكان يقال له السهلة. وبعث جاسوسا يعلم له الخبر. فجاء (١٨) وأخبر بقربهم ، يعني الغلمان. فأمر أن تضرب مصاف المطوعة والعيارين من باب السهلة إلى باب القهندز ففعل ذلك.

وأقبل الغلمان يركضون ويشتمون محمد بن أحمد. وقصد باب السهلة منهم نحو ألف مملوك ، فلما نظروا إلى أهل البلد والمطوعة (١٢١١) والعيارين عليهم السلاح ، صاحوا عليهم وقالوا ما لكم والجمع؟(١٩) تفرقوا فإن الأمير السيد إن وافى ، وأنتم على هذا الحال، نالكم منه ما تكرهون. فقال الناس لهم تقدموا إلى المشايخ، فإن أمرونا بالرجوع ، رجعنا. فتقدموا إليهم فإذا الخيل مصفوفة والبنود منشورة والمشايخ وقوف على خيولهم، كل واحد مع أصحابه. فبلغوا إلى أحدهم ، وهو أبو يعقوب إسحق بن إبرهيم ، شيخ البلد و أستاذها في عمل السلاح ، وله في البلد أكثر من ألف تلميذ. فصاح عليه فارس التركي ، وهو من كبار مماليك إسمعيل والد أحمد ، وقال يابا يعقوب متى كان لأهل بخارا عادة في الخروج على الملوك ؟ لولا أنك رجل شيخ لأنزلت بك ما أنت أهله . فصاح إسحق على غلمانه، خذوا عبد السوء قاتل(٢٠) مولاه و خذوا أصحابه. ورفع يده فضرب رأس فارس(٢١) بدبوس كان معه فنكسه ونكس أصحابه الغلمان الذين كانوا معه وركب المطوعة دوابهم ولبسوا سلاحهم وكشفوهم بأجمعهم وحبسوهم في دار الحطب وأقاموا النفاطين فوق حيطانها ورسموا لهم أنهم إذا تحركوا أو نطقوا فاضربوا عليهم نارا.

ووقف الناس على حالهم وإذا بطائفة أخرى من المماليك قد وصلت. ففعل بها مثل الأولى (٢٢) حتى حبسوا أربعة ألف مملوك في دار الحطب ومن وراءهم (٢٣) لا يعلم بما كان منهم. ثم وافى أبو الحسن الكاتب في نحو ألفي غلام وعماريات الأمير أحمد و جنائبه (٢٤) بين يديه وعليه لباس أحمد وعلى رأسه القلنسوة السمور الإسمعيلية. فلما بلغ

١٣ MS. جا.
١٤ MS. اللذين.
١٥ MS. ليلا.
١٦ MS. *passim* احيد.
١٧ MS. جا.
١٨ MS. جآ.
١٩ MS. للجمع.
٢٠ MS. القاتل.
٢١ MS. بارس.
٢٢ MS. الأولي.
٢٣ MS. وراهم.
٢٤ MS. جنايبه.

محمد بن أحمد موافاة أبي الحسن الكاتب (ب١٢١) قال لصاحب جيش المطوعة يابا محمد أخرج من السهلة مع جماعة (من) (٢٥) الفتيان وقف خارج الباب بين النهرين حتى يدخل فيمن *أتى* مع (٣٦) الملك ، فإذا دخل إلينا ووصل هو إليك ، فلا يفوتنّك ، فإنه صاحب الفعلة وإن سمعت حركة من عندنا فلا تلفت إليها فيأخذه ملاك (٣٧) الأمر.

فخرج صاحب الجيش ومعه أربعة ألف فارس وألفا راجل وضرب المصاف ما بين النهرين. فلما وافى الغلمان ورأوا جمع المطوعة (٣٨) أنكروا أمرهم. وكان على المقدمة سيمجور الدواتي وبندار، وكان من أعقل المماليك وأحزمهم رأيا . فأحس بالشر فقال لبندار والغلمان تقدموا فإني واقف في مماليكي مع صاحب الجيش فإن كان لنا فهو ما يحب وإن كان علينا كفيتك أمره. فقالوا له نعم الرأي. فتأخر ووقف مع صاحب الجيش وقال له يابا محمد أرى شركا منصوبا . فقال ما كل ما ترى إلا فرحا بالأمير. فقال سيمجور على أن لي ذمة الله ورسوله أنا وأهلي ومالي. فقال صاحب الجيش إن كان الأمر كما تزعم فمر مماليكك بالترجل وبنزع (٣٩)السلاح وادفعه الى أصحابي. وتعرف كل مملوك منهم من استعار سلاحه وفرسه ليرده إليه. فأجاب سيمجور إلى ذلك وكان معه من مماليكه خمس مائة مملوك وكان فقيها مناظرا على مذهب الشافعي رحمه الله.

ووقف سيمجور مكانه واليا وبين يديه غلامان. فكلما مر قائد من المماليك قال له بالتركية تقدم فإني أكفيك هذا، يعني صاحب الجيش. فيتقدم فينكسونه المطوعة بين باب السهلة والقهندز وهم هنالك مع محمد بن أحمد. ثم يحبسونه في دار الحطب هو وغلمانه.

(ا١٢٢) وأقبل أبو الحسن الكاتب وعليه القلنسوة. فلما صار بين النهرين وحاذى صاحب الجيش، قال السلام عليك يابا محمد و قال صاحب الجيش لا سلم الله يا عدوه ، وعلاه بالدبوس فوقعت الضجة وصاح الغلمان الذين وراءه وأمراءه (٣٠) فبادر إليه المطوعة ونكسوه عن دابته وطرحوا غلا (٣١) في عنقه وعدوا به. وتفرق الجيش في طلب من تأخر من الغلمان فأخذ عن آخرهم وحبسوا. فوكل محمد بن أحمد بدورهم وبعث من ساعته الجمازات صحبة تابوت (٣٢) تحمل الأمير الشهيد أحمد بن إسمعيل. وصلب أبا الحسن الكاتب على سور القهندز ساعة من النهار ثم أنزل وحبس وكان يصلب كل يوم مدة أربعين يوما ساعتين من النهار وكذلك الغلامان القاتلان ثم قتلوا وصلبوا و تركوا سبع سنين حتى فرخ العصافير في أجوافهم.

ولما وصل الرسل بجثة الأمير أنزل بها دار الإمارة وغسلت وكنفت وحمل نعشه ليصلى عليه. وخرج القواد الأحرار حفاة يبكون وأخرجت المماليك وأطلقوا للصلاة عليه. فلما وضع التابوت في المصلى قام محمد بن أحمد وقال أيها المسلمون والأولياء، عندي لكم

[٢٥] MS. جماعة .... الفتيان.

[٣٦] The passage here italicised may have been rewritten in a second hand, although this is not entirely clear from the microfilm version of the manuscript used for this edition. An alternative reading might be ... فيمرالي مع.

[٣٧] The reading adopted here is *mallāk* (s. *mālik*).

[٣٨] MS. ورأوا بجمع المطوة.

[٣٩] MS. تبرع.

[٣٠] MS. اميراه.

[٣١] MS. جلا.

[٣٢] MS. ياقوت.

رأي أنا ذاكره قبل الصلاة على هذا الميت وإنفضاض الناس من هذا المحفل، فإن كان صوابا ساعدتم عليه وإن لم يكن عندكم صوابا قلتم غيره. ثم استدعى صاحب الجيش سرا وقال له امض الى البلد وخذ المطوعة ووكّل بكل ناحية من البلد شيخا وإجمع نساء (٣٣) الأجناد والمماليك الموكّل بدورهم وعيالاتهم في مكان واحد (٣٤) وخذ خيولهم و أسلحتهم فأعطها للمطوعة ورتب راجلهم على القهندز (ب ١٢٢) وفارسهم بين السهلة وبينه واثبت حتى يأتيك أمري فامتثل ذلك.

ثم قال محمد بن أحمد إن هذا الأمير الشهيد رحمه الله توفي ولم يخلف ولي عهد ولا يترك في رقابنا بيعة لأحد ولا بد للمسلمين ممن يدبرهم والرأي أن لا يتفرق هذا الجمع حتى يبايع هذا الرجل. فقال له مشايخ البلد وأهل العلم قد أصاب الأمير. فقال لهم اختاروا من تشاؤا. فقالوا يختار الأمير وننظر نحن بعد ذلك. فقال إن للأمير الشهيد في رقابنا صنائع وإني أرى لو ترك جروا مثلا لحفظناه فيه فكيف وقد ترك خمسة بنين يقر بهم العين والرأي أن يبايع أحدهم. فقال المشايخ والأولياء الأحرار الرأي ما رأى الأمير وسكت الأتراك. فقال لهم محمد بن أحمد ما لكم صمتم وأنتم أرباب المملكة؟ فقال بغرا الكبير صدقت أيها الأمير ولكن لو صلينا على هذا الميت ودفناه ثم رجعنا إلى البلد وتشاورنا لكان أولى.(٣٥) فقال محمد لا يجوز أن ينصرف الناس إلى منازلهم إلا بعد مبايعة. فقال بغرا هو ذا، أنت الحاكم على المسلمين والمتصرف في أمورهم إلى أن يتفقوا على من يولّونه أمرهم.

وكان محمد بن أحمد يداري الأتراك ويشاغلهم حتى يرد رسول أبي محمد صاحب جيش المطوعة بالقبض على عيالتهم وخيولهم وتأهب أهل البلد لحربهم. ثم قال لقاضي(٣٦) البلد، وهو أبو ذر، ولأبي سهل شيخها إختاروا عشرة من مشايخ الفقهاء وعشرة من مشايخ المحدثين وامضوا بنا إلى البلد لننظر من نبايعه من أولاد الأمير ففعلوا ومشوا بأجمعهم إلى القهندز واستخلف محمد بن أحمد (١٢٣١) على الجنازة بعض أصحابه. ثم مضوا إلى دار الإمارة ودخلوا على والدة الشهيد أحمد وقال لها محمد بن أحمد أحضري (أولادك؟) (٣٧) وكان الأكبر أبو الفضل العباس عليلا لا يرجا فاتفقوا على نصر بن أحمد فبايعوه بين يدي جدته وحمله محمد بن أحمد على عاتقه. فقال له لصغر سنه ،إلى أين بي تريدون ؟ تقتلونني كما قتلتم أبي؟ فبكى ابن أحمد وقال بل نجعلك يا سيدي أميرا. وانتهى به إلى الجنازة وأجلسه أمام النعش وبيده سيف مصلت.

ونادى معاشر المسلمين إن لأميركم الشهيد خمسة بنين أكبرهم العباس وهو عليل لا يرجا فلم يرى القاضي مبايعته وقد بايعنا الأمير نصر بن أحمد وهو ابن إثنتي عشرة سنة، صحيح العقل، حافظ (٣٨) لكتاب الله، عارف بالفرائض ، حسن الأدب، فما ترون؟ فأجابه أهل البلد والمشايخ والأولياء الأحرار بالطاعة والسمع وقال الأتراك إن هؤلاء موالينا ولنا في إمرهم نظر حتى نشاور سيدتنا، يعنون والدة الأمير الشهيد. فقال محمد بن أحمد إني قد بايعت الأمير أبا الحسن مولى أمير المؤمنين. ألا من كان عازما على البيعة فليبايع. فأول من بايع أبو الحسن علي بن عبد الصمد العارض ثم الأمير حمويه بن علي ثم محمد بن أحمد بن جيهان ثم محمد بن أليسع ثم بايع الناس أجمع إلا الأتراك ومعهم أبو الحسن الكاتب القاتل، أحضر الجنازة ليحسر، وأخذوا يدارون لأنفسهم ليرجعوا بلا

---

٣٣ MS. نسا.
٣٤ MS. في كل مكان واحد.
٣٥ MS. اولي .
٣٦ MS. القاضي.
٣٧ MS. illegible at this point.
٣٨ MS. حافظا.

بيعة لأن هواهم مع العم الكبير إسحق بن أحمد بن أسد وهو إذ ذاك أمير سمرقند وعنده أهله وبنو عمه وأجناده متوافرون.

(ب١٢٣) فقال القاضي لسيمجور الخوارزمي يابا علي إنك من أهل العلم وما ينبغي لك أن تخلف عن هذه البيعة لأن الله من عليك بأسلاف هذا الأمير وهداك على يديهم إلى الإسلام وجعلك بهم من ذوي الأمر. فصاح عليه بغرا الكبير إنك شيخ قد خرفت. ما لك والأتراك؟ عليك بأصحابك ودعنا حتى نتشاور فيما بيننا كما تشاورتم و صاح الأتراك وارتفعت الضجة. فقال محمد بن أحمد لصاحب جيش المطوعة أظهر ما رتبت لك.

فأحضر جماعة من أولاد الأتراك ونساءهم (٣٩) وأوقفها فوق القهندز وخرجت كتائب (٤٠) المطوعة وأهل البلد. ونادى مناد أمر الأمير محمد بن أحمد أن يقتل من خرج من الأتراك من غير مبايعة ولمن قتله ماله. فلما رأت الإتراك الجد بايعوا بأجمعهم كارهين بعد العصر وصلوا على الشهيد أحمد إصفرار الشمس ودفنوه عند المغرب. وأمر ابن أحمد بأن لا ترد للأتراك دوابهم ولا سلاحهم إلى ثلاثة (٤١) أيام إلى أن يحلفوا يمينا أخرى.(٤٢)

ثم كتب من ليلته كتابا إلى سمرقند لحضرة إسحق بن أحمد، عم الشهيد وبعث الكتاب من الغد وأحضر الإتراك وأمرهم باليمين فقام فيهم مامراج وهو من أجل غلمان إسمعيل الماضي. فقال أيها الأتراك إنكم لم تقبلوا مني يوم قتل مولانا واليوم لا أعرف لتخلفكم عن اليمين وجها. إحلفوا لهم بعدد المطر وورق الشجر حتى يخلصوا أولادكم وأموالكم. فحلفوا عن آخرهم (٤٣) وكملت البيعة ووضع محمد بن أحمد المال.

واجتمع بعد ذلك أبو منصور قراتكين و يلبغ (٤٤) وبغرا الكبير وغيرهم (١٢٤ا) وحلف بعضهم لبعض أنهم يكونون يدا واحدة. ثم قال قراتكين لمحمد بن أحمد أيها الأمير إنك ما ظفرتم بنا إلا بمساعدة أهل بخارا وكذلك نريد أن تساعدونا في حرب من يحاربنا وإنكم طرحتمونا في أمر الله تخلصا منه. فقال ابو سهل شيخ البلد علي الرجال وعليكم الأموال. إن قبلتم عشرة ألف فعلي مثلها فطابت نفوس الأتراك وقاموا بأجمعهم فسلموا على نصر بن أحمد بالإمارة وقبلوا الأرض.

Translation

(fol. 119a/line 13) Aḥmad b. Ismāʿīl's death came about as follows. Having come to seek his (Aḥmad's) protection, Ibn Qārin, the lord of Jabal Dunbāwand,[45] remained at his court for many days without being presented to the amir. He complained about this to K.ndātakīn (?) b. K.ndājūr (?) al-Daylamī, one of Aḥmad's generals, who asked

٣٩ MS. نسايهم.
٤٠ MS. كتايب.
٤١ MS. ثلثة.
٤٢ MS. اخري.
٤٣ MS. اخرهم.
٤٤ MS. يبلغ.
45 W. Madelung identifies Ibn Qārin as Shahriyār b. Bādūspān, Ispahbad of Lāpūr and descendant of the Qārinwandid ruler Māzyār who was executed in Baghdad in 224 A.H. (Madelung, *op. cit.*, 177–178).

him if he had brought anything for the senior courtiers. Ibn Q̲ārin replied that he had not and he (the general) explained that this was the reason he had not been admitted. "Then what am I supposed to do?" he asked. K.ndātakīn said that he would go to Abu'l-Ḥasan the secretary and find out from him what he should do in order to gain admittance.[46] He came to the secretary and put this question to him. The secretary said that the sum of 6000 dinars was required in order to gratify the senior courtiers. When the Daylamī told him this, Ibn Q̲ārin borrowed 6000 dinars from some merchants and handed it to K.ndātakīn who (fol. 119b) passed it on to Abu'l-Ḥasan. On the third day after taking the money, he brought Ibn Q̲ārin before the amir. Aḥmad was delighted to see him: he received him with honour, showed him favour and provided him with lodgings. Then he said to Abu'l-Ḥasan "Find out from him whether he would prefer to return to his own country or stay at our court." When asked by Abu'l-Ḥasan, Ibn Q̲ārin chose to return to his country. Aḥmad publicly presented him with robes of honour fit for a king, ten purses of coin and ten fine horses with jewelled saddles. He then saw him off, having assigned to him an escort to accompany him to the borders of his territory and written letters to his governors, (instructing them) to provide lodging for him and look to his needs. He sent him on his way, full of gratitude.

The governor of Marv, who has previously been mentioned in this book, was Muḥammad b. ʿAlī, known as Ṣuʿlūk.[47] When Ibn Q̲ārin

[46] Ibn Isfandiyār gives Abu'l-Ḥasan the epithet *dihqān* (*Tārīkh-i Ṭabaristān*, 271); Gardīzī names him Abu'l-Ḥasan Naṣr b. Isḥāq (*Zayn*, 150).

[47] Muḥammad b. ʿAlī Ṣuʿlūk (or al-Ṣuʿlūkī) was the son of ʿAlī b. al-Ḥusayn al-Marwarrūdhī (also al-Marwazī), governor of Marv, who had formed an alliance with Ismāʿīl b. Aḥmad the Sāmānid against ʿAmr b. al-Layth the Ṣaffārid before Ismāʿīl's decisive victory over ʿAmr at the battle of Balkh in 287 A.H. Muḥammad and his three brothers, Husayn, Aḥmad and Manṣūr, served the Sāmānids as generals and administrators: for their common descent from ʿAlī b. al-Ḥusayn, see de Goeje, "Die Iṣṭakhrī-Balkhī Frage", 54, note 1. Muḥammad and Aḥmad later achieved notoriety by reason of their conversion to Ismāʿīlism. During Ismāʿīl's reign, Muḥammad was initially appointed governor of al-Rayy and then Ṭabaristān (Gardīzī, *Zayn*, 148: Ibn Isfandiyār, *Tārīkh-i Ṭabaristān*, 266). Ibn Ẓāfir's statement that he was governor of Marv just prior to Aḥmad's death is puzzling: if he was the governor of Ṭabaristān who was defeated by the Zaydī, al-Nāṣir al-Uṭrūsh, at the battle of the Būrūdh River in Jumādā II 301 A.H., (as Ibn Isfandiyār has it), he would not have had time to take up the governorship of Marv in the interval between his defeat and Aḥmad's death, both of which events occurred in the same month. Perhaps Ibn Ẓāfir has mistaken Muḥammad for one of his three brothers: misattribution of their *kunyas* is common in the literary sources. The origin of the

arrived in Marv, Muḥammad accommodated him in his own residence. He (Muḥammad) asked him how he had found the amir (*al-amīr al-sayyid*)[48] and Ibn Qārin replied that he had bought an audience with him (by paying) 6000 dinars. "Whom did you pay?" asked Muḥammad. The reply came, "Abu'l-Ḥasan the secretary." The intelligence officer (for the city of Marv) immediately sent a letter reporting this without Ibn Qārin's knowledge. When Aḥmad received it, he replied at once, ordering that, wherever he might be reached (on his journey), Ibn Qārin should leave everything he had with him to be sent on to his country and return with five slaves. After this, Aḥmad rode off to hunt down a lion which had been causing injury to people on the banks of the Jayḥūn river.

The messenger overtook Ibn Qārin while he was (still) in Marv and took him back to Aḥmad b. Ismāʿīl, who was on the hunting expedition. When he met him, Aḥmad said, "Abū Manṣūr, we have caused you anxiety by bringing you back." He told him to put his hand on his head and he did so. "Now swear," he said, "how much did you forfeit at my court?" Ibn Qārin replied, "6000 dinars, but if I had had to forfeit my children in order to see you, it would have been a small loss." "Who took this from you?" asked Aḥmad. "Abu'l-Ḥasan the secretary" replied Ibn Qārin. (fol. 120a) After he

---

nisba al-Ṣuʿlūkī, which is only applied to Muḥammad and not to his relatives, is unknown: it is most likely a personal sobriquet, perhaps with the meaning of "bandit" or "highwayman". There is no known connection between Muḥammad al-Ṣuʿlūkī and the Nīshāpūrī family of Shāfiʿī *ʿulamāʾ* who bore the same *nisba* (see Samʿānī, *Ansāb*, vol. viii, s.v. "al-Ṣuʿlūkī"). Ibn Ẓāfir's earlier mention of him occurs in his chapter on the Ziyārids (fol. 112a), where he is incorrectly identified as the Sāmānid general who quelled a revolt in Ṭabaristān in 901 A.D.

[48] *Al-amīr al-sayyid* is the title found on Sāmānid copper coinage from the reign of Aḥmad's successor, Naṣr. Its earliest appearance is on a *fals* of Samarqand dated 304 A.H., before which year the names of the ruling Sāmānids were preceded by the simple title *amīr* (Davidovich, "Novuie dannuie po istorii Samanidov", nos 83–89, 116). The use of the title on two *fulūs* of Samarqand which were apparently struck by Naṣr's eponymous great-uncle, dated 280 A.H., cannot be taken as evidence for its earlier use on the coinage (*Ibid.*, nos 5–6). The two *fulūs* cited by Davidovich postdate Naṣr I's death by one year and the *duʿā* which follows Naṣr's name in their legends (*aʿazzahu Allāh*) first appears on the copper coinage in the reign of his successor, Ismāʿīl b. Aḥmad, and continued to be used on the copper coinage in the reigns of his successors. The reverse die used to strike these two *fulūs* was probably engraved in Naṣr II's reign and muled with an obsolete obverse die (bearing the date) from the coinage of his great-uncle. Nevertheless, Ibn Ẓāfir's use of the title with reference to Aḥmad, both here and below (fol. 121a) suggests that the Sāmānids were known by the title before it was incorporated into the legends of their copper coinage.

had given him another gift, Aḥmad summoned Abu'l-Ḥasan and said to him, "(He was) a stranger who left the comforts (*niʿma*) (of his own country) without fear—for we have no designs on his lands—and came to us, bearing valuable gifts. To treat him as you treated him, makes me think that you have forgotten how you came to me, wearing a cloak which was not worth even six dirhams! I shall call you to account for this when we return to Bukhārā!"

The lion-hunt had meanwhile brought Aḥmad to a district called Farabr, where he spent the night.[49] Realising that if he returned to Bukhārā the next day, Aḥmad would punish him, Abu'l-Ḥasan plotted to kill him. The *ghilmān* (slaves) joined the conspiracy after he had given his word that he would pay allegiance to Aḥmad's uncle, Isḥāq b. Aḥmad, increase their stipends, and promote every one of their captains to a governorship. He ordered the Keeper of the Privy Purse and the Master of the Wardrobe to kill him and promised them a great deal of money. They then entered the amir's tent and cut his throat.

In (his) book *Akhbār Khurāsān* al-Wazīr Abu'l-Qāsim al-Maghribī says that Aḥmad had two tame lions which lay at the entrance of his sleeping chamber every night so that no-one could harm him. On this evening however he neglected to place them at the entrance of his tent and was killed. He was murdered in the year 301 after a reign of 7 years. He was one of the most handsome of men and a person of exemplary conduct. After his murder, he was gived the honorific title of "The Martyr". His eldest son was Abu'l-ʿAbbās al-Faḍl; the others were Abu'l-Ḥasan Naṣr b. Aḥmad, Abū Zakarīyā Yaḥyā, Abū Isḥāq Ibrāhīm and Abū Ṣāliḥ Manṣūr.

Abu'l-Ḥasan Naṣr b. Aḥmad b. Ismāʿīl

(fol. 120b) Ghars al-Niʿma mentions in his history that (Naṣr's) companions gave him the title *al-muʾayyad* (The [Divinely] Assisted) during his lifetime; after his death he was known as *al-saʿīd* (The Fortunate).[50]

[49] Farabr was a town on the main road from Āmul to Bukhārā, two stages (*marḥalas*) from Bukhārā (Iṣṭakhrī, *Masālik al-mamālik*, 334f.).

[50] Ibn Ẓāfir is probably mistaken in attributing the title *al-muʾayyad* to Naṣr, on the authority of Thābit b. Sinān (here erroneously called Ghars al-Niʿma, see below note 69): he is in general an unreliable source for Sāmānid titulature. The numismatic evidence demonstrates that the title was adopted by his son, Nūḥ, who was

As soon as the *ghilmān* had murdered him, they made haste to inform Abu'l-Ḥasan. He seized the (royal) treasury and made good his promises to the elder *ghilmān* and those who had actively participated in the murder. He then ordered them to ride quickly to Bukhārā before the news reached the city and to take over the citadel, the governor's palace and the treasuries, so that Muḥammad b. Aḥmad, Aḥmad b. Ismāʿīl's deputy in Bukhārā, should not find out what he had done.[51] They set off in haste, taking Aḥmad's corpse with them in a litter in their baggage train. But the younger *ghilmān*, who had not pledged allegiance (to Isḥāq b. Aḥmad), went ahead and agreed to send a messenger to take the news to Aḥmad's mother. They dispatched one of their number to her and he brought her the news. She then sent the messenger on to Muḥammad b. Aḥmad and Sākin, the Rūmī eunuch, who was a loyal counsellor to his masters. When he heard the news, Muḥammad b. Aḥmad hastily mounted his horse, rode to the gate of the citadel and made it secure. He mobilised the *muṭṭawwiʿa* (local militia) and sent a thousand of them to guard the governor's palace and the treasury.[52] He ordered the *ʿayyārūn* (civilian levies) to take up their weapons, brought out (their) banners and marched them out to a place known as al-Sahla.[53] He

---

the first of the Sāmānids publicly to proclaim such a title, on his coinage, in the form *al-malik al-muʾayyad*.

[51] There is some confusion in the sources about the name of Aḥmad's governor of Bukhārā. The manuscript gives it as محمد بن احيد. However Ibn al-Athīr names him Aḥmad b. Muḥammad b. al-Layth and Narshakhī tells us that he had been Ismāʿīl b. Aḥmad's chief of police in Bukhārā (*Kāmil*, vol. viii, 78: Narshakhī, *Tārīkh-i Bukhārā*, 15 = tr., 11 and note 45). But in a passage dealing with the events of the year 261 A.H., Ibn al-Athīr gives the same name, Aḥmad b. Muḥammad b. al-Layth, to a military officer who briefly acted as commander of a Sāmānid army occupying Bukhārā just prior to Ismāʿīl al-Sāmānī's arrival in the city. This commander he identifies as the father of Abū ʿAbdallāh ibn Junayd (variant readings for Junayd are *ḥ.m.d* and *ḥ.y.d*) (*Kāmil*, vol. vii, 281). Whatever the correct version of the *ism* of the military officer active in Bukhārā in 261 A.H. it is likely that it was his son, rather than he, who was governor of Bukhārā in 301 A.H.

[52] *Al-muṭṭawwiʿa* is here translated as "militia", rather than "volunteers", in order to reflect the fact that this corps of troops was probably part of a standing army, drawn from the inhabitants of Bukhārā; see Treadwell, "The role of the *mamlūks* in the early Sāmānid state" (forthcoming).

[53] Al-Manīnī, the Ottoman commentator on al-ʿUtbī's *Kitāb al-yamīnī*, says of Ṣadr al-Afāḍil, an earlier commentator on the same text, that he described al-Sahla as "the open space (*al-saḥrāʾ*) behind Tell Abī Ḥafṣ al-kabīr (up to) the Mawālī river." He added that the Sāmānids' palace was in the fortified compound (*al-ḥiṣār*) near al-Sahla (Manīnī, *Al-fatḥ al-wahbī*, 165). This corresponds to the Jū-yi Mūliyān estate which was purchased by Ismāʿīl b. Aḥmad from a local landowner (Narshakhī, *Tārīkh-i Bukhārā*, 39 = tr. Frye., 27–29).

then sent out a spy to gather information. The spy returned with the news that they, meaning the *ghilmān*, were approaching. (Muḥammad) ordered that the *muṭṭawwiʿa* and the *ʿayyārūn* should be drawn up in ranks between the Sahla gate and the Citadel gate and his command was carried out.[54]

The *ghilmān* arrived, running forward and shouting abuse at Muḥammad b. Aḥmad. About a thousand *mamlūks* (slaves) made for the Sahla gate and when they saw the local people, the *muṭṭawwiʿa* (fol. 121a) and *ʿayyārūn*, (all) bearing arms, they shouted at them "How is it that you are assembled here? Disperse! If the *amīr al-sayyid* arrives to find you here like this, he will give you cause to regret it." The citizens replied, "Go forward to our leaders: if they order us to withdraw, we will do so." They made their way towards them and found the cavalry drawn up in rows, (their) banners unfurled and the city elders mounted on their horses, each one of them with his retainers. They approached one of them, Abū Yaʿqūb Isḥāq b. Ibrāhīm, the city elder and Master of arms manufacture, who had more than one thousand apprentices in the city. Fāris al-Turkī, one of the senior *mamlūks* of Aḥmad's father, Ismāʿīl, shouted at him, "Tell me, Abū Yaʿqūb—since when have the people of Bukhārā been accustomed to taking up arms against their kings? Were you not an elderly man, I would give you your just deserts." Isḥāq shouted to his *ghilmān* (attendants?), "Seize this evil-doer, who murdered his master, and his companions." Then he raised his hand and struck Fāris a blow to the head with a mace he was holding and forced him and his slave retainers who were with him to dismount. The *muṭṭawwiʿa* took their horses and weapons and searched them all before confining them within the timber yard. They stationed naphtha-throwers on the walls (of the compound) and instructed them to shoot fire at them if the prisoners moved or spoke a word.

The citizens held their positions until another group of *mamlūks* arrived. They disposed of them in similar fashion to the first. They now held 4000 *mamlūks* captive in the timber yard, while those who were behind them still had no knowledge of their fate. Then Abu'l-Ḥasan the secretary drew near, wearing the amir's clothes and the tall Ismāʿīlī sable cap,[55] leading a company of some 2000 *ghulāms*, the amir's baggage train and surplus horses. On hearing of his

[54] See Barthold for these gates: *Turkestan*, 100–102.
[55] The *nisba* "*ismāʿīlī*" refers to Aḥmad's father, Ismāʿīl.

approach, (fol. 121b), Muḥammad b. Aḥmad said to the commander of the *muṭṭawwiʿa* army, "Abū Muḥammad, take a group of young soldiers with you out of al-Sahla and wait beyond the gate between the two rivers until he enters (*with those who have come?*) with the king. When he (i.e. Abu'l-Ḥasan) comes in to where I am and (the other) reaches you, do not let him give you the slip, for he is the perpetrator of the crime. If you hear a commotion from our direction, pay no attention to it, so that those responsible may apprehend him."[56]

The commander marched out with 4000 cavalrymen and 2000 foot-soldiers whom he deployed between the two rivers. When the *ghilmān* drew close and saw the *muṭṭawwiʿa* assembled before them, they rebuked them. The leaders of the vanguard were Sīmjūr, the Pencase Holder,[57] and Bundār, one of the most intelligent and prudent of the *mamlūk*s. Sensing that something was amiss, Sīmjūr told Bundār and the *ghilmān* to go forward while he and his *mamlūk*s remained with the commander. "If he is for us," said Sīmjūr, "all well and good: if he is against us, then I will take care of him for you." They approved of his plan, so he remained with the commander and said to him, "Abū Muḥammad, I see that a trap has been laid." "What you see is nothing but festivities in honour of the amir", said the commander. Sīmjūr replied, "(I will join you) on condition that (you give) me, my family and my property (a guarantee of security) in the name of God and his Prophet." The commander replied "If you are telling the truth, order your *mamlūk*s to dismount, remove their weapons and hand them over to my men." Every one of the *mamlūk*s knew who had taken his weapons and charger so that they might be returned to him. Sīmjūr, who had 500 of his *mamlūk*s with him,

---

[56] This passage is corrupt (see note 26 to the edition). The general sense however is clear: Muḥammad b. Aḥmad prepared a trap for Abu'l-Ḥasan which was to be sprung once Abu'l-Ḥasan reached him and Aḥmad's corpse reached the commander's forward position.

[57] This appears to be the famous Abū ʿImrān Sīmjūr *al-dawātī*, former slave of Ismāʿīl b. Aḥmad and founder of the Sīmjūrid line of governors of Khurāsān. In Ibn Ẓāfir's text he is given the *kunya* Abū ʿAlī and the *nisba* al-Khwārazmī (see fol. 123b), neither of which are attested in other sources. Perhaps Sīmjūr was a Khwārazmian by origin, rather than a Turk, as is commonly believed to be the case. See Muqaddasi, *Aḥsan al-taqāsīm*, 285–6, for the perceived similarity between Khwarazmians and Turks in physical appearance and military abilities and the practice of passing off Khwārazmians as Turkish *mamlūk*s in the slave markets. All our sources, with the exception of Ibn Ẓāfir, locate Sīmjūr in Sīstān as governor of the province at the time of Aḥmad's death (see for example Ibn al-Athīr, *Kāmil*, vol. viii, 79).

agreed to this proposal. He was a learned man of the school of al-Shāfiʿī (may God have mercy on him) and skilled in disputation.

Sīmjūr remained at the head of his troop with two *ghulāms* standing before him. As each of the *mamlūk* captains filed past him, he said to them in Turkish, "Go forward: I will take care of him (meaning the commander) for you." So they went forward to the *muṭṭawwiʿa* who forced them to dismount between the Sahla gate and the citadel, where they were stationed with Muḥammad b. Aḥmad. They confined each one of them with their *ghilmān* in the timber yard.

(fol. 122a) Then Abu'l-Ḥasan the secretary approached, wearing the *qalansūwa*. As he came in between the two rivers and drew level with the commander, he greeted him, "Peace be upon you, Abū Muḥammad." The reply came, "I give you no greeting, enemy of God!" He raised his mace against him and a tumult ensued. His *ghilmān* and amirs who were behind him began to raise their voices. The *muṭṭawwiʿa* rushed towards him, pulled him off his horse, threw a shackle around his neck and ran away with him. The army dispersed in pursuit of the *ghilmān* who had not yet arrived, took them all captive to the last man and imprisoned them. Muḥammad b. Aḥmad posted men to mount guard outside their houses and immediately dispatched fast camels to accompany the coffin of the martyred amir Aḥmad b. Ismāʿīl (to Bukhārā). (In the following days) Abu'l-Ḥasan the secretary was gibbeted on the walls of the citadel for a while every day before being taken down and returned to prison. He and the two *ghulām* murderers were gibbeted for two hours every day for forty days. They were then executed and their corpses hung on the walls where they remained for seven years. Small birds eventually nested in their skeletal cavities.

When the amir's body had been brought to the governor's palace by the messengers, it was washed and shrouded and his bier was moved (to another place) so that prayers might be said for him. The freeborn captains came out, barefoot and weeping, and the *mamlūks* were released from their confinement so that they might pray for him. When the coffin had been put down in the prayer-ground, Muḥammad b. Aḥmad stood up and said, "(Hear me), Muslims and partisans (of the Sāmānid dynasty), I have a proposal which I will put to you before we pray for the dead and disperse from this gathering. If it meets with your approval, you will help me to carry it out; if not, then you may suggest an alternative." Meanwhile he secretly summoned the army commander and told him "Go to the city, take the *muṭṭawwiʿa* and station one of their leaders in every quarter and bring together the women-folk and families of the soldiers and *mamlūks* whose houses are under guard, in one place. Hand over their (the Turks') horses and weapons to the *muṭṭawwiʿa* and deploy the infantrymen around the citadel (fol. 122b) and the cavalry between al-Sahla and the citadel." "Then," he said, "stay put until you receive my command." The commander did as he was told.

Muḥammad b. Aḥmad said, "This martyred amir (may God have mercy on him) died without having left an heir apparent or pledging us to pay allegiance to a successor. Muslims must of necessity have someone to govern them. I believe that we should not leave this gathering until the pledge of allegiance has been sworn to that person." After the city elders and the scholars had expressed their approval of what he had said, he told them to make their choice of whomever they wished (to appoint as amir). But they said, "Let the amir (Muḥammad) make his choice and we will consider the matter afterwards." Muḥammad said, "We are obliged to the martyred amir for the benefits he bestowed on us. If he had left but one single young child we would have reserved his right to have him succeed him. But he is survived by five sons who are satisfactory in this respect. I believe that we should pledge allegiance to one of them." The elders and freeborn partisans concurred with his decision, but the Turks remained silent. Muḥammad b. Aḥmad addressed them, "You are the lords of the kingdom, yet you say nothing." Then Bughrā the Elder spoke up "What you say is right, O amir, but it would be more fitting if we first prayed for the dead and buried the amir, then returned to the city and consulted among ourselves." (Muḥammad) said, "No-one will be permitted to return to his dwelling until we have made our pledge of allegiance." Bughrā answered, "So be it—until a successor has been agreed upon, you have jurisdiction over the Muslims and you manage their affairs."

Muḥammad was cajoling the Turks and distracting their attention until Abū Muḥammad's messenger returned (with the news that) their families and horses had been seized and that the citizens were prepared for war. Then he said to Abū Dharr, the (senior) *qāḍī* of the city and Abū Sahl, the (senior) *shaykh*, "Choose ten of the most eminent jurists and Traditionists and let us go to the city and decide to which of the amir's children we should make the pledge of allegiance." They did so and then, after Muḥammad b. Aḥmad had assigned some of his men to take charge (fol. 123a) of the funeral, they all went together to the citadel. Then they went to the governor's palace and entered (the chamber of) the mother of the martyred amir. Muḥammad b. Aḥmad bid her bring forward (her [grand]sons). The eldest, Abu'l-Faḍl al-ʿAbbās was a sickly child for whom there was no hope of recovery. They therefore agreed upon Naṣr b. Aḥmad and swore allegiance to him before his grandmother. Muḥammad b. Aḥmad picked him up and put him on his shoulders, but the child in his youthful innocence said "Where are you taking me? Will you kill me, as you killed my father?" Ibn Aḥmad wept (on hearing this) and told him "No, my lord, we have appointed you amir." They took him to the funeral and seated him before the bier with an unsheathed sword in his hands.

Then he called out, "O gathering of Muslims, the martyred amir had five sons, the eldest of whom, al-ʿAbbās, is sickly with no expectation of recovering his health. For this reason the *qāḍī* did not deem it right that he should succeed. We have therefore sworn allegiance to the amir Naṣr b. Aḥmad, a twelve year old, who is sound of mind, has the Qurʾān by heart, knows the religious duties and is well educated. What is your opinion?" The Bukhārans, their elders and freeborn leaders, declared their acceptance, but the Turks said "These are our lords and it is our right to have a say in their affairs and consult our Lady." They meant by this the mother of the martyred amir. Muḥammad said "I have sworn allegiance to the amir Abu'l-Ḥasan, Client of the Commander of the Faithful. Let those who have decided to swear allegiance (come forward and) do so." The first to pledge allegiance was Abu'l-Ḥasan ʿAlī b. ʿAbd al-Ṣamad, the Inspector of the army, then the amir Ḥamūyah b. ʿAlī, Muḥammad b. Aḥmad b. Jayhān, and Muḥammad b. Alīsaʿ.[58] After this, the people swore allegiance *en masse*, with the exception of the Turks and the murderer Abu'l-Ḥasan the secretary who had been brought to attend the funeral in order that he might repent (for his crime).

[58] ʿAlī b. ʿAbd al-Ṣamad was the *ʿāriḍ* (see, among others, Gardīzī, *Zayn*, 148, where he is called Abu'l-Ḥasan ʿAlī b. Muḥammad). Ḥamūyah b. ʿAlī was a general in Ismāʿīl's army: he had helped to negotiate the settlement in the civil war between Naṣr I and his brother, Ismāʿīl (Ibn al-Athir, *Kāmil*, vol. vii, 281), and later served as one of Naṣr II's generals. Muḥammad b. Aḥmad b. Jayhān (= al-Jayhānī) the great wazir of Naṣr's reign, is said by al-Thaʿālibī to have held the office of wazir late in Aḥmad's reign (*Yatīmat al-Dahr*, vol. ii, part 4, 62). He acted as wazir to Naṣr from 301–310 A.H. when he was dismissed on charges of heresy. Muḥammad b. Alīsaʿ al-Ṣughdī led Naṣr's army against his cousin, Ilyās b. Isḥāq b. Aḥmad (Ibn al-Athīr, *Kāmil*, vol. viii, 133).

The Turks began to dissemble in order to return without paying allegiance, because they inclined towards (Naṣr's) great-uncle, Isḥāq b. Aḥmad b. Asad, who was at the time the amir of Samarqand. He commanded a large army and lived in the city with his immediate family and other relatives.

(fol. 123b) The *qāḍī* spoke to Sīmjūr al-Khwārazmī, "Abū ʿAlī, you are a man of learning and it is not right that you should abstain from taking the oath of allegiance, for God showed you favour at the hands of the amir's forebears and guided you to Islām through them. By means of them he made you a man of consequence." Then Bughrā the Elder shouted at him, "You are a senile old *shaykh*! What business do you have with the Turks? Stick to your own kind and let us consult among ourselves just as you had the chance to consult!" As the Turks began shouting and causing a commotion, Muḥammad b. Aḥmad told the commander of the *muṭṭawwiʿa* to execute the order he had given him. He brought out a group of the Turks' sons and wives and stood them on the walls of the citadel. The *muṭṭawwiʿa* regiments and the citizenry marched out and a herald proclaimed "The amir Muḥammad b. Aḥmad has given the order that any Turk who leaves without first swearing allegiance will be killed and his property given to the man who kills him." When they understood the gravity of the situation, the Turks all grudgingly swore allegiance after midday and prayed for the martyr Aḥmad in the late afternoon. He was buried at sunset. Ibn Aḥmad ordered that their horses and weapons should not be returned to the Turks for three days until they had sworn another oath.

That night Ibn Aḥmad wrote a letter to Samarqand, to the court of Isḥāq b. Aḥmad, the uncle of the martyred amir and sent it the next day. He then summoned the Turks and ordered them to swear an oath. Mām.rāj, one of the most eminent of the *ghilmān* of the late Ismāʿīl, stood up amongst them and said "Turks, you did not accept (my recommendation) on the day of our master's murder and today I can see no way in which you can abstain from swearing this oath. Swear to them (as many oaths as there are) raindrops and leaves on the tree, so that they will release your children and your property." Every one of them, to the last man, gave his oath and the pledge of allegiance was completed. Then Muḥammad gave up their property.

After that Abū Manṣūr Qarātakīn, Yalbugh, Bughrā the Elder and others gathered together (fol. 124a) and swore oaths to each other that they would act together as one. Then Qarātakīn said to Muḥammad b. Aḥmad, "O amir, you only got the better of us with the assistance of the people of Bukhārā. Likewise, we want you to help us fight those who are waging war against us. For you cast us into this matter, in order to be rid of it yourself." Abū Sahl, the *shaykh* of the city said, "I will provide the men, if you provide the money. If you accept ten thousand then I will provide a similar number." The Turks' minds were put to rest by this and all arose, saluted Naṣr b. Aḥmad as amir and kissed the ground (before him).

Commentary

The passage under consideration here is of interest to historians of the Sāmānid period for two reasons. First, it presents a unique account of the rivalries of two of the most powerful interest groups involved in the politics of the early imperial Sāmānid state, the Turkish *mamlūk*s and the Bukhārans. Secondly, the style of the narrative is unique, both within the context of the Ambrosiana manuscript and the historiographic corpus of the early Sāmānid period. Its frequent use of dialogue is exceptional, as is the close detail of its narrative. Both features suggest that the passage was carefully constructed by its author(s), who had in mind not only to describe the course of events in the few days surrounding the death of Aḥmad, but also to use the narrative to present a less directly perceptible, but nevertheless potent, message about the role of the Turks in the history of early 4th century Transoxania. A detailed study of the authorial agenda will have to await further consideration, since it is a complex subject.[59]

The identity of the author(s) of the passage remains a matter of speculation which can not be satisfactorily resolved. The narrative precision and unimpeded flow of action, underpinned by the careful construction of the dialogue, suggests that the original story, regardless of later refinements and accretions which might have found their way into the present text, was unitary, rather than composite. The important question is whether it derives from the mainstream tradition of early Sāmānid historiography, which as Barthold and others have

[59] See Treadwell, "The role of the *mamlūk*s in the early Sāmānid state."

conclusively demonstrated, was drawn in large measure from al-Sallāmī's (d. circa 350 A.H.) *Kitāb wulāt Khurāsān.*[60] It is certainly true that Ibn Ẓāfir, or rather his immediate sources, derived some of their information on the Sāmānid state up to the middle of the 4th century A.H., from sources based on Sallāmī's work.[61] But most of the details of our passage are found in no other source and the most important element of the story, the regicides' failed attempt to seize Bukhārā and impose on its population their chosen successor, Aḥmad's uncle, Isḥāq b. Aḥmad, has no parallels whatsoever.

Many of the sources other than Ibn Ẓāfir which mention Aḥmad's death identify his assassins as his *mamlūk*s and give the date of his death as the month of Jumādā II 301/January 914: beyond that they have little to say on the matter.[62] Gardīzī and Ibn al-Athīr, the two most complete sources on early Sāmānid history which represent the mainstream tradition, give further details about the circumstances of Aḥmad's death. They both mention that shortly before he died, Aḥmad received news of the defeat of his governor of Ṭabaristān by a Zaydī army. He was so distressed by the news that he decided to return that evening to the campsite where he had spent the previous night. He had ordered the campsite to be burned when he had left it and his return was interpreted as an omen of his own terrible fate. Furthermore, he is said to have beseeched

---

[60] See Barthold, *Turkestan*, 21 for Gardīzī and Ibn al-Athīr's dependence on Sallāmī. Further evidence for Ibn al-Athīr's reliance on Sallāmī is presented by Frolova, "K voprosu ob istochnike svedenii Ibn al-Asira".

[61] Compare Gardīzī, *Zayn*, 145 and Ibn Ẓāfir, *Duwal*, fol. 116b for very similar accounts of the estimation of Sāmānid military power given to ʿAmr b. Layth the Ṣaffārid by his generals after their first military defeat by the Sāmānid army. Another passage which is common to Ibn Ẓāfir and the mainstream tradition occurs within the text of the present passage: see fol. 123a for the scene in which the young Naṣr asks the governor of Bukhārā who has come to pledge allegiance to him whether he intends to kill him as he had his father. In addition to these examples of *verbatim* correspondence there are many similarities in content for the early Sāmānid period.

[62] Ṭabarī, *Taʾrīkh al-rusul waʾl-mulūk*, vol. iii/4, 2289 (Ṭabarī does not give the month of his death, but says that Aḥmad was murdered by one of his most favoured Turkish *ghulām*s who, along with two other *ghulām*s fled and escaped arrest): Ibn al-Athīr, *Kāmil*, vol. viii, 77 (23rd Jumāda II): Gardīzī, *Zayn*, 149–150 (21st Jumāda II): Mīrkhwānd, *Tārīkh rawḍat al-ṣafā*, vol. iv, 38–39 (23rd Jumāda II): Narshakhī, *Tārīkh-i Bukhārā*, 128–129 = tr. 94–95 (11th Jumāda II): Qazvīnī, *Tārīkh-i guzīda*, 378 (3rd Jumādā II): Juzjānī, *Ṭabaqāt-i Nāṣirī*, vol. i, 206: Samʿānī, *al-Ansāb*, vol. vii, 26–27: ʿArīb, *Tabarī Continuatus*, 45: Khwāndamīr, *Tārīkh ḥabīb al-siyar*, vol. ii, section 4, 356 (23 Jumādā II). The news of his death reached Baghdad in Shaʿbān (ʿArīb, *Tabarī Continuatus*, 45).

God to take his life if He intended to take his kingdom away from him.[63]

If not by Sallāmī, or a source used by him, our passage was very likely originally written by a contemporary of the events described, who was most likely a native of Transoxania, and probably a native of Bukhārā. This is evident from his intimate knowledge of the topography of the city and the immediacy of his reporting of events. The only possible known candidate for its authorship would be Narshakhī, the author of the *History of Bukhārā*, presented in 332 A.H. to the amir Nūḥ b. Naṣr.[64] His work survives in several manuscripts of an abridged Persian translation of the Arabic original and it is therefore difficult to pinpoint similarities in style between his work in its original form and our passage.[65] Nevertheless there is little evidence that Narshakhī was the author of our passage. Like all other sources on the early Sāmānids, he has much more to say about Aḥmad's father, Ismāʿīl, the founder of the imperial Sāmānid state, than Aḥmad himself, to whom he devotes but a single page in the edited version of his history.[66] Moreover, his extended treatment of Ismāʿīl's biography is stylistically distinct from our passage: it does not make use of dialogue to the same extent, neither is its narrative structure as precise. The balance of opinion must therefore tend towards seeing Ibn Ẓāfir's passage as coming from a different pen than Narshakhī's.

Although we cannot identify the original source for the story, we do know something about the intermediate transmitters of the story, from whom Ibn Ẓāfir probably took his account. The same problem arises at this level of the transmission of the text as earlier: Ibn Ẓāfir nowhere says which of these intermediate sources, if any, transmitted the bulk of the story. But his text does offer a few hints. The three authors he cites in his sections on the reigns of Aḥmad and Naṣr are Thābit b. Sinān al-Ṣābī (d. 365 A.H.), Abu'l-Qāsim al-Ḥusayn b. ʿAlī al-Wazīr al-Maghribī (d. 418) and al-Farghānī,[67] all

[63] Gardīzī, *Zayn*, 149–150: Ibn al-Athīr, *Kāmil*, vol. viii, 77.

[64] Barthold was correct in his tentative conclusion that Muḥammad b. Sulaymān b. Aḥmad al-Bukhārī (d. 312), identified by Ḥajjī Khalīfa as the author of a history of Bukhārā, did not exist. Ḥajjī Khalīfa was mistakenly referring to al-Bukhārī's namesake, Muḥammad b. Aḥmad al-Bukhārī al-Ghunjār (d. 412). Frye notes that the earlier Bukhārī is also mentioned in the *Taʾrīkh Samarqand* (Frye, tr. *The History of Bukhārā*, introduction, note 8).

[65] Frye, *The History of Bukhara*, xii. The translation was made in 522 A.H. and the abridged version in 574 A.H.

[66] Narshakhī, *Tārīkh-i Bukhārā*, 128–9 = tr. 94–95.

[67] Ibn Ẓāfir, *Duwal*, fol. 120a and fol. 125b. For Thābit see *EI* (2nd ed.), s.v.

of whom lived in the 4th century A.H., but none of whom was a native of Eastern Iran.

Thābit b. Sinān is the only one of these three who is cited by Ibn Ẓāfir with reference to the history of another 4th century Iranian dynasty. He is quoted as a supplementary source to the history of Thābit's nephew, Abū Isḥāq Ibrāhīm b. Hilāl al-Ṣābī's *Kitāb al-Tājī*, from which Ibn Ẓāfir took his account of the death of the first Ziyārid king, Mardāwīj b. Ziyār, in 323 A.H.[68] Thābit is twice quoted in Ibn Ẓāfir's chapter on the Sāmānids, although in both instances Ibn Ẓāfir incorrectly names him Ghars al-Niʿma, the last of the triad of Sabean historians.[69] He cites him as a source on the genealogy and titulature of the Sāmānid dynasty:[70] there is no way of knowing however that he did not supply more information than this. The chronology of Thābit's history, which is said to have begun with the events of the year 295 A.H., would have allowed Ibn Ẓāfir to use him as a source on Aḥmad's reign (295–301 A.H.).[71]

Of the two remaining intermediate sources, al-Wazīr al-Maghribī is cited twice, first as the source for the tale of the two lions who normally guarded Aḥmad's sleeping quarters but were absent on the night of the murder, and secondly, on Naṣr's age at the time of his accession.[72] Both citations occur outside the narrative body of our passage, in concluding remarks situated at the end of the sections on Aḥmad's and Naṣr's reigns respectively. Both these details are found in the accounts which use Sallāmī as a source on the Sāmānids.[73] Given the evidence summarised above to the effect that our passage

"al-Ṣābī": for al-Wazīr al-Maghribī, see *ibid.*, s.v. "al-Maghribī": for al-Farghānī, father and son, see *ibid.*, s.v. "al-Farghānī". The latter is the *nisba* of both Abū Muḥammad ʿAbdallāh b. Aḥmad b. Jaʿfar (d. 362 A.H.) author of the *Ṣilat* (var. *Mudhayyal*) *ta'rīkh al-Ṭabarī*, and his son, Abū Manṣūr Aḥmad (d. 398 A.H.), author of a further continuation known as *Ṣilat al-ṣila*.

[68] Ibn Ẓāfir, *Duwal*, fol. 4b.

[69] Ibn Ẓāfir makes a similar mistake in alluding to the work of Ghars al-Niʿma's father, Hilāl b. Muḥassin, in his chapter on the Buyids (see Madelung, "Yemenite historical manuscripts", 178, note 13).

[70] Genealogy (Ibn Ẓāfir, *Duwal*, fol. 115b): titulature (*ibid.*, fol 120b). Thābit provides a unique item of information on Sāmānid titulature, to the effect that the kings were given posthumous sobriquets in addition to the regnal titles they bore during their reigns.

[71] Khan, *Studies*, 149.

[72] See Ibn Ẓāfir, *Duwal*, fols. 120a and 125b. The first citation is from a previously unknown history of Khurāsān, entitled *Kitāb akhbār Khurāsān*.

[73] See for example, Gardīzī, *Zayn*, 150 (which mentions one lion rather than two) and gives his age at his accession as 8.

falls outside the mainstream historiographical tradition, we must conclude that Maghribī was not a major source. The author Farghānī is quoted once only, in the sentence which contains the second citation from Maghribī, as contradicting Maghribī's calculation of Naṣr's age, which Farghānī gives as 12 rather than 8.[74] In the narrative body of our passage, Ibn Ẓāfir gives Naṣr's age as 12, with no reference to where he found this information.[75] The likelihood is, therefore, that Farghānī supplied at least that part of our text describing Muḥammad b. Aḥmad's selection of Naṣr as successor.

Thus far we have established that there are two different accounts of these events, one which originates with Sallāmī and a second which occurs in Ibn Ẓāfir's history. There are in addition two others, both of them independent of one another as well as the two just mentioned. They are the accounts of Ibn Isfandiyār and the later Persian sources, Juzjānī and Qazvīnī. The most detailed is in Ibn Isfandiyār's *Tārīkh-i Ṭabaristān*, which was written between 612–613 A.H. He is the only source other than Ibn Ẓāfir who says anything about the secretary's role. He tells us that the secretary had already been reprimanded once by Aḥmad for taking bribes but paid no heed to the warning and was subsequently apprehended again for the same crime: fearing for his life, he bribed four *ghilmān* to kill the king. They murdered Aḥmad together with one of his eunuchs and a Turkish *ghulām* and fled the scene, but were soon caught and put to death. The slaves were thrown to the lions and the secretary was forced to eat his own flesh until he died from the torture.[76] In common with all other sources than Ibn Ẓāfir, Ibn Isfandiyār has no knowledge of the regicides' march on Bukhārā and the subsequent struggle over the succession to Aḥmad. He casts the whole tragedy as the result of Abu'l-Ḥasan's duplicity. Neither does he mention the burning of the campsite before Aḥmad's murder which is common to all the main sources derived from Sallāmī. Thus it may be deduced that his source was different to both Sallāmī as well as Ibn Ẓāfir's. Ibn Isfandiyār also makes an error in his chronology when he says that at the time of his murder, Aḥmad was leading an army to Ṭabaristān to avenge the defeat suffered by his governor of that province at the

[74] Ibn Ẓāfir, *Duwal*, fol. 125b.
[75] Ibn Ẓāfir, *Duwal*, fol. 123a.
[76] Ibn Isfandiyār, *Tārīkh-i Ṭabaristān*, 271.

hands of the Zaydī army led by al-Nāṣir al-Uṭrūsh.[77] Although Aḥmad would not have had time to mobilize a large force to retake the province before his death, Zaydī successes in Ṭabaristān may have been the cause of Shahriyār b. Bādūspān's (Ibn Qārin) decision to seek refuge at Aḥmad's court in Bukhārā. As Ibn Isfandiyār says, Shahriyār was an old enemy of al-Uṭrūsh, the Zaydī general and future *dāʿī*.[78]

It is only the later Persian historians, Qazvīnī, the official of the Īlkhānid government whose patron was the famous wazir Rashīd al-Dīn, and Juzjānī (b. 589 A.H.), basing themselves on unknown sources, who allude to the grievances which Aḥmad's *mamlūks* harboured against their king.[79] Qazvīnī tells us that the *mamlūks* turned against Aḥmad because he spent all his time with members of the scholarly class, thus presumably neglecting his own *mamlūks*.[80] Juzjānī says that the *ghilmān* were eager to avenge the deaths of several of their peers whom Aḥmad had executed for misconduct.[81] The significance of these allusions to *mamlūk* discontent will be considered in their place.[82]

In summary it should be noted that although they add points of detail to Ibn Ẓāfir's account, none of these sources deals with the events surrounding Aḥmad's death and the succession of Naṣr in the same detail as Ibn Ẓāfir. These sources only take up the story after Naṣr's succession, beginning with the Bukhārans' successful campaign to defeat the Turks' candidate for the succession, Isḥāq b. Aḥmad. The existence of four different accounts of the transfer of authority from Aḥmad to his young son raises the question as to whether Ibn Ẓāfir, or one or more of his sources, was selective in his choice of material and if so why?

---

77 If Ibn Isfandiyār's date (Jumādā II 301 A.H.) for the battle on the River Būrūdh (in which the Zaydīs defeated the army of Sāmānid governor) is correct, Aḥmad would not have had time to mobilize an army of 40,000 troops, which Ibn Isfandiyār says he was leading towards the province when he was murdered (Ibn Isfandiyār, *Tārīkh-i Ṭabaristān*, 270).

78 Ibn Isfandiyār, *Tārīkh-i Ṭabaristān*, 270.

79 Of the earlier authors, only ʿArīb (d. *circa* 370) refers to the *mamlūks*' disaffection but does not elaborate on its cause: he notes that Aḥmad had given his *ghilmān* cause to fear him and that they plotted against him for this reason (ʿArīb, *Tabarī Continuatus*, 45).

80 Qazvīnī, *Tārīkh-i Guzīda*, 378. Khwāndamīr has a report to the effect that Aḥmad kept the company of the *arbāb al-faḍl wa kamāl* and did not allow his *ghulāmān* into his presence (Khwāndamīr, *Tarīkh ḥabīb al-siyar*, vol. ii, 365).

81 Juzjānī, *Ṭabaqāt-i Nāṣirī*, vol. i, 206.

82 See note 59, above.

This article is offered to Edmund Bosworth on the occasion of his 70th birthday, in gratitude for his many contributions to the medieval history of Islamic western Central Asia, and in the hope that he will continue to lead the field in this area of study.

Bibliography

ʿArīb, *Tabarī Continuatus*, ed. de Goeje, 1897.
Barthold, W., *Turkestan down to the Mongol invasion*, London, 1958.
Davidovich, E.A., "Novuie dannuie po istorii Samanidov (klad mednuikh monet ix–x vv. iz Samarkanda)", *Srednyaya Aziya v drevnosti i srednvekove (istoriya i kul'tura)*, ed. Gafurov, B.G. and Litvinsky, B.A., Moscow, 1977, 112–125.
Frolova, O.B. "K voprosu ob istochnike svedenii Ibn al-Asira o pravlenii Samanidov (10 v.) ve Srednei Azii", *Á la mémoire de l'academicien I.J. Krackovskij, Recueil d'articles*, Leningrad, 1958, 36–43.
Frye, R.N., *The History of Bukhārā*, see Narshakhī.
Gardīzī, *Zayn al-Akhbār*, ed. A. Habibi, Tehran, 1347.
de Goeje, "Die Iṣṭakhrī-Balkhī Frage", *ZDMG*, vol. xxv, 1871, 42–58.
Ibn al-Athīr, *al-Kāmil fi'l-ta'rīkh*, ed. C.J. Tornberg, revised and reprinted, Beirut, 1965–67.
Ibn Isfandiyār, *Tārīkh-i Ṭabaristān*, ed. A. Eqbal, Tehran, 1320.
al-Iṣṭakhrī, *Kitāb al-masālik al-mamālik*, ed. M.J. de Goeje, Leiden, 1870.
Juzjānī, *Ṭabaqāt-i Nāṣirī*, ed. A. Habibi, Tehran, 1343.
Khan, M.S., *Studies in Miskawayh's contemporary history*, Chicago, 1980.
Khwāndamīr, *Tārīkh ḥabīb al-siyar*, vol. ii, ed. Huma'ī, Tehran, 1954.
Madelung, W., "The identity of two Yemenite historical manuscripts" *Journal of Near Eastern Studies*, vol. xxxii, nos. 1 and 2, (1973), 175–180.
al-Manīnī, *Al-fatḥ al-wahbī ʿalā ta'rīkh abī naṣr al-ʿutbī*, vol. i, Cairo, 1869.
Mirkhwand, *Tārīkh rawḍat al-ṣafā*, vol. iv, ed. Sabuhi, Tehran, 1338–9.
al-Muqaddasī, *Aḥsan al-taqāsīm fī maʿrifat al-aqālīm*, ed. M.J. de Goeje, Leiden, 1906.
Narshakhī, *Tārīkh-i Bukhārā*, ed. M. Razavi, Tehran, 1351.
———, *The History of Bukhārā*, trans. R.N. Frye, Cambridge, 1954.
Qazvīnī, *Tārīkh-i guzīda*, ed. Nawa'i, Tehran, 1339.
al-Samʿānī, *Kitāb al-ansāb*, ed. A. al-Yamanī, 13 vols., Hyderabad, 1962–82.
al-Thaʿālibī, *Yatīmat al-dahr*, vol. ii, Cairo, 1934.
al-Ṭabarī, *Ta'rīkh al-rusul wa'l-mulūk*, ed. M.J. de Goeje *et al.*, Leiden, 1879–1901.
Treadwell L., "The role of the *mamlūks* in the early Samanid state" (forthcoming).

LOVE-RELATED CONVENTIONS IN SAʿDI'S *GHAZALS*

Ehsan Yarshater

Conventions of love-poetry differ from culture to culture. If we approach Persian love-poetry with the expectations derived from Western, Far-Eastern, or Indian poetry, both its climate and its conventions appear rather odd. We find sweethearts armed with bow and arrows, or wielding swords and daggers; sweethearts who are involved in bouts of drinking; disdainful, quarrelsome, and contemptuous sweethearts who have a host of lovers, among them the poet, a selfless and imploring one whose love and admiration for the beloved knows no bounds, even when the upper lip of the latter begins to be covered with a budding moustache or his face with a fuzzy beard.

Odd as these features may appear, they are readily understandable once we recall that the typical beloved in classical Persian poetry is a youth, a teenager rather, who is often a soldier or is being trained as one.

It is well-known that such youths were bought as slaves or acquired as war booty (a custom dating back to the first century of Abbasid rule, and in Persia to at least Samanid times), and then trained as pages or soldiers to serve their owners, mostly rulers and dignitaries. The standard histories of Persian literature, however, have generally ignored the implications of the beloved's gender and occupation, and the ways in which the phenomenon influenced the development of the conventions of the Persian *ghazal*. Neither Browne, nor Rypka, nor Ṣafa, nor Arberry concern themselves with this question. Only de Bruijn has addressed the question, succinctly, in his article in the *Encyclopedia Iranica*, s.v., "Beloved."

Earlier, I have discussed the subject and its impact on Timurid poetry.[1] Here, I should like to examine the reflections of the beloved's gender in the *ghazal*s of Saʿdi, the accomplished Persian lyric poet who, with Hafez, set the example for subsequent *ghazal* writers.

Saʿdi inherited a set of poetic norms which were born of certain

[1] In my "Persian Poetry under Shāhrokh" *Šeʿr-e fārsī dar ʿahd-e Šāhrokh*, Tehran, 1955, 153–60.

social circumstances, the most conspicuous of which was the practice by Persian local ruling houses of including a slave contingent in their armies, following the Abbasid model. The temperament, bearing, manners, armor, and occupation of the young men or boys who were bought or recruited and could also serve as the subjects of love poetry shine through Sa'di's *ghazals* as well as those of his predecessors. The following lines, for instance, imply the soldierly occupation of the poet's sweetheart and the slave status of at least some of them:

Gholām-e ḥalqe-ye simin-e gušvār-e to am
Ke pādešāh-e gholāmān-e ḥalqe dar gušī.[2]

I am the slave of the silver ring of your earring,
You, who are the king of the ring-in-ear slaves.

or

Čun kamān dar bāzu ārad sarvqadd-e sīmtan
Ārezuyam mīkonad k'āmāj bāšam tir rā.

When the cypress-figured, silver-bodied [beloved] takes up the bow to his arm
I feel the wish to be the target of [his] arrow.

or

Kamān-e sakht ke dād ān laṭif bāzu rā
Ke tir-e ghamze tamām-ast ṣeyd-e āhū rā.

Who gave a hard bow to that tender-armed one?
The arrow of his coquettish glance is enough to hunt deer.

or

To xod be jowšan-o bargostovān na mohtāji
Ke ruz-e ma'reke bar xod zereh koni mu'rā.

Indeed you have no need of mail and armour,
For you will make for yourself a chain mail of your hair.

or

[2] The quoted verses can easily be located in Foroughi's edition of *Ghazaliyyāt-e Sa'di* or in most other editions as the *ghazals* are generally arranged alphabetically according to rhyme and within each rhyme according to the first word of each first line.

Gar dast be šamšir bari ʿešq hamān-ast
K'ānjā ke erādat bovad enkār nabāšad.

If you resort to sword [my] love remains the same
For where there is devotion there would be no disavowal.

The expected indulgence of such youths in drinking is referred to in a number of lines, e.g.,

Fetne bāšad šāhedi šamʿi be dast,
Sar gerān az khāb-o sarmast az šarāb.

It is a tumult a beau with a candle in hand
Heavy-headed with love's slumber and intoxicated with liquor.

or

Duš ey pesar mey khorde'i, čašmat govāhi midahad
Bāri ḥarifi ju ke u mastur dārad rāz rā.

Boy! You have drunk wine, your eyes attest it,
Regardless, seek a partner who would keep the secret hidden.

A famous and exceptionally musical line of Hafez depicts the sweetheart of the poet as a drunkard, with hair disheveled, shirt buttons undone, sweating, singing happily, with a jug of wine in hand:

Zolf āšofte-ʷo khoy karde-ʷo khandān lab-o mast,
Pirahan čāk-o ghazal-khān-o ṣoraḥi dar dast.

Tresses disheveled, perspiring, lips smiling, inebriated,
Shirt open wide, singing *ghazal*s, with a jar of wine in hand.

The martial profession of the *maʿšuq*, or the beloved, affected the imagery of Persian lyric poetry from its inception. Metaphors such as *kamān-e abru, nāvak-e mozhgān, peykān-e ghamze, khadang-e ghamze, zereh-e mu, kamand-e zolf, laškar-e gham, tir-e negāh*, and the frequent use of military terms and arms and armor, such as *peykār, meydān, tigh, selāḥ, khanjar, kheyl, khašm, ḥeṣār, zenhār, darāvikhtan, asir šhodan* and *gereftan, panje endākhtan, tigh-barkešidan*, and *khun-rikhtan* in the lyrics, more than expected, find their explanation in the gender of the beloved and his profession, as does the use of "turk" in the sense of a male beauty. Notice, for example, the military terms and images in the following lines:

Bandevār āmadam be zenhārat
Ke nadāram selāḥ-e peykārat.

I came to your refuge like a slave
For I have no weapon to fight you.

Khadang-e ghamze az har su nehān andākhtan tā key?
Separ andākht ʿaql az dast-e nāvakhā-ye khuninat.

For how long shooting arrows of twinkling glances?
The intellect threw down its shield in the face of your sanguinary arrows.

Hesār-e qalʿe-ye bāghi be manjaniq madeh
Be bām-e qaṣr bar afkan kamand-e gisu rā.

Do not give to catapults the walls of a garden fort
Throw [instead] the lasso of your tresses to the roof of the tower.[3]

Mā separ andākhtim gar to kamān mikaši
Gu del-e mā khoš mabāš gar to bedin delkhoši.

We threw down the shield, if you draw your bow
Let our heart not be happy, if this makes your heart happy.

We must also add to this category the terms and images of hunting and the polo game, both activities in which favored youths engaged:

Khāham andar pāy-aš oftādan čo guy
Gar be čowgānam zanad hič-aš maguy.

I wish to throw myself at his feet like a polo ball;
If he hits me with his polo stick, do not forbid it.

Ān ke del-e man čo guy dar kham-e čogān u'st
Mowqaf-e āzādegān bar sar-e meydān-e u'st.

He who my heart is like a polo ball in the curve of his polo stick
The station of the nobles is at his race-ground.

Several observations may be made here. First is the openness of the homoerotic feelings in the lyrics, in spite of religious prohibitions, as is evident from lines such as:

Bā javāni sar khᵛoš-ast in pir-e bi tadbir rā
Jahl bāšad bā javānān panje kardan pir rā.

[3] I.e., You do not need catapults to gain entrance to a fort; your long tresses can be used as a rope to climb up to the roof of the fort.

This witless old man is merry with a youth,
It is folly [though] for an old man to wrestle with the young.

or

Khoš miravad in pesar ke barkhāst
Sarvi-st ke miravad čonin rāst.

Gracefully walks this youth who rose,
He is a cypress, who walks so straight.

Calling the object of their love a youth (*javān*), a boy (*pesar*), or referring to *khaṭṭ*, the onsetting hair on the beloved's face, is quite common among poets of the classical and post-classical periods. Shams-e Qays quotes[3a] a *qaṣide* from Naṭanzi, of which the first line reads:

Ey pesar nik ze ḥadd mibebari kār-e jamāl
Bā čonin ḥosn ze to ṣabr konam? in't mohāl.

O boy, you carry the business of beauty beyond limit;
With such beauty you demand my patience? Impossible.

and there are poems with *pesar* as their *radif* (e.g. a *ghazal* by Loṭf – Allāh Nishāburi, of the 15th century).[3b] As late as our own century, a major *qaṣide* by Iraj, the pro-emancipation and anti-veil poet, addresses a youth on the verge of puberty to whom he was attached, with the following *matla*ʿ:

Fekr-e ān bāš ke sāl-e degar ey šukh pesar
Ruzegār-e to degar gardad-o kār-e to degar.

Be mindful that next year, O jolly boy,
Your fortune will reverse and your affairs change.

It is also interesting to note that the Arabic words used for the beloved, i.e., *ma*ʿ*šuq*, *maḥbub*, and *ḥabib* are all masculine nouns. It is only rarely that the feminine *ma*ʿ*šuqe* is used.

A second point that attracts our attention is that love in Persian *ghazal*s is asymmetrical. There is almost a total absence of mutual affection and reciprocal love; none of the tender feelings that might develop in the heart of the beloved are discussed, and the lover shows little concern for the moral, intellectual, or spiritual qualities that might arouse amorous sentiments in a lover. Nearly all we hear

[3a] Tehran ed., 326.
[3b] See Yarshater, 1953, 155.

about is the incomparable physical beauty of the beloved. Love is generally born at first sight and is almost totally dependent upon visible qualities. There are no descriptions of the development and the degrees of love. Love is presented as sudden, complete, all-consuming, almighty, and, usually, unrequited. There are, to be sure, some lines, even entire poems, that describe moments of union (*veṣāl*) as opposed to ages of separation (*ferāq*), like Sa'di's well-known *ghazal* that begins with:

Yak emšabi ke dar āghuš-e šāhed-e šekaram
Garam čo 'ud be ātaš nehand gham nakhoram.

This one night when I am in the embrace of the sweet beauty
I care not if they put me like incense[4] on fire.

or Hafez's line:

Didār šod moyassar-o bus-o kenār ham
Az bakht šokr dāram-o az ruzegār ham.

Meeting with him became attainable, as did kisses and embraces,
I am grateful to fortune and to destiny.

But, even in such exceptional instances, it is only the lover's joy and delight we hear about; of the beloved's feelings on such occasions we seldom hear a word.

The general attitude of the beloved is one of disinclination and reluctance; faced with the lover's desire, his reaction ranges from disdain to protest and to anger. The lover often complains of the beloved's temper, his ill-treatment, oppression (*jafā*), and vituperations:

Be 'ešq-e ruy-e neku del kasi dahad Sa'di
Ke eḥtemāl konad khuy-e zešt-e niku rā.

(Only) he would give his heart to a pretty face
Who can bear the ugly humour, O Sa'di, of the pretty ones.

or

Sa'diyā gar dar baraš khāhi čo čang
Gušmāl-at khord bāyad čun rabāb.

O Sa'di, if you want to have him in your embrace like a lute,
You shall have your ears rubbed (hard) like a rebeck.

or

[4] Lit. "aloe's wood."

Bā jowr-o jafā-ye to nasāzim če sāzim
Čun zahre-ʷo yārā nabovad čāre modārā'st.

What shall we do if we do not put up with your tyranny and abuse?
When the gall and daring are lacking, the remedy is discretion.

or

Saʿdi az akhlāq-e dust harče barāyad nekust
Gu hame došuām gu, k'az lab-e širin nekust.

O Saʿdi, whatever comes from the beloved's conduct is good,
Even if it is all insults, which are lovely from sweet lips.

or

Tondiyy-o jafā-ʷo zešt-khu'i
Harčand ke mikoni neku'i.

Hot temper, abuse, and ill-humour
Though you commit, you are (still) beautiful.

Foḥš az dahan-e to ṭayyebāt-ast
Zahr az qebal-e to nušdāru'st.

Insult from your mouth is delicious,
Poison from you is antidote.

or

Vagar to jowr koni rāy-e mā degar našavad
Hazār šokr begu'yim har jafā'i rā.

If you maltreat (me), my[5] thoughts will not alter,
I will utter a thousand thanks for each abuse.

or

Zahr az kaf-e dast-e nāzeninān
Dar ḥalq čonān ravad ke jollāb.

Poison from the hands of the lovely ones
Goes down the throat like julep.

or

Saʿdi az akhlāq-e dust harče barāyad neku'st
Gu hame došnām gu ka'z lab-e širin doʿāst.

---

[5] Lit. "our."

O Saʿdi, whatever issues from the beloved's disposition is fine;
Let it be all insults, they are prayers from such sweet lips.

or

Došnām karam kardi-yo gofti-yo šenidam
Khorram tan-e Saʿdi ke barāyad be zabānat.

You conferred upon me insults, you spoke and I listened;
Happy (is) Saʿdi's person, whose name passes to your tongue.

And the lover tolerates all this abuse and tyranny on account of his love, a love that despite its ardor and intensity is not always confined to a single *maʿšuq*. Poets often proclaim that they are enraptured by beautiful ones—in plural—as if to say they are in love with love or with anyone who manifests charm and beauty:

Saʿdi ze kamand-e khubruyān
Tā jān dāri namitavān rast.

Saʿdi! from the rope of the beautiful ones
You will not be able to free yourself as long as you live.

or

Yār gerefteam basi, čun to nadideam kasi
Šamʿ-e čonin nayāmada'st az dar-e hič majlesi.

I have befriended many beloveds, (but) I have not seen anyone like you;
No such candle has (ever) entered the door of an assembly.

or

Nazar bā nikovān rasmist maʿhud
Na in bedʿat man āvardam beʿālam.

To desire the lovely ones is a known custom;
This is not an innovation that I brought to the world.

A corollary of the lover being attracted to beauty wherever it is found is that he condones the same on the part of other admirers, and as a result admits, in spite of his keen jealousy, that others are in love with his beloved, or, as the favorite expression of the poet's goes, "there are many hearts fettered in the chains of his curls." He even complains that the beloved is kinder to his rivals:

To rā nādidan-e mā gham nabašad
Ke dar kheyl-at beh az mā kam nabāšad.

You care not if you do not see me[6]
For there is no shortage [of people] in your camp[7] better than me.

or

Emšab ke bazm-e ʿārefān az šamʿ-e ruy-at rowšan-ast,
Āheste tā nabovad khabar rendān-e šāhed-bāz rā.

This evening, when the banquet of [us] the wise ones is illuminated with the candle of your face,
[Keep] quiet! so that the beau-loving debauchees do not get wind of it.

or

Ey velvele-ye ʿešq-e to bar har sar-e ku'i
Ruy-e to bebord az del-e mā har gham-e ru'i.

O you, the tumult of whose love resides in every lane,
Your face freed me from caring for any other.

or

Gar dust rā be digari az man farāghat-ast
Man digari nadāram qā'emmaqām-e dust.

If the beloved is free of my care because of other (lovers),
I have no other to take the place of the beloved.

or

Bā došmanān movāfeq-o bā dustān be khašm
Yāri nabāšad in ke to bā yār mikoni.

Friendly with (my) enemies and angry with (your) intimates,
It is not friendship what you do with your friends.

An outgrowth of the beloved's gender and his occupation are the lines that refer to the beloved's travel away from home and the poet's longing for his return. In the static society of medieval Persia there were scant opportunities for women to travel; but young men could be sent out on expeditions or could accompany their journeying masters. In the poetry of Hafez the beloved's absence due to travel is a recurrent theme e.g.:

Khāk-e rah-e ān yār-e safar karde biyārid
Tā čašm-e jahānbin konamaš jāy-e eqāmat.

---

[6] Lit. "us", modest form for me.
[7] Lit. "horsemen, army."

Bring the dust from the road of that journeying sweetheart,
So that my world-seeing eyes become its place of residence.

or

Duš āgahi ze yār-e safar karde dād bād
Man niz del be bād deham, harče bād bād.

Last night the wind brought the news of the journeying friend,
I, too, shall waste away my heart[8] (for his love), come what may.

or

Ān safar karde ke sad qāfele del hamrah-e u'st
Har kojā hast khodāyā be salāmat dāraš.

That journeying (sweetheart), who is accompanied by a hundred caravans of hearts,
O God, keep him safe wherever he is.

In the poetry of Saʿdi, however, there is a dearth of this theme, either because Saʿdi did not believe in love on credit, or, as is more likely, because the Salghurid rulers of Fārs were able, exceptionally, to maintain peace and stability in the province during the time that encompassed the main period of Saʿdi's literary activity. Hafez, on the other hand, lived during a turbulent period of Fārs, when it was repeatedly subjected to the wars between various predatory princes.

Before I proceed with a discussion of the nature and origin of love as portrayed in Persian *ghazals*, I should like to point out that on occasion there are also traces of heterosexual love in some lyrics, where we find direct or implied allusions to it. Notice, for instance, the following line of Saʿdi:

Gomān barand ke dar bāgh-e ʿešq Saʿdi rā
Nazar be sib-e zanakhdān-o nār-e pestān-ast.

They think that in the garden of love, Saʿdi has his eyes on
The apple of the chin and the pomegranate of the breasts.

or, a number of lines in which women's cosmetics such as *vasme* (i.e., the blue for the eyebrows) or ornaments such as *khakhāl* or anklets are mentioned, e.g.:

V'ān vasme bar abrovān-e delband
Yā qows-e qozaḥ bar āftāb-ast?

[8] A pun on *bād* "wind."

And is that the blue on those charming eyes
Or is it the rainbow in the sun?

There are also a number of lines in which the veil (*neqāb*) of the *maʿšuq* is mentioned; one would naturally assume that they refer to women, e.g.:

Agar to barfekani dar miyān-e šahr neqāb
Hazār moʾmen-e mokhles dar afkani be ʿeqāb.

If you should throw off the veil in the middle of the town,
You will throw a thousand sincere believers into the torment (of hell).

or

Ḥeyf bāšad bar čonān tan pirahan
Ẓolm bāšad bar čonān ṣurat neqāb.

It is a pity (to have) shirts on that body,
It is an injustice to have a veil on that face.

or

Gar to paričehre napuši neqāb
Towbe-ye ṣufi be ziyān mibari.

If you, fairy-faced, should not wear the veil,
You will make the Sufi forfeit his repentance.

I must say, however, that I am somewhat puzzled by the lines referring to the veils as their context sometimes encourages us to assume a male subject. For instance, the second line that I have just cited occurs in a *ghazal* (contained also in Prof. Zipoli's volume on Saʿdi)[9] which includes also the following line:

Fetne bāšad šāhedi šamʿi be dast
Sar gerān az khāb-o sarmast az šarāb.

It is a tumult a beau with a candle in hand
Heavy-headed with slumber and intoxicated with liquor.

This reminds us of a *ghazal* by Khāqāni that begins with:

Mast-e tamām āmad-ast bar dar-e man nimšab
An mah-e khoršid ruy, v'ān šah-e yāqut lab.

---

[9] Zipoli, Riccardo and Manoukian, Setraj, *Saʿdi: Concourse and lexical repertories of 1000 lines*, Venice, 1992, 18.

Fully drunk he has come to my door,
That sun-faced beauty,[10] that ruby-lipped king.

and contains the following line:

Gar na šabasti rokhaš key šavadi bi neqāb
V'ar na meyasti saraš key šavedi bi šaghab.

If there were no nights, when would his (?) face become free of veil?
If there were no wine, how could his head become free of brawls?

or a *qasida* by Mas'ud-e Sa'd of which the *matla'* is:

Be gāh-e raftanam az dar dar āmad ān delbar
Ze bahr-e jang miyān baste-ʷo gošude neqāb.

I was about to leave when the sweetheart entered the door,
Girded for a fight and having opened his (?) veil.

Perhaps the poets sometimes mix their sweethearts! Furthermore, the number of references to the veil appear to me to be somewhat more than can perhaps be justified by the male gender of the *ma'šuq*. The contexts, it must be admitted, are generally inconclusive in this respect, as a result of the fact that classical Persian poetry is so abstract and non-specific when it comes to the identity of the beloved, and is so stereotyped and stylized in its convention. For example, we can hardly be absolutely certain that Anvari is visited by a female *ma'šuq* when in the *nasib* of a panegyric he says:

čun vālehān ze jāy bejastam davide piš
Begreftamaš kenār-o barandākhtam neqāb.

I sprang up like madmen, running forward,
Took him (or her?) in my embrace and threw off the veil.

Or the use of *ma'šuqe*, a feminine word, in a line of Hafez:

Didi delā ke ākhar-e piri-yo zohd-o 'elm
Bā man če kard dide-ye ma'šuqe-bāz-e man?

Did you notice, O (my) heart, that despite my old age, learning, and ascetic piety
What my philandering eyes did to me?

But such traces are too rare to contradict the overwhelming evidence that the beloved addressed by the classical poets is male. Even in

[10] Lit. "moon."

the line that I just quoted from Hafez, *maʿšuqe-bāz* could be a frozen construct for a philanderer, particularly since other lines of the *ghazal* point to a male *maʿšuq*, e.g.:

> *Mast-ast yār-o yād-e ḥarifān namikonad*
> *Yād-aš be kheyr bād sāqi-ye meskin-navāz-e man*;

> (My) sweetheart is intoxicated and does not show remembrance of (his) partners
> May the memory be blessed of my kindly[11] Saki;[12]

as one would not expect a drunken *maʿšuqe*, nor a female *sāqi*. It should also be noted that there is one manuscript which has *maʿšuq* instead.[13]

In any event, it would not be correct to say that since gender is not distinguished in the third-person singular of Persian pronouns, the poet may be understood to refer to either a female or a male beloved. The correct way to understand Persian lyrics is that they are, as a rule, addressed to male sweethearts. Due to the grammatical ambiguity of Persian pronouns with respect to gender, however, the modern reader can often interpret the poems as referring to women.

Our conclusion with regard to the love climate of Persian lyrics is amply confirmed by the 13th century anthologist Jamāl Khalil of Sharvān who compiled a selection of 4125 quatrains, providing thereby a good sampling of the themes treated by Persian *robāʿi* writers (which are essentially the same as the themes of the *ghazal*). The *robāʿis* are divided in this anthology into categories according to subject. In the section on *maʿšuq* we find the following subdivisions, which in fact reads as a summary of what I have been discussing: "On his clothing," "On traveling, farewell, and return," "On offering kisses and withholding kisses," "On his falling in love," "On speaking, not speaking, bitter retorts, and his insults (*došnām-e u*)," "On his oppression (*jafā*) and his stone-heartedness (*sangdeli*)," "On the wine-drinking of the *maʿšuqe*." The most revealing, however, is a small rubric called "On *nesāʾiyyāt*" or women-related (*robāʿis*), a collection of only 125 quatrains that have been considered distinct by the compiler since they have a woman as the subject of love. But

[11] Lit. "kind to the indigent." The poet remembers a more caring beau.

[12] Lit. "wine-server." It refers to youths who served wine in banquets at court and in the homes of dignitaries; by extension it refers to a sweetheart.

[13] Ed. Khānlari, 801.

of these, only a few can be said for certain to refer to a woman (i.e., when an item such as an anklet, necklace, kerchief, collyrium [*sorme*], rouge, and *vasme* [the blue for the eyebrows] is mentioned); the others are vague, and might refer to either sex. Even if all of these 125 quatrains were about women, they would constitute only 1/33 of a total of 4125 quatrains—a negligible portion.

This again finds confirmation in the literature. The author of the *History of Ṭaberestān*[14] relates, as does the author of *Qābus-nāme*,[15] that the Ziyarid Prince, Sharaf al-Maʿāli imported a slave from Bukhara. He was so handsome that the 70 year old prince, realizing the consequences of his falling in love with him, ordered his vizier to take the boy away, seek a wife for him, and not let him be seen by the prince until a beard had grown on his face.

Various aspects of the practice could be gathered from other literary sources, such as Saʿdi's *Golestān* (chap. five), and of course also from the facetiae, notably those by Saʿdi and Zākāni, where pudency is no longer an obstacle.

Now we may take up the question of the nature of homosexual love as reflected in Persian poetry. The first instinct, particularly among those who have their eyes on mystical *ghazal*s, may be to regard love in Persian *ghazal*s as only Platonic. The poems themselves, however, do not support such a view. On the contrary, there is clear evidence that homoerotic love was thought of as having a physical basis; in other words, what the poet was craving was not simply abstract love and companionship, but also physical satisfaction. Setting the *hazliyyāt* or the facetiae aside, however, the atmosphere of Persian love poetry is generally free from vulgarity and grossness; the poet's desire for physical intimacy is, therefore, most often expressed only by longings for embraces and kisses, e.g.:

Duš dar khābam dar āghuš āmadi
V'in napendāram ke binam joz be khāb.

Last night in my dream you came to my embrace,
I do not believe that I can see this except in dreams.

or

[14] 146–7.
[15] 83.

Be khāb duš čonān didami ke zolfeynaš
Gerefte budam-o dastam hanuz ghāliye bu'st.

Last night I dreamt that I was clasping his tresses
And my hands have still the aroma of *ghāliye.*[16]

or

Marā rāḥat-e zendegi duš bud
Ke ān māhruyam dar āghuš bud.

For me the pleasure of life was last night,
When that beauty[17] was in my embrace.

or

Mard-e gostākhi niyam tā khoš dar āghušat kašam
Buse bar pāyat zanam čun dast-e bālā'im nist.

I am not a rude man so as to draw you happily to my embrace,
I kiss your feet (instead) as I have no high hand.

or

Če delhā bordi ey sāqi be sāq-e fetneangizat
Darighā buse čandi bar zanakhdān-e delāvizat.

How many hearts did you sweep away, O Saki, with your seditious calves,
Alas, I would wish (only) a few kisses to your charming chin.

or Hafez's line:

Labaš mibusam-o dar mikašam mey
Be āb-e zendegāni bordeam pey.

I keep kissing his lips and sipping wine:
I have discovered the water of life.

Only rarely more daring desires are expressed, as in the following two lines from Hafez:

Šab-e qadri čonin ʿaziz-o šarif
Bā to tā ruz khoftanam havas-ast.

---

[16] A perfume made of musk, ambergris, and some other ingredients.
[17] Lit. "the moon-faced one."

Vah ke dordāne'i čonān nāzok
Dar šab-e tār softanam havas-ast.

On the Qadr night, so honoured and so noble,
To sleep with you till daytime I desire;

Oh! a pearl bead so delicate
To bore during the dark night I desire.

The *Nozhat al-Majāles* cites a number of quatrains referring to the poet and his sweetheart being in a bathhouse (*garmābe*), of which one begins with the following line:

Būdim be garmābe man-o šamʿ-e Čegel.
U dast be gel dar zad-o man dast be del.

We were in the bathhouse—I and the Chagelian beauty[18]
He reached for the (washing) clay and I grasped (my) heart.

From the lines I have cited, it should be clear that what I have been describing is hardly the Western variety of love between consenting male adults, but resembles rather pedophilia. The age range of the beloved may be gauged from such lines by Hafez as:

Delbaram šāhed-o ṭefl-ast-o be bāzi ruzi
Bekošad zāram-o dar šarʿ nabāšad gonahaš.

My sweetheart is a beauty and a child, and I fear that one day
He will kill me miserably and he will not be accountable.

or

Čārdahsāle boti čābok-o širin dāram
Ke be jān halqe be guš-ast mah-e čārdahaš.

I have an idol, fourteen years old, nimble and sweet,
The full moon[19] is truly his slave.[20]

or

ʿĀšeq-e rūy-e javāni khoš-o nowkhāsteam
V'az khodā šādi-ye in gham be doʿā khāsteam.

[18] Lit. "candle."
[19] A metaphor for beauty.
[20] Lit. "ring-in-the-ear."

I am in love with a youth, jolly and newly grown,
And I have beseeched God in prayer for the happiness of this heartache.

or this line of Saʿdi:

Ruz-e bāzār-e javāni panj ruzi biš nist
Naqd rā bāš ey pesar, k'āfat bovad ta'khir rā.

The market day of youth is no more than five days;
Adhere to the here and now, O boy, as there is risk in delay.

Of course we have more accurate knowledge of the prevalence of homoerotic love from literary and historical sources, more particularly from the Mirror for Princes genre. *Qābus-nāme*, for instance, gives us reliable information on the topic. Its fourteenth chapter is on the falling in love (*'eshq varzidan*, lit. practicing love), and it is entirely about homoerotic love, as if heteroerotic love did not exist. The next chapter is about making love (*andar tamattoʿ kardan*) which includes practical advice on lovemaking, such as the following, which is the author's idea of moderation in the enjoyment of love—moderation being the hub of most of his recommendations: "But do not keep your inclination confined to either boys (*gholāmān*) or women, so you can have a share from both and so none of the two (sexes) would become inimical to you."

However, considering the variety and complexity of human emotions, and the effect of circumstance, sublimated affections without bodily desires no doubt did develop in lovers' hearts as some of Saʿdi's lines seem to indicate; e.g.:

Jamāʿati ke nadānand ḥaẓẓ-e rowḥānī,
Tafāvoti ke miyān davāb-o ḥeyvān-ast,

Gomān barand ke dar bāgh-e ʿešq Saʿdi rā
Naẓar be sib-e zanakhdān-o nār-e pestān-ast.

A people who do not know spiritual pleasures
And the difference between man and beast

Think that in the garden of love Saʿdi
Is enamoured of the apple of the chin and the pomegranate of the breast.

Or the following line which points to the beloved's chastity:

Pākize ruy dar hame šahri bovad valik
Na čun to pākdaman-o pākize ru bovad.

The pretty-faced[21] are found in every town, but
Not chaste and pretty like you.

As to the origins of the expression of love in a manner that blatantly contradicts Islamic precepts, one's first surmise is that it must follow a national trend or tradition rooted in pre-Islamic Persia. But although the mention of sodomy in the *Vidēvdād*[22] among the grave sins for which there is no atonement attests to the existence of homosexuality in ancient Persia, we fail to find any literary trace of it in extant Middle Persian literature. The *Šāhnāme*, the chief depository of ancient Iranian lore, and other heroic epics written in its imitation such as *Bahman-nāme, Kuš-nāme*, and *Borzu-nāme*, are totally devoid of it also, as are Ṭabari and Balʿami, Thaʿalebi and Dinawari, *Fārsnāme* and *Mujmal al-Tawārikh*, as well as popular prose epics like *Dārāb-nāme* and *Firuzšāh-nāme* that contain pre-Islamic elements. And Gorgāni's *Vis o Rāmin* and Nezami's romances *Khosrow o Širin* and *Haft peykar*, like *Šāhnāme*'s romantic episodes are all eminently heterosexual love stories.

We might consider the Hellenistic period of Persian history and think of the phenomenon as a Greek legacy; but, again, were this the case, it would show itself in Sasanian tradition before passing to the Islamic period.

As the New Persian poetry adapted itself to the forms, meters, and on occasion the content of Arabic poetry, one might think that here perhaps the key to the question could be found. But then the pre-Islamic and Umayyad Arabic poetry discourages this assumption. It is only with the Abbasids and the introduction of Persian-inspired ideas by *mawāli* poets like Abu Nowās that such novel themes were broached.

Thus, we are left only with Central Asia as a possible source of the tradition. The availability of slave funds in the region on the one hand, and long distances to be covered by nomadic hordes during raids away from base, on the other, may have encouraged the practice. But this is a mere hypothesis and careful research is required to confirm it.

The possibility that Sogdian and Bactrian Buddhist monasteries, where innocent attachments between older and younger monks may have initiated the trend also suggests itself. The universal use in Persian poetry of the word *bot* "idol" (< Buddha) for a beauty points

[21] Lit. "clean-faced."
[22] VIII, 31–2.

to the influence of the Buddhist culture in the areas where New Persian poetry originated. But again, these are surmises in need of evidence. If we knew more than we do about the Kushans and their culture we could be clearer about their possible impact on this issue.

I have mentioned physical and visible beauty as the basis of love in Persian poetry, its one-sidedness, and the fact that such loves, lacking a firm foundation in explicit moral or spiritual qualities, may have been transient, if passionate. I should make it clear, however, that this by no means detracts from the intensity and depth of amorous feelings as expressed in Persian poetry. The very reluctance of the beloved, the religious stricture against homosexual love, and the difficulty of access because of the *raqib* (that is, guardian or supervisor, and later, rival) which resulted in *ferāq* or separation, and finally the social stigma (leading to *rosvā'i* "infamy" and *bad-nāmi* "public disgrace") make the expression of yearning in Persian poetry one of the most profound.

THE MUSICAL SETTING OF THE MAWLAWĪ LITURGY

Yaqub Zaki
(James Dickie)

Traditionally, the Mawlawī *samāʿ*, with its peculiar turning motion, goes back to the moment when Mawlānā Jalāl al-Dīn Rūmī danced to the beat of the goldbeater's hammer; but, as attested in the *Manāqib al-ʿArifīn* (*Outstanding Deeds of the Sages*) of Eflaki Dede, Mawlānā's followers met to induce spiritual states by whirling at certain times and in certain places. Organised ritual dates, however, from the time of Sultan Walad, who founded the Mawlawī order in memory of his father so that the initiatic techniques and spiritual method imparted by him should not be lost. Under his leadership the *ṭarīqa* developed set forms and strict rules for group performance of their liturgy.

The Seljuq patronage of Mawlānā and his father, Bahāʾ al-Dīn Walad (d. 1231), known as Sultan al-ʿUlamāʾ, did not cease with the demise of the dynasty, for it was taken up by the Ottomans, indeed to such a degree that the Mawlawiyya became the establishment order of the Ottoman régime, closely linked to the judiciary, which contained the administrative cadres of the empire, but also attracting to its ranks poets, musicians, composers and the intellectual segment of society generally. So close was the association with the régime that the investiture of the Ottoman sultan was the hereditary privilege of the reigning head of the order, who travelled from Konya to Istanbul to officiate at the ceremony whenever a new sultan succeeded. There was in fact an overlapping of the two institutions. Of the 38 Ottoman sultans no fewer than 18 were Mawlawīs, including the composer sultan Salīm III, who was responsible for a notable setting of the liturgy.[1] Court composers like ʿIṭrī (1036–1124 A.H.; 1625–1712 C.E.) would compose secular music for court performance and religious music for the Yeni Kāpı Mawlawī-khāneh. He was frequently summoned to perform at the court of Mehmet

[1] Apart from Salīm III other famous sultans who were Mawlawī include the founder of the dynasty Osman Ghāzī and Sulaymān the Magnificent. Fātiḥ's wife was the great-granddaughter of Rūmī's sister, so all subsequent sultans belonged to Mawlānā's bloodline.

IV (d. 1692). Of his 27 surviving works five are of a religious nature. He composed the setting for the *Bayram tekbiri* (used on both ʿĪds); he is commemorated for this, the contribution to Islamic music for which he is most remembered, on his tomb outside the Edirne Gate in Istanbul in the Martyr's Park, not far from the Yeni Kāpı *tekke* and the quarter where he was born. Iṭrī aimed at synthesising a Mediterranean music out of the national styles of foreigners purchased at the slave-market at Istanbul. In contradistinction to popular *ṭarīqa*s like the Bektashiyya, which made use of folk melodies and folk instruments like the *sāz*, Mawlawī music is intellectual, engaging the mind and emotion simultaneously.

Membership of ʿAlawī cults was, particularly in eastern Anatolia, frequently a form of social protest. Sufism is a very complex phenomenon which ranges through a diversity of expressions; in antinomian guises (*ḥurūfiyyāt*) it could function as a vehicle of political dissent. Sunni orders, however, affected classical musical forms. The Mawlawī order in particular was the cradle of Turkish art music; the lodges of this order were the conservatoires where art music developed. An extensive repertoire came into being, both of a religious and a secular nature, as a composer had to cater for both kinds of audience. Thus the Mawlawī order is often referred to as "the music school of the Ottoman dynasty", and Jeffery Somers in an article published at the time of the World of Islam Festival in London in 1976 affirmed that it:

> was . . . the rise of the Sufi (dervish) orders which gave music a new liturgical position. This music was to influence the rise and course of classical music in many Muslim countries.

The Mawlawiyya was politically strong from the 15th to the 17th centuries. During this time it was influenced by secular *maqām* music. This accounts for the entry into its liturgical repertoire of secular forms like *peshrev* and *taqsīm*. The same author goes on:

> Most of the orders encouraged music, and many of their members composed not only religious music for the use of their brotherhood but often classical music as well. This gave classical music in the Islamic world a meditative quality, so that the spiritual states evoked are closely related to the inspired state of the Sufis.[2]

[2] Somers further adds that this "was yet another link through Sufism to the spirit of the Koran." Earlier in the same article he had pointed out in an equally insigh-

A Mawlawī novitiate lasts 1001 days for the duration of which the postulant learns to play the instrument of his choice or practises singing or dancing.[3] When finally admitted to the order, a dervish's function will depend on the nature of his experience whilst still a novice. The *tekke* provided a well-rounded education, turning out poets, artists and calligraphers. This was the milieu from which most of the great Turkish composers, including the court musicians, emerged. The Yeni Kāpı Mawlawī-khāneh in particular was a centre of excellence. Although a tolerant *ṭarīqa*, the Mawlawiyya are the most aristocratic of the orders; this élitist character is reflected not only in their royal, or rather imperial, connexions but in their music, which is to the taste of sophisticated court circles. The court attended performances of the *samāʿ* at Yeni Kāpı, and there is even a royal tribune (*hünkār maḥfil*) in the refectory where the sultan dined whenever he attended the *samāʿ*. The Yeni Kāpı *tekke* was the largest of its kind in the whole empire; standing without the Edirne Gate, it was to all intents and purposes the capital's conservatoire. ʿIṭrī, who was born in 1625, enrolled there but studied composition under the famed Ḥāfiẓ Post (d. 1694), who was an initiate of the Khalwatī order, to which Ḥāfiẓ Kamāl (d. 1621) also belonged; whilst ʿUthmān Dede (d. 1730) was shaykh of the Galata Mawlawī-Khāneh, and Ismāʿīl Dede Efendī (d. 1846), known as Büyük-Dede, or even just "*the* Dede", divided his time between the Yeni Kāpı *tekke* and the court. Ṣāliḥ Dede Efendī (d. 1886 or '88) was born at Beshikṭāsh, where his father was shaykh of the Mawlawī-khāneh. He became *nayzānbāshī* in two other *tekke*s, besides playing in the imperial orchestra. The same *tekke* at Beshikṭāsh also witnessed the birth of Shaykh Ḥusayn Fakhr al-Dīn Dede Efendī (1854–1911). Ḥāfiẓ Kumrāl was a dervish in the Khalwatī *tekke* in Scutari. There was even one female Mawlawī composer, Dilḥayāt Hānum, who lived in the latter part of the 18th century.

The ceremony assumed its present form in the late 15th and early 16th century. During Rūmī's lifetime there were no rigid rules; the dervishes would make use of any text to hand; not till the time of Sultan Walad (d. 1312) were Mawlānā's poems incorporated in the

tive passage that the "Koran . . . is both the visual and aural base for Islamic art. The rhythm of its metre, the form, flow and proportion of its calligraphy are fundamental. The cantillation of the Koran is the very foundation of Islamic music." (*Country Life*, May 20, 1976, 1302).

[3] Properly speaking, "dancing" is a misnomer, for only one step is involved. The art of revolving (*dawr*) is more than physical; it is related to the faculty of meditation.

liturgy, as were, subsequently, Sultan Walad's own. Eventually the liturgy was standardised around a very restricted repertoire which included, in addition to Rūmī and Sultan Walad, poems by Jāmī one of whose verses adorns the entrance to the Konya *tekke*:

> This place has become the Kaʿba of lovers; any arriving incomplete are completed here.

As both Rūmī and his son played the *rabāb*, it is safe to assume that this instrument accompanied the earliest performances of the ritual, probably with the addition of kettledrums (*qudūm*) to accentuate the rhythm and the *nay* to support the melody.[4] Later, two more percussive instruments were added, *ḥalīla* (cymbals) and the *bandir*, or *mizhar* (frame drum),[5] the latter usually reserved for private performances. The *kamānja Rūmiyya, ʿūd* and *qanūn* are all subsequent additions, whilst the *ṭanbūr*, which recommended itself by its accuracy of tone (24 frets), timbre contrast and additional drone, is an innovation belonging to this century. As the instrumentation became standardised the ceremony assumed its definitive form. The principal instruments are the *nay* and the *qudūm*; the orchestra is led by the chief flautist and chief drummer. As many as eight different types of *nay*, varying in size, are used; examples are on view in the Mevlana Museum in Konya. The *āyīn* begins with a beat on the drum on a signal to the drummer from the shaykh on his *post* (sheepskin seat) at the opposite end of the *samāʿ-khāneh.*

According to the late Ulvī Ergunner, there are 66 extant settings of the ritual, 28 of them outstanding.[6] The three earliest, which date from after 1450, are anonymous but their quality is very high.[7] Known as *beste-i qadīm* ("ancient melody"), they are in the Panjgāh, Dugāh and Ḥusaynī modes. The first, which is undoubtedly the earliest extant setting of the Mawlawī liturgy, was recorded in Konya in 1968 by Anthology in collaboration with the Society for Ethnomusicology. Dating from the 15th and 16th centuries, these three

[4] Mystics compare the way the flautist's breath brings or, rather, restores the reed to life with God's animating the inert clay by breathing into it of His spirit (Quran, 15:29; 38:72). Rūmī also used the *nay* as a symbol for the individual emptied for self (*nafs*) and tilled with the divine spirit.

[5] Pronounced *mazhar* today and consequently often written that way.

[6] Personal Communication.

[7] There are, however, two compositions, a *peshrev* and a *sāz semāʿī* attributed to Sultan Walad which are the earliest examples of Turkish classical music extant. The *peshrev*, though secular, may have been used liturgically. If so, this would make the earliest extant Mawlawī composition.

settings formed a prototype to which all subsequent settings of the *āyīn* conformed; the earliest, however, of which the identity of the composer is known is that of Kochek Muṣṭafā Dede, who died in 1683. Probably the best known setting is that by the greatest of all Ottoman composers, Muṣṭafā ʿIṭrī (1640–1712), which is in the *maqām* Segāh. After this date, settings of the *āyīn* proliferate: 12 in the 18th century, 42 in the 19th and 8 in the present century. As a rule, music, at least in the classical sense, tends to be the last art to develop in any great civilisation. After the early compositions referred to, the second phase opens with ʿIṭrī:

Composer	*Maqām*
Buhūrīzādeh Muṣṭafā ʿIṭrī	Segāh
Quṭbünnayī ʿUthmān Dede	Rāst, Chārgāh, ʿUshshāq and Ḥijāz
Ḥāfiẓ ʿAbd al-Raḥīm Shaydā Dede	ʿIrāq
Muṣāḥib Sayyid Aḥmad Aga	Ḥijāz, Nihavend (2 settings)
Sulṭān Salīm III	Sūzidilārā

Composers of the third period comprise:

ʿAlī Nuṭqī Dede	Shawqīṭarab
Naqshī Dede	Shaṭṭarabān (same as shadd-ʿarabān, a transposition of the scale of ʿarabān onto a new pitch without alteration of the intervals
Zakāʾī Dede Efendī	Māye (a collective name for 3 *maqāms*, Iṣfahān, Sūẓinā, Ṣabāzemzeme (a composite *maqām*) Sūzidilāra
Dede Efendī	Ṣabā
Bolahenk Nurī Bey	Karajigar, Pūselik
Aḥmad ʿAynī Bey	Dilkeshīde, Pūselik-ʿashīrān, Rūy-i ʿIrāq
Ḥusayn Fakhr al-Dīn Dede	ʿAjam-ʿashīrān (compound of ʿAjam and ʿAshīrān)
Zakāʾīzādeh Aḥmad Efendī	Müsteʿār, Bayātī-pūselik (composite, starting in Bayātī and ending in Pūselik)
Raʾūf Yekta Bey	Yegāh (a very ancient *māqām*)
Ḥāfiẓ Kamāl Efendī	Nikrīz
Saʿd al-Dīn Heper	Ḥiṣār-pūselik (a compound *māqām*, only two or three centuries old)

Etem Üngör's compilation contains 58 settings, but there are at least 66, besides 16 more known to have existed and which might turn up some day. Down to the closure of the *tekke*s by official order in 1925 (edict of September 2) there had been composed some 70 settings, of which 50 exist in modern transcription. But according to other sources there are over 100 settings, some of them fragmentary.[8]

The *samāʿ* features both vocal and instrumental music. The *naʿt* (*lauds*), with which the ceremony begins, is unaccompanied. This is followed by a *taqsīm*, a solo improvisation on the *nay*, the purpose of which is to establish the *maqām* underlying the following sections. Although a solo performance, the other flautists may hold a drone, the sound of which imparts an otherwordly character to a section of the liturgy which is essentially meditational. Occasionally the *ṭanbūr* accompanies the *nay*, and where two *nayzān*s are very much in sympathy a double improvisation is possible. There follows a *peshrev* (prelude), which is instrumental, whilst the four *salām*s, the core part of the ceremony, are mainly choral with orchestral accompaniment. Two ensemble pieces at the end, the *son peshrev* (postlude) and the *son yürük semāʿī*, as well as the closing (*son*) *taqsīm*, are purely instrumental. The ceremony is therefore cyclical, like the groundplan of the hall (*samaʿ-khaneh*) where it takes place or the *post* on which the shaykh (*postnīshīn*) sits, which is red in allusion to Mawlānā's death at sunset and thus embodies the dawn-to-dusk cycle, or the mystical circle of completion that underlines the choreography of the *āyīn*.[9] The commencement of the *peshrev* is the signal to the dervishes that the *āyīn* is about to begin. They thump the floor and stand up, casting off their cloaks to begin the triple circumambulation of the floor (*dawr-i Waladī*) to a marching rhythm before passing serially into the first *salām* as each one passes the *post*, to receive the blessing of the shaykh, which is the point of transition between the two kinds of movement involved, from the cyclical (*dawrī*) to the pivotal (*miḥwarī*). In the *salām* pivotal and cyclical are combined, for the dervish, or *ʿāshiq*, athirst for the rapture of union, pivots simultaneously around his own axis (self) and the universe's.

[8] I owe this information to Naīl Kesova whose notes on the subject we translated for the programme notes for the Sadler's Wells performance in 1974.

[9] See the present author's "The Mawlawi Dervishry in Cairo", *Art and Archaeology Research Papers* 15 (June 1979), 9–15, which in spite of the title is really a study of the cosmology underlying the design of Mawlawī *samaʿ-khaneh*s (ceremonial halls).

Mawlawī music shares the basic characteristic of all Turkish art music: an identifiable modal pattern, both melodic and rhythmic. The music is melodic and linear, utilising both *maqāmāt* and *uṣūllar*. There is also *düzen*, or melodic rhythm, which at the start corresponds with the *uṣūl* but promptly develops an independent existence. Mawlawī music belongs to the classical *maqām* tradition linked to the Arab and Persian modal system but with significant divergences, as Turkish modes sometimes differ from their Arabic and Persian namesakes in the composition of their intervals. A *maqām* is a scale-based melodic mode, differing from a *rāga* in that it has no allegorical meaning and is not linked to a particular time of day. *Maqāmāt* have been described (by Oransay) as "composition rules" but could just as well be described as "interpretational guidelines": as interpreter, the musician need not adhere too strictly to the rules. The *maqām* determines the tessitura, melodic direction and cadences; it begins and ends on the same tone, producing a melodic arc; it has a dominant and, usually, a middle tone and cadential tone before the *finalis* (keynote). Arel lists 553 *maqām*s but less than a hundred are used. Some musical theorists refer to Rāst as the basis of all Turkish musical theory whilst others reserve this honour for Chārgāh. In the Mawlawī rite, Rāst is *de rigeur* for the *naʿt*, with which the ceremony habitually begins, because this portion of the liturgy has become standardised in the setting by ʿIṭrī, which utilises this particular *maqām*, one of the oldest and certainly the most important in Turkish music. Therefore it is necessary for the *nayzān* to interpose a *taqsīm* at this point to establish the *maqām* of the following sections and effect a transition. Prior to ʿIṭrī the *naʿt* was in the *maqām* of the *āyīn*.

However, the core ceremony, the four *salām*s, does not always adhere strictly to a single *maqām*; modulations are allowed; the skeletal nature of Turkish composition makes for modulatory derivations, leaving the performer free to interpret the composer's notation as he sees fit. For example, starting in Ṣabā, a musician can modulate to Bestenigār (a composite *maqām*, formed by the addition of *segāh* to the bottom of the scale of Ṣabā) and end in Evich, with transitional passage inserted, or modulate from ʿAjam-ʿashīrān to Ṣabā, ʿAjam-ʿashīrān's closest neighbour in the modal system. The fixed tessitura of the notation are usually transposed downward by a 4th in performance to suit the singers but are also transposed in ensemble passages. The ensemble passages at the end, *son peshrev* and *son* *yürük semāʿī*, can be in different (but preferably related) *maqāms* from the four *salāms*. Thus in the UNESCO recording, the *salāms* are in Rūy-i ʿIrāq, which is the same as Segāh (the preferential mode for religious music) but for the addition of a final note on F, whilst the postlude (*son peshrev*) and the *son yürük semāʿī* are in *Faraḥnak*, which is obtained by transposing onto the tonic F sharp, the note which connects Segāh with Rūy-i ʿIrāq. This way the entire composition exhibits a modal unity. The Anthology recording is, as already observed, in Pānjgāh, a *maqām* made up of tetrachords and pentachords from other *maqāms* but similar to the Rāst of the *naʿt*, with the same variable intervals, whilst the two closing passages are in Segāh. The compatibility of the *maqāms* used for a single composition guarantees a uniformity of style in conformity with the cyclical structure of Turkish music as exhibited in the *peshrev* with its intermezzos (*taslīmāt*) marking the end of each movement (*khāneh*) or the *āyīn* with the same number of movements and ritornellos.

Except for the *taqsīm*, which is free from set rhythm, the rhythm is guided by a predetermined rhythmic mode (*uṣūl*); but both ensemble and chorus can depart from the rhythm in the same way as modulations are tolerated within a *maqām*. The rhythm implicit in the melody, i.e. the *düzen*, is made explicit by the percussive elements of the ensemble. An *uṣūl* comprises (a) primary beats, which determine the duration of the cycle, (b) rhythmic groups, binary or tertiary, depending on whether they contain two or three beats, and (c) an accent system. *Düm* is the strong accent, *tek* the weak, *düme* is strong-weak. A Mawlawī drummer uses two differently tuned kettledrums. Again, the best account is that by Jeffrey Somers:

> [The rhythmic accompaniment] has patterns which are based on the same units as those used in Arabic poetry. These are accented by the strong beat (*düm*), the light beat (*tek*) and the silence or rest (*suqūṭ*), one of the three accompanying each musical syllable. The repetition of the rhythmic unit gives an ordered sequence of beats similar to poetry. Rhythmic units reflect the vowels and consonants of the written word, which gives the possibility of the transcription of poetry.[10]

The Sufi orders have always used music, particularly rhythm, to support their spiritual exercises (*dhikr*), but in the Mawlawi rite rhythm is used not only to assist the movements of the dervishes but to

[10] *Loc. cit.*

translate into measured time the texts (*Mathnavī*, *Dīvān-i Shams-i Tabrīzī*, *Dīvān-i Jāmī*) used for the libretto. *Uṣūl*s are chosen out of a range of over 40 for their symbolic properties. Prescribed *uṣūllar* (rhythmic patterns) are used for different stages of the ritual. The threefold circumambulation of the floor is known as *dawr-i Waladī* after Sultan Walad. It is accompanied by a prelude (*peshrev*), and for this the *dawr-i kabīr* (Great Circle) *uṣūl* is invariable. A *peshrev* is an overture (Pers. *pesh*, before, and *raftan*, to go) used to introduce cycles of both sacred and profane compositions. So as to be coterminous with the triple circumambulation it sometimes has to be repeated with all four *khāneh*s (movements) as much as two and a half times. The foursquare rhythm of the *dawr-i kabīr* forms a metre suitable for marching. Though not sung, the *peshrev* counts as a processional; the *son peshrev* however cannot be accounted a recessional. The Great Cycle has 28 primary beats; these beats and 14 isochronous rhythmic groups make up a complete cycle. Unlike the prelude (*peshrev*) the postlude (*son peshrev*) has only one *khāneh*, and this is in *velvelī düyek* rhythm, with a rhythmic pattern of eight beats with signatures of 8/8 and 8/4. *Uṣūllar* from the 40 or more available to the performer can be combined to produce *velvelī* (tumult, din).

For the first dance movement (*birinjī salām*) the *dawr-i revān* (Ambling Circle) *uṣūl* is standard. This has 15 beats, fourteen on the right-hand drum, one on the left-hand drum. The tempo of the second movement (*ikinjī salām*) is in sharp contrast to the first: this movement is very short but taken at a slow pace and usually in the *evfer* rhythm, which has a limping or stumbling motion. The third movement (*üchünchü salām*) is the longest and most complex: it has various sections, mostly modifications of the *dawr-i kabīr*, whence it passes to the *aksak* (limping) rhythm and ends on *yürük semāʿī* to speed up the dancers before the close. This last rhythm has a three-part *uṣūl* of the *semāʿī* class as its basis. The *peshrev* is in four sections, each ending with a *taslīm*, or ritornello. The *taslīm* is always taken at a fast tempo.

As the music intensifies with the accumulation of beats towards the end of the third and fourth *salām*s the revolutions of the dancers speed up. One reason for the introduction of an intermezzo (*tarannurum*) is to ease the transition to the succeeding section. Thus a decreasing tempo, with syncopated effect, introduces the slow second *salām*. Syncopation is also present in the quick *yürük semāʿī* of the third section as well as in the final (*son yürük semāʿī*). The fourth (*dördünjü*) *salām* reverts to the slow tempo of the second. The *peshrev* is in tumultuous (*velvelī*) rhythm, and the *son yürük semāʿī* takes its name from the fast rhythm (*yürük*: rapid) in which it is composed; its purpose is to accelerate the motion of the dancers toward a finale. *Yürük semāʿī* is a rhythmic pattern with six beats to the bar. There follows a final (*son*) *taqsīm* on the *nay* free from rhythm. Like the introductory *taqsīm*, the other *nayzāns* can hold a drone whilst the soloist improvises.

When the *son yürük semāʿī* brings the dancers to an abrupt stop, they withdraw to one side of the hall. *Tilāwat al-Qur'ān* (Quranic recitation) follows, whereafter the shaykh petitions God silently, calls for the recitation of the Fātiḥa, then pronounces the blessing:

> May the grace (*ināyat*) of God and the zeal of men be present with us and watch over us, likewise the spirit of holy Mawlānā, the insight of Shams-i Tabrīzī and the nobility of Imām ʿAlī,

ending *hū delīm hū*. In this last *hu*, indicative of *ḥaqīqa* (He, It, the ultimate reality) all present join with elongated unison. Before exiting, the shaykh greets the *semāʿ-zānbāshī*, whereupon the *semāʿ-zānbāshī* and *darāwīsh* respond, drawing out the final vowel of *barakātuhu* after the manner of the previous glissando. A similar exchange is made between the shaykh and the orchestra. The shaykh then turns and bows toward the vacant *post* before leaving by the gate in the balustrading reserved for himself.

Mawlawī music contains the most valuable compositions in the Turkish repertoire from the point of view of art. Composing a setting for the Mawlawī liturgy was never a task to be embarked on lightly; a composer needed to be endowed with a creative talent matched only by the intensity of his inspiration. Before sitting down to compose he had first to prepare himself spiritually for the task with prayer, fasting and meditation; from so daunting an enterprise the composer of average endowments would flinch.

The core ceremony, the *āyīn*, goes back to Sultan Walad. Besides *āyīn*, it is also known as *muqābala* (meeting, encounter) from the moment when each two dervishes confront one another across the *post*. The *āyīn* is a *dhikr*, for, as they revolve, the dervishes silently invoke the name of God at each turn as they put the right foot down (the left serves as the axis of gyration). The participant gradually recedes from the phenomenal world the closer he draws toward gnosis (*maʿrifa*). The *dhākir* is transported to a state of ecstasy; it is, say those who have experienced it, as if with the first gyrations all the sorrows of the world were laid plain to view but as the gyration proceeds a sense of rapture supervenes, so that a feeling of indescribable happiness is felt. The second *salām* brings the *dhākir* to the brink of *fanā'* (annihilation to self). The third brings awareness of *fanā'*, whilst in the fourth they become consubstantial with the universe by turning in an orbit around a mystical axis. The four parts of the *āyīn* form stages in a mystical progression; they correspond to the four synoptic spheres that make up the universe: the first *salām* represents the *'ālam-i nāsūt*, the phenomenal world; the second the *'ālam-i malakūt*, the realm of sovereignty or invisible world, the third, the *'ālam-i jabarūt*, the highest heaven and the fourth the *'ālam-i lāhūt*, or court of heaven i.e. next to the godhead. When, in the last *salām*, the *postnīshīn* moves off the *post* to gyrate slowly down the unmarked equator line (coincident with the *qibla*), holding the right hem of his robe with the right hand, until he reaches the centre, where he turns briefly before returning to the *post*, this means that for a brief duration the two axes, Rūmī and his living representative, coincide.

This is the importance of *silsila*, because the shaykh is linked to the founder of the order through an unbroken *silsila*. A *silsila* in *taṣawwuf* is what a dynasty is to politics or a *madhhab* to jurisprudence, that is, a valid and irreplaceable channel for the transmission of authority. In this case the authority is not political or legal but spiritual. Herein lies the significance of the *post*. When the *post* is spread on the floor by the *post-naqībī* and the shaykh takes up his stance on a fleece inherited from his immediate predecessor in the *silsila*, this guarantees his authority; otherwise, the unwary aspirant (*'āshiq*) could be entrusting his soul to a black magician. The *post* is the visible and tangible proof of his authority: herein lies the significance of his role as *post du'a'sı*, when the *pīr* is petitioned by the inheritor of his *post*. This act, together with the recitation of the *Fātiḥa* and some verses from the *Mathnavī*, opens the ceremony even before the lead singer chants the *na't*. It is also important that the ceremony be performed in the setting designed for it. This is more than just a question of aesthetics or liturgical propriety; at the *tekke* in Konya the *āyīn* was executed in full view of Rumi, whose grave is visible from the dancing floor. A similar arrangement obtains in Damascus and at Karamān (the Umm Sultana *tekke*, where Rūmī's mother is buried) as well as in Nicosia. This way the *silsila* is physically present, and the dancers are exposed to the *baraka* their graves emit.

INDEX OF NAMES

INDEX OF PLACES